A HISTORY OF
PHILOSOPHICAL SYSTEMS

BOOKS BY VERGILIUS FERM

The Crisis in American Lutheran Theology (1927)

What Is Lutheranism? (1930), EDITOR

Contemporary American Theology, Theological Autobiographies,
VOLUME I (1932), EDITOR

Contemporary American Theology, Theological Autobiographies,
VOLUME II (1933), EDITOR

First Adventures in Philosophy (1936)

Religion in Transition (1937), EDITOR

First Chapters in Religious Philosophy (1937)

An Encyclopedia of Religion (1945), EDITOR

Religion in the Twentieth Century (1948), EDITOR

What Can We Believe? (1948)

Forgotten Religions (1950), EDITOR

A History of Philosophical Systems (1950), EDITOR

A HISTORY OF PHILOSOPHICAL SYSTEMS

EDITED BY

VERGILIUS FERM

COMPTON PROFESSOR
AND HEAD OF THE DEPARTMENT OF PHILOSOPHY
IN THE COLLEGE OF WOOSTER

NEW YORK
THE PHILOSOPHICAL LIBRARY

COPYRIGHT, 1950, BY
THE PHILOSOPHICAL LIBRARY, INC.
15 EAST 40TH STREET, NEW YORK, N. Y.

PRINTED IN THE UNITED STATES OF AMERICA

A HISTORY OF
PHILOSOPHICAL SYSTEMS

INTRODUCTION

THERE ARE already many excellent texts in the history of philosophy. In justification of another volume, it may be pointed out that this one has been planned on different lines: a cooperative work by many minds and with an emphasis upon periods of thought and upon broad characterizations of schools or systems.

Those who have joined in this venture are especially qualified in the particular field or subject upon which they have written. Invited to participate by reason of the special study each has given to his subject in which he has already gained reputation among professional philosophers or by reason of courses he is now giving in the particular subject in college, university or graduate-school, each author gives to his article the weight of mature thought and authority. It is becoming increasingly clear that no one historian can be expected to deal with the whole range of philosophic thought in full competence where the specialization of scholarship is bringing to light fresh data and interpretations and in view of the many ramifications of the complicated subject-matter. Philosophers like all research-specialists turn to definite areas for study and a history of so vast a field must take into consideration the results of this scholarship. A cooperative volume thus justifies itself.

By "systems" is here meant not necessarily those types of thought which may be characterized as "symphonic." If so, many philosophies would necessarily have to be omitted. Rather, by "systems" is here meant the general trend or course of thought of a particular time, school or group of thinkers. While references, of course, are made to classical and less-well-known names of the philosophical hierarchy with attention paid to their individual thought, the main purpose of the volume is to direct attention not to the thinkers as such but to the main patterns of thought represented by them and their school. Questions of detailed analysis and technical points of dispute have been passed by in the interest of an over-all exposition of the various currents of thought. Each writer has had in mind

INTRODUCTION

plain exposition rather than a defence of some particular view at the expense of it. This is historical writing as it should be. To his topic, however, he has applied a sympathetic treatment because his study of it naturally has grown out of a particular interest and liking for it.

The aim throughout has been to reach students who already have some acquaintance with the general subject of philosophy, particularly those who have been fortunate enough to have had at least a semester's work in "introduction" and who aspire to move in the direction of a "major" in the field. Should the reader have had no previous study of philosophy, a competent teacher will help him see the many implications and ramifications of thought embedded in the discussions. It may be safely asserted that graduate-students in philosophy will find here a fresh and invigorating review of historical material so organized as to present perhaps more clearly the outline of systems in all their variety and in their historical setting.

Thus, in claiming a distinctive approach in the literature in its field, this volume aspires to take its place in the ranks at least as a worthy supplement to the standard historical works written along more conventional lines.

Some of the technical details in shaping this volume may be mentioned: page-footnotes are avoided and notes at the end of the chapters are provided for reasons which are apparent to the users of text-books; a bibliography has been appended to each topic to make for guided independent study; year dates appear again and again to give the student a chronological sense and to make each chapter more or less independent in such matters of the others; readability has been set as an ideal in exposition even though certain topics do not lend themselves easily to popularization; and, an index has been prepared so that the student may tie together the thought of particular philosophers and various schools mentioned in scattered places because they play into more than one topic.

In a subject so expansive as the history of disciplined thought about fundamental meanings of the world, it would not be difficult for the expert to notice the omission of some area of inquiry or of some more or less major philosophical name. Such omissions are inexcusable in encyclopedias. The purport of this volume, of course, is not encyclopedic but rather to give an historical sense and appreciation of systems. The expert, however, will not fail to see that

INTRODUCTION

all the subjects here treated are in themselves an integral part of that total picture of which a student of the history of philosophy may be expected to have some degree of knowledge—including topics which are now engaging the interests of contemporary philosophers.

The editor has found his professional colleagues most helpful in making suggestions in the planning of this work. Without exception the prospectus to this book has met with the most cordial enthusiasm on the part of everyone having a part in it, giving evidence to the claim that there was a place for just such a volume on the student's and even the professor's philosophical book-shelf. Credit, however, for the general idea of the book belongs to D. D. Runes, Ph.D., president of The Philosophical Library and a philosopher in his own right, who, in a New York City office in the spring of 1949, set forth the idea to the editor and gave him the commission to carry it, in whatever way seemed best, to its execution.

To the student-reader it may be said: If you will pursue these chapters thoughtfully, seeking an understanding acquaintance with the material contained in them in terms of the broad outlines of systems in their historical perspective, you may be assured that you will have reached a clearing which will bring light to what may have been an experience of clouded confusion of conflicting and unrelated thoughts and thereby have attained your own philosophical majority.

VERGILIUS FERM

The College of Wooster

TABLE OF CONTENTS

INTRODUCTION v
VERGILIUS FERM

PART I

ANCIENT AND MEDIEVAL

Chapter Page
1. THE STORY OF INDIAN PHILOSOPHY 3
   SHRI KRISHNA SAKSENA, PH.D.
   Formerly Head of the Department of Philosophy in Hindu College, Delhi and now Deputy Director (Editorial) of the Publications Division, Ministry of I. & B., Government of India

2. ZOROASTRIAN PHILOSOPHY 19
   IRACH J. S. TARAPOREWALA, PH.D.
   Retired Director of Deccan College Post-Graduate and Research Institute, Poona, India

3. BUDDHIST PHILOSOPHICAL SYSTEMS 33
   CLARENCE H. HAMILTON, PH.D.
   Professor of History and Philosophy of Religion and Christian Missions, The Graduate School of Theology, Oberlin College

4. CHINESE PHILOSOPHY (CONFUCIANISM, MOISM, TAOISM, LEGALISM) 44
   H. G. CREEL, PH.D.
   Professor of Early Chinese Literature and Institutions, The University of Chicago

5. ANCIENT JEWISH PHILOSOPHY 57
   SAMUEL S. COHON, D.D.
   Professor of Jewish Theology, Hebrew Union College

Chapter	Page
6. THE BEGINNINGS OF GREEK PHILOSOPHY	70

GORDON H. CLARK, PH.D.
Professor and Head of the Department of Philosophy, Butler University

7. EARLY GREEK MORALISTS — 82

PAUL R. HELSEL, M.A., B.D., PH.D.
Professor of Philosophy, The University of Southern California

8. PLATONISM — 93

JAMES H. DUNHAM, M.A., PH.D., LL.D.
Dean Emeritus and Professor Emeritus of Philosophy, Temple University

9. ARISTOTELIANISM — 106

HENRY VEATCH, M.A., PH.D.
Associate Professor of Philosophy, Indiana University

10. HELLENISTIC AND ROMAN SCHOOLS OF PHILOSOPHY — 118

GORDON H. CLARK
(As Above)

11. ALEXANDRIAN PHILOSOPHY — 131

EUGEN KULLMANN, PH.D.
Lecturer in Philosophy, The Graduate Faculty, The New School for Social Research (New York City)

12. EARLY CHRISTIAN PHILOSOPHY — 144

VERGILIUS FERM, B.D., M.A., PH.D.
Compton Professor and Head of the Department of Philosophy, The College of Wooster

13. ARABIC AND ISLAMIC PHILOSOPHY — 158

EDWARD J. JURJI, PH.D.
Associate Professor of Islamics and Comparative Religion, Princeton Theological Seminary

Chapter		Page
14.	MEDIAEVAL JEWISH PHILOSOPHY EMIL L. FACKENHEIM, PH.D. *Lecturer in Philosophy, University of Toronto*	171
15.	EARLY CHRISTIAN SCHOLASTICISM RICHARD J. THOMPSON, M.A., PH.D. *Assistant Professor of Philosophy, University of Notre Dame*	185
16.	REVIVED ARISTOTELIANISM AND THOMISTIC PHILOSOPHY ARMAND MAURER, L.M.S., M.A., PH.D. *Assistant Professor of Philosophy, Pontifical Institute of Mediaeval Studies*	197
17.	SCOTISM AND OCKHAMISM ARMAND MAURER *(As Above)*	212

PART II

MODERN AND RECENT

18.	RENAISSANCE PHILOSOPHIES PAUL OSKAR KRISTELLER, PH.D., DOTT. IN FIL. *Associate Professor of Philosophy, Columbia University*	227
19.	EARLY MODERN RATIONALISM ALBERT G. RAMSPERGER, PH.D. *Professor and Chairman of the Department of Philosophy, University of Wisconsin*	240
20.	EARLY MODERN EMPIRICISM DOUGLAS N. MORGAN, PH.D. *Assistant Professor of Philosophy, Northwestern University*	253
21.	THE PHILOSOPHY OF THE ENLIGHTENMENT CHARLES FRANKEL, PH.D. *Assistant Professor of Philosophy, Columbia University*	266

Chapter	Page
22. KANT'S CRITICAL PHILOSOPHY	280

NEWTON P. STALLKNECHT, M.A., Ph.D.

Professor and Chairman of the Department of Philosophy, Indiana University

23. CLASSICAL GERMAN IDEALISM, THE PHILOSOPHY OF SCHOPENHAUER AND NEO-KANTIANISM 291

ALBAN G. WIDGERY, M.A. (Cantab)

Professor of Philosophy, Duke University

24. DIALECTICAL MATERIALISM 306

SIEGFRIED MARCK, Ph.D.

Professor of Philosophy, Roosevelt College

25. ENGLISH AND AMERICAN ABSOLUTE IDEALISM 315

G. WATTS CUNNINGHAM, M.A., Ph.D., D. Litt., LL.D.

Sage Professor Emeritus of Philosophy and Dean Emeritus of the Graduate School, Cornell University

26. POSITIVISM 329

CHARLES FRANKEL

(*As Above*)

27. PERSONALISM (INCLUDING PERSONAL IDEALISM) 340

EDGAR SHEFFIELD BRIGHTMAN, M.A., S.T.B., Ph.D., Litt. D., LL.D.

Borden Parker Bowne Professor of Philosophy, The Graduate School, Boston University

28. PHENOMENOLOGY 353

DORION CAIRNS, Ph.D.

Professor of Philosophy, Rockford College

29. EARLY PHILOSOPHIES OF EVOLUTION 365

RAY H. DOTTERER, M.A., Ph.D.

Professor Emeritus of Philosophy, Pennsylvania State College

Chapter		Page
30.	VITALISM ARTHUR BERNDTSON, Ph.D. *Assistant Professor of Philosophy, University of Missouri*	375
31.	PRAGMATISM DONALD S. MACKAY, B.D., Ph.D. *Professor of Philosophy, University of California*	387
32.	EXISTENTIALISM HELMUT KUHN, Ph.D. *Professor of Philosophy, University of Erlangen*	405
33.	THE NEW MATERIALISM ROY WOOD SELLARS, Ph.D. *Professor Emeritus of Philosophy, University of Michigan*	418
34.	VARIETIES OF NATURALISM VERGILIUS FERM	429
35.	PANPSYCHISM CHARLES HARTSHORNE, M.A., Ph.D. *Professor of Philosophy, The University of Chicago*	442
36.	CONTEMPORARY THOMISM DONALD A. GALLAGHER, M.A., Ph.D. *Assistant Professor of Philosophy, Marquette University*	454
37.	LOGICAL POSITIVISM GUSTAV BERGMANN, Ph.D., J.D. *Associate Professor of Philosophy, State University of Iowa*	471
38.	SEMANTICS GUSTAV BERGMANN *(As Above)*	483
39.	A BRIEF HISTORY OF GENERAL THEORY OF VALUE STEPHEN C. PEPPER, M.A., Ph.D. *Professor of Philosophy and Chairman of the Department of Art, University of California*	493

Chapter		Page
40.	RECENT SCHOOLS OF LOGIC ALBERT E. AVEY, M.A., Ph.D. *Professor and Chairman of the Department of Philosophy, Ohio State University*	504
41.	RECENT EPISTEMOLOGICAL SCHOOLS LEDGER WOOD, Ph.D. *Professor of Philosophy, Princeton University*	516
42.	PHILOSOPHY OF THE SCIENCES A. CORNELIUS BENJAMIN, M.A., Ph.D. *John H. Lathrop Professor and Chairman of the Department of Philosophy, University of Missouri*	540
43.	RECENT SCHOOLS OF AESTHETICS VAN METER AMES, Ph.D. *Professor of Philosophy, University of Cincinnati*	552
44.	RECENT SCHOOLS OF ETHICS GLENN NEGLEY, M.A., Ph.D. *Professor of Philosophy, Duke University*	563
45.	PHILOSOPHIES OF HISTORY ELIZABETH FARQUHAR FLOWER, Ph.D. *Assistant Professor of Philosophy, University of Pennsylvania*	574
46.	PHILOSOPHIES OF CULTURE HORACE L. FRIESS, Ph.D. *Professor of Philosophy, Columbia University*	588
47.	PHILOSOPHIES OF RELIGION VERGILIUS FERM	598
	INDEX	610

LIST OF CONTRIBUTORS

VAN METER AMES
ALBERT E. AVEY
A. CORNELIUS BENJAMIN
GUSTAV BERGMANN
ARTHUR BERNDTSON
EDGAR SHEFFIELD BRIGHTMAN
DORION CAIRNS
GORDON H. CLARK
SAMUEL S. COHON
H. G. CREEL
G. WATTS CUNNINGHAM
RAY H. DOTTERER
JAMES H. DUNHAM
EMIL L. FACKENHEIM
VERGILIUS FERM
ELIZABETH FARQUHAR FLOWER
CHARLES FRANKEL
HORACE L. FRIESS
DONALD A. GALLAGHER
CLARENCE H. HAMILTON
CHARLES HARTSHORNE

PAUL R. HELSEL
EDWARD J. JURJI
PAUL OSKAR KRISTELLER
HELMUT KUHN
EUGEN KULLMANN
DONALD S. MACKAY
SIEGFRIED MARCK
ARMAND MAURER
DOUGLAS N. MORGAN
GLENN NEGLEY
STEPHEN C. PEPPER
ALBERT G. RAMSPERGER
SHRI KRISHNA SAKSENA
ROY WOOD SELLARS
NEWTON P. STALLKNECHT
IRACH J. S. TARAPOREWALA
RICHARD J. THOMPSON
HENRY VEATCH
ALBAN G. WIDGERY
LEDGER WOOD

Part I

ANCIENT AND MEDIEVAL

CHAPTER ONE

THE STORY OF INDIAN PHILOSOPHY

SHRI KRISHNA SAKSENA

INDIAN PHILOSOPHY is, perhaps, the earliest recorded thought of man. Its four thousand-odd years of history embracing the multitudinous phases of intense enquiry cannot possibly be done justice to in the short space assigned for the purpose. Only a bird's-eye-view of this vast panorama is, accordingly, possible in the following survey.

The Vedas

The *Vedas* (2500-2000 B. C.) which embody divine truths, are believed to have been revealed to the super-consciousness of the seers. They represent the fountainhead of Hindu philosophical thought. Each of the four *Vedas, Rig-Veda, Yajur-Veda, Sāma-Veda* and *Atharva-Veda,* has three main divisions: 1) *the Samhitās* (sacred texts), 2) *the Brāhmaṇas* (commentaries) and 3) the *Āraṇyakas* (forest-books). The *Rigveda Samhitā* is the oldest record of Hindu philosophical thought.

To begin with, man looks outside. His first thoughts therefore relate to the sequence of natural phenomena in which he sees the causes of vicissitudes of his everyday life. The early *mantras* (hymns), thus, contain a religion of nature-worship, in which the various powers of nature like fire (*agni*) and wind (*vāyu*), which influence human life, are personified as gods, whom it is a man's duty to propitiate. *Varuṇa* and *Indra* are the chief among them, the former being conceived as a symbol of omniscience and righteousness. The gods being righteous are believed to uphold *Rta* or the physical and moral order in the universe. The relation of man to gods who are conceived as originating and sustaining the world is one of utter dependence. Man, it is maintained, must lead a righteous life to please the gods who are good. In Vedic religious thought the unreality of the universe is never suggested. In fact, worldly prosperity and the joys of everyday life are constantly stressed. Transmigration is not directly referred to though the soul is conceived as immortal.

In later hymns and the *Brāhmaṇas*, the development of thought takes three distinct lines: monotheism, monism and ritualism. Identity in the conception of different gods suggests monotheism. A supreme God is, however, not yet conceived, though an attempt is made to discover a common power behind all the gods. God *Prajāpati* is such a power. The monistic tendency traces the world not to a creator but to a single primal cause, diversifying itself into the universe, which anticipating the later *Upaniṣadic* Absolute is described as *Tat Ekam* or "That One." Here, therefore, the focus of attention turns from the concrete and the external to the abstract and the internal, which is, later followed up in the *Upaniṣads*.

Ritualism, representing the effort to gain the favor of the gods through sacrificial gifts culminates in the *Brāhmaṇaṣ*. It is just another way of looking at the concept of *Rta* according to which a correct sacrifice inexorably brings its own good result.

The Upaniṣads

The *Upaniṣads* (700-600 B.C.) literally mean 'secret teaching.' Forming the concluding part of the Vedas, they are also called the *Vedānta* and *Āranyakas*—or the *forest books*. They mark a distinct step beyond the *Brāhmaṇas*. Of the major *Upaniṣads*, about ten are the most celebrated, the *Brihadāraṇyaka* and the *Chāndogya* being the most important among them. Their exalted idealism and lofty teachings have had a lasting influence upon the Indian mind. Much of the subsequent Indian philosophy in one way or another draws its inspiration from the *Upaniṣads*.

In the *Upaniṣads* the stress is, not on the traditional performance of action (*Karma-mārga*), but on the knowledge of the ultimate truth as a means to the final liberation of man. (*Jñāna-mārga*) Apart from this shift in emphasis, the *Upaniṣads* inaugurate a new era of "looking within" for the reality of the Universe as against the Vedic perception of the *Puruṣa* as a macrocosmic reality.

Thought is here devoted chiefly to the concept of the *Ātman* and the *Brāhmaṇ*. The quest after *Brāhmaṇ* as the all-pervasive spirit springs from the desire to discover a supreme Controller of Man and Nature. By a process of progressive elimination, this ultimate reality is found by the *Upaniṣads* to be none other than Man's own Self—which is, therefore, also the *Brāhmaṇ*. This alone is real. But the problem is: if the *Ātman* alone is real, what happens to the reality of the external world? Though the universe is a reality, say the *Upaniṣads*, the real in it is the *Ātman* alone. The most pervading thought, in fact, is that the *Ātman* is the only reality, though at places we also find the pantheistic thought which identifies the universe with the *Brāhmaṇ*, and the theistic thought which looks upon the *Brāhmaṇ* as the Lord of the Universe.

The *Ātman* is characterized as transcendental and beyond the reach of the senses and the intellect. It is a pure, subject-object-less Consciousness. Sometimes it is identified with *Brāhmaṇ*, as in the sayings, *That thou art* (*tat tvam Asi*) and *I am Brāhmaṇ* (*Aham Brāhma asmi*). But the meaning is that the *Ātman* alone underlies Man and Nature and not that there are two realities which are one. Demonstrating that it is *not this, not this* (*Neti, Neti*), the indescribability of the *Brāhmaṇ* is also stressed.

Next to the doctrine of the *Ātman* and its realization is the doctrine of transmigration. The significance of the doctrine is that it points to desire and not to *Karma* as the cause of rebirth. *Karma* only forms the connecting link between desire and rebirth, for "whatever a man desires he wills, and whatever he wills he acts." Desire is annihilated by Self-Knowledge. *Mokṣa* (emancipation) is, therefore, the state of infiniteness to which a man attains when he realizes his own Self. Transmigration naturally ceases for such a knowing man. He transcends limits and is happy, for the Infinite is bliss, just as the finite is pain. Emancipation is not the attainment of something that is not: it is only the true knowledge of the Self that ever is.

The Epics and the Bhagvad-Gītā

A few centuries of thought that separate the Vedic period from the later systems are embodied in the epic of the *Mahābhārata* containing the *Bhagvadgītā* of Lord Krishna and some minor *Upaniṣads*. The continuation of Vedic monotheism, the emergence of two new creeds (*Śaivism* and *Vaiṣṇavism* glorifying the Vedic deities of *Śiva* and *Vishnu* respectively), the concept of *dharma* as predominantly ritualistic, and various other notions of *Bhakti* (devotion) and divine grace (*prasāda*), these are the chief philosophical features of this period. During this period the concepts of *Karma* and *Mokṣa* grow finer. The *Gītā*, second only to the *Upaniṣads* in philosophical importance, advocates *niṣkāma-karma* or performance of duty without thought of consequences. According to the *Gītā* one's own duty (*sva-dharma*) is relative to one's social status. Every duty is as good as every other; only it is to be done in a spirit of non-attachment (*Karma-Yoga*). Duty in the *Gītā* is, however, conceived in the absolutist as well as in theistic terms, the latter forming the basis of *Bhakti-Yoga* or dedication of all work to the Lord.

The Chārvāka

This heterogeneous material could not perhaps long remain without systematization. Hence the transition to systems. First comes the *Chārvāka* or the *Lokāyata, i.e.*, the commonsense philosophy—restricted to the world of common experience. This is regarded as one of the heterodox or non-Vedic systems as it neither believes in revelation nor in the authority of the *Vedas*. Things, it maintains, have no transcendental essence: they are what they appear to be. Only the perceived elements—earth, water, fire and air—are real. Supersensible entities, like God, soul and the divine origin of the Vedas are ridiculed. Perception being the only source of knowledge, life is to be taken as it is, a mixture of pain and pleasure. It is vain to strive after a painless existence: wisdom consists only in maximizing the balance of pleasure over pain. Yet the system does not recommend a purely animal living. It may be taken as an earlier counter-part of Western Epicureanism.

Jainism

Another non-Vedic religion is Jainism derived from the word *Jin* meaning the conquest of life's suffering. It is older than Hinduism or Buddhism. Its founder was *Riṣabha*, the first *Tirthānkara* (a perfect soul), Lord Mahavīra being the last of a series of *Tirthānkaras*. Its two well-known sects are the *Śvetāmbaras* (the white-clad) and the *Digāmbaras* (the sky-clad). Their central philosophy, however, is the same.

Jain metaphysics is both dualistic and pluralistic. The animate and inanimate, or the *Jīva* and *Ajīva*, are both treated as eternal, independent and numberless. The *Jīva*, meaning only the individual soul and not the supreme Self of the *Upaniṣads*, is always mixed up with matter except when liberated. It may be mobile or immobile as in stones but *Cetana* (consciousness) is its chief quality. It is by nature ever active to perfect itself: and the *Tirthānkaras* are just these perfect souls. Most of the functions of God are attributed to the *Jīva's* potential power. It may be *mukta* (liberated) or *baddha* (in bondage). In the former case, it has the usual characteristics of perfect knowledge, power and bliss.

The Ajīvas are five in number—*Pudgala* or Matter, *Ākāṣa* or Space, *Kāla* or Time, and *Dharma* and *Adharma* (principles of movement and rest), the last two being peculiar to Jainism.

Karma is described as the soul-energy that links the soul with the body. The Law of *Karma* is said to operate inexorably. Normally, every soul is mixed up with matter through *Karma*: this is bondage. Liberation consists in finally extinguishing *Karma*. Therein lies the perfection of Man. Jainism is, in fact, the religion of the Perfect Man. No more perfect or higher being like God is visualized for the origination or maintenance of the universe: hence the atheistic touch in the system. To attain this spiritual perfection, non-injury to all life is recommended. *Ahimsā*, the supreme ethical principle, is, however, not mere non-injury but also positive love for all. Right faith (*Samyag Darshan*) and right knowledge (*Samyag Jyāna*) are made basic to right conduct (*Samyag Cāritra*). The ideal conceived is the supreme happiness of all creatures.

Jain logic gives us the distinctive theory of the manyness of reality and the difference of viewpoints, known as the *Anekāntavāda*. Every proposition is held to be only partially real or unreal or both real and unreal from different points of view. Jain logic, therefore, prefixes propositions with the *may be* or *Syad*. Knowledge is classified into five kinds, viz., *Mati* or perceptual knowledge, *Sruti* or scriptural, *Avadhi* or clairvoyant, *manahprayāya* or telepathic, and *Kevala Jyāna* or absolute knowledge.

7

A HISTORY OF PHILOSOPHICAL SYSTEMS

Buddhism

Buddhism, founded by Lord Buddha (563 B.C.), is the revolt of reason against the transcendentalism of the *Upaniṣads* and the excessive ritualism of the Vedic age. Early Buddhism was a gospel of hope though later it took a negative turn. Through self-effort and concrete moral goodness (*dharma*) the individual is advised to realize his spiritual nature and annihilate suffering. Buddhism, as it later asserted itself, can be summed up as follows:

Life is suffering. Suffering has a cause. This cause can be eliminated and there is way or *mārga* to the elimination of suffering. The cause of suffering is ignorance (*avidyā*), which consists in not knowing the nature of the Self as a composite of body (*rūpa*) and mind (*nāma*) and as ever-changing. All things including the Self are just aggregates (*Saṃghata*). Ignorance causes cravings (*tṛṣṇā*) which, being unsatisfied, cause rebirth. In *nirvāṇa*, (emancipation), the *nāma-rūpa* is completely annihilated. *Nirvāṇa*, or a state of serene composure, comes to the worthy (*arhan*) who has broken through the cycle of birth and death (*Saṃsāra*) by following the Eight-fold path of discipline stressing right conduct (*Śīla*), right knowledge (*Prajñā*), and right concentration (*Samādhī*).

The two schools of the *Hīnayāna* (lower) and the *Mahāyāna* (higher), into which Buddhism gradually split itself both entertain the theory of momentariness (*Kṣana-bhangvāda*). At every moment, everything is changing itself into something else, and identity is only an illusion. Even the Self is defined as a continuous succession of ideas. Facts of memory and moral responsibility can be explained by similarity which the different appearances of the Self bear to one another. External objects are, therefore, a series (*santāna*) of unique particulars. Universals are dismissed as ideal superimpositions upon the object. This refusal to admit unity and universality as real, is in direct opposition to Jainism.

Mahāyāna Buddhism is represented by two idealistic schools,—the *Yogācāras* and the *Mādhyamikas*.—The *Yogācāras* whose *Vijñāna-vāda* (theory of the sole reality of ideas) maintains that knowledge points to no objects beyond itself and explains an object (including the Self) as a mere series of ideas, resembles closely the modern subjective idealists. The *Mādhyamikas* who deny both the external objects and the Self are like the modern nihilists. The latter

A HISTORY OF PHILOSOPHICAL SYSTEMS

school is also called the *Śūnyavāda* or the doctrine of the void which, however, does grant a sort of reality to the subject and object and seems to suggest that the ultimate reality is called *Śūnya* because it is incomprehensible and not because it is non-existent.

In spite of common ethical practice, the ethical teaching, however, of the two schools is not the same in some respects. While the *Hīnayāna* scheme of individual perfection is virtually the same as in Canonical Buddhism, Mahāyāna Buddhism maintains that the ideal man or the Bodhisatta attains his own perfection through social channels.

The Six Systems

While later Indian thought seems to diverge from the original source and diversifies itself into a number of conflicting systems, it would, perhaps, not be correct to regard them as independent schools of thought. They are more in the nature of an elaboration of different aspects of the same thought. The six well-known systems of Indian philosophy are an amplification of the monistic, the dualistic and the pluralistic trends of the traditional Hindu thought. We shall briefly note them in convenient pairs.

The Nyāya-Vaiśeṣika

The two systems of the *Nyāya* and the *Vaiśeṣika* are generally summarized together. Their basic books are: the *Vaiśesika Sūtras* of Kaṇāda with the glossary by *Prasasta Pāda,* and the *Nyāya Sūtras* of Gautama with the commentary of *Vātsyāyna.* Gangesa in 1200 A.D. gave the system its prevailing logical character.

This system is both realistic and pluralistic. It acknowledges the external world as independently real and no other substances (*Dravyas*)—earth, water, air, fire, *akāsa,* space, time, self and manas —as ultimately real. Separate reality of universals (*Sāmānya*) of qualities (such as odor, sound, knowledge, *dharma, adharma, karma* or movement), *abhāva* (non-existence), and *Samavāya* (a relation of one sided dependence) are also fully recognized. The physical universe is conceived as consisting of numberless atoms—(inferred from the divisibility of objects) and the three all-pervading entities —*akasa,* space and time. Every atom is regarded as unique (*visesa*).

N.V. believes in the causal theory of origination or *ārmabha-vāda*, i.e., atomic aggregation can produce something new and distinct. It does not believe in the pre-existence of the effect in the cause (*Asat-kāryavāda*) as in the *S. Y.* system.

God is conceived only as an efficient cause, or the Being who manipulated the external atoms into creation. Individual selves vary in their past deeds or *Karma*. The world serves the dual rôle of enabling the individual to reap the fruits of his *karma* and also of freeing him from its shackles. The vast variety of the world is made to argue for God's infinite power and wisdom.

Reality of both Self and God is postulated on the basis of introspection and inference. The *Ātman*, or the individual self, is an eternal spiritual principle although psychically featureless. Knowledge or consciousness appears only when certain external features co-operate with the Self through the medium of the *manas* or the mind. The Selves are many and fundamentally distinct.

Nyāya-Vaisesika Epistemology

Nyāya-Vaisesika epistemology is as realistic as its metaphysics. It lays down four *Pramānas* as the valid means of knowledge. They are—(a) perception, (b) inference, (c) analogy, and (d) authority. Perception, it is said, reveals objects directly and inference indirectly. Knowledge is true if it works in practical life; the pragmatic criterion, however, constitutes only a test and not the essence of truth which lies in correspondence. Even error has an objective basis. A rope exists; it only appears as something different—a snake—in erroneous perception (*anyathā-Khyāti*). Side by side with this realistic epistemology, a transcendental (*alaukika*) form of perception which enables the Yogin to perceive atoms and moral merit (*dharma*) is also recognized.

Mokṣa or the ultimate end is conceived as the transcendence of pleasure and pain on the part of the self. This is, however, achieved only after death. Liberation consists in realizing that the Self is neither the body nor the *manas*. Right knowledge, detached living and meditation upon the ultimate truth (*Yoga*) are prescribed as means to liberation.

A HISTORY OF PHILOSOPHICAL SYSTEMS

The Sānkhya-Yoga

The two systems of the *Sānkhya* and the *Yoga,* founded many centuries before Christ by Kapila and Pātañjali respectively, are dualistic in thought, recognizing two independent, ultimate and eternal principles, *viz.,* the *Puruṣa* and the *Prakriti* as the transcendental essences of the conscious and the unconscious of our everyday life. While the system is dualistic, in its concept of the Puruṣa, it is a bulwark of idealism. *Puruṣa* is regarded as pure spirit, inactive and unchanging, while *Prakriti* is unconscious, active and everchanging. The system is, however, not free from the difficulties of a satisfactory relationship between the two mutually exclusive and independent principles.

The everchanging and the primordial *Prakriti* which modifies itself into twenty-four evolutions of increasing grossness, along with the unchanging *Puruṣa* constitute the matrix of our universe. *Prakriti's* modifications are successively the *mahat, buddhi* (mind), and the *Ahankāra* (principle of individuation), from which are derived the five fine elements (*Tanmātras*) and the five gross elements of ether, air, light, water and earth, which, in turn, give us the ten senses and the *manas.* Evolution is regarded as *Prakriti's* self-modification for the sake of *Puruṣa.* The evolutions of the *Prakriti* are regarded as potentially present in the cause; for nothing new can really be produced. This theory of the potential presence of the effect in the cause is known as *Satkāryavāda.* Though the system recognizes just one ultimate spiritual principle, it somehow provides for many selves or individual *Jīvas* also. The *Jīvas* are the results of the *Puruṣa's* contact with *Ahankāra* and the *ling-śarīra* or the subtle body. It is the *Jīva* that needs liberation from suffering. The *Puruṣa,* linked only temporarily with *Prakriti,* is ever free. Knowledge involves the *jīva,* the object, and the activity of the internal organ (*antahkarana*) which links the illumining *Puruṣa* with the object. Thus objects are only mediately known. Highest knowledge, called the *Viveka-jnāna,* is intuitive and consists in a clear discrimination of the *Puruṣa* from the *Prakriti.*

Yoga here means the discipline required for the restoration of the original and free status of the individual Self, *Viyoga* or separation of the *Jīva* from the true self being regarded as the prime cause of suffering.

To the *Sānkhya* aim of discrimination (*viveka*) between *Puruṣa* and *Prakriti*, the Yoga adds an eight-fold psycho-physical discipline for the re-attainment of the *Puruṣa's* originally pure nature (experienced in the state of *asamprajnāta Samādhi*). This means complete transcendence of life's suffering whether psychological (*Ādhyātmika*), environmental (*Ādhibhautika*) or supernaturally-induced (*Ādhidaivika*).

God is rejected on grounds of logic and life's sufferings, though Yoga admits Him as an aid to spiritual realization. In fine, *Sānkhya-Yoga* is an exalted idealism without theistic implications wherein the wonderful harmony of the *Puruṣa* and the *Prakriti* are supposed to discharge the functions of God.

The Mīmāmsā

Mīmāmsā, literally meaning systematic investigation, stresses reflection or *vicāra*. The *Pūrva* and the *Uttar mīmāmsā* are based upon the *Brāhmaṇas* and the *Upaniṣads* respectively. The earliest literature of the *Pūrva mīmāmsā* known as Jaimini's *Sūtra* (about 300-200 B. C.) has been interpreted differently by Kumārila Bhatt and Prabhākar Miṣra. *Mīmāmsā* believes in plurality of souls and material ultimates and is both pluralistic and realistic.

The *Mīmāmsā* envisages a vague kind of modified pluralism inasmuch as Reality is described as "identity in difference." Five categories, *i.e.*, substance, quality, action, universals and non-existence are admitted. The Self is regarded as all-pervading and eternal. Two kinds of universals, abstract and concrete, are recognized. Otherwise, the categories are generally conceived in the *Nyāya-Vaiśeṣika* fashion.

Mīmāmsā has some notable contributions to make in the field of epistemology. The Self is supposed to be known in all knowledge although only as an object. For instance, in "I see a table" both the "I-notion" and the "table-notion" are apprehended. Knowledge is a changing activity of the Self which, in knowing, manifests itself as well as the object. Objects are known directly; the Self, indirectly. According to *Mīmāmsā* epistemology, all knowledge is intrinsically valid; all error is either due to outside interference in the apparatus of knowing or to conflict with another bit of knowledge. Prabhākara attributes error to some omission (*akhyāti*) and Kumārila, to commission (*Khyāti*).

According to *Mīmāmsā*, mere knowledge (*jyāna*) does not lead to *Mokṣa* without detached performance of duty (*Karma*). The Vedas, it is maintained, determine *dharma* (religious duties). *Sanyāsa* or retirement from life is not prescribed; performance of Vedic rites is deemed capable of achieving the cherished goal. In short, the *Mīmāmsā* discipline consists in doing the obligatory deeds and avoiding the prohibited ones which are the direct cause of birth and suffering.

The Vedānta (*Absolutistic*)

The *Uttar Mīmāmsā* or the *Vedānta*, as it is popularly known, is the *Upaniṣads* systematized, and represents the cream of Indian thought. The *Upaniṣads*, the *Bhagvad Gītā* and the *Sūtras* of *Bādarayaṇa* form the base of the *Vedānta*. It may be classified as absolutistic representing Brahman or the ultimate reality as an impersonal principle, and theistic or representing the ultimate Reality as a personal God. The Absolutistic Advaita is represented by Śankara while the theistic type is represented by Rāmānuja and Mādhva.

Śankara (788-820 A.D.) maintained that the *Upaniṣads* really teach unity, their inclusion of diversity being only expository. The real, he held, is one, eternal and of the essence of pure '*cit*' called the Brahman. The Absolute is changeless. The change attributed to the *Brahman* and the world is only apparent. Nothing else is. Yet the *Brahman* is not always realized as such. Thus something other than the *Brahman* also is; *i.e.*, the world also appears, but it is illusory as it is neither real nor unreal. It is of the nature of the "serpent in the rope" which is neither existent nor non-existent. The Absolute appears as the world just as the rope appears as a serpent. Thus the world has another kind of reality though not the absolute reality. The Absolute appears not only as the world but also as the individual Self. This is due to the delimiting adjuncts of the Self like the internal organ (*antah-karaṇa*) and the rest. The true Self is to be seen shorn of its conditionings. Just as one light appears different through different shades, even so the individual Self, when seen *sub*-

specie aeternitatis, is Brahman itself. Thus *Brahman* alone appears both as the objective universe and as the individual Self.

The Māyā

The appearance of the world and the plurality of the individual selves—if these are appearances—have to be adequately explained. This is done by the concept of *Māyā*—or the principle of Nescience. The existence of *Avidyā* in ourselves cannot be denied. As *Avidyā* dissolves and true *Vidyā* or the knowledge of the *Brahman* dawns, the Brahman is more and more revealed. On a complete realization of true knowledge, nothing remains but the *Brahman*. Not only is the world and the plurality of the selves destroyed but along with it *Avidyā* also disappears. *Māyā* also is both real and unreal, *i.e.,* it is practically real but ultimately unreal. That is why it is called *Anirvacanīya* or indescribable. This admission of the principle of *Māyā* in *Advaita Vedānta* has evoked persistent objections from non-*Advaitic* systems, but the *Advaitists* have never regarded it as a vulnerable point in their metaphysics.

Advaita, however, is not subjectivism, for according to Advaita epistemology, all knowledge points to an object beyond it. Even error has an objective counterpart. The appearance of the snake in the rope is not real, but it is not wholly unreal either, or else it could not appear at all. Error is thus the apprehension of that which is neither being nor non-being hence it is inexpressible *anirvacanīya*. Ultimate truth is not only coherent, but also all-comprehensive. "All this, verily, is *Brahman*." (*Sarvam khalvidam Brahma*). Man's ultimate aim is to know that he himself is *Brahman*. The ego is a blend of the Self and the non-Self. Any objectification of the Self is *Avidyā* or the individual's share of *Māyā*. To know oneself as Brahman and as completely dissociated from the non-self is true knowledge and Man's complete emancipation.

Vedānta-Theistic

As if by a natural rebound against the Absolutism of Śankara, the theistic tendencies of *Śaivism* and *Vaiṣnavism* tried to reassert themselves and in the *Viśiṣṭādvaita* of Rāmānuja (1100 A. D.) we find a powerful attempt to synthesize *Vaiśnavism* with *Vedānta*.

The effort is embodied in Rāmānuja's commentaries on the *Vedānta-Sūtra* and the *Gītā*.

The world and the soul, says Rāmānuja, are to the *Brahman* what the body is to the soul. Neither can exist nor be conceived without Him (*Aprathak-Siddhi*). In the *Upaniṣads*, it is contended that all the three are distinct and eternal, though of unequal status and inseparably associated. The one Brahman, however, informs and sustains both Matter and Soul: hence monism (*advaita*). The embodied is one: the embodying, many: hence qualified monism (*Viśistādvaita*).

In theistic *Advaita, Prakriti, Jīva* and God are conceived as important substances. Out of *Prakriti* whose nature and evolution is conceived largely in the *Sāmkhya-Yoga* fashion, the world evolves under the guidance of God. But the world is an adjunct, and not a transformation of Him. Though atomic, the Jīva can perceive far-off things because it possesses "attributive intelligence (*dharmabhūta-jnāna*, also attributed to God). It is essentially sentient and self-revealing. The souls are intrinsically happy: only past deeds (*karma*) compel them to transmigration and suffering. God is self-existent, all-knowing and all-powerful. He is the sole unchanging cause of the universe.

Knowledge, it is maintained, always reveals a complex object. Hence the falsity of conceiving *Brahman* as *Nirguṇa* or featureless. Knowledge is necessarily true, even erroneous apprehension being true so far as it goes.

The end of life is to attain to the perfectly free and blissful world of *Nārāyana*. *Prapatti* or complete self-surrender to Him, and *Bhakti*, or loving meditation based upon highest knowledge, are the means to it.

The Dvaita

This doctrine, like *Viśistādvaita*, is theistic and identifies God with *Nārāyan* or *Vishnu*. But it is more explicitly pluralistic inasmuch as individual souls and physical objects are both treated as distinct from one another. *Bheda* or uniqueness, according to this system, is manifold. There is a difference between God and Soul, between the different Souls, between Soul and Matter, and between the discrete material objects. The majesty of God is taken as the basis of His being distinct from the world which He completely controls. God is the only independent entity recognized: hence It is no ordinary pluralism. He is conceived as the all-controlling personality. The evolution of *Prakriti,* conceived as the ultimate source of the physical world, is explained through the theory of *Sadāsat-Kārya-Vāda,*—that before its production, the effect is both existent and non-existent in the cause.

Knowledge, it is maintained, is due to a transformation of the internal organ (*manas*) and not of the self. All knowledge, even erroneous, points to an object beyond itself. Truth is correspondence with outer reality or the apprehension of an object just as it is (*Yathārtha-Vāda*).

The aim of life is described as the dispelling of ignorance (*avidyā*) which obscures the true nature of the Self and God. When that is achieved, life is all bliss, although it is strictly proportionate to the intrinsic worth of each self. The means recommended for the attainment of this state of perfect bliss are the knowledge of God from scriptures and *Bhakti* or love of God, which in turn leads to Grace (*prasāda*), the crowning cause of Salvation.

Conclusion

A survey of India's philosophy, however rapid, will show that in spite of occasional lapses into inconsequential dialectic subtleties, the constant aim has been to interpret life in the concrete and to find basic means for the deliverance of man from the ills of life. This deliverance lies in the realization of the spiritual nature of man and the unity of all life. "No other path is known to the sages." This Indian emphasis on *Mokasa* as the ultimate goal of life has often been misunderstood in the West, and Indian philosophy has consequently been accused of being other-worldly and its ethics as world-negating. Nothing could be farther from the truth, for there is no other world. There is only one world—the world of the spirit and there is just one way or *Marga*—the way of *Dharma*. Hindu philosophy, therefore, seeks to attain here and now the highest perfection. It emphasizes that human aspirations should be based upon the fundamental principles of *Dharma,* wherein one's good does not clash with the good of another.

The story would be incomplete without a reference in these

modern times to *Brahmo Samaj,* founded by Ram Mohan Roy
(1772-1833), which sought to revitalize Indian society with the
age-old principle of Vedic unity; the *Arya Samaj,* founded by
Swami Dayananda (1824-1883), reorienting the Hindu faith on the
basis of Vedas philosophically interpreted; Sri Ramakrishna Paramahamsa (1836-1886), who, speaking from the depths of realization, stressed the divine solicitude for man and his illustrious disciple,
Swami Vivekananda (1863-1902), who first transplanted Indian
spirituality on Western soil; Sri Aurobindo Ghosh (1872-) whose
poetical profundity is reminiscent of the Vedic seers and whose
message of a synthetic integral *yoga* has opened up fresh possibilities
of harmonizing man's varied experience; and finally to Sri Ramana
Maharishi (1891-), whose very existence is a demonstrable
transcendence of Space and Time and a living equation of the
Ātman with the Brahman. In most of these men the Vedantic
temper prevails. If the Vedantic principle of the fundamental oneness of life—as was so admirably pursued by Gandhiji in his daily
life—becomes the basis of our conduct, the much coveted peace may
yet be within our reach. This is, as Tagore said, the quintessence
of India's spiritual philosophy, *Sāntam, Sivam, Advaitam* (Peace,
Goodness and Unity of all beings).

BIBLIOGRAPHY

I

Aitareya Upaniṣad
Brahma Sūtra of *Bādarāyana*
Brahma Sūtra Bhāsya—Śankarāchārya
Brhadāranyana Upaniṣad
Bhagavad Gītā—Sankara Bhāsya
Chāndogya Upaniṣad
Iśa Upaniṣad
Kona Upaniṣad
Katha Upaniṣad
Mīmāmsā Sūtra—Jaimini
Māndukyopanisad—Sānkara bhāśya
Mundaka Upaniṣad
Nyāya Bhāśya—Vātsāyana
Nyāya Sūtra—Gautama
Praśna Upaniṣad

A HISTORY OF PHILOSOPHICAL SYSTEMS

Rāmānuja bhāsya on Brahma Sūtra
Sābara Bhāsya on Jaimini Sūtra
Sānkhyapravacana Sūtra—Kapila
Sankhya Kārikā—Isvara Krana
Sloka Vārttikā—Kumārila
Taittirīya Upaniṣad
Vaiśesika Sūtra—Kanāda
Yoga Sūtra—Patanjali
Yoga Bhāśya—Vyāsa

II

S. Das Gupta, *A History of Indian Philosophy*, 3 vols. (London, 1932).
———, *Indian Idealism* (Cambridge, 1933).
S. Radhakrishnan, *Indian Philosophy*, 2 vols. (New York, 1927).
———, *Eastern Religions and Western Thought*.
M. Hiviyanna, *Outlines of Indian Philosophy* (London, 1932).
A. A. Macdonell, *India's Past* (Oxford, 1922).
R. D. Ranade, *A Constructive Survey of Upanisadic Philosophy* (Poona, 1926).
S. C. Chakravartty, *The Philosophy of the Upaniśads* (Calcutta, 1935).
Aurobindo Ghosh, *Essays on the Gita* (Calcutta, 1922).
Jagmanderlal Jaini, *Outlines of Jainism* (Cambridge, 1940).
Rhys-Davids, *Letters on the Origin and Growth of Religion as Illustrated by Buddhism* (London, 1906).
P. Deussen, *Religion and Philosophy of India* (Edinburgh, 1906).
———, *The Systems of the Vedanta*.
T. M. P. Mahadevan, *The Philosophy of Advaita* (London, 1938).
Various Authors, *Vedanta for the Western World* (London, 1948).
R. Guenon, *Man and his Becoming according to Vedanta* (London, 1945).
A. B. Shastri, *Post-Samkara Dialectics* (Calcutta, 1936).
Chatterji and Datta, *Introduction to Indian Philosophy* (Calcutta, 1939).
M. Hiviyanne, *Essentials of Indian Philosophy* (London).
R. Guenon, *Introduction to the Study of Hindu Doctrines* (1945).
J. Davies, *Hindu Philosophy* (London, 1894).
Ramakrishna Century Committee, *The Cultural Heritage of India*, Vol. I. (Calcutta).
Complete Works of Swami Vivekananda, 7 Vol. (Advaita Ashram, Mayavati, Himalayas, 1922).
Swami Nikhilananda, "Hindusim" in *Religion In The Twentieth Century* (New York, 1948), edited by Vergilius Ferm.
Shri Krishna Saksena, "Jainism" in above cited work edited by Vergilius Ferm.

CHAPTER TWO

ZOROASTRIAN PHILOSOPHY

IRACH J. S. TARAPOREWALA

ZOROASTER had been renowned throughout the ancient world of Greece and Rome as one of the greatest Sages of the world, and he was thus known to tradition all over Europe right up to the year 1771. In that year was published the first authentic translation of the Zoroastrian Scriptures by the Frenchman Anquetil du Perron.[1] Nearly a century and three quarters have passed since this first publication and during this period much solid work has been done by great and devoted scholars in interpreting these ancient writings scientifically and critically.

We need not go into the question of the date of Zarathushtra. (Throughout this essay I have used the Iranian name of the Prophet—ZARATHUSHTRA.) It is enough to state that he was contemporary with the Sages of the earliest Vedic Hymns of India. It is not the date that matters so much as the message that he gave to mankind. The Prophet of Ancient Iran was proclaiming the Eternal Truth (which has been proclaimed by all the Great Teachers and Saviours of Humanity). He speaks of the Eternal Laws of Life laid down since the Dawn of Creation. His is a message addressed to all mankind of every age and every clime and not merely to the people of Ancient Iran at a particular period of their history. On account of this message Zarathushtra has been reckoned among the Saviours of Humanity from remote antiquity, and, indeed, his message has a lesson for even our 20th century.

Of course there had been great Prophets and Teachers before Zarathushtra who had taught mankind the Eternal Law of God. As always happens in the history of every Prophet, human beings have exceedingly short memories. Religious Teachers teach us how to lead the true spiritual life, always a most difficult task. So human beings easily slip into ritualistic observances and ceremonial, which are ever so much easier to follow. And as time passes we notice that this message of Spiritual Life gradually gets more and more dim, and at the same time the name of the Teacher is more frequently invoked and with ever-growing vehemence. The net result is that men remember the Messenger but *forget the Message*. The ceremonial and ritual branch out variously and give rise to mutually warring factions. And priests find a satisfactory means of livelihood by multiplying the ceremonial.

Such was the state of "religion" in Iran just before the advent of Zarathushtra. Thinking men and women were distracted amidst the warring factions each upholding its own special deity as the only Redeemer. This confusion is very finely described in the opening verse of the First GĀTHĀ (Chant) of Zarathushtra, where distracted humanity (poetically named "the Soul of the Cow" or "the Soul of Mother-Earth") [2] approaches the Supreme Creator and complains to Him about the evils that encumber our Earth:

> To You the Soul of Mother-Earth complained:
> "Wherefore Ye gave me birth? Who fashioned me?
> Passion and rapine, outrage everywhere,
> And violence enmesh me all around;
> No other help than Yours I see, Ye Lords;
> Reveal to me a strong One who can save." [3]

The Supreme Lord thereupon asks the great "Angels" around Him if they could name any soul who could undertake this task. They are unable to do so and so the Lord Himself names ZARATHUSHTRA as the one person He would choose because he is "the only one who kept all Our Commands." After some hesitation the "Soul of Mother Earth" accepts this Saviour.

After this "Prologue in Heaven" the Prophet is born upon earth in the Royal Family of Iran, and he takes up the task and delivers his message—the message of the Eternal Law of God. This message is contained in the Five GĀTHĀS of Zarathushtra. These Five Gāthās (or Chants) constitute the oldest portion of Zoroastrian Scriptures and are rightly regarded as the fountain-head of Zoroastrian Religion. These Chants have to be interpreted in the light of their own contents. Unfortunately the earlier commentators have brought down the whole of this message to our earthly level, and so the Teaching has been interpreted as the fostering of agriculture and the care of cattle.[4] But we must not for a moment forget that the Gāthās are *spiritual* in their contents and are to be interpreted as such. "Read the things of the flesh with the eyes of the spirit, and not the things of the spirit with the eyes of flesh."

Fully realising the impossibility of reconciling the mutually hostile worshippers of the various Powers of Nature Zarathushtra swept them all aside as of secondary importance. He was well aware of the ancient Aryan tradition that saw "the One Reality" behind all these deities, the Supreme Being, whom "the wise call by many names." He therefore enjoined the worship of the One Supreme Lord and of none besides. That Supreme Being was called AHURĀ-MAZDĀ. This name is a *double* name. It signifies "the Lord of Life (and) the Lord of Creation," in other words the Supreme Lord of Spirit as well as of Matter. The so-called "dualism" of Zoroastrian Teaching is clearly seen in this double name of the Supreme. The dualism of Spirt and Matter is the basic fact in our world. The Prophet has recognised this basic fact and at the same time he has recognised that *both* (Spirit and Matter) have come from the One Source, had One Creator. The Supreme Ahurā-Mazdā creates and sustains both Spirit and Matter.

Necessarily this Supreme Being is formless, and so must be intangible to any of our senses, and incomprehensible to our human mind. So Zarathushtra "revealed" (or explained) Him in His various "Aspects." The whole of his Gāthās revolve round the Prophet's teaching about the AMESHĀ-SPENTĀ (the "Holy Immortals"). They are not merely "personified attributes" of the Godhead (as many scholars have hitherto assumed them to be), neither may they be compared to the "Archangels" as understood in other religious systems. They are best understood as "Aspects" of the Supreme, or as "Rays" from the central Luminary. The greatness and depth of the Prophet's mind is evident from the names as well as from the arrangement of these "Holy Immortals." They are six in number, and the most remarkable point about them is that three of them are *masculine* in their nature and attributes and three are *feminine*. They represent respectively the Father-side and the Mother-side of the Godhead. What is more, these six together with the Supreme constitute a HEPTAD. In the Gāthās these Seven have been invoked more than once as *"the Mazdā-Ahurās* (in the *plural* number), thus emphasizing the fact that they all are "Aspects" of the same Supreme Lord. In several of the later Texts it has been clearly stated that these Seven are ever "of one accord" and that their "thoughts and words and deeds are identical." The three Holy Immortals on the Father-side have been described in great detail by the Prophet in his Gāthās. This helps the ordinary human being to understand clearly and correctly the essential "Aspects" of the Supreme.

There has also existed a very ancient "Sacred Verse," which tradition says is pre-Zoroastrian.[5] This verse has been regarded as the most sacred in all Zoroastrian Scriptures. In it the three "aspects" of the Father-side have been mentioned by name. This verse is famous by the name AHUNA-VAIRYA. The First Gāthā of Zarathushtra is a sort of detailed explanation of this Sacred Verse and it is named Gāthā AHUNAVAITI in consequence.

The first "Aspect" or "Ray" of Ahurā-Mazdā is named ASHA. This name has been translated as "Righteousness." It has to be understood in the higher spiritual sense as used by Jesus in his "Sermon on the Mount." The name implies TRUTH, the ETERNAL LAW OF GOD. Truth is assuredly an "aspect" of God, when one realizes Truth one would also know what God is. Lord Tennyson in the last stanza of his great poem *In Memoriam* has spoken of

> That God, which always lives and loves,
> One God, one law, one element,
> And one far-off divine event
> To which the whole creation moves.

This is very close to the idea of Asha as given by Zarathushtra.

Asha, therefore, stands for Truth, which is indeed God Himself. To search for Truth, to strive to realize it, is one of the ways to approach God. In one of the later Texts (which orthodox Zoroastrians recite at dawn) the aspirant prays: "Through the Supreme Truth, through the Highest Truth, may we catch a glimpse of Thee, may we come near to Thee, may we be in union with Thee." This indicates the "one far-off divine event, to which the whole creation moves."

A HISTORY OF PHILOSOPHICAL SYSTEMS

ASHA VAHISHTA (the Supreme Truth) is also the name given to the Sacred Fire, which is kept ever-burning in Zoroastrian Fire-Temples. Nowhere in the Avesta Texts is the Fire (ĀTAR) to be understood in the sense of physical fire. It is always the Inner Fire of the Supreme (the "Son of Ahurā-Mazdā") found in the heart of every human being. The Gāthā is quite clear on this point:

> Thine Inner Fire, Ahurā, to see
> We yearn;—He blazes mightily through Truth,
> He has Thy Strength; our Goal and Hope is He;
> He lights the Faithful clearly through Life,
> But, Mazdā, in the hearts of Infidels
> He sees the hidden evil at a glance.

The Fire in the Fire-Temples represents also the Divine Spark within each human being, a Spark of the Great Fire, who is God Himself.

The realization of Asha demands the pursuit of Spiritual Knowledge, and in the Gāthās very often the name also implies the "Path of Knowledge." It is a strenuous pursuit, demanding one-pointed devotion.

The second "Aspect" or "Ray" of Ahurā-Mazdā is VOHU-MANŌ. The name is usually translated as "Good Mind," but that seems to miss the essential point. There is an obsolete Aryan verb, *vas-*, to love,[6] from which is derived the first half of the name (*Vohu*). In later Texts the word *vohu* does mean "good." But in the Gāthās it does not necessarily imply mere "goodness." The rendering "Good Mind" is somewhat colorless, but "Loving Mind" is something far more definite. Vohu-Manō is, in short, the LOVE "aspect" of the Supreme. God *is* Love. In the very first prayer Zarathushtra utters in the Gāthās he expresses the wish:

> Fain would I, Mazdā-Ahurā to You
> Reach up through Vohu Man', devoted Love.

There are a few favoured souls amongst us, to whom "God has whispered in the ear," who can love the invisible, intangible God in the abstract. The average man, however, needs something visible, on which to pour out this love. The Love for God can be best expressed as Love for our Brother-Man. This is the fundamental teaching of all great religions.

As a matter of fact on reading the Gāthās we get the impression that the whole teaching is based on Vohu-Manō or Love. And it may be noted that in the later Texts Vohu-Manō definitely stands in the first place, immediately after Ahurā-Mazdā, though in the Gāthās Asha occupies that position.

Vohu-Manō implies not merely love of man, but his activity covers the whole of living creation. In later Theology his special province is the animal kingdom, particularly the creatures who are useful to man.[7]

The cultivation and the realization of Love is best possible in the lives of wedded pairs upon earth. Hence wedlock has always been regarded as *holy,* for it is the first step along the Path to God. In a later Text we read that a married person is dearer to Ahurā-Mazdā than an unmarried one. There is a beautiful verse in the Fifth Gāthā which brings out this ideal of wedded bliss: [8]

> These words I speak to maidens truly wed
> And to their comrades young; bear them in mind,
> And understand them deep within your Souls;
> Bring down Vohu-Man' in your lives on earth;
> Let each one strive the other to surpass
> In Asha's Truth, in Vohu-Manō's Love;
> Thus each one surely shall reap rich rewards.

In the later Texts this idea of Love seems to have developed in another direction. Zoroastrians are enjoined to recite their prayers five times a day. With each of the five divisions of the day [9] one "Lord" of a "social unit" is associated. These Lords are, in order: 1. Lord of the House; 2. Lord of the Village; 3. Lord of the Province; 4. Lord of the Country; and 5. the Supreme Teacher of Religion (Zarathushtra). These five Lords represent ever-widening circles of duties and love. The last—the Supreme Teacher (Zarathushtra) enfolds the whole of humanity in his loving embrace.

Realizing thus both Truth and Love, one is not to rest content with his own attainment. He has to translate the Truth and the Love he has attained into Action—into loving SERVICE of Humanity. That is the third "Aspect" of the Supreme—His KSHA-

A HISTORY OF PHILOSOPHICAL SYSTEMS

THRA. The name means "Power" or "Strength" of the Lord. This Strength is derived from the Lord Himself and is inspired by Love. Hence in the Gāthās the name Kshathra often has the adjective *Vohu* attached to it. The action or service done must be inspired by love. Such service brings as reward "the Kshathra of Ahurā" Himself. In other words the highest reward for service is power to render greater service.

Thus the Father-side of the Supreme is summed up in these three "Aspects." In human life these are best expressed by the three verbs—*to know, to love, to serve.*

The Mother-side also shows three "Holy Immortals," but in the Gāthās they are not treated in so much detail as the three on the Father-side. The first of the Mother-side is the most important as she is closely associated with Asha.

ĀRMAITI (usually translated "Piety") is the first "Aspect" on the Mother-side. Her name really implies "correct mental attitude." She represents firm, unshakeable FAITH in God's Eternal Law and Justice. She is implanted and dwells within the heart of each human being. She stands by and "resolves our doubts" as they arise. Zarathushtra admonishes us to keep our ears open to her whisper in our hearts. In later theology Ārmaiti represents the firm solid Earth, typical of the inner firm Faith which nothing can shake. The Zoroastrian, when initiated into the Faith, "chooses" Ārmaiti as guide through life. And after death the body is left in her loving arms and the soul passes into her protection.

The names of the remaining two "Holy Immortals"—HAURVATĀT and AMERETĀT—mean PERFECTION and IMMORTALITY. They represent the ultimate goal of human life and endeavour. These two are regarded as Twins, always together, because the attainment of Perfection must bring Immortality and the conquest of death. They represent the reward a man earns through his efforts to tread the Path of Asha. They bring as rewards "spiritual strength" and "life renewed," which are also regarded as the two precious gifts of Love.

Such is the wonderful and poetic Teaching about the Holy Immortals, through which Zarathushtra strives to give mankind some idea of the essential nature of the Supreme Power. We may sum up this Teaching thus: "Every human being must strive to understand the Eternal Law of Truth and Righteousness (Asha) and must try to realize it in his daily life. In order to do this he must cultivate Love—universal Love—(Vohu-Manō) and realize it deep within his Inner Self. This Truth and Love thus realized must be next translated into Acts of Service (Kshathra). All through one must hold fast to firm unshaken Faith (Ārmaiti)—Faith in the essential divinity and goodness of all creation. And thus one attains to Perfection and Immortality (Haurvatāt and Ameretāt), and becomes perfect as our Father in Heaven is perfect and conquers death.

Besides the Holy Immortals and the Fire, Zarathushtra has mentioned another "deity" in the Gāthās. He is SRAOSHA. The name signifies "Obedience" (to the will of the Supreme). In the Gāthās he is called "the Greatest Servant" of the Supreme. The Obedience here implied is not the blind and slavish obedience of the fanatic, but the *willing* obedience of the understanding mind. In later theology Sraosha ranks next after the Holy Immortals.

Zarathushtra emphatically maintains that each one of us must discover the Truth *for himself*. He has certainly claimed to be the Teacher appointed by Ahurā-Mazdā, but he has never said that a person should follow a particular course of life and conduct because *he* had said so. His own words are quite clear and precise:

> Hear with your ears the Highest Truths I preach,
> And with illumined minds weigh them with care,
> Before you choose which of two Paths to tread,
> *Deciding man by man, each one for each.*

This is the Charter of Spiritual Liberty for all mankind. Man is given absolute freedom in the choice of the Path he wants to tread, because he possesses the most precious gift of God—MIND—which enables him to distinguish Good from Evil.

The Problem of Good and Evil has been solved by Zarathushtra in a unique manner. And that constitutes Zarathushtra's greatest contribution to the religious thought of the world. His Teaching is best given in his own words:

> The First created were the Spirits Twain,
> As Twin Co-workers they reveal themselves,
> Yet in each thought and word and deed these Two

> Are ne'er agreed;—one's Good, the other Bad:
> And of these two the Wise do choose aright,
> The Unwise choose not thus—and go astray.
>
> And when together did the Spirits Twain
> Foregather at Creation's early dawn,
> LIFE did One make, the Other made NOT-LIFE;
> And thus Creation's purpose is achieved;
> Dark is the mind of those that cling to False,
> But brightly shines the mind that holds to Truth.

Zarathushtra has said in so many words that *both Good and Evil have been created by Mazdā*. The essential character of these Twin-Spirits is revealed in what they have "made"—LIFE and NOT-LIFE. The *negative* form of the latter is full of deep significance. The Evil Spirit is the Spirit of Eternal Negation. Goethe in his *Faust* has described Mephistopheles in words which might have been taken straight from the Gāthās. Mephistopheles is the Spirit that evermore denies. He claims as his own domain "all elements which ye Destruction, Sin or briefly Evil name." And further Mephistopheles says that he is "part of that power that still produceth good while ever scheming ill."

This is exactly what Zarathushtra has taught. The Plan of God is that ultimately every Soul shall attain Perfection and Immortality. But this is to be achieved *by each one's own effort*. And *the initial choice is left absolutely free to each human soul.*

This freedom of choice necessarily implies *full* responsibility for all one's thoughts and words and deeds. And here we find the LAWS OF KARMA (of Action and Reaction) stepping in. Zarathushtra calls them "the Laws of Happiness and Pain," because, as he has explained,

> Falsehood brings on age-long punishment,
> And Truth leads on to fuller, higher life.

The twin Spirits indicate the fundamental difference between Life and Matter (Not-Life), between things heavenly and things mundane. The Arch-Deluder (the Evil One) is ever at hand to delude mankind when their ears are filled with loud songs of the earth, which drown the whispering of Ārmaiti in their hearts. Lured by the Deluder, and blinded by earthly glitter, men become deaf to the call of Asha and of Vohu-Manō and dash away along the Path of Wrath and Hatred; [10] and thus do they "pollute our mortal life." But the inexorable Laws of Happiness and Pain never spare any one, for "none may deceive the Omnipotent Lord." After death Souls have to pass over the "Judgment-Bridge," where their earthly lives are reviewed and rewards and punishments meted out. There, at the "Judgment-Bridge," the Inner Selves of sinners "shall chide them as they fall." Punishment for evil is but the natural result of evil done—it is the Law of God. Evil does triumph very often for a time, but in the long run frustration awaits the follower of Untruth and all his triumphs are "brought to naught by Truth." From that moment shall his mind retrace its steps, for

> Then, Mazdā, Lord of All, Thy Law Supreme
> Shall be revealed to them by Vohu-Man',
> Then, O Ahurā, shall they learn, indeed,
> To give all Falsehood into Asha's hands.

Then, indeed, shall Love replace Wrath and Hatred in their hearts.

After years of frustration, tribulation and mental agony experienced in this "Abode of Untruth" (our earthly existence) the Soul at last learns the great lesson that Hatred is conquered by Love alone. Once that lesson is learnt the upward progress towards the Realm of Light, the Abode of Vohu-Manō, is assured. Thus even the worst sinner must, and ultimately does, attain Perfection and Immortality. There is hope for all; none shall be left out.

In India, as a natural corollary to this Law of Karma, the idea of reincarnation has been stressed. But no such stress on repeated lives on earth is found in any of the Zoroastrian Scriptures. In fact only one verse (out of 239) in the Gāthās, and, indeed, out of all the Avesta Texts, might be interpreted as speaking clearly of a return to this "Abode of Untruth." [11] So we may assert that the idea of repeated births upon earth is nowhere emphasized in any Zoroastrian Scriptures. This doctrine of rebirth, though quite logical and though undoubtedly very comforting in our moments of distress, still does certainly tend to make a person somewhat slack. One is apt to imagine that with several lives still to come there need not be any occasion for strenuous effort. Zarathushtra has all through laid great stress on *constant strenuous action*. In one of the Gāthā verses he says quite clearly: [12]

> Within the space of this ONE life on earth
> Perfection can be reached by fervent Souls,
> Ardent in zeal, sincere in their toil.

We can therefore conclude that we may *infer* the teaching about reincarnation from the other teachings of Zarathushtra, but the idea of rebirth is not at all emphasized anywhere in the Avesta Texts.

The Three Commandments of Zarathushtra—good thoughts, good words, good deeds—are often mentioned in the Gāthās. And of the three *deeds* are specially stressed:

> Who strives to understand and reach true Life,
> Should preach the Laws of Mazdā to mankind
> Better by acts of Service than by words.

As long as the high ideals of Zarathushtra's Gāthās remained a living inspiration to the nation, so long Iran continued to prosper; and she became the Mistress of the Ancient World. But as happens with every nation, in course of time these high ideals were forgotten. The prosperity following in the wake of a huge empire and the consequent riches that gather-in Iran led to the decay of Iranian character. The pure and vigorous teaching was gradually replaced by superstition and ritual. In the final phases of Zoroastrian Religion in Iran under the Sasanians (226-642 A.C.), the religion became full of complicated ritual and superstitious fear. This fear was perhaps necessary in preventing evil, but the Teaching of Love in the Gāthās was far superior, inasmuch as it *inspired good*. In later Zoroastrianism this fear has become an obsession. Human life from birth to death (and even beyond) meant an unceasing struggle against the demon hosts, and was regulated accordingly. This fear was the prime cause for the crumbling of the huge fabric of the Sasanian Empire at the first touch of the desert Arabs inspired by the fresh and vigorous gospel of Muhammad.

After the Arab conquest the "official religion" of Iran changed but not the spirit of the nation. The Arabs had conquered Iran but not her spirit. Islam became the "official faith" of Iran, but Iranian Islam was very different from Arabian Islam. The spirit of Iran blossomed forth in the wonderful mystic poetry of the Sufis, which reminds one of the teaching about Vohu-Manō as given by Zarathushtra.

The Zoroastrians who emigrated to India (over a thousand years ago) have until now continued to practise the customs and rituals of the Sasanian days. Until within living memory practically all the ancient rituals were observed and enforced rigorously. The impact of Western thought, however, has profoundly modified these old ideas of Sasanian days.

The Zoroastrians both in Iran and in India had stuck to the traditional Pahlavi interpretation of the ancient Avest Scriptures right up to the sixties of the last century, when the great Zoroastrian scholar, K. R. Cama, taught some of the learned priests of Bombay the critical and philological methods which he himself had learned from Western Iranists. Cama's labours helped considerably in removing many superstitions which had continued through many generations. Cama's pupils in their turn trained a new generation of scholars in India who have been working to reinterpret the Sacred Literature of their own religion in the light of the latest researches of Western scholars. Many of these younger scholars themselves have received training under Western masters. It is now established that the fountain-head and core of Zoroastrian Faith is certainly to be sought in the Gāthās of Zarathushtra. The labours of many scholars have enabled us to separate the original teaching of the Prophet from the later accretions that have grown up around it. Of course the majority of the Zoroastrians still cling to the old "orthodox" ways, but the younger people have begun to appreciate more and more clearly that the true teaching is to be found only in the Gāthās. A clear movement has been inaugurated emphasizing a return to the Gāthās, and in it lies the best hope for the future of Zoroastrians all over the world.

NOTES

1. *Le Zend-Avesta*, ouvrage de Zoroastre, traduit en Français sur l'original Zend, 3 vols. (1771).

A HISTORY OF PHILOSOPHICAL SYSTEMS

2. This is an ancient Aryan fancy. The same word (*gāv*) is used to indicate "cow" as well as "earth." The same imagery has also been employed extensively in the Scriptures of India.

3. This translation, as well as other verses given elsewhere, are from my book on *The Gāthās of Zarathushtra* (Text with a free English Translation) (Bombay, 1947).

4. This has been more or less the traditional interpretation of the Pahlavi commentators of the Sasanian days (3rd and 4th centuries of Christ). An interval of at least fifteen centuries separates these commentaries from the Prophet. This was long enough to have made the later writers forget the true inner significance of the Gāthās. And they naturally interpreted these ancient documents in the light of the beliefs they themselves held and the ritual and ceremonial they themselves followed.

5. Many scholars (notably Bartholomae) have thought that this "Sacred Verse" was composed after the time of Zarathushtra. I personally am inclined to hold the traditional view that it represents "the First Word of God."

6. This Aryan *vas*- remains unchanged in Sanskrit, but changes to *vah*- in the Avesta. The verb itself is not found in any text either of Iran or of India. Both several derivatives are known in both lands. In India the derivatives of the verb seem to have been "degraded" in sense, and there is an implication of "illicit attachment" in some of the derivatives.

7. On days sacred to Vohu-Manō (the 2nd, 12th, 14th and 21st of each month) orthodox Zoroastrians, though normally meat-eaters, abstain from flesh.

8. This verse is from the Fifth Gāthā, which has been regarded by many scholars to be a "Wedding Hymn."

9. The day of 24 hours, beginning at midnight.

10. Desire for the joys of earth leads a person to strive to gain them. When frustrated in this attempt, Wrath and Hatred arise in his heart against those who have thwarted him.

11 and 12. It would be fair to state here that other scholars have translated both these verses very differently.

BIBLIOGRAPHY

This is a short list meant for the general reader. Most of the books represent the views of older scholars.

C. BARTHOLOMAE, *Die Gatha's des Awesta* (Strassburg, 1905).
E. BENVENISTE, *The Persian Religion According to the Chief Greek Texts* (Paris, 1929).
S. D. BHARUCHA, *A Brief Sketch of Zoroastrian Religions and Customs* (Bombay, 1906).

A HISTORY OF PHILOSOPHICAL SYSTEMS

S. J. BULSARA, *The Religion of Zarathushtra* (Bombay).
M. N. DHALLA, *History of Zoroastrianism* (New York, 1938).
————, *Zoroastrian Civilization* (New York, 1922).
L. H. GRAY, *Foundations of Iranian Religion* (New York, 1929).
C. HUART, *Ancient Persia and Iranian Civilization* (New York, 1927).
A. V. W. JACKSON, *Zoroaster, the Prophet of Ancient Iran* (New York, 1899).
————, *Zoroastrian Studies* (New York, 1928).
H. LOMMEL, *Die Religion Zarathushtras nach dem Avesta dargestellt* (Tübingen, 1930).
A. MEILLET, *Trois Conferences sur les Gathas* (Paris, 1917).
J. J. MODI, *The Religious Ceremonies and Customs of the Parsis* (2nd ed. Bombay, 1937).
J. H. MOULTON, *Early Zoroastrianism* (London, 1913). This contains an English version of the German translation of Bartholomae.
H. S. NYBERG, *Die Religion des alten Irans* (Leipzig, 1938).
Sacred Books of the East Series—There are three volumes (iv, xxxi and xxxiii) of translations from Avesta Texts and five volumes (v, xxiv, xxviii, xxxvii and xlvi) of translations from Pahlavi Texts).
I. J. S. TARAPOREWALA, *A Few Daily Prayers from the Zarathushtrian Scriptures* (Bombay, 1939). The text is in Gujarati script with an English Translation and notes.
————, *The Gathas of Zarathushtra*. Text, in Roman script, with a Free English Translation (Bombay, 1947). (A larger edition with full grammatical and critical notes and a glossary is being printed.)
————, *The Religion of Zarathushtra* (Madras, 1938).
————, "Zoroastrianism" in *Religion In The Twentieth Century* (New York, 1948), edited by Vergilius Ferm.
A. S. WADIA, *The Message of Zoroaster* (London, 1912).

CHAPTER THREE

BUDDHIST PHILOSOPHICAL SYSTEMS

CLARENCE H. HAMILTON

BUDDHISM BEGAN as a religion, a way of salvation and deliverance, not as a philosophy. In the oldest literature its founder, Gotama Buddha (B.C. 563-483), is represented as taking note of the impermanence and misery of existence, seeking a way of release, and finding it in what are called the Four Noble Truths and the Noble Eightfold Path. "What have I specifically taught? I have taught of Ill, of its origin, of its cessation, and of the path that leads to cessation." [1] When asked by disciples whether the world is eternal or not eternal, finite or infinite; whether life and body are distinct entities; whether a truth-finder exists or does not exist after death, and how?—he set all such speculative questions aside "because they do not conduce to weariness with mundane things, to passionlessness, to purgation, to tranquillity, to insight, to full enlightenment and to Nirvāṇa." [2]

Gotama and his disciples lived, however, in an environment of religious and philosophical debate. Rivaling Indian teachers did discuss speculative questions. Converts coming from Brahmanism, Jainism and other disciplines could not divest themselves of intellectual problems, and later Buddhist teachers tended to deduce answers by reasoning from the basic postulates of Buddha's own early teachings. Moreover, exigencies of debate with non-Buddhists caused them to develop theories, psychological, cosmological and metaphysical, in addition to the ethical dogmas relating to deliverance from suffering. All professed their ideas to be consonant with the basic meaning of the founder. The variety of systems that unfolded with the passing centuries, however, shows that no one interpretation fully gained the field. Meanwhile each school of thought contributed some characteristic insight to the process of further reflection.

During the first three hundred years of Buddhism in India the community, according to common tradition, split into eighteen schools, each named for some particular doctrine or emphasis for which its members contended. Extant lists of these vary, but groups which eventually proved most important philosophically were four in number. Their positions attained clearest formulation later during the second, third and fourth centuries A.D. By name these groups are known as the Vaibhāṣikas, the Sautrāntikas, the Mādhyamikas (or alternatively Śūnyavādins) and the Vijñānavādins. The first two adhere more closely to the older conservative tradition in Buddhism called Hīnayāna or Little Vehicle (*i.e.*, Lesser Way of Salvation). The last two represent a more liberal speculative tendency of the Mahāyāna or Great Vehicle (*i.e.*, Great Way of Salvation) which arose during the first century A.D. Interest attaching to these systems of thought lies in the fact that they represent attempts by able thinkers to furnish theoretical basis for concepts which in the oldest Buddhist literature were axiomatic and taught dogmatically. If the Enlightened One taught the ultimate truth and way of salvation, as they believed, it was of utmost importance to understand his ideas thoroughly.

In its earliest forms Buddhist literature consisted of (1) Discourses (*Sūtras*) or Dialogues of the Buddha with his disciples, and (2) Rules of Discipline (*Vinaya*) laid down for his monastic community. In both Discourses and Rules of Discipline ideas are didactically expounded for purposes of simple practical instruction. On the basis of these, later scholastic reflection developed classifications of terms and debated meanings which in time gave rise to (3) Treatises, more definitely philosophical. The Treatises constitute the Abhidharma literature, to which class writings of the speculative schools belong.

At the outset we may note that in one respect our first two schools, the Vaibhāṣikas and Sautrāntikas, classify together. In main doctrine both are Sarvāstivādins, *i.e.*, those who hold to the proposition "All things are existent" (*śarvam asti*). This proposition arises from a difficulty with which reflection is faced in meditation on the principle of universal impermanence. Everything is transitory and perishing, Buddha had taught, and all ill arises from attachment to the impermanent; renounce the impermanent, therefore, and be at peace. But how is this to be understood? Does it mean that the realm of the existent is nothing but unreality and illusion, or does it apply only to things composite? The Sarvāstivādins chose the second alternative. They could accept the dictum "Decay is inherent in all component things," whether individual persons or outer objects, but they maintained that the elements or factors of existence which enter into compounds are ultimate realities, dynamic and effective in their action. In analysis the Sarvāstivādins detected no less than seventy-five of these ultimate factors (*dharmas*), the majority being material and mental elements, with some few, as in the case of space, being neither one nor the other. In these matters both Vaibhāṣikas and Sautrāntikas partake of the same tradition. Both agreed that understanding the elements of existence was essential to gaining final release from Ill.

Vaibhāṣika Philosophy

The character of their understanding, nevertheless, was different. The Vaibhāṣikas based their thinking on the Treatises (Abhidharma literature) of the Sarvāstivādin school, more especially upon a great commentary on this literature called the Vibhāṣa which was compiled, in the judgment of Louis de La Vallée Poussin, in the latter part of the second century A.D. Hence the name Vaibhāṣikas or adherents of the Vibhāṣa. On the other hand, the Sautrāntikas regarded as authoritative only the Discourses (*Sūtras*) of the same school, whence their name Adherents of the Sūtras (*i.e., Sautrāntikas*).

For the Vaibhāsikas the explanation of the universal transitoriness of things lies in the interactive relations between the elements of existence. On the material side are ultimate atoms which combine into molecules and larger aggregates. On the mental side are forty-six kinds of mental properties; some of which are present in all mental functions, good, bad or neutral; others which are present only in good states of mind; still others which are operative in undesirable or evil mental states. On this view, an individual person is a complex compound of physical and mental energies which are always in process, arising and passing away under the law of causation. What is called a person has no existence apart from the elements of personal life. The elements are real and discriminable, yet without root in any fundamental substance or self, and acting always under the control of strict causality in the world process.

This dynamic conception of real factors of existence in both world and individual led the Vaibhāṣikas to maintain the reality not only of present factors but of those of the past and future as well. Because the present is the result of former actions the past still exists as conditioning the present. Because present and past actions condition a conceivable future, the future exists as the coming result. This is the special interpretation which the Vaibhāṣikas give of the slogan that "everything exists." "Those who maintain that everything, past, future and present, exists are advocates of universal existence." [3]

Thus where Buddha himself had taught the doctrine of impermanence the Vaibhāṣikas by their analysis showed its source in the ceaseless operation of the elements of existence. But Buddha had also taught concerning the sorrow and suffering involved in existence and proclaimed a way of release. How is this to be understood? Here the Vaibhāṣikas point to the unrest and turmoil represented by the continual operation of the elements. Certain elements called *kleśas* or passions stain and defile other elements in the life process, giving rise to emotions of wrath, envy, jealousy, anguish, etc., and to harmful actions such as hypocrisy, deceit, trickery or arrogance. This is the problem set by the untamed restlessness of the energies of existence, which restlessness must somehow be suppressed and overcome if the stream of life is to become pure and calm.

Two ways of quieting the unrest are recognized. One is by understanding the character of the elements which are the components of personality. Such understanding can suppress the working of harmful and vicious elements. The second method is the practice of mystical concentration. This is thought to bring about cessation of the unrest of the remaining elements until the ultimate calm of Nirvāṇa is attained—an indefinable state no longer troubled by the world of existence.

A HISTORY OF PHILOSOPHICAL SYSTEMS

Sautrāntika Philosophy

In their rationalizing of Buddha's teaching the Sautrāntikas, in many respects, held ideas in common with the Vaibhāṣikas. At points, however, they differed markedly. Thus they opposed the Vaibhāṣika notion that past, present and future objects are all equally existent. They quoted sūtras to sustain the more common-sense view that past and future things may be thought about without thereby making them existent now. They also opposed the idea, taken for granted by the Vaibhāṣikas, that outer objects are perceived directly by the mind. Such objects are real and known, they held, but through a process of inference which is eventually validated by satisfactory dealing with the object.[4]

More important for the practical problem of deliverance from the painful unrest of existence is the Sautrāntika conception of the individual. The self is not some permanent metaphysical substance as commonly held, but a series (*samtāna*) of constantly changing states, born and perishing from moment to moment. Each of the successive states arises from a complex of causes in the previous elements of the series. Recognizing this momentariness, both in the flux of conscious states and in the appearances of outer objects, it is possible to become freed of the delusion of permanent entities and from attachment to them. Through attention to causes which bring on states that are right and good, the changing series which is the individual may be purified of evil moments and brought to the state of ultimate rest. It can be seen that in these two theories of (1) the self as a series, and of (2) momentariness (*kṣaṇika* = existing only for a moment) the Sautrāntikas give their reasoned explanations of Buddha's original dogmas of impermanence and suffering, and their conception of the process of deliverance.

In general, for both Vaibhāṣikas and Sautrāntikas we may say that in pure philosophy they represent an early attempt to think in terms of process and change instead of substance and fixity.

Mādhyamika Philosophy of the Void

The foregoing schools are Hīnayānist. With the Mādhyamikas we come to the first of the great systems of thought in the more freely developed Mahāyāna branch of Buddhism. This is largely due to the dialectical genius of Nāgārjuna who lived in the second century A.D. As early as the first century A.D. there were those who regarded Buddha's doctrine of impermanence as meaning the utter emptiness and unreality not only of composite things but also of all phenomena in whatever form. In the Perfection of Wisdom (*Prajñāpāramitā*) Sūtras and the Diamond-cutter (*Vajracchedika*) the view is asserted dogmatically and repetitiously, "All things are void." The affirmation is addressed to insight and not to reason, however, and it was Nāgārjuna who supplied the reasoned basis for the view.

The system derives its name from Buddha's original teaching that his doctrine represented a Middle (*madhyama*) Way between extremes, ethically between self-indulgence and asceticism, reflectively between all metaphysical alternatives. Nāgārjuna, however, was not content with a naive faith in metaphysical agnosticism. Using the weapon of dialectical logic he sought to prove that all things are necessarily void, empty of any metaphysical entity or substrate whatsoever. It is not merely because things are in state of continual flux as the older Buddhism had taught. It is because every particular determination whether of sensation, perception or thought can be shown by analysis to contain contradictions which make it impossible to accept it as finally real. On this basis Nāgārjuna finds illusory, not only the world of common experience, but also all the concepts by which earlier thinkers had sought to understand and explain the problem of life. With reasoned arguments against every alternative of thought he denies in his Mādhyamika Śāstra the validity of cause and effect, of past, present and future, of elements of existence (so important to the Hīnayānists), of origination, of passing away, of transmigration, of karma, of any essence of anything, and even of Nirvāṇa however conceived. Everything, in short, is empty of what is taken to be its own proper nature. Hence the basic proposition "All is śūnya (empty)" which gives the Mādhyamikas their second name of Śūnyavādins.

Such universal negativism, in the end, points beyond itself. Destructive dialectic may indeed shatter all determinations of sense and knowledge in conventional, relative experience. To that task Nāgārjuna chose to limit himself. But it does not finally exclude an intimation of transcendent or absolute truth. It simply shows how impossible it is to grasp the ultimate in the relative terms of existence.

Later philosophers of the school tended to give more recognition to the reality of ultimate truth, though admitting with Nāgārjuna that every particular conception of it is necessarily false. As Candrakīrti (7th century) put it, "the true nature of reality is not perceptible." [5] Śāntideva (latter half of the 7th century) while admitting that transcendent truth is beyond the domain of intelligence yet saw it more positively as the final reality in light of which the world of relative existence is but dream and illusion.

The Vijñānavādins

The second great school of Mahāyāna philosophy developed a more positive metaphysical conception. Here the names of two brothers are important. Asanga and Vasubandhu, according to Noël Péri and Louis de La Vallée Poussin, lived in the first half of the 4th century A.D. Of the two, Asanga the elder is more notable in religious expression, while Vasubandhu the younger is the more powerful in intellectual statement. Between them they expounded an impressive system of absolute idealism which remains to this day a subject of study in the Far East. They and their followers are called Vijñānavādins because they are those who say that the ultimate reality of all things is consciousness (*vijñāna*) only.

The school was not without antecedents. In some earlier scriptures, notably the Saṃdhinirmocana and Lankāvatāra Sūtras, the oldest parts of which go back to the third century A.D., idealistic utterances are found, though in brief, unsystematic form. Taking these germinal insights, Asanga and Vasubandhu expanded their interpretation with reasoned, systematic exposition.

As expressed in his work known as Mahāyāna-sūtrālamkāra, Asanga's thought takes its departure from the negative conclusions of the philosophy of the Void. With Nāgārjuna he recognizes the non-substantiality (*nairātmya*) and illusoriness of the world of phenomena, including both outer objects and inner self. This, however, is simply clearing the way for insight into the reality beyond, or better, within which these appearances occur. For this reality is the all-inclusive receptacle consciousness (*ālaya-vijñāna*) whose activity gives rise to everything. Phenomena are nothing but thought events, so to speak, taking place in universal consciousness. That consciousness is the ocean, of which phenomena are the waves. In its pure essence it is undifferentiated, without distinction of subject and object, self and other, and without discrimination of particular things. Attainment of the true Buddhist goal, therefore, which is enlightenment or Buddhahood, consists in realizing, as in the state of mystical concentration, the undifferentiated calm of pure consciousness in itself. For Asanga this is no isolated individualistic aim. He is eloquent in praise of the selfless compassion for all ignorant, suffering creatures which leads the enlightened ones to labor for the enlightenment of all. To that high end the Vijñānavādin will seek to rid himself of all passions, all obstructions of false notions, all illusions of particularity. For these are the sources, thinks Asanga, of the unrest and wandering amid the delusions of the world.

The younger brother gave Buddhistic idealism its completest intellectual statement. Vasubandhu was at first a Sarvāstivādin realist, writing an outstanding exposition of that philosophy in his Abhidharmakośa. After being converted to Asanga's view, however, he composed treatises to establish the conception that all phenomena, whether outer or inner, whether of subject (*ātman*) or of objects (*dharmas*) are mental representations (*vijñapti*) only. These treatises are in Twenty Stanzas (*Viṃśatikā*) and Thirty Stanzas (*Triṃśikā*) respectively, following the Indian practice of putting philosophical propositions into mnemonic verse for purposes of comment. They became famous in both India and the Far East, evoking numerous commentaries through the centuries of later Buddhist history.

In his Treatise in Twenty Stanzas Vasubandhu defended the proposition that "the three worlds (*i.e.*, the universe) are mental representations only." He answers objections of other thinkers, Budhist and non-Buddhist, shattering their arguments with a dialectical power worthy of the great Nāgārjuna. The conclusion reached is that the concept of representation-only (*vijñaptimātra*) is alone tenable, though to know it truly is possible only to those who attain Buddhahood.

In the Treatise in Thirty Stanzas Vasubandhu presents his positive conception. With Asanga he holds that everything emerges into the world of existence by development within the receptacle consciousness, but he analyzes the process to show how this is so.

In itself the all-inclusive consciousness is likened to a vast storehouse or granary containing "seeds" which are results of previous actions and potentialities of future actions. That is, it is the receiver of all effects, the source of all causes. As developing itself in action, however, the store-consciousness (*ālaya-vijñāna*) manifests itself, first as thinking (*manas*) which gives rise to the general distinction of subject and object, then specifically as the six kinds of consciousness by which the differentiated world of perceived objects appears. The six kinds are intellective consciousness (*mano-vijñāna*) which thinks intelligible objects, visual consciousness which beholds visible objects, auditory which hears the audible, olfactory which smells odors, gustatory which tastes flavors, and finally tactual consciousness which is aware of tangibles. All forms of consciousness are rooted, however, in the one basic consciousness of which they, together with their objects, are simply developments. Thus the vast world of perceived outer objects, spread out in space and time, and the world of inner subjective states discriminated by introspection, are both to be regarded as representations only. Thus the elements of existence (*dharmas*), regarded as real in the Hīnayāna systems, denied as unrealities by the Mādhyamikas, are now seen as active manifestations or functionings, not independent entities apart from consciousness.

After the time of Asanga and Vasubandhu their idealistic system of philosophy long remained a subject of study in India, especially at the University of Nālandā. When in the T'ang Dynasty the famous Chinese pilgrim-scholar Hsüan Tsang traveled and studied in India (A.D. 629-645) he found no less than ten important commentaries on Vasubandhu's Treatise in Thirty Stanzas. On returning to China he combined them in translation into one inclusive commentary called Ch'eng Wei Shih Lun (*i.e. Vijñaptimātratā-siddhi*) or Treatise Establishing Representation-Only. In the Far East this work has been studied by Buddhist scholars to our own day.

The Decline

After the four speculative schools described above had achieved their climactic formulations no comparable new lines of development appeared in Indian Buddhist philosophy. As great traditions the four schools continued to have representatives who debated their classic problems with one another and with non-Buddhist philosophers down to the twelfth century. Such advance as there was took place in the field of logic and the most able thinkers were primarily logicians. The great names are Dignāga, Dharmakīrti and Ratnakīrti. Their work falls in the fifth, seventh and tenth centuries respectively. By the twelfth century Buddhist philosophical activity had practically ceased in India and Hindu thinkers took over the field.

In China, Japan and Tibet the philosophical literature of both Hīnayāna and Mahāyāna Buddhism was translated gradually into the respective languages. This transferred the traditional debates into new settings but they went on largely in terms of problems connected with assimilating the older patterns of thought from India. New sects which arose were more creative in religious ideas and practice than in philosophy. Whether under impact of science and modern knowledge generally Buddhism will achieve some new synthesis of thought comparable to the systems of its creative past is a question which only the future can answer.

NOTES

1. Majjhima Nikāya, Sutta No. 63. Translated by Lord Chalmers in *Further Dialogues of the Buddha*. Vol. I, p. 307.
2. *Idem*, p. 306.
3. From Yaśomitra's Commentary on the Abhidharmakośa, as given in Th. Stcherbatsky's *Central Conception of Buddhism*, p. 78.
4. Dasgupta, *A History of Indian Philosophy*, Vol. I, p. 152.
5. R. Grousset, *Les Philosophies Indiennes*, Tome I, p. 314.

BIBLIOGRAPHY

SURENDRANATH DASGUPTA, *A History of Indian Philosophy*, Vol. I (Cambridge, 1922).
RENE GROUSSET, *Les Philosophies Indiennes* (Paris, 1931), 2 vols.
CLARENCE H. HAMILTON, *Wei Shih Er Shih Lun,* or The Treatise in Twenty Stanzas on Representation-Only by Vasubandhu. Tr. from the Chinese (New Haven, 1938).
A. BERRIEDALE KEITH, *Buddhist Philosophy in India and Ceylon* (Oxford, 1923).
ÉTIENNE LAMOTTE, Samdhinirmocana Sūtra (Paris, 1935).
WILLIAM M. MCGOVERN, *A Manual of Buddhist Philosophy* (London, 1923).

A HISTORY OF PHILOSOPHICAL SYSTEMS

Louis de La Vallée Poussin, *L'Abhidharmakośa de Vasubandhu.* Traduite et annotée (Paris, 1923–5), 3 vols.

―――, *Vijñaptimātratāsiddhi; La Siddhi de Hiuan-Tsang.* Traduite et annotée (Paris, 1928-9), 2 vols.

―――, *Le dogme et la philosophie du Bouddhisme* (Paris, 1930).

S. Radhakrishnan, *Indian Philosophy.* Vol. I (London, 1923).

Otto Rosenberg, *Die Probleme der Buddhistischen Philosophie* (Heidelberg, 1924).

Th. Stcherbatsky, *The Central Conception of Buddhism* (London, 1923).

Daisetz Teitaro Suzuki, *Studies in the Lankavatara Sutra* (London, 1930).

E. J. Thomas, *The History of Buddhist Thought* (London, 1933).

Yamakami Sogen, *Systems of Buddhistic Thought* (Calcutta, 1912).

Ananda Kentish Coomaraswamy, "Buddhism" in *Religion In The Twentieth Century* (New York, 1948), edited by Vergilius Ferm.

CHAPTER FOUR

CHINESE PHILOSOPHY
(CONFUCIANISM, MOISM, TAOISM, LEGALISM)

H. G. CREEL

THE CHINA into which Confucius (551-479 B.C.) was born stood at a low ebb in its history. Political decentralization was almost complete; not only were the feudal states independent of control by the king, but their rulers often had little authority within their own states. As a result, war and lawlessness were general. The traditional religion and ethics were in decline. The hereditary aristocrats oppressed the common people at will; their autocracy was believed to be justified by the fact that their ancestors were mighty spirits in heaven.

While Confucius may have had aristocratic forebears, he grew up in humble circumstances and had to earn his living, as a young man, at menial tasks. Thus he became well acquainted with the sufferings of the people, which he vowed to try to abolish. Preaching his doctrines, he attracted about himself a number of students, and thus became, it is believed, the first private teacher in Chinese history. Some of his disciples obtained important political posts, but although it was the life-long dream of Confucius to put his philosophy into practice, he was never given any office carrying real authority.

Confucius conceived the happiness of the whole people to be the end toward which all efforts should be directed. Thus he condemned needless war and denounced the oppressive actions of the aristocrats. While he did not demand that the hereditary rulers give up their thrones, he insisted that they should turn over the administration of their governments to men chosen, from the whole people, purely on the basis of their virtue and capacity, without regard to birth or wealth. In order that the best talents might become available for this purpose, he advocated that every person should be educated who was intelligent enough and industrious enough to profit by it.

The religion of Confucius consisted only of a faith that somewhere in the universe there is a power which is on the side of the right. He divorced ethics and politics from every kind of religious dogma. In fact, he did not treat any belief as beyond question, and was always ready to discuss his own views and admit they might be wrong. In education he did not emphasize the imparting of specific doctrines, but tried to equip his students to think for themselves. In his insistence that men's emotions must be educated as well as their intellects, he is at one with the most modern psychiatric theory.

Confucius has influenced every subsequent development in the history of Chinese thought. Yet not even Confucianism is identical with the philosophy of Confucius. Even his immediate disciples did not always understand him, and those who transmitted his teachings transmuted them, in some respects, as well. Confucius had been a reformer at heart, and a teacher only incidentally, but very soon most Confucians were primarily scholars and teachers, academic if not pedantic in character as well as in profession. The Master had taught that ceremonial forms are only "the outward and visible sign of an inward and spiritual grace," but very soon a large proportion of the Confucians were devoting their attention to the minutiae of ceremonial usages.

* * *

Mo Tzŭ (*c.* 480-*c.* 390 B.C.) studied with Confucians as a young man, but turned violently against Confucianism and founded a school of his own. He blamed the Confucians for their emphasis on ritual, and declared that the lavish funerals which they advocated would impoverish the whole people. In this respect he had a valid point, although it is clear that Confucius personally did not advocate such funerals. Mo Tzŭ also charged the Confucians with scepticism with regard to religion, and with believing that the spirits of the dead are not conscious beings. He denounced the Confucian emphasis on family ties, asserting that each individual should love all others equally. The Confucians preached a cosmopolitan sympathy, declaring that "all men are brothers," but they considered the family to be the cradle of ethics, and believed that in order to be a good citizen a man should first be a good son. Mo Tzŭ, however, advocated "universal love," which should embrace every human being whatever without the slightest difference of degree. This has sometimes been compared with Christian love, but there is a distinction in that Mo Tzŭ's "universal love" appears to be purely intellectual, without any emotional element. Rather than appealing to emotion, Mo Tzŭ seems to have depended upon rational argument, to persuade men that it is to their mutual interest to love each other equally.

Like Confucius, Mo Tzŭ was tremendously concerned with the sufferings of the men and women around him. Since he lived in a part of China that was perennially a battleground, he was naturally concerned especially with the evil of war, which he attacked in several ways. One was his doctrine of universal love—"when the feudal lords love each other there will be no more war." Another was his argument that war is unprofitable, that in the long run the vanquished and the victor alike must lose far more than can be gained by any campaign. In case such persuasion should fail, he also made an extensive study of the tactics of defensive warfare and taught them to his disciples, seeking to strengthen the defense so greatly that successful offense would be impossible.

Mo Tzŭ declared "utility" to be the necessary justification of every course. In fact, his philosophy was no more utilitarian than the Confucian, but some of his ends were different. He believed these five goods to be especially desirable: enriching the country, increasing the population, bringing about good order, preventing aggressive war, and obtaining blessings from the spirits (the desire to increase the population probably stemmed from the fact that in Mo Tzŭ's day much of China was not overpopulated, but underpopulated). To attain these ends, Mo Tzŭ was willing to sacrifice almost everything else. Clothing, food, and shelter should be such as is necessary, but not in any respect gratifying to the senses. All must marry, whether they wish to or not, in order to increase the population. Nothing not useful in Mo Tzŭ's terms was to be tolerated. He particularly opposed music, since it required an expenditure of time and created nothing tangible. The Confucians laid great emphasis on music. Like Plato, they believed that the right sort of music could play an important rôle in the development of character; they also valued it as providing necessary relaxation. But Mo Tzŭ had no use for relaxation. Since music interfered with men's work, it must go.

To bring about good order, Mo Tzŭ advocated "identification with the superior." He believed that men had at first lived in an anarchic condition like Hobbes' "state of nature," from which the chief deity, Heaven, had rescued them by appointing an emperor. The emperor had chosen his subordinates, who had chosen their subordinates, and this process was followed until a whole hierarchy was established. Mo Tzŭ said that it was the duty of each subordinate wholly to identify his will with that of his superior, thinking precisely as the superior thought. At the same time, if the superior were in error, it was his subordinate's duty to remonstrate with him (there would seem to be some difficulty in harmonizing these two duties).

Thus while Confucius had divorced politics from metaphysics, and declared that the only valid title to a throne was solid achievement in promoting the welfare of the people, Mo Tzŭ reaffirmed the religious basis of sovereignty and bolstered the traditional doctrine of the almost absolute power of the ruler by philosophical argument. Yet Mo Tzŭ was quite as much interested in the welfare of the people, and opposed to despotism, as Confucius had been. Mo Tzŭ believed that despotism would be curbed by his principle that the emperor must, in his turn, identify himself with Heaven, thus acting only as Heaven wills. But how could one know what Heaven willed? By observing the phenomena of nature, Mo Tzŭ said. If Heaven was pleased with a ruler's conduct, then all his concerns would prosper. But if he acted wrongly, Heaven would show its displeasure by causing unseasonable weather, blighting his crops and herds, sending epidemics and hurricanes, and so forth. Mo Tzŭ's ideal state was, therefore, a theocracy, and he paid great attention to the various duties toward the spirits, such as sacrifice.

Mo Tzŭ organized his school, in accordance with his conception of the state, along strictly hierarchical lines; his was in fact the only philosophical group having a formal organization in ancient China. Mo Tzŭ disciplined his students severely, and demanded obedience of them even after they had gone out into the world as officials. His power as leader was handed down to a series of successors, who evidently held it for life; they are said to have wielded the power of life and death over their followers. We have only slight knowledge of the history of the school after Mo Tzŭ's time.

In the book called *Mo Tzŭ* chapters forty through forty-five are largely given over to the discussion of questions of a logical and dialectical nature; these are believed to have emanated from later Moists, rather than from Mo Tzŭ himself. It is true that Mo Tzŭ proposed certain tests to be applied to propositions, but in general he cannot be said to have been a very logical thinker. He argued, for instance, that fate cannot exist because "no one has ever seen fate or heard fate."

In its early centuries the Moist school flourished and was a principal rival of Confucianism. In a famous revolt against totalitarian rule in 209 B.C. both Confucians and Moists took part prominently, and we find the Moist mentioned as a group as late as the first century B.C. Shortly thereafter they disappear from sight, and interest in Mo Tzŭ has henceforth been virtually extinct except as it has been slightly revived in recent times.

Confucius is sometimes said to have been intent solely upon reviving the usages of antiquity. In fact, however, his concern with the past was neither so great nor so exclusive as it has been represented. But after his death the Confucians became more and more traditionally minded, and ascribed to the past a great many practices which were, in fact, what they hoped might be done in the future. It is improbable that any of these convenient traditions were consciously invented as willful deception, but there is no doubt that their usefulness caused them to multiply rapidly. Thus it was said that Yao and Shun had been two ideally virtuous emperors of remote antiquity, who had not transmitted their thrones to their sons, but instead had sought among all their subjects, no matter how humble, in order to appoint the most virtuous individual as heir. If we examine the literature from any time earlier than that of Confucius, however, there is no mention of such traditions, nor even of the names of Yao and Shun. But Mo Tzŭ, as a child of his age, believed thoroughly in these traditions, and considered them to be a sovereign guide for conduct. "Any doctrine," he said, "or any action that is in accord with those of the sage-kings [such as Yao and Shun] is to be practiced."

* * *

The same sentiments were voiced in almost the same words by Mencius (c. 390-c. 305 B. C.), who was an outspoken critic of Mo Tzŭ's teachings. After Confucius, Mencius is the most famous of all Confucians. In contrast to the near-poverty of Confucius, he traveled from feudal court to feudal court with a great retinue of attendants and disciples, and was supported by lavish gifts from the rulers. This was not because these nobles were deep students of philosophy, but because they were engaged in a vast struggle to determine which one of them might swallow up all of China into his domain and proclaim himself emperor. They hoped that philosophy could help them in this undertaking, and each of the philosophical schools claimed that it, and it alone, owned the secret of success. For this reason a large number of philosophers were maintained in luxury at the various courts.

Naturally, this did not promote humility among the philosophers. Mencius asserted that the worth of the scholar is greater than that of any ruler, and that one who is "benevolent, just, high-principled and faithful, and takes an unwearying joy in being good," has a kind of nobility more exalted than that of the most blue-blooded aristocrat. Paradoxically, and perhaps for personal reasons, Mencius at the same time had a great deal of respect for hereditary rank, and a sentimental interest in the institutions of feudalism. This fact is in part responsible for the statement which is frequently made that Confucianism as such championed feudalism, which would be difficult to prove in general terms.

Much more than in the case of Confucius, we have a relatively full account of the thought of Mencius; perhaps it is for this reason that his ideas seem more fully worked out. In his program for the renovation of the state he advocated beginning with such fundamentals as economic organization. Some of his economic measures, such as diversified farming and the conservation of natural resources, sound very modern. As a true Confucian, however, he believed that no material considerations were comparable in importance with moral values, and he went so far as to assert that a people who lived under a good government, and were instructed by the proper sort of education, would need nothing more than sharpened sticks to defeat the well-armed but unenlightened troops of a militaristic tyrant.

Mencius argued against the Moist position that action should be dictated by the motive of "utility" or "profit." Thus when a certain ruler asked for advice which would profit his state, Mencius pointed out that if each of the ruler's subjects took personal profit as his aim the state would be torn by dissension and the ruler's very life would be endangered. Yet Mencius was not really opposing a utilitarian ethics, but only warning against a narrow, personal, and immediate estimate of utility as opposed to a broad, social, and ultimate view of "enlightened self-interest."

The most celebrated of Mencius' doctrines is that man's nature is good, rather than being evil or morally indifferent. He declared that human nature "is endowed with feelings which impel it toward the good. That is why I call it good. If men do what is not good, the blame does not lie in the basic stuff of which they are constituted. All men have the feelings of sympathy, shame and dislike, reverence and respect, and recognition of right and wrong. These feelings give rise to the virtues of benevolence, righteousness, propriety, and wisdom. These virtues are not infused into me from without; they are part of the essential *me*."

Psychology played a very important part in the philosophy of Mencius. He himself admitted that his psychology was not easy to understand, and for us after two thousand years it is extremely difficult. There is no doubt, however, that it would reward much greater study than has yet been given to it; I. A. Richards has opined that "it is possible that Mencius anticipates some of the educative prescriptions of Freud." In man's mental constitution Mencius distinguished between *ch'i*, which we may very roughly identify as the emotional nature, and *chih*, which corresponds to the rational faculties. Mencius believed that the rational faculties must remain firmly in control of one's conduct, but at the same time that the emotions must not be repressed, but cultivated. This was a sharp difference with Mo Tzŭ, who had advocated that the emotions be "eliminated."

Mencius believed that to repress the emotions was both impossible and dangerous, for this leaves them uncultivated, lying in wait to assert themselves and overwhelm one in a crisis. Instead they should be recognized as a great potential force for good, if educated and properly channeled. Thus Mencius told rulers that their love for valor, wealth and sex were not evil, but capable of good. They should cultivate valor not in vainglorious wars, but in protecting their people. Their love of wealth should cause them to see that each of their subjects enjoyed an economic competence. Their love of sex should cause them to see to it that all of their people have the opportunity to marry and make a home.

Although men's natures are such as to predispose them to become good, Mencius recognized that environment causes some of them to become bad. It is necessary, therefore, that they be educated, and the content of this education should be the morality laid down by the sage-kings of old. Thus we get an emphasis on tradition and authority which diverges considerably from that of Confucius. At the same time, Mencius' belief in the goodness and completeness of man's original nature caused him to make some statements which remind us of the mysticism of the Taoists.

* * *

Taoism is the most enigmatic of all Chinese philosophies. Traditionally it has been supposed to have been founded by an individual known as Lao Tzŭ, an older contemporary of Confucius and the author of the work known either as the *Lao Tzŭ* or as the *Tao Tê Ching*. There is no mention of any such person, however, until we come to works written long after the time of Confucius. Furthermore, the book called *Lao Tzŭ* contains anachronisms which indicate that it can hardly have been written earlier than the time of Mencius, if that early, and shows variations which seem to rule out the possibility of a single author. Some critical scholars now believe that the person called Lao Tzŭ lived later than the time of Confucius, while others consider him a fictitious invention; few still accept the traditional view.

The other most famous Taoist, Chuang Tzŭ (*c.* 365-*c.* 290 B.C.), is believed to have been a real person although we know very little about him. The book called *Chuang Tzŭ*, however, shows a variety of style and a multiplicity of points of view which indicate that it contains writings by more than one author. Some scholars have tried to show that the *Lao Tzŭ* is an earlier work, and sets forth a more original type of Taoism, than the *Chuang Tzŭ*, while others would reverse this chronology. Both books are so composite, however, that either case is difficult to prove.

Taoism was in essence a revolt of the individual. The rulers tried to dominate and exploit their subjects for their own ends. The Confucians and the Moists sought to enlist men in a crusade against this exploitation. But the Taoist asserted the right of the individual to go his own way and live his own life as he pleased. It may be that Yang Chu (*c*. 395-*c*. 335 B.C.) was the first philosopher to take this position. Mencius said that Yang Chu had a great following, and that "though he might benefit the whole world merely by plucking out one of his hairs, he would refuse to do it." As fully developed, the doctrines of Taoism included elements from both Confucianism and Moism, despite the fact that they were its detested rivals. It has been alleged that it owes something to ideas imported from India, but while this appears possible it has not been clearly demonstrated.

The central concept of Taoism is that of "the Tao." For Confucius, the Tao was the right way of action, an exalted ideal. The Taoists, however, conceived the Tao to be the totality of all things, the absolute. It was the basic, undifferentiated stuff from which all things have been generated. The farther man gets away from this primal state, the less good and the less happy he is. The ideal, then, is to recognize one's oneness with the Tao, and to achieve the calm which comes from knowing that no matter what becomes of one he must remain, no matter how transformed, within the great totality of all things. One should therefore accord with, not rebel against, the laws of nature. *Wu wei,* "doing nothing," does not mean doing nothing at all, but not straining, doing nothing forced or unnatural. By following this course, the Taoists say, one actually accomplishes more. They use the illustration of an archer, who will carelessly display his best skill when nothing is at stake, but if offered a rich prize to hit the mark will become tense and nervous, and miss it.

They apply this doctrine to politics, and conclude that it is a mistake to try to govern men. "I have heard," the *Chuang Tzŭ* says, "of letting mankind alone, but not of governing mankind successfully." Men like the Confucians and Moists may sincerely wish to benefit the people, but their meddling will only make things worse.

This leaves us with an emphasis on self-knowledge and contentment for the individual, and with a political philosophy which is essentially anarchistic. The Taoist books excoriate martial vainglory and military exploits, and damn oppressive government no less violently than do the other philosophies. Above all they are sceptical of every dogma, sometimes even making fun of their own ideas. These elements would seem to constitute the proper essence of Taoism, and certainly it is they which have most deeply affected the

Chinese mind. The Taoist emphasis on man's oneness with nature has inspired Chinese art, and has given to the Chinese people much of the poise which has made it possible for their culture to endure. By its universal scepticism, its doctrine of the relativity of all values, and its magnificent insistence upon the worth of the individual, Taoism has contributed essential ingredients to the Chinese spirit.

There is another aspect of Taoism, however, which is in some respects logically incompatible with what we have considered thus far, and which would seem to be a perversion of the essential Taoism. It appears impossible to prove that it is a later addition, however, for we find it in the *Lao Tzŭ* and the *Chuang Tzŭ* mingled, almost inextricably, with the rest. This other aspect of Taoism probably originated in a breakdown of contentment. It is all very well to talk of being perfectly quiescent, being content with the lowest position in the world, caring nothing for the opinions of mankind, and so forth, but in fact human beings get tired of this. However, the Taoist reasoned, being absorbed in the Tao he could not be hurt because he recognized no hurt; one who cannot be hurt is impregnable; and one who is impregnable is more powerful than all of those who would hurt him. Thus the Taoist sage is the chief and the most powerful of all creatures, imbued with the majestic power of the Tao, the universe, itself. It is all very well to talk of anarchism, of letting all things go spontaneously, but when they get off the right track should not the omniscient sage put them back? Thus we read in the Taoist works of the methods by which one may "get control of the world," and how the Taoist sage should rule, "emptying the people's minds and filling their bellies, weakening their wills and strengthening their bones." Sometimes we are told that he treats the people as ruthlessly as do the powers of nature.

As Taoism became popular it was infused with a variety of popular superstitions. The *Chuang Tzŭ* claimed (quite without foundation) that Confucius had been converted to Taoism in his old age, and Taoism succeeded in infiltrating Confucian thought to a very considerable degree.

* * *

The last great Confucian thinker of the early period, Hsün Tzŭ (*c*. 300-*c*. 230 B.C.), was little influenced by Taoism and was explicit in his denunciation of superstition; he declared that rather than fearing omens and ghosts, men should be afraid of bad government and disorder. Hsün Tzŭ had perhaps the most incisive mind of all the Confucians, and in many directions he developed to fruitful conclusions theories which his predecessors had merely suggested. Yet Hsün Tzŭ could not, of course, escape the pressure of the circumstances of his day. He served as an administrative official of the government in a troubled age; this experience made it impossible for him to share the view of Mencius that men are by nature good. On the contrary, Hsün Tzŭ asserted that "the nature of man is evil; his goodness is only acquired training."

As the remedy for man's natural depravity, Hsün Tzŭ prescribed study, and by study he meant intensive application to certain prescribed books, or "classics." Confucius believed that mere book learning was useless, unless it were supplemented by independent critical thinking on the part of the student. But the easier method of dependence on the letter of books had been gaining ground, and in Hsün Tzŭ we find the tendency toward bibliolatry which has remained with Confucianism ever since. Undoubtedly Hsün Tzŭ as an official was attracted by the fact that the classics provided an authoritative standard which the government could use to maintain order. He specifically advocated government with a rather heavy hand, and it is not surprising that his two most famous students were Legalists.

The Legalists are so called because they emphasized the rôle of law and administrative apparatus in government. Confucius had insisted that men cannot be governed effectively by coercion, but only by means of education which makes them willing participants in the political process; this tended in the direction of democracy, and reflected the paramount concern of Confucius with the sufferings of the people. The Legalists, however, were primarily champions of the authority of the ruler, and were desirous of re-establishing the order which had been impaired by progressive decentralization. They lived, and their doctrines flourished, chiefly in states in the northwest, on the periphery of Chinese culture, where the autocratic authority of the prince had been relatively less challenged by the dangerous new doctrines. Although they opposed feudalism, as limiting the authority of the sovereign, they regarded with horror the idea that all men are essentially equal, and opposed the wide dissemination of education by the Confucians and others. They embraced much of Taoist metaphysics, and believed like the Taoists in "weakening the people's wills and strengthening their bones."

The Legalists did not compose an organized school. There is considerable divergence in emphasis between some of the books which are called Legalist, and considerable doubt of the authenticity of parts of them. Shang Yang (c. 390-338 B.C.), a scion of the ruling house of the state of Wei, held office in the far western state of Ch'in, where he reorganized the state along totalitarian lines and laid down some of the principles of Legalism. By economic reforms, by breaking up the unity of the patriarchal family, by offering rewards to make the people inform against each other, and by strengthening the army, he sought to mould Ch'in into a well-disciplined state capable of conquering all of China.

Han Fei Tzŭ (c. 280-233 B.C.) was the ablest of the Legalist philosophers. A member of the ruling house of the state of Han, he was a student of Hsün Tzŭ. Han Fei proposed a system of utter totalitarian despotism. His purpose was to make the ruler rich and powerful. According to his doctrines the people are to be used purely as means, and their good will is not of the slightest importance; a ruler should be neither oppressive nor benevolent. The ruler must hold all power himself, keeping his ministers and all his subjects in such fear that they will not dare to do wrong. Every individual must be compelled to live only for the state.

Another pupil of Hsün Tzŭ's, Li Ssŭ (c. 280-208 B.C.), assisted the ruler of Ch'in to conquer all of China and establish a totalitarian empire based on Legalist principles. Twelve years later both Confucians and Moists took part in a great revolt in which the Chinese people repudiated Legalism as the basic philosophy of government. Under the Han (B.C. 206-220 A.D.) there was elaborated the pattern of Chinese government which survived in its essentials until 1911. Although in large part Confucian, it bears clear traces of the influence of each of the other philosophies as well.

* * *

Of the four philosophies, only Confucianism and Taoism continued as definite schools. In addition to being deeply affected by popular superstitions, Taoism took over from Buddhism an elaborate apparatus of religious practices, priests, and temples. At some periods Taoism was the dominant influence at the Chinese court. Confucianism, though not unscathed, has suffered much less from the inroads of superstition. Despotic emperors have found its critical approach to political, social, and economic problems distasteful, and have tried to make it subservient to themselves, or to divert it into channels of innocuous pedantry. Yet such efforts have never been more than partially successful. During the early centuries of the Christian Era Confucianism was often overshadowed, as an intellectual discipline, by the logical and metaphysical complexities of Taoism, and, especially, Buddhism. In the Sung dynasty (960-1126 A.D.) this disadvantage was overcome by a group of philosophers of whom the most famous was the brilliant Chu Hsi (1130-1200). The "Neo-Confucianism" which they developed met the challenge of Buddhism by supplying the metaphysics and cosmology that had been absent from classical Confucianism, but retained its emphasis on the moral and political problems of this world.

BIBLIOGRAPHY

FUNG YU-LAN, *A History of Chinese Philosophy.* Tr. by Derk Bodde (Peiping, 1937).
E. R. HUGHES, *Chinese Philosophy in Classical Times* (New York and London, 1942).
ARTHUR WALEY, *Three Ways of Thought in Ancient China* (London, 1939).
———, tr., *The Analects of Confucius* (London, 1938).
———, *The Way and Its Power* (London, 1934).
JAMES LEGGE, tr., *The Chinese Classics.* Vol. I, *The Confucian Analects,* etc., Vol. II, *Mencius,* 2nd ed. rev. (Oxford, 1893-1895).
———, *The Texts of Taoism* (*Sacred Books of the East,* Vols. XXXIX-XL) (London, 1891).
H. G. CREEL, *Confucius, the Man and the Myth* (New York, 1949).
I. A. RICHARDS, *Mencius on the Mind* (London, 1932).
Y. P. MEI, tr., *The Ethical and Political Works of Motse* (London, 1929).
———, *Motse, the Neglected Rival of Confucius* (London, 1934).
H. H. DUBS, tr., *The Works of Hsüntze* (London, 1928).
———, *Hsüntze, the Moulder of Ancient Confucianism* (London, 1927).
J. J. L. DUYVENDAK, tr., *The Book of Lord Shang* (London, 1928).
DERK BODDE, *China's First Unifier* (Leiden, 1938).
J. P. BRUCE, tr., *The Philosophy of Human Nature by Chu Hsi* (London, 1922).
———, *Chu Hsi and His Masters* (London, 1923).
CHAN WING-TSIT, "Confucianism" in *Religion In The Twentieth Century* (New York, 1948), edited by Vergilius Ferm.

CHAPTER FIVE

ANCIENT JEWISH PHILOSOPHY

SAMUEL S. COHON

1. *The Law and the Prophets*

WHILE NO formal philosophy appeared in ancient Israel, philosophical reflection emerged as a function of religion. It was awakened through the wrestle of the national religion with the notions of Semitic paganism from which it broke away. Survivals in Genesis, in several Psalms, in Job and in the apocalypses of the Bible show that the mythological world-view of the Semites claimed the mind of Israel as well. The legends of creation, of the Garden of Eden, of the Flood, etc., were disengaged from the grosser elements of Babylonian mythology, and were recast in the mold of the advancing religion of Israel. Like the Babylonian so the Jewish thinkers sought to discover how the world came into existence, how death originated, why man is given to sin, how civilization began, etc. Their answers were fitted into the pattern of the national religion.

The channel of reflection, too, was religious. Revelation, while non-rational, discloses the partial application of intelligence to experience. The transformation of divination into prophecy was in itself a triumph of reason as well as of religion. Tests of true as distinguished from false prophecy, like those of Deuteronomy 13.1-3; Jeremiah 23.25 ff. and Ezekiel 33-34, derive from experience. Amos (*c.* 750 B.C.E.), for example, while speaking under divine compulsion rather than as an independent thinker, regards man's thought as divinely derived and advances a number of analogies to substantiate his claim. Direct appeals to reason appear in Jeremiah 10.2-16; Isaiah 40.26; and Psalm 94.8. The very nature of Yahwism as a covenant religion stimulated reflection. The prophets persistently demanded of their people that they put their confidence in the superiority of their God, with whom their fortunes were bound up, over all other deities, and strove to adduce reasons for their claims. The mind thus sought to justify its beliefs and to define their contents.

The greatest achievement of the prophets in the realm of religion, which has definite philosophical significance, is the doctrine of ethical monotheism. Unlike the Greek philosophers, who arrived at their theistic ideas through speculation on the multifariousness of nature, they discovered God's unity and uniqueness through their intuitive insights and moral experience.

Amos sees God operating in the world process and in the affairs of men. His justice, like a builder's plumbline, is applied to all nations, whether they be his own covenant people or their foes, punishing the cruel oppressors and those who disregard his laws of humanity. Righteousness, representing the will of Yahweh, reveals alike his character and the bond of his relation with men.

The universality of God's retributive justice is a fundamental conviction of all the prophets. Hosea (c. 740-735 B.C.E.) modified it by insisting that God tempers his justice with all-sustaining love (*Hesed*). Sinful men and nations can be restored to God's mercy by turning away from their evil ways and returning to God in wholehearted repentance. The reconciliation between God's grace and justice remained a permanent problem in Jewish theology.

The early presentations of God unhesitatingly use anthropomorphic terms. With the growing refinement of religious thought, they were used more guardedly as harmless poetic figures of speech, without which it is hardly possible to convey the idea of his personality. Isaiah (c. 738-700 B.C.E.) declares that God is spirit and not flesh. His angel choir sings of God's holiness, *i.e.*, of his mysteriousness and transcendence and also of his ethical nature. His glory fills the whole earth. The second commandment prohibits all sensuous presentation of him. While stressing that God's thoughts are not like man's thoughts nor his ways like man's ways, the Jewish thinkers continued to conceive of him as personal, exercising his will, his wisdom, and his might in the government of the affairs of men and in shaping the course of nature.

Ethical monotheism supplied a philosophy of history. In the light of God's retributive justice, Isaiah interprets the events of his day. The world conquering power of Assyria appeared to him as an instrument in the hands of God for executing punitive justice upon the wicked nations. With the completion of the task assigned to it, Assyria itself will come under God's judgment. History thus ceases to be a meaningless succession of events and assumes the form of an unfolding drama in which God is both the author and the leading actor. The nations and their leaders, while strutting on the world stage in boastful pride, are marionettes who move in accordance with the way in which the invisible hand pulls the strings. In the parable of the potter, Jeremiah (c. 626-585 B.C.E.) 18.1-11 represents God shaping the destinies of the nations as the potter molds the clay to fashion the vessels of his desire. When they fail of their missions, he subjects them to correction until they conform to the divine pattern of conduct. The goal to which all history moves is the establishment of God's kingdom on earth. This belief furnished the basis for the messianic hope.

The prophetic conception of God and of history furnished Deutero-Isaiah (6th century) with the answer to the riddle of existence and of national destiny. He views the world in terms of creation and purpose. The vast universe reveals to him the creative and ordering power of God. "Lift up your eyes on high, and see who created these." He displays a wisdom that is unsearchable. In the light of the prophet's insight, the idols of the nations, manufactured by craftsmen, fade into insignificant "nothings." Even the dualistic world-view of the Parsis is rejected as inadequate to account for the cosmic drama. One will dominates the entire process of existence and guides the history of the nations in ways that are unfathomable. God is the first and the last, and besides him there is no one comparable to him. He forms light and creates darkness. Good and evil derive from him. The creator of the earth also "gives breath to the people upon it, and spirit to those that walk in it." He summons the generations from of old, and charges Israel with the exalted mission of witnessing unto him before the nations of the earth, a task that involves suffering and perseverance, but calculated to bring salvation to all humanity.

The Priestly Code (c. 500 B.C.E.), which forms the framework of the Pentateuch, recasts the history of the world and of Israel from the standpoint of the cosmological conception of God. Its presentation of deity is less anthropomorphic than in the older documents of the Pentateuch. While he appears to men at important moments in history, no details of his likeness are ventured. He merely speaks and his word translates itself in visible forms of creation. By his fiat he called heaven and earth and all their hosts into being. Creation culminated in man who was fashioned in the divine image and entrusted with dominion over all other creatures. The kinship of the human race is emphasized, despite its many divisions. The Priestly writer traces the beginnings of the theocratic institutions of Israel, the Sabbath, circumcision, the tabernacle, the sacrifices, the priesthood, and the festivals. He pays strict regard to chronology and to genealogy and to the different names under which God revealed himself to the Patriarchs and to Moses. And he holds out the ideal to Israel to be a kingdom of priests and a holy people.

All thinkers of the Bible regard life as coming from God, and therefore possessing absolute value. While accepting the sovereignty of God as an unquestionable dogma, they held with equal firmness to the belief in man's freedom of choice. Life and death, weal and woe are set before him, and he must choose wisely that it may be well with him. This motive of ethical and spiritual conduct marks the thinking of the entire Deuteronomic school of writers.

Three important consequences followed the development of the doctrine of ethical monotheism. The nation, which formed the basis of all ancient thought and value, was purged of overweening pride and self-centeredness. The original idea of the chosen people was invested with spiritual value. Choice spelled consecration to a world mission. Instead of using God as the instrument of political power, Israel became the instrument of God, his servant people. Further, in the light of the ethical nature of God, the older idea of national responsibility was replaced, in the thought of Jeremiah and particularly of Ezekiel, with the doctrine of individual accountability for character and deeds. In addition, the advanced theology produced a purer form of worship. Instead of approaching God by means of magic, or seeking to win his favor through sacrifices, men were taught to consecrate themselves to him through righteous lives. While the sacrificial cult remained until the fall of the second Temple in 70 C. E., the center of gravity was shifted to ethical conduct as the most acceptable way of obeying God.

II. Wisdom Literature

A practical philosophy was developed by the sages of Israel. Unlike the prophets, they claimed no supernatural authority for their utterances. Occasionally they ventured to probe the mysteries of Providence, but their main concern was with human conduct and with righteousness; and their appeal was to reason, to conscience and to tradition. The chief medium of their instruction was the *Mashal*, the pointed, terse, self-evident and self-illustrated enunciation of truth. It was broader than the common variety of proverb. Instead of being "the coinage of the popular mint," it was the creation of literary artists for didactic purposes.

The book of Proverbs (compiled *c*. 4th century), the product of many minds and many ages, forms a manual of instruction in practical ethics covering almost every phase of personal and social conduct. Beside the maxims of common-sense prudence, seasoned with humorous and sarcastic turns, there are penetrating observations on human vices and virtues. They appeal not to the Jew as Jew, but to the Jew as man. The individual soul is made to mirror universal experience. National issues, ritual prescriptions, messianic hopes, and the condition of the soul after death find no room in their reflections. Their primary aim is to lay down universal precepts for rational living on earth. The religious philosophy which animates the sages is the conviction that man lives and moves in the presence of God, and that moral probity forms the most acceptable way of honoring him.

From "a prudence taught by observation of this world's laws," wisdom developed into the unfailing light by which man may guide his conduct so as to find favor in the eyes of his fellowmen and of God. Wisdom was further recognized as transcending human experience, constituting an attribute of God himself and figuring as his directing principle in the creation and preservation of the universe. The cosmical conception of wisdom reaches its climax in its personification as God's cherished companion from the beginning, and as man's surest and best guide (Proverbs 3.19-20; 8; 9). This idealization of wisdom sustains an affinity to Plato's theory of Ideas.

The *Mashal* in its most extended form appears in the book of Job, which was written about 400 B.C.E. This drama of the suffering soul forms one of the finest creations of the poetic genius and one of the most searching analyses of God's ways with men. A traditional hero of faith is utilized by the unknown author to examine the accepted dogma of monotheism that God's retributive justice operates along ethical lines, that goodness is rewarded with happiness and evil is punished by misery. Contrary to the comforting belief, he finds that gladness is not always the portion of the upright, nor life, prosperity and honor the lot of the lover of God. Through his personal experience, Job demonstrates not only the illusory character of the orthodox view, but also its utter uncharitableness.

Beginning with a plaint concerning his own misery, Job is driven by the attacks of his dogmatic friends on his personal integrity, to a defiance of their pious lies about Providence. From the reflections about the unmerited suffering that befell him, he advances to the problem of the universal wretchedness of man. With merciless realism he unfolds the tragedy of undeserved pain and of triumphant evil, which sharply contradict the belief in the justice of God. The faith of the mystery cults in resurrection of the body, which had newly flashed upon the horizon of Judaism, in the light of which the balance of the divine scales of justice was postponed to the hereafter, carries no conviction with Job. If such a faith were authenticated, the sufferer could wait for his vindication after death, but what proof is there that when man dies, he will live again?

Yet, though baffled by the universal disorder, Job neither doubts the value of righteousness nor does he swerve from his confidence that his integrity will be vindicated in the end. His faith in God and the consciousness of his innocence are the two fixed stars in the firmament of his religion. In their light, he looks with contempt upon the greed, the violence and the injustice of the wicked, and gathers courage in his trial. But mystery veils all existence, which no human eye can penetrate.

The very limitations of the human mind suggest a practical way out of man's perplexities. In his reply to the patriarch out of the storm, God demands: "Where wast thou when I laid the foundations of the earth? Declare if thou hast understanding." Is it only the presence of evil that puzzles the mind of man? Is not the manifest abundance of goodness just as mysterious? In a world so filled with wonder, how can finite man contend with the infinite Creator? Humility and reverence befit him as he contemplates the unknown.

Without solving the problem of the theodicy, Job succeeded in using honest doubt to vindicate faith. God cannot be judged by human standards, and man is better than his creeds.

The enthusiasm for wisdom, so characteristic of Proverbs and Job, is wanting in Ecclesiastes (*c.* 200 B.C.E.) Their confidence in moral and religious values is replaced in the reflections of this work, with the sombre thought "Vanity of vanities, all is vanity." Less poetic than Job and more analytical than Proverbs, it deliberates on the whole course of nature with extraordinary calm. The gloomy views of the world-weary sage are stimulated by the deep demoralization of the upper classes of his day, the self-seeking of the leaders, and the wide suffering of the masses. His weakened religious fervor probably reflects the influence of Greek scepticism.

Though he recognizes the hand of God in shaping the affairs of men, the author of Ecclesiastes lacks the feeling of fellowship with God. The heavens have no cheering message for him. The skies and the sea only spell meaningless monotony. The dull round of daily sunrise and sunset, of veering winds, and of streams that ever flow into the sea without filling it, have their analogy in human life. Generations come and go, without seeming goal or purpose. No prophetic vision of "the end of days" kindled his imagination. Neither was his mind fired by the sense of mission, which the prophets had assigned to his people in the world drama. He appears to have written before the national spirit was aroused by the Maccabean struggle for independence. He lives in the immediate moment, and seeks happiness in and for himself. The sole object of his inquiry is, as it was for the Greek thinkers, what constitutes the highest good for the individual.

This sage spurns the sensualists who seek life's meaning in the crude pleasures of feasting, carousing and licentiousness. The tides of his ancestral faith ran too high in his soul to permit him to drift into egoistic hedonism. Wisdom, too, does not seem to him an unmixed blessing, for in much wisdom there is much grief. Neither does moral idealism quiet his hunger, for no discernible relation seems to exist between righteous and unrighteous action. Good men die despite their goodness, and bad men live despite their badness. Indeed, man has no preeminence over the beast. They perish alike, and the destiny of their spirits is equally uncertain. Under the circumstances, the wisest course for man is to make the best of his lot, to discharge his tasks with all his might, and to enjoy life while he may, for the very opportunity and power to enjoy are God's gift to man.

This sceptical work probably was saved for the Bible canon by the identification of the author with Solomon and by the interpolation of the text with pious glosses that mitigate its heterodox opinions. Such was not the fate of the far more orthodox book of The Wisdom of Jesus ben Sira, known as Ecclesiasticus (so named because of its use in the Church), which forms part of the Apocrypha.

Having come under the influence of the better side of the Greek spirit, Ben Sira (*c.* 175 B.C.E.) was equipped to warn his people against the seductions of decaying Hellenism. The distinctive feature of his teaching is his identification of wisdom with the Torah, which found its abode in Israel. Of divine origin, the Torah concerns itself with the practical needs of men, with fearing God and fulfilling his commandments. As the consummation of wisdom, it helps man master his inclinations. In contrast to the profitlessness of (Greek) speculation, the Torah endows men with long life, patience, faithfulness and resignation to God's will. Wisdom is both an attribute of God and man's Highest glory. Man grows in God-likeness by pursuing wisdom and eschewing folly, wickedness and pride. The choice between wisdom and folly is wholly within man's power. Consequently sin comes not from God but from man. If he but will it, he can pursue the good.

Ben Sira's common-sense philosophy shows itself in his attitude toward medicine. The art of healing, originally forming part of the priest's task, was set up as an independent profession. Hence the opposition to medicine, in some religious quarters. Ben Sira spurns the opposition, and counsels that in sickness one should consult a physician and make use of medicine, for they serve as God's instruments of healing.

Contrary to the Epicurean view, Ben Sira teaches that God is not indifferent to man's actions. However, he cannot be bribed by sacrifices. The piety that recommends itself to this sage is of the prophetic type, consisting of a spiritualized ritual combined with good will and good deeds. Men should enjoy the pleasures which life offers, but "remember that death will not delay." The author knows nothing of the judgment of the soul after death or of a resurrection. Limiting himself to the common-sense view of the religious teachers of the Bible, he frees life of the dismal shadows which it began to assume in apocalypticism, and teaches man to meet the inevitable lot of all flesh with courage. Death is not an unmitigated evil. It is a bitter thing for the healthy and the prosperous, but a welcome friend to the hopeless sufferer.

III. Hellenistic Judaism

It was through its Hellenistic expression that Judaism joined the main stream of philosophy. It began with the translation of the Hebrew text of the Pentateuch into Greek, known as the Septuagint, about the middle of the third pre-Christian century. Designed to meet the religious needs of the Jewish community in Alexandria, which adopted Greek as its vernacular, the Septuagint aims to gain the esteem of the Greek speaking world in general. Accordingly, it frequently paraphrases expressions which call for interpretation, tones down anthropomorphisms, and removes phrases which sound harsh to Greek ears.

This apologetic tendency comes to full light in the Letter of Aristeas (first pre-Christian century), which tells the story of the preparation of the Septuagint, and glorifies the Jewish law and Jewish wisdom, through the mouth of an esteemed Greek scholar. It formed part of the extensive effort of Alexandrian Jewish thinkers to win the gentile world away from idolatry to the truths of Judaism. To this end they set out to demonstrate the superiority of the Torah not only over the pagan cults but also over the current philosophical systems. Unlike human wisdom which is liable to error, the Torah, revealed by God, is perfect. They sought to establish their claim by employing the allegorical method which had been current for some time among the Greeks, to rationalize their ancient myths in the light of their new knowledge. The Torah, they assumed, has an external and an internal meaning. The latter, they took to be in accord with the pure teachings of the Greek philosophers. Accordingly, they viewed the narratives of the Bible as allegories with ethical, psychological and philosophical content. Even the ceremonial laws of the Pentateuch, they invested with rational purpose.

Seeking a secret spiritual essence beneath the external forms of the Bible, they gave the ethical aspect of Judaism primacy over the ritual, and the universal over the particularistic. The very distinctiveness of the Jewish people was viewed as a phase of their universal mission. They are "men of God," "people who see God," a kingdom of priests laboring for the salvation of humanity from the thraldom and degradation of idolatry. Like the people so their leaders were pictured as blameless men. From the Letter of Aristeas to the writings of Philo, Moses is presented as a culture hero who discovered the art of writing and transmitted it to the Phoenicians, who in turn gave it to the Greeks. He was further acclaimed as the founder of philosophy, medicine, statecraft and industry. Plato and Pythagoras drew upon a translation of the Torah before the Septuagint for their wisdom. Indeed, Plato was "but Moses speaking Attic Greek." This conception of Moses reappears in Josephus and came to be shared by the Church as well as the Synagogue. Second only to Moses, Solomon represented the highest philosophy and science.

The Wisdom of Solomon (*c.* 50 B.C.E.), the most attractive book of the Apocrypha, utilizes Platonic and Stoic ideas to counter the scepticism of Ecclesiastes and to reformulate the teaching of Judaism. Its philosophical core is the conception of Wisdom (7.22-8.1), which occupies a position midway between Proverbs 8 and the Logos of Philo. Since Wisdom penetrates and orders formless matter of which God fashioned the world, all things may be said to be good. Evil is but seeming. In reality the forces of the world work together for the consummation of justice and of goodness. Man was made for immortality, but, yielding to "the envy of the devil," he brought death into the world. However, only sinners experience death. The righteous, while dying physically, live on spiritually. Their suffering while on earth is but disciplinary. They are tested like gold to ascertain their worth, that God may reign over them forever. Thus the author utilizes the Platonic doctrines of the pre-existence of the soul and its immortality, and adjusts them to the Jewish belief in the final judgment connected with the inauguration of the reign of God.

Hellenistic Judaism found its foremost exponent in Philo-Judaeus of Alexandria (*c.* 20 B.C.E.-54 C.E.). A devout Jew, he set himself to reshape Platonic and Stoic teaching, in the pattern of Jewish belief and tradition, for the intellectual elements of Jewish and Graeco-Roman society. His writings are mostly homiletical expositions, in the philosophic spirit, of the ideas of God, the Logos, creation, ethics, psychology, etc., and refutations of idolatry, superstition, materialism and scepticism. (For Philo's teaching and influence on general philosophy, see the chapter on Alexandrian Philosophy.)

IV. Rabbinic Judaism

Space permits indicating only a few highlights of the thought currents of Palestinian and Babylonian Judaism from Ben Sira to the redaction of the Talmud (*c.* 500 C.E.).

Josephus (37-110 C.E.), for apologetic reasons, compares the sectarian divisions in Judaism of the latter half of the Second Commonwealth with the Greek philosophical schools. Actually, these sects differ from one another along the line of religious doctrine and ceremonial practice. Only incidentally do some philosophical interests emerge among them.

The Sadducees represented biblical orthodoxy in its more enlightened form, rejecting the eschatological views of the apocalypticists, including angelology and resurrection. Their position probably approximated that of Ben Sira.

The Pharisees held to a more progressive conception of religion. They refused to regard revelation as completed and exhausted in the *Written Law*. In their view, revelation represented a continuous process in which *Oral Tradition* supplements Scripture. With the apocalypticists (Isaiah 24-27; Daniel; Enoch, etc.), they set their sights on the world to come, to rectify the injustices of this life. Their eschatology included beliefs in the resurrection of the body, judgment after death, heaven and hell, and the advent of the Davidic Messiah. They transformed Judaism from a religion centered in the Temple and the sacrificial cult into a religion based on the study of divine word, worship through prayer, and the practice of charity and brotherliness.

As a party name, Pharisaism disappeared soon after the fall of the Temple (70 C.E.). But its spirit and purpose have continued in Rabbinic Judaism, as embodied in the Talmud and in the Midrashim. This vast literature consists of two strands, both of them connected to the Bible by means of a hermeneutic system. One of them is the authoritative *Halachah* (Law, civil and ceremonial). The other is *Haggadah* (Lore, homiletical and mystical). The first is closely knit by strict logical rules and high ethical principles. The second exhibits the free play of the imagination. Though it lacks inner harmony and consistency, it presents a body of more or less unified opinion. The rabbis kept the Torah vital for the passing generations, by means of the Halachah and the Haggadah. Through these they defended the doctrinal contents of Judaism against the attacks of Gnosticism and other alien creeds, utilizing also ideas familiar to us from the philosophical schools.

BIBLIOGRAPHY

The Bible Literature:
J. A. BEWER, *The Literature of the Old Testament in its Historical Development* (2nd ed., New York, 1933).
R. H. PFEIFER, *Introduction to the Old Testament* (3rd ed., New York, 1941).
A. S. PEAKE, ed., *Commentary on the Bible* (London, 1920).

Theology:
J. P. PETERS, *The Religion of the Hebrews* (Boston, 1914).
W. O. E. OESTERLEY and T. H. ROBINSON, *Hebrew Religion: Its Origin and Development* (2nd ed., New York, 1937).
A. B. DAVIDSON, *The Theology of the Old Testament* (New York, 1904).

Wisdom:
T. K. CHEYNE, *Job and Solomon, or The Wisdom of the Old Testament* (London, 1887).
W. T. DAVISON, *The Wisdom Literature of the Old Testament* (London, 1894).
D. B. MACDONALD, *The Hebrew Philosophical Genius* (Princeton, 1936).

Apocrypha:
R. H. CHARLES, *The Apocrypha and Pseudepigrapha of the Old Testament in English*, 2 vols. (Oxford, 1913).
E. J. GOODSPEED, *The Apocrypha: A New Translation* (Chicago, 1938).
W. O. E. OESTERLEY, *An Introduction to the Books of the Apocrypha* (New York, 1935).

Hellenistic Judaism:
N. BENTWICH, *Hellenism* (Philadelphia, 1919).
MAX RADIN, *The Jews among the Greeks and Romans* (Philadelphia, 1915).
EMIL SCHUERER, *History of the Jewish People in the Time of Jesus Christ*. Eng. tr. 5 vols. (New York, 1886-1890).

A HISTORY OF PHILOSOPHICAL SYSTEMS

Pharisaism:
R. T. HERFORD, *The Pharisees* (New York, 1924).
———, *Judaism in the New Testament Period* (London, 1928).
L. FINKELSTEIN, *The Pharisees, the Sociological Background of their Faith.* 2 vols. (2nd rev. ed., Philadelphia, 1939).
J. Z. LAUTERBACH, *The Pharisees and their Teachings*, Hebrew Union College Annual VI:69-139 (Cincinnati, 1929).

Rabbinic Judaism:
M. MIELZINER, *Introduction to the Talmud* (3rd ed., New York, 1925).
H. STRACK, *Introduction to Talmud and Midrash* (tr. from 5th German ed., Philadelphia, 1931).
G. F. MOORE, *Judaism in the First Centuries of the Christian Era,* 3 vols. (Cambridge, 1927-1930).
A. COHEN, *Everyman's Talmud* (London, 1932).
R. T. HERFORD, *Pirke Aboth* (3rd rev. ed., New York, 1945).
C. G. MONTEFIORE and H. LOEWE, *A Rabbinic Anthology* (London, 1938).

CHAPTER SIX

THE BEGINNINGS OF GREEK PHILOSOPHY

GORDON H. CLARK

IN CONTRAST with the Eastern modes of thought, the beginnings of Greek philosophy were rather strictly scientific. It was astronomical phenomena and cosmological speculation that first attracted attention: witness the reason for selecting 585 B.C. as the beginning of this new era.

The Milesians and Heraclitus

Long before the time of Thales—a citizen of Miletus, in the district of Ionia, on the west coast of Asia Minor—Chaldaean astrologers had listed data on the positions of stars and planets. As Thales studied these tables he thought he discerned a pattern or regularity in the occurrences of eclipses, and he ventured to predict a solar eclipse that occurred May 28, 585 B.C. Some scholars disparage this as merely a lucky empirical guess; but if it was the discovery of an astronomical regularity or natural law, Thales may be credited with distinguishing Greek philosophy and science from the aimless observations and disjointed information of the Eastern wise men. When a law is formulated, man's wonder at the phenomena is supposed to be satisfied, and nature is said to be explained and understood. Thales is also credited with the discovery of several theorems of geometry and with diplomatic, engineering, and economic exploits. If there is a difference between science and philosophy, it is that the regularities of a science are relatively restricted, whereas the more general principles, called philosophic, apply to wider areas. Thales' more general speculations concerned the constitution of the universe. What is the world made of? Are there many elements or is there but one? And if one, what is it? These questions dominated the entire Pre-Socratic period; they are still live issues today; and if Thales' answer seems crude to twentieth century sophisticates, his motivation and procedure may prove as profound as any contemporary inspiration.

As a matter of fact, Thales taught that all things are made of water, and we may imagine reasons that might have convinced him. One no doubt would be that water is known as a liquid, a solid, and a gas; and these various forms seem to suggest that water is capable of all the transformations a universal substratum must undergo if it is to produce the objects of our world. Since, too, a general theory must attempt to explain biological phenomena as well as physics and astronomy, another reason for selecting water might have been its indispensability to life. And a little ingenuity can invent other considerations. But Anaximander (610-545?), Thales' successor, in addition to specific contributions to science, saw a difficulty in Thales' general cosmology. If water were the basic substance, he thought, fire could never come into existence, for there is an essential antagonism between their peculiar qualities. For the same reason, if the substratum were fire, the existence of water could not be explained. Therefore Anaximander assumed a Boundless that was not peculiarly wet or dry, cold or hot, but rather indeterminately both wet and dry, cold and hot. Thus the matter of the universe was Boundless, not merely because it extended throughout infinite space, but also and mainly because it was not bounded, limited, or defined by any quality. This original substance produces the world and its contents by a swirling motion that separates the four qualities out of the chaotic mass. This swirl also explains the revolution of the stars and planets.

The third member of the Milesian school, Anaximenes (*c.* 590-525), could not be persuaded to look for the universal substratum beyond the range of experience. He therefore selected air. Air is not only more necessary to life than is water, but also it seems to solve a troublesome astronomical enigma. If with Thales the planet earth is supported on water, one naturally wonders what the water rests on. To say that the earth is situated in the middle of the universe and therefore has no reason to move in any direction, as Anaximander taught, smacks of speculative magic. Air on the other hand does not fall when unsupported and may therefore be thought capable of supporting the earth and the planets. Anaximenes also described more particularly the process by which the substratum changed into other things with their different qualities. Condensation, as when air from a tire blows on the palm of the hand, causes cold; and rarefaction, as when one breathes gently against the palm, produces warmth. Thus, the generation of qualities is explained by an explicitly mechanical process.

The selection of water or air may be a curious ancient matter of unimportance; the dim recognition of mechanical law and the advances in astronomy are substantial contributions to the early history of science; but beyond this the Milesian world-view presupposed some basic principles of philosophic generality that are pertinent in any age. There is, obviously, the assumption that the universe is made of one stuff. Fifth century Greece or nineteenth century America may have held to ninety-four elements, but the Milesians and the twentieth century look upon gold, iron, lead, and so on, as transformations of an original, homogeneous substance. In the next place, this substance has no cause, origin, or beginning. It always was and always will be. And, third, the changes and transformations of this substance, the growth and dissolution of plants and planets, occur spontaneously. There is no cause of motion before, behind, or above the original substance. Nature itself is the principle of motion and life. The details of Milesian science have been outmoded a long time, but naturalism is a philosophy with contemporary advocates.

Heraclitus (530-470), since he lived in Ephesus, was not literally a Milesian; but his views were in fundamental harmony with the preceding three. The difference lay in his emphasis on the importance of change. "One cannot step into the same river twice, nor touch mortal substance twice in the same state, but by quickness and speed of change it disperses and again comes together, draws near and withdraws. . . . Into the same rivers we step and we do not step; we are and we are not." When in any place the change is even and regular, as in a stream without a ripple, the appearance is one of stability; but thoughtful consideration will conclude that all things flow, and that permanence is an illusion.

Thus emphasizing the speed, the continuity, and the universality of change, it was natural for Heraclitus to select fire as his single and original element because fire is the quickest and most mobile of all substances. The fire undergoes transformations in measure and in rhythm to produce the things of the world and the course of their history. Every day and every summer the proportion of light, warmth, and combustion increases; every night and every winter the proportion is reversed. And there seems to have been also a cosmic periodicity in which cosmos follows cosmos in eternal succession.

Since each thing and each person has only his own brief day, lyric poets may have lamented the perishing flower of youth and voiced a pessimistic desire for permanence; Anaximander, too, may have suggested the injustice of the antagonism among qualities; but Heraclitus thought that strife was natural and that life is a struggle. "War is the father of all, the King of all; some he set forth as gods, some as men; some he made slaves, some free. . . . To God all things are fair and right and good, but men suppose some things wrong and others right." This attitude is possible because the original and everlasting fire is God who rules the world by wisdom. A pawn may lament its being sacrificed in a gambit; but the player is producing a noble game. Thus the world is governed by a Logos, a Reason, a Law, and this is the fire itself. This pantheism, as it may be called, is essentially one with the Milesian hylozoism: if all is to be explained by one substance, this substance must account for life and mind as well as for rocks and stars. But can anything visible and tangible provide a satisfactory explanation?

The Pythagoreans and Parmenides

It was on the eastern extremities of ancient Greece that philosophy began. The next development was located in the extreme west—southern Italy. And in outlook also, the two schools were equally far apart. The earlier philosophy, with slight exceptions in Heraclitus, was mainly physical and non-religious; Pythagoreanism, placing less confidence in tangible water and fire, was a religious and mathematical school.

The religion, however, was not Homeric. The Olympian deities may have had some dramatic majesty, but their scandalous conduct provided no moral incentive. The ancient heroes may have been grand in epic poetry, but the dismal prospect of Hades, to which everyone, good, bad, and indifferent, was doomed, produced less and less enthusiasm. The ritual, largely social and civil rather than personal and vital, became increasingly perfunctory and slowly lost its hold on the people. In competition, mystery religions, promising to their initiates a happy, personal communion with the gods both now and hereafter, and later threatening punishments to the immoral, were active in the fifth century and influenced the Pythagoreans. Homeric thought, appalled at the hopelessness of death, celebrated the glories of life and action; but the Pythagoreans were able to reverse the theme and, emphasizing the immortality of the soul, to teach that the body is a tomb. Purification from evil, freedom from incarceration in the body, recovery of the soul's pure divinity, is to be accomplished partly by rites and practices that today would be dismissed under the disparaging epithet of taboos, and partly by moral and political activity in accord with aristocratic principles; but mainly salvation is to be attained through knowledge. Thus religion becomes the motivation of philosophy.

Under this general outlook, the more immediate, one might say the more scientific explanation of the cosmos is not to be sought in water or fire. In Anaximander and in Heraclitus there had been dim gropings after a principle of equity or measure. There was a periodicity, a law, a mathematical proportion. The Pythagoreans, standing in awe of their own success in geometry, and noting that the most perfect musical chords are expressible in the simplest fractions, and also believing that the distances between the planets correspond to the musical scale, quickly came to the conclusion that not water but number is the key to the universe. The number series originates from the one, perhaps in conjunction with two or the indefinite dyad. All numbers are either odd or even; certain numbers are prime, perfect, square, oblong, or triangular. A theorem was discovered relating prime and perfect numbers. The common categories of thought are listed in a table of opposites under the distinction between odd and even. For example, under odd are found right, male, rest, and good; under even are left, female, motion, and evil. Numerical analogy was still further extended with the result that justice, the square deal, is the number four, and marriage is the number five because it is the combination of the first even and the first odd number.

Another western school, the Eleatic, also in southern Italy, was dominated by Parmenides (515-440). It occurred to him that no matter how keen an observer's eyes were, no matter how much water and fire he saw, if he talked nonsense, his theory could not be true. Truth must be tested not by the senses, but by reason and logic. Whatever cannot be thought, whatever is self-contradictory and inconceivable, cannot be. The previous philosophers had all asserted the inconceivable and impossible; in one way or another they all had said that what is not, is.

The assertion that fire is water or that water is fire, is patently false. Water simply is not fire. It is not a question of physics; it is pure logic. Water means one thing and fire means something else. They are not equivalent concepts, and it is always false to say that one thing is a different thing, or that it is something that it is not. There seems to be one predicate, however, that is attributable to water, and to fire as well. Could not Thales have said that water is existent? The answer is negative for the same reason. The concept of existent is not the equivalent of the concept of water, and to speak the truth one must say water is not existent. Well, at least water is water. Here the two concepts are identical. But once again the answer is negative because the *is* indicates existence, and since water is nonexistent, it is false to say that water is, regardless of the concept used as predicate. Only what is, is. Being alone exists. The logic of the argument depends on defining the verb *to-be* as meaning equivalence and existence.

It follows that there is only one Being. In fact, the aim of reducing the cosmos to one substance is common to all the preceding philosophers. Parmenides merely draws out the logical implications. There is only one Being, homogeneous, indivisible, unchangeable, eternal, and solid. If, indeed, Being is not one, but on the contrary there are several Beings, they must differ among themselves. The point or points of difference must be with respect to Being or with respect to nonbeing. But how could they differ with respect to Being, since they are alike in being Being? Can likes differ in respect to their likes? And yet the differences should exist in some respect. Yet they cannot exist by reason of nonbeing, for nonbeing is not, and would not permit of differences' existing. It follows therefore that what people call many things are not different, but the same. Being therefore is not many, but one.

Indivisibility and homogeneity are consequences of the nonexistence of difference. Similarly it is unchangeable, for there is nothing for it to change into. It is eternal, for it cannot have come from something else because something else, other than Being, is nonbeing, and nonbeing does not exist for Being to come from. Nor could it have come from the same thing, for the same thing is Being itself, which already exists and does not have to come. Origin therefore is inconceivable. *Ex nihilo nihil fit.*

Since empty space is pure nothingness and cannot exist, Being must be solid, perfected on every side like a well-rounded sphere. A homogeneous body, without differences, could not be greater in one place and less in another. It is equal throughout, and only the spherical shape satisfies these requirements.

Pluralism

Thus Parmenides brought to its logical conclusion the original theme of Thales that the world can be explained in terms of a single physical substratum. But however logical Parmenides' arguments were, many of his contemporaries were not so willing to trust reason and repudiate sense. If corporeal monism implies the solid immobility of Being, there must, they thought, be something wrong with corporeal monism. Since the world is obviously physical, visible, tangible, or corporeal, the trouble must have been concealed under the idea of monism. The world cannot be one stuff. By this line of reasoning there arose the school of Pluralists. It will be seen that the history of philosophy is not a haphazard development. Pluralism did not arise in a vacuum, but rather it was inevitable among men who had inherited this particular tradition. And the development of pluralism is not haphazard, either. If the world is not one, but many, there are just three possibilities. Each must be tried in succession. The world may be composed of beings that present a finite number of original qualitative differences; or there may be an infinite number of qualitative differences; or, third, the world may be composed of beings, numerically infinite, which are qualitatively identical. If pluralism fails, it will not be until after the three forms have been elaborated and examined.

Empedocles of Sicily (495-435), studying Parmenides' arguments, was convinced that qualitative differences could not originate from one stuff. Therefore he posited four original differences. Like the nineteenth century chemists he held that the world was composed of a finite number of elements. Instead of ninety-some, he thought four would do: earth, air, fire, and water. As an artist with a few basic pigments can produce all the colors of a great painting, so four elements can account for the amazing variety seen in the world. What ordinary people call origin is merely the mixing, or chemical combination, of the elements. A particular example is given in a passage that seems to analyze bone into two parts water, four parts fire, and two of earth, or in modern formula, $W_2 \, F_4 \, E_2$. This type of "explanation" was later criticized incisively by Plato in his dialogue *Theaetetus*. Empedocles went to considerable length in describing the formation of the solar system, the origin of life on this planet, and being particularly interested in medicine he studied the details of biology and the processes of sensation.

While chemical combinations might come and go, each element in itself remained fixed and unchangeable. They were in effect pluralistic miniatures of the Parmenidean Being. But the more the characteristics of Parmenidean Being were applied to them, the more another difficulty emerged. If they were fixed and stable, how could motion be explained? Clearly something other than immutable atoms must be sought. Somewhat as Newton in modern times spoke of attraction and repulsion, so Empedocles explained motion by assuming the principles of Love and Hate. Love combines the elements into things and Hate explains their dissolution. But if Love and Hate are not the fifth and sixth elements, what are they? Apparently Empedocles was embarrassed. The earlier hylozoism had not seemed to need any additional moving principle because matter itself is alive or spontaneous; but when Empedocles was forced to reject this philosophy, he was in fact straining after the distinction between the animate and the inanimate. And it is not surprising that this first attempt lacked precision.

Anaxagoras (500-428), the first philosopher to visit and to be banished from Athens, thought that four qualitatively different types of element were not enough and that two moving principles were too many. Four elements are not enough because origin is inconceivable; and if the world is to contain an infinite variety, the infinite variety must have always existed. The world cannot produce novelty, for this would mean that an existent (quality) had arisen from a nonexistent (quality). Mechanical rearrangements of these qualities bring some of them to our attention at one time and others at another time.

Since every combination involves the separation of elements

from other groups, one moving principle is sufficient. This principle is Mind or Intelligence. Anaxagoras sharply distinguishes it from the infinite elements, and later Socrates hoped that this Mind could be taken for a God who directed the world wisely for the Good. But Anaxagoras had not exploited his idea, and, to Socrates' chagrin, gave only mechanical explanations of the world process.

Mechanism rather than teleology was the dominating inspiration in pluralism, and Democritus (460-360) gave it a systematic exposition that in principle cannot be improved upon.

Atoms and void are the terms in which the world is to be explained. The void is necessary for the atoms to exist in and move in; accordingly this nothingness, called empty space, *is*—regardless of the scandal to Parmenides. The atoms, on the other hand, are not empty but full. They are continuous, indestructible, simple, unchangeable, particles of matter that differ infinitely in size and shape. They do not differ qualitatively because strictly they have no qualities. Weight or specific gravity as well as color, temperature, taste, and so on can be attributed only to combinations of atoms and not to any atom individually. The atoms are real or natural; the qualities exist only by convention, that is, in relation to percipients. Some attempt was made to describe the different mechanical patterns that produced the various qualities.

To form a world the atoms must move. What causes an atom to move? Love? Hate? Mind? No, Democritus' answer is that an atom moves because another atom hit it. And this atom was in motion because a previous atom had started it in this direction. Therefore there is no need of a moving principle in a mechanistic system. Aristotle later objected that while this explains the particular speed and direction of every motion, it does not explain motion. Democritus thought it was not necessary to explain motion in general if every particular motion was accounted for. Because the several motions are produced by mechanical collisions, it follows that all events occur by necessity. There is no purpose in the universe, no providence, no teleology. The regularity of astronomy and the apparent design in biology are not evidences of any directing Mind; they are merely one chance arrangement that occurs during an infinite time in which all possible arrangements must be realized.

A HISTORY OF PHILOSOPHICAL SYSTEMS

Zeno

To avoid the motionless acosmism that Parmenides had inferred from the principle of corporeal monism, the pluralists asserted that Being is many and that nonexistent (empty) space exists. Did they thus save the appearances? Had they succeeded in justifying motion? Zeno (490-420), the faithful and brilliant disciple of Parmenides, tried to show that they had not.

To demonstrate the absurdity of motion, Zeno tells a story. An Eleatic tortoise challenges Achilles, the track star of antiquity, to a race, on condition that he, the tortoise, be given a head-start. At the crack of the pistol they're off. But when Achilles reaches the point from which the tortoise started, the tortoise is no longer there. In the meantime he had gone ahead a short distance. Then when Achilles reaches the point at which the tortoise was when Achilles was at the point from which the tortoise started, the tortoise is no longer there. In the meantime he had gone ahead a short distance. And so on. Every time Achilles arrives at the point at which the tortoise was, the tortoise is no longer there. Since this happens every time, at no time does Achilles overtake his philosophic rival.

Is this absurd? Does it contradict our senses? But which are we to trust, sensation or reason? Then someone objects that since Achilles runs one hundred times as fast as any philosopher, he will overtake his slow friend in exactly so many seconds. This is not just sensation, it is mathematics.

However—suppose Achilles or an atom is to traverse a distance of so many yards or a time of so many seconds. Before he can reach the end, he must pass the halfway point; or can one conceive him somehow to escape this necessity? And before he arrives at the halfway point, he must pass the quarter mark. And before he runs a quarter of the distance, he must complete an eighth. And so on. It follows, therefore, that before he can even start to run, he must exhaust this series. Unfortunately, this series is inexhaustible. Consequently Achilles cannot start. Motion is impossible.

Another illustration also will show that motion is inconceivable. Rest, the absence of motion, can be described as that condition in which the extremities of a body are coincident with two fixed points in space. Take an arrow at any moment of its supposed flight. Its extreme points are coincident with two given points of space—since it is in space. Therefore, at every instant of its "flight" it is at rest. Motion is inconceivable.

Space, too, is an absurd conception. Democritus thought that there had to be space for an atom to exist *in*. But if existence requires something for the existing object to exist *in*, and if space exists, then space must exist *in* something—a superspace. And the superspace must exist in a supersuperspace. And so on until it is seen that one should never have begun. The first "space" was absurd.

Furthermore, the assumption that there are many atoms is also absurd. If Being were many, it would have to be both infinitely small and infinitely large. It would have to be infinitely small because every plurality is a collection of unities. A unity is indivisible, and therefore can have no magnitude. A sum of zero magnitudes is zero. And thus a world constructed of unitary atoms would have neither length, breadth, nor thickness. But if the atoms exist, they must have magnitude. To have magnitude, however, the south pole of each atom would have to be separated from the north pole by a finite extent. This third part in turn would have to be separated from the north and south poles by other extended parts. And so on. This requires an infinite number of extended parts, with the result that each atom would be infinitely extended.

The Greek thinkers, faced with this refutation of atomism, could choose one of three possibilities. They could agree that Being alone exists and that Being is one. A few did so, and for them philosophy had accomplished its task. It had found the truth. Or it might be argued that the pluralists had made a different mistake. They had seen the culmination of corporeal monism, rejected the monism and kept the materialism. Someone might now try to reject the materialism and keep the monism. But such a person, so hardy as to suggest that reality is spiritual and not material, would have to be a genius as great as Plato. There is a much easier choice that can be made. The great minds of early Greece with all their scientific acumen, so it may be concluded, have failed to find any truth. The reason for their failure is simply that there is no truth to be found. Knowledge is impossible. This conclusion is a welcome relief after such arduous philosophizing; and, besides, it offers great opportunities to ambitious young men. Thus there arose in Greece the movement known as Sophism.

A HISTORY OF PHILOSOPHICAL SYSTEMS

BIBLIOGRAPHY

John Burnet, *Early Greek Philosophy* (New York, 1930).
Martin, Clark, Clarke, and Ruddick, *A History of Philosophy* (New York, 1941).
Milton Nahm, *Selections from Early Greek Philosophy* (New York, 1934).
Léon Robin, *Greek Thought* (London, 1928).
E. Zeller, *Outlines of Greek Philosophy* (London, 1931).

CHAPTER SEVEN

EARLY GREEK MORALISTS

PAUL R. HELSEL

THE ETHICAL conceptions of the Greek moralists germinated in the views of earlier thinkers while the conditions of their own time brought these ideas to maturity. For a century and a half philosophic reflection had been preoccupied with the origin of the material world but underneath the surface a different current of thinking was going on which in time was destined to come to light. This situation is understandable if one adopts an evolutionary point of view for thought as illustrated by Lewis Mumford where he says "that the person is an emergent from society, in much the same fashion that the human species is an emergent from the animal world." [1] W. G. Greene implies this development where he claims that "the whole trend of Greek thought is from an external toward an internal conception of life" [2] and Werner Jaeger reenforces this claim by the observation that "other nations made gods, kings, spirits: the Greeks alone made men." [3]

One should not suppose that philosophic speculation created the moral problem as a historical event. On the contrary, the moral situation is as old as man. Prior to the rise of philosophic reflection morals existed in a natural state and their expression in literature was in some such form as myth, poetry or legal procedure. A line from Homer (*fl.* 850 B.C., or earlier) illustrates practical morality at this early stage: "through blindness of their own hearts, [men] have sorrows beyond that which is ordained," [4] or this from Hesiod (*fl.* 8th century B.C.) "long and steep is the path that leads to her [virtue] . . . ; but when a man has reached the top then she is easy to reach, though it was hard before." [5] After struggling with the problem of moral evil, Theognis (565-490 B.C.) concluded that, "by teaching never shalt thou make the bad man good," [6] and Simonides (556-467 B.C.) meditating upon the Athenian dead at Plataea reflected that "if to die nobly is the greatest part of virtue, on us of all men Fortune has bestowed this lot." [7] Finally, the morality of nature as opposed to the standards that men erect was highlighted by Antigone where Sophocles (495-406 B.C.) described her as subordinating the laws of man to a higher authority: "Justice enacted not these human laws." [8]

Also the reflective movement converged at nuclear conceptions which implemented the historical shift from cosmological considerations over to the anthropic-moralistic issues, thereby facilitating the philosophic handling of the ethical problem. Pythagoras (582-507 B.C.) put forth the idea that the principle of individuation was a balanced equilibrium that ordered the universe, imparted health to the body and the quality of goodness to the soul. In the opinion of Parmenides (*fl.* 475 B.C.) his predecessors had never faced the problem of change, so he demanded how the existent non-exists and the non-existent exists? In Parmenides' own answer to this query the principle of logical consistency first came to the fore. Inasmuch as he considered that the alternatives of his quandary involved a contradiction, he felt that the selection of either one would necessitate the rejection of the other. This loyalty of Parmenides to the principle of logical consistency made a contribution to later reasoning that should be ranked along with the consequences of the alternative which he chose. In his denial of change Parmenides severed the universe into exclusive portions and subsequent thinkers have labored ever since to connect it together again. Parmenides sorted things into two classes, one of thought objects out of reach of the senses and liable to the charge of mental creations; the other of the tangible and demonstrable objects of man's senses. Parmenides thus awakened reflection to the persistent fact that the world is relative. To the principle of consistency he added a second one, that of identity in the sense of uniting thought and being.

Another nuclear conception that prepared the way for the shift to the moral issue, was put forward by Heracleitus (*fl.* 500 B.C.) who believed that the universe was a concourse of ceaseless change, everything flows. This idea of change may be imagined to imply a pulverized universe of discrete entities succeeding one another.

When the notion is carried over into human society the collective idea may be likewise broken down into individual units each with its own natural and self-justifiable idiosyncrasies. At the same time Heracleitus understood that it was impossible to derive knowledge from external change. Therefore he sought the principle of explanation within himself.

Finally, the events of the fifth century B.C. transformed the basic characteristics of civilization in a manner similar to what is going on in our own day. In the first half of the century the two most powerful nations of the civilized world, Greece in the west and Persia in the east, engaged in a crucial conflict from which neither one ever recovered. Nicholas P. Vlachos draws the analogy. He says that "the Hellenic World War had its counterpart in our own World War." [9] As a consequence of the Hellenic world conflict traditional sanctions became suspect and in their stead new theories of society, government, philosophy and religion were advanced. Some ideas were re-thought while others that had been growing now ripened because of the favorable condition of the times. In the days of the old aristocracy noble blood and the deeds of heroes had furnished the moral bases of the state and society and had been regarded as characteristics of the highest virtue. But after the defeat of the Persians and the incoming of the liberal democracy of the Periclean age new privileges were extended throughout a larger portion of society. Many of the old bars were let down, particularly those of the law courts, so that inherited and legal lines of demarcation were swept away. Replacing the earlier characteristics of birth and noble deeds as goals of mortal striving, service to the state now depended upon intellectual attainment. This change set up a different kind of requirement, one that replaced the uncontrollable course of natural inheritance and valiant deeds by the demands for mental effort.

The Sophists spearheaded this movement. In fact, they embodied the rising emphasis that was now coming into prominence upon the new conception of man in whatever form—mind, intellect, reason. For the first time and during the age of Pericles, Anaxagoras from across the Aegean introduced philosophy into Athens. But according to Anaxagoras mind served only a limited purpose; it was a principle of philosophic or scientific interpretation. However, the times were ripe for the Sophists to break the narrow limits of the speculative idea of man and to liberate it for practical service throughout society generally. The one who did this more than anyone else was Protagoras (481-411 B.C.), the founder of the Sophist movement. Little is known of his life or writings but his famous dictum has been preserved: "Man is the measure of all things, of things that are, that they are, of things that are not, that they are not." [10] This statement released such a weight of natural authority which up to this time had been neglected, that notwithstanding its limitations something which the dictum denotes carries over into our own day.

The Sophists instigated a rift among the views of Greek thinkers. The distinction is understandable when it is studied in the light of practical experience. Early Greek conceptions of the development of man contained the two familiar aspects: nature and nurture. Thucydides (471-400 B.C.) had understood that foresight and wisdom were natural endowments and he thought that it was futile for instruction to offer acquired characteristics as substitutes for innate qualities.[11] Hesiod, on the other hand, emphasized the human capacities that were subject to training.[12] When the people become confused, if one should come forth on whose tongue Zeus has poured sweet dew and from whose lips flow gracious words and should settle the cause with true judgments, that one would be a prince. The Sophists took up what Hesiod had emphasized and concentrated their efforts upon the training of those traits that were susceptible of education. But in the estimation of the Sophists education should be practical, not an end in itself; they linked it up with the fortunes of the state and deliberately undertook the task of teaching political virtue, an attempt that was to meet with stubborn opposition. The Sophists defined their profession as an art, a term which misleads us today. As their method developed we would define it as a skill or technique. But in his best moments Protagoras apparently hoped to include more than mere skill in the conception of his own task. He seemed concerned with promoting a basic culture which although called political, yet it resembles more our idea of statecraft or statesmanship. Protagoras is represented by Plato as making this distinction where Protagoras explains to Socrates that "the other Sophists are in the habit of insulting their pupils; who, when they have just escaped from the arts, are taken and driven back into them by their teachers. . . . ; but if he [Hippocrates] comes to me, he will learn to order his own house in the best manner, and he will be able to speak and act for the best in the affairs of the state." [13] It would seem then that the distinction between the original intention of Protagoras and the practise of his later followers illustrates the historical transformation that often accompanies movements of this kind. When a founder of a movement passes and his influence wanes then the structure of the movement comes to light and the disciples emulate its weaknesses which at first were concealed by the dominance of the leader.

Inasmuch as Periclean democracy guaranteed "equal justice to all alike in their private disputes," [14] and as the citizens were supposed to represent themselves personally at the courts of law, opportunity was thus created for trained assistance. This assistance supplied the occasion of service where the individual Sophists might tie into the practical needs of Greek society. One might suppose, too, that their expectations of success would set their goals to be achieved. This practical situation, then, dictated in advance the kind of preparatory training that should be selected for the work at hand. Naturally the training should be organized about rhetoric and the determination "to speak well"; these would vie for first place with all other factors, even with the justice of the issue on trial. This performance "suited the Greek passion for form so well that it actually ruined the nation by overgrowing everything else like a creeping plant." [15] The sophistic profession, on the other hand, heightened the general consciousness as to the importance of the forms and means of expression. The Sophists created the need for the study of grammar, rhetoric and dialectic. Treatises on syntax, theories of meaning, examination of letters and syllables, grouping of words, the principles of argumentation, defending and attacking both sides of an argument and the beginning of logic are representatives of the intellectual discoveries and achievements of the sophistic movement which have supplied much of the structure of Western learning and culture.

But the sophistic movement was so constituted as to contain something of a direct ratio between its method of achieving success and the disclosure of its faults. It attempted success by the skillful manipulation of the form and means of expression. Often those who practised this technique went to unjustifiable lengths to win their point. An oft-cited instance of this excess is the litigation between Protagoras and Euathlus where the practical intention of Euathlus appears to have been the termination of the suit in a logical impasse and thereby to win a verdict that would dissolve him of further responsibility.[16] But such success is won at the cost of principles which are basic to social welfare and brought to light ideas of earlier thinkers which the Sophists now organized into a new social outlook that at an earlier time was little suspected.

It has been explained how Protagoras had introduced the principle that everything is relative; that the senses may testify to one situation while thought may dictate another. It would follow, then, that the world of affairs is different from what it appears to be because knowledge involves relationships. Moreover, upon the adoption of an assumption as a starting point of the thought procedure, logical consistency necessitates that one shall follow through the connected steps of its consequences with unflinching loyalty. In addition to this loyalty Parmenides had identified thought and being but later the sensationalistic theory of knowledge had united perception and thought. Therefore the substitution of perception for thought in the formula of identification seemed both possible and natural with the resulting doctrine embraced by the Sophists that perception and being are one. Again Heracleitus had implied a pulverized existence, a notion that when divorced from the rest of Heracleitean thought accommodated itself to the idea of self-ruled social units, each according to the Sophists having the privilege of exercising its own unique traits and characteristics without let or hindrance. Now when such ideas are refashioned, when they are set in a changed social milieu and are welcomed by practical conditions, when being released from their earlier meanings and universalized throughout society generally, and when they are actuated by unrestrained, human drives determined upon success at the cost of making morals as well as knowledge relative, then a sophistic condition obtains against which men of another view feel that they must speak out.

Possibly there was no more outspoken and stronger opponent of the Sophists than Socrates (467-399 B.C.). However long society had practised the distinction between nature and nurture or convention, Archelaus (*fl.* 450 B.C.) had first at Athens put the difference in formal expression and thereby had made it current in the thought of the time.[17] Plato (427-347 B.C.) used the distinction as a means of new classification.[18] Whereas the Sophists in the realm of convention sought affluence by the cultivation of the human capacities educable along the lines of rhetoric, logic and social practises, the first concern of Socrates and Plato was for nature. An instance of the method that they used generally occurs in the conception of the origin of the state. Plato put it in the form of a question: "for we cannot suppose that States are made of 'oak and rock' and not out of the human natures which are in them, and which in a figure turn the scale and draw other things after them?"[19] Aristotle (384-322 B.C.) also observed the same principle of distinction in his reference to language: "the limitation 'by convention' was introduced because nothing is by nature a noun or name."[20]

The schism between the Sophists and their opponents, notably Socrates, Plato and Aristotle, was uncompromising; it resulted from two different world views. The deeper thinkers conceived of the universe, including man, as one interconnected whole with interlocking relations all grounded in and derived from an underlying nature, physical, living, human, social, philosophic and religious. The Sophists, on the other hand, neglecting nature as the starting point of investigation, grounded everything in convention. Two outstanding characters of Plato's Dialogues illustrate this view. From Thrasymachus' insistent contention that justice is the interest of the stronger, by matching method with method Socrates forced Thrasymachus to drop back into "gentleness" and by mute inference Thrasymachus permitted Socrates to speak for them both in the conclusion, "I know nothing at all." [21] The second character is Callicles who held that it is man's nature to do injustice and reap the rewards while to suffer injustice is both a disgrace and an evil. Therefore, "if there were a man of sufficient force, he would . . . break through . . . all this, . . , and the light of natural justice would shine through." [22] Finally, the crowning charge that Socrates makes against the Sophists is what Erdmann calls "the sophistic formula": [23] they "made the worse appear the better cause," [24] all because, as Plato explains, they are "bent upon giving them [citizens] pleasure, forgetting the public good in the thought of their own interests." [25] Aristotle even denies the Sophists a place among the philosophers due to their failure to grasp the true nature of things: "sophistic is Wisdom which exists only in semblance . . . is what appears to be philosophy but is not." [26]

A HISTORY OF PHILOSOPHICAL SYSTEMS

Socrates was born among the Sophists, he was educated by the Sophists, he used the method of the Sophists, but Socrates was not a sophist. This statement contains the kernel of Socratic morality. Not concerned with physical nature Socrates nevertheless headed the movement that wished to investigate the nature of human behavior and the narration of his attempt in this respect will be an explanation of the Socratic method and the Socratic principle.

The Socratic method was made up of two parts: the negative and the positive. The negative aspect is more newsworthy because of its dramatic setting; without the negative part of Socrates' work it is possible that he might have remained unknown like many of his fellow-citizens. It was upon this activity that he established his reputation, arrayed his enemies against him and at the last inspired the charges of the indictment upon which he was tried with the resulting verdict of ostracism or death.

The negative aspect of the Socratic method is basic to any thoroughgoing investigation. The dictum, "know thyself," was already ancient in Socrates' day but denoted little more than a pious epigram in comparison with the searching application it received at his hands. In Greek history no one before him had been so relentless in exploring the realm of the self for the purpose of peering into its being. Naturally the preparatory work consisted of the uncovering and rejecting of the accumulations of time, heredity, habits and opinions. In other cultures certain men were devoted to a similar task. Hebrew-Jewish prophets purged themselves in Midian, in the Temple, along the Chebar, in the wilderness and in Arabia to expel the useless accumulations which they had collected and to prepare themselves for their creative work. In English culture Francis Bacon bemoaned the fact that mankind was wedded to the idols of the cave, the tribe, the market-place and the theater. If men would desert these idols then they could acquire new outlooks. Finally, Descartes by the *Cogito ergo sum* insight swept from his mind the useless paraphernalia of French culture that had hindered this intellectual quest.

It appears, then, that Socrates hit upon a universal principle. Before the mind is capable of acquiring new truth, false accumulations of tradition, prejudice, career and ignorance must all be faced and expelled by denial and confession. Irrespective of the employment to which they subjected it, Jesus and Socrates adopted the same method. What Jesus denoted by repentance and Socrates by the negative aspect of his method, for both a change of mind was meant. If by the conversation with Socrates, Thrasymachus had actually willed a change of mind equal to the change of his conduct from conceit over to mute silence when for both of them Socrates confessed their ignorance as to the nature of justice, such a change of mind would have been recorded as a conversion both by Jesus [27] and by Socrates.[28]

After one by a confession of ignorance has purged his nature of inherited prejudice, traditional illusions and blinding presuppositions, preparation has then been made for the positive aspect of the Socratic method. Inasmuch as the kind of knowledge in which he was interested excluded factual accumulations of what now passes for scientific knowledge and involved morals and religion, Socrates held that the acquiring of knowledge was a cooperative enterprise. The Socratic method made no provision for mass classroom procedure where an instructor is compelled to act as if knowledge is conveyable in a single direction. The Socratic method was informal and conversational. However skillful Socrates may have been as a conversationalist, he never supposed that he was in possession of a body of knowledge that he wished to transmit to the listener. Whatever theory of knowledge prompted it, his continual effort was to elicit truth by the pooling of ideas, a creative result which slavish mind could never accomplish.

Socrates' reliance upon this method was grounded in what is called the Socratic principle: the validity of the moral self-consciousness. It was this principle that differentiated Socrates from the Sophists and kept him from being a sophist. The sophistic dictum, "man is the measure of all things," located the source of all things in man. In regard to the distinction between nature and convention, the Sophists stood firmly on the side of convention, which, however beneficial, has its ultimate source in man. This view cuts the vital cord of nature and theoretically opens the door for the entrance of all kinds of unnatural aberrations. Socrates was the first one to work at this distinction and headed the movement that attempted to discover human nature, a curiosity that caused him to pry into all kinds of moral and religious questions.

Moreover, in undertaking the investigation Socrates believed in a criterion upon which he could rely. This criterion was an inner

A HISTORY OF PHILOSOPHICAL SYSTEMS

monitor, or voice which came to him when he was yet a child and to whose checks he was loyal throughout his entire life. It was as if life could be compared to a game of athletics like basket-ball. The rules are outlined in advance of the game and as long as the activity of the players falls within them the game proceeds. But when the activity of the players falls outside the rules, the playing ceases. Now Socrates believed that he lived in a world that had rules or laws. These laws had been prescribed by an infinite intelligence and were ordered for the ongoing of life. When the activity of living fell outside the prescribed laws a cosmic impasse forbade the "game" to go forward. But different from the experience of players in an athletic contest, Socrates held that prior to the incorrect act "a kind of voice . . . always forbids . . . me to do anything which I am going to do." [29] By heeding the checks and changing to a course of life that did not encounter a warning Socrates concluded that he could live a life in harmony with what nature intended.

NOTES

1. Lewis Mumford, *The Condition of Man*, p. 61.
2. W. G. Greene, *Moira*, p. 9.
3. Werner Jaeger, *Paideia*, I, xxiii.
4. Homer, *Odyssey*, I, 33.
5. Hesiod, *Works and Days*, 290.
6. Theognis, *Elegiac Poems*, I, 437.
7. Simonides, "Epithets" (*Greek Ethical Thought*, Hilda D. Oakley, editor, p. 17).
8. Sophocles, *Antigone*, 451.
9. Nicholas P. Vlachos, *Hellas and Hellenism*, p. 126.
10. Kathleen Freeman, *The Pre-Socratic Philosophers*, p. 348.
11. *Thucydides*, I, 138.
12. Hesiod, *Theogony*, 81 ff.
13. Plato, *Protagoras*, 318E.
14. *Thucydides*, II, 37.
15. Werner Jaeger, *op. cit.*, I, 313.
16. *Diogenes Laertius*, IX, 56.
17. *Ibid.*, II, 16. *Cf.* Ernest Barker: "It was he [Archelaus] who first drew the famous distinction between *physis* and *nomos* in the world of human affairs." *Greek Political Theory*, p. 53. Also, J. Burnet declares that "in the great controversy about Law and Nature he [Protagoras] is decidedly on the side of the former." *Greek Philosophy, Pt. I*, 114.

18. Plato, *Gorgias* 482E, *et al.*
19. Plato, *Republic* 544D.
20. Aristotle, *De Interpretatione* 16a27.
21. Plato, *Republic* 354B; *cf.* also 336B ff.
22. Plato, *Gorgias* 484; *cf.* also 482E ff.
23. Johann Eduard Erdmann, *A History of Philosophy* I, 70.
24. Plato, *Apology* 18C, *logon* is often translated reason; *cf.* also Aristotle, *Rhetorica* 1402a23 and John Milton, *Paradise Lost*, II, 113.
25. Plato, *Gorgias* 502E.
26. Aristotle, *Metaphysics* 1004b19, 26.
27. *Matthew* 18:3, *et al.*
28. Plato, *Republic* 533D.
29. Plato, *Apology* 31D.

BIBLIOGRAPHY

JOHN BURNET, *Greek Philosophy, Part I,* 105-192 (London, 1928).
KATHLEEN FREEMAN, *The Pre-Socratic Philosophers,* pp. 341-423 (Oxford, 1946).
R. D. HICKS, "Protagoras," in Hastings' *Encyclopaedia of Religion and Ethics,* X, 409-10 (New York, 1930).
———, "Sophists," in Hastings' *Encyclopaedia of Religion and Ethics,* XI, 687-692 (New York, 1934).
WERNER JAEGER, *Paideia,* I, 283-328 (Oxford, 1939).
———, *Paideia,* II, 13-76 (New York, 1943).
HILDA D. OAKLEY, *Greek Ethical Thought,* pp. vii-xxxviii; 1–89 (London, 1925).

CHAPTER EIGHT
PLATONISM

JAMES H. DUNHAM

THE PHILOSOPHY of Plato, sometimes called Platonism, is the first attempt of Western thought to organize a critique of pure reason as the instrument for obtaining scientific knowledge. Before his day reflection had devoted its efforts to a study of the facts of nature as presented to ordinary observation. The men of Miletus agreed that causality was the problem demanding immediate attention. What was the first and all-embracing cause? They answered the question in various ways, either by pointing to the primordial elements, earth, air, fire or water, or by constructing in mind an indeterminate substance which contained the properties of the several elements but without specific form. But cause implies effect, and between the two, change or motion must intervene. Hence a new analysis was made by Heraclitus (*c*. 545-475 B.C.). Nothing, he said, remains the same, everything is in flux; opposites clash, hot and cold, large and small, swift and slow, good and bad, and an attunement of conflicting tendencies must be effected. This is done by assuming a *logos,* a law of change regnant in the entire world. Meantime in Italy a new doctrine was taught. A permanent substance exists, says Parmenides (*b*. 539? B.C.), which cannot be moved, divided or dissolved, nor can it abide unfinished. If motion is a phenomenon in nature, it is confined within her own limits; if individuals appear, they are factors in the majestic whole. The One is dominant and the Many are phases of the whole, which is the antithesis of the Ionian postulate.

It was clear to the discerning mind that the major concepts of human thinking, one and many, same and different, like and unlike, must undergo rigid examination by a method which will reveal their basic meaning and the exact relations between them. The sponsor of the method was none other than Socrates (*c.* 470-399 B.C.), the son of Sophroniscus, a teacher of repute in the capital city, a man of acute intelligence and of unimpeachable integrity. His personal interests, by his own testimony and by the tradition of the Academy, lay outside the area of physical research. He confined his studies to the formulation of the logical definition, with its application to moral and political problems. He was the first disputant to distinguish sharply between universal and particular judgments. He brought every argument, says Xenophon (430- post 355 B.C.), back to the underlying principles. Yet he was careful to test every conclusion by reference to appropriate examples. Aristotle (384-322 B.C.) insists that Socrates would allow no definitional concept to stand apart from its own object, as his successor did, and thereby established the new logic on a thoroughly inductive basis.

With such a precedent as this before him Plato (428-348 B.C.), the disciple, took up the task of perfecting the method, in order to make it the standard guide for the settlement of every question whether in the physical sciences or the broad field of moral jurisprudence. Every object, he teaches, has two constitutional aspects, its matter and its form. Matter being limitless, as he says in the *Philebus,* is capable of being divided into a multiple of units each exhibiting the same form. Form, in its turn, expresses the integral meaning of the object, and a given form retains the same content wherever it is recorded. But despite the distinction between them, form and matter belong to the same individual. Nevertheless, because of his strong emphasis on the importance of the idea or form, Plato seems, at times, to wrest it from its residence in the object and install it in a new field of existence. He does this, Aristotle complains, by framing a hypothetical series, the first term concrete, the second abstract. Thus, Socrates is a concrete individual, a man, when we first study him; then he becomes an abstract object, the essential principle of manhood (*Met.* 1040a9). How can he be both? The issue is fundamental and must be met. Are Plato's ideas concrete individuals, separated (a dangerous word, says Natorp) from their objects in the real world and therefore existing by themselves? Or, are they conceptualized properties of their objects and therefore inseparable from them? Sometimes Plato speaks of them as "supersensibles"; but by that term he means precisely what we mean when we say that concepts cannot be seen, heard or felt, nor can they be represented by the idioms of physics. Ideas, he holds, are the instruments used to identify an object or relation or as we now say, *event*. Prof. J. A. Stewart puts it succinctly: "Ideas are ways of thinking"; they are, therefore, "in us not in the external world." Aristotle, to all intents and purposes, expresses the same opinion when he writes, "I call the essence of an object a *substance* without corporeality"; and again, "Ideas cannot be substances in the primary sense since they qualify an object. At the same time if ideas are not universals but individuals standing apart from their objects, they cannot be known; for science deals only with universal or abstract terms" (*Met.* 1032b15; 1003a7). We may sum up the discussion as follows: ideas belong to objects but can only be comprehended by the methods of logical analysis. That this is Plato's teaching will appear with convincing force when we study the Divided Line in the Sixth Book of the *Republic*.

The Deduction of the Universal Ideas

Ideas and their primordial images are part and parcel of the cognitive process; that is to say, they belong to the natural habits of thought. In order to reach their final form ideas must pass through what Nettleship calls the four stages of intelligence, corresponding to the four sections of Plato's Line. Two of these are products of the imagination, namely, sense-perception and belief, and the remaining two, of the faculty of reflection, namely, judgment and the principle of reason. The first registers the direct contact between the mind and objects in the external world by means of an image or "likeness" (*eikon*). This may appear as the shadow of a projected body, with its contour and size; again as a figure mirrored in a pool of water or on a polished plate, its lines, angles and colors being clearly defined. In certain cases the image may emphasize a particular quality, *e.g.*, whiteness, enabling us to detect its principal features. The *Theaetetus* dialogue is the expert's laboratory for the analysis of such rudimentary experiences. It is made plain at once that we must go beyond the first section of the Line, if we are to obtain the notion of a "steady" image. Perception by itself can never produce knowledge; the contention of Protagoras was false and misleading. For consider the following facts:—we must have a second supporting sensum, if we are to know what *white* as a simple sensation involves.

But the next percept emerging from what seems to be the same situation may yield an altogether different result, either because there is a change in the situation or a change in the attitude of the percipient. We can only conclude that accuracy in perception comes through a long and arduous process of education (*Th.* 184-6).

The problem of perception is much more difficult when we are obliged to decide whether certain facts in nature can actually be perceived. Can we, for instance, form a distinct image of either motion or power? Both appear to confront our organic senses with the same appeal that individual bodies make. But Plato shows with inconfutible evidence in the *Theaetetus* (181, sq.) that motion itself cannot be perceived but only bodies in motion, and in the *Sophist* (247) that power is not a substance, a real thing, but the ubiquitous attribute of substance, hence capable of becoming a predicate in the judgment—"real things have their distinguishing marks, chiefest of which is dynamical power."

The second step in the pursuit of knowledge is the identification of an image as having a fixed content to be accepted as its true and only meaning. The image has now a "greater degree of truth" because we are surer of its relation to the external object. This brief statement of the matter in the *Republic* (510A) comes into clearer light in the *Theaetetus,* when he examines the mental function, memory, which makes knowledge possible. We have here the first historical analysis of the principle of association which has its consummation in the *Treatise of Human Nature* by David Hume. The process of forming a concept is extremely complex and full of insidious perils. The mind, says Plato, is like a wax tablet receiving impressions from many widely separated sources (*Th.* 194,5). Hence, error easily tracks its pathway. The percept may not be distinct in form or well-defined in substance. It may become entangled with unrelated or confused materials. It may have been communicated to a mind not trained to assimilate its particular kind of sensation. But granted the presence of an unclouded mind, in the Cartesian sense, every new image of equivalent content will be automatically referred to the original image, and together they will constitute an enduring notion. This Plato calls its *eidos*, that which has been, so to say, officially seen. Still at this early stage it is only a belief, as contrasted with ascertained knowledge, and it may be *wrong*. Later when he has placed it in a psychological judgment, he thinks it may have a greater chance, though not a guaranteed certainty, of being right. For such judgments, which are not yet controlled by logic's laws, are subject to two natural tendencies, either to make a judgment about something which does not exist, or to mistake one existing thing for another. The only escape from such a tragedy is obedience to the system to be outlined in the third section of the Line.

At this point, then, we turn from sense to reflection, from routine memory to the *noetic* faculty of mind. This does not imply that we break all ties with sensible experience, as Aristotle had charged. Every universal idea, concrete or abstract, every form of predication, has some surviving feature of the original sense-datum. The problem now is, how shall we determine the meaning which the mature idea is to carry? The method he adopts is Grecian. Its name highlights all modern scientific inquiry, but the mode of approach is different. Hypothesis, to us, signifies a tentative formula set up to account for the operation of certain forces in nature in ways not yet known. Controlled experiment and the readjustment of physical conditions are usually involved. If the formula fails, it is discarded and another substituted. For the Greek, however, the hypothesis was a primordial judgment accepted as true, often called "prior knowledge," although no logical proof can be adduced. Thus, given the properties of a triangle, we can through the use of parallelism as the middle term, arrive at the conclusion that its interior angles are equal to two right angles.

The method requires us to develop two points, the nature of the given judgment and the manner in which its implications can be unfolded. It is assumed at the outset that every judgment, when valid, is the union of related and complementary ideas; that is, they must be logically negotiable. Plato said the subject must "participate" in the predicate; we say the predicate is implied in the subject. Aristotle listed a group of fundamental ideas which he called categories. Plato distinguished predicates that dealt with existence, and those that denoted value, the former represented by the physical sciences, the latter by ethics and aesthetics. We confine our attention just now to the former. In general, Plato and Aristotle agree that every real thing must have attributes, but existence itself cannot be an attribute. The attribute tells us what the object is, it puts it into the class to which it belongs. Thus the star is a heavenly body emitting rays of light from its distant orb, pursuing its course in a steady geometrical curve, and maintaining a fixed relation to neighboring bodies and to the constant earth. The idea of star is embodied in this definition, and conversely when the terms of this definition are satisfied, we call the body a star. However, when the terms are not fulfilled, as in the sun or planet or meteor, the body cannot be classified as a star. This is the essence of the Socratic method, the genus, a heavenly luminary, the differentia, the properties that belong to the star. In short, the logical definition becomes the basis of all scientific analysis, where ideas have a fixed and unchanging connotation. That is the reason why the Greeks when they wished to formulate a scientific law, determined upon the class to which the situation conformed, and then wrote out the definition of the class as the sum and substance of the law.

But the logical predicate does something more than preserve the identity of the idea; it shows how from the specific idea a great company of cognate ideas may be developed. The instruments used here are the antitheticals—same and different, like and unlike, motion and rest in physics, equal and unequal in mathematics. The purpose of these categories is to clear away all materials that do not lend themselves to a better understanding of the subject under consideration. Thus the contrasting concepts motion and rest made an enormous appeal to scientist and layman alike, in an age when the position of the earth in the system of nature was a question of heated debate. For the majority of observers the earth was the symbol of complete quiescence, while the heavenly bodies were in uninterrupted movement. Some hinted, however, that the earth might be in motion, and Plato lets Timaeus say that "the earth, our nurse, goes to and fro in its path round the axis which stretches right through the universe" (*Tim.* 40). In our day when the relativity of motion has become almost a fixed dogma in physics, and absolute rest an inconceivable formula, we might dispense with that type of logical predication. But we cannot exclude the more abstract categories, like and unlike, same and different. If it be asked, whence comes the authority attaching to such predicates, the answer is found in the *Theaetetus* (186): "they are things which the mind itself undertakes to judge for us, when it reflects upon them and compares them with one another." Beyond that it would seem Plato does not care to go. If anthropology had been even a rudimentary science in his day, he might have extended his investigations further; but even if he had possessed the cultural data we have now assembled, it is quite possible that his conclusion would not have been changed.

It remains to examine the second phase of the hypothetical method—how truths latent in the original judgment can be unfolded. The classical report is made in the *Sophist,* and Plato gives the name *division* to its particular form. We start with a recognized genus, *e.g.,* animal, and then cite the differential properties belonging to its several members. Plato proposes to handle the supreme issue in philosophy in the same manner. He asks, what properties can be alleged to be the dominant attributes in the fundamental substance. At first the battle is between the gods and the giants, the Formists and the Materialists, the Italians, Pythagoras (*fl.* 532 B.C.) and Parmenides, on the one side, and the Ionians, Anaximander (611-*c.* 547 B.C.) and Heraclitus on the other. The latter insist that substance is composed of corporeal things, things that you can crunch and crumble in your hands. But Plato objects: substance is not sheer inert stuff; it is matter crowned with motion; it is force, energy, dynamic action. It has the essence of soul, and is found in human beings, where its power is expressed in intelligence, goodness, justice, *real things* because they display irresistible energy.

The opposing camp, the Formists, contend only with ideas; they say that action and reaction in the human body, the coming and going of sensory images, all belong to the sphere of becoming, which has no enduring quality. Then Plato speaks again: are we to infer that change, life, soul, understanding have no place in the realm of reality? Must the soul of man stand apart in "solemn aloofness, devoid of intelligence"? In point of fact, are the two sets of combatants, Materialists and Formists, the only claimants to the definition of substance? No; there is a third member of the supreme genus: substance includes both change and stability, "all that is changeless and all that this is in process of changing." That synthesis is the master concept and frames the only incontrovertible theory of substance. The method of division has passed into the stately order of the Dialectic (*Soph.* 246-53).

There is also another species of division which answers one of the age-long problems of philosophy. Here the members are two, a positive term and its contradictory. The former is again divided in the same manner, and the process goes on until the indivisible is reached. Thus, substance is organic and inorganic; organic is sensible and insensible, and the division proceeds until the individual, Man, appears. It is this method which teaches us the meaning of non-being. Non-being is no longer a term in ontology, as with Parmenides, it is a term in logic. The negative judgment is often more inclusive than the affirmative. For inorganic substance embraces astronomy, physics, chemistry, and the allied sciences, a vast electorate from which to choose the desired member (*Soph.* 255-58).

The Idea of the Good

The third section of the Line has uncovered the following cardinal items: (1) that every object has its own specific idea which is the law governing its activity; (2) that every idea is related to other ideas by fixed and coördinate predicates, ultimately expressed in mathematical symbols, the true language of science (*Philebus*, 25, 26); and (3) that no breach or hiatus can occur in substance since every negation is only another form of significant determination. For most scientific operators the inquiry ends at this point, but not for Plato. For him, as for Immanuel Kant (1724-1804), the shores of truth are girt by a wide and stormy ocean, the "natural home of illusion." He had traveled three-fourths of his Line, mastering problems that had mocked the skill of a myriad of earnest scholars. He felt sure that the human mind had yet another faculty, *nous*, the pure reason, which was concerned neither with concrete images nor the "bloodless categories," as Bradley (1846-1924) called them, and he intended to push on until he apprehended it, the "first principle of the whole." This idea he defined as the Good. Here no formal method was needed, only direct intuition, and then the instant penetration into subordinate truths as a matter of course (*Rep.* 511B). For as the eye can discover no object except by the light of the sun, so the mind can comprehend none of the elements of knowledge without the interpreting support of the Good.

What is the Good? In every mature language it is the property, single or manifold, apart from which no object in nature or mind can be what it is. In his study of the human eye, its structure and function, Plato first expounded its physical purpose, namely, sight, and then proceeded to itemize the extraordinary facts that sight makes possible—the invention of numbers, the development of the concept of time, and the appreciation of the nature of the whole. Thus the *eidos* of an object—what it means, is exactly equivalent to its primary purpose—what it can do. In fine, the good of an object is its overshadowing purpose, the second point in every definition. But this is not all; the good can explain the nature and character of the human percipient who is called upon to assess the value of the object before him. Plato examines this question at length in the *Philebus* dialogue. What is the Good, the *summum bonum*, for man, for society, indeed, for the entire constituted cosmos? Aristippus (*c.* 435-356 B.C.) said, pleasure, agreeable feeling; Socrates retorted, ordered knowledge eventuating in superior wisdom. Restricting our thought for the moment to the experiences of the citizen in the state, the good must satisfy the needs of his physical constitution and fulfill the highest aspirations of his moral nature. Can the play of emotion even when long sustained or some brilliant achievement in the conquest of truth, can either of these by itself promote the end in view which is nothing less than the making of a rounded life? The complete good must contain certain ingredients which Plato recites in detail: the harmony of our native interests—to see, to know, to cultivate the affections, to associate ourselves with the movements of the visible world, to find our true place in the community of the social group; then to join to harmony the grace of symmetry, where variations of temper are subject to rational control, all excesses being forbidden: and finally, to see to it that the good embodies the truths that have been won by analysis and experience, and so far as possible, installed as the accepted statutes of government. (*Phil.* 65-67).

The Metaphysical Aspects of the Good

It is obvious from the foregoing argument that a world in which reason rules is the only kind which Plato conceives as possible. But how can we apply the term *reason* to a physically organized universe? In the *Phaedo* Plato makes Socrates chide Anaxagoras (*c.* 464-428 B.C.) for saying that reason is the cause of motion, when motion is the sign of the activity of matter, and nothing else. Later, in the *Timaeus* he allows the Theban physicist to construct a world through the Demiurge by copying the timeless ideas as "patterns," and then endowing it with a comprehensive and authoritative soul. Some scholars, Burnet amongst them, find here the key to Plato's religious system:—God is distinct from the universe, presides at its creation and engraves upon it the characters of his own intelligence. But the dialogue hints more than once that the whole argument is problematical and does not reach a satisfactory conclusion (48B). There is nothing in this dialogue or any other (before the *Laws*) to show that Plato did not believe matter to be uncreated and eternal. Certainly, this was the tradition in the Academy; for Xenocrates (396-314 B.C.), his nephew and successor as head of the Academy, says explicitly that Plato did not teach the creation of the world "in time" (a phrase used for convenience of exposition) but was concerned solely with the study of its phenomena in due and proper order, "things logically first, and then things scientifically allied with them."

But there is another definition of reason which the philosopher cordially endorsed—the world can be understood by men of trained intelligence. This implies that the good exists in total nature and we can analyze it in the same way that we analyze the good in man. The world is presented as an individual, the Supreme Unity, whose *matter* (in the technical sense) is the complex of all substances, together with the motions appertaining to them, and whose *form* is the order and harmony of the whole. The structural concepts are three, time, space and cause. Time is the "enduring essence" of the world; it cannot be confined to days, months and years, its natural divisions, but is "the moving image everlasting." Time is a continuum, it has no beginning and it will have no end. It is the central index of the harmony of motion. Scarcely less significant is space which establishes the internal relations of the cosmos, and denotes continuity, expansion, and the unified whole. Plato lets Timaeus call it the "receptacle of all becoming," which appears to mean that the "planes" of individual bodies would have no "home," were they not connected by the unseen but coercive factor of space. Hence space guarantees the *order* of nature and forbids us to accept the theory of void which would destroy the symmetry of the system.

The third property is that of Cause, as important to Greek as to modern science. Two types are distinguished, the material and the efficient on the physical side, the formal and final on the mental. Take an analogy. The statue of Athena in the Parthenon has marble and the chisel of the artist as its physical causes, the charm of the goddess and the sense of beauty as immaterial causes. But it will not escape our attention that a double aspect attends every causal process, (1) what originates the action, *aitia*, and (2) what certifies to its operation, *ananke*, necessity. Still we must be extremely careful not to identify the Greek notion of cause with the concept of mechanical law employed by modern science. For Plato allows Timaeus to introduce the idea of a "wandering cause," which has troubled commentators more than it should. If it did not refer to the peculiar orbits of the planets, it might be due to the thesis accepted by all Greek observers, that the purpose of the whole always dictates the actions of its parts. Or, did Plato cast an eye to the far future and discern the strange "jumps" of the electrons and Heisenberg's principle of indeterminacy?

It follows from these reflections that the "divine philosophy" had an intimate connection with the concepts of the natural sciences. The adjective *divine* (*theion*) is the synonym for the extraordinary, chiefest, most distinguished, an appropriate term for Plato to use, when he examined the operations of the visible universe. Here are his words: "the philosopher who holds converse with divine and universal ideas, does by such experience become part of the divine and universal order, so far as his nature permits" (*Rep.* 500B). Thus the idea of the Good is a logical instrument sharp enough to cut away the rubbish which commentators who follow Aristotle have allowed to gather about Plato's religious theory. It suggests, too, that the commonplaces of the *Laws* should not supplant the seasoned arguments developed at the zenith of his power. The idea of the good is the symbol of the perfect whole, whether in the rounded character of man or in the seamless periphery of the cosmos. Parmenides, we said, conceived of a single substance defined by negative terms. Pythagoras postulated an original One out of which sprang an interminable series of abstract numbers. Plato interpreted the world with the skill of an expert aesthetician as well as with the ingenuity of a practised physicist. Its orderly processes, its harmonious movements, its infinite parts contributing to the solidarity of the whole, all testified to its teleological structure, a purpose that defines the specific function of every segment down to the most minute grain of sand.

But if the good is the symbol of the perfect whole, it is also the guarantor of the indiscerptible unity of substance. The Greeks of the

Periclean age reveled in the conceit that being and one are the same, a fancy confirmed by the *Parmenides* dialogue with logical precision. There was need in Plato's day of establishing this unity with all the authority that philosophy could summon. For the pluralists were at work with as much energy as in the days of Empedocles (*c*. 490-430 B.C.) and Democritus (*b*. 470 or 460 B.C.). They broke substance into pieces and left no place for a substantive whole. Then Plato, having erected the Good as the loftiest principle in logic, converted it into the solidifying property of nature. The good is the essence of reality; in fact, it exceeds even the essential property in dignity and power (*Rep*. 509B). Take another analogy. The picture on the wall is a composite whole, with its figures, colors, lights and shades, gathered about the radiant center; but it is also a federal unity endowed with a common meaning and penetrated by an infallible intuition of beauty. The world which our philosopher viewed possessed a unity which could be nothing short of that reality which men call divine.

The destiny of man is inevitably bound up with the fortunes of the universe. For Plato the world had no beginning and could have no end. Can the same be said of its integral units? In particular, is there any foundation for the Hellenic belief that the soul of man will survive when the body perishes? The subject is debated in the *Phaedo* dialogue but no decision is reached. Even when the idea of immortality is supported by strong public sentiment, it is accepted only with a kind of "reluctant confidence" (107B). In the light of so much uncertainty as to its destiny, two theories as to its nature have grown up. The first holds that there are two distinct substances, body and soul, united for a few years in a single personality, and enjoying all the rights of self-expression. When the body dies, the soul proceeds to its appointed goal.

The other theory is more complex. Man is an individual having matter and form as every other object in nature. Plato raises the question whether desire and emotion are separate faculties or merely modes of the same type of behavior, which is the way the body functions (*Rep*. 439, *sq*.). But whether the same or different, one point is certain, both are distinguished from the "logistic" faculty, reason, the sole expression of the form, and are wholly subject to its decisions. How? By force of ideas, hardened into judgments. The meaning of manhood does not lie in desire or emotion but in the capacity to think out the proper way of acting. Reason belongs to man, the person, and cannot be separated from him. It does not come into his mind "from out-of-doors," as Hardie translates Aristotle's phrase. It is the universal aspect of man's behavior, the *good* of his nature. Socrates, a man of superlative intelligence, drinks the hemlock, and as an observable figure disappears, but the quintessence of his ideas, his soul, persists through untold ages. Immortality inheres in ideas, and in ideas only. This is the implication of the Divided Line reaching its climax in the idea of the Good which is now established as the Genus of Reason operating in the intellect of man and in every other form of excellence in the real world.

NOTES

The Dialogues of Plato referred to in the text and their abbreviations:—
The Republic (Rep.), Phaedo (Phaed.), Timaeus (Tim.), Theaetetus (Th.), Parmenides (Parm.), Sophist (Soph.), Philebus (Phil.).

The Greek Text of Plato's Dialogues is edited by John Burnet, and the traditional translation is by Benjamin Jowett. Other translations are by Francis M. Cornford.

Aristotle's *Metaphysics*. Translation by W. D. Ross (Oxford, 2d Edition, 1928).

Ritter and Preller, *Historia Philosophia Graeca*. Quotation from Xenocrates, Section 330.

The author is indebted to the owners of the copyright (Temple University, Oxford U. Press) of his *The Religion of Philosophers*, for permission to use certain sentences of the text without the identifying quotation marks.

BIBLIOGRAPHY

J. BURNET, *Greek Philosophy*, Pt. I. Thales to Plato (London, 1924).
F. M. CORNFORD, *Plato's Theory of Knowledge* (London and New York, 1935).
F. M. CORNFORD, *Plato's Cosmology* (London, 1937).
W. A. HARDIE, *Study of Plato* (Oxford, 1936).
C. RITTER, *The Essence of Plato's Philosophy*, Translated by A. Allen (New York, 1933).
J. A. STEWART, *Plato's Doctrine of Ideas* (Oxford, 1909).
A. E. TAYLOR, *Plato: The Man and His Work* (London, 1936).
E. ZELLER, *Plato and the Older Academy* (London, 1888).
J. H. DUNHAM, *The Religion of Philosophers*, Chap. II (Philadelphia, 1947).

CHAPTER NINE

ARISTOTELIANISM

HENRY VEATCH

ARISTOTLE (384-322 B.C.) in the present day enjoys the dubious distinction of being a classic: nearly everyone respects his name, and almost no one reads what he wrote. True, Aristotle's writing is crabbed and difficult, so that if one were casually to take up an Aristotelian text, one would probably put it down again none-the-wiser: one simply would not know what the man was talking about.

Nor is this the only disability from which the unhappy Aristotle currently suffers. For it is the settled and almost unanimous opinion of latter-day intellectuals that even if one were to read Aristotle and were to understand him, one would still be none-the-wiser. For what is there of importance in Aristotle any longer? True, what he said may have been important for the ancient Greeks in their day and for some medieval monks in theirs, but it certainly is of no particular importance for us in ours.

In consequence, Aristotle tends to be consigned to a fate which, for a philosopher, is almost worse than that of not being read at all. That is the fate of being read only as a line or as a paragraph or, perhaps in Aristotle's more celebrated case, as a chapter in what is now fashionably known as the "history of ideas."

But is it possible ever to understand a philosopher thus? To be sure, as historians or anthropologists or perhaps even as Freudian psychologists we may gain a kind of understanding of a philosopher merely by looking at him in a museum case. But we can hardly come to understand him as a philosopher in this way. For philosophy, or at least Aristotelian philosophy, professes to be science, in the sense that it offers a descriptive and explanatory account of the nature of things and of reality. But scientific knowledge insists on being judged as contemporary, for it will only talk about things as they are and are now. Consequently, if we are ever to understand Aristotle as a philosopher, we must necessarily think of him as talking about reality, and about reality as it is and as it now appears to us to be. But this is only another way of saying that even in order to understand Aristotle as a figure in the past, we must needs try to see him in the present.

And yet no sooner do we attempt to see Aristotelianism in the present than we seem to become hopelessly entangled in anachronisms. Thus for one thing in the present, almost everyone considers that the only way to get any real positive knowledge of the world round about us is through the so-called natural sciences. And as for philosophy, its function would seem to be at best a merely critical one, and at worst a merely logical one. That is to say, so far from providing any knowledge of the observable phenomena of the world, philosophy is thought to be concerned with no more than determining the epistemological conditions of our experience of phenomena, or perhaps with no more than the logico-linguistic apparatus for talking about such phenomena.

But clearly, any such perspective is utterly alien to Aristotle. That there was no such thing as modern science in Aristotle's day goes without saying. Instead, for him philosophy was science, and science philosophy. Hence to understand Aristotelian philosophy is to understand it as a scientific description of the real world. But this would seem to be simply impossible any longer.

Accordingly, if what Aristotle had to say does not seem to make much sense if we try to fit into the current critical or positivistic frame of reference, perhaps we would do better to treat Aristotelianism as if it were simply "metaphysics." And this is what we do do by and large now-a-days.

And yet such a treatment of Aristotle is scarcely calculated to do him much justice either. For by "metaphysics" people have generally come to understand both a certain type of method and a certain type of subject matter. As for the method, it is supposed to involve some such thing as *a priori* synthesis and construction, in contrast to the more humdrum empirical description characteristic of the natural sciences. And as for the subject matter of metaphysics, this is supposed, almost by definition, to be made up of entities lying quite beyond the reach of observation and experience, all else being considered to be within the province of the natural sciences.

Now to convince ourselves that Aristotle was hardly a metaphysician in this sense, we have only to recall Aristotle's determined and unremitting criticism of Platonism. Thus as regards knowledge, Aristotle sharply rejected the Platonic doctrine of *anamnesis*—a rejection which means, translated into modern terminology, that Aristotle recognized no knowledge as being *a priori,* or prior to sensory experience and independent of all reference to such experience.

Likewise, as regards the notion that the proper objects of metaphysics transcend the world of sense, there is a certain sense in which this might be said to be true of Aristotelianism. And yet in the usual sense in which this is understood today, it simply is not true of Aristotelianism at all.

Instead, most of the basic Aristotelian notions—form, matter, substance, the soul, the four causes, being, potency, act, etc.—are to be understood primarily in the context of the changing world of nature which we observe round about us. Indeed, once again one might say that the principal thrust of Aristotle's criticism of the so-called Platonic theory of Ideas is that the latter errs in the direction of being too "metaphysical," in the modern sense: it dislocates the proper and primary objects of philosophy, transporting them from the real world of change with which our senses acquaint us, and placing them in a supposedly other-world of Ideas.

No, rather than being "metaphysical," Aristotle would consider that the first (though, to be sure, not the only) function of philosophy is to provide a straightforward description of the observable, changing world in which the human being finds himself. Indeed, historically, one might say that Aristotle thought of himself as confronting an unhappy and, in his eyes, an unnecessary dilemma, which all previous Greek philosophy had fallen afoul of—the dilemma of change *vs.* intelligibility. For it appeared to Aristotle as if his philosophical predecessors had either held fast to the changing sensible reality of the natural world, only to fail to make such changing being intelligible through adequate causal description, or they held fast to principles of intelligibility, only to squint at or to lose from sight altogether the concrete changes of nature.

Accordingly, to meet this dilemma and to exhibit the intelligibility of changing being, Aristotle insists upon the recognition of at least two basic principles in all change—form and matter.

Thus, form as the principle of determinateness in things is also the source of their intelligibility. In other words, it is in virtue of a thing's form that that thing is what it is and does what it does. At the same time, a thing's form is certainly not all that it is. On the contrary, as is clear simply from experience, the green leaf is not merely green; it is also able to become red. Or an atom of oxygen is not just the form or nature of oxygen as such; it also has the potentiality for being combined with hydrogen to form water.

In this sense, then, one may say that things in the natural world, in addition to being what they are in virtue of their forms, are also able to become other and different from what they are in virtue of their matter. For by matter is meant the source or principle of potentiality in things, and specifically of potentiality with respect to new and different forms. Hence change is to be understood as the process of actualizing any such potentiality for a new form.

Moreover, given these hylomorphic principles, a causal explanation of change becomes possible. Thus if one wants to know the causes of any given change, one must recognize the matter as a cause in the sense that it underlies the whole change and actually receives the new form. Likewise, the form is a cause in the sense that it provides the new determination; it is in virtue of it, the form, that the changed thing is actually different from what it was. At the same time, that the thing should become different, that its matter should actually receive the new form or determination, requires an agent or efficient cause. For that the marble should become a statue is explained neither just by the marble, nor just by the statue, but by the activity of the sculptor. Moreover, that an agent should act in a certain determinate way and give rise to a certain determinate effect means simply that that agent is ordered to that effect as to an end; and that its efficient activity comes to an end and terminates in that effect. Thus the activity of the sculptor, *qua* sculptor, culminates in the completed statue, and not in the process of photosynthesis, or in a legal transaction, or in the geological phenomenon of faulting.

Nor is it hard to see what would happen to the whole enterprise of rendering change intelligible, if one were to try to dispense with either the formal or the material principle.

Thus if one were to let the forms go, intelligibility would go as well. For if there are no forms, nothing will have any determinate characteristics. And if things are neither this nor that, there will be no determinate efficient causes acting in determinate ways to produce determinate effects. In short, without formal causes, there will be no efficient or final causes either; and the world of nature will be reduced to a mere Heraclitean flux, utterly opaque to intelligence and understanding.

On the other hand, if one tries to dispense with the material principle, then some sort of Parmenideanism would seem to become the order of the day. For forms as such are incapable of change. Greenness, for example, just as such can never either be or become other than itself. But then if there is no matter in which new and different forms may be received or actualized, and if forms themselves never change, then change itself must be declared an illusion. And if change is thus shuffled off, the efficient and final causes no longer have any function to perform and disappear altogether. Instead, the whole burden of explanation comes to be carried simply by the formal cause, and the resulting type of explanation turns out to be essentially mathematical.

Or as an alternative, one might try to play the hopeless game of sacrificing the material cause, retaining the formal cause, and yet at the same time trying to save the appearances of change. But the consequence is inevitably the replacement of change by something quite different, *viz.*, succession. For if matter as the principle of potentiality be excluded, and if it be impossible for any form as such ever to change or become different from what it is, the only way to save the appearances, so far as change is concerned, is to suppose that one form ceases to be and another form succeeds it, simply *ex nihilo*.

Unfortunately, however, such a succession of atomic formal occurrences quite defies intelligibility. For the formal cause in such a case can do no more than explain the properties of a form, but not its occurrence. And as for the other causes, they simply are not available for explanation. For an efficient cause cannot act in a determinate way without something to act upon. And without matter there is nothing that it could act upon, since only matter is susceptible of being changed by an agent. Indeed, in desperation, or perhaps in ignorance, thinkers have sometimes tried to identify the agent merely with the preceding event or occurrence—"a cause is that which precedes its effect in time"—, as if an agent could act without anything to act upon, or could produce an effect after it had itself ceased to exist.

In short, the main Aristotelian thesis in regard to the physical world is clear: unless we recognize in things both a formal and a material principle, we cannot possibly make the fact of change intelligible.

And yet this is not the whole story so far as Aristotelianism is concerned. For it must never be forgotten that in explaining change, Aristotle thinks of himself as explaining changing *being*. That is to say, it is not just an intelligible pattern or order of events that Aristotle is trying to discover in experience; instead, he is trying to understand how change can *be,* or, if you will, how that which is or has being can change.

Accordingly, "after the *Physics,*" Aristotle's editors placed the *Metaphysics* which undertakes the study of being just as such, or *qua* being. Moreover, no sooner does one thus turn to an examination simply of the being of things, or what it means for them to be, or in what senses we say of them that they are, than it immediately becomes apparent that being is said in many senses. For instance, our common human experience would certainly indicate that such things as quantities, qualities, actions, passions, relations, *are*. But in just what sense are they? Again, from experience we recognize that they are in a very different sense from substances. For a quality can only exist as the quality of something. Likewise, the quantity, "six inches long," obviously cannot exist just as such: there must always be something that is six inches long. But not so substances: a man, for instance, or an atom or a tree, does not have to be *of* anything, in the same way as a quality must needs be the quality of something.

Moreover, besides this difference between being in itself and being in another, Aristotelian metaphysics also recognizes the difference between being able to be and actually being. Also in the case of any being it is obvious that it is what is: it has a "what" or an essence through which it is intelligible. In consequence, we may regard any being as a "what" that is either in itself or in another, either actually or potentially.

But now regarding these basic distinctions of Aristotelian physics and metaphysics—form and matter, the four causes, substance and accident, act and potency, being and essence—we may ask: Are these mere "metaphysical" distinctions in the modern sense of the word? It would hardly seem so. For Aristotle would certainly think of all these distinctions as arising out of the world of experience and as ever having a locus in the world of experience. Indeed, it is directly *in* the observable changing things of nature that we actually *find* these distinctions between matter and form, substance and accident, etc.

True, the analogical character of many of these basic notions is such that they can be made to transcend the mere being of the natural world and so be used in the description of any being whatever—for example, of the unmoved mover of the *Physics,* of the active intellect of the *De Anima,* or of the divine, self-thinking thought of the *Metaphysics*. But still, on an Aristotelian basis there is no possible way of ever reaching or knowing about such beings outside the world of nature, save in so far as they are causally connected with things in the natural world. And the metaphysical concepts and principles that we employ in order to understand and describe such transcendent beings arise only by abstraction from what we experience and are freed only in virtue of their analogous character from exclusive application to what we thus experience.

And yet even so, the thesis of Aristotelian empiricism may seem simply fantastic to modern readers. For by what possible empirical test or means of verification can one determine the truth or falsity of statements about substance, or about act and potency, or about formal and material causes, etc?

However, all such criticisms quite obviously proceed from a very different understanding of empiricism from the Aristotelian. And specifically, the difference would seem to center around the notion of the function of reason or intelligence in an empirical philosophy. Thus accustomed as we are to the perspective of modern positivism, we quite naturally think of "experience" as involving sense data on the one hand and reason on the other; and the rôle of reason is thought to be one of ordering or arranging these data in such ways as will enable us to talk about them and make predictions about them.

But in Aristotelian empiricism the rôle of reason is quite different. True, Aristotle is just as insistent as anyone that human knowledge can only be based on the data of sense. Nor would he, like Socrates in the *Meno,* attribute to sense only the stimulus to knowledge, while suggesting that the reality which we actually come to know must lie outside the sense world altogether. No, for Aristotle that which we ultimately come to know and understand through intelligence is the very same thing that was originally presented to us in sensation. And yet, while it is only in sense experience that we come to know the *real,* it is only through our rational faculties that we come to *know* the real, in the sense of understanding it and knowing it for what it is. Hence for Aristotelianism the rational faculties do not have a mere ordering function with respect to sense data, but rather an actual descriptive function with respect to real things.

And having said this much, we must also say more. For it now becomes apparent that the distinction between Aristotelian empiricism and the more modern forms of empiricism goes far beyond a mere difference of opinion as to the respective rôles of sense and reason in empirical knowledge. Rather the real point of difference would seem to be that Aristotelian empiricism is not just an empiricism but also a realism. For Aristotle would consider that it was the task of knowledge to understand things as being and in their very being. But this means that things necessarily present themselves in experience as being either in themselves or as accidents of a substance, and as being what they are and having their own natures and essences, and as being able to change, in addition to being what they actually are, etc. Indeed, such are simply some of the senses in which things may be said to be and can only be understood as being.

On the other hand, in the critical perspective of modern positivism, and even to a certain extent of modern natural science itself, it is not the being of things that one is concerned with trying to understand. Instead, knowledge and understanding are thought to involve simply the discovery in sense data, or perhaps even the projection upon sense data, of certain intelligible types or patterns of order. However, merely to devise a pattern or order for events does not as such explain how such events can *be.* In consequence, the modern positivist tends to rule out all questions as to the being of things as irrelevant or even meaningless, and his resultant philosophical performance becomes a venture in empiricism minus realism.

Moreover, it is precisely the context of realism that provides the key to an understanding of Aristotelian logic, particularly in its contrast with modern mathematical logic. For Aristotelian logic is a thoroughly realistic, or, as the Scholastics would say, an "intentional" logic. What it proposes to investigate are the tools or instruments of knowledge—concepts, propositions, syllogisms, etc. And these tools are thought to be such that their whole being consists simply in their being adapted to the disclosure of being. Indeed, so completely are these logical entities given over to the intention or representation of what is or is real, that there can be no proper understanding of them in themselves without some understanding of what it is that they are fitted to represent—*viz.*, being. In this sense, then, Aristotelian logic necessarily presupposes metaphysics (as that which makes the peculiar nature of logical entities intelligible), just as in another sense, of course, metaphysics presupposes logic (as the *organon* or instrument of all knowledge, including the knowledge of being *qua* being). Thus, for example, concepts are thought of as instruments for getting at the "what" or essences of things. Propositions, in turn, are the means whereby we can grasp essences as they really *are* in things. And finally the syllogism, with its middle term, is but a device for disclosing the *causes* for things being, and being as they are.

In contrast, mathematical logic, so far from being concerned with instruments and devices for the intention of being, would rather seem concerned simply with exhibiting possible types of relation and ordered structure. Nor would it seem to make much difference whether one conceives of such relational patterns as being themselves real, or as being creatures of *a priori* analytic judgments, or as being mere logico-linguistic conventions; in any case, when such relational types or "logical molds" are put to use for purposes of acquiring scientific knowledge, they turn out to have only an ordering function with respect to sense data or events, and not an intentional function with respect to being.

Nor is such a consequence surprising from the Aristotelian point of view, so long as logic submits to the attraction of mathematics and tends to become simply a mathematical logic. For according to Aristotle, mathematics is to be contrasted with both physics (*i.e.* the philosophy of nature) and metaphysics, in that it considers its objects in abstraction from their being or existence. And further, since these objects of mathematical investigation are not themselves intentions, like logical entities, but rather are only possible objects of such logical intention, it is little wonder that a so-called mathematical logic should hardly be appropriate for the representation and intention of the real, or even for representation and intention at all.

Finally, in passing from a consideration of the Aristotelian theoretical sciences, such as physics and metaphysics and even, in its own way, logic, to a consideration of the Aristotelian practical sciences of ethics and politics, we venture to suggest that even in this sphere the guiding principle for a right understanding of Aristotle is that same philosophical realism which we have made the central theme of our whole discussion.

And yet our thesis might seem at least initially much less plausible in this case. For while in the theoretical sciences the objective of the scientist is simply to see and describe the real, in the practical sciences the objective would seem to be, not to know the real as it is, but rather to make or do that which still has no being, but which merely might be or ought to be. Thus it is often said that ethics, for example, is concerned only with what ought to be, and not with what is. And from this it is often concluded that the proper subject matter of ethics is the ideal and not the real, and that the proper method of ethics could hardly, therefore, be one of empirical observation and description.

But such a conclusion would be thoroughly misleading if applied to Aristotelian ethics. For in an Aristotelian context, just as potentiality pervades the whole natural world, so also it is present in human nature. And this fact makes quite intelligible how a given human being might well be able to become more than he actually is, or how the very capacities of his nature might not have been brought to perfection or fully realized. Nor does it thus become intelligible merely how such a discrepancy between potency and actuality in the case of human beings can be; it also becomes intelligible how from an observation of human beings, one can come to recognize what the full perfection of human nature involves, as well as the extent to which given individuals either succeed or fail to attain such perfection.

And yet for all that, it might be objected that a practical science, even in Aristotle's eyes, is concerned with doing and making; and what is done or made by human design could hardly be said to come about by nature. Instead, by its very definition it would seem to be something artificial.

However, Aristotle would undoubtedly want to make a distinction here. For while it is true that both the productions of human art and the perfecting of human nature require the intelligent, purposive agency of human beings, and hence do not result merely from the ordinary processes of nature, still there is a difference between the two cases. For art involves a making, and ethics involves a doing. And the difference between them is that the process of making anything results in a thing made which is other than its human artificer, and which as such is quite literally an artefact; on the other hand, the deeds and actions of a man result not in any extrinsic and independently existing artefact, but rather in the perfection of the man himself, *i.e.*, in the natural perfection of a natural being. In other words, whereas the end or goal of human life is achieved not just by the processes of nature, but rather as a result of human purpose and planning, still the end which is thus achieved is none other than that demanded by human nature itself.

In short, in matters ethical quite as much as in matters physical and metaphysical, the basic thrust of Aristotelianism as a philosophy is unmistakable. For it is ever the observed changes of the world of nature (and among them the behavior and actions that are within the control of human nature) which Aristotle takes as his primary data and which he seeks to make intelligible, and intelligible in their very being. Such, indeed, is the uncompromising realism that distinguishes Aristotelianism alike from the Heracliteanism and Parmenideanism of the ancient world, as well as from the critical positivism and the "metaphysics" of today.

BIBLIOGRAPHY

For English translations of the Aristotelian texts, the most usable and the most readily available edition is that of R. P. McKeon, *The Basic Works of Aristotle* (New York, 1941).

For the standard studies of Aristotle, both general and special, that still are of not too technical a nature, the reader might profitably consult the brief, but excellent, annotated bibliography given in the above-mentioned McKeon edition.

A HISTORY OF PHILOSOPHICAL SYSTEMS

For some comparatively recent and highly suggestive treatments that are oriented, not so much toward a mere historical account of what Aristotle said, as toward a philosophical appraisal of Aristotelianism even in its contemporary significance, the reader is referred to the following:

R. P. McKeon, *The Philosophy of Aristotle* (Chicago, 1940). This has so far been circulated only in mimeographed form. It is available at the University of Chicago Bookstore.

W. A. Wick, *Metaphysics and the New Logic* (Chicago, 1942). Contains a very illuminating discussion of the different metaphysical perspectives of Aristotelian logic and modern logic.

J. Wild, *Introduction to Realistic Philosophy* (New York, 1948). A brilliant and comparatively comprehensive modern statement of Aristotelian natural philosophy, psychology, ethics, and politics.

CHAPTER TEN

HELLENISTIC AND ROMAN SCHOOLS OF PHILOSOPHY

GORDON H. CLARK

SO GREAT was the genius of Plato and Aristotle that the Hellenistic age which followed them seems by contrast to be one of decadence. The impression is heightened by the political misfortunes of the Greek states, first weakened by the Peloponnesian war, next subjugated and united in the brief career of Alexander, and then abandoned to a century of miserable decay until Rome moved in.

The philosophy of the time, however, was not so dismal as the general picture. Even the disadvantage of a comparison with Aristotle does not obscure the originality and vigor of Epicurus (340-270 B.C.), Zeno (334-264 B.C.) and Chrysippus (277-206 B.C.); and when one remembers that only fragments, and no complete volumes of philosophy remain as witnesses of two centuries, it may be suspected that the intellectual life of the early Hellenistic age was far from dormant.

If the Presocratic period had a dominant interest in science, and if Plato and Aristotle gave their best efforts to epistemology, the later age may be said to be characterized by its attention to ethics. The rapidly darkening political scene and the loss of the optimistic faith in the Homeric deities pressed home the problem of personal living. How should a man conduct himself in this vale of tears—or if not of tears, at least of events beyond his control? What would the Wise Man do?

Two schools of Socratic inspiration, the Cynics and the Cyrenaics, were forerunners of the more important movements. The Cyrenaic motif is that nothing but the inward feelings of pleasure and pain are true or important. Pleasure is good and pain is evil. Convention and prejudice lead people to praise wealth or virtue, but nature teaches that only the feeling of the moment should be considered. The Cynics also repudiated the conventions of society for a life according to nature, but to them this meant a disregard of luxury and pleasure, an independence from wealth and possessions, and an acceptance of a sort of hobo-asceticism. The well-known stories about Diogenes of Sinope (413-327 B.C.) are illustrative. Although the members of these two schools may have had some elements of epistemological and cosmological theory, the intellectual foundations of their ways of life were too weak for permanence, and the main thrust of their recommendations had to receive a more stable basis at the hands of the Epicureans and Stoics.

The Epicureans

Zeno founded Stoicism and Epicurus launched his school at approximately the same time, 300 B.C.; both schools continued active for five centuries and faded from view under the brilliance of Neoplatonism. Since the Epicureans, instructed with catechetical fidelity, did not deviate from their master's doctrine, while the various Stoic writers show considerable variation, development, and originality, it is convenient to discuss Epicureanism first.

In common with Stoicism, Epicurus' main problem was to secure independence of the vicissitudes of time and to live contentedly in a disordered society. The scholar's devotion to speculative truth, unless with Spinoza's geometrical ethics it led to blessedness, was a disappointing ideal. We have but one life to live: we must make the best of it. To promote happiness, therefore, is the sole aim of philosophy.

Happiness, unlike Aristotle's meaning of the term, consists in pleasure; but unlike the thoughtless Cyrenaics also, pleasure is not defined as momentary sensual stimulation, but rather as the absence of pain. To be sure, the pleasures of licentiousness are not bad: "No pleasure is a bad thing in itself, but the means which produce some pleasures bring with them disturbances many times greater than the pleasures." "If the things that produce the pleasures of profligates could dispel the fears of the mind about the phenomena of the sky and death and its pains, and also teach the limits of desires and of pains, we should never have cause to blame them."

The happy life, therefore, is not one of physical pleasure only but also and more so of a tranquil mind.

Since these things are true and their opposites are false, the Epicureans had to construct the outlines of an epistemology, here omitted. And for similar reasons their ethical theory could not dispense with physics and the other traditional divisions of philosophy. To avoid frustration, one must understand the limits that the universe sets. This does not mean that every detail of physics is important. The exact motions of the sun and the planets and whether the moon is self-luminous or shines with a borrowed light are obscure matters that do not affect our pleasure. What is needed is a general cosmology that will banish superstitious fears.

According to Epicurus and his faithful expositor Lucretius (94-55 B.C.), the chief cause of human misery is religion. Because of religion men have committed impious deeds of sacrifice; because of ignorance they fear death; and because of superstition they fear divine punishments after death. To live in contentment, therefore, it is necessary to accept as one's first and basic principle the proposition that "nothing is ever begotten out of nothing by divine power." To implement this principle Lucretius describes a world that has resulted, not from any purpose, but from the collisions of atoms in empty space. He goes to some length in giving a materialistic explanation of mind, of soul, of sensation, and the phenomena of life. With this theory he aims to show how groundless is the fear of death and divine punishment. Since sensation, feeling, pleasure, and pain pertain to living bodies, and since the life or soul is itself a collection of atoms, the event of death is merely the dispersion of the atoms. The collection that had been the self no longer exists and can therefore no longer feel. "Accustom thyself to believe that death is nothing to us . . . A right understanding that death is nothing to us makes the mortality of life enjoyable, not by adding to life an illimitable time, but by taking away the yearning after immortality. . . . Foolish, therefore, is the man who says he fears death, not because it will pain him when it comes, but because it pains him in the prospect. Whatsoever causes no annoyance when it is present, causes only a groundless pain in the expectation. Death, therefore, the most awful of all evils, is nothing to us, seeing that, when we are, death is not come, and, when death is come, we are not."

A HISTORY OF PHILOSOPHICAL SYSTEMS

Not the cause perhaps of so much actual misery as religion, but theoretically as evil is the theory of naturalistic necessitarianism, destiny, or fate. The legends of the gods offer some faint hope that we may prosper if we observe the rituals, but necessity or fate, deaf to all entreaties, destroys moral responsibility, makes praise and blame meaningless, and leaves nothing under our control. One might at first think that the Epicureans with their materialistic, atomistic, ateleological physics would defend rather than repudiate mechanical necessity. But strange to say they took human freedom as a fact to which physics must be made to conform. Man is free; man is composed of atoms; therefore atoms are free. A great deal of the time they move because of the force and direction of colliding bodies; but sometimes they move spontaneously, for no cause at all. If this were not so, not only would human freedom be impossible, the world itself would be impossible. At first all the atoms were falling straight down in the infinite void; since there was neither medium nor friction, they fell at one speed and could not collide; to produce a world one or more atoms had to swerve from the straight course; and the resulting collision and vortices eventually produced this world of things and free men. Accordingly "we must remember that the future is neither wholly ours nor wholly not ours, so that neither must we count upon it as quite certain to come nor despair of it as quite certain not to come."

Of lesser importance but of wider popularity are the detailed practical maxims that Epicurus gave for everyday life. Some of them are pointed denials of Stoic teaching. Hatred, envy, and contempt are evil and irrational motives. The wise man will not fall in love, nor will he marry and raise a family unless special circumstance make it prudent to do so. He will feel gratitude towards friends and show it by word and deed. He will not take part in politics, become a mendicant, or commit suicide, though not all of these sins are equal. Illness, and even torture, will not destroy the happiness of the wise man, for "continuous pain does not last long in the flesh; on the contrary, pain, if extreme, is present a very short time, and even that degree of pain which barely outweighs pleasure in the flesh does not last for many days together. Illnesses of long duration even permit of an excess of pleasure over pain in the flesh." And tranquillity of mind is more important than pleasure or pain in the flesh.

A HISTORY OF PHILOSOPHICAL SYSTEMS

The Stoics

After Zeno had founded Stoicism, Cleanthes presided over the school (264-232 B.C.), and then Chrysippus in a term of twenty-six years (232-206 B.C.) reorganized the movement, systematized its doctrine, and greatly increased its influence. Two men of the middle period should be mentioned for establishing Stoicism in Rome: Panaetius of Rhodes (180-110? B.C.), and Posidonius (130-50? B.C.). Roman Stoicism is chiefly exemplified in Seneca (4 B.C.-A.D. 65), Epictetus (50-130), and the emperor Marcus Aurelius (121-180).

That the Stoic temper differs radically from the Epicurean, giving rise to the English connotations of those adjectives, may be seen first in some of the detailed advice for everyday living. For example, the Stoic wise man will take part in politics (in fact, Stoicism both directly and indirectly contributed to Roman law); he will marry and raise a family; he will not groan under torture, and in general he will suppress emotion as irrational, neither showing pity nor as a magistrate relaxing the penalties fixed by law; and, since one falsehood is just as false as any other, it follows that all sins are equally great, and all men who are not perfectly wise are arrant knaves. However, if life grows too burdensome, he may commit suicide.

The Epicurean withdrawal from political and domestic obligations in favor of an easygoing avoidance of trouble and the Stoic acceptance of social responsibility both spring from the common search for happiness. But the search led the two schools in opposite directions partly because the Stoics had the more vivid, realistic, and even pessimistic view of the evils of life. Most men are vicious fools. Only a few, and these in their old age, attain wisdom. These wise men have all the virtues; the others have none at all, for there are no degrees in virtue: one who drowns in a foot of water is just as dead as if he had drowned in a hundred. Since wisdom and foolishness, virtue and vice, happiness and misery are mutually exclusive and incompatible, there can be no gradual progress in morality. A man becomes wise instantaneously by a total transformation of his character. The history of the school shows a tendency to tone down the rigor of some of these particularities, but in all its course Stoicism remained more rigorous than any of its rivals.

The good life, the life of a wise man, is a life according to nature. Not everything in nature is according to nature; there are Cynics, Epicureans, and the feebleminded. These diverge from type. The nature to follow is the universal nature, rational nature, human nature, for reason in man is essentially the same as reason in the universe.

To desire the moon is irrational. Frustration, the disappointment of desire, can be avoided by governing desire. "Require not things to happen as you wish, but wish them to happen as they do." "Some things are under our control, while others are not under our control. Under our control are thinking, choice, desire, aversion, and, in a word, everything that is our own doing; not under our control are our body, our property, reputation, office, and, in a word, everything that is not our own doing." Since our bodies are not under our control, pleasure is not a good and pain is not an evil. There is the famous story about Epictetus, the slave. As his master was torturing his leg, he said with great composure, "You will certainly break my leg." When the bone broke, he continued in the same tone of voice, "Did I not tell you that you would break it?" The good life, therefore, does not consist of externalities, but it is an inward state, a strength of will, and self-control. As Marcus Aurelius says, "Everything is opinion, and opinion is in your power. Suppress your opinion when you wish, and like a ship that rounds the cape, you will find calm, everything still, and a waveless bay."

Inasmuch as the Stoics interpret their slogan "a life according to nature" to mean "a life according to reason," thus using reason to connect human nature with universal nature, they might be expected to take a less pessimistic view of the extent of human depravity. And in fact they are optimists. For them the universe is rational in all its details.

"All things intertwine one with another, and the bond is sacred, . . for the cosmos, composed of all things, is one, and there is one God who pervades all things. . . ." "Universal nature initiated the formation of the cosmos. Since that time, either every event occurs as a consequence, or else [an impossibility] even the most important matters, on which the universal spirit bestows its particular attention, are irrational."

The seeming inconsistency arises from assuming that a world perfect and rational in its entirety cannot contain factors which, viewed in themselves and apart from the whole, are evil. No doubt most men are knaves, but it is as irrational to make a beautiful world without vice as it is to paint a great picture without dark colors. This pessimistic view of mankind is therefore consistent with a universal optimism, just as the more superficial optimism of the Epicureans has the pessimistic background of a purposeless materialism.

The Stoics, too, were materialists, for nothing is real that does not occupy space. It is interesting to note that Plato in the *Sophist* had argued: materialism is false because virtues exist. The Stoics reply: virtues exist, therefore they are bodies. Materialists they professed to be, but their physics was neither atomistic nor ateleological. Under the inspiration of Heraclitus, they composed their universe of an eternal, intelligent fire. This fire, reason, or God permeates everything, so that—and this follows also from the fact that virtue is a body—two bodies occupy the same place at the same time in a "complete mixture." With this go theories of space, of growth, and logical theories of expression and meaning that ill accord with materialism; and it may be surmised that their attempts to account for the nonmaterial factors of the universe prepared for their eclipse in the later light of Neoplatonic spiritualism.

However that may be, God or Reason permeates and controls every thing and every event. The world and its history are governed by Fate. Logic as well as physics supports this position. Every proposition, *e.g.*, Scipio will capture Numantia, is either true or false. If it is true, the event must happen; and if it is false, it cannot possibly happen. Opponents of determinism argue that if everything is fated, there is no use in exerting oneself, for the event will happen anyway. The Stoics, insistent on moral exertion, reply that Scipio will not take Numantia *any way,* but in one way only; for it is true not merely that he will take Numantia but that he will take it by marching his army against its walls and laying down a siege.

The opponents, now forced to admit that exertion may be predetermined, continue by asserting that determinism is incompatible with responsibility. If a man can do only what is fated and has no free choice, he can neither be praised nor blamed, and the concepts of good and evil become meaningless. The answer to this objection may be found in the Stoics' strong insistence on the power of volition. Volition may not be "free," but volition exists and some things are in our power. Perhaps it is fated that I shall irrationally desire the moon. Then I must choose to desire it, and I am evil. Or it may be fated that I shall desire wisdom. I choose it then, and I am virtuous. These things are in my power or choice in a way that a thunderstorm or a broken leg is not in my power. They are, therefore, to be referred to their proximate cause: my will, or, me. Thus determinism does not make good and evil meaningless, nor does it destroy responsibility. What it does is to reject the freedom of irrationality and to base responsibility on volition.

Skeptics and Academy

Both the Epicureans and Stoics were dogmatists; that is, they believed that truth could be had and that they had it. During this Hellenistic age there was also a group of skeptics: men who knew they had found no truth and who were certain that there was none to be found. Some of the more important names are Pyrrho (365-275 B.C.), Arcesilaus (315-240 B.C.), Carneades (219-129 B.C.), Aenesidemus (between 80 B.C. and A.D. 130), and Sextus Empiricus (c. 200 A.D.).

Although Pyrrho was a contemporary of Epicurus and Zeno, it was a century and more later, when the epistemology of these two schools had been well examined, that Skepticism became more prominent. Plato, in opposition to the skepticism which the Sophists deduced from Presocratic science, had founded the possibility of knowledge on an intellectual intuition of supersensible Ideas. Aristotle also, even though he gave a fundamental rôle to sensation, had his abstract Forms and Active Intellect. In reaction the Epicureans and Stoics based all knowledge on sensory images. In particular, the Stoics, admitting that it is often possible to confuse real images with fancies, or accurate images with inadequate distortions, asserted that there is one type of image, the "comprehensive representation," that forces our assent to it and about which we cannot be mistaken. This is the criterion of truth.

The skeptics of this age with some help from the earlier Sophists riddled this theory, and modern skeptics have found little to add to their arguments.

There exists no criterion of truth, they maintained, either in sense or reason, for if the alleged criterion is a special type of image, it would have to assure us that it was this type and at the same time inform us of the nature of its object. But no specific differences can be discerned among images. Images in dreams are as real to us while we are dreaming as sense images are when we are awake, and, since we can dream we are pinching ourselves to see whether we are awake, it is impossible to know whether we are dreaming now or not. Then, too, we see Castor and think we see Pollux, which shows both that the same thing (Castor) can produce two images (at one time of Castor, at another of Pollux), and also that two things (the twins) can produce the same image. There is, therefore, no criterion in sense, and if reason is based on sensation, no criterion can be found in reason either.

There are other arguments. Animals have organs that differ from men's, and they sense differently. Why then should we assume that our senses better reveal nature than those of a dog or a fish? Even among men there are notably different reactions to the same object; and for that matter the senses of any individual contradict one another. Further, we see objects as they appear to us and in a particular surrounding; no object is ever isolated; with the result that every object is known only in and by its relations, and nothing is ever known as it really is in itself.

And, finally, all science is based on hypotheses. To prove an hypothesis, one must have recourse to another, and so on to infinity. Or, to escape an infinite regress, one may go around in a circle. Or, to escape the circle, one may make an initial assumption—an elaborate form of begging the question. Truth, therefore, is impossible.

But there is a difficulty. The Epicureans and Stoics had pursued logic and physics as means to the good life. Now, if nothing is true, is it not just as good to sift arsenic on one's cake as powdered sugar? There is the amusing story of the skeptic who taught that "it makes no difference." One day he jumped back quickly to avoid a collision with a four horse chariot. His disciples chided him because of his inconsistency—he should not have jumped back because it made no difference. "On the contrary," he replied; "I jumped back because it made no difference."

In words a skeptic may profess suspension of judgment, but the ordinary activity of living, or of committing suicide for that matter, shows that a judgment has in fact been made. Accordingly the skeptics advised conformity to convention—why be an iconoclast if it is not true that idolatry is wrong? Or, they went a little further and posited "the reasonable," or "the probable" as a practical criterion. Carneades is credited with escaping the difficulty with a thoroughgoing skeptical solution. Men act for no reason at all; it is not a question of truth and knowledge; action springs from natural urges and does not require an opinion. On the other hand Carneades is also said to have advised "the preferable." It then becomes a problem to pass from what is doubtful, uncertain, or even untrue, to what is preferable or probable.

It was on this point that St. Augustine later centered his famous argument for truth. If it is possible to arrive at a probability or at an approximation to truth, there must be true knowledge of the principles of probability and a true judgment by which to determine approximation.

The New Dogmatism

The despite in which the Epicureans were popularly held and the eclectic deterioration of the Stoics contributed to the prominence if not the dominance of skepticism just before the beginning of our era. But the heart of man, not to mention the mind of man, cannot be satisfied with negativism, suspension of judgment, and indifference to life. Dogmatism, therefore, was bound to revive.

The first of these dogmatic stirrings was Neopythagoreanism. During Plato's life-time the original school disintegrated, though the Orphic cults in Italy seemed to have retained some memory of earlier days. By 100 B.C., however, there was an active revival, setting in motion some three centuries of writing and teaching. The names of most of the writers are unknown (P. Nigidius Figulus was a friend of Cicero, and Sotion lived in the reign of Augustus), and none of them is philosophically eminent. Nor is the theory of the school thoroughly unified. The individual authors wander in different directions and incorporate into the general Platonic background various elements from the Stoics and the Peripatetics.

The unit and the dyad, identified as form and matter, were their basic principles, but some taught that the unit was the moving cause and God, while others, anticipating Plotinus, placed the One above all motion. Although they paid serious attention to mathematics, their interest centered in a mystical and metamathematical symbolism that cannot be much more than a curiosity today. But they seem to have made one innovation which adds coherence to Platonism, and which, independently thought out by Philo Judaeus (30 B.C.-45 A.D.) and accepted by Plotinus (204-270), made the Platonic philosophy seem favorable to Christianity. In the *Timaeus* Plato himself posited three eternal and independent principles: the Ideas, the Demiurge, and Space. This arrangement makes the Demiurge, *i.e.,* the maker of the universe or God, inferior to and bound by the Ideas. A Hebrew or Christian monotheist could not accept such a view, and within paganism the urge to some form of monism was too strong to find it comfortable. The Neopythagoreans, though the historical evidence is not too clear, seem to have been the first to derive their Numbers from God. Thus the Ideas become the thoughts of God, the contents of the Divine Mind, and so philosophic unity is combined with divine supremacy.

Plutarch, (50-120 A.D.) also, though not a Neopythagorean, contributed to the revival of Platonism. He was not a philosopher of the first class, but he was an extremely well educated and representative man of his time. His literary production was voluminous, and he suffers from the injustice of achieving popularity by his *Lives* rather than by his philosophical, religious, and moral discourses.

In opposition to the Neopythagoreans, who took Plato's account of the formation of the world to be a pedagogical device expressing in temporal terms what is really a logical relationship, Plutarch interpreted Plato to mean that the world had a first moment. To this end he exegetes the *Timaeus* in detail. A great deal of his motivation comes from the problem of evil, and he selects certain Platonic passages for emphasis. Since God is good, Plato is right in saying that he cannot be the cause of everything. To explain evil it is necessary to assume an independent, evil principle. In the *Politicus* the great catastrophe that occurs when God lets go the rudder of the universe cannot have been caused by a neutral matter (though Plato seems to say so); and in the *Laws* there is a definite allusion to an evil world-soul. This type of dualism, Plutarch notes, is the more plausible because all philosophers, however much they praised monism, were forced to concede a plurality of principles.

As the goodness and transcendence of God are accentuated, Plutarch finds it necessary to supply mediators to preserve God from defiling contact with a wicked world. By this device he could support the popular religion of his day and point the way to a happy, a blessed life. Man is composed of body, soul, and reason. When death frees the soul from the body, the soul together with the reason journeys to the moon, there to function as a mediator-demon. But as reason is superior to the soul, there occurs in the moon a second death by which reason is freed, and, leaving the soul in the moon, it returns to its source and home, the sun.

With Plutarch this chapter must close. Peripateticism, the school that Aristotle founded, in this age was of minor importance. Other material is more literary and cultural than strictly philosophical. There are also the curious religious tractates of Hermes Trismegistus (written by different authors at different times, *circa* 150 A.D.), but these depend in part on Christian as well as mystical sources. The next part of the main story therefore is the Alexandrian philosophy.

BIBLIOGRAPHY

SOURCES

CICERO, *De Natura Deorum*
———, *De Fato, De Finibus, etc.*
———, *Academica*
DIOGENES LAERTIUS, *Lives of Eminent Philosophers,* Books VII, X.
EPICTETUS, *Discourses*
LUCRETIUS, *De Rerum Natura*
MARCUS AURELIUS, *To Himself*
PLUTARCH, *Moralia*
———, *De Facie*
———, *De Animae Procreatione*
SEXTUS EMPIRICUS, *Adversus Mathematicos*
Translations of these sources may be found in *The Loeb Classical Library,* Bohn's *Classical Library,* or in particular editions.

SECONDARY MATERIAL

E. VERNON ARNOLD, *Roman Stoicism* (Cambridge, 1911).
EDWYN BEVAN, *Stoics and Skeptics* (Oxford, 1913).

A HISTORY OF PHILOSOPHICAL SYSTEMS

EMILE BRÉHIER, *Chrysippe* (Paris, 1910).
———, *La Théorie des Incorporels* (Paris, 1908).
VICTOR BROCHARD, *Les Sceptiques Grecs* (Paris, 1887).
GORDON H. CLARK, *Selections from Hellenistic Philosophy* (New York, 1940).
WILLIAM L. DAVIDSON, *The Stoic Creed* (Edinburgh, 1907).
LÉON ROBIN, *Greek Thought* (London, 1928).
FARRAND SAYRE, *Diogenes of Sinope* (Baltimore, 1938).

CHAPTER ELEVEN

ALEXANDRIAN PHILOSOPHY

EUGEN KULLMANN

NEOPLATONIC philosophy will be considered in the following as an attempt to give the sum of Greek thought at the turning point of the epochs. This attitude toward a synthesis not only originates from the general trend of Hellenism, but it is also in conformity with the course of Greek philosophy itself. To understand the meaning of the Neoplatonic Way requires the background whence this philosophy emerges, transmitting a great many issues to the ages to come.

Three complexes of thought intertwined have helped in moulding the Neoplatonic system: Unity as in the selfsame source; Unity as in tensed participation; Unity as in a continuous movement. Neoplatonism as a form of thinking is an ever possible adventure of the mind to reduce the apparent differences, without eliminating them, into a Unity, with which they are gradually connected: *Ex Uno Plura.*

A. Thematic Background

I. Unity as in the Selfsame Source

Confidence in Being as ever abiding in spite of the surging appearances is the characteristic attitude of the Pre-Socratics. Being is the All encompassing One. There is nothing beyond it, nothing whereinto Being could change. It is not limited but by itself. It is infinitely finite. What is experienced as contradictory has its common principle beyond the reach of perceptual experience. Whatever is thus experienced is by a relative negation: this is so and not so. Being simply is. Whatever epithets are ascribed to it are but marks to signalize it, yet they do not cover Being. In symbols only it may be betokened, or in a symbol of symbols, like the *Apeiron* (Infinite) of Anaximander (6th cent. B.C.) and the *Logos* (the comprising comprehensive sense) of Heracleitus (536-470 B.C.). Even this has been renounced by Parmenides (6th-5th cent. B.C.), leaving the symbols to the attributes of Being; whereas Being is beyond even a symbolic representation.

II. Unity as in Tensed Participation

Plato (428-7-348 B.C.) goes farther. Being is not the ultimate. Being is caused by the idea of the Good, he announced not without a feeling of amazement in the *Republic* (509 b): "The Good is not only the author of knowledge to all things known, but of their being and yet the Good is not Being, but far exceeds Being in dignity and power." Being is no more the *arche,* the principal source, but becomes issued by an *arche* which as highest idea is beyond the reach of Being. Strangely enough, Plato attributes being to the ideas, yet the coordinating idea of the Good leaves even Being behind. This makes the dialectic of the ideas and Being, as discussed in a series of antinomies in the dialogue *Parmenides.* The case concerns the primacy either of the Idea or of Being, and Plato hardly arrives at a positive conclusion. These deliberations of the *Parmenides* are frequently commented upon by Plotinus (204-270 A.D.). To overcome the antinomies and, of course, also from out of his "Weltgefühl" Plotinus holds that the One is beyond Being—this would be the Platonic conception—yet also above all Good. The Platonic dialectic between the intelligible and the sensible as being by participation in the former, was one starting point to Plotinus for his own adventure into the *Epekeina* (Beyond), so deeply inherent in man.

III. Unity as in a Continuous Movement

A substitution somehow of the idea of the Good seems to be the Aristotelian *Telos* (the Turning End), being already related to the Good by Plato (*Gorgias,* 499 e). The continual motion toward the *Telos* renders the whole a gradation from the lower to the higher, which is the relative *Telos* of its respective lower component and moves in turn toward a yet higher *Telos.* The highest *Telos* as "Pure Form" is not involved in any sort of movement, yet it moves everything, being lovingly desired by everything (Aristotle *Metaphysics,* 1072 B). Thus the *Telos* being "Thinking of Thinking" (*ib.*) establishes just by being what it is the continuity of motion from the things toward it. For the Neoplatonic concept of a continuous "Shining forth" from the "One" to the "One" through the interconnected spheres this has become of great significance. Moreover, Plotinus' theory of the *Nous* (Mind) fills the Aristotelian *Nous* with the Platonic ideas. The Plotinian terminology is greatly indebted to Aristotle and this has its systematic reason. The same is to be said concerning the Aristotelian manner of *pragmateia* (treating a subject-matter in a gradual approach to its meaning), largely adopted by Plotinus.

B. Early Neoplatonism

I. Neopythagorean Trend

The great bearing which the teachings of the Pythagoreans (reputed founder, Pythagoras, 6th cent. B.C.) had on Plato is obvious from such Dialogues as *Gorgias, Phaedo* and *Timaeus*. The old Plato, in whom several momentous tendencies toward the Neoplatonic approach can be found, was to a large extent a Pythagorean, who was inclined to transform the theories of ideas and soul into the Pythagorean scheme of numbers. His concept of the *Monos* (Oneness) and "Dyos" (Twoness) as positive and negative poles in antithetic tension exerted a great influence on the Neoplatonic outlook and were among the factors gradually elaborating the Neoplatonic Way as one of a Unity over a duality.

II. The "Alexandrian World-Scheme": Philo

Philo (20 B.C.-50) sees philosophy centered on *Theologia,* pointing out that what theology wants to account for is "beyond Oneness," thereby unknowable. He raises the problem of how the "Infinite God" could be mediated in the finite. The "ideas" which are *dynameis* (powers) are those mediating agencies related (by Philo) to the Biblical "angels" (messengers). Another mediator is the Biblical *Ruach* (*Pneuma, i.e.,* the breathing spirit in the Septuagint) which is understood to be the All-permeating *Logos* (Heracleitus, *Stoa!*). The *Logos* is the "place" of the ideas. Most distant from God is matter. Due to this distance, especially felt in the human soul, there is a longing for a "union" with "God-Oneness and -Beyond Oneness" in an *ekstasis,* where the soul would "stand out from herself" and thus thinking would be no more with its division into thinker and thought. The ascent culminates in this *unio mystica,* as depicted by Philo and Plotinus, who probably was familiar with Philo's thought.

III. Plutarch

That the distance from the "Oneness" to the many may result in an almost antithetic conception of the universe—owing to ethical implications—we learn from Plutarch (48-125). But he also knows a neutralized third force in between matter. Mediation is ever characteristic of Neoplatonic philosophy. The extreme to the One Good God is the Evil World Soul. Here Plutarch follows a suggestion by the old Plato (*Laws,* 896 e) that the Evil in our soul is due to the Evil World Soul. Whatever is destructive in nature comes from it.

Even as *Theologia* was the consummation of philosophy for Philo so likewise was it for Plutarch. To him "to philosophize together" means "to be human(e) together" and thus to step up from the lower to the most high.

IV. Numenius

A man of the second century, Numenius was considered by some people of the third century to have anticipated to some extent the philosophy of Plotinus. His thinking seems to center on the *Timaeus.* Accordingly, he assumes a trinity in the divine order. The "First God" is the Good and as "Thinking of Thinking" the *arche* of Being. The "demiurgic" Second God is Good by participation in the First, shaping the formless matter eternal after the pre-existent paradeigmatic ideas, as contained in the First and thus the principle of Becoming. His product, the World, is the "Third God," even as Plato at the conclusion of the *Timaeus* had called this "kosmos" "somewhat like a visible God." Momentous is the manifoldness of ideas as already contained in the "First God." How can the principle of the many be already in the One? This was a question which stimulated Plotinus.

A HISTORY OF PHILOSOPHICAL SYSTEMS

C. Plotinian Philosophy

I. Ammonius Saccas

Ammonius, "the sackbearer" (175-242), is traditionally said to have been the inaugurator of Neoplatonism in the stricter sense of a school. Like Socrates he would talk to those who joined him in pondering on Heaven and Earth. He did not write, nor had he been anyone's student. One of his intentions, we are told, was to reconcile Aristotle with Plato: how the material could be combined with the *Eidos* (forming principle) without the latter losing its independent essence. How could this ever have been possible? And, if so, what conclusions should be drawn? This twofold quest in the one proposition outlines our summary of Plotinus. The "How" implies the eternal history of the universe, how the "One" abiding in itself is stepping down. This is the *egressus,* the first half—and as some Plotinian scholars hold "the greater half" of the story. The second then: This being so, what does it mean to me? How can I, a single one, a lonely soul return to my homeland? This is the "Way Up."

II. The Life of Plotinus

The life of Plotinus, as described by his disciple the Tyrian Melekh (his Greek name: Porphyry [233-300]), reflected his philosophy. He would never talk about his family or country; he seemed to be ashamed of being in the body—so Porphyry has recorded. When Amelius, his favorite disciple, once asked him, if he would consent to sit to a painter, he replied so piercingly: "Is it not enough to have to bear the image in which nature has wrapped me, without consenting to perpetuate the image of an image, as if it were worth contemplating?"—As in the "Allegory of the Den" a twilight is hovering on the Plotinian road from light to light.

Plotinus was born at Lykopolis in Upper Egypt about 204. Having gone through the public school of his town, he continued his education in Alexandria, attended lectures on philosophy, but was disappointed by them, until he found, at the age of 28, Ammonius, "the man, I was looking for" (as he later told his disciples). He studied with him for ten years. After the death of Ammonius, Plotinus joined the Emperor Gordianus in his expedition against

Persia. He intended to get more directly familiar with the wisdom of the Iranians and perhaps of the Brahmans, of which he had heard already much talk in Alexandria, the eastern metropolis in those ages. In Mesopotamia the Emperor was assassinated and Plotinus managed to reach Rome in 244. Plato had made his journey to Egypt and three journeys to Sicily while Plotinus turned Eastward only to arrive in the West!

In Rome he met Amelius, who studied with him 24 years, and became a friend of Emperor Gallienus (reign, 253-268) and his wife Salonina. Shy by nature, he was a beloved teacher to his students and a devoted guardian to orphans.

Together with his friends he would read and discuss the classic writings of Greek philosophy and also those of contemporaries, always with special reference to Plato and Aristotle. He would encourage them not to refrain from interrupting his lectures by raising worthwhile objections; then he would show the point in its context with the subject-matter. He meditated while he was lecturing. To philosophize meant to him mutual meditation, but above all a silent conversation of the "Single One" with the "Single One" (*Enneads* VI, 9, 11, 51 ed. by Bréhier). Shortly after the Emperor's death, he left Rome for a country house of one of his students in Campania, where in his younger years he once had planned a model town "Platonopolis," designed after the *Republic*. Gradually his delicate health was failing and he realized the symptoms of final departure. His friend and physician Eustochius was sent for. When he had arrived, the gentle nature of Plotinus was just given to say these words of welcome and farewell: "I was waiting for you, that you might help to bring the Divine in me to the Divine in the All."

His biographer has preserved for us these words of the Plotinian way of life, as he has also arranged the lectures of his master and published them in six books, each containing nine essays, hence *Enneades, i.e.,* "Ninenesses." Plotinus had started writing some of his treatises, when already fifty years old. Being engaged in renewed meditating he never revised them, a fact which is manifest to those who seriously study the difficult *Enneads* in the original. The subject-matter of the first book is mainly ethics, of the second "physics," of the third metaphysics. The fourth book concerns the soul, the fifth the Mind, the sixth the One and its spheres.

A HISTORY OF PHILOSOPHICAL SYSTEMS

III. The Plotinian Philosophy

a. The Egressus

1) The "One"

You cannot say: The "One" is. Even its "Oneness" is perhaps only accidental (*En.* VI, 8, 11). It is the last unconditioned, whither we arrive questioning backward. It is absolutely simple, a selfsameness of possibility and actuality and yet beyond both. Beyond any possible differentiation, it thinks not, for thinking, even as "Thinking of Thinking" implies a distinction,—thus Plotinus argued against Aristotle (*En.* VI, 7, 37). It is what it is, its own cause. Hence it is free, whereby this unconditional freedom is its absolute necessity. This Freedom-Necessity Plotinus calls in a metaphoric way *Bulesis* (Rational Will, *En.* VI, 8, 21, 14). It wills ever itself. It is, as the Parmenidean "Being," "One, unshakeable, ever perfect." Yet it is beyond its "Oneness." Identical with itself it is at one together, "good" in this absolute sense. All this, Plotinus implies, is metaphoric transference of a *logos* (meaningful word) to an unwordable. His successors stressed this still more emphatically.

2) Nous and Ideas

The "One" "willing itself" is its own revelation. This "will to itself" "ever producing itself" is the *Nous,* "ever productive thinking" of an "ever productive thinking," the latter being the ideas. The "One" with its "consciousness" through the *Nous* in the "mirror" of the ideas is the *Aion* (the "Ever"). The *Nous* in its fullness of the ideas is the eternal logical presence of what successively shines forth and thus constitutes *Chronos* (Time). Eternity and Time do not have different contents but they are what they are in the order of either a static "coexistence" or a dynamic "subexistence." To describe somewhat analogically the "Ever" in its *Eklampsis* (Shining forth) and the *Eidola* (images) thereof (*En.* IV, 5, 7, 61) on the temporal screen, to betoken the oscillations from yonder to here, Plotinus applies and elaborates the "Five Categories" of Plato's *Sophist* (pp. 255 *sqq.*), namely "Essence," "Difference," "Identity," "Motion" and "Rest," adding consequently as the sixth category the *Nous,* their supporting principle (*En.* V, 1, 4). This issue of the "categories" as some other topics in Plotinus is not, however, without inconsistencies.

3) Psyche

What is the cause of this Temporal? In the intelligible cosmos, *i.e.,* the *nous,* there is not only a distinction between thinking and its object as its explication, but these "ideas" are *paradeigmata* (models) of the sensible things. Their manifoldness has its principle in the intelligible world. Moreover, these ideas are *dynameis* (powers), as Philo taught. Why can the ideas be the moving forces of the sensible world? Because they are besouled, and the Soul is the principle of motion (so conceived from Thales [6th cent. B.C.] on). The ideas have two countenances, one reflected to the *Nous,* the other eternally moving toward the infinitely indefinite void. And the totality of these faces turned downward, the light in its back and night indifferent beneath, is the Universal Soul. Still contained in her ideal home, the Universal Soul shines forth her borrowed light like the moon (*En.* V, 6, 4, 17). Looking back to the pure actuality of the *Nous* she receives the ideas thereof and after this *Eikon* (primordial image) she actuates forming the void matter. Thus the Universal Soul is extending into a twofold direction, in receptive contemplation toward the higher she is *Psyche* in the pregnant sense; as forming power irresistibly moving toward the potentially lower she is *Physis,* productive Soul. From the *Psyche* the Gods emanate; from the *Physis* the daimons. Thus Plotinian theology interpreted popular religion.

The Universal Soul mediates between what is Eternity and what becomes Time (III, 7, 13). Extending herself, she leaves her "shadow" behind (IV, 3, 9, 45 *sqq.*) and this is "Space." There is no absolute Space; space is a function of the Universal Soul. Ever being what it is (*ib.*) the Universal Soul moving on, evolves Time, which is potentially as infinite as the actual march of the Soul.

Each void touched by the Universal Soul is her offspring. There are countless individuations of the Universal Soul, to which all the many are related. Such an effluescence is the individual Soul, her miniature issue, the *psyche* in it turned to the heights, the *physis* in it acting toward matter.

4) Hulē

"Matter" (*hulē*) is the last step downward (I, 8, 7). It is ever related to the Universal Soul and thus indirectly to the "One." The "One" would not be, what it is, were matter left alone (II, 9, 3). Matter is receptive, as Plato and Aristotle had assumed. The Soul moving toward the potential matter may impose on it any form the Soul desires. Matter is all-transformable. Thus matter in itself would be a negative infinity. As such, matter is not, since it is ever contacted by the rays of the "good infinity," the "transfinite" "One." Matter in the strict sense is *Asomaton* (bodiless, *En.* III, 6, 7). To state the paradox: Matter is immaterial; it is, strictly speaking, only as an "idea of matter" in the intelligible world, an idea of what cannot be. Here Plotinus continues Parmenides' "Being of the 'Non-Being,' " following the Democritean and Platonic identification of this "Non-Being" with the "Void."

As the remotest from the "One," matter is thus the remotest from the "Good." "Good" is the will to self-limitation. This was the Platonic tradition, especially from the *Philebus*. Matter as formless, indefinite, is so, owing to the "absence of the Good" (II, 4, 16). This is "Evil," not something actual, but "privation" from something (V, 9, 10). As the "One" is *apoion* (without a quality) so matter likewise. The "One," due to its "abundance," is a "peaceful well, never exhausted" (III, 8, 10). (The analogy of "emanation" is somewhat misleading for the Plotinian outlook.) Thus the "One" cannot be defined, being so rich. Matter in turn is "poverty" (V, 9, 10). From "abundance" to "poverty" this is the *egressus*.

Yet simultaneously the mediating powers move upward on the rungs of the cosmic ladder, longing in love for the yonder.

b. The Regressus

Whereas the eternal "way down" issues from the "One," the return is the response of a single soul only, who encounters the Universal Soul beaming in herself. It has been by the Universal Soul, that I have entered this sensible world; so by rightly using her part in me, I shall be able "to stand out of it" again. In analogy this possibility may be empathically transferred to all the many. Primarily, it is the most inward situation throughout the spheres, "Flight of the Single One to the Single One."

This thought significantly concludes the *Enneads*. Yet it is the "single One," the "God-Oneness" in me turned back to itself. Not an individual "existential" person, but a "divine part" is brought back to the whole in the intelligible world.

1) In Action

The *regressus* is possible indirectly and approximately by the *physis* of the Soul, in action. Immediately, however, it is by the *psyche* of the Soul, in contemplation.

Action is toward the world. Even ethical action hinders from purely contemplating the Divine. Action can at best be only a preparation as *katharsis* (purification), separating from matter's bondage. Plotinus is only conditionally interested in moral actions—whether they are of a positive influence on man in his society. This would concern transitoriness only, whereas the ascent concerns eternity. Only the Soul can be elevated. Her earthly ties cannot enter, from whence they did not actually arise. They have become, touched by the Soul. They decay, when no more ruled by the Soul. For the Soul has built her matter (and not is the Soul received by matter) which becomes only through the Soul's shining.

In connection with ethics, Plotinus deals somewhat sketchily with society and history. Everything is radiated, in the void refracted, and personal action dies out in the twilight. To be a person is a tragic attempt of the Soul to render matter sufficiently strong to respond conformably to her claim. Thus dwelling in the dusk, the Soul nostalgically adventures to fly on the rays toward the light of her Source.

2) In Contemplation

The goal of contemplation is to understand the "One." Its relative form is sensation. Since the Soul does not perceive points, but things as configurations, the Soul has the faculty of uniting the manifoldness of a sensible thing. Those sensations are reflected by the individual Soul and this "bending back" (*En*. I, 4, 10) is "consciousness." Even as the external thing as objective being is lit up by the world soul, so, likewise, the sensible thing subjectively is "relit" by the individual soul. To know is to reproduce. Logic is ontological.

In "reflection" the continuity occurs between sensation and

thinking. Thinking is a wandering from the many to the "One" by an intuitive comprehension of the whole ladder of light. Thinking is toward what is in the light—and this is the *kalon* (beauty). Hence there is more than "aesthetic" meaning of "beauty" (*En.* 1, 6) in Plotinus' metaphysics of cognition. Only the "beautiful" soul will visualize "beauty." The artist having perceived an idea in its light, wanting to express it outwardly, must fall short. As the soul is finally to fail in the world here, so, too, the artist will fall short. The "Void" refracts the shining beauty. Only in a "clairobscure" may beauty be suggested. Accordingly, one could dare to say: The best works of art are those not created externally.

The greatest and highest contemplation is that *theoria* which acts upon what it contemplates (III, 8, 3) toward the transfinite "ONE" Then all things become a *parergon theorias* (an incidental work of contemplation, *En.* III, 8, 8). He who has contemplated the "one" shies from talking about it and reveres it in *euphemia* and in *siope* (due silence, *En.* III, 8, 4, 3). This *theoria* (vision of the Divine) may reach its peak, when "consciousness" is glowing back in the "One" and is burned away in it. This is *ekstasis* (VI, 7, 35). At times Plotinus was granted this anticipation of Eternity—so we are told by Porphyry. The "One" has been devolved into the "One."

D. Proclus

Proclus (410-485), born in Constantinople, was the head of the Athenian Academy which had for 915 years been the living monument for Plato until, in 529, the Emperor Justinian had ordered it closed. Proclus considered himself to be simply a Platonist, as did Plotinus. The subtle architect of what later was called "Neoplatonism," he made this "cyclical *energeia*" (his term), the foundation of his system. He points out (*Elements of Theology,* ed. by Dodds, proposition 35): "Every effect remains within its cause (*Mone*, Remaining), then stands forth from it (*Prohodos*, Standing forth) and finally returns to it (*Epistrophe*, Return)."

This triadic scheme has often been compared with Hegel's triadic dialectic, "thesis, antithesis, synthesis," in which the "Universal Mind" unfolds itself. Neoplatonism is the background of "German Idealism." Mediaeval Philosophy cannot be understood without an appreciation of its Neoplatonic heritage.

Putting One "yonder," Proclus intended to suggest the "wholly otherness" of the "God-Oneness." The words of Berkeley (1685-1753): "Dwindling in sense and growing in expression," match the thought of Proclus. Philosophy becomes analogy, a breathing out into the realm of the awesome from whence it has begun:

"Yonder of Yonder! what else is it rightful to call Thee? . . .
Sole Unknowable Being, since Thou art the cause of all knowing.
All things existing, the speaking and speechless together, proclaim Thee.
All things existing, the knowing and nescient together, adore Thee.
All keen desires, all painful passions are yearnings
Only for Thee. To Thee prayeth the All; to Thee all,
Sensing Thy token within, utter a praise, which is silence. . . ."

(Proclus, *Hymn to God*)

BIBLIOGRAPHY

A. Neoplatonism in General

P. E. MORE, *Hellenistic Philosophy* (Princeton, 1923).
M. THEILER, *Die Vorbereitung des Neuplatonismus* (Berlin, 1928).
TH. WHITTAKER, *The Neoplatonists* (Cambridge, 1928).
ED. ZELLER, *Die Philosophie der Griechen in ihrer geschichtlichen Entwicklung*, III, 2 (Leipzig, 1921, 5th ed.).

B. Philo

F. H. COLSON and C. H. WHITAKER, *The Works of Philo,* in the original and in translation (Loeb's Class. Lib., 1929 *sqq.*), 9 volumes.
H. LEWY, *Selections from Philo* (Oxford, 1947).
E. BRÉHIER, *Les idées philosophiques et religieuses de Philon d'Alexandrie* (Paris, 1925, 2nd ed.).
E. R. GOODENOUGH, *An Introduction to Philo* (New Haven, 1940).
H. A. WOLFSON, *Philo* (Cambridge, 1948, 2nd rev. printing), 2 volumes.

C. Plotinus

E. BRÉHIER, *Plotin, Ennéades, texte et traduction* (Paris, 1924-38), 7 volumes.
K. S. GUTHRIE, *Plotinos,* complete works in chronological order grouped in four periods (London, 1918).
S. MACKENNA, *Plotinus* (London, 1917-30).
G. H. TURNBULL, *The Essence of Plotinus,* Extracts from the six Enneads and Porphyry's Life of Plotinus, based on the translation by S. Mackenna (New York, 1934).

A HISTORY OF PHILOSOPHICAL SYSTEMS

E. Bréhier, *La philosophie de Plotin* (Paris, 1928).
F. Heinemann, *Plotin* (Leipzig, 1921).
W. R. Inge, *The Philosophy of Plotinus* (London, 3rd ed., 1948), 2 vols.
P. O. Kristeller, *Der Begriff der Seele in der Ethik des Plotin* (Tübingen, 1929).
B. Switalski, *Plotinus and the Ethics of St. Augustine* (New York, 1946), IX-XXIX Bibliogr.

D. Proclus

E. R. Dodds, *Elements of Theology*, revised text with translation, introduction and commentary (Oxford, 1933).
L. J. Rosán, *The Philosophy of Proclus* (New York, 1949), pp. 245-260 Bibliogr.

CHAPTER TWELVE

EARLY CHRISTIAN PHILOSOPHY

VERGILIUS FERM

THE HISTORIAN knows well that there has been no one Christian philosophy. There have been many called by that name. Even the sacred literature grown up unconsciously around Paul (d. *c*. 62) and others is a plural literature showing various interpretations and reflecting various cultural environments. It is commonplace now to speak of the religion *of* the founder and the religion *about* the founder; those ideas of the Jewish group (with all their varieties); those of the Hellenistic group; views of the Apostolic Fathers; the Alexandrian school; the Christian Gnostics; the ante- and the post-Nicene Fathers; and so on through the complexities of ongoing history.

The Apostolic Fathers and Early Christian Apologists

Beginning with the simple estimates of the Christian way at looking at life on the part of the first followers-of-the-followers, the story grows exceedingly complex as other cultures are met and their philosophies embraced. The writings of the so-called Apostolic Fathers reveal interests mainly in a way of life and less in matters of cosmic speculation: the *Shepherd* of Hermas (*c*. 140), the *Didache* (*c*. 150), Ignatius (early second century) and others. A system of theology was lacking and perhaps not needed. Certainly the founder offered no *system* of ethics nor *system* of philosophy. It may be said that, if he were all that was claimed of him by later generations, he had the wisdom to appreciate the course of human events as one which produces changes of emphases and outlook, thus necessitating various interpretations in line with the prevailing culture. Even the sacred scriptures—from the simple reportings of Mark to the more complicated late-first (or early-second) century Gospel—attest to the changing modes of thought which come even in a generation.

In the face of growing syncretisms throughout the Roman empire the so-called Apologists began to sharpen distinctions. They represented, on the whole, non-Jewish Christian converts trained to think in Hellenistic terms. Justin Martyr (100-c. 167) began the serious task of accommodation and discrimination: making the religion seem respectable to the Greeks by embracing their current philosophy; and, at the same time, carving out for his own religious thought something that might well be considered distinctive, *i.e.*, the logos as the central principle of revelation in the person of the founder. A philosopher by profession, Justin gave honor to it as the discipline of the understanding of truth. His contacts (he claimed) had been many: with Stoicism, with Peripateticism, with Pythagoreanism, with Platonism, with Judaism. His conclusions came step by step through the philosophies he studied to the top of the ladder to the supreme philosophy of his religion. Christianity was not so much a synthesis as *in itself* the fulfilment of the best found in other philosophies.

Tatian (middle of the second century), another Apologist, famed for his widely used harmony of the gospel writings (*Diatessaron*), declared himself a philosopher and freely criticized Heraclitus, Zeno, Plato and Aristotle. Theophilus (writing about 190), the first to use the concept of God as Trinity in Christian literature (God, Logos and Wisdom), defended the doctrine of free-will, the antiquity of Christian truths (before the time of its historic founder) and criticized Plato and other ancient Greek thinkers.

Other second century Apologists include the writings of Quadratus, Aristides and, later, Melito, Athenagoras, Minucius Felix—all of whom hammered away on the contradictions and defects of current philosophies, their moral and religious weaknesses, and turned to the sacred literature of their own for their authority and faith.

Anti-Gnostic Fathers

Four stalwart names now appear giving a distinctive philosophic note to Christian interpretations. Collectively, these four men (particularly the first two) are sometimes known as the Anti-Gnostic Fathers.[1] They are: Irenaeus and Tertullian in the West; and

Clement and Origen in the East. The latter two are singled out as illustrious members of the Alexandrian School.

To Irenaeus (b. *c.* 130) may be ascribed the distinction of being the first Christian thinker who gave to the Christian religion a *system* of belief. His principal writing, *Against the Heresies* (*c.* 180), was definitely written against the complexities of Gnostic speculations—a writing widely read. He examined in detail all the heresies he could find and then attacked them as inherently absurd and inconsistent— Gnostic thought (he charged) being full of incompatible elements. Moreover, these heresies do violence to the sacred writings, to Paul and the apostles, to the rule of truth (*regula veritatis*) of the Christians and to the thought of the custodians of truth, the bishops and the church. When Irenaeus attacked Gnosticism he was in many, if not most instances, attacking fellow-Christians; for many Hellenistic Christians had taken over phases of the faith of Gnosticism.

In general, the Gnostics believed that the world has not been created by a good God but rather by a Demiurge, a fallen aeon or spirit. God (or Profundity) is above and beyond description, from whom issues a realm of pleroma filled with (masculine and feminine) aeons or entities. The evil in the world is due not to the ultimate reality but to the dramatic falling away of a cosmic aeon. Redemption from the throes of evil was the main note of Gnostic thought. Revealed knowledge (*gnosis*) through the logos which proceeded out of Profundity offers a way of escape of spirit from the darkness of this physical world. Christian Gnostics tended to interpret the founder of their faith as possessed by a high aeon for the brief period of his ministry. Carpocrates, Basilides and Valentinus (the latter two elaborate speculators) were among the important figures of second century Christian Gnosticism. It was an abhorrent thought to think that this world with all its evil could have issued from a good God; thus the Jewish creator-god was the Demiurge, an altogether inferior being; or, the act of creation was the work of lesser angelic beings.

Latin theology began in West North-Africa separated by mountains and desert from the East and Asiatic North-Africa. Carthage was second only to Rome in the development of a Western type of Christian thought. As such, Carthage was to Western thought what Alexandria was to Eastern. It was in Carthage where Tertullian was born (*c.* 160). A brilliant and vehement thinker, lawyer, rhetorician, satirist, prolific writer and dialectician, his influence upon early Christian thinking was enormous. He was a heresy-hunter, writing bitter polemics against anyone who disagreed with him and singling out the heresies of Gnosticism and Marcionism.

According to Marcion (100-160?), too many Christians had tied their thinking to traditional Judaism and its sacred literature. The God who creates the world so dramatically depicted in the Old Testament was not the real God but the Demiurge; the religion of law (Judaism) was inferior to the religion of Paul who outgrew his legalistic Pharisaism. A simpler type of scripture should be selected to avoid the old errors. Accordingly, Marcion proposed ten selections from the Pauline letters which would have the place of honor, together with an abridged form of the Lukian gospel together with his own selected writings. These would constitute the canon. Thus Marcionism with its rash anti-semitism plus a selected canon looked toward a revised Christian outlook. From the middle of the second century until its close [2] this school of thought constituted a major threat to the slowly growing self-conscious Catholic Christianity.

It was Marcionism that Tertullian denounced in five volumes of writings and, before that, all forms of heresies. Against them he took his stand upon the scriptures. To argue with authorities, he held, was to deny them. A philosopher is always in quest of something; the believer, on the other hand, has ended his quest even though what he believes may be absurd. It is utter obedience that makes for real virtue if one believes in divine laws. How can one be virtuous and at the same time question what is itself a good? Turning toward Athens is the spirit of the philosopher; surrendering to the authority of Jerusalem is the way of the believer. Thus did a spirit of antirationalism enter into Catholic orthodoxy and a rule of faith take the seat of honor. Tertullian, like all the others, could not, however, be consistent with such dogmatism; for all through his life he sought to make a reasonable case for his position and thus, in spite of himself, became a religious philosopher. In the area of philosophy he was poorly trained; moreover, he was always curbed by the nature of his temperament. A legal mind wants things settled. A genuine philosopher sees questions still to be wrestled with.

Tertullian's psychology of the soul is reminiscent of the Stoic doctrine of corporeality. The soul, he said, has form although immaterial: length, breadth and thickness; it permeates and directs both the mind and the body. Even God is corporeal, possessing a form which thus explains forms of the created world. Like Plato, he believed in (and argued in circularity for) the soul's immortality because of its simplicity and indivisibility. How a soul could be both corporeal and indivisible did not seem to bother him. God, he said, created *ex nihilo;* a creation out of nothing reveals a power greater than a creation out of something already there. The whole drama of the life of man was for him a preparation for a secure post-existence. To the sovereignty of God man must bend completely since man is condemned to torment because of inherited sin and guilt. The way of salvation is fixed by penitential hardships, by diligent observation of the commandments of God, by submission to the ordained sacraments. To attain a place in that "other world" is man's *summum bonum.*

The Alexandrian School

Important for the development of early Christian philosophy was the contemporary school of thought which emanated from Alexandria in North-Africa in the East. Often referred to as the Alexandrian School, this type of Christian thought was eminently speculative and embedded in Greek thinking. Alexandrian thought was not confined to a city but rather reached out far beyond its borders. Leaders of this school were Pantaenus (d. 202), Clement (*c.* 150-*c.* 213) and Origen (d. 254?).

Pantaenus is the earliest of the teachers of the theological school at Alexandria concerning whom there is information. Christian practice developed what is called "catechetical schools" directed to the training of those outside the faith. During the second and third centuries numbers of writings were used as materials for "Christian education." Among them were: parts of the *Didache*, Justin Martyr's *First Apology,* Irenaeus' *Epideixis*, Tertullian's *Lectures for Catechumens,* Hippolytus' *Canonens,* Cyprian's *Testimonia*, Origen's *Contra Celsum* and Lucian Martyr's *Didascalia.* The grand consummation of this type of literature was later reflected in the *Apostolic Constitutions* and in Augustine's *De Catechizandis Rudibus.*

President of this theological college (*c.* 190), following Pantaenus, was the Anti-Gnostic Father Clement, a figure who never fails to attract philosophical minds. Set in the midst of a metropolitan city, this denominational school could boast of proximity to famous scholars, great libraries, contact with university atmosphere, a cosmopolitan population, a commercial center. Its own supporting organization was democratic, relatively free from ecclesiastical domination. At Alexandria, Greek and Oriental thought met and fused, provoking a breadth of interpretation of its faith and a catholicity of outlook upon others.

Clement was the quiet literary scholar: urbane, easy-going, broad-minded, widely read. Three of his major works, the *Protrepticus* (Exhortation), the *Paedagogus* (Instructor) and the *Stromateis* ("Carpet-Bags") are extant. From his writings we are made sure that the New Testament canon was virtually completed in his day.

Quite unashamedly, he sought alliance with the philosophers—certainly to be preferred over the rhetoricians. Philosophy, he said, was to the Greeks what the Jewish law was to the Jews; both philosophy and Jewish law were preparations for the Christian faith. As Tatian before him, Clement affirmed that the Greek philosophers had taken over much from Jewish thought; Plato borrowed from Moses. But gold is gold whether in the hands of borrowers or thieves. Do not be frightened, he said, when you find truth in unsuspected places. There is but one river of truth although many rivulets. Even the Greeks possessed divine truth. Philosophy is to be used as an ally to theology.

With Philo (*c.* 20 B.C.-50 A.D.) and the later Platonists in the background, Clement speculates about God. Far removed from the world, without characteristics and with full transcendence, stands God—was the teaching of Philo. For Clement also God is changeless and timeless, an Absolute, beyond space and description, a pure being—to be apprehended only by pure thought abstracted from the limitations of sense. Thought may move toward God by the analysis of subtraction of characters (*e.g.,* not color, not shape, not extension, not any qualification) to the place where no characterization whatsoever is possible. Man's anthropomorphic images of God misrepresent God. And yet, God is creator and a beneficent providence, first-cause. Creation included time, hence creation did not take place in time. This phase of God's nature comes to light through the logos (a Philonic conception and vaguely in Plato) through which the Absolute enters into the sphere of the relations of creation. It is the logos that is the creative and guiding power, inspirer of both prophets and philosophers, making manifest what is hidden in the nature of God. The logos is both transcendent and immanent, as divine as God. The Absolute God has been made manifest by the logos as the Son of God and the Son of God was the founder of the Christian faith.

Thus Clement was a Christian Neoplatonist,[3] heavy in emphasis upon the doctrine of the logos; this logos reflected Plato's supreme idea and the Stoic's immanent principle.

Besides the emphasis upon speculative theology tied to Greek philosophy and to Philo, another characteristic shows itself in the Alexandrian school of thought: the ingenuity with which allegorical interpretations developed to accommodate tradition to the changing modes of thought. By means of allegory the Stoics thus could understand ancient Greek writings; by the same means the later Greeks thus made rational their traditional myths; the Jews, notably Philo, so could understand their scriptures; and so Clement and Origen their sacred literature; and, finally and later, Augustine interpreted very conveniently portions of the New Testament literature. Clement employed allegory in the search of esoteric truths believing that the mark of attainment to higher knowledge or *gnosis* came by way of such insight. Deeper meanings are concealed to those who have only literal eyes. Redemption of man thus comes by way of illumination and enlightenment (a Greek doctrine so explicitly taught by Socrates). Men need only to be shown the way to the good life and they will follow after it, for man has the divine image in his rational make-up. No taint of original sin mars this divine nature in man. But the logos is needed for illumination.

Thus, in Clement Christian philosophy was made reasonable for the times, generous in its receptivity to allegedly alien truths, catholic in its appraisal of the multiple paths to divinity and a *rapprochement* between the fields of the theologian and the philosopher. The Christian faith for him was an intellectual adventure for those capable of it. It was not a religion reserved only for the rank and file (whom he called "simple believers"), not to literal fundamentalists whose strait-jacket thinking would prevent the use of reason.

It was Origen (185-251? or 254?), Clement's pupil, who succeeded him at Alexandria, who developed a system of Christian philosophy on a larger scale, more complete than heretofore. A prodigious student, fiery temper, scholar of tremendous applications, ascetic, voluminous writer, lover of the philosophers, Origen was a controversial churchman in and out of the good graces of office. His commitment to tradition was stronger than that of his teacher. With great patience he gave himself to the task of editing an authoritative text of the Old Testament scriptures, the *Hexapla*, containing the Hebrew with Greek transliteration and four Greek versions. Besides commentaries on certain New Testament gospels and letters he wrote *De Principiis*, a monumental work on systematic theology, *Contra Celsum* and *De Oratione*. Under Clement and Ammonius Saccas (who taught at Alexandria in the first half of the third century, teacher of Plotinus) he learned the Platonic philosophy and he set out to wed the Christian faith to it. His anti-Gnostic thought is seen in the guiding principle of his thinking: nothing is to be believed as unworthy of God. Thus, those Christian Gnostics who would have difficulty believing that the world could have been created by a good God (good Jewish cosmogony) he denounced. And to help him in his cause he allegorized the scriptures. In allegorizing he made famous the three senses of interpretation: 1) the bodily, somatic, or literal; 2) the psychic or moral; and 3) the spiritual or allegorical—highest of all. All of Origen's speculations were grounded in the belief that the scriptures were standard or the basis for all speculation.

Origen's God was less abstract than Clement's although incomprehensible apart from the revelation of the creative divine logos or sophia (wisdom) from God, the latter subordinate [4] to God and yet of the same substance (*homo-ousios*). The Son is eternally generated from God, so also the third hypostasis in the Trinity, the Holy Spirit. The Son is the divine logos joined to a created spirit which in turn was joined to a human soul. It is the Son of God through whom the nature of God is revealed and the way of salvation made open. All beings, archangels (with very fine bodies), angels down through man and to arch-fiends (with very coarse bodies) will ultimately be saved (universalism). The physical world was created *ex nihilo*. Men have, as spirits, pre-existed. Common man can be expected only to follow the pathway of faith (*pistis*); but educated man will rise to knowledge (*gnosis*) or to the level of philosophy. Here he will think through by deductive analysis the truth of the scriptures and tradition and go on through further processes of reasoning to new levels of truth.

A HISTORY OF PHILOSOPHICAL SYSTEMS

Augustine and Augustinianism

The period following the one just considered offers some well-known names in the history of Christian thought. But, on the whole, they are of less interest to our present purposes than the last great name (which we shall presently consider) of the ancient period of Christian philosophy.

The one stalwart figure, Plotinus (205-270), Neoplatonist *par excellence,* belongs to this interval. Plotinus' influence upon Eastern Christian philosophy was immediate and, thanks to Augustine, the sweep of his mystical emphasis became entrenched in Western Christian thought. (A special section in this book is devoted to Neoplatonism.)

Controversies within the Christian church were thick and heavy on technical points of Christology and the nature of God conceived as somehow three-in-one. Nicea saw in 325 the first great ecumenical gathering of the church to settle a major dispute of theology; but it was not settled there because of the divisions of political parties, of alliances and deep differences of outlook not capable of resolution by verbal resolutions. The Trinitarian controversies continued to rage past 381 (the date of the so-called Niceno-Constantinopolitan creed). Even Augustine was called upon to make more or less final pronouncements on the Trinitarian formula, even though after more than a quarter of a century work upon the subject (written in fifteen volumes, *De Trinitate*) he confessed that we cannot understand it too clearly!

Augustine (354-430) is an important figure in the history of early Christian philosophy for many reasons: his personality, his varied background and interests, the multitude of his writings over a period of more than forty years, his public office, and the times. The times must not be overlooked: Augustine witnessed the crumbling of the long dominant Roman empire. In his famous *City of God* he saw in the splendor of the Catholic church the anchor for a crumbling world and the destiny of the saved.

There is no Augustinian "system" for a very simple reason: there is no one Augustine. His personality was a criss-cross of many currents, much like Paul before him, like Luther and George Fox after him. He fits no one mould; he is now this and now that. Schools of thought of different types which followed looked back to him quite capable of quoting him to their advantage but each taking only the side which suited its purpose. A failure to see this multiple type of personality is to fail to understand original Augustinianism.

This explains why he is sometimes called an eclectic; he had tried to satisfy his mind with one system and then another, retaining the imprint of each. Always a sensitive mind he was open to conversions. His psycho-autobiographical *Confessions*, written later in his life, retells his crisis experiences within his divided self. The cross-currents of his mind made him rich in experience. He was sensuous and spiritual-minded; critical and naive; a mystic and a critical analyst; at times a philosopher free to speculate and again a subject devoutly loyal to his tradition and church; he encouraged speculation and he pointed to a revelation given once-for-all; he employed rational arguments but insisted that faith has priority over reason; evil he viewed as a negation and again as something very positive; the world is for him good and yet it is condemned to wretchedness; he was a pre-scholastic and he was a child of child-like acceptance; he insisted on the necessity of the sacraments and yet he taught a direct communion with the Divine; he sketched a plan of visible church-rule and still taught the invisibility of the universal and real church in so far as it possesses the indwelling spirit; he was conservative and progressive; he put emphasis upon a social order and yet remained an individualist; he observed the events of physical nature and sounded the depths of man's own inner nature.

What came to be called Augustinianism is the selection of those facets of his thought which lent support to the growing orthodoxy. Extreme Augustinians forgot to remember, if they did remember, the heterogeneous character of the man and his thought.

The historian particularly interested in the development of philosophy will naturally pick out certain phases of Augustine's thinking as of special interest. He finds in him some notable discussions pertaining to philosophy.

It may be said that Augustine—and Tertullian and Origen before him—in the sweep of his religious imagination presented a more or less comprehensive philosophy of history which came to be widely adopted but different from the one taught before. He examined the traditional notion that cosmic history moves in cycles by a succession of returning periods. For him this made the cosmos greater than the God who created it. How can the Creator be subject to such monotonous Fate? Moreover, the meaning of history for him revolved about the history of man's redemption (not a new thought, of course); but it had a beginning in God, a climax in a definite period when God became incarnate in Jesus Christ (a unique event) and an end that is to come in the last Judgment. It is not a repetitive process but an ongoing drama in which the Creator creates free restless beings who are to find their way by the help of Divine grace—although (inconsistently!) the Divine grace for Augustine was irresistible and thus fore-ordains men, some to salvation and some to damnation (double predestination) to the equivalent of the number of those fallen angels, no more and no less.

Again, Augustine's notion of the soul is of interest to the philosopher. Each soul is a unique spiritual entity, now holding to the doctrine of its special creation and now holding to the traducianist view that it is derived from the soul of its parents—the former view becoming the one chosen by Catholic orthodoxy. His "proofs" of the soul's existence anticipates Descartes' *cogito ergo sum:* to doubt the existence of the soul, he said, is to assert it, for to doubt is to think and to think is to exist. Souls are thinking beings.

Again, Augustine held to the doctrine of creation *ex nihilo* at a given moment chosen out of the deliberate free-will act of the Creator. Both the world and time thus had a definite beginning. What God wills to do is, however, inspired by God's knowledge of what is good.. (Tertullian had argued that the will of God wills and the good is derived from that will.) God's intellect is thus the primary motive to creation. For Augustine the will is free in the sense of self-determination (without external compulsion) even though only one alternative may present itself.

Again, the problem of theodicy (evil in relation to a good God) looms large in his thought. As a good traditionalist, he looked to the story of the fall of Adam for one of his theories. Man originally possessed a perfectly free-will and a holy inclination to do the right. The *possibility* to do wrong was in Adam but only became actual under a test. When Adam did fail to make the better choice sin originates *ex nihilo,* possibility becomes a permanent actuality. Thus "original sin" enters by way of perversion passed on from Adam to the sons of man (traducianism). The root of evil lies in this inheritance, corrupting not only human nature but nature itself (thus cursed). Helpless is man without Divine grace. On this question

A HISTORY OF PHILOSOPHICAL SYSTEMS

Augustine fought the more moral views of his contemporary Pelagius (d. *c.* 420) whose notion of grace was that of *aid* to do the right and who rejected the doctrine of transmitted original sin. Each man, argued Pelagius, is an Adam to himself, making for his own choices. Pelagians held that a thousand sins did not render the power of the will to do the right less impotent if it chose (an extreme Pelagianism). Another theory crops out in Augustine's thought revealing elements of the teachings of Manichaeism to which cult Augustine gave his one-time allegiance. Manichaeism was a syncretistic religion with mixtures of Zoroastrianism, Buddhism, Hinduism, Judaism, Neoplatonism and Christianity.[5] Mani (b. *c.* 215) taught the typical doctrine of Zoroastrianism of the eternal struggle between good and evil; the latter, he thought, became expressed in nature and in the body of man and part of his soul. Man is thus caught in a cosmic battle between principalities good and principalities bad. Procreation of the body is a procreation of more evil; sexual lust is this strong manifestation of evil desiring to perpetuate itself. Original sin thus for Augustine became identified with sexual lust and the volcanic eruption of the powers of darkness. On the other hand, another theory shows Augustine's contact with and high regard for the Neoplatonic view that evil is a lack, not something positive—thus absolving God since it lacks the attributes of existence as such. And still another theory: evil is *permitted* by God for the sake of a larger good—so said Augustine.

The theodicy which came to prevail in the history of Western Christian philosophy is a modification of Augustine's doctrine of the self-determination of the will. Man is thus a sharer in the drama of creation; though man is responsible for evil God creates the good. Created in the image of God, man reflects that image in self-determination. Thus moral decisions are possible and a moral cooperative plan of the created world follows. This, of course, is not purely Augustinian but it was selected out of the complex patterns of his solution. For Augustine, of course, man was made the center of the solution; the problem of dysteleology in physical nature is not solved other than by the tacit view of physical nature as, in the Neoplatonic sense, of less consequence than that of the realm of spirit.

Augustine atoned for this slight upon physical nature by his insistence that God continually sustains it out of His goodness, explaining miracles as well as natural events. The created world is in evolutionary process but these processes are natural and, at the same time, supernaturally directed.

Like those of his predecessors in the tradition, Augustine remarked little about physical nature—except to speculate on its spherity (uninhabited on the other side), to remark that astronomy offers only idle speculation—all such speculations tending only to divert attention from what ought to be of prime interest: man's concern over the destiny of his soul and the glorification of his Creator.

With Augustine the Platonic tradition became secure as the dominant Christian philosophy for the church. For him Platonism and Catholic Christianity were in essential harmony. Plato, he had confessed, was the Christ of the philosophers.

NOTES

1. The Gospel of John is an earlier Anti-Gnostic writing.
2. By the end of the second century, the main body of the New Testament had been canonized. The rabbis at Jamnia in the second century settled, finally, the canon of the Jewish scriptures.
3. Bigg believed Clement to have been the real founder of Neoplatonism. *Op. cit.* in Bibliography.
4. Origen's doctrine of subordination was later appealed to by the heretical Arians who were unwilling to use the term "homoousios" (a Gnostic term). The term became the hot-spot in the controversy before, at and after the Council of Nicea.
5. See the chapter "Manichaeism" by Irach J. S. Taraporewala in *Forgotten Religions* (New York, 1950), ed. by Vergilius Ferm.

BIBLIOGRAPHY

For Primary and Secondary Source material many of the books here listed furnish excellent bibliographies.

R. SEEBERG, *Text-Book of the History of Doctrines,* tr. by C. E. Hay, 2 vols. (Philadelphia, 1905).
K. LAKE, ed., *The Apostolic Fathers,* Vol. I (Loeb Classical Library, 1913).
C. BIGG, *The Christian Platonists of Alexandria* (2nd ed., 1913).
E. R. GOODENOUGH, *The Theology of Justin Martyr* (Jena, 1923).
H. HAUSHEER, *The Genius and the Influence of St. Augustine* (Iowa City, 1922).

A HISTORY OF PHILOSOPHICAL SYSTEMS

G. P. FISHER, *History of Christian Doctrine* (reprint, New York, 1922).
A. C. MCGIFFERT, *The God of the Early Christians* (New York, 1924).
———, *A History of Christian Thought* (New York, Vol. I, 1932; Vol. II, 1933).
S. J. CASE, *Makers of Christianity* (New York, 1934).
K. S. LATOURETTE, *The First Five Centuries* (New York, 1937).
G. WEISS, *Urchristentum* (Eng., tr., 1938).
I. EDMAN and H. W. SCHNEIDER, *Landmarks for Beginners in Philosophy* (New York, 1941). Selections from Augustine.
E. J. GOODSPEED, *Early Christian Literature* (1942).
VERGILIUS FERM, ed., *An Encyclopedia of Religion* (New York, 1945).

CHAPTER THIRTEEN

ARABIC AND ISLAMIC PHILOSOPHY

EDWARD J. JURJI

THE MOST crucial event in European history, since the Punic Wars, was the triumph of Moslem arms in the eighth century, a hundred years after the death of Mohammed. Roman antiquity came to a halt and while Europe was only beginning to be Byzantinized, the Middle Ages fell upon her. In a series of military assaults, delivered upon Egypt, Iran, Mesopotamia, North Africa, Spain, and Southern France, Islam shattered the Mediterranean unity which the Germanic invaders had left intact.

Although unable to consolidate the entire Mediterranean world, the Arab conquerors encircled it on the East, South, and West. Only the North lay outside their control. Culture in the vast domains that fell to them became oriented as time passed towards Mecca and Medina, Damascus and Baghdad.

Almost simultaneously, a new Christian civilization—neither Greek nor Latin but Nordic—was struggling to be born. Its chief representatives, Frank, Anglo-Saxon, and German, were, however, blockaded and circumscribed by their geographic isolation from the old centers of culture in the Mediterranean world. But the decadence of the Merovingian monarchy which gave birth to the more truly Germanic Carolingian dynasty was a straw in the wind indicating the coming importance of the North. By A.D. 800, the establishment of Charlemagne gave proof of the new trend in European history and culture. A new Europe would emerge under Teutonic auspices and Christendom, though battered by its Moslem adversary, will reconstruct a new Roman Empire and regain the Greek heritage aided by what the Arab philosophers were able to transmit.

A HISTORY OF PHILOSOPHICAL SYSTEMS

The intellectual contribution which the Arabic-Islamic civilization made to the new West did not exactly originate in the Arabian Peninsula. Prior to the universalization of the Arab cultural themes —largely due to the participation of Syrian, Jewish, and Iranian converts—the Arab mind had had a narrow horizon. It had not proceeded farther than the odes and oracles of pre-Islamic times. In the path of philosophy hardly anything more than the wisdom lore of Arabia was known. The propounding of maxims and aphorisms, the crystallization of wisdom hammered on the anvil of experience, these were the closest approach made to philosophy.

Within this restricted area, the pre-Islamic Arabians boasted a repository of keen observations of nature centering in the life and fate of man. They had nothing like a systematic philosophy concerned with ultimate reality, the nature of existence, a theory of knowledge, an exploration of the meaning of truth, ethics, and immortality. Confronted by what seemed as the enigmatic and inscrutable will of God, they expressed themselves in terms tantamount to a complete resignation. Within their peculiar categories, however, the Arabians achieved a reputation in the ancient Semitic world, as the Old Testament proves. Thus Agur, son of Jakeh (Prov. 30:1) and Lemuel (Prov. 31:1) are two Arabian kings who like Job—tribesman of the Bene Qedem—were noted for wisdom. The Koran (31:11-12) reproduces the name of the sage Luqman, paragon of wisdom among the ancient Arabs.

This oral tradition of wisdom is not the sub-soil of that later Arab philosophy which radiated from the centers of Islamic culture and exerted a decisive influence upon the medieval thought of Europe. The philosophy which Islamic writings enshrine is traceable to the Greek studies of Syrian Christian scholars who worked at such centers as Edessa, Nisibin, and Jundishapur. Having acquired classical philosophy and science from the Syrians, the thinkers of Islam fashioned them into a new synthesis observing the demands of their own era with its cosmopolitan society wherein diverse Oriental and Occidental traditions mingled together under the banner of the Caliphate. This was an era when Asia Minor was a Christian country with Constantinople as capital and when the Iberian Peninsula together with Sicily were the home of Islamic cultural effervescence. In those times it was hardly accurate to speak of the Moslem East and the Christian West.

A HISTORY OF PHILOSOPHICAL SYSTEMS

Throughout the tenth century, the progress of Western culture was surpassed by the more rapid strides of the Islamic peoples. In the thirteenth century, after the crusades and the Mongolian invasion of Western Asia, Europe began to breathe more freely and it attained intellectual equality with the Islamic world. Only with the coming of the Renaissance in the fifteenth century and the geographic expansion attendant upon the discovery of the New World did the Christian West attain that cultural ascendancy which it has ever since retained and enlarged.

Key Figures and Schools

For the origins of Arab philosophy, then, we must turn to the advanced civilization of the Near East which became subject to the political authority of the Arabs in the seventh century. The Hellenization of Western Asia had proceeded since the days of Alexander the Great (356-323 B.C.). Alexandria and Antioch attained fame as the centers of Greek culture. With the spread of Christianity, interest in the classical heritage deepened. In order to comprehend the Bible, ecclesiastical canons and decrees, and the writings of the Church Fathers, the Christians of Syria had to learn the Greek language and literature. They accomplished this in their oldest school founded at Edessa by St. Ephrem (*ca.* 306-373) in A.D. 363 and closed in 489 when a number of its scholars migrated to Sassanid Persia where they established their two celebrated academies at Nisibin and Jundishapur. It was in the schismatic Church of the Nestorians and that of the Jacobites, therefore, that Arab philosophy was rooted.

The seventh-century Moslems were hardly in a position to appreciate the true meaning of Greek logic and philosophy. Their capacity for philosophical discipline and inquiry was improved, however, as converts from Christianity and Judaism began to swell their ranks. By the eighth century, the first Islamic school of philosophy, that of the Qadarites, made its appearance in Syria partly as a reaction against Koranic determinism. Its major concern with the problem of free will became a primary tenet of the rationalist Mutazilite school which came to its own under the early rulers of the Abbasid Caliphate (750-1258) of Baghdad. The dynamic Greco-Syriac ideas were already beginning to register in the theological controversies which stirred the Moslem world.

A HISTORY OF PHILOSOPHICAL SYSTEMS

The Abbasid Caliph al-Mamun (786-833), himself a sympathizer with the Mutazilite rationalists, instituted in Baghdad the first bona-fide school of higher learning, known as the House of Wisdom. It was the most notable development in the realm of the intellect since the founding of the Alexandrian Museum in the early third century B.C. Here the translation of Greek texts into Arabic was pursued with resolution. The Nestorian physician, Hunayn ibn-Ishaq (Joannitius, 809-873), assisted by his son Ishaq and his nephew Hubaysh, figured as the chief translator. Plato's *Republic*, Aristotle's *Categories, Physics, Magna Moralia,* and *Hermeneutics*, were among the classics rendered. The response which these works evoked in the scientific and philosophical circles was reëchoed in the halls of Islamic theology.

The orthodox Islamic reaction to the philosophical trend in theology was spearheaded in the tenth century by abu-al-Hasan al-Ashari (873-935) of Baghdad. A native of Basra, he had started life as a pupil of the Mutazilite school acquiring the rhetorical skills and scholarly acumen of its disputatious doctors. Then he executed an about-face and declared theological war against his former masters. He evolved a new dialectic (*kalam*) receptive to Greek reason but thoroughly grounded in Koranic thought and primarily poised to strike at the strongholds of heresy. The Mutakallimun (dialecticians) were Islamic speculators who subordinated philosophy to revealed religious truth.

A harmony of faith and reason, religion and philosophy, was the goal of the philosophers. It was attempted by their ranking representatives, the Arab al-Kindi (d. *ca.* 873), the Turk al-Farabi (*ca.* 870-950), and the Persian ibn-Sina (Avicenna, 980-1037). The achievements of these men who lived in the Near East were climaxed in ibn-Rushd (Averroës, 1126-98) whose career belonged to the annals of Spanish Islam. The most subtle minds in Islamic philosophy, these four dedicated themselves to the creation of a colossal syncretism in which Plato and more particularly Aristotle prevail. Beneath the surface of their work was a revolt against orthodoxy.

Although the philosophers of Islam generally coined their phrases in simple style and used the then widespread Arabic idiom, they won neither the confidence of the average intelligent Moslem nor the endorsement of the theologians. Their very name *falasifa* (philosophers) came to denote heresy. Like the billowy current belts that traverse the ocean, always preserving their own coloration and direction without ever vanishing in the expansive waters that encompass them, the Moslem philosophers may be said to have passed through Islam without ever becoming fully integrated in its basic thought pattern.

Akin to the philosophers in the antipathy they drew from orthodoxy, were the Brethren of Sincerity, a secret philosophical school of Basra and Baghdad encyclopedists (*ca.* 970). These Brethren deviated from the course of conservative religion in favor of Pythagorean speculation and endeavored to compile the then existing knowledge on a philosophical basis. More effective in the long run, however, were the Sufis (mystics) who in the twelfth century created the beginnings of a vast reorganization is Islamic life corresponding to the monastic orders of medieval Christendom. Although influenced by the Brethren in his early career, al-Ghazzali (Algazel, 1058-1111)—Islam's greatest theologian—turned in his maturity to Sufi mysticism and enunciated in his major works the fundamental affirmation that religious knowledge must inevitably depend upon Revelation.

The Essence of Arab Philosophy

The great authority attached to the Moslem philosophers, especially Avicenna and Averroës, stamped them as the expositors of Aristotle. The Stagirite was not, however, their only master. In al-Kindi's so-called *Theology of Aristotle,* Plotinus (Books IV-VI *of the Enneads*) in Aristotelian disguise contributed to the philosophers' conception of God and His relation to the universe. The pantheism and monism of Plotinus were, of course, a far cry from Aristotle's dualist theism.

Arab speculation was steeped, nonetheless, in practically the entire content of Greek thought: From the Sophists, who gave the first impulse to logical analysis of what was involved in description and definition, to Socrates whose important contribution to knowledge included designating the concept as part of the essence; and from Plato, who objectified the concept by raising it from the world of shadows to that of the particulars, to Aristotle who offered an analysis of thing as well as of thought and was hailed in the medieval and Islamic world as the unrivaled First Teacher.

It must be emphasized, however, that although research in the field of Arab philosophy seems to suggest that it was a coat of many colors, the stage has not been reached as yet when a full-orbed history of this subject can be written.

The evidence leaves no doubt that the lines were sharply drawn between the Arab philosophers and their orthodox opponents in the controversy concerning the knowledge of God, creation, prophecy, and the immortality of the soul. Although the philosophers affirmed the unity of God, they contended that matter was eternal and thereby seemed to reject His rôle as Creator. They asserted, furthermore, that God's knowledge extends only to the general laws of the cosmos and not to individual things and persons, all of which in the opinion of the orthodox was a repudiation of the omniscience of God and of prophecy. Equally repugnant to the pious was the theory of the intellect whereby the philosophers, in line with Peripatetic precept, taught that the human soul was only a faculty of the intellect capable by virtue and information of union with the active intellect which emanates from God. To admit this was to deny the immortality of the soul, in the view of the believer.

The orthodox Mutakallimun rose to the defense of the Islamic faith. Their apologetic seemed to center in the problem of creation. Against the Aristotelian idea that the universe is fixed and matter eternal, they advanced a theory of particles (atoms) based on Democritus. It upheld the view that the energy of God is in perpetual action, vitalizing the very particles of the created objects which, therefore, live and move and have their being by the constant flow of divine life. Thus bodies come into existence or die through the aggregation or sunderance of the particles. Not only Space, but Time also, was allegedly made up of small individual moments. The creation of the world, once established on these grounds, it was an easy matter for the apologists to confirm the existence of the Creator, the validity of prophecy, and the immortality of the soul.

That the science of Aristotle triumphed over the Democritean theory of particles, espoused by the Mutakallimun, and over the Platonic concepts current in the Moslem world, is not essential to the understanding of Arab philosophy in its world-wide relations. What is of the essence is that since the Arabs introduced Aristotle to Spain in the tenth century, he became for medieval science what Newton's physics is to the modern age. Not within the orbit of Islam, therefore, but in Christian philosophy and theology must be discovered the transformation wrought by the readmission of Aristotle into the bloodstream of Western science and religion.

Until Arab thinkers rescued Aristotle from obscurity in the West, Augustinian theology had had for its philosophical framework the theory grounded in Plotinus and Plato, namely that the sensed world is not real and that the sensed self is but the symbol of the more ideal and immortal soul beyond. With the entry of Aristotle into the sphere of Christian theology, a new approach to ultimate reality was deemed necessary.

Aristotelian science began from the thesis that the real world is the sensed world. Ideas and concepts which did not originate in sense perception did not constitute part of reality's core. By the chemical constituents of all things—earth, air, fire, and water—was meant the qualified bits of the total manifold of nature. The four qualities of these primary constituents were grouped in two pairs—hot-cold and wet-dry. Hence the doctrine of opposites.

Fundamental to Aristotelian physics was the doctrine of positive forms, perceived, for instance, when cold water is indicated by a cold hand, and the doctrine of forms by privation, as when a cold hand may be described as not hot. Being and becoming do not involve *creatio ex nihilo* but rather the shift in forms, a combination of forms by privation.

Therefore, to be is to possess sensed properties which are actualized in concrete nature as positive forms. Thus, the soul of man was identified with the rational body. When the dissolution of the human body occurred, the soul passed from positive form to the status of form by privation. God was likewise identified with the cosmos as the Unmoved Mover, the Rational Principle, approximately but never completely actualized in matter. Once the logical character of Aristotle's forms was conceded, the eternity of God and the immortality of man followed in neat order.

Peculiarities of Arab Philosophy: Avicenna and Averroës

Aristotle emerged in Arab philosophy as the ideal guide of a movement which drew its authority from his works, whether authentic or apocryphally ascribed to him. From these works arose the problems which exercised medieval philosophy and endowed it with special meaning. Yet the writings of Arab philosophers, the more carefully they are scrutinized, turn out to be less the works of exegesis and commentary and more—if their objectives and results are recalled—an expression of calm inquiry, a definite step in that philosophical quest which knows no end. With few exceptions, Arab philosophy was guided by the standards of the great Stagirite not in order to discover what he actually taught but rather for the purpose of probing the structure of reality. This was the chief peculiarity of that intellectual development represented above all by Avicenna and Averroës.

Avicenna

Having supplanted al-Kindi, al-Farabi was in turn supplanted by Avicenna (980-1037), the primate of Arab philosophy. Born in Afshana, near Bukhara, and buried in Hamadhan, he was the greatest scientist of Eastern Islam and the Latins knew him before they were acquainted with Averroës. Attracted to Greek philosophy in childhood, Avicenna, who also devoted himself to the Koran, soon mastered Porphyry, Euclid, and Ptolemy, as well as what was available of Plato and Aristotle. Despite the tyranny which he once endured, he was a frequent counsellor of princes and his career was one of comparative ease dominated throughout by a multiplicity of scientific and metaphysical concerns. In addition to his medical *Canon,* which Gerard of Cremona translated into Latin, his *Healing,* planned on encyclopedic lines, contained the logic, metaphysics, physics, and philosophy by which his name became deservedly celebrated.

Although the *Healing* dated to Avicenna's younger days, the main positions which he defended in it were not abandoned in the writings of his more mature years. Moulded by Greek insights, this work had the distinction of reconciling Aristotle and Plotinus in a simple refreshing manner. The central theme, to which everything else seemed subsidiary, was that of being. There lay Avicenna's chief contribution to the making of medieval philosophy.

Like Aristotle, he strove to construct a special science, metaphysics, which would make being as such its main concern. And more worthy a concern could not have been chosen, for among the diverse phenomena of existence, the most compelling single item is always that of existence itself whose secret is the challenge and despair of intelligent men everywhere.

Avicenna interpreted being in the light of empirical psychology and relied on concepts drawn from the Neoplatonic theory of emanation. Classified as vegetable, animal, and rational, the hierarchy of being was apexed by the First Principle, the sovereign and indivisible One who is God. From the First Principle emanated the First Intelligence. The world of ideas loomed as a series of pure intelligences which animated the celestial bodies. The highest body to be thus animated was the sphere of fixed stars. From this emanated a soul which animated the planets of which the Moon was considered the lowest. From the soul and body of the Sphere-Moon sprang the Active Intelligence which gave rise to the human soul and the four elements. An existence of necessity and an existence of possibility, furthermore, dominated the entire realm of being.

This world of being involving a series of intelligibles—upon which the entire structure of ultimate reality and theology was predicated—became part of the Western scholastic tradition. Trends in that direction appeared when Albertus Magnus (*ca.* 1193-1280) and his contemporaries adopted the intelligibles of Avicenna and referred to them as intellects under the general heading of *intentio*.

Averroës

Born in Cordova and buried in Marrakesh, Averroës (1126-1198) for twelve years was judge in his native city, an office once filled by his father and grandfather. Belonging to a famous Hispano-Arab family, his career fitted into the period of the Almohades who from their court at Marrakesh ruled all North Africa to the borders of Egypt, as well as Spain. Like Avicenna, Averroës combined several scientific and philosophical pursuits, including medicine and metaphysics. But in him the philosopher-commentator dwarfed the physician. Among his philosophical works, which were rebuked by the Moslem divines, was the *Incoherence of Incoherence*, a reply to the attack on rationalism which al-Ghazzali had embodied in his *Incoherence of the Philosophers*.

Since Averroës did not know Greek, his commentaries on Aristotle were based on the earlier Baghdad translations. Actually, these commentaries were new metaphysical explorations rather than expositions of Aristotle. With one exception, the so-called commentaries of Aristotle are not extant in the original Arabic but are preserved in Hebrew. From Hebrew, the Latin translations of

Averroës, begun in 1220 by the British-Sicilian Michael Scotus, opened Hellenic philosophy more fully to Western Christendom.

Averroës sought to reconcile Islamic dogma with the results of philosophy. In his defense of the eternity of the world, which precluded *creatio ex nihilo*, he incurred the enmity of Moslem theologians. The thirteenth-century Church was also compelled to proscribe his doctrine. Banished to Lucena, near Cordova, because of this teaching, he had to submit to a painful hearing and to the burning of his books save those on medical, metaphysical, and astronomical subjects. Although his last years were mostly spent in disgrace, he was able, nonetheless, to enunciate his themes with a clarity that made them well-nigh unforgettable in the annals of Western thought.

His doctrine on the eternity of the world did not explain creation as the result of a single act but as a movement which is rendered every instant in an ever-changing cosmos. Though eternal, the world has a Prime Mover who Himself is eternal and who is constantly endowing creation with dynamic. The two forms of eternity are, therefore, to be differentiated since the one is with, the other without, cause. Averroës drew another important distinction between soul and intellect, making the latter the superior kind of soul if only because of its absolute freedom from matter.

It has already been noted that Arab philosophy—culminating in Averroës—was the most impressive body of speculative thought known to the medieval civilization of the Mediterranean basin. Despite the controversy and hostility which his name and works called forth, he was able to orient the minds of his age in a new direction. His underlying purpose had to do with the supreme authority of speculative knowledge based on experience. It bore fruit in the philosophical and rational trends of subsequent centuries.

Within the confines of this philosophical knowledge, he discovered a measure of certitude which informed his epochal reply to al-Ghazzali. The basic conception to which he appealed was that the noble does not exist by virtue of the less noble but vice versa. Consequently, he affirmed that the less noble beings had no value apart from participation in that magnificent harmony wherein the more noble creatively joins. He went on to propose that we live in the beatitude of the spheres which in their turn live by the power of the Supreme Mover. In laying the foundation of his philosophical certitude, Averroës discussed the four causes—matter, form, efficiency, and action—in relation to the eternity of God. And describing the energy which bestows perfect actuality upon being, he adduced an entelechy which was expanded to embrace within its sweep the cosmic and rational spheres as well as the existential and practical.

Influx Into Western Thought

This Arab philosophy reached the Latin West through diverse channels. Primary among these was the Hebrew channel. What the Jewish writers had derived from their study of Arabic and Islamic philosophy was now transmitted to Christian Europe. When Archdeacon Gundisalvus of Seville was commissioned in the early twelfth century by Raymond, Archbishop of Toledo, to make translations of Avicenna he was assisted by Avendeath (*ca.* 1090-1165), a convert from Judaism. Their translation of Avicenna's *On The Soul*—a commentary on Aristotle's great treatise—exercised considerable influence in the West. Maimonides (1135-1204) formulated the evidence for the existence, unity, and incorporeality of God with the aid of the Aristotelian metaphysics embedded in Avicenna's writings; his attack on the Mutakallimun was freely utilized by Thomas Aquinas (1227-1274). Much of the text of Averroës, as it was known to the medieval schoolmen, came through Hebrew. At Paris especially, the main themes of Arab philosophy on providence, immortality, and creation were found unsatisfactory.

Taking the two foremost Arab thinkers singly, it would seem that the influence of Avicenna in the West passed through three distinct stages: First, there was an epoch of about a hundred years, starting with the initial translations and closing with the strong reaction of Guillaume d'Auvergne, Bishop of Paris, who devoted most of his voluminous writings to the refutation of Averroism. Second, the stage launched with the Pontifical decree of 1231 which permitted the study of Aristotle and implicitly his Arab commentators. This lasted broadly until about 1260 when the scholastic philosopher Albertus Magnus—earliest of the great Dominican philosophers and teacher of St. Thomas Aquinas—made his compilations. Third, the stage which assured Avicenna a well-defined position in the Thomist system of thought. Accorded him by the commentators on Thomas Aquinas, this position of Avicenna gave him a reputation which persists in Western thought till the present.

A HISTORY OF PHILOSOPHICAL SYSTEMS

Citations from the authoritative doctrines of Avicenna on being appeared during the fourteenth century in the commentary on the Book of Wisdom penned by Meister Eckhart (*ca.* 1260-*ca.* 1327), the Dominican contemporary of Dante (1265-1321). Here the distinction between being and essence was brought out in veritably Aristotelian fashion. Thereafter, the influx of Avicenna into Western thought was inextricably linked to the works which gave an exposition of Thomist philosophy. Among these, the brilliant commentary on the Aquinian *De Ente et Essentia* is noteworthy; it was delivered by Cardinal Cajetan (1469-1534) at the Academy of Padua in the school year 1493-1494. Likewise, the Spanish-French theologian John of St. Thomas (family name, John Poinsot, 1589-1644) made frequent references to Avicenna in the lectures, which he gave at Alcala and Madrid in 1630-43, published as recently as 1930 in Turin under the title *Cursus Philosophicus Thomisticus.*

Averroës—the Commentator *par excellence*—had a markedly different career in the West. His interpretation of Aristotle aroused the suspicion of the scholastic theologians. He was understood to mean that man was the union between body and soul, that the soul was the form of body, and that the intellect was another substance in contact and communion with the soul. To Christian thinkers, all this sounded heretical and was utterly inadmissible. Christianity promised man an individual immortality, not the immortality of a substance outside himself. That the Christian and Averroist doctrines were incompatible is shown in the anti-Averroist pronouncements of the Italian Franciscan theologian St. Bonaventura (1221-1274) as well as in those of Albertus Magnus and Thomas Aquinas.

Intent upon saving both the Platonic immortality of the soul and the Aristotelian unity of the human composite, Christian philosophers were naturally drawn to Avicenna. He seemed to offer the elements of a solution. His exposition of the pseudo-Aristotelian *Theology* had the effect of reconciling Plato and the Stagirite in a synthesis which had an appeal to Christian minds. The Christian philosophers recognized in him those elements of Platonism which were already incorporated in their tradition since St. Augustine. Precisely this, together with those Aristotelian concepts which Christians were able to accept, occasioned the influx of Arab philosophy into Western theology. The trend was unmistakable: Avicenna was accepted after an attempt was made to rid him of incongenial views, and having reduced his principles to agree with St. Augustine, it was possible to admit his interpretations as part of a necessary Aristotelianism.

BIBLIOGRAPHY

E. R. BEVAN and C. SINGER, editors, *The Legacy of Israel* (Oxford, 1928).
C. BROCKELMANN, *History of the Islamic Peoples,* tr., by J. Carmichael and M. Perlmann (New York, 1947).
G. G. COULTON, *Medieval Panorama* (New York, 1938).
C. G. CRUMP and E. F. JACOB, editors, *The Legacy of the Middle Ages* (Oxford, 1926).
C. DAWSON, *The Making of Europe* (New York, 1945).
T. J. DE BOER, *The History of Philosophy in Islam* (London, 1903).
E. GILSON, *The Spirit of Medieval Philosophy,* tr., by A. H. C. Downes (New York, 1940).
A. M. GIOCHON, *Introduction à Avicenne: Son Epître des Définitions* (Paris, 1933); *La Philosophie D'Avicenne Et Son Influence En Europe Médiévale* (Paris, 1944).
A. GUILLAUME, "Philosophy and Theology," *The Legacy of Islam,* ed., by T. Arnold and A. Guillaume (Oxford, 1931).
P. K. HITTI, *History of the Arabs,* 4th ed. (London, 1949).
M. HORTEN, *Die Metaphysik Avicennas* (Leipzig, 1913).
I. HUSIK, *A History of Mediaeval Jewish Philosophy* (Philadelphia, 1941).
J. MARITAIN, *The Angelic Doctor,* tr., by J. F. Scanlan (New York, 1931).
F. S. C. NORTHROP, *The Meeting of East and West* (New York, 1946).
H. PIRENNE, *Mohammed and Charlemagne,* tr., by B. Miall (New York, 1939).
G. QUADRI, *La Philosophie Arabe Dans L'Europe Médiévale,* tr., by R. Huret (Paris, 1947).

CHAPTER FOURTEEN

MEDIAEVAL JEWISH PHILOSOPHY

EMIL L. FACKENHEIM

I.

IN THE context of mediaeval culture, the chief importance of Jewish philosophy lies in its mediating function between Muslim and Christian thought. Jews played a major rôle as translators who made Arabic writings—often translations or paraphrases of Greek works—available to Latin scholars. But their function was more than formal. Muhammedan, Jewish and Christian thinkers all faced the problem of relating a revealed religion to philosophy; hence the solution found by Jews could affect the thinking of Christians. Thus Maimonides (1135-1204), the greatest Jewish thinker, was able to influence Thomas Aquinas (1225?-1274), the greatest Christian thinker of the Middle Ages.[1]

But mediaeval Jewish philosophy must be viewed in its inner unity as well as in its merely external historical rôle. Here one fact is of crucial importance: philosophy is not an autonomous growth in mediaeval Judaism, but is forced upon it by the Islamic environment mediating the Greek heritage. The very language in which the earlier Jewish thinkers wrote is Arabic, Hebrew being used only after translators had made it a tool fit for philosophic expression. By and large, a pure philosophy never developed in mediaeval Judaism. Until the end of the twelfth century only Isaac Israeli (*ca.* 850-950), the first of mediaeval Jewish philosophers, and Solomon Ibn Gabirol (*ca.* 1020-*ca.* 1050? 1070?) wrote general philosophic works. While in the latter Middle Ages such works became more common—especially in the form of commentaries and subcommentaries on Aristotle—, the central interest of mediaeval Jewish philosophy remained confined to the task of reconciling Judaism, as a revealed religion, with philosophy, a product of natural reason.

One may thus speak of mediaeval "Jewish" philosophy in a quite specific sense. Greek or British philosophy are "Greek" or "British" in the restricted sense that they may be historically intelligible only within their respective cultures; but their claim to truth is presumably universal, and the evidence they offer universally accessible. Mediaeval Jewish philosophy is "Jewish" rather in the sense in which mediaeval Latin philosophy is "Christian": here universal reason is only one of two sources of truth; the other is extra- (though not necessarily anti-) rational,—a body of revelations available only to the followers of a particular faith.

To the superficial observer it seems obvious that no genuine contribution to philosophy can arise from such a situation. For wherever reason plays its rôle unchecked by revelation, we can expect nothing specifically "Jewish," but simply the Aristotelianism and Neoplatonism characteristic of all mediaeval thought, whether written in Arabic, Hebrew or Latin. And wherever revelation does curtail reason we can expect no philosophy at all, but simply orthodox apologetics with philosophic trimmings. If the superficial observer is right, mediaeval Jewish philosophy has, as such, no contribution to offer the history of philosophy; it offers at best a few philosophic ideas discovered accidentally in a situation hostile to genuine philosophy.

But the truth is that the characteristic contributions of mediaeval Jewish philosophy arise precisely from the situation which constitutes it as a distinctive entity. Philosophy here is not an activity without presuppositions, but "the recognition of the authority of the revelation is the presupposition of all philosophizing." [2] Great liberties may be taken in interpreting its true *content;* but the *fact* of revelation constitutes a commitment prior to all philosophy. It is obvious that this is a condition to be found nowhere in ancient or modern philosophy.

Problems of profound philosophical significance arise from this situation: (i) Prior in its claims to all philosophizing, the revelation (more precisely: the revealed Law) can hardly remain indifferent to the very activity of philosophizing. The philosopher-under-the-Law will be driven toward interpreting his philosophical activity as commanded by the Law. To the ancients philosophy was the ultimate arbiter not only of truth but also of its own value. The value of philosophical activity now tends to be measured by extra-philosophical criteria: the prophet stands above the philosopher. In other words, philosophy requires a theological foundation.

(ii) But theology also requires a philosophical foundation. Reason is inherently unable to prove the *fact* of the revelation,—for if it could the revelation would cease to be supernatural—; but the *possibility* of revelation must be subject to rational proof. For if what is a supernatural fact is rationally impossible, no ground is left for any genuine reconciliation between reason and revelation, and only one alternative remains to the total rejection of either of them: the so-called "double-truth-theory," according to which a doctrine may be at once naturally true and supernaturally false, and vice versa. But this theory is overwhelmingly rejected in mediaeval Jewish philosophy, which shuns a wholly anti-rational position.

(iii) The above two problems, novel to mediaeval thought, arise from the very situation in which mediaeval Jewish philosophy develops. Other problems are less fundamental but no less influential: specific theological doctrines, of Biblical or post-Biblical origin, now become problems for philosophic justification. Some of these doctrines prove to be an inspiration to philosophy outlasting the specific mediaeval setting. The most important of these would appear to be the Biblical doctrine of creation.[3]

Mediaeval Jewish philosophy may be divided into three periods, according to the philosophy from which they draw their chief inspiration: Kalam, Neoplatonism and Aristotelianism. This division is inaccurate in several respects: the three types of thought do not follow each other in strictly temporal order; no thinker follows purely one type of thought, without combining with it elements of another; some thinkers—notably Jehudah Hallevi (*ca.* 1085- shortly after 1141)—do not fit into any of these types. This division is therefore of limited validity, made largely for purposes of convenience.

II.

Kalam is a movement in Islam arising from the need to reconcile certain doctrines of the Koran with the requirements of an enlightened faith. The anthropomorphisms of the Koran were found to be incompatible with the concept of divine unity, and its doctrine of predestination with divine justice. Kalam developed into a rational defense of the major doctrines of Islam, such as the existence and unity of God, creation, providence and immortality. The rationalist was subsequently opposed by an anti-rationalist school. The former held that God and His creation were subject to the laws of reason. The latter which denied this used rational argument for dialectical purposes only.[4] In Judaism, Kalam developed only in its rationalist form, its most significant representative being Saadia Ben Joseph (882-942). A religious and communal authority as well as a scholar, Saadia saw his philosophic task in the refutation of the sectarian and skeptic views which had originated between the seventh and ninth centuries.

Saadia sets out by defining the relation between reason and revelation. Much of the doctrinal and moral content of the revelation is also rationally attainable; here the revelation, far from being superfluous, serves a paedagogic purpose. Only the select few can find these truths by purely rational means, and even these only after long labors and many errors. Other parts of the content of the revelation are rationally altogether unattainable: in moral matters, reason can only provide principles but not practical applications; and the ceremonial Law, given to Israel over and above the moral Law, escapes all rational deduction. The fact of the revelation cannot be proved rationally but only historically: the entire people of Israel, standing at Mount Sinai, cannot have been mistaken.

Saadia follows the Kalam-pattern in proving the existence of God from the temporal origin of the world. If the world can be proved to have a beginning in time, the existence of a Creator follows as a matter of course; for something can come into being *ex nihilo* only by reason of supernatural *creatio*. Four proofs are offered for the temporal origin of the world; the last is most interesting: on the assumption of the eternity of time, the occurrence of any actual "now" would involve the impossibility of an infinite time already passed.

This Bible- (or Koran-) inspired starting-point with creation is of far deeper philosophic significance than might appear. Creation is the *absolute* giving of existence—and the world is *per se* radically contingent; reason is *created* reason—and is as such limited to the understanding of the created world: these and other doctrines, here implicit, were to be of lasting effect, even beyond the confines of mediaeval philosophy.

Saadia follows Kalam in his treatment of the divine attributes. Life, wisdom and power are real attributes of God, but they do not introduce a real multiplicity into His nature; they appear as many only to our finite viewpoint. He rejects, on the one hand, any real multiplicity in God (partly in polemic against the Christian Trinity), and, on the other, the Neoplatonic radicalism which regards any positive description of God as an illegitimate introduction of multiplicity into His nature.

In his theodicy, Saadia asserts free will and its compatibility with divine omniscience. The world is governed by the law of reward and punishment, and this law extends to life after death. Saadia maintains the substantiality and immortality of the soul—though he does not achieve the notion of pure spirituality—and upholds the doctrine of resurrection.

Saadia thus follows mostly the pattern of thought set by Kalam. But his thought is not free from different admixtures. He rejects the atomism of Kalam in favor of Aristotelian notions, and there are Platonic as well as Aristotelian elements in his psychology.

Kalam was soon superseded by more sophisticated philosophies. But the questions Kalam had first posed—under theological influence—remained of profound and lasting influence, even if its answers were found inadequate.

III.

Neoplatonism interprets reality as a succession of emanations from a God conceived as Absolute Unity. These emanations are related among themselves, and all to God, as is logical consequent to logical ground: the posterior is wholly dependent on the prior, while the prior is wholly independent of the posterior. Increasing dependence means both increase in multiplicity and decrease in value. The One is prior to the realm of intellect because the multiplicity of ideas first appears at that level; but, again, that realm is prior to the realm of sense at which appears the multiplicity of sense-objects. Soul—endowed with self-movement—may be anywhere—enslaved below or soaring high. It may be lost in the multiplicity of sense-objects and passions; liberated from these and elevated to contemplation of the world of intellect; or even united in ecstasy with the One Itself.

This system commends itself to the mediaeval Jewish philosopher in many points but is suspect in almost as many. Hence it is eagerly embraced but also immediately modified. On Neoplatonic grounds the philosopher can assert the strict unity of God required by monotheism, against what appear to be compromises in Kalam: but in so doing he also removes all positive attributes from God and deprives Him of His personal character; he is forced to regard the Biblical attributes as merely negative in significance, *i.e.*, intended to reveal only the essential unknowability of God. Neoplatonic emanationism appears to support *creatio ex nihilo* in that it makes the world stem completely from God; there is here no prime matter independent of the creative act of God: but what in the Bible is a free act of creation here becomes the necessary metaphysical relation of ground and consequent. Neoplatonism further commends itself for its sharp distinction, both in reality and value, between the spiritual and the sensual; it helps combat materialism and such forms of religious skepticism as may be based on it: but it also implies the superiority of contemplative withdrawal from the world, to the life of moral action in the world. And that is a type of ethics and piety quite alien to traditional Judaism which centers in a revealed Law demanding moral practice in the world.

These tensions are reflected in the writings of mediaeval Jewish Neoplatonists, almost all of whom make some attempt to limit the sphere of validity of their philosophic principles. Isaac Israeli (*ca.* 850-950) sets the course. While accepting the emanationist principle as valid within the cosmic hierarchy, he rejects it as explaining the relationship between the cosmos as a whole and God. God has created the world freely, and the ground of creation is not a logico-metaphysical necessity but the goodness of God. Hence ethics, too, can be given a traditional rather than a Neoplatonic foundation: it is founded in obedience to the will of a God providentially concerned with man, rather than in the desire—of a soul imprisoned in matter—to ascend to mystic union with God. Bahya Ibn Paquda's (11th or 12th century) connections with Neoplatonism are far slighter still. Some traces of it are evident in his concept of God as strict unity, and in his view that the central task of the good life is liberation from the senses. But the God he proves is the Creator-God, and his proofs are those of Kalam; and the chief motivation of his ethics is not contemplative ascent to the impersonal One, but gratitude to the personal God. A much more radical Neoplatonist is Joseph Ibn Zaddiq (died 1149). He departs far enough from traditional theology to assert, with Neoplatonism, that the individual human souls have their origin in the World-Soul. Nevertheless he, too, seeks to combine free creation with emanation, and even to justify the temporal beginning of the world, a doctrine certainly underivable from Neoplatonic principles.

The great exception is Solomon Ibn Gabirol (known in the Christian Middle Ages as Avicebron, *ca.* 1020-*ca.* 1050? 1070?), celebrated poet and the profoundest of mediaeval Jewish Neoplatonists. His poetry proves abundantly that his traditional religious convictions are genuine; but his *Fountain of Life* does not mention Judaism in a single word; characteristically mediaeval Christians could regard it as the work of a Muslim. Gabirol's problem is strictly metaphysical: the derivation of reality from a First Principle, in terms of multiplicity gradually emanating from unity. Traditional Neoplatonism involves an unexplained transition at that level in the emanation-chain where matter first appears: above it, there are non-material entities of increasing multiplicity in essence; below it, unformed matter accepting increasing degrees of formation. Gabirol's systematic mind finds in this break a serious problem. He solves it by positing matter of a sort—intelligible matter—even at the spiritual levels of reality, thus seeking to understand the whole chain in terms of matter and form.[5] In the structure of reality the higher level, while existing independently, is always undetermined (matter, genus) relative to the level immediately below it which thus requires a new principle of determination (form, specific difference) for its actualization. Gabirol's doctrine unifies the emanation-chain but poses a new problem. Neoplatonism must affirm that from the Absolutely Simple only a simple being can directly emanate; hence the first emanated being is simple in nature, possessing duality only indirectly, in that it is related to both itself and the source of its emanation. But Gabirol is compelled to explain how two principles—matter and form—can emerge directly from the First Principle. To make this metaphysically possible he abandons necessary emanation at the first step in favor of a free divine will which, though simple, is yet able to create more than one entity. Gabirol's doctrine of the divine will is obscure and difficult; but it would be a mistake to see in it an accommodation to theological teaching: there is no evidence that it arises from any but philosophical exigencies.

IV.

Jehudah Hallevi's (*ca.* 1085-shortly after 1141) position within Judaism is similar to that of al-Ghazzali within Islam: in defence of revealed religion, he criticizes not merely specific philosophic doctrines but philosophy as a whole. In the quarrels of the metaphysicians he sees evidence of the inherent uncertainty of the whole discipline, contrasting it with the historically-documented certainty of the revelation at Mount Sinai. The roots of metaphysical uncertainty lie in human nature: all merely natural striving after God is finite and incomplete. Only where God actively descends to reveal His will can this uncertainty be overcome; but the God of the philosophers dwells above, unmoved. These differences between religion and philosophy are reflected in the attitude toward God assumed by their followers. The philosopher makes God a mere object of contemplation, whereas the follower of Abraham strives for passionate communion with God. The truly good life is not philosophic contemplation but that immediate and super-rational relation with God achieved in its highest form by the prophet. For the ordinary man the good life consists in prayer, good works and the love of God. Jehudah Hallevi lifts the historical covenant between God and Israel above all universal determinations: Israel possesses a super-rational capacity which is actualized by the practice of the divine Law and life in the Holy Land. The rationalist thinkers tend to regard the ceremonial as inferior to the moral Law, ascribing to it a largely paedagogic function in the service of the latter; Jehudah Hallevi sees in its very irrationality proof of its super-rationality.

But the sharpness of Jehudah Hallevi's opposition to both universalism and rationalism is mitigated. There is no difference between Israel and the nations as regards the moral Law, and in the messianic age all differences will disappear. Moreover, he himself uses philosophic arguments for the existence and unity of God, and some Neoplatonic notions. Thus he is not a radical critic of philosophy as such; he merely wishes to point out the limitations of its achievement and value in comparison with the religious life.

V.

From the beginning of the twelfth century Aristotelian gradually supplant Neoplatonic notions. Largely owing to the influence of Muslim philosophers, Aristotelianism now earns the prestige of greater philosophic soundness; but it scarcely fulfills the requirements of personal religion any better than Neoplatonism. Positively characterized as highest Thought, Aristotle's God may seem closer to that of the Bible than the Neoplatonic bare One. But He thinks only Himself; and even if this self-thought is interpreted as involving indirectly all that it produces, it still embraces only form, to the exclusion of matter. As the ultimate formative principle, God does not create matter. But matter is the principle of individuation. Hence at the very best the Aristotelian God can know the species only; and His providence can extend no further. But this makes Aristotelianism compatible with Biblical religion only if it can be fundamentally reconstructed.

Precisely such a reconstruction is attempted by Moses Maimonides (1135-1204), the greatest of mediaeval Jewish thinkers. His *Guide for the Perplexed*—as is indicated even by its name—is not a philosophic system, but a systematic treatment of those problems which must be solved if the principles of philosophy are to be reconciled with the principles of the revealed Law of Judaism.[6]

Maimonides' proofs for the existence of God are those of Aristotle and Avicenna. His concept of God is Neoplatonic, and he states the doctrine of negative attributes in classic form. All qualities attributed to God in truth merely remove contrary imperfections. Even "existence" means only "lack of all non-being," and "unity," "lack of all multiplicity." God is the unknowable cause of the most perfect actions, and we refer to His works, not His nature, when we give Him positive attributes.

Maimonides' crucial departure from "the philosophers," in defence of the foundations of the Law, occurs in his treatment of creation. He grasps this with unsurpassed clarity: given the necessary nexus between God and the world which is asserted by both Aristotle and Neoplatonism, all "arbitrary" divine interference with natural law becomes in principle indefensible. Individual providence and miracles become impossible, above all the crucial miracle of revelation—the very root of the Law itself. Maimonides urges that the philosopher can prove the validity of natural law only *within* the world; that it is therefore philosophically permissible to hold that God has created the laws of nature as well as nature itself; and that if this is the case His act of creation cannot be understood in terms of these laws. He points out certain insuperable difficulties in the emanation-theory which vanish on the assumption of free creation. But he does not hold that creation can be proved philosophically. On strictly rational grounds, the laws of the cosmos may be regarded as either absolute or the product of free creation.

In such a situation religious interest may decide in favor of the latter view. This view saves the foundations of revealed religion: for if God has freely created the laws of nature He is also free to suspend them temporarily, for the purpose of miracles, providence and, above all, revelation. Revelation is thus rationally possible, and faith may assert its reality without eschewing reason.[7]

Chiefly concerned with saving the principles of revealed Judaism, Maimonides often moves far from it in spirit. Although miracles are in principle possible the most sparing use must be made of them in practice. Hence providence is to be explained in "natural" terms. At the subhuman level providence looks after the species only; in man it can extend beyond that to the individual only by virtue of intellect; for this is what distinguishes man from animal. "Natural" providence for the human individual is the result of closeness to God which may be achieved by intellectual self-perfection. Prophecy, too, is to be explained as naturally as possible. With the Muslim philosophers, Maimonides interprets the human share in all knowledge as the mere achievement of receptivity; actual cognition is due to the pouring down of illumination from a higher cosmic intellect. Prophecy differs from natural philosophic illumination only in degree. Maimonides' ethics, too, is far in spirit from traditional religion. The highest end of man is the contemplation of God, the moral law largely a means to this end, and the ceremonial law largely a means to the moral law,—a mere means to a means. His departure from the spirit of Judaism is perhaps greatest in his doctrine of immortality: only the intellectual part of the human soul can be immortal, and even this is only potentially so; only those who are able to actualize their intellect by the contemplation of God acquire actual immortality.

This anti-traditional tendency in Maimonides is partly due to his reluctance to resort to supernatural explanations and miracles beyond necessity; such a necessity exists wherever the principles of revealed religion are at stake, and these he guards without hesitation. Thus while conceding the natural explanation of prophecy he yet relates it directly, if negatively, to God's supernatural intercession. In each case, God may supernaturally prevent the occurrence of prophetic illumination; hence wherever a prophecy takes place it is at once subject to natural explanation, and directly related to the divine will. Moreover, the prophecy of Moses does not submit to any natural explanation; it is an absolute miracle. Maimonides also seeks to mitigate the exclusiveness of his doctrine of immortality; he is well aware that according to Judaism a share in the world-to-come is not restricted to an intellectual elite. But his principles make immortality dependent on the acquisition of religious truth; hence he can uphold the traditional conviction only by laying down a minimum of truth—his celebrated thirteen articles of faith—as condition of immortality; whoever lacks the rational capacity to understand their truth must accept them as a dogma.

The most radical of mediaeval Jewish Aristotelians is Levi Ben Gerson (or Gersonides, 1288-1344). Returning under the influence of Averroës to a more genuine version of Aristotelianism, he makes God highest Form, insisting that positive attributes may be ascribed to Him without impairing His unity. To think otherwise is to confuse secondary beings—which possess their attributes derivatively—with God who possesses His attributes *primo et per se*. Gersonides rejects emanationism and is thus forced to admit the existence of uncreated prime matter. But he plays down its importance as the barest potentiality; moreover, he derives all forms from God and interprets the formation of matter as a free and creative, not a necessary, process. Divine knowledge, too, must stop short of matter. God can exert providence over the species only, and over the individual only in so far as it is a member of the species. The individual human being can as such become subject to providence only by acquiring a share in the intelligible world. Gersonides follows philosophical exigencies much more closely and with much less autonomy than Maimonides. For instead of confronting religion and philosophy in their principles he attempts to achieve the reconciliations needed by the minute analysis of specific doctrines.

In the fourteenth century the conviction grows that Aristotelian philosophy must be opposed in principle if the true character of Judaism is to be preserved. By far the profoundest of the critics of Aristotle is Hasdai Crescas (1340-1410). His critique of Aristotle's *Physics*—which anticipates modern notions of space and infinity—is sweeping and fundamental, not piecemeal or confined to details.[8] The same fundamental opposition to traditional philosophy characterizes the rest of his thought. Like Gersonides he ascribes positive attributes to God, subjecting the doctrine of negative attributes to subtle criticism. But unlike the former he rejects the positive attributes of the Aristotelians. These are product of a false intellectualism. If God is highest Thought, His creative activity cannot be made intelligible as flowing from His nature; He then perforce dwells above unmoved, indifferent to the creation. God is primarily Goodness and Love, not Thought; and His Love is directed on the world, not Himself. Philosophic ethics, too, suffers from a false intellectualism. The highest goal of man is not intellectual self-perfection but the love of God. To make that goal a reality is the deepest purpose of the revealed Law. Far from confined to an intellectual elite, the Law, and with it the highest human goal, is accessible to all who earnestly concern themselves with it. For only few may possess the intellectual capacity for philosophic knowledge; but all have the emotional capacity for the love of God. Immortality does not depend on the intellect; the soul—much more than mere intellect—is essentially immortal. Like Maimonides, Crescas reaffirms Biblical voluntarism against the necessitarianism of the philosophers. But Maimonides is concerned with reconciling philosophically the principles of the Law with those of philosophy, prepared to assimilate in detail a great deal of philosophical intellectualism; Crescas primarily attacks the intellectualist values of the philosophers, concerned with upholding the voluntaristic values of Jewish tradition.

The fifteenth century no longer produces original contributions in the field of Jewish philosophy. Such writers as Joseph Albo (died 1444), while widely read, are more significant for their attempts to systematize the essentials of Jewish belief than for independent philosophic efforts. Mediaeval Jewish philosophy exerts a deep influence on such post-mediaeval philosophers as Spinoza (1632-1677), Moses Mendelssohn (1729-1786) and Solomon Maimon (died 1800). But the discussion of these influences would exceed the bounds of the present survey.

A HISTORY OF PHILOSOPHICAL SYSTEMS

NOTES

1. Cf. J. Guttmann, *Die Scholastik des 13ten Jahrhundert in ihren Beziehungen zum Judentum und zur juedischen Literatur* (Breslau, 1902).
2. Cf. Strauss, *op. cit.* p. 47. This work should be consulted for all problems discussed in this section.
3. For similarities in Islamic and Christian philosophy, *cf.* chs. XIII, XVI, XVII.
4. Further on Kalam, *cf.* ch. XIII.
5. There are traces of a doctrine of intelligible matter in Plotinus and even Aristotle. For a position within Islam similar to Gabirol's, *cf.* E. L. Fackenheim, "The Conception of Substance in the Philosophy of the Brethren of Purity," *Mediaeval Studies*, vol. V (Toronto, 1943), pp. 115 ff.
6. Cf. L. Strauss, "The Literary Character of the Guide of the Perplexed," *Essays on Maimonides*, ed. by S. Baron (New York, 1941), pp. 37 ff.
7. Cf. E. L. Fackenheim, "The Possibility of the Universe in al-Farabi, Ibn Sina and Maimonides," *Proceedings, American Academy for Jewish Research* (1947), pp. 39 ff.
8. Cf. Wolfson, *op. cit.*, an exhaustive treatment of this subject.

BIBLIOGRAPHY

(a) *General Histories*

J. GUTTMANN, *Die Philosophie des Judentums* (Munich, 1933).
I. HUSIK, *A History of Mediaeval Jewish Philosophy* (Philadelphia, 1941).
S. MUNK, *Mélanges de Philosophie Juive et Arabe* (Paris, 1859).
G. VAJDA, *Introduction a la Pensée Juive du Moyen Age* (Paris, 1947).

(b) *Texts in English Translation*

SAADIA, *The Book of Beliefs and Opinions*, tr. by S. Rosenblatt (New Haven, 1948).
BAYHA IBN PAQUDA, *The Duties of the Heart*, ed. and tr. by M. Hyamson (New York, 1925-47).
JEHUDAH HALLEVI, *Kitab al-Khazari*, tr. by H. Hirschfeld (London, 1906).
MAIMONIDES, *The Guide for the Perplexed*, tr. by M. Friedlaender (London, 1928).
JOSEPH ALBO, *Sefer ha-'Ikkarim*, ed. and tr. by I. Husik (Philadelphia, 1929-30).

(c) *Selected Standard Works*

S. MUNK, *Le Guide des Égarés*, 3 vols. (Paris, 1856-66). Edition and translation of Maimonides' work, with extensive notes.

A HISTORY OF PHILOSOPHICAL SYSTEMS

M. STEINSCHNEIDER, *Die hebraeischen Uebersetzungen des Mittelalters* (Berlin, 1893). Bibliographically invaluable.

L. STRAUSS, *Philosophie und Gesetz* (Berlin, 1933). A profound analysis of the principles underlying mediaeval Muslim and Jewish philosophy.

H. A. WOLFSON, *Crescas' Critique of Aristotle* (Cambridge, Mass., 1929). Edition and translation of pt. I i & ii of Crescas' *Or Adonai*, with exhaustive introduction and a wealth of notes on mediaeval physics and metaphysics.

For further bibliographic information see the histories of Guttmann, Husik and Vajda.

CHAPTER FIFTEEN

EARLY CHRISTIAN SCHOLASTICISM

RICHARD J. THOMPSON

THE PERIOD which extends from St. Augustine (354-430) to the second introduction of Aristotle into the west is a much abused period in the history of human thought. Since the Renaissance it has been customary to call it the "Dark Ages" and dismiss it from consideration. And there is much that justifies the name. There are long spans of time in which philosophy is but a word in a book, eras in which the most notable feature is the dearth of speculation, and still other periods in which the distinction between philosophy and sophistry seems not to have been made. Yet in these centuries one finds extraordinary philosophic achievements, genuine philosophical insights, and often a very real understanding of what it is to philosophize. It is thus a period of extremes, of magnificent syntheses and puerile sophistries, of learning and ignorance, of light and shadow: it is, in short, a period of human history.

In it one may, even through the dimly lighted intervals which occur, decipher a pattern of thought, a certain regularity which justifies generalization. It may be said that, from Boethius (480-524) on, the intellectual enterprise of the men of this period, like that of St. Augustine before them, was devoted to the effort to make their faith intelligible, provided it be remembered that this faith was, for all of them, a consequence of a Revelation which could never be entirely intelligible in this world. The example of St. Augustine was always before them, both in his effort to develop a synthesis of faith and reason, and in the philosophical vocabulary and conceptual lexicon which he had put at the service of his faith. For the reason which seeks an understanding of the content of faith is not a naked reason; it is a reason clothed with a philosophical garb which it inherited from a non-Christian and frequently anti-Christian tradition.

Let the reader be warned from the beginning that he shall seek in vain for precise and finely detailed distinctions between the sciences which issue from faith and those which issue from reason. Such precisions come much later and they are the fruit of a diligent and philosophical analysis of the nature of demonstration which the men of this period could not even attempt. It is, therefore, hardly fair to these men to judge their work according to the accepted divisions of philosophy and theology; certainly they were able to draw the line between the things of faith and the things of reason, but they did not attempt to erect autonomous sciences on these diverse bases. They were rather concerned with the unity of their faith and their reason; they would start with faith and, in its light, develop an intellectual construction which was almost a continuation of that faith. With Augustine, they read in Isaiah: "Unless you believe, you shall not understand," and with this text in mind they began their speculations, the conclusions of which are neither purely philosophy nor purely theology, but a blend of the two which has been aptly called a "Christian Wisdom."

That there are genuinely philosophic notions embedded in this wisdom is evident to anyone who reads the thinkers of this period, and it is with these notions that we are primarily concerned. Now these notions did not come exclusively from St. Augustine, nor were they the product of the individual genius of each thinker in the period. For the most part they came from the later Platonists, and it is here that one finds the source of almost all that is philosophical in early Christian Scholasticism. Aristotle was known in only a part of the Organon; Plato was known only through Macrobius (fl. *c.* 400), who wrote a commentary on the *Dream of Scipio,* which forms a chapter of Cicero's *De Republica* and which is, like the commentary, full of echoes of Plato's *Republic,* and through Chalcidius (fl. *c.* 315), who made available a part of the *Timaeus.* But if there were no works of Plato, there were plenty of Platonists: Plotinus (203-269); Porphyry (233-305), student, biographer and editor of Plotinus; Origen (*c.* 184-253); the Greek Fathers; the Pseudo-Dionysius (fl. *c.* 500); and St. Augustine.

Though the men to be considered do not profess a common doctrine, since each philosophizes in a manner and a spirit appropriate to himself, they are all confronted with a common problem. Stated in its simplest terms, which are borrowed from Boethius, it was the problem of joining together, if possible, faith and reason. But, as we have indicated, the reason to which faith would be joined was, inevitably, a reason formed by a neo-Platonic tradition of thinking. We may grant the existence of a multitude of neo-Platonisms, widely varying; yet they all share a common source and possess a number of doctrines in common. A glance at these will throw some light on the intellectual context within which early Christian thinkers worked.

The neo-Platonic conception of the universe begins with the positing of a sovereign Principle, the One or the Good, which is Cause and Source of all else without being itself limited by any definition. From it issues, eternally and necessarily, usually by way of emanation, Intellect or Mind, to which the name Being properly applies, since Being begins only with the order of essence, and Mind is, as it were, the locus of all intelligibles, of all essences. From Mind proceeds the Soul of the World, an eternal principle of human souls and of inferior forms, which is an utterance of the eternal Mind as the Mind is the eternal knowledge of the One. This hierarchic development continues down to the information of matter, through man, who is possessed of a divine principle, his soul, the prisoner of the body, and who reverses the emanative process and returns himself and all things, through knowledge, to the eternal principles, achieving his true nature only in the intelligible order. Thus man must reject the sensible order of things and perfect himself both intellectually and morally by the unique route of asceticism. Hence, metaphysically, the only realities, the only true beings, are the definable essences; epistemologically, the only valid objects of knowledge are the separated forms; psychologically, sensation and the body play an unsatisfactory and even ignoble part in the acquiring of knowledge.

Now such a doctrine has obvious appeals for a Christian. It presents him with a rational scheme in which there is a God as cause and end of the world, a world of unity and order, peopled with beings of unequal degrees of perfection. It justifies his belief in Providence; it corroborates his faith in the immortality of the soul; it strengthens him in his efforts towards sanctification. But it does so only when certain rectifications have been made in it, for it is a doctrine in which a God necessitated by His goodness does not create freely, in which Ideas are subordinated to God and in which man is much too immediately continued with a God from whom he does not really differ in kind. What use the Christian confronted with this manner of thinking can make of it is the burden of the remainder of this chapter.

Anitius Manlius Severinus Boethius, "the last representative of the ancient philosophy," by one account, "the first of the Scholastics," by others, belongs to the neo-Platonic tradition in a more unusual sense than later men to be considered, for he would attempt the typically Platonic task of reconciling Plato and Aristotle, to the advantage of Plato, who was, it seems, the founder of both the Academic and Peripatetic schools. A somewhat less exacting assignment set for himself was that of transmitting all the works of Plato and Aristotle to the Romans. His untimely death prevented the execution of most of his program, although he did translate Porphyry's *Introduction to the Categories of Aristotle* as well as parts of the Organon, write commentaries on them, write theological treatises, and compose the famous *Consolation of Philosophy* while in prison awaiting death. Boethius' failure to introduce his Christianity within this last work has caused some doubt to be cast upon the genuineness of his faith, but it is not difficult to see this work as that of a Christian who is using his faith negatively to avoid error. By his translation, his commentaries and his original works, Boethius bequeathed to Scholasticism much of its terminology and many of its definitions; in his theological works he set an example of method for the later Middle Ages; in his logical works he transmitted to succeeding philosophers the enduring problem of the universals. Often criticized for his caution in the solution of this problem, Boethius was much bolder than the logician (Porphyry) from whom he had received it, for he made it clear that the Aristotelian answer that he was proposing in his commentary was by no means satisfactory to him, and in both the *De Trinitate* and the *Consolation,* he preferred to consider the universals as pure forms, somewhat on the order of Platonic Ideas. It would seem, too, that the Boethian distinction between *esse* (form) and *id quod est* (essence) is possible only for one who identifies being and intelligibility, who equates unparticipated *esse* with intelligibility in the pure state. Finally, Boethius recognizes in the ineffability, the incomprehensibility, of God a natural limit set for human reason in its consideration of things divine.

Social and political upheavals followed on the death of Boethius, and it was not until the Carolingian Renaissance that learning began again to be pursued for its own sake. In this revival of learning the most important philosopher, by far, was John Scotus Eriugena (*c.* 810-877), a man whose intellectual daring was to lead to condemnations, in spite of his unflagging effort to integrate a philosophic interpretation of the universe with his Christianity. Scotus could say with Augustine: "Unless you believe, you shall not understand," and he could accept the Augustinian identification of the true religion with the true philosophy; but whereas for St. Augustine this had meant that the Christian religion contained whatever was true in philosophy because it was the religion, for Scotus it seemed rather to mean that the Christian religion contained all truth because it was a philosophy. There is another aspect of thought by which he separated himself from his predecessor. St. Augustine had been concerned with the relations of faith and reason; Scotus dealt with the relations of authority and reason, for there was at his disposal, in addition to the deposit of faith, an enormous amount of exegetical literature handed on from the Fathers. No matter what is contained in it, and no matter who may have been its author, it in no way constrains the intellect to its acceptance; reason, accepting Revealed Truth in its entirety, is free in respect of any and all authoritative interpretations of that Truth, all of them having to be submitted to the judgment of *vera ratio,* the reason of John Scotus Eriugena himself. And it is important to note that this reason was formed by Scotus' contact with neo-Platonism, resulting from his translations of the Pseudo-Dionysius and of Maximus Confessor.

An essential character of Platonism is the notion of dialectic, the ascending from individuals to generals, and the descent from the general to its species. Scotus adapts this intellectual program to a conception of nature in which all things descend from their cause and are ultimately reunited with it. This involves a typical hierarchic structure, which Scotus elaborates in his *On the Division of Nature,* in which we have these distinct elements: the nature which creates and is not created; the nature which is created and which creates; the nature which is created and which does not create; the nature which is not created and which does not create. Here is God as uncreated cause (first division) and as uncreated end (fourth division); the second division, the created and creating nature, is the Ideas in God, which, since they have proceeded from a principle, are subordinated to God, and can in a sense be called created; the third division is the universe of things modelled on the Ideas.

Our knowledge of God is scarcely to be called knowledge. The ineffability of God permits us to speak of Him affirmatively: He is good, and negatively: He is not good. But neither affirmation nor negation is permissible in the strict sense, for God is the cause of being and the cause of intelligibility and is consequently beyond being and beyond intelligibility. Thus He is hyper-Being, hyper-Good. It is only by the hierarchically ordered Ideas: Good, Essence (*i.e.,* Being in itself), etc., that God is even self-intelligible. Each Idea is a self-revelation of God (a *theophany*), and it is by these Ideas that God, as it were, puts Himself within the order of being, creates Himself, limits Himself with the bonds of essence, begins to be. The intelligible Ideas are true beings, and God, in order to be said to be, has to reveal Himself within these Ideas. And what is true of God is *a fortiori* true of creatures; they are not, except as they are in the Ideas. "Man is a certain intellectual notion eternally produced in the divine mind." To be is to be intelligible.

In the hierarchic ordination of things which results in the production of the physical world, the higher principle contains what is present in the lower, for the divine illumination which is the self-revelation of God proceeds in an orderly manner through all the divisions of nature. Thus, man, placed on the boundaries of the spiritual and the material orders, communicates perfections from above to things below him. Possessing, by knowledge at least, all inferior perfections, and being joined to the intelligible universe by his intellect, he is a true microcosm. His own perfection is intellectual, and is to be found in a union with God, a union in which man is able to restore all things to God in such a way that all things are one in Him without losing their own identity.

Whatever be the problems arising out of the work of Scotus, and they are many, involving allegations of pantheism, rationalism, etc., there are some matters which are beyond doubt: his sincere faith; his neo-Platonic formation; and his obscurity.

There was little that was original in the two hundred years which followed the death of Scotus. The teachings of the Fathers and the songs of the poets were handed on; the old models were preserved but they did not inspire each that was new or important. There was, indeed, a frequent rejection of the world with its philosophic and literary blandishments. Yet there was a revival of dialectics, best understood as a technique for handling concepts apart from their function in a philosophic system. Identified with reason itself, it was considered by some to be the activity by which man renewed himself in the image of God.

Notwithstanding the generally unphilosophical character of the eleventh century, it was the century of St. Anselm (1033-1109), famous for his struggles with the English kings and for his "ontological" argument for the existence of God. Like his predecessors, Anselm makes no rigid distinction betweeen philosophy and theology but, like them again, his formula: *fides quaerens intellectum,* faith seeking to understand, implies an understanding of what it means to believe and what it means to know. Like Eriugena, Anselm has an enormous confidence in the ability of human reason to arrive at truth, for, among other things, he will demonstrate the necessity of the Trinity by necessary reasons. Yet, unlike Scotus, who seems to be a philosopher handling the problems of a religious metaphysics, Anselm gives the impression of a theologian using metaphysics to solve problems of Christian doctrine.

Restricting the discussion to St. Anselm's proofs for the existence of God, we find that they are of two orders. The proofs of the first order, from the *Proslogium,* are Augustinian and even Platonic, for they are based upon our awareness of inequalities and gradations in this universe, inequalities which can be explained only in terms of a sovereign Good, Being or Nature, in which the unequal goods, beings or natures participate. The arguments are cogent, St. Anselm assures us, but they are several and complicated, and so he feels compelled to offer a proof which is both single and simple. This is the second order of proof, the "ontological" argument, which still echoes in our culture.

The proof is too familiar to bear repeating.[1] Arguments for and against its validity have occupied the attention of the most eminent philosophers and theologians. Unfortunately, most of these discussions have abstracted the proof from the context of Anselm's thought and have failed to locate it in the mind of the Anselm of history. In the first place, it must be noted that there is no problem for him concerning the origin of his idea of God. Whether its origin be his faith or his reason, the only problem is the worth, the knowledge-value of the idea. Now Anselm knew two kinds of dialecticians: the nominalists, for whom the universal is but a word, having no real object; and the realists, who terminate their knowledge in things. Anselm was enough of a Platonist to subscribe to the realistic position. Thus the knowledge one has of God is not by an idea which is no more than a word; it is by a concept which permits us to grasp the very entity which is its object. From this point of view, which involves the Platonism of Anselm—further implied in his frequent use of the phrase *vere es,* Thou *truly* art, to express the very nature of God—and the contemporary situation in dialectics, the "ontological" argument may be seen as something other than a brilliant *tour de force.* It is in no sense a method of having being come from thought, precisely because if there were no such being there would be no such thought. It is vain to represent to him, as the contemporary Gaunilon did, that one could use such an argument to prove the existence of a perfect island, for the idea of the island does not compel the intellect to posit its existence. The island is known by a *vox,* a word, whereas God is not represented by such an idea, for He is present to thought by a knowledge which terminates in a nature, a nature which demands existence in order to be properly that nature.

The death of St. Anselm occurred at the beginning of a century which was marked by a new renaissance. Schools flourished in Paris, Orleans, Laon, Chartres, Melun, Bologna, and throughout western Europe. Law, theology, belles-lettres, philosophy: these became matters of vital concern. Of the many schools the most important were those at Paris and at Chartres. The schools of Chartres were the home of twelfth century Platonism, a synthesis derived from various sources and extending into various fields, including theology, metaphysics, cosmogony and grammar. In theology and metaphysics the most illustrious representative of Chartres was one of its chancellors, Gilbert of LaPorrée (1076-1154). Obscurities in the text and in his manner of expression make him difficult to follow, but the Platonic background of his thought is evident in his discussion of the Ideas, the only genuine (*sincerae*) substances, from which corporeal things come to be as from their exemplars, possessing only images of these ideal forms. Yet, since this image is the formal determination within the thing by which it is, one can ultimately assign the existence of a given order of things to their ideal exemplar as to their *esse*. Once again, then, the Ideal, the intelligible, is one with Being. Humanity and the being of man are one and the same.

This study of early Latin Scholasticism can be closed with a brief glance at a Parisian philosopher who, by his rejection of Platonism, marks the introduction of a new method of thinking. The thirteenth century will differ from the twelfth largely by the introduction of Aristotle, accompanied by his Arabian commentators. This introduction posed fresh problems for Christian theologians and philosophers, since it put a new system of concepts at their disposal. These fresh problems do not concern us, but they are foreshadowed by the work of a thinker whose greatest dependence was not upon the Platonists but upon Aristotle. Unfortunately for our philosopher, his Aristotle was the Aristotle of the Organon, not the Aristotle of the *De Anima* and the *Metaphysics,* for most of his theological and philosophical embarrassments arose from his use of a logic which was not rooted in psychology and metaphysics. The philosopher was Peter Abailard (1079-1142), famed throughout Europe for his skill in dialectics, in which science he was sure he had discovered the laws governing all human thought. Thus he had an instrument of universal application, which he applied with equal vigor and unequal success to logical and theological problems.

In logic Abailard abandons the realism of the Platonic tradition. Marshalling a variety of arguments against his contemporary realists, he concludes with the assertion that universality, the characteristic by reason of which the same term can be predicated of several things, can in no wise be anything real but must of necessity belong to the term, the word which is so predicated. This word signifies no essence, nothing real, but it does make known a *status,* a state, *e.g.* "to be man." We have here a denial of Plato, not in the name of Aristotle, but in the name of a logic conceived as the unique method of knowing all objects, whatever they may be. The denial has curious consequences. Since the object of the universal idea is nothing real, it follows that the most genuine and valid knowledge that can be had is not of the universal, the abstracted form of Aristotle, the *verum ens* of Platonism, but is of particular things. So much for Aristotelian science.

The dialectical mind can be seen at work again when Abailard gathers together a multitude of texts from the Fathers in order to reconcile opposed or apparently opposed views. Though this gathering of texts is not original with Abailard, his precisions on the methods to be employed, as well as his example in his *Commentary on the Epistle to the Romans,* influenced the compilers of *Sententiae* in his own century and played a part in the development of the *quaestio* form in the following century. In Ethics, Abailard argues, logically and plausibly, from the inwardness of morality pointed out by the New Testament to the complete indifference of the external act, and further arouses his more traditionally minded contemporaries, already disturbed by his theological opinions.

In his interpretation of the relations of faith and reason, Abailard admits the priority of faith, but he insists that there can be no science of theology without the help of philosophy, understood, of course, as dialectics. For the opinion of the theologians of the twelfth century on his interpretation and its consequences there is the verdict of two councils, both of which condemned him. Yet his errors were not due to a desire to break with tradition, but were due rather to a lack of prudence in statement, and to a conceit which drove him to a solution of problems with which, as a logician, he was inadequately prepared to deal.

The influence of Abailard, personal and philosophic, extends beyond his own century and is seen in the logical speculations of the thirteenth. But the exaggerated respect for dialectics declines somewhat, both because of the set-back at the hands of the councils, and because in Spain a flourishing school of translators is making available to the West the treasures of Greek and Arabian thought.

The past does not die. In Paris the Victorines repeat and develop the psychological and mystical content of St. Augustine; Amalric of Bènes (fl. 1200) gives a pantheistic interpretation of Eriugena; dialectics, not as the whole of science now, but as a valuable tool of the intellect, continues to occupy an important place in the curricula of the schools.

But a new spirit is abroad in Europe. Platonism is no longer the only source of philosophic inspiration. Aristotle is entering the scene, and though he brings with him a host of Arabians whose Aristotelianism is suspect, he brings also a new way of regarding things, a new method of conceptualizing reality. It will be the task of thirteenth century scholasticism to integrate these new insights to Christian thought, as it had been the task of the earlier scholastics to attempt the formation of a solid synthesis of Platonism and Christianity.

NOTES

1. For those who are unfamiliar with St. Anselm's proof for the existence of God from the *Monologium*, it is paraphrased here. It opens with a prayer, which is as necessary to the argument as anything which follows. In the prayer, Anselm retreats within the inner chamber of his mind to commune with his Creator. Then, seeking an understanding of God, he finds that God is that than which nothing greater can be thought of—*aliquid quo majus cogitari non valet.* Does such a nature exist? Its existence has been denied, for the fool has said in his heart that there is no God. Yet the fool, in denying that God is, at least admits that he has knowledge of the nature whose existence he denies, and this nature has existence in his knowledge. Thus there are two ways of knowing: to know an object as it is in thought, and to know an object as it is in reality. But for an object to exist only in thought is for it to have an inferior kind of existence, since this existence in thought is certainly not as great and as perfect as existence in reality. If, therefore, that than which nothing greater can be thought of exists only in the understanding it is inferior to that which exists in reality. But it is impossible that a being than which nothing greater can be thought of have something greater than itself. And so there is no doubt that there is a being than which nothing greater can be thought of, and it exists both in the understanding and in reality. Indeed, so truly does it exist that it cannot be thought of as not existing, for, if it were so conceived, it would be inferior to that which must be thought of as existing. Anselm concludes: "So truly dost Thou exist, O Lord my God, that Thou canst not be thought of as not existing, and rightly. . . . To Thee alone, therefore, does it belong to exist more truly than all other beings. . . . For whatever else exists does not exist so truly." Thus God is and is truly, because we can conceive nothing greater than He, and because we cannot conceive Him as not existing.

BIBLIOGRAPHY

F. UEBERWEG, *Grundriss der Geschichte der Philosophie,* Bd. II, *Die patristische und scholastische Philosophie,* ed. by B. Geyer (Berlin, 1928).
E. GILSON, *La Philosophie au Moyen Age,* 2nd ed. (Paris, 1944).
———, *Reason and Revelation in the Middle Ages* (New York, 1938).

———, "Sens et Nature de l'argument de saint Anselme," in *Archives d'Histoire Doctrinale et Littéraire du Moyen Age,* t. IX (1934), pp. 5-51 (Paris, 1934).

———, "Logicism and Philosophy" (Abailard's logic), ch. I of *The Unity of Philosophical Experience* (New York, 1946).

M. DeWulf, *History of Mediaeval Philosophy,* tr. by E. Messenger, vol. I (New York, 1935).

R. Arnou, "Platonisme des Pères," in *Dictionnaire de Theologie Catholique,* ed. by Vacant, Mangenot and Amann, t. XII, cc. 2258-2392 (Paris, 1935).

Boethius, *The Theological Tractates and the Consolation of Philosophy,* tr. and ed. by H. F. Stewart and E. K. Rand. Loeb Classical Library. (Cambridge, Mass., 1936.)

H. Bett, *Johannes Scotus Eriugena. A Study in Mediaeval Philosophy* (Cambridge, 1925).

St. Anselm, *Monologium, Proslogium,* etc., tr. by S. N. Deane (Chicago, 1926).

J. G. Sikes, *Peter Abailard* (Cambridge, 1932).

Brief translations from Boethius, Scotus Eriugena, Anselm and Abailard are found also in R. McKeon: *Selections from Medieval Philosophers,* vol. I (New York, 1929).

CHAPTER SIXTEEN

REVIVED ARISTOTELIANISM AND THOMISTIC PHILOSOPHY

ARMAND MAURER

IN THE thirteenth century, Western mediaeval civilization reached its apogee. With relative peace and prosperity at home and fruitful relations abroad with the neighboring Greek and Arabian cultures, the arts and sciences flourished to an extent hitherto unknown in Western Europe. The newly-created universities in France, Italy and England became centers of intense intellectual activity to which the youth of Europe, eager for knowledge and adventure, flocked in large numbers.

One of the most decisive influences exercised upon the scholars of the time was the discovery of the main writings of Aristotle. The thought of the early Middle Ages was largely inspired by the Scriptures and the Fathers of the Church, especially St. Augustine. Its classical elements were for the most part drawn from the humanist tradition of writers like Cicero and Seneca, and its philosophical inspiration was deeply Neoplatonic. Little was known of Aristotelianism save the logical treatises, and they were not all possessed until the middle of the twelfth century. During the first half of the thirteenth century, however, Aristotle's works on natural philosophy, metaphysics, psychology and ethics were translated into Latin, along with Arabian and Greek commentaries. In these writings the mediaeval world was confronted with a scientific and philosophic vision of the universe far superior to any it had known before. The effect of the discovery was truly exhilarating, and as the writings spread through the universities a profound revolution took place in the mediaeval mind, the effects of which are still felt in our day.

The reaction to the new philosophical literature was mixed. At first ecclesiastical authorities at Paris looked upon it with suspicion, for it contained doctrines contrary to the Faith. To prevent the spreading of these errors, a local council in 1210 forbade the public and private teaching at Paris of Aristotle's natural philosophy and metaphysics, along with the commentaries on them. In 1215 the prohibition was renewed. However, this did not forbid or prevent their being read in private, and their popularity grew rapidly in the second quarter of the thirteenth century. In 1231, Pope Gregory IX, who was himself a lover of learning, temporarily renewed the earlier prohibition and then named a council to examine the writings of Aristotle and to correct any errors found in them. By this action he hoped to make them suitable for use in the Christian world; but his commission failed to produce any positive results, possibly because of the death of William of Auxerre, its most distinguished member. By 1255 the tide had turned so strongly in favor of Aristotle that the Faculty of Arts at Paris placed almost all his works on the curriculum. The entrance of Aristotelianism into Christian thought was by then an accomplished fact, and now the only question was whether he would be the servant of the Faith or its master and destroyer.

There was a special danger to the Faith because Aristotle's works were read at first in Latin translations made, for the most part, from Arabic versions. What is more, the writings of the two great Arabian followers of Aristotle, Avicenna (980-1037) and Averroës (1126-1198), were translated and used to interpret the many enigmatic statements of the Stagirite. As a result, the Christians first saw Aristotle's philosophy through Arabian eyes and interpreted in such a way that it contradicted the Faith on important points of doctrine. A serious effort was needed to make new translations of Aristotle from the original Greek and to compose new commentaries free from Arabian interpretations. By the 1260's the need for this was acute because of the rise of an heretical Averroism in the Faculty of Arts at Paris, and once more the Papacy took action. In 1263, Urban IV reminded scholars that the decree of 1231, which seems to have become a dead letter, was still in force. But, not content to play a merely negative rôle in the issue, he set about to accomplish in his own way what Gregory IX had intended to do in 1231. St. Thomas Aquinas (1224/5-1274) was summoned to the Papal Court where he began his voluminous commentaries on Aristotle. William of Moerbeke was at the Court, too, and at St. Thomas' request made a new translation of the Aristotelian works directly from the Greek to serve as a basis for the commentaries. More than anything else, this combined effort of William of Moerbeke and St. Thomas, under the patronage of Pope Urban, turned a potentially hostile Aristotle into an ally of Christian wisdom and made possible a vital and fruitful assimilation of his thought.

If we cast a glance over the doctrinal history of the thirteenth century, we can see that opinions differed widely as to the worth of Aristotelianism and the possibility of its being used by Christian scholars. To begin with, there was a group whose main ambition was to continue and to develop the Augustinian heritage of the early Middle Ages. These traditionalists looked upon Aristotle and his Arabian commentators with suspicion or even hostility. True, they would not refuse to make use of the new philosophical vocabulary and even on occasion to adopt some of the new notions; but these never occupied the center of their thought, which in all its essentials remained attached to Platonism and Augustinianism. Their attitude is illustrated well by St. Bonaventure's saying, that Aristotle spoke the language of science and Plato the language of wisdom; while St. Augustine, under the inspiration of the Holy Spirit, spoke both languages. Like St. Augustine himself, they insisted on the primacy of Faith over reason, but they so conceived that primacy as to cast doubts on the ability of reason alone to solve the main problems of philosophy. If anyone thought otherwise, they simply pointed to the grave errors, from the Christian point of view, in the current versions of Aristotelianism. As theologians, they viewed their work as an attempt to understand better the contents of Revelation. This does not mean that they were uninterested in rational thought; quite the contrary. But their philosophical speculation was contained within their theology and it never developed autonomously as philosophy. As heirs of St. Augustine, moreover, the type of rational thought to which they were accustomed was Neoplatonism, and that is why they showed a lukewarmness to Aristotle and a preference for those writers who, like the Arabian Avicenna, were themselves under the influence of Neoplatonism.

William of Auvergne (1180?-1249), Bishop of Paris, is an interesting case of this type of theologian. A critic of Aristotle and Avicenna, his interests were clearly on the side of St. Augustine; yet his philosophy contains a large dose of Avicennism. Of course, he found much to reject in the Avicennian philosophy: the necessary emanation of the universe from God, the eternity of the world, the interposing of a series of Intelligences between God and man, the last of which is man's immediate origin, the source of his knowledge and his final beatitude. Yet there were aspects of Avicennism which struck a sympathetic chord in the Parisian theologian. For Avicenna, we do not acquire truth from the sensible world but through contact with a superior cosmic Intelligence which illuminates the minds of all men with ideas. This Intelligence is, in Avicenna's view, the Agent Intellect of which Aristotle wrote. Now, as a good disciple of St. Augustine, William of Auvergne was equally convinced that truth is to be obtained through an interior illumination of the mind and not from sensible things. He was ready to agree with Aristotle that we abstract universal ideas from the sensible world, but for him this is simply an occasion for the mind's turning inward to God, the true source of its wisdom. God thus becomes the Agent Intellect of human minds through a fruitful combination of the philosophies of Avicenna and St. Augustine, which has recently been given the name of "Avicennian-Augustinianism."

This theme was developed in different ways in the thirteenth century. Roger Bacon (1210/15-?) not only considered God the Agent Intellect of our minds, but he looked upon all human knowledge as a kind of divine Revelation. For St. Albert the Great (1206-1280), all true knowledge presupposes grace of the Holy Spirit. St. Bonaventure (1221-1274) would not go to the extreme of saying that a special help of God, such as grace or revelation, is needed for human knowledge, since that would destroy it precisely as *natural* knowledge. At the same time he did not think that man's created faculty of knowing is capable of grasping the truth by itself or with the ordinary influence which God exercises upon nature. One of his disciples, Matthew of Aquasparta (1240-1302?), tried to make his thought more definite by saying that the divine illumination by which we know the truth is a *more special* help than that which God generally exercises over nature, although it is still a general one. However this is to be understood, it is clear that

Matthew of Aquasparta's point is substantially the same as that of his fellow Augustinians: The light by which we judge the truth is not a created faculty of man but a divine illumination, so that, strictly speaking, it is not our own weak reason that is the cause of the truth of our knowledge but God Himself.

This theory of knowledge goes hand in hand with a definite conception of the soul and man which was shared by the Augustinian school of the thirteenth century. If the soul does not find truth through the perception of matter but by an interior and upward glance towards God, it is because it is a spiritual substance which is only at home in a spiritual world. The soul may be called the form of the body, and even a substantial form, but care is always taken to ensure its independence from matter. St. Bonaventure, for instance, would not say that the intellectual soul is the only substantial form of the body. Before it is informed by this soul, the body has already been completed by several other substantial forms which confer on it its organic and vital perfections and activities. There is a gap, therefore, between the intellectual soul and matter which for St. Bonaventure is the guarantee of its spirituality and immortality. If St. Albert somewhat closed the gap by asserting that there is but one substantial form between the soul and matter—the form of corporeity,—in his own way he too was bent on assuring the soul's independence. The soul, he tells us, can be considered either in itself, as an intellectual substance, or as a form exercising the function of animating a body. The first view, defining the soul's very nature, he attributed to Plato; the second, describing one of its external and accidental functions, he assigned to Aristotle. Here St. Albert was simply following Avicenna, who had already tried to reconcile the two Greek philosophers in this way. What neither Avicenna nor St. Albert could see was how the soul can be essentially the form of the body. A substance by definition, its relation to another substance such as the body could not be more than extrinsic and accidental. Now this indeed safeguards the independence of the soul from matter; but it is difficult to see how, under these circumstances, man is anything more than an accidental aggregate of soul and body.

If soul and body are so radically distinct for St. Albert, it is because each is thought of as an essence which by definition differs from the other. Indeed, the Avicennian world is composed of essences of this sort, each of which corresponds to a definition and includes only what is contained in its definition. Whatever is outside the definition is accidental to it. When we define "man," for instance, we mention "rational" and "animal," but we do not say that he is individual or universal. Individuality and universality are accidental to the essence of man as such, so that it can be individual in Peter and Paul and universal in the concept we form of it in our mind. Moreover, although the definition of a thing tells us *what* it is, it does not say whether it exists or does not exist. Consequently, existence itself is not included in the essence of a thing but is accidental to it. At least this is true of everything except God, who is pure existence.

The extension of metaphysics in the thirteenth century to include problems of existence as distinct from those of form or essence was due mainly to the initiation of Avicenna. William of Auvergne adopted his view of the accidentality of existence and used it to explain the contingency of created being. For, he reasoned, if God *is* existence, all other things must *receive* existence as an accident of their essence. Existence, then, is given to them as a free gift and they are contingent in their very being. St. Albert expressed these same views, which St. Thomas Aquinas was to use and transform for his own purposes.

Since the Avicennian interpretation of Aristotle was known to Christian scholars in the second half of the twelfth century, its influence preceded that of Averroism, which became known about 1230. Within the space of thirty or forty years, however, a new movement gained prominence under the aegis of Averroës, called "Latin Averroism." Unlike the Avicennian movement which flourished among the theologians, the Averroist found its devotees among the professors of philosophy at the University of Paris. Averroës had rebuked Avicenna for destroying the purity of the Aristotelian philosophy by mixing his Mohammedan religion with it. It was his aim to return to the pure thought of Aristotle, whom he considered the very model of human perfection and whose doctrine he treated as synonymous with philosophy itself. For him, to philosophize meant simply to comment on the words of Aristotle. The Latin Averroists, like Siger of Brabant (1253?-1281/84) and Boethius of Dacia, also wanted to be philosophers, and for them, too, this meant to return to the philosophy of Aristotle, generally as interpreted by Averroës.

Now, this attitude was bound to lead them into difficulty, for Averroism included doctrines contrary to the Faith. Among others, it taught the eternity of the world, the unicity of the intellect for all men, the denial of divine providence and personal immortality. When rebuked by the theologians for their heterodoxy, they did not deny the truth of Revelation; they simply made it clear that they were pursuing their work as philosophers, not as theologians. Siger said: "When we philosophize we seek the thought of the philosophers rather than the truth." Far from teaching a double truth, as is sometimes claimed, one theological and the other philosophical, and in contradiction with each other, Siger definitely asserted the superiority of revealed truth over philosophical reason. This is precisely the opposite of Averroës' own view, for he had exalted reason over Revelation.

Both Averroës and Siger of Brabant, however, claimed the right to philosophize apart from religion. "We have nothing to do with the miracles of God," Siger protested, "since we treat natural things in a natural way." The Averroist movement thus had as its aim the separation of philosophy from theology and the freedom of the human reason to pursue its work without any control from religion. Boethius of Dacia illustrates this attitude in a little work on the philosophical life ("the best state possible to man"), in which he outlines a natural moral order separate from the supernatural order of grace and beatitude.

In 1270 and 1277 there were violent reactions to Latin Averroism on the part of the traditionalist Augustinians. Its doctrines were condemned by the Bishop of Paris and the leaders were called up before the ecclesiastical court. Siger of Brabant fled the University of Paris and took refuge at the Papal Court where he died about 1284.

In the fourteenth century, Averroism developed further in the direction of rationalism in the philosophy of John of Jandun (d.1328), who exalts the rights and dignity of reason at the expense of Revelation. Marsilius of Padua (d.1336/43), his political collaborator, applied his separation of reason and Faith to the political domain and advocated the separation of Church and State. Dante himself, having placed Siger of Brabant in Paradise along with St. Albert and St. Thomas, reflects this Averroist separation of the spiritual and the temporal orders in his *De Monarchia*.

St. Thomas Aquinas differed from both the Augustinians and the Averroists in his attitude towards Aristotle. The thirteenth-century followers of St. Augustine tended to remain loyal to their master and to the Neoplatonism he had espoused in whatever touched the very essentials of their thought. What they accepted from the Stagirite always remained more or less on the periphery of their philosophy and did not penetrate to its very center. The Averroists, on the other hand, seemed to look upon him as philosophy incarnate. Now, it was St. Thomas' decided conviction that the Augustinians' fear of Aristotle was unfounded. He believed that when the Aristotelian texts were freed from their Arabian contamination, they revealed a philosophy which was sound in its principles and which could be of immense service to Christian wisdom. At the same time he was clearly aware of the insufficiencies of that philosophy and the need of developing and enriching it in the light of reason and Christian truth. Philosophy for him is not the mere understanding of what Aristotle had said. Rather, it is a specific manner of comprehending reality—a comprehension which admits of ever-increasing depths. "The pursuit of philosophy," he wrote, "is not to find out what men have thought, but what the truth of the matter is." Like the Averroists, he realized the importance of studying the philosophy of Aristotle, but because his gaze was turned towards truth he could use that philosophy without becoming its slave.

Unlike the Augustinians of his century, who tended to depreciate the power of the human reason to attain truth without Faith or a special divine illumination, he was confident that an autonomous philosophy based upon experience and the light of the human intellect is possible. He was convinced, moreover, that this philosophy would be in accord with Faith, since the light of reason and the light of Faith come from the same source, God. A theologian by vocation, he himself never developed such a philosophy, but was content to express his most personal philosophical thoughts in the context of his theological *Summae*. Yet he laid down the principles of an autonomous philosophy and on occasion showed us how they were to be developed. In his philosophical works, such as "On Being and Essence" and "On the Unity of the Intellect against the Averroists," we see him approach problems of his day as a philosopher without appealing to Revelation. At the same time he had no intention of separating philosophy from the light of Faith in the manner of the Averroists; as if a philosopher who is also a Christian should not on that account be a better philosopher. In ordering the relations between reason and Faith, St. Thomas thus kept a wise balance, upholding the rights of reason against those who disparaged its claims, while opening it to the influence of the higher light of Revelation against those who would close it within itself.

One of the achievements of Aristotle was to show, in contradiction to Plato, that the changing physical world bears within itself an element of stability which can serve as the object of true knowledge. The human mind need not turn to a world of Ideas in order to find truth. St. Thomas maintained essentially the same position against the Augustinians, who fixed the certitude of human knowledge in its contact with divine Ideas. He saw clearly the essential bond between Plato and St. Augustine on this point. "Augustine," he said, "followed Plato as far as the Catholic Faith permitted." In place of the separated Ideas, he continues, Augustine held that there are Ideas in the divine mind through which we judge of all things illumined by the divine light. Of course Augustine did not mean that we see the divine Ideas themselves in this life, for that would be impossible. But those supreme Ideas impress themselves on our mind, and by sharing in their light we can have true knowledge. When St. Thomas wrote this he was not only thinking of the Bishop of Hippo, but also of his mediaeval disciples whose doctrine of divine illumination revealed their essential allegiance to Augustinianism. To his way of thinking, however, to deny that the human mind can know the truth by its own natural light is to detract from its perfection and therefore from the perfection of God who is its author. As a Christian he knew well enough that the Psalmist says: "The light of thy countenance, O Lord, is signed upon us." But what is this light save the one received by the soul at its creation and which Aristotle described as the Agent Intellect?

St. Thomas thus recognized that the natural object of our knowledge is to be found in the sense world and that we are by nature adequately equipped to apprehend it. Starting with a knowledge of this world of sense, we have to raise ourselves slowly and with great difficulty to a knowledge of the Source of our existence and our last End, whose essence in this life escapes our comprehension, but whose existence is attested by His manifest effects in the world about us.

St. Thomas' empiricism in epistemology is closely associated with his view of the intellectual soul as the immediate substantial form of the body. If the intellect were a spiritual substance accidentally joined to matter or separated from it by another substantial form, its dependence for knowledge upon the senses and the sense world would be equally accidental and remote. Knowing, in the most perfect sense of the word, would be a journey of the soul within itself where it would find its own spiritual nature and the wider spiritual world with which it is in communion. But for St. Thomas such an angelic or quasi-angelic mode of knowing is not natural to man precisely because in his case it is not an intellect or soul that knows, but rather a man whose intellect is by nature the substantial form of a body. Under these conditions the gaze of the intellect is naturally turned outward to the material world, and the senses become the only channel of natural knowledge.

The Augustinians were afraid to admit that the soul is so closely allied to matter for fear of losing sight of its spiritual nature and immortality. Were not the Averroists there to warn them that if the soul is the immediate substantial form of the body it is simply another material form which cannot survive death? One way of avoiding this conclusion is to say that the soul and body are only accidentally united, or that one or more substantial forms are present in matter before the intellectual soul informs it. But St. Thomas was convinced that both explanations lose sight of an important fact. Each of us is aware that it is he himself who knows, and not just a part of himself. Experience demands, therefore, that we find a mode of union of soul and body which will permit us to attribute the act of knowing, not to the intellect or soul, but to the entire man. Now we could not say that the whole man, body and soul, knows, if the soul is simply the mover of the body or uses it as its instrument. In either case knowing would be properly the act of the soul. The only mode of union satisfying the datum of experience is the one described by Aristotle as a union of substantial form and matter. For in this case soul and body are but two incomplete principles uniting to form the complete substance of man. Consequently, *that which* thinks is the substantial reality of the whole man and not his soul alone, although he does so by means of his intellect.

Granted this, it remains for St. Thomas to explain more precisely in what sense the soul is incomplete. If the soul is looked at from the point of view of essence or nature, it appears deficient and in need of the body, for it is only a part of the complete essence of man. But from the point of view of existence, this is not true. As a substantial form the human soul has a complete act of existing (*esse*), and since it is a spiritual form, its act of existing is itself spiritual. When it informs the body it communicates to it that act of existing so that there is but one substantial existence of the whole composite. For St. Thomas, therefore, the unity of man does not consist in a combination or assemblage of various parts or substances, but in his act of existing. It is no wonder, then, that he denied the presence of several substantial forms in man. If a substantial form gives substantial existence, several forms of this kind would give man several existences and his unity as a substance would be destroyed.

St. Thomas' solution of the problem of man's unity shows us how he used Aristotelian notions while surpassing them with his own principles. Aristotle himself explained the constitution of man and all corruptible things in terms of form and matter, but he never thought to express their being or unity in terms of act of existing. Indeed the Greeks always tended to view being as form, and that is why form generally occupied the center of their philosophical discussions. Aristotle did not differ from Plato on this point. He merely substituted the Unmoved Movers for the Ideas and definitely located the forms of sensible things in the things themselves. What is new in St. Thomas' metaphysics is the notion that a being is primarily an act of existing (*esse*); so that his world is one of individual acts of existing rather than one of forms or essences. The form of each being is that whereby it is *what* it is; the principle, in other words, which specifies and determines it to be of a certain *kind*. In addition to form there is a further and ultimate act which makes it to be or *to exist*. This is the act of existing, which St. Thomas describes as "the actuality of all acts" and the "perfection of all perfections." It is that which is most profound in any being, its metaphysical nucleus, so to speak, the root-cause of all its perfections and of its intelligibility.

St. Thomas upheld his doctrine of being in the face of widespread opposition from his contemporaries. On the one hand, philosophers like Siger of Brabant wished to return to the Aristotelianism of Averroës who had hardened and fixed it against any development. Siger reminded St. Thomas that Aristotle had written about form, matter and the composition of the two; he had never mentioned an *esse* distinct from them. On the other hand, he faced the opposition of those who admitted *esse* as a distinct metaphysical principle but simply as an accident of essence. This had been the view of William of Auvergne and St. Albert, who traced the notion to Avicenna. For St. Thomas, however, this was still to look upon being as primarily essence or form and to reduce the rôle of existence to an accidental determination of essence. In maintaining the primacy of the act of existing over essence, St. Thomas stood alone in his century and indeed in the whole Middle Ages, a prophet not for his own age but for the ages to come.

St. Thomas' new doctrine of being was bound to have an influence on his notion of God and indeed upon the whole of his metaphysics. All the theologians of the Middle Ages knew that God is Being, for He revealed to Moses that His proper name is "He who is." (*Exodus,* iii, 13.) But the statement is open to different interpretations. St. Augustine, St. Anselm and their thirteenth-century followers like Alexander of Hales and St. Bonaventure, interpreted it to mean that God is pure *essence,* emphasizing by this term His supreme knowability and unchangeableness. For St. Thomas, however, to say that God is "He who is" means that He is the Pure Act of Existing. God is neither a static essence, nor a special kind of actuality like Aristotle's Pure Act of Thought. He is the infinite Act of Existing, including within Himself the absolute fulness of being with all its perfections. What we call "essence" in other things in God is nothing but His Act of Existing, or, to put it another way, God's essence is identical with His existence. A creature is nothing but a limited participation in the Act of Existing of God, and its essence marks off the measure of that participation. In all created things, therefore, there is a real distinction between essence and act of existing.

Our human intellects are entirely inadequate to penetrate the Act of Existing which is God. We can know *that* He exists, but we cannot comprehend His essence so as to know *what* He is in Himself. There are certain things which we can deny of Him, such as change, composition and passivity, for these are incompatible with

His absolute perfection. We can thus have some negative knowledge of God. We can also know Him by analogy with His creatures, for there must be some resemblance between Him and His effects. But since the distance between the Creator and His creatures is infinite, we know that any perfection that we attribute to God—such as existence, goodness, intelligence, unity, freedom—is in Him in an infinitely more perfect manner than in creatures. Consequently, we have no positive knowledge of God as He is in Himself, but only as He is represented in creatures.

Since God is infinitely perfect He has need of nothing. If He creates a universe, it is not because of any necessity on His part, but because in His supreme goodness He wishes it to share in His own perfection. Creation is thus a free act of God and the expression of His liberality. Moreover, as the Infinite Act of Existing, it is only natural that His proper effect in creating should be to give the universe its very existence. And since without existence it is nothing, creation is *ex nihilo,* from nothing. St. Thomas' view of being as primarily act of existing thus enables him to give to the doctrine of creation its true existential import, which is somewhat obscured in a metaphysics which looks upon being as primarily essence.

The thirteenth century witnessed a lively debate on whether the world is eternal. The Averroists, following Aristotle, thought that the eternity of the world could be rationally demonstrated. Theologians like St. Bonaventure were equally convinced that reason could demonstrate the contrary. St. Thomas saw no reason why God could not, if He willed, create a universe which always existed in the past and always will exist in the future. Reason cannot prove the eternity or non-eternity of the world, for whether it is eternal or not depends solely on the divine will. Only by the revelation of that will in Scripture do we know that in fact our universe began in time. But even if God created a universe endless in time, it would still be a *created* universe, eternally contingent and dependent on the creative influx of existence from God.

The universe is thus an expression of God's will, but it is above all a manifestation of His intelligence. The creative act which establishes all beings as dynamic centers of existing also confers on them their natures by which they are centers of definite activities. Now, these activities are not aimless. Coming from the Divine intelligence, creatures act in view of an end, which is to achieve their own perfection and in so doing to resemble God. Thus all beings come from God and tend back to Him as their final end.

Now, beings tend to this end in different ways and attain it with different degrees of perfection. Some things unconsciously tend towards it by the activities of matter, but they manage to achieve it only in a very imperfect way. Man also attains his final end and his beatitude by activity, but by that activity which most befits him as a human being, namely, an act of the intellect. Secondarily, he attains it by the activity of his will, enjoying the good possessed. By his spiritual intellect man can know all things, even the universal good or God, and nothing short of that will satisfy him. He discovers the traces of God in nature and yearns to know His very essence. But by his natural powers alone he cannot see God face to face. His loftiest speculations fall far short of that goal and fail to satisfy his deepest longings.

For St. Thomas Aquinas, therefore, man's ultimate happiness is unattainable by his natural powers. In a word, it is supernatural. But we have a free will by which we can turn ourselves to God who infallibly offers us His supernatural help to reach the happiness lying beyond our grasp. Not only has He made a Revelation of Himself to man and established an order of grace by which man can begin, even here on earth, to live a supernatural life. In the Incarnation He himself has become man in order that we might not despair of a union with Him in Heaven. Thus for St. Thomas the supernatural crowns the natural and grace completes nature, not by doing violence to it, but by fulfilling its deepest aspirations and needs.

BIBLIOGRAPHY

MAURICE DE WULF, *History of Mediaeval Philosophy,* Vol. 2, 3rd English ed. trans. by E. Messenger (New York, 1938).
ETIENNE GILSON, *Le thomisme* (5th ed., Paris, 1944).
————, *La philosophie au moyen âge, des origines patristiques à la fin du XIVe siècle* (2nd ed., Paris, 1944).
————, *The Spirit of Mediaeval Philosophy,* trans. by A. H. C. Downes (London, 1936).
————, *The Philosophy of St. Bonaventure,* trans. by Dom I. Trethowan (London, 1938).
————, *Reason and Revelation in the Middle Ages* (New York, 1948).
————, *Being and Some Philosophers* (Toronto, 1949).

A HISTORY OF PHILOSOPHICAL SYSTEMS

MARTIN GRABMANN, *Thomas Aquinas, His Personality and Thought,* trans. by Virgil Michel (New York, 1928).

JACQUES MARITAIN, *St. Thomas Aquinas, Angel of the Schools,* trans. by J. F. Scanlan (London, 1933).

RICHARD MCKEON, *Selections from Medieval Philosophers,* 2 vols. (New York, 1930).

HANS MEYER, *The Philosophy of St. Thomas Aquinas,* trans. by Rev. F. Eckhoff (St. Louis and London, 1945).

ANTON PEGIS, *The Basic Writings of St. Thomas Aquinas,* 2 vols. (New York, 1945).

A. D. SERTILLANGES, O. P. *The Foundations of Thomistic Philosophy,* trans. by G. Anstruther, O.P. (St. Louis, 1931).

FERNAND VAN STEENBERGHEN, *Aristote en Occident, les origines de l'aristotélisme parisien* (Louvain, 1946).

PAUL VIGNAUX, *La Pensée au Moyen Age* (Paris, 1948).

CHAPTER SEVENTEEN

SCOTISM AND OCKHAMISM

ARMAND MAURER

THE ECCLESIASTICAL condemnation of Aristotelianism and Arabian philosophy in 1277, which even included some of the theses of St. Thomas Aquinas, had a deep influence upon the subsequent development of mediaeval thought. Of course, opposition to Greco-Arabian philosophy was nothing new to the thirteenth century. Its opening decades had seen the newly-translated works of Aristotle and Averroës prohibited; but their vogue spread, and in the years that followed a reconciliation was attempted, with varied success, between Christian dogma and the "new learning." The heresy of Latin Averroism at the end of the century only confirmed the suspicion of the traditionalist theologians that any Christian who accepted the essentials of Aristotelianism must arrive at conclusions contrary to the Faith. The great condemnation of 1277 expressed their renewed reaction to Aristotle and left an even deeper impression on subsequent scholars of the inadequacy of philosophy and pure human reason. If, as has been claimed, the fourteenth century is a period of criticism, it is above all a period of criticism, in the name of theology, of philosophy and the pretensions of pure reason.

The attitude of Duns Scotus (1266-1308) towards Aristotle and philosophy in general is seen in his doctrine of the object of human knowledge. According to the Greek philosopher, the human intellect is naturally turned towards sensible things from which it must draw all its knowledge by way of sensation and abstraction. As a consequence, the proper object of our knowledge is the essence of a material thing. Now, Duns Scotus was willing to agree that Aristotle correctly described our present way of knowing, but he did contest that he had said the last word on the subject and that he had sufficiently explained what is in full right the object of our knowledge. Ignorant of Revelation, Aristotle did not realize that man is now in a fallen state and that he was describing the knowledge, not of an integral man, but of one whose mode of knowing was radically altered by original sin. Ignorance of this fact is understandable in a pagan like Aristotle, but it must have seemed inexcusable to Scotus in a Christian theologian like St. Thomas. The Christian, Scotus argues, cannot take man's present state as his natural one, nor, as a consequence, the present servitude of his intellect to the senses and to sensible things as natural to him. We know from Revelation that man is destined to see God face to face. Now this would be impossible to achieve if the adequate object of his knowledge were restricted to the essences of material things, for God is not contained within their scope. To be open to the vision of God, the intellect must have an object broad enough to include Him, and the only one that satisfies this condition is *being*. Being, therefore, in its full indetermination to material and immaterial things is the first and adequate object of the intellect.

When as a theologian Duns Scotus made this decision, he was not only assuring the human intellect's capacity for the beatific vision; he was also making metaphysics as a science possible by marking out its proper object. Natural philosophy moves in the realm of finite mobile being and theology in that of infinite being. Metaphysics, on the other hand, has for its object being as being, or the pure undetermined nature of being. For Scotus this is not a logical universal. It is a reality, and the most common of all. Taken simply in itself, the notion of being abstracts from all the differences of beings. That is why it is, for the metaphysician, univocal, having one and the same meaning when applied to all things. Only in its finite and infinite modes is being analogical.

Being has consequently a univocity in Scotism which is not found in Thomism. For St. Thomas did not treat of being as if it were a nature or essence; rather it is for him *that which is,* at whose center is an act of existing. And since every act of existing is irreducible to every other, there is a radical *otherness* in every being which the work of abstraction can never erase. That is why in the philosophy of St. Thomas being is, for the metaphysician, not a univocal, but an analogical, concept.

It was the Arabian philosopher, Avicenna, who taught Scotus to conceive of being as an essence in an absolute state, *natura tantum,* and at the same time suggested to him his solution of the classic problem of universals. The Scotist nature, like the Avicennian, is simply what the definition of it signifies. Now, neither individuality nor universality is included within the definition of any nature. When I define "humanity," for instance, I mention its essential parts, "animality" and "rationality," but I do not say whether it is individual or universal. Indeed, in itself it is entirely indifferent to being one or the other or both at the same time. It can be individual in real existence and universal in the mind and still remain basically the same nature, for these modalities are entirely accidental to it. Suppose that the nature were of itself universal. Then it could never be individual; but as a matter of fact it is individual in the world of existing things. On the other hand, if it were by its very nature individual, it could never be universal, but it is universal in the mind. Consequently, the nature in itself must be "absolute," abstracting from both individuality and universality.

In Scotism the absolute nature does not exist as such. Humanity, for instance, does not exist except in individual men and in the concept which we form of it. But it is not on that account simply a conceptual entity. Scotus says that it is a real being. This real being is contracted or limited by an "individual difference" or "haecceity" which renders the nature individual. Following upon this contraction of the essence or nature, the individual is actualized by existence, which (at least in creatures) is the ultimate act of a thing, related to it simply as a mode of being.

If this is true, it is evident that essence plays the primary rôle in Scotist metaphysics. The metaphysical nucleus, so to speak, of an individual thing is an essence which is limited by different modalities which are purely accidental to it. That is why Duns Scotus' metaphysics has justly been called "essentialist," in distinction to the "existentialist" metaphysics of St. Thomas,[1] in which the metaphysical center of an individual thing is an act of existing and its essence is but a limitation on that act. Because they do not agree in their notions of being, the two metaphysics are fundamentally different. To confuse them and to equate Scotism with Thomism is simply to invite misunderstanding in both doctrines.

On the other hand, seen in its own light, the metaphysics of Duns Scotus is entirely intelligible. He carefully distinguishes between two orders of real beings: the order of things (*res*) and the order of realities or formalities (*realitates, formalitates*) which are in things. Things are such that one can exist in separation from the other, if not naturally (like Peter and Paul), at least by the omnipotence of God (as matter can exist apart from form). Realities or formalities, however, cannot possibly exist separately. They are only formally non-identical, in the sense that one is not contained within the formal definition of the other. In Peter, for example, rationality is not contained within the definition of animality and his individuality as Peter is not contained within the definition of humanity; otherwise there could be no animality which is not rational and no humanity other than Peter's.

What is characteristic of the philosophy of Duns Scotus is that he attributed reality even to these formalities. They are not simply abstractions of the mind; they are abstract from each other even before the mind considers them. Each has a real being of its own and a real unity distinct from that of individual things. Peter and Paul, for instance, are each numerically one. But in them there is present humanity, animality, substance, etc., each of which is formally non-identical with the others and constitutes a real being with its own specific or generic unity. True, Scotus always maintained that individual things are most worthy of being called "real," and that their numerical unity is "major unity." Still, formalities are also real, and their generic or specific unity is for him a real "minor unity" and not simply a unity in the conceptual order. Scotus conceived of an individual thing, then, as a coming together of many formalities or natures of this sort, all of which are made individual or concretized by an "individual difference" or "haecceity." But even though these formalities are individualized in things, in their own order they remain common or universal. That is why Scotus can say, paradoxically, that only individual things exist, but that there is something common in reality which is not *of itself* individual. This means simply that in the order of existing things there are only individuals: there are no existing universal *things*. But in the order of formalities or essences there are common natures which guard their commonness within their own order even when they are individualized in the order of things.

The reason why Scotus says that there are common natures in reality is to assure a suitable object for knowledge. The primary object of knowledge and science is not individual things but universals. Now, there are two kinds of science: one which concerns conceptual entities, namely logic, and another, such as physics and metaphysics, which concerns real being. Since the object of both kinds of science is universal, there must be two kinds of universals: the complete universal, which is the product of the intellect and the object of logic, and the incomplete universal or common nature which is the object of the sciences of real being.

The world of Duns Scotus is thus peopled not only with individual things but also with real common natures which the intellect has merely to seek out to read their intelligible messages. In such a world even the senses can perceive a reality which is in a way universal. According to Scotus, the object of sensation is not properly an individual thing as individual, but a reality common to all the sensible objects in one genus, the whiteness, for instance, of all white things. Under these circumstances there is no need of an abstractive process of the intellect, in the Thomistic sense, by which the intelligible object, bearing the stamp of singularity in a sensible image, must be rendered universal and actually intelligible in order to be known. For the object present to our cognitive faculties is a common nature in which, as a recent historian put it,[2] the Agent Intellect can read, as in an open book, the intelligible object from which the concept will be born.

By his realism of common natures Duns Scotus placed himself in the long line of mediaeval Christian Platonists, all of whom agree that in some way there is universality or community outside the mind corresponding to our universal concepts. Of course, historical Platonism is realized in very different forms. The rather crude realist philosophies of Boethius, John Scotus Eriugena and William of Champeaux are a far cry from the refined realism of Duns Scotus; yet we can see the same Platonic inspiration behind them all. And just as early mediaeval Platonism aroused the unrelenting criticism of Abailard, so the Platonism of the fourteenth century found an even more formidable adversary in William of Ockham.

A student at Oxford in the first decade of the fourteenth century, William of Ockham (1290?-1349/50) became acquainted with Scotism either from the Subtle Doctor himself or, more likely, from his immediate disciples. But he was a student with an independent mind, and while listening to his teachers he formed his own philosophy in opposition to them. Ockhamism thus grew out of a criticism of contemporary doctrines, and especially of Scotism, whose founder, he says, surpassed all others in subtlety of judgment.

Duns Scotus had accepted the Avicennian metaphysics of essence, but there was much in the Arabian's philosophy which as a Christian he rejected. For one thing, according to Avicenna God is not a free creator; all things flow from Him in a definite hierarchy with all the rational necessity with which conclusions are drawn from premises. Now, necessity enters the Avicennian world—and the world of Greek and Arabian philosophy in general—precisely because it is a rational world of intelligible essences. For even though existences or facts are contingent, essences are necessarily what they are. The problem which Scotus faced was to reconcile the freedom of God and the contingency of created things with the fact that there are intelligible essences in the universe and ideas in the divine mind. His solution was to assert the transcendence of God as infinite being above all essences, and to teach a radical voluntarism according to which all things—in a way even the divine knowledge—are subject to God's will.

Now William of Ockham was equally certain that God is all-powerful and the free creator of the world. Like Scotus, he did not think this could be proved by natural reason; but he knew it to be true by Faith, for we say in the first article of the Creed: "I believe in God the Father Almighty." The only question for Ockham was: Can the omnipotence and liberty of God and the contingency of the world be saved in the way Scotus tried to do it? Ockham was convinced that they could not; an essential reform would have to be made in Scotism and every trace of intelligible essence removed from it if the danger of necessitarianism was to be avoided.

At the same time, Ockham was a shrewd logician and a man who loved clarity and simplicity of thought. An explanation, to his mind, should always be in as simple terms as possible, or, to put it another way, we should not posit a plurality without necessity. This principle of thought, which has come to be called "Ockham's Razor," is not original with him. It was a common dictum of the time and is traceable to Aristotle. What is new is the devastating way Ockham used it in accordance with his theological aims and his basic metaphysical and logical notions.

In Ockham's criticism of Scotism and other contemporary philosophies, one of his first aims is to eliminate common natures and universals from reality, and in doing so he proceeds as a logician. When terms are used in propositions, he reminds us, they serve as substitutes for things. This function of terms standing for things in propositions the schoolmen called supposition (*suppositio*). Now, there are three ways in which a term can exercise this function. In the first place, it may stand for the word itself, as when I say "Man is a word." Here "man" stands for the word "man" taken materially. Consequently, this kind of supposition is called material supposition. Secondly, a term may stand for individual things, as in the proposition "Man runs," for it is the individual person who is signified as running. Hence the name of this kind of supposition is personal supposition. In still a third way, a term may have a simple supposition, as when we use "man" in the proposition "Man is a species."

Now, the point which particularly interested Ockham was the meaning of simple supposition. What precisely does "man" stand for in the last proposition? Peter of Spain, whose treatise on logic served as a text book for the schoolmen, thought that it stood for and signified a universal thing. Obviously this is to prejudice the debate over universals in favor of realism. For if he is correct, there is a universal thing which the common term signifies and for which it can stand in a proposition. Ockham, however, had another view on the matter. For him, in simple supposition the common term simply stands for a concept in the mind and properly speaking signifies individual things. This was also giving an answer to the problem of universals, this time in favor of nominalism or conceptualism. If Ockham is right, there is nothing common or universal in reality; universality abides solely in the mind and nothing is real except individual things.

We can see how thoroughly Ockham was convinced of this by reading his treatise on universals in his commentary on the *Sentences* of Peter Lombard. There he arranges the various realist doctrines according to the degree of reality they attribute to universals and then proceeds to refute them one by one. The burden of his criticism is generally the same. If a universal is outside the mind and realized in things, it is either one (and then we cannot understand how it is multiplied in individuals), or it is many (and then we cannot understand how it is one). In either case we end in absurdity, and it is better to admit that universals are simply in the mind and have no reality whatsoever. They are present in things neither actually, nor virtually, nor potentially. They are strictly in no way in things.

If this is true, the common natures so dear to Scotus lose their status as realities and the complicated structure of being built upon them is eliminated. For one thing, there is no need of an haecceity added to nature to account for individuality. Every individual is individual in itself and not in virtue of an added principle. Moreover, the Scotist formal distinction is banished from philosophy along with the realities which are its basis. The only kind of distinction left in reality is real distinction, in the precise Scotist sense of a distinction between individual things, one of which can exist without the other. Ockham admitted formal distinctions only in theology, for instance between the three Persons and the Divine Essence, although for him this is contrary to the ordinary laws of logic. A logical distinction, such as Ockham conceived it, is simply one between concepts without any foundation in an individual thing. The distinction between the various concepts the intellect forms of a thing has thus no meaning as far as the individual itself is concerned, for they all signify one and the same reality. That is why, for him, the concepts we form of God are all equal in signification. If we distinguish between the divine intellect and will, for example, this is purely a distinction between concepts which signify the same indistinct divine reality. We can say, then, that God knows by His will or wills by His intellect, for the two concepts have precisely the same meaning when predicated of God. The same is true of all universal concepts predicated of an individual thing. Consequently, an individual in the Ockhamist sense is absolutely impervious to distinction; it is by definition "the indistinct."

If real being is thus radically individual, what is a universal, and what relation has it to things? A universal, for Ockham, is simply a sign which stands for many things. Now signs, he tells us, are either conventional and artificial, like written or spoken words, or natural, like the noise an animal makes to signify its feelings. There are universal artificial signs outside the mind, but on analysis they are found to be simply individual things whose signification is purely conventional. Within the mind, however, we find natural signs or terms which are our universal concepts. Their signification is not conventional but natural, since they are produced in us in an obscure way by nature itself as likenesses of things. That is why the concepts of men are alike while their languages differ. As to the exact reality of these concepts, Ockham, after some hesitation, seems to have taken the stand that they are simply our acts of understanding.

We know already that, for Ockham, concepts can have no foundation in reality save individual things. But how can they be a basis for *universal* concepts? If there are no common natures in reality, is not our conceptual and abstract knowledge completely out of contact with it? In the twelfth century, Abailard, faced with the same problem after his criticism of the realism of William of Champeaux, resorted to the notion that God created things with a common status or condition which accounts for the resemblances among them. Consequently, even though things do not share a common essence, they can be designated by a common name because of their common status. Ockham adopted a similar solution although it was more radical. It is evident, he said, that there is a greater similarity among some things than among others. Plato, for instance, is more like Socrates than he is like an animal. Accordingly the mind forms a concept of the species "man" which signifies both men but not the animal. Then it can form a more universal concept of the genus "animal" because of the common likeness of all three. The difficulty with this solution is that Ockham has really no intelligible explanation for the likenesses of things. They are not alike because they share in a common nature. Neither are they alike because they were created by God according to a common idea or model. Abailard had resorted to the divine ideas to explain the common status of things, but this was not acceptable to Ockham for the good reason that he did not think God's mind contained distinct ideas; the divine ideas, in his view, are simply the individual things which God creates. As a result, the likenesses of things are purely factual. They can be experienced but not rationally explained.

Once Ockham shifted the interest of philosophy from common natures to individual things, a new theory of knowledge was inevitable. The primary object of the senses and intellect can no longer be a common reality, as in Scotism, but individual things. Following the terminology of Duns Scotus, Ockham distinguished between intuitive and abstractive knowledge. Intuitive knowledge, he says, is always concerned with a singular thing as existing and present to the observer. Abstractive knowledge, on the other hand, tells us nothing about the existence or non-existence of things, but concerns abstract ideas or representations. Now, for Ockham, all our knowledge begins with an intuition of the senses and this is followed by an intellectual intuition. Abstractive knowledge comes afterwards and depends on them. Thus he insists as strongly on the primacy of the individual in knowledge as on its primacy in being.

Although sensible intuition is at the origin of all our knowledge, absolutely speaking it does not guarantee the existence of its object. There can be an intuition of a non-existent thing, and even a judgment of its existence, without the actual presence of the object. This doctrine of Ockham's comes as a surprise in view of his definition of intuition; yet we can easily see what led to this conclusion. God, who is omnipotent, can always do alone what He does by secondary causes. Now, Ockham says, when we see a star, God produces our intuition of it using the star as a secondary cause. He can, then, supernaturally conserve our sight of the star without the star. Of course, Ockham never doubted that in the normal course of events the object perceived is really the cause of the intuition. What is in question is simply what God is, absolutely speaking, capable of doing, not what He in fact does. It may be objected that the Ockhamist God, for all His omnipotence, cannot do what is contradictory, and the intuition of a non-existent thing is contrary to the very notion of intuitive knowledge. Faced with this objection, Ockham admits in one place that such a cognition would not be a true intuition, but rather an assent lacking evidence and belonging to the realm of faith, although the assent would be of the same kind as the evident judgments based on intuition. What Ockham does not explain, however, is how we could for all practical purposes distinguish between our knowledge of existing and non-existing things, and he thus opens the way to idealism and skepticism even though he himself does not enter upon it.

We are witnessing here the final result of Ockham's attempt to rid theology and philosophy of Greco-Arabian necessitarianism. Scotus thought that he could do it and still retain the divine ideas and common natures with the necessity which they introduce into the world, if they were subordinated to the divine will. Ockham would not concede even this much. While keeping Scotus' voluntarism, he abolished ideas from God's mind and common natures from things, with the result that he had nothing left but an omnipotent God governed by no law save that of contradiction, and a morcellated universe of individual things, no one of which has anything in common with any other. In such a universe God can act in a very arbitrary way. He can, if He wishes, make it meritorious for us to hate Him. Hatred of God, theft, adultery are bad only because of the will of God, not for any intelligible reason. So, too, God can make fire cool, just as easily as He makes it heat, for there is no necessary connection between cause and effect. The nominalist universe of Ockham is thus a world of *fact* rather than one of intelligible necessity, a world of things to be experienced rather than one of intelligible natures to be understood. Such a world, it is true, would prove interesting to the experimental sciences which were soon to set out on their brilliant career. It was barren soil, however, for philosophy such as it was known to the schoolmen of the thirteenth century.

Scotism and Ockhamism spread widely in the fourteenth century. Followers of the Subtle Doctor, like Francis of Mayronne (d. after 1328) and William of Alnwick (d. 1334), continued and developed his thought. Through them and subsequent Scotist commentators his teaching took deep root in the later Middle Ages, especially in the Franciscan Order of which he had been a member. Indeed, certain Scotist themes, such as the univocity of being, formal distinction and common nature, continue to have an influence in our own time.

Ockhamism also had a marked success in the fourteenth century and its influence was felt in many of the doctrinal developments of the later Middle Ages. Its influence is seen, for example, in the tendency of that period towards probabilism and skepticism in philosophy and especially in natural theology. Continuing a trend of both Scotism and Ockhamism, an increasing number of theses regarding God and the soul, considered rationally demonstrable in the thirteenth century, were regarded as merely probable from the point of view of philosophy. At the same time, the tendency to separate the domains of philosophy and theology gained momentum, leading in some circles to a more positivist theology of Sacred Scripture and to fideism and mysticism. Ockhamism was also influential in the domains of logic and experimental science. In its wake a school of natural scientists arose at Paris, devoted to the nominalist logic and emphasizing the need of immediate experience; and its investigations were to prove important for the development of modern science. For example, John Buridan's (*c.* 1350) studies of *impetus* foreshadowed the theories of Galileo and Descartes. His disciple, Albert of Saxony (d. 1390), exercised an influence on the development of statics, as did Nicholas Oresme (d. 1382) on that of astronomy. The exact indebtedness of modern science to William of Ockham is still in dispute. There can be little doubt, however, that his nominalism and radical empiricism were influential in laying the grounds for its beginnings in the fourteenth century.

NOTES

1. In calling St. Thomas Aquinas' metaphysics "existential" there is no intention of using the word as it is applied to the thought of such moderns as Jean Paul Sartre or Gabriel Marcel. It is simply used to express the primordial importance of the act of existing (*esse*) in that metaphysics.
2. E. Gilson, "Avicenne et le point de depart de Duns Scot," *Archives d'histoire doctrinale et litteraire du moyen âge*, vol. 2 (Paris, 1927), p. 146.

BIBLIOGRAPHY

PHILOTHEUS BÖHNER, O.F.M., "The Realistic Conceptualism of William Ockham," *Traditio,* vol. 5 (New York, 1947), pp. 307-335; "The Notitia Intuitiva of Non-Existents according to William Ockham," *Traditio,* vol. 1 (New York, 1943), pp. 223-277.

MAURICE DE WULF, *History of Mediaeval Philosophy,* vol. 2, 3rd English ed. trans. by E. Messenger (New York, 1938) (for Scotus); "Histoire de la philosophie médiévale," vol. 3, 6th ed. (Louvain et Paris, 1947) (for Ockham).

ETIENNE GILSON, *La philosophie au moyen âge, des origines patristiques à la fin du XIVe siècle,* 2nd ed. (Paris, 1944).

―――――, "L'Objet de la Métaphysique selon Duns Scot," *Mediaeval Studies,* vol. 10 (Toronto, 1948), pp. 21-92.

―――――, "Avicenne et le point de départ de Duns Scot," *Archives d'histoire doctrinale et littéraire du moyen âge,* vol. 2 (Paris, 1927), pp. 89-149.

―――――, *The Unity of Philosophical Experience* (New York, 1947).

MAURICE GRAJEWSKI, *The Formal Distinction of Duns Scotus* (Washington, D. C., 1944).

ROBERT GUELLUY, *Philosophie et théologie chez Guillaume d'Ockham* (Louvain et Paris, 1947).
ERICH HOCHSTETTER, *Studien zur Metaphysik und Erkenntnislehre Wilhelms von Ockham* (Berlin and Leipzig, 1927).
JOHANNES KRAUS, *Die Lehre des Johannes Duns Scotus von der Natura Communis* (Freiburg, Schweiz, 1927).
RICHARD MCKEON, *Selections from Medieval Philosophers*, vol. 2 (New York, 1930).
ERNEST MOODY, *The Logic of William Ockham* (New York, 1935).
ANTON PEGIS, "Concerning William of Ockham," *Traditio*, vol. 2 (New York, 1944), pp. 465-481.
―――――, "Some Recent Interpretations of Ockham," *Speculum* (Cambridge, Mass.), vol. 23, n. 3, July, 1948, pp. 452-463.
C. L. SHIRCEL, O.F.M., *The Univocity of the Concept of Being in the Philosophy of Duns Scotus* (Washington, D. C., 1942).
STEPHEN TORNAY, *Ockham: Studies and Selections* (LaSalle, Illinois, 1938).
A. B. WOLTER, *The Transcendentals and their Function in the Metaphysics of Duns Scotus* (Washington, D. C., 1946).

Part II

MODERN AND RECENT

CHAPTER EIGHTEEN
RENAISSANCE PHILOSOPHIES

PAUL OSKAR KRISTELLER

THE TRADITIONAL interpretation of the Renaissance as a revival of ancient civilization after a long decay has been the subject of much recent controversy, yet the period which extends roughly from the middle of the fourteenth century to the first few decades of the seventeenth certainly possesses its distinctive though complex physiognomy. Whereas its achievements in political and religious history, in the arts and in literature are rightly famous, its contributions to the history of philosophy are less widely known. A brief survey of the major trends of Renaissance thought is necessarily quite tentative, due to the limitations of our knowledge, and also to the unusual diversity not only of schools and currents, but also of individual figures, of conditions in various places and at various times, of religious sympathies, and of institutional and professional traditions. Even the borderlines between philosophy and the other areas of civilization were not always too clearly drawn, and the mutual influences and correlations add to the difficulties of our task.

The first major current of Renaissance thought, Aristotelianism, is closely linked with the teaching traditions of the medieval universities where Aristotle's works had been introduced during the thirteenth century as the standard textbooks of logic, natural philosophy, metaphysics and ethics. This situation remained basically unchanged during the Renaissance, and consequently not only the professional students of philosophy but also those of theology, of medicine and to a lesser extent of law had a thoroughly Aristotelian background. What these Aristotelian philosophers had in common was not merely the knowledge of Aristotle's writings, but also a precise terminology, the use of the inherited literary forms of the commentary and of the question, the "scholastic" method of reasoning *pro* and *con* through an accumulation of separate arguments, and the preference for a number of specific problems traditionally discussed on the basis of Aristotle's works. Within this general framework, Renaissance Aristotelianism includes a great variety of different schools and opinions. Among the traditions inherited from the preceding period, Thomism was still largely limited to the fields of metaphysics and theology, and to the members of the Dominican order; yet the prestige of Aquinas was rising also outside of the circle of his strict followers, his doctrine was often adhered to by the thinkers of the new Jesuit order, his *Summa* began to replace Peter Lombard's *Sentences* as a textbook of theology, and the period produced important commentators of his writings, such as Thomas de Vio Cajetanus (1470-1534). On the other hand, Scotism was at least as influential; and the "Modern Way" of Ockhamism as it had developed at Paris and Oxford during the fourteenth century remained quite predominant in the fields of logic and of natural philosophy beyond the end of the fifteenth century. "Latin Averroism," an ambiguous term by which scholars sometimes denote the use of Averroës' commentary on Aristotle, sometimes the acceptance of particular doctrines such as the unity of the intellect for all mankind, remained an important current throughout the Renaissance. On the other hand, the study of Aristotle was modified after the fifteenth century through the use of his Greek text, of new Latin translations of his works, of the writings of his ancient Greek commentators, and through the influence of different ancient and contemporary philosophical ideas. (The trend which emphasized the Greek commentator, Alexander of Aphrodisias, is often referred to as "Alexandrism.") These group names fail to give an adequate idea of the great variety of ways in which Aristotelian notions were interpreted and combined with each other and with those of different origin.

From the French and English universities where this Aristotelianism flourished until the end of the fourteenth century and where its later history is still imperfectly known, its center shifted during the fifteenth and sixteenth centuries to Italy, Germany and the Iberian peninsula. Hispanic "Neoscholasticism" which had its main centers at the universities of Alcalà, Coimbra and especially Salamanca, produced important Aristotelian commentators in the sixteenth and early seventeenth centuries. Francis de Vitoria (1480-1546) was the first famous member of that school which culminated in the Jesuit, Francis Suarez (1548-1617), whose *Disputationes metaphysicae* have remained the most influential and most systematic work of scholastic philosophy after Aquinas. Whereas Aristotelianism in Spain and Portugal was closely linked with Catholic theology, its place in the university curriculum of Protestant Germany was firmly secured by Philip Melanchthon (1497-1565), and it thus provided the academic background of philosophy down to the times of Leibniz and of Kant. At the Italian universities among which Padua attained greatest prominence in the sixteenth century the emphasis was on logic and natural philosophy rather than on metaphysics, and philosophy was studied together with medicine rather than with theology. The Italian Aristotelians tended to separate the truth of religious faith and the results of natural and rational investigation, a notion which has been rather inadequately labeled as the "theory of double truth" and which is neither as insincere nor as absurd as it is often represented. Thus Pietro Pomponazzi (1462-1524), the most famous of the Italian Aristotelians, attempted in his treatise *On Incantations* to give natural explanations for supposedly miraculous phenomena, and argued in his treatise *On the Immortality of the Soul,* which became the starting point of a long and violent controversy, that immortality cannot be proven on rational grounds but is merely an article of faith. Jacopo Zabarella (1532-1589) was important not only as an excellent commentator of Aristotle, but also for his logical theory of two complementary modes of knowledge, the resolutive method which proceeds from effects to their causes, and the compositive method which returns from the causes to their effects, a distinction which appears to have influenced Galileo's doctrine of the physical hypothesis.

The second major intellectual movement of the Renaissance, classical humanism, was in its core and origin literary and scholarly rather than philosophical. The term "humanism," when applied to that period, should be freed of modern connotations. In the Renaissance, a "humanist" was a teacher of the "humanities," and these were understood to include the study of Latin and Greek, of grammar, rhetoric, poetry, history and moral philosophy. The movement originated in Italy early in the fourteenth century and later spread to the other European countries where it reached its climax in the sixteenth. The humanists occupied the chairs of the humanities at the universities, dominated in the secondary schools which they thoroughly reorganized, and held an important place in the chanceries, courts and other educated circles of the time. The pervasive classicism which characterizes Renaissance civilization in all its aspects is largely their work. Their literary production includes translations, commentaries, orations, letters, poems and historical writings as well as philosophical treatises, and many of the latter are popular and amateurish in character. Nevertheless, Renaissance humanism exercised a deep influence on the history of philosophical thought, and some of its representatives achieved philosophical significance. To the philosophical literature of the Renaissance, the humanists contributed not merely higher standards of clarity and literary elegance, and the methods of philological and historical criticism, but also the forms of the epistle, of the dialogue and of the essay. Humanist emphasis on man was expressed by its earliest great representative, Francesco Petrarca (1304-1374) and gave rise to several treatises on the dignity of man. Humanist flair for the literary expression of direct and concrete personal experience acquired philosophical significance in Michel de Montaigne (1533-1592), who considered his own individual self as the main subject matter of his philosophizing.

Humanist interests produced or influenced an extensive literature on education, on the method of history, on rhetorical and poetical theory, on moral and political problems. Still more important was the Greek philosophical source material made accessible and popularized through the scholarly activity of the humanists. The Middle Ages had known practically all of Aristotle, some writings of his commentators and of Proclus, and part of Plato's *Timaeus* in Latin translations. Renaissance humanism not only improved the knowledge of these same sources through a study of the Greek text and through new Latin translations, but also made available in editions, in Latin and vernacular translations, the whole remainder of Greek philosophical literature: The Greek commentaries on Aristotle, Plato and the Neoplatonists, Plutarch and Epictetus, Diogenes Laertius and Sextus Empiricus, to mention but some of the most important and influential sources. Thus resulted a gradual change in the reading material of the student and writer, which left its impact on the literature and thought of the period and even on the Aristotelian school. Due to the general prestige of classical antiquity, ancient and pseudo-ancient quotations and ideas circulated widely and contributed to a body of eclectic philosophical reasoning that is much richer and more diversified in origin and content, though perhaps less organized, than the philosophy of the preceding period. For humanism as such was held together by a common cultural program and ideal, but not by specific philosophical or theological convictions, and a classical training could be combined in each case with a great variety of ideas and of opinions. Outside of Italy, humanism is represented by such great figures as Desiderius Erasmus (1467-1536), Sir Thomas More (1480-1535) and Juan Luis Vives (1492-1540). They are all characterized by strong religious and theological interests and by the tendency to formulate political ideals based on moral standards. Vives is also notable for his attempt to substitute a complete encyclopedia of humanist learning for the traditional body of the medieval arts and sciences (*De tradendis disciplinis*).

In the field of logic, the anti-Aristotelian bias of many humanists led to some characteristic attempts at a reform of the traditional system. The tendency was to simplify logic, and to treat it in close connection with rhetoric. This tendency began with the *Dialectic* of Lorenzo Valla (1407-1457) and found its strongest and most influential spokesman in Peter Ramus (1515-1572) who devised a new system of "natural" logic that taught the methods of discovering arguments and of applying them to the solution of particular problems. Ramus' logic found many followers, and his doctrine became the basis of many courses in logic that were offered in Protestant Germany, in Great Britain, and in early America throughout the seventeenth century.

The humanist view of history was dominated by the conception that learning and eloquence, poetry and the arts, had flourished among the ancient Greeks and Romans but had declined in the successive "Dark Ages," and that it was their own task to revive or to bring back to light those arts and sciences. This view which also underlies the modern term "Renaissance" was applied to the field of philosophy as well. It is against this humanist background that we must understand the revivals and restatements of ancient philosophies that occurred during the Renaissance. Not only Aristotelianism which in its core was a heritage from the Middle Ages was now modified by a new emphasis on the original text and doctrine of Aristotle and of his Greek commentators, as we have seen, but also the other schools of ancient philosophy, which had been neglected during the Middle Ages and for which the source material was now for the first time made available to the West through humanist scholarship, were revived and restated by serious followers. Epicurean ethics was defended by Valla and others, and Democritean physics as transmitted by Epicurus and Lucretius was again taken seriously by Pierre Gassendi (1592-1655) and others, and influenced the conceptions of early modern science. The moral philosophy of the Stoics found prominent defenders in Justus Lipsius (1547-1606) and in Guillaume Du Vair (1556-1621) who prepared the way for a broad Stoic trend in the seventeenth century. Also the position of ancient Scepticism was taken up by a number of thinkers with a humanist background, of whom we may mention especially Montaigne and Francisco Sanchez (1550-1623). All these restatements are not mere repetitions of ancient doctrines, to be sure, but contain some differences of selection and of emphasis as well as significant additions from other ancient or Christian sources and original contributions on the part of the authors. Yet the conscious orientation toward authoritative ancient wisdom is always apparent.

Renaissance Platonism may be considered as one of those revivals of ancient schools of philosophy that occurred in the wake of the humanistic movement. Yet it deserves separate consideration since it had elements and sources different from humanism, and a speculative metaphysical content of its own. It was linked with the theological and mystical traditions of medieval Augustinianism, and not as foreign to the terminology and method of the Aristotelians as its name might suggest. Unlike Aristotelianism and humanism, Platonism had no institutional basis in the universities or schools of the time. It was cultivated at the Platonic Academy of Florence (founded 1462) and in many smaller groups and circles in the sixteenth century; but its appeal was mostly of a more individual and personal nature before it degenerated into a kind of social and literary fashion. Renaissance Platonism began with Georgios Gemistos Plethon (1389-1464) who utilized the teachings of Plato and of ancient Neoplatonism for an allegorical explanation of pagan mythology and for an attempted political reform of the declining Byzantine Empire. The debate between him and his opponents on the differences and the relative merits of Plato and Aristotle was continued by his pupils on Italian soil.

More influential was the work of Marsilio Ficino (1433-1499), leader of the Florentine Academy, and of his circle in which his friend Giovanni Pico della Mirandola (1463-1494) occupied an independent place. Ficino gave to the Western world the first complete Latin translations of the works of Plato and of Plotinus, and accompanied them with extensive commentaries. His *Platonic Theology* provided an authoritative summary of Platonic doctrine in which Plato's own teachings are blended with Neoplatonic, Christian and original elements. The major concern of his philosophy is the contemplative life which he interprets as an inner ascent, through various degrees, of the human intellect and will toward the ultimate vision and enjoyment of God. Since this goal cannot be fully attained during the present life, Ficino is prompted to postulate the immortality of the soul, a doctrine that thus becomes the main theme of his *Platonic Theology*. Drawing upon ancient and Christian theories of love and of friendship and upon the works of Dante and of other Tuscan poets, Ficino linked the spiritual love between two human beings to the inner quest of the soul for God, and coined the term "Platonic love" for this relationship. This "philosophy of love" which he developed in his commentary on Plato's *Symposium* had a wide repercussion in Academic lectures and discussions, in the love poetry of the later Renaissance, and in a long series of treatises on love, which include the *Dialogues on Love* of Leone Ebreo (*c.* 1460-1530). Assigning to the soul the central place in the hierarchy of five substances (God, Angelic Mind, Rational Soul, Quality and Body) and stressing the universal aspirations of man and the ties that link him with things both above and below his own station, Ficino gives a metaphysical setting to the humanist doctrine of human dignity whereas Pico in his famous *Oration* emancipates man completely from the objective hierarchy as a world of his own and bases his dignity on his freedom to choose whatever form of life or existence he may wish to assume. The harmony between Christian theology and Platonic philosophy, which Ficino assumed and in which he included the apocryphal doctrines attributed to Orpheus, Pythagoras and Hermes Trismegistus, was broadened by Pico to include the entire school of Aristotle, the Arabic philosophers, and the Jewish Cabala. Although Ficino defended the superior truth of Christianity, he considered all religions as forms of a religion natural to man and directed toward one true God, and Pico asserted that all religious and philosophical doctrines contain at least some true statements and thus have a share in one universal truth. These ideas imply not only a philosophical justification for the eclecticism of the sixteenth century, but they also contain the seeds of later theories of tolerance and of natural religion.

The greatest thinker of the fifteenth century, Nicolaus Cusanus (1401-1464) defies classification, but may be considered a Platonist. He received some impulses from Italian humanism, but was more deeply indebted to the traditions of German and Dutch mysticism. He conceived God or the absolute maximum as the infinite in which all opposites coincide and which hence cannot be known through ordinary processes of reasoning that apply only to the finite, but must be approached through an indirect and negative method which Cusanus calls "learned ignorance" (this is also the title of his major work). The universe which is created by God consists of particulars each of which is a different manifestation or "contraction" of the one infinite that is their common model or "Idea."

As the sixteenth century went on, the humanist belief in the authority and superiority of the ancients gave way to a rising pride in modern achievements. Encouraged by this trend, the so-called philosophers of nature attempted to replace the natural philosophy of Aristotelianism by new, original constructions. Many of these thinkers made definite contributions to the progress of scientific inquiry in various fields, but at the same time were deeply concerned with the pseudo-sciences of astrology, alchemy and magic and clung to the belief that the world was animated as a whole and pervaded by occult forces and affinities. Theophrastus Paracelsus (1493-1541) was not only an ingenious and successful physician but also the author of a strange philosophical system in which sulphur, mercury and salt constituted the main principles of material reality and which found many followers in Germany, England and other countries. Jerome Cardan (1501-1571), distinguished writer on medicine, mathematics and other subjects and author of an interesting autobiography, eliminated fire from the traditional group of four elements. Francesco Patrizzi (1529-1597), an avowed Platonist in metaphysics, distinguished between mathematical and physical space, and considered space, light, heat and fluidity as the principles of corporeal things. Bernardino Telesio (1508-1588) accepted heat, cold and matter as basic causes of natural events and defined space and time as empty receptacles. His theory that sensation is an attribute of all material things was further developed by Thomas Campanella (1568-1639) who explained all things outside of God through a mixture of Being and Non-being. Long imprisoned for his fantastic political schemes and prophecies, he is best known as the author of the *City of the Sun,* an influential utopia. Giordano Bruno (1548-1600) who after a wandering life through most of Europe was imprisoned and burned by the Inquisition, was the boldest and most ingenious among the Italian philosophers of nature. In his metaphysics which was influenced by Neoplatonism and Cusanus and which may have been known to Spinoza, he described God as an infinite substance of which Matter and Form or Soul are the two basic aspects, and all particular things mere accidents or temporary manifestations. In his natural philosophy which presupposed Lucretius and the Copernican theory he emphasized the spatial infinity of the physical universe, distinguished between the one comprehensive universe and its many worlds or planetary systems and considered the earth merely as one of the many stars, thus anticipating many features of later cosmology.

A special place on the borderline between Renaissance and modern philosophy belongs to Sir Francis Bacon (1561-1626). In his *Novum Organum* he gave a new logic of pure induction, describing a cognitive method that proceeds from properly controlled empirical observations through various degrees of generalization to universal principles which will not only give us a theoretical explanation of phenomena but also increase our power to subject nature to human use. In the *Advancement of Learning* Bacon described the system of the sciences and formulated a program for future progress in the various fields of knowledge, comparing the expected discoveries on the "intellectual globe" to the geographical discoveries of the fifteenth and sixteenth centuries. Bacon did not make any definite contributions to the particular sciences or understand the method of mathematical physics, but he became the prophet of modern science in its purely empirical and technical aspects. His emphasis on useful knowledge that would enlarge the reign of man over nature connects the Renaissance notion of the dignity of man with the social and practical ambitions of modern technology.

The picture of Renaissance thought would not be complete nor could its influence on later developments be understood without some mention of those ideas which appeared in other areas of Renaissance civilization but had a more or less direct bearing on philosophy as well. Among the theological questions discussed as a result of the Protestant and Catholic Reformation, the relation between free will, grace and predestination is of definite philosophical significance. This problem was debated between Luther and Erasmus, and within the Catholic Church, it gave rise to the Molinist and Jansenist controversies. Outside the established churches, antitrinitarianism found significant expression in Michel Servetus (1511-1553). Religious mysticism flourished in the Low Countries far into the fifteenth century, where the so-called *Devotio Moderna* produced the famous *Imitation of Christ* by Thomas à Kempis (1380-1471). In the sixteenth century, Catholic Spain had several noted mystical writers, whereas Protestant Germany had its school of "theosophy" culminating in Jacob Boehme (1575-1624). The religious wars and persecutions stimulated some new thought on the relations between Church and State and on religious tolerance.

The humanistic movement produced not only many treatises on education but also had its repercussions in the theory of history where Jean Bodin (*c*. 1530-1596) developed a cyclical view, and in legal thought where the conceptions of international and of natural law were formulated by Hugo Grotius (1583-1645). Humanistic was also the background of Niccolò Machiavelli (1467-1527) who used examples from ancient history for the discussion of contemporary political problems because he considered human nature to be always the same. His aim is to view the state and political actions not as they should be but as they are, taking the method of a physician for his model. A comparison between his *Prince* and his *Discourses* shows that he did not favor despotic over republican government but that it was his intention to detach the rules of political necessity from those of private morals. Although he did not deny the validity of the latter entirely, the dangers of his theory lie exactly in this separation. His brilliantly written works were hotly debated throughout the sixteenth century and later, and he found successors who modified and partly tempered his views in the theorists of the *raison d'état* and in Thomas Hobbes (1588-1679). On the margin of the humanist movement, we also find a large body of moralistic literature written for the courtier or the man of the world. In the fields of rhetoric and poetics which belonged to the proper domain of the humanists, Aristotle acquired an authority as never before whereas Plato's doctrine of divine madness found occasional defenders. Also the discussions on the relative merits of Latin and vernacular or of various ancient or modern writers were not without general interest. Treatises on music reflected not only the changes that were taking place in musical practice but also the general philosophical currents of the time. Among the visual arts, painting, sculpture and architecture became dissociated from the applied arts and crafts, and the treatises on these arts began to supplement the merely technical instruction with general philosophical considerations. The links which the artistic development of the time had established between architecture and engineering, between sculpture and the geometry of proportion, between painting and perspective as well as anatomy explain the type of the artist who is also a scientist, as most brilliantly embodied in Leonardo da Vinci (1452-1519) whose scattered notebooks contain a large amount of observations and theories relevant to the various natural sciences. In the sciences themselves notable progress was made especially during the sixteenth century. Technology and navigation made advances, and geography profited from the recent journeys and discoveries. Biology and natural history developed largely within the tradition of Aristotelianism, whereas medicine and especially anatomy were furthered by the work of many distinguished physicians, from Andreas Vesalius (1514-1564) to William Harvey (1578-1657). In mathematics, the solution of cubic equations was found, algebraic notation was simplified, and the introduction of the logarithm was not far off. Still more fundamental were the developments in astronomy and physics. Nicolaus Copernicus (1473-1543) formulated the heliocentric theory which was widely debated, Tycho Brahe (1546-1601) added many astronomical observations and discarded the traditional conception of chrystalline spheres, and Johannes Kepler (1571-1630) established his famous laws of planetary motion. William Gilbert (1540-1603) propounded the first modern theory of magnetism. Galileo Galilei (1564-1642) made not only notable contributions to astronomy and formulated some of the fundamental laws of mechanics, but was also of direct importance to philosophy through his description of the methods of the experiment and of the hypothesis, and through his insistence that physics should henceforth be based on mathematical, quantitative analysis. Thus mathematical or experimental physics took the place of the qualitative natural philosophy of the Aristotelians. To understand this new physics in its existence, methods and results, and to put philosophy upon an equally solid foundation—this was the task taken up by Descartes. It marks the end of Renaissance thought and the beginning of a new period in the history of Western philosophy.

In the history of philosophy, the Renaissance was a period of transition and of fermentation rather than of synthesis or of lasting achievement. Yet many of its ideas are of great intrinsic interest, and they gain in importance through the influence which they exercised in many subtle ways upon the later development of European thought. Certainly without a knowledge of the major trends of Renaissance philosophy, the difference, say, between Aquinas and Descartes cannot be fully understood.

BIBLIOGRAPHY

The following primary sources are easily accessible in English translations:

ERASMUS, *Praise of Folly;* TH. MORE, *Utopia;* M. DE MONTAIGNE, *Essays;* TH. CAMPANELLA, *City of the Sun;* F. BACON, *Works.*

The Renaissance Philosophy of Man (PETRARCA, VALLA, FICINO, PICO, POMPONAZZI, VIVES) (Chicago, 1948), ed. by E. Cassirer, P. O. Kristeller and J. H. Randall, Jr.

LEONE EBREO, *The Philosophy of Love,* tr. by F. Friedeberg-Seeley and J. H. Barnes (London, 1937).

J. BODIN, *Method for the Easy Comprehension of History,* tr. by B. Reynolds (New York, 1945).

N. OF CUSA, *The Idiot* (San Francisco, 1940).

LEONARDO DA VINCI, *The Literary Works,* ed. and tr. by J. P. Richter (Oxford, 1939).

A HISTORY OF PHILOSOPHICAL SYSTEMS

G. GALILEI, *Dialogues concerning two new sciences,* tr. by H. Crew and A. de Salvio (Evanston, 1939).

J. BURCKHARDT, *The Civilization of the Renaissance* (London, 1944).

H. O. TAYLOR, *Thought and Expression in the Sixteenth Century* (New York, 1920).

W. K. FERGUSON, *The Renaissance in Historical Thought* (Boston, 1948).

P. O. KRISTELLER and J. H. RANDALL, JR., "The Study of the Philosophies of the Renaissance," *Journal of the History of Ideas,* II (1941), 449-96 (for further bibliography).

G. DE RUGGIERO, *Rinascimento, Riforma e Controriforma* (Storia della filosofia, pt. 3) (Bari, 1937).

F. UEBERWEG, *Grundriss der Geschichte der Philosophie,* III (12th ed., Berlin, 1924).

E. GARIN, *La filosofia* (Milan, 1947).

G. GENTILE, *Il pensiero italiano del rinascimento* (3rd ed., Florence, 1940).

E. CASSIRER, *Individuum und Kosmos in der Philosophie der Renaissance* (Berlin and Leipzig, 1927).

E. RENAN, *Averroès et l'averroïsme* (3rd ed., Paris, 1866).

J. H. RANDALL, JR., "The Development of the Scientific Method in the School of Padua," *Journal of the History of Ideas,* I (1940), 177-206.

CH. E. TRINKAUS, *Adversity's Noblemen: The Italian Humanists on Happiness* (New York, 1940).

W. H. WOODWARD, *Studies in Education during the Age of the Renaissance* (Cambridge, 1906).

N. A. ROBB, *Neoplatonism of the Italian Renaissance* (London, 1935).

E. A. BURTT, *The Metaphysical Foundations of Modern Physical Science* (New York, 1936).

E. W. STRONG, *Procedures and Metaphysics* (Berkeley, 1936).

L. THORNDIKE, *A History of Magic and Experimental Science,* vols III-VI (New York, 1934-41).

CHAPTER NINETEEN

EARLY MODERN RATIONALISM

ALBERT G. RAMSPERGER

BY THE time that René Descartes (1596-1650) was born the new influence of the preceding two centuries had taken effect. The Copernican astronomy had displaced the earth from the center of the universe and Galileo had formulated the laws of mechanics which experiment, not scripture, would confirm. A conflict of ideas and doubts about one's beliefs sometimes lead to scepticism and disillusion but the times were favorable to confidence in the power of human reason and if Descartes makes a show of doubting all that had previously passed for knowledge it is only in order to rebuild it on a firmer foundation of reason.

In the *Discourse on Method* Descartes tells us that of the subjects he had studied in his youth, mathematics pleased him most because in it conclusions were demonstrated with certainty. He was a soldier in his early twenties, and it was probably during one of the quiet interludes between military campaigns, when he had time for reflection, that there came to him an intuitive vision of a new branch of mathematics. We owe to Descartes the analytic geometry by which geometrical figures, laid out upon "Cartesian" coordinates, can be expressed by algebraic equations. For example, the points on a circle of radius r, whose center is at the intersection of perpendicular axes x and y, have a locus determined by the equation: $x^2 + y^2 = r^2$. Might it not be possible, by using the right method, to give to all our knowledge the same certainty that is enjoyed by mathematics and yet not limit it to the meagre structure that has heretofore been built on so excellent a foundation? Descartes devoted his life to carrying out such a program.

The truths of mathematics do not by themselves assure us that anything having the extensional properties of a circle, say, actually exists, and our dreams and illusions warn us that we cannot take it for granted that our senses report to us really existing objects. Do we then know that anything at all exists? Perhaps all that we see is only a dream. But even so, says Descartes, I who think I see, or I who dream, must exist every time I do so, and whenever I try to doubt this, it's as clear and distinct to me as a mathematical demonstration that I reaffirm my existence as a doubting or thinking being—not, be it noted, as a physical body.

In his attempt to doubt all that might be in the least uncertain, Descartes has here found a starting point in establishing what exists and what its true nature is. He has also found a criterion by which to judge the certainty of any proposed affirmation. He will accept as true that, and only that, which is as clear and distinct as the existence of himself, whose essence is thinking. Here we have the principal thesis of all rationalism: the "natural light" of reason, or rational intuition, distinguishes the true from the false and if we can build a structure of knowledge in which every step is such that we cannot think it otherwise, we are in no danger of falling into error, provided our memory of the earlier steps is not faulty.

There is some question as to just how Descartes understood his basic truth, "I think, therefore I am." Descartes retained the scholastic conceptions of substance and essence. Consequently, although thinking was essential to his being, a particular thought or act of thought was not all that he was; the thought was but an attribute which belonged to himself, the thinking substance, who might also have other thoughts. This point is worth noting, for some critics of Descartes would maintain that though any instance of doubt or of thought is *ipso facto* proof that something exists, it does not follow that this proves the existence of the mind or soul to which this thought along with others belongs.

Having satisfied himself of his own existence as a thinking substance Descartes inquires how he, an imperfect being, could think of a being more perfect than himself. It was intuitively evident to Descartes that for anything to exist, though it be only an idea, there must be a cause whose reality and perfection is at least as great as the effect. The greater cannot proceed from the less. It follows that there must exist a being whose actual perfection is no less than that of Descartes' idea of perfection—in a word, God exists.

Descartes also accepts as valid a famous argument, previously used by Anselm and others. The so-called ontological argument runs as follows. Just as it is in the very nature and meaning of a triangle that the sum of its angles must equal two right angles, so there is implied in the idea of a supremely perfect being that such a being must exist, for it would be an imperfection to lack existence. Or again, as Descartes says, I can conceive a mountain only by also conceiving a valley, though I need not conceive that either actually exists. But the idea of a perfect being constrains me to think that such a being exists as necessarily as the idea of a mountain constrains me to think of a valley.

The important point in these two arguments for the existence of God is that existence is deduced purely from a consideration of certain ideas. In the first, it is argued that there is such a measure of reality in the idea of a perfect being that it calls for an actually existing perfect cause of that idea. In the second, the very meaning of "supremely perfect being" is asserted to include existence. This is a typical example of the rationalist's confidence in the power of the intellect: pure reason can find in its clear and distinct ideas the grounds for asserting what exists beyond those ideas and beyond the thinker who has them.

Having proved the existence of a perfect God whence all his powers derive, Descartes believes he has assurance that no malevolent demon could deceive him into thinking that something which he clearly and distinctly perceives, is true if in fact it is false. It should be noted in this connection that if the natural light of reason is not its own guarantee of truth, but depends for its reliability upon God, then Descartes' argument can be charged with circularity, for the existence of God was itself established only by employing that same principle of rational clearness and distinctness which God is now called upon to validate.

Only after he has proved the existence of himself as a thinking substance, and the existence of God, can Descartes proceed to a proof of a material world. He finds that in addition to those ideas and truths which are innate and which constitute the essence of his mind, there are others, such as those of color, or hunger, or external shapes—adventitious ideas he calls them—which come to his mind from some other source. Now it could be that the cause of these ideas in no way resembles them and that he is completely deceived as to the nature of the object whence they seem to come. In fact, supposing there are material bodies, of which his own body with its sense organs is one, the ideas resulting from the interaction of the body with the mind would vary with the conditions of the sense organs and not correctly represent external objects. When it is now asked, however, whether there is anything which is essential to the existence of matter, that is, some character without which matter would not exist at all, Descartes' natural light of reason tells him that extension is such a character and if God had made him so that he would be deceived in this, then God would be a deceiver. Since this would be contrary to the nature of a perfect being, it is certain that matter, whose sole essence is extension, exists. Where there is extension there is matter; nature is a plenum differentiated into parts by motions. Since the moments of time are discrete, Descartes believes that God must re-create the world from moment to moment, giving to the parts that succession of locations which we call the laws of mechanics.

We have here the pattern for much of the later development of physical science. Given a certain arrangement of matter expressible in mathematical terms, and the laws of motion, we have all that is necessary to make a world and to determine by mathematical calculation all that will happen there. Even living things, in so far as they are bodies without minds or souls, are mere mechanical automata and Descartes believed that all earthly creatures except man are but complicated machines. Whatever objections may be brought against such a view, it had the merit of leading physicians to understand the processes in the body as instances of physical laws, not as the working of hidden powers, and rapid advances in the physical sciences in the 17th and 18th centuries testify to the fruitfulness of interpreting the world in mathematical terms and explaining its changes by mechanical laws rather than by qualitative powers or final causes.

From a philosophical standpoint Descartes must be credited—if credit it be—with setting many of the problems with which later philosophers had to struggle. If man is a combination of two distinct kinds of substance, matter and mind, how can they influence one another? Can a series of motions terminating in the brain produce ideas in the unextended mind, which Descartes thought to be located at a point in the pineal gland? And even if one were to grant that there are innate ideas and intuited truths which are certain, is it not questionable whether these other ideas coming into the mind from an external source could yield knowledge having the same kind of certainty as a demonstration in mathematics? Descartes himself recognizes that these ideas which involve the action of the bodily senses are confused. As materials for the imagination to which a will, unchecked by reason, may give assent, they lead to error. But is our knowledge of nature then limited to the general principles of geometry and mechanics? Knowledge of the actual state of the material world in its particular parts and motions seemed to depend upon the interaction of body and mind and how that could take place or yield true ideas could not be explained.

The Dutch philosopher Geulincx (1625-1669) tried to solve the difficulties of this metaphysical dualism by modifying Descartes' position on the relationship between matter and mind. Instead of supposing that motions can cause ideas or that the will can cause motions in matter, it is supposed that God has so ordered the sequence of ideas in the mind that the corresponding states of matter are not the causes of the ideas but only the occasions for the occurrence of the ideas. The causality, therefore, really resides in God. Following this suggestion Nicole Malebranche (1638-1715) maintains that we do not know bodies; rather we know the ideas of bodies in God.

One might say, paradoxically, that no man has ever been committed more passionately to the life of reason than Benedict Spinoza (1632-1677). He was excommunicated from his own Jewish community in Amsterdam because his intellectual integrity would not permit him to recant his heretical views. He rejected a teaching post that might distract him from his studies, and chose instead to eke out a bare existence as a grinder of optical lenses while he devoted himself to philosophy.

In his most famous work, the *Ethics,* Spinoza starts with a set of definitions and axioms, as though he were presenting a system of geometry. The propositions of his philosophical system are then set forth as deductions from the definitions and axioms. Having defined God as a substance of infinite attributes, he is then able to prove that there must be one and only one such substance, that matter and mind are merely two of the attributes that express the nature of this substance, and that a particular man is a mode or part of

God manifesting himself in a series of thoughts, that is, as a thinking being, and as a succession of bodily states, that is, as an extended or material being. In place of the Cartesian conception of minds, bodies, and God as distinct substances, Spinoza's God constitutes all that there is. If one possessed an adequate and also a complete conception of God—something which is in fact impossible for a finite being—one could deduce everything that the world contains, whether it be the system of ideas that is unfolded in that deduction or the bodies which are the objects of those ideas. God and nature are ultimately one and the same. All truths follow necessarily from the nature of God as a thinking being, but approached from the standpoint of God as an extended being it is equally true that one state of the universe as a complex arrangement of bodies follows from another by necessary laws. "The order and connection of ideas is the same as the order and connection of things."

From these assumptions it follows that man's actions, like everything else in the universe, are completely determined, and the belief that we are free arises only from ignorance of the causes of the desires that motivate us. When we judge something to be good and others bad, or when we praise or blame men for what they do, we imply that circumstances might have been otherwise and that men could have acted differently. Our loves and our hates are directed to the persons whom we imagine to be the free causes of our joys and our sorrows. All good and evil is relative to our human standards. Things come to be good because we desire them; they are not desired because they are intrinsically good. To the extent that our reason can disclose that the causes of what befalls us flow inevitably from the nature of God, we cease to be in bondage to our passions, for to understand is to accept, and in that acceptance there is no longer any hatred or fear.

Spinoza defines an adequate idea as one which, in so far as it is considered in itself without reference to the object, has all the properties or internal signs of a true idea. This means that a clear idea is its own guarantee of truth and whether there is or is not an existing thing which is the object of a given adequate idea, is to be found in the idea itself, which will either involve the existence of the object or logically exclude it as impossible.

It must be remembered that ideas are not, according to Spinoza, caused by the body even though a bodily state corresponds to every idea. The ideas which we call sense perceptions and images are liable to error because, just as a body affected by other bodies is not expressing either its own nature or that of the affecting body but a combination of the two, so the images which constitute the corresponding mind are wanting in the distinct ideas required to exclude or to establish the existence of the purported object. Yet, as finite and limited modes, we must proceed from where and what we are. We cannot approach the world from the standpoint of God, who is at once the total system of ideas that expresses the eternal truth about reality and who at the same time is the whole system of nature embracing space and time, as though the structure of cause and effect were a timeless, infinite series of logical antecedent and consequent. We must proceed from the parts to the whole. As bodies we are particular modes, created according to the laws of nature, and successively affected in many ways; as minds we must proceed by adding to each idea the idea of its cause, fit them into a wider context, which is to say "refer them to God." Thus we may have some glimpse of the "total face of the universe" *sub specie aeternitatis*. It will still be God as a system of modes, not God as infinite substance, but it is enough to inspire that intellectual love of God which comes only from this joyous realization that in the life of knowledge God himself is expressing one facet of his nature. To be able to identify himself with this, is for Spinoza not only preferable to any worldly good; it is preferable to the traditional immortality conceived as the endless existence of the human person, enjoying the favor of God.

It is interesting to compare some of the views of Descartes and Spinoza with those of their English contemporary Thomas Hobbes (1588-1679). Though Hobbes was forty-four when Spinoza was born, his productive years were after the age of fifty, and he outlived Spinoza by two years.

Hobbes was a materialist. In a set of objections to Descartes' *Meditations* he argued that thought is an action of bodies and that the only action of bodies is motion. Now since human beings, or a society of human beings—the "body politic"—are but groupings of bodies it should be possible from a knowledge of the basic properties of these organized bodies to deduce the laws of human behavior and of societies just as the laws of inanimate bodies are deduced from the definitions of space, time, force, and power. The

A HISTORY OF PHILOSOPHICAL SYSTEMS

desire for self preservation is the basic trait that characterizes all men. In his original state of nature each man must fight against every other to survive and to satisfy his needs. He departs from that state only because there is more peace and security if he gives up his natural right to fight his own way, provided others will give up theirs. A social order therefore arises as a contract in which absolute power is delegated to a sovereign. Henceforth any rebellion against the decrees of the monarch is a breach of the social contract, and calls for whatever measures the monarch decides to take to protect his subjects from a return to a state of nature.

By maintaining a complete determinism which has no room for free will, Hobbes agrees with Spinoza and disagrees with Descartes. Desires are but "accidents" of bodies and good and evil are therefore relative to the individual. Spinoza found a rational basis for altruism in his metaphysical doctrine that man is only a mode whose welfare depends upon his relationship to other men and ultimately upon finding his place in the total scheme of things which is God. Since, for Hobbes, each body is a separate substance, pity for another comes of imagining one's self in another's shoes. Obedience to the laws of the state promulgated by the sovereign, may come to be regarded as though such conformity were a good in itself, but its rational basis lies in the interest of the individual in maintaining the social contract.

Gottfried Wilhelm Leibniz (1646-1716) was the brilliant son of a Professor of Philosophy at Leipzig. Among the learned men of his time whom he met on visits to France, England and Holland were Malebranche, Arnauld, Boyle, Huygens, and Spinoza. He learned much from Spinoza, and borrowed a manuscript copy of the *Ethics* only to denounce Spinoza's philosophy later because it denied personal immortality and taught that everything follows necessarily from the nature of God, not from his will.

Like most rationalists Leibniz put a high value upon mathematics. His original contribution in this field was the invention of the infinitesimal calculus. The fact that Newton worked it out quite independently at about the same time illustrates the fact that important advances are likely to occur when the intellectual climate is propitious and the stage of scientific knowledge calls for them.

Leibniz's positive conclusion that reality consists of spiritual substances is better understood when one understands why he denies that extension can be the essential attribute of substance. Anything extended is made up of parts, but if it is real, its reality cannot depend on the accidental fact of being composed or collected in a certain way. It is the elements that must be the real substances. Seeking these elements by division we must fail to find them precisely in so far as a thing still has extension and is therefore merely an aggregate. Leibniz concludes a real substance must have real properties or predicates other than extension. Substances, then, are unextended subjects characterized and individuated by predicates. The best example would be a soul such as ourselves, our perceptions being the predicates that make us what we are.

Leibniz calls these spiritual substances monads and the universe consists of an infinite number of them, distinguished from one another, not by being at different places, but by having different perceptions. Since space is itself only a pattern of perceptions, monads cannot be in space. It follows that there is no "outside" to any monad; each monad is a world to itself and it can in no way interact with or be influenced by any other monad.

There is a metaphysical sense in which we can say that a tree that we see is made up of monads or that we see and speak to a friend. Corresponding to each discriminable element in our perceptions there is a monad whose own perceptions differ from ours as they would if there really were a spatial world viewed from the perspective of that monad. Thus it is not altogether false to speak of our perceptions as though we were perceiving other substances. We find in ourselves the evidence of what other monads are, which is to say, what they perceive "from their point of view." The physical world is only a multiplicity of phenomena, yet these are "well founded" for they are objective in two senses: (1) they correspond to a multiplicity of metaphysical substances or monads, whose perceptions repeat, in a way appropriate to the "position" of each monad, the perceptions of every other monad and (2) the laws of order and relationship among phenomena are the same for every monad. While no monad causes any change in any other, Leibniz believed that every one is so created from the start that by a "pre-established harmony" what is passive in it corresponds to, and in that sense is explained by, what is active in other monads.

Instead of conceiving the constituents of nature as extended atoms, we come closer to the truth if we conceive them as points of force manifesting their reality as activity; for example, as kinetic energy or as resistance to penetration. There are all grades of monads from the barest ones that compose inanimate things to those whose perceptions are clearest. These "high grade" monads are souls. The soul of a human being is the dominant monad of the group that composes his body and unlike the inferior monads acts purposively.

Despite his view that God has created each monad so that in the concept of that individual is contained everything that will ever happen to it, Leibniz tries, not very convincingly, to find a place for freedom by distinguishing between necessitation and God's foreknowledge. We are free to do as we choose but God knows that we shall choose in conformity with our pre-established nature and with the place we must fill in the best of all possible worlds.

Leibniz's logic is the counterpart of his metaphysics. Everything can be stated in propositions of the subject-predicate form since there are no real relations between subjects, and all true propositions are analytic, that is, every predicate is contained in the meaning of the subject. There are, however, two considerations which stand in the way of deducing *a priori* all that exists. God was not *logically* necessitated to create a world with just these monads. Secondly, we do not possess such a complete concept of any existing monad (ourselves, or correlatively any other monad) that we can see *a priori* all that it contains. Consequently we must distinguish between two kinds of truths: (1) necessary truths of reason whose denial would involve a contradiction and which must therefore hold in any possible world and (2) contingent truths of fact whose subject is not defined so as to imply either its existence or the predicates which are in fact asserted of it. So far as purely logical meaning is concerned, a contingent truth might have been false. There must, however, be a sufficient reason for its truth. This is to be found in the sequence of efficient causes that account for a thing being as it is rather than otherwise. Ultimately the sufficient reason lies in God who willed that, out of all the logically possible worlds, this particular one should exist.

It is not easy to reconcile this conception of God freely willing the actual world from consideration of what is best, with the view, also expressed by Leibniz, that the actual world is that one which realizes the maximum possible reality. This leaves to God no alternative but to create an infinite number of monads differing from one another by infinitesimal steps so that together they achieve the maximum reality that is logically compossible. Do, then, all truths become for God necessary truths, and does the principle of sufficient reason merge with the principle of non-contradiction?

When we survey this movement of thought from Descartes to Leibniz we find that it fails in its principal aim, namely, to show that reason can, at least in principle, establish with certainty the nature of existence. Descartes, Spinoza, and Leibniz all rely upon the ontological argument to prove the existence of God. The fallaciousness of this and other arguments for God's existence was later to be shown by Kant. Nor can reason by itself, with or without assuming the existence of God, give us knowledge of nature. Descartes seemed to think (erroneously) that the laws of mechanics are among the truths intuited by the natural light, yet for knowledge of the behavior of matter he must turn to experiment and to the "adventitious" ideas which matter, according to his dualistic view, conveys to the mind by the senses. On Spinoza's general principles everything follows rationally and necessarily from the nature of God, yet human beings, as he notes, come to know more of God as they know more of particular bodies and the causes that relate mode to mode. Leibniz's metaphysics and logic should have made him as much a rationalistic determinist as Spinoza, yet he is aware of the difference between knowledge of logically necessary truths and knowledge of fact. Unfortunately he does not use the distinction to advocate the need for empirical enquiry and experiment but to make room for free will.

Perhaps it is not unfair to say that the rationalists generally assumed that the cause and effect connection between existing things and events is the same as the logically necessary connection between premises and conclusion. Consequently they thought that only a lack of clarity and adequacy in our ideas stands in the way of demonstrating with certainty what must be true of the world. It remained for the empiricists, and especially David Hume, to disclose the weakness of that assumption.

A HISTORY OF PHILOSOPHICAL SYSTEMS

BIBLIOGRAPHY

English translations of Descartes

The Philosophical Works of Descartes, 2 vols. Trans. by E. S. Haldane and G. R. T. Ross (Cambridge, 1911).
Descartes: Selections, ed. by R. M. Eaton (New York, 1927).

Commentaries on Descartes

A. B. GIBSON, *The Philosophy of Descartes* (London, 1932).
S. V. KEELING, *Descartes* (Boston, 1934).
KUNO FISCHER, *Descartes and His School* (New York, 1887).

English translations of Spinoza

Spinoza: Selections, ed. by John Wild (New York, 1930).
Spinoza: Writings on Political Philosophy, ed. by B. A. G. Balz (New York, 1937).
The Correspondence of Spinoza, ed. by A. Wolf (New York, 1927).

Commentaries on Spinoza

H. H. JOACHIM, *A Study of the Ethics of Spinoza* (Oxford, 1901).
JOSEPH RATNER, *Spinoza on God* (New York, 1930).
LEON ROTH, *Spinoza* (Boston, 1929).
H. A. WOLFSON, *The Philosophy of Spinoza*, 2 vols. (Cambridge, Mass., 1934).

English translations of Leibniz

Leibniz: Discourse on Metaphysics. Trans. by G. R. Montgomery (Chicago, 1902).
The Philosophical Writings of Leibniz. Trans. by Mary Morris (New York, 1934).
Leibniz: New Essays. Trans. by A. G. Langley (New York, 1896).
Leibniz: The Monadology and other Philosophical Writings. Trans. by R. Latta (New York, 1898).

Commentaries on Leibniz

H. W. CARR, *Leibniz* (Boston, 1929).
BERTRAND RUSSELL, *A Critical Exposition of The Philosophy of Leibniz* (Cambridge, 1900).

A HISTORY OF PHILOSOPHICAL SYSTEMS

On Hobbes

Leslie Stephen, *Hobbes* (New York and London, 1904).
John Laird, *Hobbes* (London, 1934).

General

S. H. Mellone, *The Dawn of Modern Thought* (London, 1930).

CHAPTER TWENTY

EARLY MODERN EMPIRICISM

DOUGLAS N. MORGAN

I

EARLY MODERN empiricism was early in date, modern in inspiration and context, and progressively empirical in tone and temper. It developed out of the quixotic philosophy of the science of Francis Bacon (1561-1626), through the probing critical analysis of Locke (1632-1704), Berkeley (1685-1753), and Hume (1711-1776), to the transcendental criticism of Kant (1724-1804). No pair of centuries in the history of human thought has taught us more of what man can know and how he can know it.

Bacon had seen something of what physical science could do, and boldly dreamed that all men's knowledge might make similar progress, if only his curiously deductive induction be followed as a method. We who know are real, and the things we know are real, Bacon taught. "Experience" is the only medium through which we may know things; and if we are to know *things, facts,* instead of merely finding echoes of ourselves in things, we must first cleanse our knowing minds of all illusions. Then sense will be able to transmit undistorted images to the mind, and perfect, boundless, certain knowledge will be achieved. Then only can man claim empire over the forces of nature. Physics was to Bacon's dream what mathematics was to Descartes' (1596-1650): a model for true and usable knowledge about man and his world.

Locke, also practically motivated, set out to ascertain the origin of our ideas, to determine the evidence, test the certainty, and survey the boundaries of human knowledge. He proposed to do this not by looking to the apparently limitless things which man may know, but rather by inspecting the knowing process itself, asking what kinds of truths it could capture and certify. He saw that the knowing process, the "understanding," can itself be understood only in terms of its possible objects. So he inquired into the nature of the things we know, and of the language in which we phrase our knowledge.

Berkeley, motivated by a theology, as well as by an independent interest in philosophical analysis, set out on a double task, one metaphysical and the other critical: to refute atheism by disproving the materialism which underlay it, and honestly and thoroughly to examine the implications of our thinking about substances and sciences and selves.

Hume, motivated by a moral interest [1] and a tenacious theoretical curiosity, philosophized not primarily to help people avoid mistakes in political affairs, but rather mainly to help people understand what they are doing in matters scientific, religious, ethical and philosophical. With Locke, he *criticized,* applying empirical calipers to men's problems, seeking to distinguish the true from the false. With Locke, he investigated the psycho-genetic origins of our ideas. But most characteristically, he did not ask with Locke "What *is* the object we know?" but rather "What do we *mean* by 'object'? 'Know'? What do we mean by 'we'?"

To make clear how these changes in the history of thought took place, suppose we put ourselves back into the mid-seventeenth century, and think together through certain of the central issues. Let us note, as we think, the continuous development of our prevailing empirical method, as well as the important shifts in emphasis within that method.

II

The immediate impetus which stimulates our philosophical thought is the impact of the wealth of new scientific knowledge, demanding both explanation and explication. Why do we so confidently accept its evidence? What does this confidence imply, with respect to the rest of our knowledge? More fundamentally, how can these earlier questions be asked or answered until we have found the source of our own knowledge, assayed it, and frankly admitted the limitations of our understanding?

Either we know what we know through having learned it in this life, or our knowledge is implanted deep within our minds at birth, or we bring our knowledge with us in some sort of subconscious portmanteau, "trailing clouds of glory from God who is our home," as a poet will put it a couple of centuries hence. Well and good for poets; but philosophers have seriously maintained such strange notions too. Plato, for example. And, more recently and less confidently, Descartes. What, we ask, is the evidence for or against the existence of these so-called "innate ideas"? What are the facts of the case? In this demand to be "shown," we have confessed our empiricism.

It seems likely that if we really did bring knowledge with us into this life at birth, babies and children should be wiser than men of experience. The facts show that this is not the case. We have thus some evidence against the ancient doctrine of recollection. Savages whose minds are not cluttered up with the impedimenta of civilization should know more truths, and more clearly, than do their civilized brethren; but they do not. More evidence against the doctrine. There is no universal agreement on ideas, even on the laws of logic, and even if there were such agreement, this would not prove innateness. To say that savages and babies and ignorant men have in their minds ideas of which they are not conscious, seems self-contradictory, as if one were to assert an understanding of that of which there is no understanding. Either the ideas are in the savage's mind, or they are not. If he is unconscious of them, it makes no serious sense to speak of the ideas as "in his mind." If he is conscious of them, he has learned them through his senses.

True, we may not yet strictly have disproved the notion of innate ideas. By ingenious patchwork, it can still be made to serve. But to what end? In the light of the evidence at hand, we have concluded that it is more probable that what man knows in truth and morals, he learns here in this life upon this earth, than that he imports his knowledge from some never-never land beyond.

Now, we ask, what is the nature of this learning? It includes *sensation* and *reflection*: seeing, hearing, touching, tasting, smelling things, and introspecting events in our own minds. Until we have sensations, our minds are blank. We grow in knowledge only by comparing, combining and separating these elements of experience. Even the most powerful mind among us can invent no single, simple new idea. What then are the "things outside" which we know, and of which we have these sensations? Here we pause.

A HISTORY OF PHILOSOPHICAL SYSTEMS

The traditional answer comes easily, for the centuries-old categories are hard to forget. A thing is a substance, in which qualities inhere. Some of these qualities are essential, some are accidental. This is what we were taught in school. It is the language of Aristotle and Aquinas. Will it serve us now? Well, once again, what is the evidence? What are the observable facts in the case?

The best evidence is the things themselves and our experiences of them, how the apple looks, feels, tastes. We find that we need a critical distinction between the two sides of this knowing-relationship. Is the redness of the apple we see a *quality* of the apple out there, or is the redness an *idea* in our minds, aroused by such a quality? We find no ground in experience for justifying a belief that quality and idea resemble each other at all; "most of the ideas of sensation being in the mind no more the likeness of something existing without us than the names that stand for them are the likeness of our ideas." [2] Indeed, what kind of an experience would it be that would allow us to compare an idea with a quality? . . . for, quite apparently, once the quality enters the mind for comparison, it becomes an idea.

Nevertheless, we do speak of the apple's having "qualities," meaning now its power of arousing sensation-ideas in our minds. And we may look, among the apple's qualities, for those which "really belong" to the apple in order to distinguish them from those qualities which are merely "adventitious." We see that the apple's color will not look the same under a microscope as it does to the naked eye, and we ask which of these two perceptions, equally "empirical," is to receive preference. Experience does not seem to be able to answer the question; perhaps the proper answer is that neither is to be preferred, and that the apple "out there" has no color, but merely has the power, under certain conditions, of arousing color-ideas "in here." But how large is the apple? It actually looks smaller, makes a smaller image on the retina of your eye, when it rests on the table in the far corner of the room, than it does when we hold it in our hand. Is the apple really the size it appears to us when we hold it and measure it with a rule? As tiny as it must appear to an elephant? Or as enormous as it must appear to a flea?

These are, for a time, perplexing notions. For we have set ourselves to answer them in terms of *experience,* and yet experience seems to give such contradictory answers. The problem is easier for those who still hold the traditional metaphysics of substance; or at least it appears easier, and indeed it *is* easier to give a verbal answer. The apple is a substance, in which inhere essential qualities. The various discordant experiences are merely accidents of seeing the real, constant apple under different conditions. The layman's language, even today, carries the subject-predicate grammar inherited from Aristotle. This fact of verbal history may be one reason why these problems continue to perplex introductory philosophy students, much as they did Locke, Berkeley, and Hume.

"Very well, if the apple is a substance, show it to us," we demand. "These experienced qualities, the flavor, the color, the odor and feel, these we observe. But they are admitted, as *experiences*, to be events in men's minds. What we wish to find is the substantial *object* of these experiences, the thing-out-there which we are experiencing when we taste and smell and feel the apple."

And if we have the courage of our empiricism, we gradually relinquish our hold on the substance-beneath-the-qualities. Slowly, at first, for the old habits of thought, the old language, are so deeply ingrained in our heritage. We first try to bring back an ancient distinction. We see that, with respect to at least some of the qualities, no one can empirically claim any more "out-thereness" than the power to produce sense-ideas: color, taste, odor. These experiences too obviously vary from man to man, from time to time, from place to place. They simply cannot, on the evidence, be an essential part of the apple. Qualities like shape and size and hardness, on the other hand, seem to be somehow different. Certainly the apple has the same shape for all men, the same basic size (it fills up just as much space), is equally hard or soft. Suppose we set aside these latter qualities (with some others, like them, amenable to qualification) and call them "primary." These, and these alone, we shall for the time being consider to inhere in the apple-out-there. The taste, the color, the odor, and some others, we shall call "secondary" and locate in the perceiving mind.

Let us note in passing that all of these existents revealed in our experience are distinguishables, particular individuals. We see and taste this apple here and now; never do we taste its essence, species or genus. Never, likewise, do we positively and uniquely know any such independent "things" as time or space or will or friendship;

these are but various ways in which simple ideas combine together, named by abstract terms.

So far, so good. We are on the road to becoming empiricists. But we cannot help asking the next natural question: "What is the stuff in which the primary qualities are said to inhere? What is substance?" At first, we give what seems to us an empirical answer: "Substance" means "that which stands beneath," and we call "substances" combinations of simple idea-qualities, considered as united in one thing. But we cannot honestly let it go at that. *What* is considered to stand beneath, and *how*? We may abandon this investigation for a while, calling the pesky substance simply a "something I know not what." Meanwhile, we are confident that all we can and do know about substances is in terms of their qualities revealed as ideas in experience. We can perceive connections and disconnections, agreements and disagreements among our ideas. We can predict and generalize on the basis of ideas in experience to more or less probably true conclusions. But *we can know no more than this,* and we need know no more. Presumably (we still feel) there is some necessary structure to our world, some set of natural and inevitable connections among things and events beneath the level of experience. As empiricists, however, we are willing forever to relinquish any hope of knowing this world beyond.[3]

But our philosophical curiosity will not let us rest. Doggedly but not dogmatically we return to our problem. Philosophers call it "matter," meaning by the term an extended, non-mental stuff that underlies the qualities which we perceive. "What *is* matter?" we ask again. "Show us some."

And here we move one more great step toward empirical clarity. We discover, to our naive surprise, that nobody can show us any. Everybody talks about a real physical matter which exists "out there" but nobody has ever seen any or touched any. The easy, lazy way out is to say that the stuff is there even though nobody has ever seen any (or ever possibly could see any); and to argue that it must be out there because otherwise how could we perceive the qualities which we do perceive? After all, the traditionalists were almost arguing, we do have a word "substance"; there must therefore be something of the sort somewhere, even though we can't find any. We must *postulate* the existence of material substance, to explain our sense experience.

"Must we?" we ask. "Why?" And then we realize that the only empirical basis anybody ever had for asserting the existence of material substance was sensation itself, the very basis of experience on which we are trying to construct our explanation of human knowledge. We cannot seriously understand what a sensation-source would be like, if it could not itself be sensed. Colors are like colors, sounds like sounds. How can the non-sensible be like the sensible without being nonsensical as well?

Heat, sweet, sound and color are all alike mental in kind. But exactly the same considerations which define these as sensible-quality ideas perceived by minds bear equally strongly against the so-called primary qualities: size and shape are similarly relative, varying, and mind-dependent. We conclude, therefore, that the things we know simply are the ideas we perceive; they do not lurk in some unknown matter.

We would not be able to recognize this mysterious material substance if we were to find any, and the postulation of it helps no whit in our understanding of human knowledge. True enough, sensations come to us whether we will or no; they are not mere mental inventions on our part. But since they are, primary and secondary qualities alike, passive and mental (or "immaterial") in nature, and since we ourselves are active minds (or "spirits"), have we not here adequate reason for concluding the existence of an active super-mind who supplies us so regularly with our sense-ideas? And why not call this super-mind God?

We have taken our earlier distinction between sensation-idea in our mind and quality in the thing known, faced our problem of "resemblance" and solved it boldly by denying the distinction, by identifying the very "thing out there" with the ideas in our minds. Having come this far along the empirical road, we may not rest.[4] Thinking anew, asking afresh, we dig again for the roots of our knowledge. Sensations? Yes, new ones and remembered ones, internal ones and external ones, simple ones and complex ones. Knowledge? Yes, relations among ideas in our minds—as in mathematics —and relations which depend on the content of the ideas related, as when we describe matters of scientific fact. Such relations as resemblance, contrariety, degrees in quality, and proportions in quantity alone can give certainty; those of identity, space, time, and causality, yield no more than likelihood or probability. The former group characterizes mathematics, the latter the physical sciences. And among the "uncertain" relations, identity, space and time are given in almost instantaneous perceptions . . . hardly worthy of the name of scientific reasoning. Causality alone will merit extended analysis.

In one bold stroke, we see that *any* claimant for the title of knowledge must be able to show its credentials. It must answer either: "I relate these ideas, and describe no facts'.' or else "I am grounded in these sensations, and describe these facts." In the former case, we have certainty at the expense of content; in the latter we have content at the expense of certainty. And there is no middle ground; any statement which cannot show its credentials is an impostor. If some dearly cherished metaphysical beliefs are thereby shown to be impostors, so much the worse for them. An honest man who seeks seriously for knowledge accepts no substitutes.

And now we put the crucial semantic and philosophical questions: Can we ultimately justify human knowledge in terms of experience? What do we mean by the central terms in our statements asserting matters of fact? What, for example, do we mean by asserting "*I* know that this *object caused* that *object* to move?"

What does *object* mean? Substance? Well, what sensation gave rise to it? How, in our reflection, do we find any substance? Surely we do not see or hear substances, nor do we find them among our emotive or voluntary ideas. Whence, then, comes the notion of *object*? We return to the facts. We find our sensations grouping themselves together. We blink our eyes as we read this page. We find sensations *after* blinking much like those *before* blinking. Our mind jumps the gap. We assume that if we had not blinked we would have had continuously similar experiences. In our pre-empirical days, we used to explain this by saying that the same real page endured through the blinking. We may still, if we like, say this . . . but now we know what we *mean* by saying so, in empirical terms. "The same real page" is explained empirically: by continuity and coherence of similar sensations, we are led to expect their continuance.

We have found the idea of *causality* to be central to the sciences, to any description of matters of fact. What do statements affirming causal sequences *mean*? How do we justify reasoning based on them? Surely we cannot explain causality in terms of the sensed qualities alone, for whichever of these qualities we pitch on, we find some object that is not possessed of it, and yet falls under the denomination of cause and effect.[5]

How are things causally related then, in experience? Quite simply, they occur together, side by side, or one follows another, over and over again. Push the button, the bell rings. Do it again. And again. You do not see or hear or feel the *causing*, yet you believe that the pushing *causes* the ringing. The fact of repetition does not ground the cause "out there." All it does is build up an associative habit "in here," so that we psychologically *expect* the next consequent sensation-set, given the antecedent sensation-set. We have found no empirical ground for our belief in a "necessary connection out there," so we explain instead how we came to such a curious belief. Not that we have found out a single new fact about nature by our analysis, but we have, for the first time, figured out what causality comes to, empirically, and given some explanation of how the idea develops in our mind. Soon we realize that no predictive inference made on the basis of causal observations can claim any more universal necessity than our own psychological expectations can guarantee . . . which is, quite strictly, none at all. "Objects have no discoverable connexion together; nor is it from any other principle but custom operating upon the imagination, that we can draw any inference from the appearance of one to the existence of the other." [6] Our criticism is cutting deep. Induction is believed, and will continue to be believed. But, unless we obviously beg the question, we as empiricists can find *no* empirical justification for induction. We must admit by the force of our own logic that no strictly empirical evidence will alone make any prediction even the slightest degree more probable than any other, let alone warrant it as certain.

Finally we face one of the most difficult problems of all. We ask for the meaning of the term "self," for the nature of our *selves* who have come thus far along the empirical highway. Who are we? As empiricists, we look for ourselves in experience, "turn our eyes inwards." What do we find? Selves independent of sensation, which are doing the experiencing? Strip away all sensations; try to catch yourself naked and unaware. Is this not impossible? Try as you will, are you not invariably confronted by some experience?

Then we are ready for the final step in our analysis: let us admit that, empirically, we *are* the experiences we say we "have." We are not unexperienceable somewhats which somehow undergo these experiences. We hold fast to our facts and know ourselves frankly for what we are: bundles of constantly moving perceptions.

III

These thoughts of ours, fully formulated by the middle of the 18th century, have remained central in our philosophical tradition ever since. Far behind them lay the dogmatic materialism of Leucippus and Lucretius, the theologized empiricism of the Middle Ages, the naivete of Francis Bacon. Ahead lies the cold criticism of the Kantians.

If this development were merely (as some have thought) a case of men changing their minds about some fuzzy philosophic notions of little intrinsic importance, the world would not have stirred. But it did stir, because it met new intellectual problems which demanded not merely the doffing of one old idea and the donning of a new one. Whole, bold, thoroughgoing new conceptions of what human knowledge is and how it works—these were called for, and supplied. New kinds of questions had to be asked and answered. Philosophy moved, in a century and a half, from Bacon's "How can we make all knowledge scientific?" through Locke's and Berkeley's "On what basis does scientific knowledge depend?" to Hume's "What is the nature, and what are the conditions, of knowledge itself?"

How rich and simple is this old idea that knowledge must be grounded in human experience, that man knows his world not by tracing its reflection in an axiomatic mental mirror, but by experiencing, and relating experiences! Yet it seems to take generations of genius to explore such a fertile idea, to apply it thoroughly and rigorously, to trace out its implications, and to shatter the noble, persistent illusion of "finding" a necessary logical order in nature by smuggling it in when no one is looking.

Locke, Berkeley and Hume had intellectual precursors, of course. Their thought was not wholly original. But they did exemplify preeminently the empirical rigor and thoroughness requisite in their day. A rationalist at heart, Locke nevertheless freed philosophy from many of its rationalistic presuppositions. For our modern world, he freed the mind from "innate ideas," at least so far as those ideas may be said to have content, to be ideas of or about the world.

The mind has remained free since Locke's time.[7] He freed things of their secondary qualities, leaving to the "world out there" merely something moving somewhere somehow. Physics since his day has confirmed his wisdom, finding that these minimal qualities suffice at least for control and prediction; and even today finding its most intriguing problems precisely in the analysis of these primary qualities. Locke recalled man's attention to language, the medium through which he thinks and speaks; tracing its sources, dissecting its structure, pointing out pitfalls of careless abstraction and verbal confusion. An old philosophical discipline, semantics, advanced with Locke, and has continued its advances since his day.

Berkeley, also inquiring into the experiential basis of knowledge, dared more than Locke. He faced squarely the question Locke raised: What, empirically, is substance? And he alone gave the ultimate empirical answer: *Substance is what it is experienced as.* To pretend to find more in the idea is to fall into confusion and contradiction. By understanding the world as mental, Berkeley did not of course deprive it of a single quality, nor did he alter its structure in the least. He saw that science studies structure and nothing else, and he saw no necessity for transforming common sense-experiences into incomprehensible and unevidenced experiences of substances which by definition lie forever beyond experience.

Hume, pushing the empirical logic relentlessly, drove home the conclusion that the very notions underlying the experience-knowledge relation: self, cause, substance: these too demand explanation, and are subject to analysis from an empirical point of view. What experiences are referred to by statements of scientific causation? How do we arrive at the idea of a cause beyond these experiences? What is the self in terms of experience?

Hume's answers to questions like these may seem extreme, perhaps radical even today. Unable to answer his reasoning, critics have levelled charges of skepticism, claiming that his empiricism if pushed far enough makes positive knowledge impossible . . . as if honest David Hume were to blame for the state of the universe. Critics have merrily rejected Hume's quaint psychology; they find "association" inconvenient, and hence call it obsolete. Were he alive today, it seems likely that Hume's philosophical position—and even his psychological position—might not be radically different than it was the year he died and the United States was born.[8]

Our debt to Hume cannot be overestimated. Directly, of course, he "woke Kant from his dogmatic slumbers." Some might say that Kant should not have gone to sleep again and dreamed up noumena, that what is true in Kant he owes to Hume, and what is false he wills to Hegel. The recessive strain in nineteenth century thought: Comte, Bentham, Mill, Peirce and James . . . all these share the temper of Hume. And the dominant strain of our own day: Russell, Wittgenstein, Dewey, Lewis . . . these too could not have thought as they have, had Hume not thought as he did.

We now know that empiricism is not a magic wand, which solves or dissolves philosophical problems with a wave. Nor is "empiricism" a magic word which will forever banish metaphysics and verbal confusion by its mere utterance. "Empiricism" is a name for a way of thinking and working with facts, a willingness to be ruled by observable evidence and to follow it wherever it may lead, an act of faith in man's common sense and in his power to know by using his senses. It is the philosophy, perhaps the only philosophy, which takes science seriously. We now see that empiricism is not unique—today we call it pragmatism and positivism and logical analysis, and other names as well—and we see that empirical postulates cannot themselves be deduced. But we know no other way of knowing truth. And not mere logical clarity, but truth, today as for Locke, Berkeley and Hume, is still the philosopher's goal.

NOTES

1. See Kemp Smith, *The Philosophy of David Hume* (London, 1941).
2. Locke's *Essay*, Bk. II, Chap. VIII, par. 7.
3. Our thoughts, thus far, have in the main been those of Locke. We turn to Berkeley for the ensuing ideas.
4. Now Berkeley gives way to Hume as model for our philosophizing.
5. Hume's *Treatise*, Bk. I, Pt. III, Sec. III.
6. Hume's *Treatise*, Bk. I, Pt. III, Sec. VIII.
7. Kant's categories, although *a priori*, are but hollow ghosts of innate ideas, purely structural and empty of content before perception.
8. Two tempting speculations present themselves: How, exactly, would Hume have answered Kant? And how would he reply to the challenges of the Gestaltists? See, for example, Chapter X in Köhler's *Gestalt Psychology* (1947).

BIBLIOGRAPHY

The principal philosophical works of these authors, in standard editions, follow:

J. LOCKE, *An Essay Concerning Human Understanding*. Ed. by Fraser (Oxford, Clarendon, 1894).

G. BERKELEY, *The Principles of Human Knowledge*. Ed. by Jessop (London, 1937).

———, *Three Dialogues Between Hylas and Philonous* (Chicago, 1935).

A. C. FRASER'S edition of Berkeley's *Works* is standard (Oxford, Clarendon, 1871).

D. HUME, *A Treatise of Human Nature*. Ed. by Selby-Bigge (Oxford, Clarendon, v.d.).

———, *An Enquiry Concerning Human Understanding* and *An Enquiry Concerning the Principles of Morals*. Ed. by Selby-Bigge (Oxford, Clarendon, 1894).

———, *The Dialogues Concerning Natural Religion*. Ed. by Kemp Smith (Oxford, Clarendon, 1935).

———, *Essays Moral, Political, and Literary*. Ed. by Green & Grose (London and New York., v.d.).

CHAPTER TWENTY-ONE

THE PHILOSOPHY OF THE ENLIGHTENMENT

CHARLES FRANKEL

THE ENLIGHTENMENT is something less and something more than a philosophical movement. It has no single school of thought, no established canon or systematic program. It produced philosophers whose influence on technical philosophy has been immeasurable; yet it was not mainly concerned with theoretical issues but with practical ones, and the interest which its leaders had in philosophy was not technical but political and humanitarian. The prevailing tone of the Enlightenment is literary, and its manner is relaxed and unacademic, attuned to the *salon* rather than the library.

There is in the thought of the Enlightenment, however, an identifiable pattern, a unity of objective and assumptions which has had a decisive effect on subsequent history. The Enlightenment represented a collective, even a co-operative, effort to reappraise European life without sectarian prejudice or ulterior purpose. The thinkers of the period made every effort to be unprejudiced, but they were not "disinterested," and did not claim to be. They were convinced that scientific knowledge is the only effective instrument for achieving human happiness, and they were interested in freeing Europe from the fantastic mythologies and fanaticisms which prevented men from being either intelligent or happy. The Enlightenment is mainly responsible for the contemporary ideal of an objective, co-operative social science, and it shaped out the main features of the contemporary "liberal" outlook to which this ideal is integral. It is the crucial period in the formation of the minds and consciences of modern liberal men.

A characteristic conception of the nature and program of "philosophy" is shared by most of the thinkers of the Enlightenment. Philosophy is an instrument for human happiness, and the struggle against error is linked with the struggle against tyranny; philosophy appeals to "the common sense of mankind" above the babel of provincialism and unilluminated egoism; it seeks universal solutions to particular problems, and is congenitally cosmopolitan, believing that "the good of all mankind" takes precedence over the interests of any nation or sect; it is convinced that in fundamental respects men are more alike than they are different, and that knowledge of moral good is easily available to any mind, provided only that it is candid and free from inherited prejudices. The point of departure for philosophy was the Newtonian vision of an Order of Nature in which everything contributed to a higher harmony, and, with few exceptions, the Enlightenment was convinced that there was a basis —a "public interest," "natural law," or "general will"—on which all men might understand each other and live in peace.

The special effort of the Enlightenment, therefore, was to find a foundation in every field, "from the profane sciences to revelation," "from music to morals," and "theology to commerce," [1] such that thinking and action could be made independent of speculative metaphysics and supernatural revelation. Religion was treated mainly as an appendage to morals and discussed as though it were a part of physics. History was written to place European life in balanced perspective among other ways of life, none of which enjoyed the special sanction of God. In politics, the conceptions of divine right and supernatural providence were replaced by "the social contract," so that governments could be evaluated as instruments of human desire. In moral philosophy the effort was to base moral codes on Natural Law or on the "well-established facts" of human psychology. In general, the eighteenth century attempted to bring together two secular traditions which had not always been in sympathy with each other—humanism and science. The classic humanistic persuasion that nothing human can be alien to a cultivated mind was given a spine and a positive program by the scientific demonstration of the reign of universal law. Erasmus had passed into Voltaire.

The symbol of this faith in the unity and vitality of enlightenment was the publication of the great French *Encyclopaedia*. Edited by Denis Diderot (1713-1784) and Jean D'Alembert (1717-1783), it successfully enlisted most of the best minds of Europe in a synthesis of the most reliable existing knowledge. Not all of its articles were of equal quality, but its attempt to be objective and nonpartisan inescapably made it the manifesto of "the party of Reason and Humanity." For, in a world of competing sects, of Jansenists and Jesuits, Protestants and Catholics, it took the singular and radical position that there was a possible point of view that did not represent the views of any particular sect. The peculiar achievement of the Enlightenment was the vision of a European culture unified on the basis of the common acceptance of scientific methods and certain inter-cultural human values.

Probably the most widespread moral philosophy of the Enlightenment, especially in France, was that based on the doctrine of "natural rights." This doctrine had its most immediate source in John Locke, whose philosophy was a paradoxical combination of an empiricist account of the origins of ideas in experience together with an optimistic rationalist confidence in the possibility of establishing morals on self-evident principles. This paradox persisted in the most representative philosophies of the eighteenth century. Philosophers such as Voltaire (1694-1778) employed an empiricist approach to show that the most cherished beliefs and institutions of the Old Regime in Europe had originated in the malice of priests and despots and had been sanctified merely by custom and tradition. In building their own positive philosophies, however, they resorted to "self-evident" rational principles which, in their view, were as clear and incontestable as the axioms of geometry. "It has taken centuries to learn a part of nature's laws," wrote Voltaire, "but one day was sufficient for a wise man to learn the duties of man."

The doctrine of natural rights held that, over and above the particular customs of any given society, there were certain universal principles whose protection is the purpose and touchstone of every society. Every individual has certain inviolable claims—to life, liberty, security from arbitrary government action, property, etc.,—which inhere in him quite apart from his social status or the function he performs in society; and they cannot justly be taken away from him unless it can be shown that, as an individual, he has violated the rights of others. These rights define the moral function of society; society does not define these rights. The most characteristic and illustrative of these rights, though not the fundamental one either in the eyes of Locke or the eighteenth-century philosophers, was the right to property, based on the "self-evident" principle that the individual was entitled to any object with which he had mixed the labor of his body.

On the whole, the doctrine of natural rights was less carefully developed or rigorously expounded than other moral philosophies of the period. This was but natural. In the first place, the very essence of the doctrine was that fundamental moral laws needed no proof, and were accessible to the minds and hearts of even the most untutored. In the second place, the great effectiveness of this doctrine as a slogan in political struggles militated against its continuing theoretical refinement. Its most dramatic application is undoubtedly the American *Declaration of Independence*. The French *Declaration of the Rights of Man and the Citizen* was also considerably influenced by natural-rights theory, though it also contains a strong Rousseauan tendency. And, as the title suggests, the French attempted to equivocate on the crucial issue as to whether the indefeasible rights of individuals were "natural" or "civil."

Though the philosophy of natural rights has been closely identified with the struggle of the middle class against mercantilism and absolute monarchy, and has been used to support the particular program of this class, its significance is not exhausted therein. It has also played a considerable rôle in the development of socialist and anarchist philosophies. And while most political and legal thinkers today have rejected the idea of absolute individual rights apart from a particular social context, many of them have tried to preserve the spirit behind the doctrine of natural rights by pragmatically reinterpreting them as "constitutional" guarantees, whose status is distinguished from other, merely statutory, rights.

The sharply individualistic strain in natural-rights philosophy was maintained in another variety of Enlightenment moral philosophy, which also made the attempt to appeal to "facts" which any candid man might recognize, no matter what his place or time. This philosophy, which came to be known as "utilitarianism" in the nineteenth century, replaced the appeal to universal "rights" with an appeal to universal physiological demands—in particular, the desire for pleasure and the aversion to pain. It represented the fusion of a number of elements: Hobbes' theory of human motivations; Locke's account of the growth of ideas by association; the translation to the anti-clerical French scene of the interpretation of virtue developed by theologically oriented British thinkers such as John Gay (1669-1745), Abraham Tucker (1705-1774), and William Paley (1743-1805); and the Lucretian epicureanism (or "libertinism") descended from Charles de Saint-Evremond (1610?-1703) and stimulated by Montaigne (1533-1592).

A characteristic and influential instance of the utilitarian theory of human motivations was *The Fable of the Bees,* by Bernard de Mandeville (1670-1733). This work argued the paradox that the self-seeking "private vices" were really "publick benefits," and that, whatever men may say, they actually appraise conduct in terms of its consequences and are disposed to accept the beneficial results of egoism. The *Observations on Man* by David Hartley (1705-1757) also contributed materially to the psychological theory on which utilitarianism was based. This work was an extended elaboration of the theory of the association of ideas which had been developed by Hobbes, and even more by Locke. In France Etienne Bonnot de Condillac (1715-1780) also elaborated on Locke's psychology and empiricist theory of knowledge. Condillac made the effort to be even more consistently empirical than Locke had been, tracing the origins of reflective thought back to the emergence of language rather than to an occult, non-empirical "power" of reflection, and he produced the most systematic and influential technical philosophy in eighteenth-century France.

The most complete and extreme statement of eighteenth-century utilitarianism in France was by Claude Helvetius (1715-1771), in his two books, *De l'esprit* and *De l'homme*. Helvetius' peculiar achievement was the substitution of the single, quantitative standard of the greatest happiness of the greatest number for a vaguely defined and indefinite number of natural rights. In effect, Helvetius drew the extreme implication from Locke's philosophy that man was perfectible if his environment was rationally controlled. "Make good laws; they alone will naturally direct the people in the pursuit of the public advantage, by following the irresistible propensity they have to their private advantage." [2]

Helvetius' utilitarianism was ultimately of great importance in the development of the radical British utilitarianism of Jeremy Bentham (1748-1832) and James Mill (1773-1836). On the whole, however, it was an extreme position which was not widely shared during the Enlightenment, even in France. The most philosophically circumspect version of eighteenth-century utilitarianism was developed in Great Britain by David Hume (1711-1776). Hume's philosophy is treated at length in another chapter, but we may note his contribution to utilitarian theory very briefly. Hume struck at the basis of the philosophy of Natural Law and Natural Rights by showing that moral judgments could not be derived either from truths of reason or truths of fact alone, but required the presence of some human preference or "sentiment." At the same time, Hume considerably enlarged the utilitarian psychology and standard of valuation by showing that "utility" was not a question of pleasure or pain alone, but required an elaborate consideration of conventions and existing social demands.

In contrast with the egoistic psychologies descended from Hobbes and Mandeville, Hume stressed the motive of "sympathy" as the source of virtuous behavior. In this emphasis, Hume was in the tradition of Joseph Butler (1692-1752), with his emphasis on benevolence and conscience, and that of Lord Shaftesbury (1671-1713) and Francis Hutcheson (1694-1746), with their conception of a "moral sense." This tradition received its most finished formulation at the hands of Hume's friend, Adam Smith (1723-1790). In his *Theory of Moral Sentiments* Smith traced moral behavior to the individual's capacity to sympathize with the feelings of others, and so to evaluate his own actions impartially. "I divide myself, as it were, into two persons: . . . I, the examiner and judge, . . . [and] I, the person whose conduct is examined into and judged of." [3]

The recognition that "moral sentiments" play an uneliminable rôle in human conduct was carried much farther by the most idiosyncratic thinker of the Enlightenment, Jean-Jacques Rousseau (1712-1778). The appeal to "moral sentiments" by Hume and Smith had been made in terms of the accepted analytic methods of the eighteenth century, and largely to support the scheme of values—toleration, cosmopolitanism, reasonableness—for which the Enlightenment stood. In Rousseau, however, analytic methods as such were rejected, and with them many of the values of his philosophic contemporaries. In his *Discourse on the Moral Effects of the Arts and Sciences*, Rousseau suggested that the rationalist morality of the philosophers only mirrored the artificial society they thought they were criticizing. In this essay, and in his *Discourse on the Origin of Inequality*, he contrasted the artifices of rationalist morality with the spontaneous morality that springs from the heart, and argued that no moral code was stable which did not satisfy man's instincts for affection, loyalty, and membership in a community. In *The Social Contract* Rousseau went on to reject the individualistic doctrine of natural rights, and to argue that all rights are social, and that what is most "natural" is most completely "social." Though Rousseau's differences from the representative thinkers of the Enlightenment have been exaggerated, and he was certainly not an advocate either of primitivism or unreasoning emotion, it is true that no one during the century did so much to enlarge the conception of human nature, or to suggest the importance of the emotional life for morals, education, and politics.

The moral philosophies of the Enlightenment probably had much to do with the notable rise in the interest in history during the period, and in the achievement of a style in history which, despite its shortcomings, remains the prototype for modern objective historiography. Though the cosmopolitan belief in the universal reign of unchanging psychological laws, unaffected by differences of custom, led to questionable historical analogies and cultural parallels, it also led to the largely successful disengagement of the European record from dependence on special supernatural revelations, and encouraged a critical attitude towards historical sources. Indeed, in *The Spirit of Laws,* by the Baron de Montesquieu (1689-1755), the effort to demonstrate how all societies can be interpreted in terms of a few, simple, and universal laws frequently led to a practical rejection of the principle that all societies have the same structure and growth, and an interpretation of the diversity of laws by reference to physical and social factors such as soil, climate, and cultural setting. Furthermore, the humanitarian orientation of historians led them to emphasize the rôle of general cultural and intellectual conditions as against exclusive emphasis on military, theological, or diplomatic history. Voltaire's histories are probably most representative in this respect, and his emphasis on the durability of the works of the mind was one of the major sources for the widespread belief in progress.

Most of the histories written during the Enlightenment were frankly pragmatic and reformist in temper, hoping to free men from slavish dependence on the past by revealing it as a record of crime and folly. Despite its concern with the diversity of facts, Montesquieu's *The Spirit of Laws*, as well as his *Persian Letters* and *Greatness and Decadence of the Romans*, were basically moralistic, hoping to provide lessons in sound policy. Similarly, the *Observations on the History of France*, by the Abbé Mably (1709-1785) was a brief for unearthing the French Constitution which had been buried by centuries of superstition and despotism. The extremely popular book, *The Philosophical and Political History of the Indies*, by the Abbé Raynal (1713-1796) is an especially good instance of Enlightenment history. It performed a dual purpose: to contrast European life with the "natural" model of some non-European culture, and to condemn the imperialist exploitation of non-European peoples by Europeans. And undoubtedly the most memorable achievement in history by the Enlightenment is *The Decline and Fall of the Roman Empire* by Edward Gibbon (1737-1794), which argued with erudition and irony that the triumph of Christianity was the signal for the victory of religion and barbarism over enlightenment and civilization.

The interest in finding a law of history, and the conviction, underscored by the historians of the Enlightenment, that the rising power of science distinguished the modern world, together led to the development of theories of progress. In France, the two principal contributors to this theory were A. R. J. Turgot (1727-1781) and the Marquis de Condorcet (1743-1794). Turgot stated in rudimentary form the law of the three stages of thought—the theological, the metaphysical, and the positive—which became the basis of Auguste Comte's nineteenth-century interpretation of history. Condorcet's *Sketch of the Progress of the Human Mind* went even farther in making the law of progress and the indefinite perfectibility of man the central principle for interpreting history. Written at the close of the century, while Condorcet was in hiding from the Reign of Terror, it is perhaps the most moving affirmation of faith produced by the Enlightenment.

In Germany, Gotthold Ephraim Lessing (1729-1781) interpreted history as the progressive education of man by religion, and Johann Gottfried von Herder (1744-1803) developed the notion of history as a completely determined series of epochs, each fulfilling a specific function and contributing to the higher stage which follows. Immanuel Kant (1724-1804), who, with Hume and Rousseau, was the most incisive critic of Enlightenment thought, also produced in his *Essay on Universal History* a representative statement of Enlightenment ideals. He argued that history exhibited the tendency towards the increasing achievement of rationality and that it moved in the direction of a "cosmopolitical" or world-government organization of mankind.

The faith in the rising power of enlightenment helps explain the fact that the most widespread political philosophy of the Enlightenment was enlightened despotism. In Great Britain, the Constitutionalist philosophies of Harrington and Locke, and the Constitutional settlement of 1688, provided the almost exclusive political tradition; and, on the continent, British liberties were looked up to as a model of progressive and enlightened government. But until relatively late in the century most continental philosophers thought that British liberties could be achieved more easily by enlightening princes than by creating or reviving long disestablished parliaments. Convinced of the universal governance of Natural Law, the philosophers simply extended this "general providence" to social affairs: the self-interest of a king was sufficient to make him serve the general interest, provided only that he be enlightened. Frederick the Great, an enlightened despot by profession, argued, for example, that the mistakes of princes were due mainly to their "want of knowledge," and held that "in our times ignorance commits more faults than vice." [4]

Actually, however, with the exception of a few apologetics such as those by Frederick himself, enlightened despotism was not so much a systematic philosophy, as a combination of faith and tactics—faith in the continued progress of reason, and a willingness to use existing political mechanisms to achieve desired reforms. A much more thoroughly developed point of view was that of Constitutionalism, represented by Montesquieu in France and, in America, by the "Federalist Papers" of Alexander Hamilton (1757-1804), John Jay (1745-1829), and especially James Madison (1751-1836). Montesquieu's reflections were stimulated by his nostalgic desire to revive the medieval French Constitution which had provided safeguards for local government, the judiciary, and the nobility against the inroads of centralized monarchy. Influenced by these preconceptions as well as by his reading of Locke and Harrington, Montesquieu misinterpreted the meaning of the Glorious Revolution of 1688, which had given supreme power to the British Parliament, and passed on to the eighteenth century the idea that the British Constitution consisted of an elaborate system of checks and balances, mitigating the danger of despotism on the one hand, and of mob rule on the other. The Federalist Papers continued in this tradition, and placed even greater stress than had Montesquieu on the economic and cultural checks and balances necessary to prevent tyranny. In general, the Constitutional tradition in the Enlightenment was noteworthy for its widening of the context of political discussion and its emphasis upon socioeconomic issues and their bearing on government.

Undoubtedly, however, the single most influential work in political philosophy during the Enlightenment was Rousseau's *The Social Contract,* a work which contains the seeds of most contemporary political positions. The idea of a "social contract" provided the most prevalent context for the discussion of political issues during the eighteenth century, and was the instrument by which it could be shown that just government rested on the consent of the governed. As in most other things, however, Rousseau adopted the reigning terms of his day but radically altered their content. *The Social Contract* completely rejected the conception of an individualistic state of nature as the norm for civil society; and it also rejected the Constitutionalist idea that a sort of "secondary" contract obtained between the community and government such that governments could be changed only under very strictly limited conditions. For Rousseau, the community as such, the people as a whole, was primary, and government was only its agent, to be changed whenever and however the community desired. Rousseau's organizing principle was the conception of "the general will," the sovereign will of the community as a whole. In addition to his private will, each individual has a general will for the good of the community itself; and since he is a member of the community, and all civilized values are shaped and sustained by it, the general will rightly takes priority over any lesser interest. In this sense a just community is one in which men are free because they are subject to their own will at its fullest and most rational. Indeed, if individuals reject the general will, they may even "be forced to be free."

The final chapter of Rousseau's book consisted of a discussion of a "civil religion" and condemned Christianity for fostering an other-worldly morality inimical to good citizenship. The nature of this discussion suggests the dominant pattern in Enlightenment thought about religion. As in most other fields, the interest was moral, and the objective was to establish a relationship between man and God that was a logical consequence of the physical order and a stimulus to sound morality.

The most characteristic and prevalent position towards religion was "Deism," which attempted to demonstrate the truths of religion without recourse to revelation. By means of "reason" Deistic philosophers such as Shaftesbury found a "Universal Harmony" in Nature, a general fittingness and concord in the relations of the part to the whole, which was evidence of the existence of a rational and benevolent God. In some cases, especially in the earlier phases of Deism, the attempt was made to demonstrate the essential rationality of Christianity and the agreement of revelation with reason. Locke, John Tillotson (1630-1694), Archbishop of Canterbury, and John Toland (1670-1722) all argued—to employ the title of Locke's book—for "The Reasonableness of Christianity." And Samuel Clarke (1675-1729), after Locke the leading philosopher in England, found that natural morality, though based on the necessary order of things, is both confirmed and strengthened by revelation.

As the Enlightenment progressed, however, it became more usual for exponents of natural religion to discard revelation entirely. *Christianity as Old as Creation,* a book by Matthew Tindal (1653?-1733) which came to be known as "the Deists' Bible," argued that natural religion was complete without special revelation, and made the essence of religion lie in a moral attitude based on the recognition of the unerring rationality of nature. Where social conditions were favorable, this worship of nature led to a kind of "cosmic Toryism" which made "all discord harmony not understood." Lord Henry Kames (1696-1782), for example, found that "even the follies and vices of men minister to the wise designs" of nature, and thought that "every thing Nature has made is good." But in France the rational Order of Nature was used to highlight human folly and waste. And Voltaire's *Candide* is the classic denunciation by a Deist of Deist complacency, either about man or about the unqualified friendliness of Nature.

Though it enjoyed a considerable vogue during the eighteenth century, there is little doubt that Deism was a failure as a version of religion. Its two major arguments for the existence of God—the argument for a First Cause and the argument for Design—were subjected to devastating criticism by the skeptical Hume and the atheistic Baron D'Holbach (1723-1789). Even more important than the validity or invalidity of its arguments, however, was the exclusively intellectualistic and moralistic context to which Deism reduced the discussion of religion. The Deists made the truth-value of religion primary, thereby placing both religion and truth under excessive strain. Furthermore, the moral message which they found in religion was largely exhausted in specific and limited ideals—for example, the elimination of religious intolerance—and there was little place in the Deist vision of the moral life for the transcendent ideals and the sense of the radical disparity between human aspirations and human capacities which have played so central a rôle in traditional religions. In the end, Deism passed into agnosticism and atheism not nearly so much by logic, as by default. Its arguments were unconvincing, but this was not nearly so important as the fact that they were uninteresting.

To find religious feeling best exemplified in the Enlightenment one must turn not to the avowed defenses of religion but to the avowed attacks upon it—to systematic atheism and materialism. The faith in the harmonious Order of Nature and the spiritual commitment to the ideal of worldly salvation for the human race seemed less ambiguous when they were clearly separated from traditional religious institutions. In the temperate, biologically oriented materialism of Diderot this faith received its most balanced expression. Holbach's more extreme *System of Nature*, the most clear-cut and general expression of eighteenth-century materialism and atheism, beautifully illustrates the religious aspect of materialism. It employs materialism as a philosophy of emancipation from the follies and fears spawned by supernaturalism; but its closing passages (which may have been written by Diderot) are a paean to Nature, "the sovereign of all beings."

In many ways the paradoxes in Holbach's book are representative of the paradoxes in the thought of the Enlightenment in general. Marx and Freud, Darwinism and the pragmatic emphasis on the rôle of ideas as instruments, have made us sensitive to the practical urgencies and local dialects in which philosophy takes shape. Undoubtedly, there was much more special pleading and *ad hoc* rationalization in the philosophy of the Enlightenment than its exponents suspected. Their universal generalizations were for the most part particular solutions elevated into cosmic necessities, and their "rights of man" were in large measure the demands of a selected class of men at a particular juncture in history.

But these platitudes of contemporary psychological and historical criticism should not distract us from noticing that it is in terms of the philosophers' own ideals of rationality that we reject their rationalizations. Their effort to think in universal terms shows how conscientiously they accepted the requirement that any proposed program for human life must be supported by more than personal caprice or mere habit and convention. The Enlightenment represents the first great effort of the secular and humanistic tradition of the West to propose an alternative to the universal hegemony of the Church. What it arrived at was only a sketch, and it was challenged in the next century by still a third alternative for the unification of Europe—the Marxian idea of the international solidarity of the working-class. But it remains likely that if any viable alternative to the unification of Europe under either the Church or the Proletariat is worked out, it will bear the indelible impress of the Enlightenment.

NOTES

1. *Cf.* Jean D'Alembert, *Oeuvres* (Paris, 1805), Vol. II, pp. 9-11.
2. *Cf.* Claude Helvetius, *A Treatise on Man,* trans. by W. Hooper (London, 1777), Vol. I, pp. 299-301.
3. Adam Smith, *Theory of Moral Sentiments* (Bohn ed., 1911), p. 164.
4. *Cf.* Frederick the Great, *An Essay on Forms of Government,* translated by T. Holcroft.

BIBLIOGRAPHY

In addition to primary sources, the following works will be found helpful:

ERNEST ALBEE, *A History of English Utilitarianism* (London, 1902).
CARL BECKER, *The Heavenly City of the Eighteenth-Century Philosophers* (New Haven, 1932).
J. B. BURY, *The Idea of Progress* (London, 1920).
ERNST CASSIRER, *Die Philosophie der Aufklärung* (Tübingen, 1932).
LOUIS DUCROS, *Les Encyclopédistes* (Paris, 1900).

A HISTORY OF PHILOSOPHICAL SYSTEMS

EMILE FAGUET, *Dix-huitième siècle* (Paris, 1890).
CHARLES FRANKEL, *The Faith of Reason* (New York, 1948).
F. J. C. HEARNSHAW, ed., *The Social and Political Ideas of some Great French Thinkers of the Age of Reason* (London, 1930).
J. G. HIBBEN, *The Philosophy of the Enlightenment* (New York, 1910).
F. A. LANGE, *The History of Materialism* (London, 1925).
HAROLD LASKI, *Political Thought in England from Locke to Bentham* (New York, 1920).
A. O. LOVEJOY, *The Great Chain of Being* (Cambridge, 1942).
A. C. McGIFFERT, *Protestant Thought before Kant* (New York, 1911).
KINGSLEY MARTIN, *French Liberal Thought in the Eighteenth Century* (Boston, 1929).
JOHN MORLEY, *Diderot and the Encyclopedists* (London, 1914).
————, *Voltaire* (London, 1923).
G. V. PLEKHANOV, *Essays in the History of Materialism*. Trans. by R. Fox (London, 1934).
LESLIE STEPHEN, *History of English Thought in the Eighteenth Century* (New York, 1902).
BASIL WILLEY, *The Eighteenth-Century Background* (New York, 1941).

CHAPTER TWENTY-TWO

KANT'S CRITICAL PHILOSOPHY

NEWTON P. STALLKNECHT

"A philosophical system cannot come forward, armed at all points like a mathematical treatise. Hence it may be quite possible to take exception to particular passages; while, nonetheless, the system, considered as a unified organic structure, need have no danger to fear."

Critique of Pure Reason, 2nd edition, preface.

TWO MAJOR themes persisted in the philosophy of Immanuel Kant (1724-1804) summarized, in his own words, as the "starry heavens above and moral law within." On the one hand, the physical universe of Copernicus, Kepler, and Newton, infinite in extent and mathematically determined in detail, as in the calculable motions of the planets;—on the other hand, the moral ideal of the autonomous human individual who can comprehend this order of nature and from within it, paradoxically enough, determine his own course of action by effective rational decision. For Kant, nature and freedom, *i.e.*, as he interpreted them, physical determinism and rational autonomy, stood in spectacular contrast and conflict. But the historical student is likely to be interested not only in the intellectual motivation but also in the logical and philosophical "style" of his author. Here we find Kant's work distinguished in several ways. We may notice its over elaborate form, or "architectonic," which is the despair of the reviewer. But more characteristic still is the conflict, often discernible, between two tendencies, which we may describe as the synoptic or speculative and the critical or methodological. Kant's critical concern for logical security, his dread of making unconscious assumptions that might prove unfounded, held his constructive ingenuity and his speculative curiosity within bounds. On the other hand, this speculative interest kept him from limiting his philosophical activity to the mere formulation of an epistemology.

Kant's chief speculative or constructive concern sprang from his desire to reconcile the scientific theories and ethical beliefs to which he was committed. This purpose stands out clearly enough, if we survey the three *Critiques* together, although it is true that isolated consideration of the *Critique of Pure Reason* or of the *Prolegomena* may somewhat overemphasize the interest in physical science and, in general, the critical or strictly methodological aspect of Kant's philosophy. Again the importance of the *Critique of Judgment* which completes the speculative phase of Kant's work, is sometimes overlooked or, at best, treated as an afterthought. Nonetheless, it is in the *Critique of Judgment* that Kant presents his theory of art and the beautiful, in terms of which he draws together the important concepts derived from his earlier work, at last, if only tentatively, reconciling a deterministic nature with moral freedom and the reality of values. In this work, Kant finds a subtle affinity between beauty and moral worth and again between beauty and the teleology of living things; and in neither case does he substitute sentiment for analysis. The human soul considered as a center of autonomous choice, the functional concert or self-supporting interplay of the organs of a living thing, the recognition of successful art considered as an organization of understanding, sense and feeling—all these are thought to point toward a "supersensuous substrate" of which the phenomenal objects open to scientific observation constitute only the surface or façade.

Viewed in this light, Kant's philosophy appears as a boldly speculative theory of value and existence. Despite Kant's usual indifference to Platonism, which was based, after all, largely on ignorance, this system stands closer to Platonic idealism than to any other type of thought. Even the cautious reserve with which Kant entertains his final hypotheses is comparable to the discretion with which Plato speaks of the form of the good in *The Republic*. Like Plato, Kant distinguishes sharply between a scientific understanding and a higher philosophical insight, and he is very cautious in defending the latter. Such caution, in both Kant and Plato, was the result of a critical methodology. In Kant's work, however, the spirit of criticism became dominant. It colored his whole thinking and, in his own eyes, characterized his philosophy. In writing the *Critique of*

Pure Reason, one of Kant's primary concerns was to maintain the highest standard of certainty and of logical rigor, equivalent in his own eyes to that of mathematics and the natural sciences. This standard of certainty was to be set so high that not even the professional skeptic could take exception to it. In this way, Kant hoped to reëstablish the prestige of philosophy which he felt had deserved the indifference with which his contemporaries regarded it.

In the *Critique of Judgment,* Kant recognizes as conceivable two basic types of intelligence: the *archetypal* or perceptive (intuitive) intelligence; and the *ectypal,* discursive or constructive intelligence. The net-work of phenomena open to our natural science is the proper object of ectypal interpretation. On the other hand, archetypal awareness being capable of "intellectual intuition" may be said directly to contemplate organized wholes as such, recognizing their unity from the start, while discerning and emphasizing their constitutive elements or functions against this background of integration. Archetypal intelligence comprehends the *one* and proceeds toward the *many* as subordinate to it. Ectypal intelligence begins with the many and works toward an approximation of the *one*. Thus, in general, wholes appear to an ectypal intelligence as composite constructs.

An archetypal awareness of things is for the most part closed to us as human beings. We cannot be directly aware of concrete wholes in their organized integrity, although we may, so to speak, postulate their existence hypothetically, if we receive some hint of their presence. We do receive such hints. There are times when we do entertain unity as predominant, as an over-all meaning or purpose evoking the significance of a variety of detail. This is especially true of esthetic enjoyment. We can thus be aware of the ideal possibility of an archetypal way of knowing even though we do not ourselves consistently apprehend things in this way.

The ectypal view of the world is analyzed at great length in the *Critique of Pure Reason.* Here Kant explores the philosophical presuppositions of Newtonian science. Thus throughout the major part of this work Kant is concerned primarily with what he calls a "theoretical" approach to our world. Theory, in this sense, is identified with *de facto* description as distinct from appreciative evaluation. Here the mind, although it does not evaluate, is nonetheless far from being a passive onlooker. It is at once a center of receptivity and a source of selective interpretation. A multiplicity or "manifold" of sensibility, a sea of impressions or sensations of every kind, constitutes the raw material from which our awareness draws its content. This raw material is an indispensable condition of mental activity. Kant's theory of knowledge centers, however, upon the notion of an *a priori* synthesis, an activity whereby the human mind orients itself by affirming certain principles in terms of which it recognizes phenomenal objects. This recognition involves the synthesis of many sensuous data (in themselves without significance) so that a unified and coördinated experience of objects may result. The principles of this synthesis are *a priori* in that they make our intelligible experience possible rather than merely recording what is experienced. They are "synthetic" in that they are not obvious or tautologous. We can, and as philosophers we often do, challenge these principles without contradicting ourselves or talking nonsense.

Consider the following statements or "judgments," which formulate such principles: *Events follow upon other events according to rules. Every event is both a cause and an effect. Nature is a system of causal relations.* These statements are generally accepted as valid, although they outrun all possibility of experimental verification. They are rendered *a priori* by their universality. They are synthetic for the simple reason that we can consistently conceive of an event without including any reference to its causal conditions. Indeed, on this latter point Hume and Kant agree.

Much of our mathematical thinking involves synthetic *a priori* judgments. These are supported by our *a priori* awareness of space and time, as unique, unitary wholes. Kant's treatment of the sensibility does not include discussion of a possible extension, volume or duration proper to the several sense data. But he does insist, and with cogency, that our awareness of the all-inclusive unities of space and time are not empirical concepts derived from sensuous data by generalization or abstraction. Thus our awareness of space and time must be classified as *a priori*. We do not learn about space by generalizing upon our acquaintance with places, nor about time by abstracting from an experience of dates and periods. Places and periods cannot be recognized as such unless we apprehend them as in contact with other places and periods in the all-inclusive and boundless unities of space and time, whose presence we cannot ignore or imagine to be absent. These unities are the pure or non-sensuous forms into which we receive the manifold data of the several senses. These forms apply to all our experience, since our experience is limited by our sensibility. We have no reason to suppose, however, that space and time enjoy any reality wholly distinct from this sensibility. These pure forms of the sensibility support the synthetic *a priori* judgments upon which traditional geometry and arithmetic seem to rest.

Kant draws an all-important distinction between phenomenal objectivity and reality. Concerning the proper spatio-temporal *objects* of our ectypal experience we may formulate synthetic judgments *a priori*. Concerning *reality* or things-in-themselves we cannot do so. Our understanding of the critical philosophy depends primarily upon a satisfactory interpretation of Kant's meaning as he develops this notion of objectivity. Objects are not to be identified with groups or clusters of sensuous data. Kant emphasized this point, concerning which he had once entertained some doubts, in his "Refutation of Idealism" (1st *Critique,* 2nd edition). To entertain data and to apprehend objects are distinct, if usually simultaneous, operations. Here the Kantian definition of object is relevant: *An object is that under the conception of which the manifold in a given intuition is united.*

The status of the phenomenal object is somewhat clarified by Kant's bold departure in theory of knowledge, a departure which he compares to the Copernican revolution in astronomy. Mind does not copy objects. It determines or distinguishes them as it synthesizes the manifold of sensibility. This is exemplified in the history of science which indicates that the inquirer must take an initiative in selecting and determining the objective area in which he is to work. Pythagoras (572-497 B.C.) (or one of his contemporaries) in geometry, Galileo (1564-1642) in physics, may be said to have introduced this type of procedure. In mathematics, it involves establishing a well-defined field of reference by asserting and strictly abiding by definitions and postulates. In physics, it involves setting up experiments and thus controlling observable data, in terms of which preconceived questions may be answered. In neither case, do we simply note down the features of an uninterpreted reality. Science is a process of putting questions to nature. The spontaneity of the human mind may be recognized most easily in the sagacity which formulates the question so that an answer is possible. The presuppositions made in formulating such questions indicate the *a priori* orientation of our theoretical activity. We put questions concerning spatio-temporal quantity and concerning causal connections. In doing so, we have advanced a concept of nature as a system of spatio-temporal objects, quantitative and causal in their relations to one another. In this way we have defined or determined the objects, or objectives of our research. Thus, from the standpoint of a critical theory of knowledge, *i.e.*, from a "transcendental" rather than an "empirical" approach, we cannot say that any given object, ready made, awaits our attention and, so to speak, requires the mind to conform to its structure.

Accordingly, the object which holds our ectypal attention is not a "thing-in-itself" or an ultimate reality, nor can it be identified with sensuous impressions or with a concept. We must remember that sense data on the one hand, things in themselves, the universe as a whole, on the other, are not genuine objects of ectypal awareness. They belong to the margins and horizons of our awareness of objects. Sense data are intuited but not conceived. Things-in-themselves are conceived but not intuited. Apprehension of an object involves both intuition and conception.

Ectypal apprehension of determinate and interrelated objects (within the space and time which are inseparable from our sensibility) is made possible by certain concepts, the categories of the understanding, in terms of which we establish a trans-spatial and trans-temporal relevance throughout the sensuous manifold. Cause and effect, whole and part, substance and attribute, are examples of the categories.

When employing his "transcendental method," whereby he "deduces" or shows the necessity of the categories, Kant argues from a principle of "this or nothing." Thus we are brought to see that if one ignores the categories of the understanding, he ignores the foundations of all consistent experience and ectypal comprehension. In these central passages of the *Critique of Pure Reason* (*Transcendental Analytic*) Kant brings the critical phase of his philosophy to its most effective expression. He tries, with the greatest ingenuity and penetration, to show that the very distinction bewteen subject and object, along with that between private imagery and public or objective phenomena, depends upon our recognition of the categories as definitions of objectivity. Kant recognizes that our conscious experience would be impossible without some tension between data or imagery on the one hand, and understood objects to which these data are more or less consistently relevant, on the other. In grasping the presence of an objective structure, as distinct from a play of sensibility, our consciousness realizes itself and maintains its continued identity. Consciousness does not consist of discrete unrelated moments of awareness, nor can we be aware only of our own subjectivity. There must always be consciousness *of* something. The *a priori*, *i.e.*, space, time, and the categories, constitutes the minimal meaning of this *something*, the *sine qua non* of humanly cognizable objectivity, and the trans-temporal connectedness of our conscious experience depends upon our recognition of the connectedness of the objects which we observe at different moments, however remote.

We have so far discussed Kant's analysis of our spatio-temporal experience and of our ectypal intelligence. We must now compare this with his notion of archetypal intelligence which as an ideal concept helps us to complete a theory of reality. Without reference to such an intelligence and to the reality which it may be thought to contemplate, Kant's philosophy is rather more a systematic and rigorous extension of Hume's (1711-1776) skeptical philosophy than an answer to it. As it stands, however, Kantian thought culminates as a speculative idealism held within the limits of a critical theory of knowledge and thus never dogmatically asserted as final.

Ectypal intelligence grasps the interrelation of phenomena. It is at home in a net-work of connectedness. But it does not evaluate and it cannot summarize or complete its vision of things. Kant never considered identifying reality with the order of our possible experience. He always insisted that our *a priori* judgments concerning space, time, and the categories are valid only as guiding principles of our spatio-temporal experience. He even argued that these principles cannot readily be rendered consistent with one another, since they tend to yield paradoxical results when we try to consider the phenomenal order as a whole, whether as infinite or finite in extension, duration and divisibility. These "antinomies" indicate an unavoidable indecision on the part of ectypal intelligence when it tries to contemplate nature as a whole. Nature, itself, cannot be entertained as an object and cannot be experienced as a unit. Here the limits of ectypal awareness are most clearly manifest.

Such intelligence begins with sensuous multiplicity and works toward the apprehension of an objective unity. But this objective unity is never intuited or exhaustively experienced. In this way, the meta-phenomenal unity, the ontology, of the realities which we pursue in cognition may well escape us. We see them as composite structures when ideally they should be apprehended as organic or global unities. But this latter view is closed to ectypal intelligence.

An analogy may help the student follow the trend of Kant's argument. Phenomenal objects may be thought to stand in relation to real things as the letters of a sentence stand to its meaning, or as the brush strokes on the canvas to the total esthetic effect of a portrait. These letters and brush strokes are genuine objects. But we may apprehend them in such a way that their intricate relations to one another are independent of any synoptic and appreciative apprehension of the whole to which they belong. The whole as such then remains unintelligible.

Thus phenomenal objects are very partial manifests of full-bodied or concrete reality. Even when conceived in systematic pattern, they constitute no more than a scheme lacking the full dimensions of real entities. It is as if we "reduced" a poem to a systematic arrangement of syllables subject to rhyme and rhythm. Like the syllables, stressed and unstressed in ordered array, the system of phenomenal objects is subject to measure. A repetitive mathematical pattern is apparent. But meter and rhyme may be understood mechanically without any reference to purposes or values. They may, indeed, be studied in isolation by a reader who completely lacks a sense of poetic value and who misses or ignores the author's intent and never feels the presence or the effectiveness of the poem as a whole. Still, syllables ordered in meter and rhyme-scheme are genuine objects, and they can help to support a continuity of experience, even though such experience fails completely to enjoy or evaluate the esthetic value of the poem itself.

So, we may conclude, nature, the incomplete system of possible ectypal awareness, reveals a secondary or superficial order, relevant to the structure of the cosmos, but not constituting its full content or its dominant values. In phenomenal nature ectypally surveyed, the good, the true, and the beautiful retreat before those humanly discernible objects which support the continuity of our experience. On the other hand, things-in-themselves may be conceived as realities open to the contemplation of archetypal intelligence. Thus beauty and the realization of value may in the end characterize concrete, ultimate reality more adequately than do the categories of the understanding. This is based on the notion that things-in-themselves are to be known, if at all, as wholes whose real nature may be manifest only in their integrity and cannot be perceived *seriatim* through their several parts or incomplete aspects. Thus certain entities are conceivable only as things-in-themselves, as genuinely metaphenomenal or ontological realities, but nonetheless as the supersensible "substrates" of systems of phenomenal objects. Among these realities may be listed: Artistic creation as embodied in a sensuous medium; the organism maintaining and fulfilling itself as a living whole, a center of self-realization through coördination; [1] and also the moral autonomy of a personality consistently maintaining its own integrity, recognizing and respecting the autonomy of others. Here the maintenance and recognition of moral freedom require a motivation that springs not from this or that desire, impulse or sympathy, but from recognition and respect for the over-all consistency, or the moral reality, of autonomous conduct, whether our own or that of another.

Our sense of beauty, our respect for moral worth and our recognition of living teleology present themselves as disparate and fleeting glimpses of things in themselves. But we cannot be quite sure of their credentials. These glimpses do not appear as indispensable foundations of our conscious experience. In this, they are less well-established than the order of phenomenal objects, subject in their full details to space, time, and the categories. On the other hand, since these insights do not limit us to an incomplete or paradoxical view of things, from which the very notion of value is omitted, they may be thought to be of greater speculative power, prompting us, for instance, to postulate our own moral freedom and to accept as a plausible hypothesis, responsibly conceived, the teleology of living things.

In Kant's philosophy, man appears as a metaphysical amphibian breathing the atmospheres of two realms, the sensible or phenomenal and the ideal or noumenal. Man is, tragically enough, more completely at ease in the former, although truly at home in neither. After all, an intelligence limited entirely to ectypal awareness would be sub-human, while the only consistently archetypal intelligence of which we can conceive is that of God, whose existence seems to us problematic. Thus Kant's philosophy may be said very accurately to epitomize the predicament of the modern spirit, which has so competently traced the interrelations of phenomena and so clearly distinguished phenomenal systems from reality itself, without being able to do more than speculate with cautious ingenuity concerning the nature of this reality through which, as free, rational, and creative individuals, we have our being. Thus despite its technical imperfections and anachronisms, and indeed because of its final lack of hard and fast conclusions, the Kantian system remains the most faithful philosophical expression or *speculum* of modern life which has yet been formulated.

NOTES

1. It seems reasonable to suggest that Kant might well have included in this list the transcendental unity of apperception, our normal consciousness, whose self-maintenance as a continuity of awareness involves a coördination of sensibility, imagination and conception remarkably similar to the unity of function maintained in an organism. Certainly our examination of the unity of apperception requires teleological assumptions comparable to those employed in the study of living things. A recognition of this fact on Kant's part would have helped him further to resolve the tensions which disturb the reader who compares the first *Critique* with the later writings.

BIBLIOGRAPHY

I. KANT, *Critique of Pure Reason,* translated by Norman Kemp-Smith (London, 1929).
———, *Prolegomena to Any Future Metaphysics,* edited in English by Dr. Paul Carus (reprint ed., Chicago, 1933).
———, *Critique of Practical Reason,* translated by L. W. Beck (Chicago, 1949).
———, *Critique of Judgment,* translated by J. C. Meredith, 2 vols. (Kant's *Critique of Aesthetic Judgement,* and Kant's *Critique of Teleological Judgement.*) (Oxford, 1911 and 1928).
E. CAIRD, *The Critical Philosophy of Immanuel Kant,* 2 vols. (New York, 1909).
E. CASSIRER, *Kants Leben und Lehre* (Bd. XI, *Immanuel Kants Werke*) (Berlin, 1923).
A. C. EWING, *A Short Commentary on Kant's Critique of Pure Reason* (London, 1938).

C. B. GARNETT, *The Kantian Philosophy of Space* (New York, 1939).
M. HEIDEGGER, *Kant und das Problem der Metaphysik* (Bonn, 1929).
N. KEMP-SMITH, *A Commentary to Kant's Critique of Pure Reason* (London, 1923).
A. D. LINDSAY, *Kant* (London, 1934).
H. J. PATON, *Kant's Metaphysic of Experience*, 2 vols. (New York, 1936).
———, *The Categorical Imperative* (Chicago, 1948).
G. T. WHITNEY and D. F. BOWERS, editors, *The Heritage of Kant* (Princeton, 1939).

CHAPTER TWENTY-THREE

CLASSICAL GERMAN IDEALISM, THE PHILOSOPHY OF SCHOPENHAUER AND NEO-KANTIANISM

ALBAN G. WIDGERY

THE IDEALIST philosophers of early nineteenth century Germany were university teachers: the most eminent philosophers of the preceding period, Descartes, Spinoza, Leibniz, Locke, Bacon, Berkeley, Hume were not. This contrast is significant with reference to differences in modes of approach and in methodology. The professional philosophers have a more definite schematism and formalism than the others, with the exception of Spinoza. The criticisms and oppositions which shook German Idealism from the dominance it had for some decades came primarily from other than professional philosophers. Philosophies cannot escape from the tests of ordinary human experience in history: as a result of such tests German Idealism has in general been abandoned. Nevertheless, one should recognize the contributions of its exponents to the development of philosophy.

The founders of Classical German Idealism were pre-eminently Johann Gottlieb Fichte (1762-1814); Friedrich Wilhelm Joseph Schelling (1775-1854); and Georg Wilhelm Friedrich Hegel (1770-1831). There are important differences in their individual systems, but they are all expressions of a fundamentally similar philosophical attitude. Though he disowned them, they were all the "children" of Kant. They were influenced by his academic formalism. More important, they accepted his contention that the primary consideration for philosophy is the nature of human knowledge. Fichte, in his chief work, *The Science of Knowledge* defined philosophy as the "science of sciences," "the science of knowledge," as transcending the sciences which are the knowledge of objects. Schelling maintained that to know things as they are is to know them as they are in and for reason. Beyond reason there is nothing. Hegel declared: "Being is thought" and that "The knowing of reason is not the mere subjective certitude, but also truth." He asked: "What is this world but the image of reason?" "Everything actual is an Idea."

Kant's philosophy has sometimes been called Transcendental Idealism, but he himself rejected its description as idealism, as he understood the term. To him, his system was Critical Philosophy. His two main problems were those of the nature of knowledge and the nature of morality. He maintained that he had shown that though knowledge involves functions of the mind in some fashion transcending experience, it is limited to experience. As contrasted with the idealism which he disclaimed, the insistence on the limitations of knowledge was to him fundamental. Reason can form general inclusive concepts, such as those of "the world," "the soul," "God," but they are simply regulative, that is, forms of ideal construction with no demonstrative metaphysical import.

Fichte, Schelling and Hegel all challenged and rejected Kant's doctrine of the limitations of human knowledge. On the basis of what he had himself admitted as to the functions of reason, they pressed beyond those limitations. The Critical Philosophy failed to satisfy their demand for ultimate unity. It appeared dualistic with its distinction, on the one hand, of the transcendent functions of thought, and, on the other, of phenomena, with sometimes an explicit reference to noumena, as unknowable things-in-themselves. They all accepted as fundamental that reality is a complete systematic unity, spiritual at least in this, that it is intelligible in and for reason. The ideal of reason must inevitably be a complete system, each and every constituent of which fits rationally with every other. Reason cannot halt at the partial and incomplete, which points beyond itself. Classical German Idealism was not truly a search for unity, but an acknowledgement of it as an ultimate implication of thought. The systematic Whole of thought was explicitly identified with reality, as stated in the Hegelian phrase: "The real is the rational; the rational is the real." The Whole was called by such terms as: the Absolute, the Absolute Idea, the Absolute Spirit, God. Hegel talked of the Absolute as "the Idea which knows itself," "the thought which conceives itself," "the reason which knows itself," "the Idea thinking itself." The last sentence of the *Encyclopedia* is of "the Idea, eternal and being for itself as Absolute Spirit, (which) is eternally active, generates and enjoys." With the initial assumption of unity the task was to show how the facts of experience are to be regarded from the standpoint of the Absolute. But though these idealists started out from the formal consideration of knowledge, following Kant with an investigation of the logical categories, they avowed eventually that the awareness of the Absolute is rather of the character of an intuitive immediacy, moral for Fichte, aesthetic for Schelling, rational for Hegel. German Idealism thus culminated in a form of mysticism. The emphasis on the unity of the whole gave it the general impression of pantheism. It may be said that there was a development through Fichte and Schelling to Hegel, in whose philosophy Classical German Idealism had its comprehensive formulation. However, instead of giving a chronological treatment of the positions of these thinkers, an attempt will be made here to co-ordinate their attitudes with regard to different aspects of experience as viewed from their general idealistic standpoint: a) Nature; b) Morality; c) the Aesthetic; d) Religion; and e) History. Their initial approach to all these was that of academic logical formalism, and they considered all with reference to the Absolute as the ultimate systematic unity.

a. *Nature*

It was Schelling who concentrated the greater part of his reflection and writing on Nature. To him, in the earlier period of his thought, Nature as the objective side of the duality of knowledge was more impressive in its extent and duration than the subjective side as found in human consciousness. He complained that Fichte never got beyond his own consciousness. The Absolute, as known by transcendent reason is something other and wider than that. It is the unity of the real and the ideal. For human knowledge there is a distinction of the objective and the subjective. Nature is the predominantly objective; spirit the predominantly subjective. Both are "posited" by the Absolute, which does so in "positing" itself. Thus, though men may suppose these distinctions of real and ideal, objective and subjective, all is ultimately identical. Schelling's early emphasis on Nature gave some the impression that his characterization of reality was essentially naturalistic. The Absolute objectifies itself as Nature, or, as he otherwise put it using the term God for the Absolute: "God affirms himself in Nature." He observed in some detail the differences in Nature, as the inorganic and the organic, and introduced the notion of process, an advance through Nature to spirit in man. Nevertheless, all this is phenomenal, for all sense experience, and finite existence in general, is only the counterpart of true being. Fichte, with little interest in the scientific study of Nature as of significance in itself, considered it as having relevance for man in being an environment and a stimulus for his moral life. For Hegel Nature and Mind were only "modes of expression for the forms of pure thought." Speaking metaphysically he could declare both that "Nature is the Absolute Idea" and that "Nature is Spirit in alienation from itself." His early treatment of Nature was to present it as no other than a duplication of the concepts of logic, a realization of its categories. He described Nature as constituted of a range of types, but with no implication of any temporal evolution. From this purely logical standpoint, he asserted that "time-difference has absolutely no interest for thought." But it was quite impossible for him to ignore the particulars in Nature. He had to admit the multiplicity of its contingencies, even though he had no way of dealing satisfactorily with them in his system. He met the difficulty by taking up the attitude that they are of little, if any, significance. "Frequently Nature . . . has been chiefly admired for the richness and variety of its structures. Apart, however, from what disclosure it contains of the Idea, this richness gratifies none of the higher interests of reason, and in its vast variety of structures, organic and inorganic, affords us only the spectacle of a contingency losing itself in vagueness." Nature "is full of freaks, a bacchantic God, who does not rein himself in and keep himself in hand." After all, the particulars were for him only a species of illusion, and in general he ignored them. German Idealism, with its central attitude, concentrated itself as regards Nature,—to quote Hegel—on its "inner harmony and uniformity." It acknowledged the problem of the knowledge of Nature in consequence of which materialistic and naturalistic conceptions were judged untenable as ignoring the functions of the knowing mind. Though it made no significant contribution to the philosophy of Nature, it kept in view the Kantian contention that the experience of Nature, and the sciences of Nature, involve fundamental epistemological problems. Its exponents maintained that the proper consideration of those problems leads beyond any form of Naturalism to the recognition of Nature as within a spiritual Absolute. Even, therefore, with regard to Nature itself, it presented a challenge to Naturalism, a challenge which must still be met.

b. *Morality*

The nature of Morality became the chief concern of Fichte. His philosophy, like that of Schelling and Hegel, was dominated by the conception of the complete unity of the Absolute. Though he used the term "the Ego," suggesting a transcendental self, for the Absolute, in and for which all is, he treated It as "impersonal" and even at times as though no other than a formal concept. There is thus some incoherence in his ethical views as related with these different attitudes. Kant, in the first formulation of the Categorical Imperative, had pointed to the universality of reason in his contention that the maxim of one's conduct should be such as could be willed to be "a universal law." Fichte maintained that it is in the "practical reason" of moral experience that one is acquainted with the ultimate nature of reality. From this he was led, on the one hand to the concept of universal Moral Order, and on the other to the acknowledgement of will as striving for perfect freedom. The striving for freedom is experienced in the individual egos of finite beings: hence Fichte came to state that the Ego, the infinite subject-object, must exist as a plurality of individuals. Even so, he still regarded them as though modes of the one substance. The pluralistic character of morality as individuals striving for freedom is thus in a realm of appearances. The moral ideal is such only in its completeness and that is in the universal Moral Order. From this standpoint morality is essentially an abandonment of selfishness, a transcendence of individuality. In his *The Way to the Blessed Life* he declared: "He who still has a self—in him assuredly there is nothing good." Each stage of morality is the realization of a wider whole than that of the particular person's own ego. His *Speeches to the German Nation* aroused German youth to unite for a comprehensive German life in opposition to the effects and conditions of the Napoleonic wars. Yet he did not idealize the State, which is concerned with external rights as *e.g.*, those of property. As distinguished from external rights, morality is of the inner disposition, a love of the good for its own sake. His ethical idealism pointed to a condition in which, with a higher level of morality, the State would not be needed even for the protection of external rights. Schelling gave comparatively little attention to ethics, but in later life he turned to an investigation of the nature and implications of spiritual freedom. With this he tended (with Fichte) to pass from logical formalism towards a voluntarism, the acknowledgement of reality as of the character of will. The moral is a development of personality. Hegel treated of the ethical and the political as intimately related in his *Philosophy of Right*. His position has frequently been misrepresented in such a way as to imply a disregard for the moral through an insistence on the dominance of the State. But it is an implication of Classical German Idealism, with its Absolute as a systematic harmonious whole, that the welfare of each goes together with the welfare of all. That was Hegel's view, and he considered the development of personality, the attainment and expression of rational freedom, as fundamental. He maintained, however, that such can be achieved only in and through social groups, as the family and the State, especially the State, which, in distinction from Fichte, he conceived as an organic spiritual whole. His essential ethical idea—preached by many later Idealists—was that in "dying" as a narrow particular person, the individual "lives" and realizes himself in the wider social whole. His own exaggerated language as to the German State of his time may have been a pandering to its dominance in the universities in his day. Classical German Idealism in general stood for an ethics of the realization of spiritual personality, of rational freedom, to be through and in social relationships.

c. *The Aesthetic*

As Fichte had considered the moral experience as transcendent, giving an apprehension of reality, so Schelling asserted this of aesthetic experience. Though philosophy may begin with intellectual reflection it must end with an aesthetic immediacy. Fundamental, therefore, for the aesthetic is the apprehension of unity and harmony, in which there is an identity of the real and the ideal. Hegel, similarly, treated the beautiful as the manifestation of the harmony of the Absolute Spirit.

d. *Religion*

In that the aesthetic involves a large measure of "external" sensuousness, it cannot be accepted as the highest form of experience: that is to be had in religion. This is most clearly stated by Hegel. Fichte's idea of the Absolute as an impersonal Moral Order, led to his being charged with atheism. His rebuttal implied a form of pantheism, with religion as the perfection of the moral in the experience of the complete harmony of the Whole. Schelling's earlier position was definitely pantheism, and he never really emancipated himself from it. With his later emphasis on freedom and personality, he presented a dynamic conception of God as striving for spiritual perfection, but with a "dark ground"—a sort of unconscious natural necessity—that involves Him in suffering. God is "making Himself," as spiritual personality. Schelling suggested that this is manifested in the religious experience of human beings. Perhaps Schelling meant that religion is the attainment of human and divine personality. That ultimately these are one is never explicitly denied: consequently men share in the evils of the "dark ground" in God. For Hegel also, although he admitted that in religion men treat God as a Spirit other than themselves, in that God is the Absolute and the Absolute is the real, religion is the Divine Spirit knowing Himself through the manifestations of finite spirits. Applied to the empirical history of religion, this is taken to mean that religion is the reconciliation of man to God. Hegel endeavored to avoid the charge of pantheism by representing it as the identification of God and the world, as the world is for us. But, as for him God is the Absolute, and the Absolute is the Whole, the treatment of the world as "appearance" does not place it in every sense "outside" of God. Classical German Idealism was in general ambiguous as to human immortality. Nowhere did it explicitly work out a definite doctrine of personal immortality as the implication of the movement of finite consciousnesses to the realization of spiritual freedom. Hegel talked of man as spirit, and as such sharing "eternity," so that immortality is a "present quality." In this, and otherwise, he acknowledged that religion with its cosmic significance transcends merely human morality.

e. *History*

Classical German Idealism culminated in the philosophy of Hegel, and it has been contended that the truly significant in that, is not the conceptions such as those already presented but his "dialectical method." But a distinction must be made between two uses of the dialectic by Hegel. One is purely logical: the "development" through formal relations for thought of the concepts within the Absolute Idea. The other is with empirical reference: "development" as actual progressive unification. The former is static and eternal: the latter dynamic and temporal. The former "a bloodless strife of categories": the latter a presentation of history. Apparently Hegel regarded these as identical. But it may be questioned whether he carried out the logical dialectic with purely rational reflection. It may be maintained, for example, that the concepts of "Being" and "Nothing" do not necessarily include that of "Becoming," so that it may be arrived at by their unification in thought. He must actually have got the concept of "Becoming" from an awareness of his own process of thinking and of changes in Nature. Opponents of and most adherents to Hegelianism have rejected or ignored Hegel's identification of the two types of dialectic, of the two meanings of "development." They have occupied themselves with development in the empirical. In one way or another they have been able to find in it movements in and through oppositions to wider wholes, as for example, in economic and political organization, intellectual and artistic achievements. But there have been and are contingencies in history which neither Hegel nor anyone else can fit into such a scheme. Hegel declared: "Reason is the sovereign of the world: the history of the world therefore presents us with a rational process." That history is an entirely rational process has been rejected as not in accordance with experience, which has led not merely to the term "rational" but also to "irrational." What Hegel did was to survey history from the standpoint of the logical dialectic and to ignore or treat as of no significance what he could not include in a rational scheme. One of the greatest difficulties for Classical German Idealism is how we are to conceive the logical system of concepts of the Absolute as "eternal Idea" together with the detailed processes of Nature and history.

* * *

A HISTORY OF PHILOSOPHICAL SYSTEMS

Though individuals or small groups followed Fichte or Schelling, as a widespread movement German Idealism was Hegelian. But Hegelianism assumed different forms, usually grouped under the descriptions of "Right Wing" and "Left Wing." In the former are included those who emphasized the concept of the Absolute and gave more attention to the logic and the metaphysics. In the latter were those who stressed the empirical and regarded his doctrines of the Absolute as logical formalism. But this distinction is not exact. It is better to recognize four lines of thought with roots in Hegelianism, but in some measure in reaction from it, sometimes so definite as to be eventually a rejection of it. Some, mainly university professors, adhered closely to the conception of the Absolute as that of which all forms of experience are modes of expression. Some, most often theologians, endeavored to present Hegelianism in theistic fashion, though still with pantheistic implications. A few retaining the idealist conception of the real as self-conscious, interpreted the idea of the Absolute not as of One Spirit, but a co-ordinated system of selves. Others, retaining little more than some aspects of Hegel's dialectic method, rejected his spiritualist metaphysics, and may be said finally to have broken entirely from German Idealism in developing forms of Naturalism.

Classical German Idealism, at first academically elaborated, came to have widespread influence as a general philosophy of life throughout Germany for half a century. Associated in no small measure with Jena, close to Weimar, it expressed the broad cultural spirit of Goethe and was a leading factor in the rise of modern Germany. But by the middle of the nineteenth century its influence had seriously waned. Some of the foremost thinkers, as Feuerbach, Strauss, Marx and Engels, explicitly rejected it. The many, concerned with the social difficulties of 1848, could find neither help nor consolation in the idea of an eternal perfect Absolute. After its decline in Germany, this idealism was continued by some thinkers, mainly university professors and theologians in Italy, Britain and the United States. In the early years of the twentieth century, at the height of German prosperity, it seemed as though there was to be a wide-spread revival of idealism essentially of the early nineteenth-century type. The protagonist of this was Rudolph Eucken (1846-1926) who drew thousands of students from all parts of Germany and many other countries, and whose books went through many editions in the original and in translations. His idealism was characterized by its comprehensiveness, as, in Hegelian fashion, he described opposing views as to be taken up into a wider all-embracing conception. According to Eucken the real oppositions are between ways of life, of which philosophies are the expressions for their defence. The alternatives are, finally, only two: naturalistic and idealistic. In his own time, in Jena, Naturalism was vigorously propounded by the biologist, Ernst Haeckel (1834-1919). Eucken maintained that Naturalism is not comprehensive enough to include the moral, the aesthetic and the religious, when these are adequately understood. Nor even the intellectual, which is involved in the sciences of Nature on which Naturalism chiefly rests. None of these cultural aspects of experience can be described in the terms of the physical sciences which he regarded as the only legitimate terms for Naturalism. On the other hand, idealism can appreciate Nature as within the spiritual life, for it is an object for the intellect, an appropriate environment for the moral, a source of aesthetic experiences and of instruments for art, and can be an inspiration to religion. The spirit of the philosophy was dynamic, appealing to the contemporary German mind. Instead of describing reality as an immutable eternal Absolute, he presented it as "a self-subsistent Spiritual Life" continuous in efforts and achievements in and through men in history. He emphasized the fact that there is no mechanical continuity of culture in history. Each age, indeed, each person, only truly receives from the past what he appropriates by his own spiritual activity. Only through the spiritual activity of the present is the culture of the past carried on and added to. The fate of Eucken's philosophy may suggest the influence of political circumstances on the history of philosophy. Before World War I, it had become an expression of the forceful buoyant life of Kaiser Wilhelm II's Germany. Had the Germans been victorious, it might well have continued to flourish in Germany and have been propagated throughout the world. It collapsed with the Germany in which it had been developed.

"Philosophy," wrote Arthur Schopenhauer (1788-1860), "is nothing but the correct and universal understanding of experience itself, the true exposition of its meaning and content." The metaphysical is "that which is related to it as thought to words." As the title of his chief work, *The World as Will and Idea* suggests, his own philosophy was in the technical sense an idealism. But he differed fundamentally from the Classical German Idealists in his view of reason, which for him was no more than a formal function: "Reason is feminine in nature: it can only give after it has received. Of itself it has nothing but the empty forms of its own operation." At the outset of his chief work, he stated: "The world is my idea—this is a truth which holds good for everything that lives and knows, though man alone can bring it into reflective and abstract consciousness." He regarded that as a fundamental teaching of Kant. Along with Kant he also took the world as idea as only appearance. It is not by theoretical reason which is concerned with the world as idea, that reality is known. What is known within is the will, objectified for each individual in his body, as the Universal Will is objectified in the world. Ultimately, the former (the individuals) are no other than the latter (the Universal Will). This fundamental conception of the unity of things, which he shared with the Classical German Idealists, was acknowledged by Schopenhauer not only from what he considered the implications of the transcendental doctrines of Kant, but also under the influence of the Indian philosophy of the Upanishads. "The world, in all the multiplicity of its parts and forms, is the manifestation, the objectivity, of the one will to live." In Indian philosophy he also found support for his pessimistic views of conscious life which he accepted on consideration of the painfulness of desire as the continuous expression of the will. "All satisfaction, or what is commonly called happiness, is always really and essentially only negative, never positive." Life alternates between the pain of unsatisfied desire and the boredom which ensues when it is satisfied. It is from these standpoints that Schopenhauer's views on nature, morality, the aesthetic, religion and history may be briefly stated. While he warned that if we wish to understand Nature we must not compare it with works of our own, he maintained that "the active principle" in it, whether organic or inorganic, is "absolutely identical with what is known within ourselves as will." Morality is essentially that co-operation with others which arises from sympathy, that is, our sharing of their sufferings. It is an eradication of egoism, for hatred and wickedness are conditioned by egoism. The good man "sees that the distinction between himself and others . . . only belongs to a fleeting and illusive phenomenon."

The aesthetic has something of the character of the universal and in the contemplation of the beautiful one is at least temporarily emancipated from the urgency of one's own desires and transcends one's individuality. Religion, in its fundamental nature, is "the denial of the will to live," the peace of the complete renunciation of all conscious desire. In opposition to the Hegelian view of history as a progressive dialectical process, Schopenhauer described it as "a heavy and confused dream," a continuous reiteration of the same experiences, only the names of the places and persons being different. In a well-known passage, he asked: "The ultimate aim of it all: what is it?" and answered: "To sustain ephemeral and tormented individuals through a short span of time, in the most fortunate cases with endurable want and comparative freedom from pain, which however is at once attended with ennui; then the reproduction of this race and its strivings." Schopenhauer's philosophy had a wide influence in the later development of voluntarism as against the rationalism of Hegel. Its pessimism provided an antidote to the professed optimism of Classical German Idealism. Yet, though it was continued in the work of Eduard von Hartmann, (1842-1906), his philosophy was not of the character to make a wide appeal. It was met by the attitude of most, even of the very old, of "the will to live," an attitude at the basis of the opposing philosophy of Friedrich Nietzsche.

The Classical German Idealist and Schopenhauer had gone beyond Kant. They had supposed that they had reached an ultimate metaphysics. In spite of their application of some fundamental principles to it, the empirical was reduced to the level of appearance, between which and the metaphysical Absolute or Universal Will there was an "ugly ditch" which could not be satisfactorily bridged. The revolt from this position among professional philosophers took the form mainly of a movement "Back to Kant." From this movement came various types of Neo-Kantianism. They all went back to Kant's view of the limitations of knowledge, and proclaimed themselves non-metaphysical. They did not necessarily deny any actuality to the metaphysical in some sense, or expound a mere phenomenalism as if phenomena exhausted reality, but proceeded on the Kantian contention that the metaphysical is beyond human knowledge. As they rejected the idealist metaphysics of Fichte, Schelling, and Hegel, they also avoided falling into a materialist metaphysics. For they regarded the functions of thought and the principles of morality, which they acknowledged along Kant's lines, as not compatible with materialism. The Neo-Kantians never became a well co-ordinated School. Some devoted themselves chiefly to detailed expositions of the works of Kant. All avoided system-making. They neglected what have been called "the great problems" of philosophy: the ultimate nature of reality, of God and immortality, freedom and the nature of evil. With them, philosophy in Germany became largely enquiries into particular problems, mostly of the theory of knowledge, especially of the natural sciences. There were, however, two groups which attempted something different and something more. The Marburg group, with Hermann Cohen (1842-1918), emphasizing the fundamental principles of ethics and Hans Vaihinger (1852-1933), expounding a theory of knowledge as giving us an "as if," developed with Albrecht Ritschl (1822-1889) a view of religious dogmas as "symbols," inaugurating one of the most important movements of Christian Theology in the late nineteenth century. The Heidelberg group, Wilhelm Windelband (1848-1915), Heinrich Rickert (1863-1936), and Ernst Troeltsch (1865-1923), with detailed consideration of the particularizing logic of history as contrasted with the generalizing logic of the natural sciences, developed Kant's ethical doctrines to a wider theory of values with a recognition of the particular persons and events of history to which Classical German Idealism had not done justice. Though the similarities and any historical connection have not yet been traced American Critical Realism has close affinities with German Neo-Kantianism.

At the time of the rise of Neo-Kantianism and of the beginning of attention to the philosophy of Schopenhauer, another idealistic system was formulated in Germany which has had a great influence on British and American thinkers, especially those insisting on the significance of individual personality, as James Ward, Borden Parker Bowne, to some extent Josiah Royce and A. S. Pringle-Pattison, and Personal Idealists in general. This was the philosophy of Hermann Lotze (1817-1881). Lotze had an acute mind and was well informed in the physical sciences and psychology (on which he wrote much, anticipating Bergson's doctrine of time). Two things gave his philosophy an appeal for those who rejected Classical German Idealism: his adequate recognition of the mechanical aspects of physical nature and his defence of the reality of individual personality. Though with a conception of one ultimate World-ground, he seemed to give his philosophy a turn towards pantheism, it was widely interpreted as theistic. His attitude was essentially teleological, maintaining in somewhat Aristotelian fashion, that the nature of reality is to be sought with reference to its "end" or purpose. Even the mechanical aspects of Nature have significance only if viewed teleologically. His writings are distinguished by their balanced judgments, and those interested in idealism today might find better support in them than in those of Fichte, Schelling, or Hegel.

BIBLIOGRAPHY

In view of the purpose of this volume, this Bibliography gives only a selection of main works, and when available, in English translation.

I. KANT, see chapter XXII.
J. G. FICHTE, *The Science of Knowledge,* trs. by A. E. Kroeger (London, 1889).
———, *The Science of Ethics,* trs. by A. E. Kroeger (London, 1907).
———, *The Popular Works of J. G. Fichte* (London, 1889).
———, *Addresses to the German Nation,* trs. by R. F. Jones (Chicago, 1922).
W. J. SCHELLING, *Ideen zur einer Philosophie der Natur* (1797).
———, *System der transcendentalen Idealismus* (1800).
———, *Philosophie der Offenbarung* (1858).
———, *Of Human Freedom,* trs. by J. Gutman (Chicago, 1936).
G. W. F. HEGEL, *Logic,* trs. by W. Wallace (Oxford, 1892).
———, *The Philosophy of Mind,* trs. by W. Wallace (Oxford, 1894).
———, *The Phenomenology of Mind,* trs. by J. B. Baillie (London, 1931).
———, *The Philosophy of Right,* trs. by T. M. Knox (Oxford, 1942).
———, *The Philosophy of Fine Art,* trs. by F. P. B. Osmaston (London, 1920).
———, *Lectures on the Philosophy of Religion,* trs. by E. B. Spiers (London, 1895).
———, *The Philosophy of History,* trs. by J. Sibree (London, 1861).
A. SCHOPENHAUER, *The World as Will and Idea,* trs. by R. B. Haldane and J. Kemp (6th ed., 1907-09).
———, *The Basis of Morality,* trs. by A. B. Bullock (London, 1903).

A HISTORY OF PHILOSOPHICAL SYSTEMS

R. EUCKEN, *The Problem of Human Life,* trs. by W. S. Hough and W. B. Gibson (London, 1910).
———, *Life's Basis and Life's Ideal,* trs. by A. G. Widgery (London, 1911).
———, *The Life of the Spirit,* trs. by F. L. Pogson (London, 1909).
———, *Christianity and the New Idealism,* trs. by W. J. and W. B. Gibson (London, 1909).
H. LOTZE, *Logic,* trs. by B. Bosanquet (Oxford, 1889).
———, *Metaphysics,* trs. ed., B. Bosanquet (Oxford, 1887).
———, *Microcosmos,* trs. E. Hamilton and E. C. Jones (Edinburgh, 1888).
H. COHEN, *Ethik des reinen Willens* (Berlin, 1907).
———, *System der Philosophie* (Berlin, 1922).
W. WINDELBAND, *Einleitung in die Philosophie* (Tübingen, 1923).
E. TROELTSCH, *Der Historismus und seine Uberwindung* (Berlin, 1924).
H. RICKERT, *Die Grenzen der naturwissenschaftliche Begriffsbildung: eine logische Einleitung in die historischen Wissenschaften* (Tübingen, 1929).
H. VAIHINGER, *The Philosophy of "As if,"* trs. by C. K. Ogden (London, 1924).

CHAPTER TWENTY-FOUR

DIALECTICAL MATERIALISM

SIEGFRIED MARCK

WHEN ONE speaks of dialectical materialism, the two terms appearing in this conception and the justification for their combination need precise explanation. Much more than other "isms" the trend of dialectical materialism is exposed to the danger of being used as a slogan of propaganda. There have been approving or disapproving interpretations which considered the propagandistic meaning of dialectical materialism its very foundation and justification.

What then does "dialectical" mean? Immediately the name of Hegel (1770-1831) comes to our mind. But by no means was Hegel the inventor of this type of thinking. It has had a long history which in Western philosophy began with Heraclitus (c. 536-470 B.C.). Hegel said that there was no sentence of Heraclitus which he would not have been able to include in his own logic. In a very different way Zeno (c. 490-430 B.C.) of the anti-Heraclitean Eleatic school developed dialectics, and still another type of dialectics was represented by Plato (427-347 B.C.). These different forms of dialectics have something in common: they are characterized by the central rôle of the opposites and contradictions for both human thinking as well as for reality. For Heraclitus "war is the father of all, the king of all." This statement was not meant as a glorification of war as a military phenomenon. Heraclitus speaks of the struggle of metaphysico-ontological opposites which he considers the core of the universe. In Zeno there is rather a negative type of dialectics than a positive one: according to this opinion, he who tries to leave the circle of the static concepts of the Eleatic school must run into contradictions. For Zeno such contradictions do not have a creative function for truth; they tend to compromise certain attempts at thinking. Finally in Plato, at least in the Plato before his dialogue *Parmenides,* the struggle of the opposites is not the core of the universe. The ideas are as static as the Eleatic being. But for Plato dialectics is a necessary method of grasping these ideas through the Socratic method of discussion. Thus the Socratic dialectic was enriched by Plato's insight in the rôle of analyses and hypotheses in the field of mathematics.

Whether dialectics is understood as something positive or negative, whether it is considered a method of human thinking or a metaphysical quality, in any case the confrontation of the opposites is the indispensable vehicle of dialectics. The acceptance of the dialectical method implies an element of dynamism and evolutionism. From the epistemological viewpoint this attitude leads to "contextualism," *i.e.*, the object of knowledge is produced in the process of knowing rather than mirrored according to the copy-doctrines.

If Hegel's dialectics was not the only outstanding type, it was nevertheless the most comprehensive. Furthermore, it became the point of departure and of permanent reference for dialectical materialism. Hegel's dialectics appeared in the framework of the metaphysics of absolute idealism, the famous catchword of which was the statement: the rational is real, and the real is rational. For the radical monism of these speculations, reason is not human reason and reality is not experiential reality. The Hegelian system is an idealistic and rational pantheism and therefore an attempt at fusing philosophy and theology. Though philosophy of religion is treated as a special division of Hegel's system, his entire system is through and through philosophy of religion. Hegel wants to trace the thoughts of the Divine Mind, and with a clarifying simplification one is allowed to speak here of God himself as the true philosopher. Of course, the history of human thought could not remain petrified at this mysticism, which was brought into rational and scholastic form. But the keen, even super-human attempt at philosophizing not only "under a certain species of eternity" like Spinoza (1632-1677), but in becoming one in human philosophizing with the Divine Mind, was one of the most exciting experiments. Its failure was a foregone conclusion, but the challenge, implied in this philosophical system, remained.

The character of the creative contradictions in Hegel's system is given in its theologico-philosophical structure: the contradictions between the absolute, infinite and Divine Mind and the limited, finite and human mind must be in the foreground. The human mind has its basis in nature, *i.e.,* in the general antithesis of mind. Since the Divine Philosopher philosophizes through the medium of the human mind, philosophy must everywhere break through the limitations of the human mind: a negative dialectics has the task of destroying continuously the barriers of finiteness. Permanent revelation of the falsities of finiteness becomes the condition of arriving at definite transcendence. In the ultimate analysis the entire finite sphere, composed of both nature and the human mind, is considered a *self-alienation* of God from himself. Then positive dialectics consists in self-reconciliation of the Divine Mind with himself. In the famous scheme: thesis, antithesis, synthesis, God appears first in undeveloped, immediate or abstract form, then He passes through the sphere of imperfect mediation, and the level of synthesis signifies perfect self-mediation and self-reconciliation. In the history of dialectics the main performance of Hegel was the fusion of the three forms of dialectical thinking, mentioned at the beginning: the Heraclitean, the Zenonian and the Platonic. Hegel combines the dialectics of things with the dialectics of thinking and so did Heraclitus and Plato. Since mind is the very essence of reality, dialectics must be both: a real metaphysical happening and a method of knowledge. Hegel also combines the positive dialectics of Heraclitus which was based upon intuition and vision with the negative of Zeno arising from analytical and polemic tendencies. In the system as a whole positive dialectics triumphs over the negativity of antagonisms. Philosophy arrives at an end and becomes saturated in the harmonious thinking on thinking of the Absolute Mind.

It seems to be a far cry from these Hegelian concepts to such Marxian ideas as class-struggle, the transformation of ideals into ideologies, economic determinism. But the so-called Hegelians of the left or "the young Hegelians," as they called themselves, thinkers like Feuerbach (1804-1872), Bauer (1809-1882) and Ruge represented the link between Hegel and the fully developed doctrine of Marxism. They began the work of putting the Hegelian system which "stood on its head" on its feet. They opposed humanistic to theological philosophy. In doing this they did not give up absolutism and monism: for them man became the *absolute* center of the universe and all standards above him were to be reduced to that of human needs and human existence The existentialists of today have emphasized the thesis that existence always precedes essence. From this viewpoint the young Hegelians too deserve the name of existentialists. In twentieth century existentialism it is more or less the religious or the anti-religious existence of man which is in the center. The young Hegelians considered the social or the historical existence of man the measure of all. Sometimes it is even the merely natural existence that becomes central and then they become outright naturalists.

The term materialism has in this context a mainly polemic meaning: it is directed against the absolute idealism of Hegel. The fundamental quality of this materialism, common to its different factions, is anti-idealism. The slogans representing this mood change: nature against mind, experience against speculation, science against dream, social reality against utopia, history against theology, man against mystification. The stream of young Hegelian existentialism discharged itself through different channels. Since Marx (1818-1883) and Engels (1820-1895) believed they had discovered the key to human life in economic categories, their materialism took the form of economic determinism. In a complete reversal of Hegelianism, the interpretation of history and of all human life moves from below to above. The substructure or the technological production forces and the social production relations determine the super-structure of political constitutions, mores and morality, ways of life, value systems, philosophies and religions. Being, interpreted as economic and social being, determines consciousness. States are no longer considered incarnations of justice or emanations of metaphysical entities in terms of the spirit of man nor of world-mind. They are instruments of economic life, more precisely, tools of the economically powerful to maintain and to strengthen their power by force and propaganda. Economic classes, *i.e.*, groups of men who play the same rôle in the process of production and therefore have the same material interests become the carriers of history. The key-statement of the *Communist Manifesto* (1848) *viz.*, that all hitherto known history is the history of class-struggles obtains its full significance when it is related to the transformation of Hegelianism. It is understandable why this philosophy of history can be called materialism.

But why is it called dialectical materialism? Two insights are obvious from the very first: 1) Hegel's theological dialectics must be eliminated from this materialistic context. 2) The concept of dialectics cannot appear without relation to the rôle of opposites and contradictions. Indeed, for Marx the real antagonism of classes shall replace the idealistic contradictions between logical and metaphysical categories. But his thesis that history always was a battlefield was not of such originality and importance that a special name dialectics, so much charged with philosophical significance, had to be coined for it. The emphasis upon the economic component in historical struggles may be original (not the thought as such), but the recognition of antagonisms as the vehicle of historical revolution is a truism. The insight into the dynamic character of history and the mutual interdependence of all social elements are not necessarily linked to dialectical thinking.

However, Marx's intentions transcended the mere passing from philosophical to empirical history. He wanted to overcome Hegel's contemplative and speculative philosophy by a revolutionary philosophy and a practical theory. Philosophy was supposed to change its substance by its very realization. Therefore the dialectics of Marxism does not evaporate into the mere clash of real forces. The struggle between such forces is rather an empirical exponent of *inner* contradictions, set with the essential structure of a social and economic system. Such contradictions are especially outspoken in the capitalistic epoch in which chronic crises occur with necessity, crises which are different from the meeting of accidentally hostile interests in the same era of history. If bourgeois capitalism produces its own and specific antagonism, this antagonism has to be understood by Hegel's dialectical concept of self-alienation in a new form. Indeed, Marxism has given a new meaning to the central concept of alienation. The alienation of the Divine Mind is now transformed into the alienation of man from himself, the self-reconciliation of the Absolute Mind through speculative thinking becomes the restoration of human totality in a classless society.

The ramifications of the category of alienation, as used by Marx, are numerous. For, alienation is the key-concept of his critique of civilization. The capitalistic system represents the apogee of "thingification" (*Verdinglichung*) of man. In the practical sphere, man has become a commodity; and in the theoretical, the social character of the most important economic phenomena is not understood and therefore the structure of capitalism is considered a "natural" necessity. "Fetishism" of commodities and man as a commodity—these are forms of alienation in the sphere of theoretical and practical reason. And Marx's criticism of this reification is still more general and radical. In the course of history, man has lost his totality through division of labor. In the long run and in connection with social dependence this division of labor has transformed man into a cog of the wheel and produced the sorcerer-apprentice-situation: man hunted and threatened by the tools which he created himself. Furthermore, the social and political institutions of man are as such endangered by reification: they suppress the very life which was their source by petrifying it and by transforming means into ends. But one finds reification not only in institutionalized ideas which are complicated by the power-situation. Reification starts with the pretense at objectivity and eternal values. Traditional value systems demand strict obedience from man, and so they restrict his immediacy. In short, there is an element of reification in the authoritarian color of all "Platonism."

Every reification, including that which led to the fateful separation of practice and theory will disappear with the establishment of a classless society. This society will restore human totality; man will return from the "abstractions" of a citizen, a manual or intellectual worker, of a follower of a philosophy or a religious faith. Total man will create the world in his image and recognize himself in all his products.

The main objection to dialectical materialism, taken strictly in its philosophical meaning, must be directed against the bringing together of validity and reification. Fetishism and idealism, man's creation of a world of forms above himself and the de-humanizing effects of a disintegrating civilization are treated on the same level by Marx. As a philosopher Marx speaks of Platonism or Christianity, as if they were already phenomena of capitalism in the phase of its "imperialistic decadence." He treats division of labor, a progressive contribution to the autonomy of man's specialized cultural performances, as if it had been man's fall from unbroken wholeness and nothing else. Both Marx's criticism of hitherto known history and his vision of the classless society suffer from elements of a romantic semi-anarchistic Rousseauanism. Such an attitude glorifies prehistorical immediacy. In Marx too, as it was the case in Hegel, such immediacy is *aufgehoben, i.e.,* preserved at the same time with its abolition. Thus the "realized philosophy" or dialectical materialism combines features of a nihilistic rejection of all existing civilizations with the optimistic belief that a change in the mode of production would transform the hitherto known man of history into a real philosopher-king. (Or should one say an anti-philosopher-king?) Man of the hitherto known history was fragmentary, aggressive, selfish, dependent, fearful. The socialistic man will be total, peaceful, solidaristic, sovereign. This sovereign will not need philosophy or religion, because he incarnates them in his own totally developed being. Using this utopian standard Marx cannot be just to the contribution each historical epoch and the social class representing it have made to a supertemporal development of the human mind.

Though it cannot be enlarged upon, the thesis could be defended that many, if not all failures in a century of Marxism have something to do with *the* mentioned cardinal mistake: to the identification of reification and autonomy. The attitude to values and to the state were the crucial points in all history of Marxism. Revisionism, Fascism and in spite of all lip-service to Marxian orthodoxy, Communism, too, were reactions against the thesis that values were nothing but ideologies, and that the state was nothing but the instrument of the ruling class. Not only sociologically, but even more so philosophically, the prognosis concerning the rôle of the lower middle-classes with their adherence to religion, nation and state was proved wrong.

With regard to dialectical materialism and its development, its orthodox defense, the loosening of its rigidity, the outright criticism of it, can be used as a primer to a survey of the numerous schools of Marxism. There have been, of course, orthodox Marxians or alleged orthodox Marxians who went through thick and thin with the line of the third Internationale. Other writers who called themselves orthodox Marxists and not only the Trotzkyites, considered Stalinism as a betrayal of revolution and of Marxism. Nevertheless, all these hostile brothers confess dialectical materialism, and all of them were opposed to that which they called "tenacious idealistic sophistries." They all fought against the wave of irrationalism which swept our century, against the resurrection of religion of supernaturalism and existentialism. For them, young Marx, the philosopher, and Marx, the economist, were one. And so they had contempt of the eclectic separation of these two elements by the revisionists. Sometimes their philosophical eagerness went so far that they almost forgot the Marxist claim that philosophy was finished through its very realization. Then a kind of re-Hegelianization of Marxism could be observed. This attitude in which the materialistic component faded in the face of the dialectical was strongly represented by perhaps the most gifted philosopher of Marxism, the Hungarian Georg Lukacs (1885-). A writer who also philosophizes in the orthodox way is Pierre Naville in France. For him dialectical materialism represents twentieth century rationalism. It is in real alliance with the development of modern science. Dialectical materialism should recognize that its true philosophical implications are opposed to all irrationalistic interpretations of modern physics by theology and "imperialism." In this country John Sommerville has written an apology of Soviet philosophy. He followed the advice of Engels and applied the three laws of dialectic: the law of contradiction, the turning of quantity into quality, and the negation of negation to specific logical and methodological problems. But such attempts rather compromised than confirmed dialectical materialism.

Orthodox partisans of dialectical materialism appeared, in general, later than those interpreters of Marx who did not pay too much attention to the philosophical writings of young Marx. This was partly caused by the fact that before the First World War the revolutionary character was considered outmoded and partly by the accidental circumstance that these writings had not yet been published. The bulk of the Marxian center which was leading in the united second Internationale between the eighties and 1914 did not make dialectical materialism the cornerstone of interpretation; on the other hand, they did not reject it. Also, those thinkers represented the center, *i.e.*, a mitigated orthodoxy, which wanted to combine in an open-minded manner elements of other philosophies with Marxism: such was the case of the Austrian socialist Max Adler (1873-1937) who combined Marx with Kant. In another way, Sidney Hook inaugurated a synthesis between Marx and John Dewey's pragmatism.

Finally the revisionists, the first speaker of whom was Eduard Bernstein (1850-1932), blamed dialectics as a catch-phrase of

Marxism and made it responsible for revolutionarism in words, refuted by the actions of the great socialist parties. Bernstein himself wanted to replace so-called scientific socialism by a critical or ethical socialism and took his philosophical cue from Kant. Much more radical revisionists of our day like Max Eastman saw in dialectical materialism the residues of the Hegelian and Germanic mind of Marx and rejected it entirely. Trends, influenced by modern psychology and all those movements in which socialism was colored ethically and religiously, pointed in the same direction.

Like other monisms dialectical materialism is unsatisfactory as such and has to be completed by dualistic and pluralistic insights. Dialectical materialism cannot overcome the necessary tension between facts and values, social reality and philosophy. But elements of a critically interpreted dialectics will be useful for socialistic thought as heuristic maxims and regulative principles.

BIBLIOGRAPHY

G. HEGEL, *Philosophy of Mind* (Oxford, 1894).
B. CROCE, *What is Alive and What is Dead in Hegel's Philosophy?* (London, 1915).
K. LOEWITH, *Von Hegel zu Nietzsche* (Zürich, 1940).
H. MARCUSE, *Reason and Revolution* (Hegel and the Rise of Social Theory), (New York, 1941).
"Dialectica," *Revue Internationale de Philosophie de la Connaissance* (1948), No. 6.
MARX-ENGELS, *Selected Works* (Moscow, 1935).
————, *The German Ideology* (New York, 1933).
F. ENGELS, *The Origin of the Family, Private Property and the State* (New York, 1942).
S. HOOK, *Toward the Understanding of Karl Marx* (New York, 1933).
————, *From Hegel to Marx* (New York, 1935).
M. EASTMAN, *Marxism is a Science?* (New York, 1935).
Aspects of Dialectical Materialism by Six English authors (London, 1937).
J. SOMMERVILLE, *Soviet Philosophy* (New York, 1946).
G. PLEKHANOW, *In Defense of Materialism* (London, 1947).
G. LUKACS, *Geschichte und Klassenbewusstsein* (Berlin, 1923).
————, *Existentialism ou Marxism?* (Paris, 1948).
M. ADLER, *Marxistische Probleme* (Leipzig, 1925).
K. KORSCH, *Marxismus und Philosophie* (Leipzig, 1930).
P. NAVILLE, *Materialism et Dialectique* (Paris, 1946).

CHAPTER TWENTY-FIVE

ENGLISH AND AMERICAN ABSOLUTE IDEALISM

G. WATTS CUNNINGHAM

THE TYPE of philosophy here under survey is that represented at the turn of the century by a group of English and American philosophers commonly called the neo-Hegelians. This group included most of the professional philosophers of the period in both countries, but for the purpose of the present discussion the most important members of the group are: Francis Herbert Bradley (1846-1924) and Bernard Bosanquet (1848-1923) in England and, in America, Josiah Royce (1855-1916) and James Edwin Creighton (1861-1924). These four thinkers are here of primary importance, because the main line of argument underlying absolute idealism received at their hands its clearest formulation and that argument is here of primary concern. But what is the doctrine?

I

As employed in the histories of philosophy, the word "idealism" refers to rather widely divergent types of philosophical doctrine such as Platonism, Berkeleianism, panpsychism, personalism, and absolutism. Among these various types, however, there is a common thesis which may be said to be the fundamental thesis of idealism as against its opposite doctrine commonly called "materialism." Loosely stated, this thesis is that both ideas and ideals are alike in last analysis fundamental for philosophical construction and not, as materialism holds, derivative and only of secondary significance. From different interpretations of this thesis, which arise out of different conceptions of the nature and context of ideas and ideals, the various types of idealism emerge. Thus, Plato's statement "the good may be said to be not only the author of knowledge to all things known, but of their being and essence"; Berkeley's "to be is to be perceived"; Bradley's "to be real is to be indissolubly one thing with sentience"; Bosanquet's "nothing can fulfil the conditions of self-existence except by possessing the unity which belongs only to mind"; McTaggart's "the only substances are selves, parts of selves, and groups of selves or parts of selves"; Royce's "to talk of Being is to speak of fact that is either present to consciousness or else nothing"; Creighton's "the real world is the world of significant individual wholes constituted by reflective experience"—all of these statements are variations on the fundamental theme, but with emphases concerning the nature of mind and its contents sufficiently diverse to carry with them divergent implications concerning the nature of "being" or "existence" or "reality."

The emphasis which distinguishes absolute idealism is, of course, that which ultimately leads to the identification of reality with what is called the Absolute. This is conceived as a "whole" or "system" or "world" which is in some sense "mental" or "spiritual" in nature. And it is one in the dual sense that (a) it systemically includes all objects that can be said to be real, and (b) it thus includes ideals as well as ideas—objects of valuation as well as objects of cognition. The fact that would fall beyond sentience, Bradley asserts in Chapter XIV of *Appearance and Reality* (1893; second edition, 1896), is "a mere word and a failure, or else an attempt at self-contradiction," and the sentience which must thus include fact must also include "every element of the universe, sensation, feeling, thought and will"; nor is it merely "the sum of things" but is, rather, "the unity in which all things, coming together, are transmuted, in which they are all changed alike, though not changed equally." And with what is here asserted other absolutists would in principle agree: whatever is real is systemically contained in the Absolute, "where we can point to reality or truth, there is the one undivided life of the Absolute."

There are, indeed, important differences among the absolutists concerning the internal structure of the Absolute and its relation to its "appearances." Thus, in the "Supplementary Essay" appended to the first series of his Gifford Lectures, published in 1899 under the title *The World and the Individual,* Royce repudiates Bradley's conception of the Absolute as a super-relational whole and urges the substitution of the conception of an "Absolute Self" which "has to express itself in an endless series of individual acts, so that it is explicitly an Individual Whole of Individual Elements." Bosanquet, for his part, tends to look in both directions but in the end leans strongly, though as I think inconsistently, towards the view of Bradley. Such differences, however, do not here concern us and may be left on one side; I have elsewhere (*The Idealistic Argument in Recent British and American Philosophy*, 1933) considered them at some length.

But, despite such differences, there is general agreement with Bradley's further assertion: "The Absolute *is* its appearances, it really is all and everyone of them. . . . We can find no province of the world so low but the Absolute inhabits it." This emphasis is recognized and constantly emphasized by all of the absolutists in their common insistence that the conception of the Absolute is empirically grounded. As Bosanquet states it, the Absolute "is simply the high-water mark of fluctuations in experience, of which in general we are daily and normally aware." In Royce's language, "the very Absolute, in all its fullness of life, is even now the object that you really mean by your fragmentary passing ideas." And Creighton urges that the "category of Absolute Mind. . . . is justified only when it is shown to be a necessary standpoint in order to enable reason to overcome actual difficulties that present themselves in human experience." Thus, for the absolutists, the Absolute is not far removed from us; on the contrary, it is everywhere present to us, the all-encompassing totality with which we are constantly in touch in all of our intellectual activities and which, as Bosanquet says, persistently drives us from pillar to post. It is not, as William James mistakenly supposed, "a marble temple shining on a hill"; it is, rather, as James would have it, inextricably involved in the dust and dirt of things. And, it may be added, the argument to which the absolutists all alike in the end appeal is designed to show precisely this.

II

As noted above, the English and American proponents of absolute idealism are commonly called neo-Hegelians. They are so called because of the assumption that the logical principles on which they build are essentially those applied by Georg Wilhelm Friedrich Hegel (1770-1831) in the construction of his own system, which is the outstanding formulation of this type of philosophy in the classical tradition.

There is no doubt, of course, that Hegel's influence on the development of English and American thought during the period under survey was not only very marked but avowedly so. In England, James Huchison Stirling's famous book, *The Secret of Hegel, being the Hegelian System in Origin, Principle, Form and Matter* (1865; second edition, 1898), written in the conviction that in this system "all the great interests of mankind have been kindled into new lights by the touch of this master-hand," was followed by translations of Hegel's more important works and by numerous expositions and articles designed to exhibit the "master-hand" in action. And contemporaneously in America Hegel was being introduced by a group at St. Louis, the so-called St. Louis school, through the medium of *The Journal of Speculative Philosophy* (1867-1893) under the editorship of the outstanding member of the group, William Torrey Harris (1835-1909; United States Commissioner of Education, 1889-1906), and also by the Concord School of Philosophy and Literature, which Harris joined in 1879 and of which he was the leading spirit for the next twenty years. In the Address to the Reader prefixed to the first volume of his *Journal*, Harris wrote: "The national consciousness has moved forward on to a new platform during the last few years. The idea underlying our form of government has hitherto developed only one of its essential phases— that of brittle individualism—in which national unity seems an external mechanism soon to be entirely dispensed with and the enterprise of the private man or of the corporation substituted for it. Now we have arrived at the consciousness of the other essential phase, and each individual recognizes his substantial side to be the State as such. The freedom of the citizen does not consist in the mere Arbitrary, but in the realization of the life which finds expression in established law. This new phase of national life demands to be digested and comprehended." To meet this demand the Hegelian system seemed to Harris and his colleagues an ideal instrument, and the main purpose of the *Journal* was to show in some detail how it was so. Nor was the "new platform" concerned exclusively with political matters but with scientific and religious as well—with "all the great interests of mankind." And the purpose was to show how these were "kindled into new lights" at the touch of the master-hand. As J. H. Muirhead writes at pages 321-322 of *The Platonic Tradition in Anglo-Saxon Philosophy:* "It was because Harris and his companions thought they saw in the Hegelian philosophy a sword with which to smite the three-headed monster of anarchy in politics, traditionalism in religion, and naturalism in science, that they found the courage to undertake and the perseverance to carry through the task of naturalizing it in America." And they succeeded well in the undertaking, as the detailed history of the movement shows. But these details lie beyond the scope of this survey.

What the four later representatives of the movement named above severally owe to Hegel is a moot question. All of them acknowledge indebtedness to Hegel, indeed, but always with important reservations; none of them seems willing to be called neo-Hegelian without qualification. In any event, however, it can be said that, though none of them makes any use of or holds in esteem the formal machinery of the dialectic which seemed so important to Hegel, the fact remains that they are all committed in principle to the basic theory which Hegel says underlies the dialectic as employed by him and which he summarily states in various passages of his writings, notably in sections 79-82 of the *Smaller Logic* (1817; second edition, 1827). Particularly are they committed to what Hegel there describes as the third 'side' or 'moment' in every "logical entity" and to which he gives the name of "the speculative stage, or stage of positive reason"—reason, that is, which, as he says in the Introduction to his *Larger Logic* (1812; second edition, 1831) is "the comprehension of the unity of opposites, or of the positive in the negative," which also "holds together in itself all abstract determinations, and is their solid absolutely concrete unity," in which "the opposition in consciousness between a subjective entity existing for itself, and another similar objective entity, is known to be overcome, and existence is known as pure concept in itself, and the pure concept known as true existence," and for which, as expressed in the Preface to his *Phenomenology of Mind* (1807), "truth is the whole" which is "merely the essential nature reaching its completeness through the process of its own development."

But the logical doctrine here schematically expressed received at the hands of our four philosophers a new formulation which is wholly independent of Hegel's quasi-esoteric terminology and which is much clearer and more convincing than Hegel's. It is this formulation with which we shall henceforth be concerned, quite without reference to Hegel. And we shall concentrate attention on the main points of agreement among the four, leaving on one side the differences which, though at times more than merely verbal and having important bearing on the varying conceptions of the Absolute above noted, fall within a common body of basic principles. Of these, space here will allow mention of only three.

III

The first is what Bradley calls an assumption about truth and reality. "I have assumed," he writes in the Appendix to the second edition of *Appearance and Reality,* "that the object of metaphysics is to find a general view which will satisfy the intellect, and I have assumed that whatever succeeds in doing this is real and true, and that whatever fails is neither." Though said to be an assumption, however, this is not arbitrary; on the contrary, it is inescapable and the alternative is ruinous. It can neither be proved nor questioned, since the proof or the question "must imply the truth of the doctrine, and, if that is not assumed, both vanish." And, except for differences arising out of various readings of the details of the intellectual process, our other absolutists agree with Bradley here.

The two assertions here made—(a) that what satisfies the intellect is true, and (b) that what satisfies the intellect is real—are distinguishable assertions. The question remains whether or not they are also separable, and this question is of fundamental importance. The absolutist maintains that they are not separable, and he bases his position on a certain view of judgment which he holds is the central activity of the intellect.

The first of the two assertions is presumably acceptable to everyone for whom truth is determinable only through the uses of reason in the sense in which "reason" is centrally involved in the process of reasoning or making inferences, since the assumption in question is at least an avowal of this position. And the sole alternative here is appeal to some sort of immediate or direct insight into truth—to mystical illumination or untutored intuition or infallible faith. To one who makes such an appeal the absolutist poses the question, How then can truth be said to be universal and what is the criterion? And this question, he thinks, is disastrous to the non-intellectualist's position.

But one might accept the first assertion and reject the second—might, that is, admit that what satisfies the intellect is alone true but maintain that such satisfaction entails no consequences with reference to the question concerning what is real. This, indeed, is done by one who identifies truth with validity and holds that validity is determinable by definition. To such an one the absolutist opposes his special theory of judgment—the theory according to which, as Bosanquet states it in the second chapter of the first volume of his *Logic or the Morphology of Knowledge* (1888; second edition, 1911), judgment is held to be "the intellectual function which defines reality by significant ideas, and in so doing affirms the reality of those ideas." For, on this theory, what is real is the subject—the logical as distinguished from the grammatical subject—of every judgment. "Every judgment, perceptive or universal," Bosanquet urges as a matter of fact (*Logic,* Vol. I. Chapter I), "might without altering its meaning be introduced by some such phrase as 'Reality is such that—,' 'The real world is characterised by —.'" And Bradley agrees, almost verbatim, in his article "On Some Aspects of Truth" (originally published in *Mind,* July 1911, and reprinted in *Essays on Truth and Reality,* Chapter XI): "'Reality is such that S is P,' may be taken . . . as a formula which expresses the nature of truth. S is P (to put it otherwise) *because* Reality is such."

This view of judgment is repudiated, for example, by epistemological dualists for whom the idea (the object of judgment) is sharply sundered from the thing itself (the real object), the former standing as the representative in mind of the latter, as also by those who maintain that the conditions of truth are determinable by initial stipulation. The absolutist, however, contends that his is the only theory of judgment which is warranted by experience and is, therefore, the only tenable view. In his essay on "Two Types of Idealism" (originally published in *The Philosophical Review,* September 1917, and reprinted in *Studies in Speculative Philosophy,*

Chapter XIV), Creighton distinguishes between what he calls "mentalism" and "speculative idealism," argues that only the latter is tenable, and concisely states the underlying theory of judgment and its empirical warrant: "This historical speculative idealism, as occupying the standpoint of experience, has never separated the mind from the external order of nature. It knows no ego-centric predicament, because it recognizes no ego 'alone with its states,' standing apart from the order of nature and from a society of minds. It thus dismisses as unmeaning those problems which are sometimes called 'epistemological,' as to how the mind as such can know reality as such. Without any epistemological grace before meat it falls to work to philosophize, assuming, naively if you please, that the mind by its very nature is already in touch with reality. Instead, that is, of assuming that there is an entity called mind, and another entity having no organic relation to mind called nature, it assumes on the basis of experience that these realities are not sundered and opposed, but are in very being and essence related and complementary. . . . If it be said that this is mere assumption, and not proof, I reply that this is the universal assumption upon which all experience and all science proceeds. It needs no proof because it is the standpoint of experience itself." And Bradley states the matter even more concisely (*Appearance and Reality*, p. 164): "No one ever *means* to assert about anything but reality, or to do anything but qualify a 'that' by a 'what.' " Thus for the absolutist, ideas are not images or copies floating "in" minds as surrogates in knowledge for something which they are supposed to image or copy; nor are they meaningless verbiage until made meaningful by definition and stipulation. Rather, they are significant characterizations, however remote, of the real world of men and things through the instrumentality of the intellectual function which he calls judging. And all of this, he thinks and urges, is but an expression of the standpoint of experience itself.

Accepting this view of judging, the absolutist further contends that one is thereby committed to the assertion that what satisfies the intellect is both true and real and, on the other side, that one who rejects the view is thereby driven in the end to embrace a nugatory truth and an ineffable reality. As Bosanquet summarily states the matter in Chapter VII of *Implication and Linear Inference* (1920), truth "is the form which reality assumes when expressed through ideas in particular minds. It is unintelligible if this unity is broken up. If you suppose a course of ideas inexpressive of reality, or a reality which has no expression in ideal form, you have destroyed the essence of truth. This is the only way of understanding the paradox about the making of truth and its discovery."

IV

When he says that reality is the subject of every judgment, however, the absolutist would have us understand that the assertion is concerned with two distinguishable "totalities." These are: (a) the immediately given complex, the datum, with which the judgment in question is directly concerned, and (b) the mediately given complex, the system, to which the immediately given complex belongs and with which, consequently, the judgment in question is inferentially concerned—"the special given complex whose consequences we desire to consider, and the total character of reality, which has to be respected and maintained in specifying those consequences" (Bosanquet, *Implication and Linear Inference*, p. 4). Thus there are two subjects in judging, the immediate and the remote; but they are elements within a single whole which is the reality towards which the judgment is oriented. This is a second principle upon which the absolutist builds, and for him it is of foundational importance.

"Let us fancy ourselves in total darkness hung over a stream and looking down on it," Bradley wrote in *The Principles of Logic* (1883; second edition, 1925). "The stream has no banks, and its current is covered and filled continuously with floating things. Right under our faces is a bright illuminated spot on the water, which ceaselessly widens and narrows its area, and shows us what passes away on the current. And this spot that is light is our now, our present." But: "We have not only an illuminated place, and the rest of the stream in total darkness. There is a paler light which, both up and down the stream, is shed on what comes before and after our now. And this paler light is the off-spring of the present." In this figure Bradley has stated the principle: the illuminated spot is the immediately given, what comes before and after is the mediately given, and the paler light which partially discloses it and is "the off-spring of the present" is the guiding light of inference from one to the other. The basis of inference is the entire content of the stream.

The essential matter here is the connection between the two givens, the data and the complex which is to guide inference. This connection has been dealt with at length by both Bradley and Bosanquet in their works on logic, and is summarily stated by Bosanquet in his *Implication and Linear Inference*: all inference "is within a connected system, and consists in reading off the implications which this system, construed as one with the whole of knowledge so far as relevant, imposes upon some of its terms." And by implication is meant the relation "which exists between one term or relation within a universal, or connected system of terms and relations, and the others, so far as their respective modifications afford a clue to one another." When Creighton says that "the logic and ideal of truth" of speculative idealism "is that of the concrete universal," he is repeating essentially what Bosanquet here says, since "concrete universal" is only another name for the implicative relationship here described and made foundational for inference. And the same in principle may be said of Royce's conception of the functional interrelationship between what he calls the "external" and the "internal" meanings of ideas.

The common doctrine, then, is that judgment everywhere moves within system, that this system is reality, that the system reaches beyond what is immediately given for judgment, and that this system is the implicative nexus which grounds inference. This is the doctrine which underlies the main argument for absolutism, described by Bosanquet as "the argument *a contingentia mundi,* or inference from the imperfection of data and premisses"—the argument which, as he maintains and other absolutists agree, ultimately "forces us to the conception of the Absolute."

Even if it were relevant to the purpose of this expository study to do so, there is here no space to inquire whether or not this contention of the absolutist is warranted. Before passing on, however, it may help to clarify issues if it is noted that, assuming that reality is the subject of every judgment in the dual sense asserted and assuming also the logical self-transcendence of the immediately given in judgment, the question remains an open one whether or not the Absolute, "the whole of reality" is involved in inference—whether or not, that is, in reading the implications within the mediately given system "construed as one with the whole of knowledge so far as relevant" one is thereby necessarily driven on to the conception of the Absolute. The contention that one is thus driven rests finally on the doctrine of the "internality" of relations—the doctrine, namely, that terms and relations are such that, in the words of Bradley, "if you could have a perfect relational knowledge of the world . . . you could start internally from any one character in the Universe, and you could from that pass to the rest." But this doctrine is at least debatable, and there seems to be considerable evidence that some relations are merely external to their terms.

In the next to the last chapter of his *Logic,* Bosanquet states the absolutist's criterion of truth as follows: "A judgment is true . . . when or in as far as its self-maintenance as a judgment is perfect. That is, in other words, when the whole system of judgments, which experience forces upon the mind which makes it, contains less contradiction in case of its affirmation than in case of its denial. Such a judgment is 'true' because on the whole it cannot be denied. . . ." This is commonly called the coherence theory of truth, and in the absolutist's opinion it is a corollary of his view of judgment: if a judgment is true in so far as it characterizes reality and if the subject in judgment is self-transcendent as above described, then the truth-value of a given judgment can be tested only by its coherence or consistency with all other relevant judgments. Thus to any objection against the theory based upon a different view of judgment, the absolutist would reply that it is irrelevant at least in the sense that it fails to consider the prior question; and such an objection is the one, frequently raised by the critics, that a consistent body of false judgments is logically possible. A similar oversight, he would also insist, underlies such an objection as that advanced by C. I. Lewis at page 339 of his Carus Lectures (*An Analysis of Knowledge and Valuation*) in the statement that "it seems never possible to be sure, in presentations of that conception, whether 'coherence' implies some essential relation to *experience,* or whether it requires only some purely logical relationship of the statements in question." So far at least as concerns the four philosophers here under survey, there is no doubt whatever on this score: for them, "the statements in question" are judgments, or expressions of judgments, and the judgments in question are "the whole system of the judgments, which experience forces upon the mind."

They would certainly assert that 'coherence' does imply an essential relation to experience and that the essentiality of the relation is guaranteed by the very nature of the judgment whose 'truth' is at issue.

V

A third principle of importance in the absolutist's construction must at least be mentioned, though there is space for little more. It is that cognition and evaluation are but distinguishable aspects of the single intellectual activity of mind and are, consequently, not separable. The criterion of truth and the criterion of value are, thus, one and the same, "the positive and constructive principle of non-contradiction" or "the spirit of the whole."

All of the absolutists insist upon this interrelationship among the cognitive and evaluative processes, and all alike urge that it is an essential characteristic of human experience. Bosanquet, perhaps more than any other, has emphasized the point especially in the first series of his Gifford Lectures which appeared in 1912 under the title *The Principle of Individuality and Value*. "If we view experience *bona fide*," he there tells us at page 39, "and follow where the connections lead us, noting the relation of incompleteness to completeness in all the responses of mind, it does not matter from what point we start. It is like going up a hill; you need only to keep ascending, and you must reach the top. You cannot study thought and not be led to will and feeling, nor will or feeling and not be led back to thought." This is the case, he further tells us, because the "spirit of the whole" or logical universal is manifest in all forms of experience. "Will and activity," we read at page 67, "mean the operation of the nature of thought through the expansion of ideas into fact"; and again, near the end of the volume at page 333, "all logical activity is a world of content reshaping itself by its own spirit and laws in presence of new suggestions; a syllogism is in principle nothing less, and a Parthenon or 'Paradise Lost' is in principle nothing more."

VI

From the preceding inadequate sketch of the absolutist's argument it is presumably evident that his position is in the end based on the doctrine of what he calls "the concrete universal"—the universal, that is, which permeates experience in all its forms and which intelligence delineates through penetration into the system of reality implicit in experience. At pages 267-268 of *The Principle of Individuality and Value,* Bosanquet summarily states this in a passage which may be quoted in conclusion as the basis of the doctrine of absolute idealism: "The positive and constructive principle of non-contradiction—in other words, the spirit of the whole—is the operative principle of life as of metaphysical thought. . . . It is this, essentially, and overlooking differences of degree, in virtue of which alone we can at all have progressive and continuous experience, whether as inference, or as significant feeling, or as expansion through action. It is this through which my perception of the earth's surface makes one system with my conception of the Antipodes, or the emotion attending the parental instinct passes into the wise tenderness of the civilised parent, and the instinct itself. . . . develops into the whole structure of social beneficence. And it is this, only further pursued, that forces us to the conception of the Absolute."

As already noted, this last assertion rests on a theory of relations as internal to their terms—a theory which is at least debatable. The crucial question, however, concerns the notion of "the concrete universal" which is, avowedly, foundational to the absolutist's doctrine. Is this conception necessitated by "the standpoint of experience" as claimed, or is it, as Bertrand Russell for example contends, merely a formulation which arises out of confusing the "is" of predication with the "is" of identity? What is at issue here is nothing less than the nature of intelligence and its implicative nexus, the nature of logic itself. And, to my mind at least, the issue runs to ground in the problem of meaning. In any event, however, to say, as Russell does, that the notion of "the concrete universal" and the type of philosophy built upon it rest "upon stupid and trivial confusions, which, but for the almost incredible fact that they are unintentional, one would be tempted to characterise as puns" (*Scientific Method in Philosophy,* pp. 39-40, note) is to make an assertion which itself surely must arise out of confusion as to what the doctrine in question really is.

A HISTORY OF PHILOSOPHICAL SYSTEMS

BIBLIOGRAPHY

F. H. BRADLEY:
>   The Principles of Logic (Oxford, 1883).
>   Appearance and Reality (London, 1893).
>   Essays on Truth and Reality (Oxford, 1914).

B. BOSANQUET:
>   Logic, or the Morphology of Knowledge (Oxford, 1888).
>   The Principle of Individuality and Value (London, 1912).
>   The Value and Destiny of the Individual (London, 1913).
>   Implication and Linear Inference (London, 1920).

JOSIAH ROYCE:
>   The Conception of God, A Philosophical Discussion Concerning the Nature of the Divine Idea as a Demonstrable Reality (New York, 1898).
>   The World and the Individual, 2 vols. (New York, 1900-1901).
>   The Problem of Christianity, 2 vols. (New York, 1913).

J. E. CREIGHTON:
>   Studies in Speculative Philosophy, ed. by H. R. Smart (New York, 1925).

Historical and Critical:
>   B. BOSANQUET, The Meeting of Extremes in Contemporary Philosophy (London, 1921).
>   H. HALDAR, Neo-Hegelianism (London, 1927).
>   G. W. CUNNINGHAM, The Idealistic Argument in Recent British and American Philosophy (New York, 1933).

CHAPTER TWENTY-SIX

POSITIVISM

CHARLES FRANKEL

"POSITIVISM" is a double-barrelled word. It stands for a certain temper of mind as well as a particular system of philosophy. As a temper of mind, positivism has a matter-of-fact orientation, and, in general, subordinates questions about what ought to be or what must necessarily be to questions of what in fact is. Positivistically inclined thinkers have usually been suspicious of theological and metaphysical doctrines as covert attempts to vindicate things as they are, and they have felt that human inquiry should be restricted to those questions to which fairly definite answers can be given. The positivistic temper of mind is primarily interested in the solution of particular problems, one by one, rather than in the construction of elaborate world-views.

The positivistic temper of mind is thus more closely attuned to the sciences than to any other department of human civilization. This does not mean, however, that positivistically oriented philosophies are exclusively, or even mainly, concerned with the natural sciences. On the contrary, there has frequently been a pronounced moral and practical pre-occupation in such philosophies. Even those positivistic philosophies which have been primarily concerned with the natural sciences have had an effect on morals and politics in freeing men from moralizing conceptions of the physical world which purported to show that the nature of things gave peculiar support to some particular scheme of human values. And, in general, positivistically inclined thinkers, like the Sophists of the Greek Enlightenment, the *philosophes* of the eighteenth century, and the American pragmatists of the first part of the present century, have not been able quite to understand why the practical

329

methods of the arts and crafts, and the matter-of-fact orientation of the sciences, should not prevail in the control of human affairs as well. By and large, positivistic thinkers have condemned vague speculation because they have wished to see intelligence applied to the alleviation of pressing human ills. Indeed, as against other scientifically oriented philosophies such as Spinoza's, for example, they have tended to think of science as a set of devices for solving particular problems, and not as a contemplative activity.

When regarded as a temper of mind, positivism is recurrent in the history of thought. Indeed, it is older than philosophy itself, for it has its roots in the arts and crafts of daily life and the common sense of the farmer, the sailor, or the woodsman about the observable regularities of nature. Ancient as are its sources, however, positivism holds a peculiar and powerful place in modern philosophy. The distinctive intellectual influence in the modern world has been the natural sciences, and the so-called "scientific outlook" is unmistakably positivistic in its affinities. The sciences have convinced all but the most stubborn or uninformed of their detractors that they are the most reliable intellectual tools we have, and their success, together with the new habits of life that have developed as a result of the widespread application of science to industry, has immeasurably stimulated and encouraged the positivistic temper. Indeed, the tremendous and unsettling impact of technology on human affairs has both created the necessity for extensive social reforms and nourished the dream that these problems could be settled if only similar positivistic methods were employed.

In short, most of modern philosophy has been wrestling with the positivistic temper of mind, as though it could neither live with it nor without it. The question of the interpretation to be placed on science, and the question of its bearing on human values, have been the most vexed issues of modern thought, and have given rise to a bewildering variety of philosophic schools of both a positivist and an anti-positivist persuasion. Among these, the so-called "Positive Philosophy," formulated by the French philosopher Auguste Comte (1798-1857), represents an extremely ambitious, and peculiarly paradoxical, attempt to systematize the positivistic temper, and to show that it should become the predominant temper of modern culture.

Comte's idea of science was a compound of ideas which the

philosophers Hume and Kant had already made current in the eighteenth century. The basis of his system was a definition of science as the study of "the laws of phenomena"—the invariable relations of coexistence and succession observed to hold between elements of experience. Comte retained, however, a quasi-Kantian belief that observable phenomena were not necessarily exhaustive of reality, but were merely all that the human mind was capable of knowing; and so he proposed that the term "cause" be dropped from the vocabulary of science and philosophy as a gratuitous provocation to useless questions. "Savoir pour prévoir," he repeated, and knowledge of the regular sequences of phenomena is quite enough to permit us to predict and control physical and human events. In short, science tells us "how" events take place, but not "why": it "describes" but does not "explain."

As recent positivists have pointed out, this distinction between scientific "description" and "explanation" is a misleading one, and it has frequently been employed by anti-positivistic thinkers to justify the subordination of scientific knowledge to some other, allegedly higher, form of knowledge. For Comte, however, it led to no such conclusion. His predominant concern with considerations of practical utility made him perfectly satisfied to restrict science to "description" and to leave the matter there. "I have a supreme aversion," he wrote, "to scientific labors whose utility, direct or remote, I do not see." [1]

Though his reflections on science, in the judgment of most later commentators, are the most worthwhile part of his work, they were thus only ancillary to Comte's main purpose. He was first and foremost a social reformer, and he was interested in science because he thought of it as an instrument for the reorganization of human life. Throughout his life he reiterated, "The head must be subordinated to the heart," and his thoroughgoing commitment to this view, though undoubtedly humane in its motivations, led him in the end to the thoroughly un-positivistic belief that the scientific outlook, "the head," lent unequivocal support to that particular set of social values which was closest to his own heart.

Like most French intellectuals of his time, Comte lived in the shadow of the French Revolution, and he was convinced that "the social problem" was to find ways and means to restore European society to stability and unity. In his thinking about this problem,

Comte was considerably influenced by the eloquent exponent of Catholic social philosophy, Joseph De Maistre (1753-1821). Comte agreed with De Maistre that the anarchic condition of Europe was mainly due to the steady incursion of the critical, incredulous, positivist mode of thinking. And while he rejected De Maistre's proposal that the Catholic Church be restored to its erstwhile position as the unifying intellectual and moral agency of Europe, he did something of much greater significance: he accepted De Maistre's initial formulation of the nature of the social problem itself. Like the traditional philosophers of the Church, Comte's controlling assumption was that institutions rest on morals, and that a stable morality rests on the general acceptance of a unified and stable body of beliefs. The peculiarly suggestive twist which Comte gave to this formulation of the issue was to argue that, under appropriate conditions, the positivist spirit might itself become the foundation for a new "organic" order of society.

For this reason, Comte rejected the program of the Utopian Socialist, Claude Henri de Saint-Simon (1760-1825), even though his own concrete social proposals were not markedly different. He was convinced that no social program could be effective without a preliminary moral re-orientation; and he never doubted that the prerequisite for this was intellectual re-organization. Comte consequently undertook to consolidate and unify what had hitherto been the random and dispersed insights of the positivist spirit by means of a systematic account of the inter-relationships of the sciences and their place in human history.

Such an attempt had already been made by the French Encyclopedists of the eighteenth century, who had made the history of the progress of the human mind the unifying frame of reference for interpreting the nature and social significance of the sciences. Comte took over many of the insights of these thinkers, particularly those of Turgot (1727-1781) and Condorcet (1743-1794), but he greatly extended and generalized them. The upshot of Comte's attempt was the formulation of two principal ideas—the hierarchy of the sciences, and the law of the three stages in the progress of the human mind.

Comte arranged the sciences in the order in which each science depends on the already established laws of other sciences. In accordance with this conception, he produced a table of the six fundamental sciences, beginning with the most abstract, mathematics, and ending with sociology or social physics. Arithmetic was basic in that it could be studied without knowledge of any other science; astronomy required knowledge of mathematics; physics, in turn, presupposed astronomy, chemistry depended on physics, biology on chemistry, and, finally, sociology on all the others. This ordering of the sciences did not mean that mankind had actually studied mathematics before other more concrete subjects; on the contrary, Comte believed that inquiry naturally begins with concrete questions, which are closer at hand. It meant, rather, that the development of a *science,* as contrasted with a mere collection of random "facts," must wait upon the development of highly abstract and general formulae by means of which these "facts" can be ordered. And, in this sense, the table of the hierarchy of the sciences showed that the development of a *science* of sociology was now possible because the studies on which it depended had now attained the status of sciences.

The emergence of sociology as a science was, for Comte, pivotal for a new understanding of the nature and rôle of the other sciences, and the fact that the time had finally arrived for the emergence of sociology meant that positive science might now develop into a Positive Philosophy which would serve as the organizing principle for society. Once sociology was established, it would react back upon the other sciences, humanizing them by showing that their function was to benefit humanity, and that service to humanity was, in fact, the moral code of the positive spirit.

Comte actually invented the term "sociology," and he regarded himself as the founder of the science. Contemporary sociology, so far as the actual content of its theories is concerned, probably owes more to such thinkers as Marx, and, in certain respects, Freud, than it does to Comte. Furthermore, contemporary sociology has expended much of its efforts in the development of precise quantitative techniques for piece-meal social inquiry, which are a far cry from Comte's far-reaching generalizations and questionable use of historical materials. In general, the distinctive sociological idea of studying a society "as a whole," the idea that all aspects of social life, intellectual, political, religious, economic, and so forth, are inter-connected elements of a "social epoch," is the product of a general historicist orientation and a pre-occupation with defining the *Zeitgeist* of societies, which was characteristic of a widespread nineteenth-century intellectual movement of which Comte was only one example. Nevertheless, Comte gave formal clarity to this general tendency, and considerable currency to the idea of sociology as a science, and to this extent his claim to be the founder of sociology is not entirely without justification.

Comte himself based his claim on the fact that he had done the two fundamental tasks which, in his judgment, were necessary in order to create a social physics. He had succeeded in formulating the method appropriate to sociology, a method which John Stuart Mill (1806-1873) later took over in his *Logic* under the name of "The Inverse Deductive Method." And he had discovered the fundamental sociological law of succession—the law of the three stages of the mind. Comte distinguished between the "Theological," the "Metaphysical," and the "Positive" stages of thought. The first stage, the "Theological," projects human emotions into the physical environment and explains events in terms of the direct volitions of gods or spirits. The second stage, the "Metaphysical," depersonalizes these gods and spirits and converts them into abstract essences, ontological beings, occult powers, and the like. The final stage, the "Positive," eschews all appeal to unobservable entities, and, in the interest of prediction and control, restricts itself to formulating the invariable conjunctions between phenomena. The Positive stage of thought is fully realized only when there is universal acceptance of the exclusive reign of unchanging and impersonal laws. Comte argued that a distinctive form of social organization corresponded to each of the three stages of thought—a military, aggressive polity to the Theological, a "juristic," defensively oriented, and nationalistic polity to the Metaphysical, and an "industrial" polity to the Positive.

Until the goal of historic progress has finally been reached, none of these modes of thought ever holds the stage completely. The Theological or Volitional mode of thought is the most spontaneous, but even at its height it has to contend with Positive types of thinking which grow up wherever knowledge of invariable relations of phenomena is necessary for survival. The Metaphysical mode of thought, indeed, is the product of the tension between the Theological and Positive modes. In effect, for Comte, metaphysics is the compromise the Theological mind makes with the Positive spirit, and it lasts only so long as the Positive spirit is too weak to make its own conception of the universe prevail in its own undiluted terms.

Comte believed that the reign of the Positive Philosophy would give rise to a Positive Religion—a "Religion of Humanity" in which the religious emotions of men would focus upon the strivings of the human race as their object, and the history of that "Grand Etre," Humanity itself, would provide a sound, "scientifically" grounded, analogue to the ancient epic of human salvation. Unlike many contemporary "humanistic" religions, Comte's Religion of Humanity contained all the trappings of organized religion—an organized priesthood, established rituals, holidays, and a claim to authority over education and morals. Indeed, his proposals went so far that he antagonized many of his most devoted disciples.

Comte's social program also caused considerable misgivings among his followers. Comte envisaged the formation of a Positivist priesthood which would have no official temporal power, but which would hold the central authority in society through its control of education, morality, and even the nature and direction of scientific research. The temporal power itself would be in the hands of the great capitalists, now humanized by the Religion of Humanity. Comte's elaborate system has been held up by many as the quintessence of "scientism." But it has in fact been more accurately described as "catholicism without christianity," and it is significant that his systematic Positivism is now mainly influential in countries with a strong Catholic tradition.

Though few subsequent thinkers of first importance accepted Comte's system as a whole, his influence on a great variety of philosophies is unmistakable. In France, P. J. Proudhon (1809-1865), the important political theorist and reformer, wrote, "My masters are Auguste Comte and Kant." A sociological and comparative approach to morality was developed by such thinkers as Emile Durkheim (1858-1917), and Lucien Lévy-Bruhl (1857-1939), which formulated a positivist theory of morality as the fundamental condition of social solidarity, and rejected the *a priori* elaboration of moral norms.

In other countries than France positivistic philosophies more or less similar to Comte's also developed and had considerable influence. In Germany, an anti-metaphysical, materialistic, and sociologically oriented version of Hegelianism was developed which culminated in the thought of Karl Marx (1818-1883) and Friedrich Engels (1820-1895). An important influence on them was Ludwig Feuerbach (1804-1872), whose materialism was strongly positivistic in tone: "Neither materialism nor idealism, neither physiology nor psychology is truth; truth is only in anthropology." [2]

In Great Britain, Herbert Spencer (1820-1903) was severely critical of Comte, but he essayed a not dissimilar positivist task—the formulation of a law of progress, and the development of a unified, "synthetic" philosophy of the sciences. The leading British philosopher of the nineteenth century, John Stuart Mill, recognized his indebtedness to Comte, especially in his philosophy of the social sciences. But he sharply criticized Comte's emphasis on methods of inquiry and neglect of methods of proof, though it should be added that his own statement of the canons of induction is susceptible to a similar criticism. Mill even more strongly disagreed with Comte's social outlook, and called it "the completest system of spiritual and temporal despotism which ever yet emanated from a human brain, unless possibly that of Ignatius Loyola." [3]

Nineteenth-century positivistic interpretations of science, subsequent to Comte's, tended to break into two wings—an idealist, quasi-Kantian version of positivism, and a critical, radically empiricist version. Hans Vaihinger (1852-1933) tried to give an idealist twist to positivism by arguing that all domains of human inquiry, science as well as religion, involve the use of "as if" statements, convenient mental fictions, and that the claim of science to provide valid "knowledge" was therefore no more justifiable than the claim of any other field. The most influential representatives of critical, scientific positivism were probably Ernst Mach (1838-1916) and Richard Avenarius (1843-1896). Mach's positivistic conception of physics is suggested by the following: "The concept of cause is replaced there by the concept of function; the determining of the dependence of phenomena on one another, the economic exposition of actual facts, is proclaimed as the object, and physical concepts as a means to an end solely." [4] Karl Pearson (1857-1936) expounded a somewhat similar view in England, interpreting science as an instrument for adapting man to his environment.

Systematic Positivism has, on the whole, not been a powerful school in American thought, but some of the most characteristic philosophic movements in America have had pronounced positivistic affinities. America has developed a radically naturalistic, and sociologically oriented, philosophy, which, like Comte's, takes its point of departure from the disparity between the state of the natural sciences and the state of social affairs, and which proposes to eliminate this disparity by extending the scientific outlook to all domains of human behavior. As exemplified by John Dewey (1859-   ), this philosophy holds a different conception of science from Comte's, and is unequivocally committed to democratic procedures, but it nevertheless bears certain striking affinities to Positivism. Probably, Dewey's most significant contributions to philosophy have stemmed from his emphasis on its social context and incidence; and Dewey's general "pragmatic" approach to the classic problems of philosophy, together with the work of George Herbert Mead (1863-1931), who conceived mind in terms of social acts, has led to the gradual rejection of epistemology, and has stimulated the development of the discipline known as "the sociology of knowledge."

Furthermore, though there is little evidence of any direct influence, the account of the history of philosophy which Dewey gives in his *Reconstruction in Philosophy* and elsewhere is remarkably close to Comte in both content and language. Dewey argues that the original material out of which philosophy finally emerges is "figurative, symbolic of hopes and fears, made of imaginations and suggestions"; and he maintains that classical metaphysics arose from "the need of reconciling the moral rules and ideals embodied in the traditional code with the matter of fact positivistic knowledge which gradually grows up." Dewey proposes that modern philosophy recover vitality by remaining faithful to positive knowledge and procedures, and he urges a "reconstructed" view of philosophy as an agency "in enlightening the moral forces which move mankind and in contributing to the aspirations of men to attain to a more ordered and intelligent happiness." [5] Dewey has even gone so far as to propose a humanistic "common faith," born out of loyalty to "the doings and sufferings of the continuous human community in which we are a link." These reflections on religion have played only the most insignificant rôle in Dewey's general view, however, and, on the whole, have been of more interest to certain of his followers than they have been to Dewey himself.

Dewey's position is systematically ambiguous on the relation of facts to values, and he sometimes gives the impression that he believes that the use of scientific method can in principle eliminate all disagreements over values. Nevertheless, Dewey certainly rejects Comte's dream of a single universally valid "scientific" morality, conceived as a set of fixed rules; and, on the whole, his conception of science is closer to that of the contemporary school known as "logical positivism" or (more properly) "logical empiricism." This school of thought is descended from the left-wing variety of nineteenth-century positivism, and its differences from Comte are suggested by the addition of the term *"logical."* In contrast with Comte's psychological and narrowly utilitarian approach, contemporary logical empiricism rejects metaphysical questions on the basis of a logical analysis which reveals them to be "factually meaningless"—that is, so formulated as to be incapable of empirical test. Thus, unlike Comte's essentially restrictive and "negative" Positivism, which sometimes acted to reject legitimate scientific questions, logical empiricism maintains that all meaningful questions are in principle answerable.

A full account of logical empiricism will be given in another chapter. It is worth noting here, however, that the recent immigration to America of most of the leaders of this school of thought, and the process of cross-fertilization with American pragmatism which has ensued, are some of the most encouraging features of the present philosophic scene, promising the development of an enlarged positivistic philosophy which will be free from the doctrinaire and visionary elements of nineteenth-century Positivism, but which will have something of its vision and humanity.

Undoubtedly, there are many who will regard such a philosophy as an upstart, which seriously impairs the traditional dignity of philosophy as the queen of the sciences. There can certainly be no question that it will lack the afflatus and high ambitions of traditional doctrines. But, however modest its ambitions, the development of a positivistically oriented and socially responsible philosophy could pose the most serious challenge to these classic points of view. For, while they are traditional, there is a sense in which they are not orthodox. Any philosopher is initially on the defensive who does not profess in theory what he practices in life; and, in one way or another, traditional philosophies have all had to make their peace with those beliefs and methods which are rooted in the daily practical experience of mankind. Contemporary positivistic philosophies are notable for the elaborate refinement of their techniques. But it is these ancient human orthodoxies to which they are fundamentally faithful.

NOTES

1. L. Lévy-Bruhl, *The Philosophy of Auguste Comte* (New York, 1903), p. 8.
2. L. Feuerbach, *Sämmtliche Werke*, ed. by W. Bolin and F. Jodl, vol. II (1904), p. 340.
3. J. S. Mill, *Autobiography* (New York, 1924), p. 149.
4. E. Mach, *The Science of Mechanics*, trans. by T. J. McCormack (La Salle, London, 1942), p. 325.
5. J. Dewey, *Reconstruction in Philosophy* (New York, 1920), Chap. 1.

BIBLIOGRAPHY

EDWARD CAIRD, *The Social Philosophy and Religion of Comte* (Glasgow, 1893).
AUGUSTE COMTE, *A General View of Positivism*, trans. by J. H. Bridges (London, 1908).
———, *Cours de philosophie positive* (Paris, 1835-52).
———, *System of Positive Polity* (London, 1875-77).
———, *The Catechism of Positive Religion*, trans. by R. Congreve (London, 1858).
———, *The Positive Philosophy of Auguste Comte*, trans. by H. Martineau (London, 1896).
ANDRÉ CRESSON, *Auguste Comte* (Paris, 1941).
FREDERIC HARRISON, *The Creed of a Layman* (New York, London, 1907).
———, *The Positive Evolution of Religion* (New York, 1913).
R. L. HAWKINS, *Positivism in the United States* (Cambridge, 1938).
L. LÉVY-BRUHL, *The Philosophy of Comte* (New York, London, 1903).
E. LITTRÉ, *De la philosophie positive* (Paris, 1845).
ERNST MACH, *The Science of Mechanics*, trans. by T. J. McCormack (La Salle, 1942).
H. MARCUSE, *Reason and Revolution* (London, New York, 1941).
J. S. MILL, *Auguste Comte and Positivism* (London, 1882).
ERNST TROELTSCH, *Die dynamik der geschichte nach der geschichtsphilosophie des positivismus* (Berlin, 1919).
HANS VAIHINGER, *The Philosophy of "As If,"* trans. by C. K. Ogden (London, 1924).
JOHN WATSON, *Comte, Mill and Spencer* (Glasgow, 1895).

CHAPTER TWENTY-SEVEN

PERSONALISM
(INCLUDING PERSONAL IDEALISM)

EDGAR SHEFFIELD BRIGHTMAN

I

THE TERM personalism was first used philosophically, but somewhat casually, by Goethe and Schleiermacher (1799); not until 1905 (H. Dreyer) and 1906 (W. Stern) was it popularized in Germany. In England it was first used by John Grote (1865). Walt Whitman introduced it in the United States (1868 or earlier). The French philosopher C. Renouvier and the American B. P. Bowne both wrote books entitled *Personalism* (1903, 1908). Mary W. Calkins extended the use of the term. Neo-Thomists (E. Gilson, J. Maritain, E. Mounier) have applied it to Thomistic social and ethical theories. Personal idealism is a synonym arising at the start of the twentieth century (Schiller, Rashdall, Howison).

In the broadest sense, personalism is a way of thinking that makes personality the key to all philosophical problems, both about value and about epistemology and metaphysics. In this sense, all theism and most idealism are personalistic. But the most typical and original personalism is idealistic (Berkeley, Leibniz, Hegel, Lotze, Bowne, Rashdall, Sorley, etc.), in the sense that all being is defined as personal consciousness. To be is to be a person or self, or some act or experience of a person or self. For "typical" personalists, personality (self, mind, or soul) is the unity of conscious experience (Kant), its *complex* unity (*unitas multiplex*, Stern). Idealistic personalists do not take the body to be part of human personality, but regard it as itself a personal activity (either of God or of systems of "monads"), which interacts with the human person and its environment. Realistic personalists, however, follow Aristotle. Since Aristotelianism is treated elsewhere, it will be presupposed in this chapter.

Personality (the idealistic personalists affirm) experiences itself as self-identical in change, especially in memory (Bergson, Bowne). It is active—in knowing, in free moral choices, and in response to stimuli. Since idealistic personalists hold all activity to be willing, personalism is a voluntarism (unlike Schopenhauer's, which asserts blind will minus rational unity). Personality is purposive and self-determining; "a self is a fighter for ends" (W. James), and these ends are its values. Personality is private. No person can experience any other's consciousness directly; yet every private person can communicate and interact with others.

A person, then, is a complex unity of consciousness, which identifies itself with its past self in memory, determines itself by its freedom, is purposive and value-seeking, private yet communicating, and potentially rational.

A distinction is often made between self and person. A self is any complex unity of consciousness; a person is a self able to develop rationality and ideal values. There are doubtless subpersonal selves that live by instinct and are unable to reason or to evaluate. It would, however, be arbitrary to assert that only human (and divine) selves are persons. Superhuman personality in God is acknowledged by most personalists (except McTaggart and Sartre). "Unconscious," "subconscious," "superpersonal," and "superconscious" are terms used to designate various levels of personality.—So much for preliminary definitions.

II

As an historical movement, personalism is difficult to delimit. Heraclitus, Anaxagoras, Plato, Aristotle, Plotinus, Thomas Aquinas, Giordano Bruno, and Descartes, for example, were all at least pre-personalists. These thinkers, however, usually included in their metaphysics some "impersonal" factors—such as non-being, matter, form, or Idea—and thus were not "typical" personalists. Considerations of space necessitate omission of the large body of genuine personalistic thought in the Orient, both in China and India. Ramanuja (d. about 1150) is an outstanding example. Dr. Albert C. Knudson has presented a useful classification of personalisms in his book, *The Philosophy of Personalism* (1927, 1949). He speaks of atheistic personalism (McTaggart), pantheistic personalism (W. Stern), absolute idealism (Hegel, Royce, Calkins), relativistic personalism (Renouvier), and "typical theistic personalism" (Bowne). He also distinguishes realistic personalism (Aristotelian Thomism, deistic dualism, and "religious realism," exemplified by such men as D. C. Macintosh, J. B. Pratt, and A. C. Garnett) from idealistic personalism (Berkeley, Calkins, Bowne, Flewelling, Knudson, Sorley, and Brightman). Panpsychistic personalism falls under the idealistic type.

The founder of modern personalism is Gottfried Wilhelm Leibniz (1646-1716), whose monadology represented the universe as consisting of simple psychic monads, ranging from the most dimly conscious types to the sublime consciousness of God. Every monad is active ("to be is to act") and all activity is conation or striving. The monads, however, do not interact, but only seem to, by virtue of a pre-established harmony. Leibniz was the father of panpsychistic personalism (H. W. Carr, Mary W. Calkins, C. A. Strong, D. Drake, A. N. Whitehead, C. Hartshorne), and has influenced all types.

Equally influential and original was Bishop George Berkeley (1685-1753), who taught that reality consists of active spirits and their passive ideas. There is no unconscious material substance; the being of matter is *percipi* (to be perceived). Material substance is unverifiable. Nature exists only in spirits, primarily in the Divine Spirit (person), and then communicated as "a divine language" to human spirits. Modern insistence on verification and specification of referents owes much to Berkeley. Bowne called his system "Kantianized Berkeleyanism."

Immanuel Kant (1724-1804) must be mentioned in any history of personalism. For him, scientific knowledge (Newton) is purely phenomenal; it consists of the data of sense organized by the categories in the unity of consciousness; the task of speculative reason is the ultimate unity of knowledge. But speculative reason does not account for "things in themselves," which produce sensation. Moral (practical) reason, however, asserts the categorical imperative of morality, and the autonomy of the moral will, and postulates freedom, immortality, and God. Kant believed that he had refuted materialism and established the validity of personal consciousness. Max Wundt holds that Kant was a Leibnizian.

Following Kant, but rejecting his view of things in themselves, the great German idealists developed phases of personalistic thought. Notable were Fichte (1762-1814), Hegel (1770-1831), Schelling (1775-1854), and Schopenhauer (1788-1860). Of these, Schopenhauer was the least personalistic, with his irrational will; Hegel, the most personalistic, with his system of dialectical development, and his principles that "the true is the whole," "the real is the rational," and spirit the ultimate definition of the Absolute. Hegelian influence spread personalism. John Caird (1820-1898), his brother Edward (1835-1908), and Thomas Hill Green (1836-1902), in Britain, and Josiah Royce (1855-1916), Mary W. Calkins (1863-1930), and W. E. Hocking (1873-   ) are personalistic absolutists, under Hegelian influence.

Others who rebelled against Hegel also contributed to personalism. In Germany, H. Ulrici (1806-1884) was a personalistic empirical idealist. H. Lotze (1817-1881) emphasized personality and value and influenced later personalists. W. Stern (1871-1938) approached philosophy through psychology. In France, personalism was often called spiritualism, and was advocated by Maine de Biran (1766-1824), V. Cousin (1792-1867), C. Renouvier (1815-1903), and very brilliantly by H. Bergson (1859-1941), philosopher of freedom and creative evolution. The British group of "personal idealists" started lively discussions about personality. In *Personal Idealism* (1902), Schiller's "Axioms as Postulates" set forth his pragmatic humanism, while H. Rashdall's "Personality, Human and Divine" defended "typical personalism" ably. Schiller's *Riddles of the Sphinx* (1891, 1910) was theistic. The personal idealists opposed absolutism on behalf of the individual. James Ward's (1843-1925) personalistic panpsychism started from physiology and psychology. F. R. Tennant has continued Ward's panpsychism at Cambridge. J. M. E. McTaggart (1866-1925) acutely defended pluralistic, eternalistic, atheistic personalism. W. R. Sorley (1855-1935) argued for personalism on the basis of objective reference of moral values. The Russian philosophical theologian, N. Berdyaev (1874-1949), counted himself a Christian personalist.

In the United States, Walt Whitman (1819-1892) stressed democratic aspects of personalism, Bronson Alcott (1799-1886) its educational applications. The "personal idealist," G. H. Howison (1834-1916), made teleology fundamental, but denied creation.

G. T. Ladd (1842-1921) taught Lotze's personalism at Yale. J. S. Bixler's (1894-   ) liberalism and theory of value have much in common with personalism, as does the theism of J. E. Boodin (1869-   ).

B. P. Bowne (1847-1910), who taught at Boston University from 1876 until his death, was a theistic, idealistic personalist, influenced especially by Berkeley, Leibniz, Kant, Hegel, Lotze, and his teacher, B. N. Martin. Among his students, A. C. Knudson (1873-   ), G. A. Coe (1862-   ), R. T. Flewelling (1871-   ), G. A. Wilson (1864-1941), H. C. Sanborn (1873-   ), F. J. McConnell (1871-   ), and E. S. Brightman (1884-   ), have written extensively. Belonging to the "second generation" of the school are writers such as P. A. Bertocci, W. G. Muelder, P. E. Johnson, L. Harold DeWolf, C. D. W. Hildebrand, L. W. Norris, W. E. Kerstetter, J. A. Fránquiz, Jannette E. Newhall, Wilbur Long, H. L. Searles, P. R. Helsel, and others. Approaching personalism through other channels are D. S. Robinson (1888-   ), J. S. Moore (1879-   ), and many others. Contemporary Neo-Thomists who call themselves personalists are J. Maritain (1882-   ), E. Gilson (1884-   ), and E. Mounier.

The greatest Anglo-American philosopher of recent times, A. N. Whitehead (1861-1947), came from a realistic tradition, but his doctrines of creativity, actual occasions, prehensions, subjective aim, and God all point to panpsychistic personalism. C. Hartshorne (1897-   ), basing his thought on Leibniz, Peirce, and Whitehead, has developed an original, if somewhat formalistic, panpsychism.

Many personalistic ideas are current in Latin America. These are reflected in the journal *Luminar* (Mexico City), in translations of personalistic works into Spanish and Portuguese, in references found in J. Ferrater Mora's *Diccionario de la Filosofía* (1941, 1944), and in the thought of such men as José Vasconcelos, Antonio Caso, and Francisco Romero. Tribute is paid to the world-wide influence of personalism by I. M. Bochenski in *Europäische Philosophie der Gegenwart* (1947). Personalism has been given a left-handed compliment by being made the object of attack in Soviet philosophical journals, Flewelling and Brightman being the chief targets.

A HISTORY OF PHILOSOPHICAL SYSTEMS

III

Let us now view personalism more systematically. While there are many differences among personalists, there are also many basic agreements, which will be chiefly emphasized in the following.

1. *Personalistic Methodology and Criteriology.* Personalists agree that philosophical truth is found only by consulting personal experience as a whole. They also agree that a grasp of the whole requires a grasp of all the parts. Personalistic method may be called analytic-synoptic. Analytic method may neglect or underestimate the properties of wholes; synoptic method may be foggy or romantic. The joint method analyzes out the parts and then relates them to the whole to which they belong. "The arrow of intelligibility" (Brightman) must eventually fly back from the parts to the total person. This method appeals to empirical coherence as its criterion. It excludes equally the procedure of Democritus, Parmenides, and Shankara, as well as of Hume, Spinoza, neo-realists and impersonal absolutists. It also rejects the demands of rationalists that philosophical first principles be confined to the self-evident and its necessary implications. Its insistence on personal experience gives it a more empirical cast. Hence the results of personalistic method enjoy coherent probability or "warranted belief," rather than necessity (Bowne, Brightman, Werkmeister).

2. *Epistemology.* The starting point of knowledge is experience or the datum self (Brightman), the total first-person experience (Werkmeister), the realm of *cogito* (which for Descartes includes all consciousness). The goal of knowledge is a coherent account of the objects to which first-personal experience refers. The person always asserts something beyond himself. There is an "other which my idea seeks" (Royce); there is self-transcendence (Bowne, Knudson, Romero); there is a dualism of idea and object (here personalism agrees with critical realism), of situation-experienced and situation-believed-in (Brightman). Actual occasions prehend others (Whitehead). The privacy of the situation-experienced in no way detracts from the publicity of the situation-believed-in (Bowne, Brightman, Werkmeister). Personalists thus escape the "egocentric predicament" (Perry) by their epistemological dualism and their doctrine of coherent probability.

The activity of the mind (person) in knowledge is basic to personalistic epistemology. Even Berkeley, with his "passive and inert ideas," required active spirits; Leibniz held everything to be active. The categories (Kant, Lotze, Bowne, Sanborn, G. A. Wilson, Knudson) are fundamental modes of personal activity. Certain categories (space, motion, for example) may apply only to the sensory phenomena; others (such as identity, metaphysical causality, and purpose) apply to the ontological realm and are called noumenal. Time is both basic and problematic.

The epistemology of personalism is experimental or empirical. Knowledge grows by the invention and testing of hypotheses. Kant speaks of his *Critique* as an "experiment of thought." Personalistic empiricism differs from traditional and recent empiricism (and positivism) by its appeal to the total unity of personality as the ultimate verifier or falsifier of hypotheses; but it agrees with empiricism and positivism in its insistence that there is no place for entities which are *in principle* unverifiable by any mind at any time. The matter of materialists and the events of naturalists are thus found less coherent than personal will as the essence of energy and substance.

3. *Metaphysics*. Typical personalists are qualitative idealists. Everything that exists is, for them, in, of, or for a mind on some level. In this theistic personalists, absolutists, and panpsychists agree. Everything is mental. Nature is a system of objects either in or for mind—God's mind, or the minds of monads, or both. All space, time, motion, sensory qualia, energy, things, universals, and values are actual or possible experiences of selves. The supposition of nonmental objects is gratuitous and incoherent. Realistic personalists, while making personality the basic being, assert also an order of nonmental being.

The metaphysics of personalism is predominantly a quantitative pluralism. That is, there are many persons and selves which are uniquely individual, private, and free; they are not parts of any other person, Absolute, or God. The many are usually thought of as dependent on the One, their Creator or Organizer. But the many spirits, monads, or persons are not identical with the God who creates and sustains them.—There is also, however, a personalistic absolutism (neo-Hegelians, W. E. Hocking, and, with qualifications, B. Blanshard) which is quantitatively singularistic and which recognizes only one universal mind, of which the seemingly many persons are phases or aspects. Absolutist monists argue that coherence requires unity and epistemological monism. Personalistic pluralists reply that the facts of error, evil, and ignorance are incoherent with absolutism (requiring the Absolute at once to believe my error and his truth); and that epistemological dualism is a better account of the structure and purpose of knowledge than is monism.

Personalistic metaphysics posits an interacting and intercommunicating universe. Interaction is postulated by all the sciences. It is especially needed for understanding the mind-body relation. It is admitted that interaction is difficult to explain on any theory. But it seems less incomprehensible on the assumption that the mutual responsiveness of mind to "matter" and of "matter" to "matter" are all cases of interpersonal communication between mind and mind. J. Ward calls it rapport; Whitehead, prehension; others may say telepathy and appeal to Rhine's ESP. Personalists view the interaction between the person and his body as basic and cogent evidence for personalism.

Personalists hold that personality satisfies the conditions of "substance" in a unique way: it combines unity and variety, permanence and change, causal activity and receptivity, actuality and potentiality, subjectivity and objectivity, mechanism and purpose, identity and creativity. Hence Bowne could say that "personality is the key to reality."

4. *Philosophy of Science*. What has been said about metaphysics indicates the main lines of personalistic philosophy of science.

Personalists have explored the psychology of personality and have developed or accepted the self psychology and the holistic methods and results of Gestalt. Personalism excludes merely analytic views of mind, such as sensationalism and association. It also excludes all forms of materialistic psychology, notably behaviorism. The mind for personalism, is not what the body does, even if the body is itself cosmic mind in action and even if it is the mind's most effective instrument of expression and interaction with environment. Practically all personalists have worked on psychology of personality. Among those who have made distinctive contributions are Lotze, Bowne, J. Ward, Bergson, G. A. Coe, H. C. Sanborn, R. T. Flewelling, F. L. Strickland, M. W. Calkins, W. E. Hocking, J. S. Moore, J. B. Pratt, W. Stern, R. F. Piper, G. W. Allport, C. Hartshorne, E. B. Marlatt, P. A. Bertocci, P. E. Johnson, and many others.

Personalism has contributed to the philosophy of biology. Personalists emphasize the combination of mechanism and purpose in life processes; the holistic principles evident in life; its evolutionary and orthogenetic development; and the systematic interactions between life processes and personality. Evolution is viewed as God's method of acting; personality is not a product of evolution, but is its constant medium. Among personalists who have contributed notably to this aspect of philosophy of science are Lotze, J. Ward, Ladd, Bowne, Bergson, and A. Korn.

Philosophy of physics was Kant's basic interest. Modern personalists have emphasized the personalistic presuppositions of experiment, methods of verification (coherence), the definition of matter and energy as volition of the cosmic mind (World Ground, as in Lotze and Bowne), and to the system of physical nature as an abstract and partial expression of the total resources of the divine person. Physics abstracts from reference to values (while presupposing the value of scientific knowledge), purpose, and personality—which must be considered in a complete philosophy. Among those who have recently contributed to a personalistic philosophy of physics in recent times are: Bowne, J. E. Boodin, R. F. Piper, A. N. Whitehead, W. H. Werkmeister, and R. M. Frye.

5. *Axiology.* Axiology or theory of value is a central interest of personalists. T. H. Green's axiom that all value is "in, of, and for a person" is typical. Personalists acknowledge no Platonic Form, no mere norm, no extra-personal state of affairs, as possessing intrinsic value. Every person, as Kant held, has "dignity"—an intrinsic worth for which there is no equivalent. Personalism has made contributions to all branches of axiology, commonly called normative sciences.

a. *Logic.* Personalistic logic, while presupposing Aristotelian, symbolic, and inductive logic, lays special stress on coherence. Rickert's description of logic as "the ethics of thought" is acceptable to personalists. The roots of personalistic logic are in Hegel, Lotze, and Bowne. Recent contributions have been made by F. C. S. Schiller, E. S. Brightman (empirical coherence), W. H. Werkmeister, and H. L. Searles.

b. *Ethics.* Personalists hold that "the true beginning of metaphysics lies in ethics" (Lotze). Kant's ethics of the good will is personalistic, as are Fichte's and Hegel's ethics. T. H. Green, H. Rashdall, and W. R. Sorley made outstanding contributions. In the

United States, personalistic ethics was developed by Bowne (the good, duty, virtue), Brightman (a system of moral laws, dialectically developed), Knudson (personalistic interpretation of Christian ethics and of problems of war and peace), F. J. McConnell, John Bennett, P. A. Bertocci (ethics of sex), W. G. Muelder, and neo-Thomists.

c. *Philosophy of Religion and Theology.* Personalists have made many contributions to philosophy of religion and theology. Idealistic and realistic personalists (except the neo-Thomists) agree in viewing theology as a branch of philosophy of religion, subject to the same methods and criteria.

McTaggart and Sartre are unique among personalists in denying a personal God, although asserting the reality of persons and their value and freedom. All of the thinkers mentioned under ethics have developed concepts important for philosophy of religion. F. R. Tennant, the ablest philosophical theologian in England, is close to personalism. The place given to objectivity of value (or, better, of norms), and the empirical tendencies of personalism, have given rise to a revision of the traditional idea of God in the direction of a denial of absolute divine omnipotence and the assertion of some sort of limitation of the divine will. Among personalists who thus affirm the finiteness of God are F. C. S. Schiller, H. Rashdall, N. Berdyaev, A. N. Whitehead, E. S. Brightman, C. Hartshorne, H. Bergson, P. A. Bertocci, and A. W. Munk. There are even traces of the idea in J. Royce. The contrary view has been ably maintained among personalists by Bowne, Knudson, W. E. Hocking, and L. H. DeWolf. Other personalists who have made contributions to philosophy of religion are H. E. Fosdick, R. M. Vaughan, H. A. Youtz, H. H. Farmer, S. P. Schilling, and many others, notably A. S. Pringle-Pattison. Somewhat less "typical," yet predominantly personalistic writers in the field are F. R. Tennant, J. B. Pratt, W. K. Wright, D. C. Macintosh, A. G. Widgery, A. C. Garnett, Georgia Harkness, E. T. Ramsdell, and N. F. S. Ferré, as well as the neo-Thomists.

d. *Aesthetics.* Modern aesthetics may be said to have its roots in the personalistic theories of Kant, Hegel, and Lotze. The aspect of axiology has been relatively neglected by recent personalists. J. S. Moore and Maritain have been active in the field.

e. *Metaphysics of Value.* All personalists except Sartre, who is peripheral, find in value experience a clue to the metaphysical structure of reality, supplementing the clues in sensory experience. Hence personalists assert "the objectivity of value," although Brightman has pointed out that values may be viewed as subjective, while their norms, as standards in the divine mind, are objective. Apart from the German idealists and W. Stern, contributions to personalistic theory of value have been made by T. H. Green, W. R. Sorley, A. Korn, W. E. Hocking, J. S. Bixler, and the neo-Thomists.

6. *Social Philosophy.* Personalism is essentially interpersonal, and therefore social. Its universe is a society of persons and other selves. Among personalists there are two main tendencies: one is toward an organic view of society, as in Fichte, Hegel, and T. H. Green; the other (more typical) is democratic and reformist, and is represented by Kant, Walt Whitman, Bowne, A. C. Knudson, R. T. Flewelling, F. J. McConnell, E. S. Brightman, J. E. Boodin, E. Mounier, and J. Maritain, as well as many others. The tendency of this latter group is to test social systems by their treatment of the individual person, and thus to emphasize political democracy, to criticize existing systems of ownership and distribution in so far as they fail to respect personality, and to make specific applications of personalism to problems of labor and management, war and peace, and the like.

7. *History of Philosophy.* Personalists have made contributions to history of philosophy. The discipline, in the modern sense, was founded by Hegel. J. Royce and M. W. Calkins have written interpretative histories of modern thought. E. Gilson has made brilliant studies in mediaeval philosophy. B. P. Bowne wrote on Kant and Spencer. Leibniz has been studied by H. W. Carr and L. E. Loemker, and Bowne by F. J. McConnell and E. S. Brightman. A. C. Knudson's *Philosophy of Personalism* treats his theme in relation to the history of philosophy. Treatments of the history of American philosophy have been written by G. C. Cell, W. G. Muelder and W. H. Werkmeister. Latin-American philosophy has been the subject of publications by E. S. Brightman and J. Fránquiz.

8. *Philosophy of History.* Like history of philosophy, philosophy of history owes much to Hegel. Personalists have only recently begun again to cultivate this field. N. Berdyaev devoted most of his lifework to it. R. T. Flewelling has undertaken a refutation of Spengler. A. W. Munk has a book in the field ready for publication, and J. H. Lavely is preparing one. B. Williams has made an investi-

gation of Berdyaev. Brightman has written one article. Much remains to be done.—In general, personalists agree on a doctrine of providence and eventual progress in history, noting its dialectical development, "the guile of reason," and the many contingencies which prevent progress from being linear. Freedom is a basic factor and goal in history. Most personalists think of history as continued in immortality, and hence reject the idea of an end of history, as a stopping place of personal-social development, and affirm inexhaustible potentialities of growth.

9. *Philosophy of Education.* Personalism in the United States was much concerned with philosophy of education. Bronson Alcott was famous for his educational theories and practices; and important contributions have been made by G. A. Coe (a pupil of Bowne's) and H. H. Horne (a pupil of Royce's). Some work has also been done by R. T. Flewelling, E. S. Brightman, and E. Marlatt.

BIBLIOGRAPHY

Journals: *The Personalist* (R. T. Flewelling, Los Angeles); *Esprit* (E. Mounier, Paris); *Luminar* (P. Gringoire, Mexico); *Philosophical Forum* (Boston University Philosophical Club); *Transformation* (London, complete in four volumes).
GOTTFRIED WILHELM LEIBNIZ, *La Théodicée* (Amsterdam, 1710).
———, *La Monadologie* (MS, Paris, 1710; publ., 1720 tr.).
GEORGE BERKELEY, *A Treatise Concerning the Principles of Human Knowledge* (Dublin, 1710).
IMMANUEL KANT, *Critique of Practical Reason and other Writings in Moral Philosophy* (Riga, 1788, etc.; tr. Beck, Chicago, 1949).
GEORG WILHELM FRIEDRICH HEGEL, *Die Phaenomenologie des Geistes* (Bamberg und Würzburg, 1807; tr. Baillie, New York, 1910, 1931).
HERMANN LOTZE, *Mikrokosmus* (Leipzig, 1856-1858).
WALT WHITMAN, *Democratic Vistas* (1871; Everyman's).
BORDEN PARKER BOWNE, *Metaphysics* (New York, 1882, 1898; Boston, 1943).
———, *Personalism* (Boston, 1908).
JOSIAH ROYCE, *The Spirit of Modern Philosophy* (Boston, 1892).
——— and others, *The Conception of God* (New York, 1902).
HENRY STURT (ed.), *Personal Idealism* (London, 1902).
CHARLES RENOUVIER, *La Personnalisme* (Paris, 1903).
WILLIAM STERN, *Person und Sache* (Leipzig, 1906).

A HISTORY OF PHILOSOPHICAL SYSTEMS

MARY WHITON CALKINS, *Persistent Problems of Philosophy* (New York, 1907, 1925).
NICHOL MACNICOL, *Indian Theism* (London, 1915).
JOHN M. E. MCTAGGART, *The Nature of Existence* (Cambridge [England], 1921, 1927).
EDGAR SHEFFIELD BRIGHTMAN, *An Introduction to Philosophy* (New York, 1925, 1951).
———, *A Philosophy of Religion* (New York, 1940).
——— (ed.), *Personalism in Theology: Essays in Honor of Albert Cornelius Knudson* (Boston, 1943).
RALPH TYLER FLEWELLING, *Creative Personality* (New York, 1926).
———, *The Survival of Western Culture* (New York, 1943).
ALBERT C. KNUDSON, *The Philosophy of Personalism* (New York, 1927; Boston, 1949).
———, *The Doctrine of God* (New York, 1930).
FRANCIS J. MCCONNELL, *Borden Parker Bowne* (New York, 1929).
JOHN WRIGHT BUCKHAM and JOHN MALCOLM STRATTON, *George Holmes Howison* (Berkeley, 1934).
EMMANUEL MOUNIER, *A Personalist Manifesto* (Paris, 1936; New York, 1938).
HARRIS FRANKLIN RALL (ed.), *Religion and Public Affairs: In Honor of Bishop Francis John McConnell* (New York, 1937).
PETER A. BERTOCCI, *The Empirical Argument for God in Late British Thought* (Cambridge, 1938).
FRANCISCO ROMERO, *La Filosofía de la Persona* (Buenos Aires, 1938).
WALTER G. MUELDER and LAURENCE SEARS, *The Development of American Philosophy* (Boston, 1940).
DEWITT H. PARKER, *Experience and Substance* (Ann Arbor, 1941).
JOSÉ A. FRÁNQUIZ, *Borden Parker Bowne's Treatment of the Problem of Change and Identity* (Rio Piedras, P.R., 1942).
CHARLES HARTSHORNE, *The Divine Relativity* (New Haven, 1948).
W. H. WERKMEISTER, *The Basis and the Structure of Knowledge* (New York, 1948).
L. HAROLD DEWOLF, *The Religious Revolt against Reason* (New York, 1949).

CHAPTER TWENTY-EIGHT
PHENOMENOLOGY

DORION CAIRNS

I

THE "PHENOMENOLOGICAL movement" started in Germany at the beginning of the twentieth century. Edmund Husserl (1859-1938) was its chief initiator; his *Logische Untersuchungen* (*Logical Investigations*), of which the first volume appeared in 1900 and the second in 1901, were its chief initial documentary source. Within the next seven years the movement had brought forth a "school," centered around Husserl at Göttingen and strongly represented at Munich. Already, however, a close observer might have noted some discrepancy between Husserl's concept of phenomenology, particularly as expressed in his current lectures, and the concepts presupposed or expounded by other leaders.

In 1913 Husserl published the first book of his *Ideen zu einer reinen Phänomenologie und phänomenologischen Philosophie* (*Ideas pertaining to a Pure Phenomenology and to a Phenomenological Philosophy*). It inaugurated a common enterprise: a *Jahrbuch für Philosophie und phänomenologische Forschung* (*Yearbook for Philosophy and Phenomenological Research*), edited by Husserl, jointly with Moritz Geiger (1880-1937), Alexander Pfänder (1870-1941), Adolf Reinach (1883-1917), and Max Scheler (1874-1928). But these collaborators and other members of the inner circle forthwith rejected what Husserl had at last proclaimed in black and white as the fundamental method and the principal insight of his phenomenology. Nevertheless, eleven massive volumes of the so-called *Jahrbuch* appeared (the last, in 1930), with only such changes in its editorial roster as were occasioned by death or the rise of new men—Martin Heidegger (born 1889) and Oskar Becker (born 1887)—to prominence in what was still generally regarded as one movement. The fact is that Husserl and most phenomenologists of the old school agreed, as their followers do today, in maintaining a number of theses which, taken jointly, characterize a distinctive type of theory.

Husserl left Göttingen in 1916 to assume the principal chair of philosophy at Freiburg, where Heidegger had become a *Privatdozent* the year before. By 1923, when Heidegger accepted a call to Marburg, the phenomenological stream running through Freiburg had taken on a new complexity and diversity. Husserl's own problematics had become richer and more systematic; while Heidegger had introduced into the local movement a new ethos, inadequately but conveniently described as "existential." Some of the changes were made conspicuous by the publication of the first half of Heidegger's *Sein und Zeit* (*Being and Time*) in the *Jahrbuch* for 1927. The author's highly original contribution, as he freely acknowledged, was founded to a large extent on Husserl's unpublished work. But Husserl's analyses seem to have been adjusted to an alien purpose; and the book contains many passages that invite interpretation as oblique criticisms of Husserlian principles. On Husserl's retirement, in 1929, Heidegger succeeded him at Freiburg. A variety of circumstances soon led to a personal estrangement, which emphasized, without clarifying, their philosophical differences and increased the tensions among their adherents. The upshot of all this has been a somewhat analogous differentiation among "Freiburg" phenomenologists in general. If we contrast a "transcendental" with an "existential" school of phenomenology, we should take note that the epithets are not co-ordinate, and that the implied theoretical differences have hardly been clarified and formulated in language acceptable to both parties.

In what follows we shall first state certain doctrines of "phenomenology" in a broad sense. Then we shall indicate the principles which characterize the transcendental phenomenology of Husserl and his closer followers and which, as a whole, are rejected by proponents of either a purely methodological or a realistic phenomenology. At the end of the chapter, since existential phenomenology is discussed elsewhere in the present volume, only a few remarks on phenomenology outside Germany will be appended.

II

The following, then, is a list of propositions that Husserl and presumably most others who have called themselves "phenomenologists" would accept, thus distinguishing themselves from philosophers of other schools.

1. The correct fundamental procedure in philosophizing is a process of attending to, and grasping, affairs that are themselves presented, then explicating them with respect to such of their determinations and relations as are likewise presented and grasped. On the evident basis established by this procedure, all philosophically legitimate primitive concepts are initially framed, and all philosophically justifiable primitive propositions are initially judged. Only by a repetition of this procedure can they receive adequate confirmation. If it should turn out that, as some have contended, the possibility of experience, or of science, or of practice, depends on antecedent conditions, then the genuineness of those conditions and the legitimacy of presupposing them would have to be demonstrated by this same process. Fundamentals must not be merely "constructed" or "postulated." They must not be accepted simply on faith, animal or spiritual, nor regarded as philosophically justifiable by the emotional comfort, moral satisfaction, or practical success, which they may bring.

2. Real individuals, purely possible or actual, exemplify ideal universals. The latter, no less than the former, can present themselves "in person." They too can be noticed, grasped, repeatedly identified, and explicated with respect to determinations and relations that are also themselves presented. To be sure, "ideating," the viewing of an ideal universal (an "essence," an "eidos"), is not precisely like the viewing of an individual. Generically, however, as viewing, graspings, or "perceivings" in a broad sense, the two processes are the same.

3. On the basis established by evident ideation, we can judge evidently true propositions about a universal and all its ideally possible exemplifications. Regardless of their truth-values, propositions about all the ideally possible instances of a universal have the sense of excluding all possible, and therefore all actual, exceptions. They point to an ideally possible verification or refutation by a grasping and analyzing of universals themselves and by an observing of the limits beyond which an entity plainly could not vary

while remaining a self-consistent member of the ideal extension of its universal essence. Phenomenologists do not deny the possibility of error in trying to establish the truth of such "eidetically universal" propositions. They do contend, however: (1) that some universal propositions are neither hypotheses nor inductive generalizations but assertions of unexceptional necessities or impossibilities; and (2) that primitive propositions of this kind can, and must, be verified or refuted by observing the relevant universals themselves and their clearly possible, or clearly impossible, instances or exemplifications.

4. "Eidetic" truths (truths about ideal essences or about their ideally possible exemplifications) make up eidetic sciences, bodies of systematic knowledge about what is essentially necessary, possible, or impossible, in particular realms of being. Moreover, the eidetic science of a realm or region is fundamental to the science of what is actually or probably the case in that realm.

5. Universals are either formal (purely logico-mathematical) or material (generic and specific). Correspondingly, ideation is either eidetic formalization (the method for grasping the logical forms exemplified in possibly existent states of affairs or in possibly true propositions) or else eidetic generalization (the method for grasping the ideal genera and species exemplified by the material contents that fill the forms of possible states of affairs or possible truths).

6. "Pure logic," the dual theory of (1) the essential forms of possible truths ("formal apophantics") and (2) the—perfectly correlative—essential forms of possible "facts" or states of affairs ("formal ontology"), is an eidetic *science,* with an observable subject-matter of its own. Its fundamental concepts and principles must be originated and legitimatized by ideation. The philosopher cannot be content with a formal logic, or a pure mathematics, that starts with merely verbal definitions, or with postulates, and operates according to arbitrary rules of the game.

7. Material eidetic sciences ("material ontologies") are also possible—as many of them as there are heterogeneous realms of possible being.

8. Everyday physical Nature, and some things and processes in it, present themselves and can be grasped, though incompletely: namely, in processes of active sensuous perceiving. To be sure, one's

perceiving of the public realm of everyday physical affairs must be founded on having a stream of coherent private sensations. But sensations function neither as parts nor as signs of the public affairs for the perceiving of which they provide the basis. (Unlike everyday Nature, the geometrically exact manifold presupposed in modern physics cannot present itself sensibly. It is apprehended by a process of idealization, founded on the perceiving of everyday Nature.)

9. Sensuous perceivings, as evidently actual or possible, establish the basis for a material eidetic ontology of everyday physical Nature. In a systematic physical science, this ontology is logically prior, not only to the factual science of everyday Nature, but also to what is usually called "physical science." The latter is science of a highly specific type. Scientists and philosophers commit a disastrous error if they set up physical science as the paragon of all science, or even if they accept the somewhat more general method of constructing and confirming hypotheses as the only, or the fundamental, scientific method.

10. The livingly present part of one's own individual stream of consciousness presents itself. It too can be noticed and (imperfectly) grasped—not, however, in straightforward acts of sensuous perceiving, but in reflective acts of non-sensuous perceiving. These and their clearly possible variants provide the ultimate basis for any psychology, including an eidetically universal psychology, a material ontology of psychic Nature. A purely behavioral "psychology" is *Hamlet* without the prince.

11. Any concrete part of a stream of consciousness (including those parts that may be, in a narrow sense, "unconscious," *i.e.*, inaccessible to a reflective perceiving) must be "intentional," *i.e.*, it must be inherently an "intending-of" (a pointing-to, a consciousness-of) "something" as beyond it. The something pointed to, or intended, need not exist nor even be possible. *Qua* "intentional object" it is purely what the conscious process intends, correctly or incorrectly, in some particular fashion, and with some degree of certainty, as something having some particular determinations. The psychologist can confine his attention to a particular conscious process, as it is purely in itself, and read off *it* its intentional object as intended in it. Nevertheless, the intentional object of a conscious process (unlike the latter's intentionality, its character as an intending) is not an inherent abstract part or moment of that process.

Thus one conscious process can intend its object as identical with the object intended by another. And more than that: No conscious process intends its object as its own exclusively. Each is an intending, not only of its "primary" object, but also of other (actual or at least possible) conscious processes as processes intending "The Same," either in the same fashion or differently.

12. "Intentionality," as the characteristic above described, sharply distinguishes psychic processes from physical (including somatic-behavioral) processes. Though every mind is necessarily connected with a body and could not exist apart from one, Nature is thus quite unambiguously "bifurcated." To be sure, one and the same natural entity may, on the one hand, be the intentional object-of a particular psychic process and, on the other hand, coexist with, and stand in a causal nexus with, that same process. But that entity's intendedness-by a psychic process is not a real relative determination, like its coexistence-with, its causativity-of, or its causedness-by, a psychic process.

13. In order to institute and develop a science of the purely psychic—a "pure" psychology, whether eidetic or empirical—the psychologist must actively disregard both the necessary and the factual relations obtaining between instances of the psychic and other affairs: for example, the temporal and causal-functional relations between psychic and somatic processes in a psychophysical individual. On the other hand, any pure psychology is inadequate to the chief feature of its subject-matter unless it describes psychic processes, not only with respect to their interrelations, their concrete parts, and their abstract moments, but also with respect to their intentional objects as intended. But this implies that physical (and all other non-psychic) affairs—along with their relations to psychic affairs—do somehow come within the scope of even an utterly pure psychology: namely, in so far as psychic processes, apart from all their external relations, are still intendings of such affairs. As the situation is rather subtle, let us describe it in another fashion: The investigator intent on developing a pure psychology must refrain from tainting his observations and theories with assertions (no matter how legitimate in other connexions) that the investigated psychic affairs are factually or necessarily related to any affairs outside themselves. He must refrain from assuming, in particular, that any psychic process is related to any of the affairs that it intends

as outside itself and perchance as related to itself. But *these* affairs, *as objects-intended-by* the psychic processes under investigation, are still to be found within the investigator's "psychologically purified" sphere of inquiry, because the investigated psychic processes are inherently qualified as intending them.

14. Valuing, even when founded on a grasping of what is valued, is not an objectivating and, *a fortiori,* is not a grasping, of the latter's value. But values of all kinds (intrinsic or instrumental; epistemic, aesthetic, moral, etc.) can be objectivated; they can also be grasped, and explicated with respect to what are then their self-presented determinations and relations. Thus an evident basis can be established, not only for valid inductive generalizations about objective values, but also for grasping the ideal universal essences exemplified by individual value-determinations; and this in turn makes possible an eidetic theory of values. The like is true, *mutatis mutandis,* with respect to conation in general, and active willing and doing in particular, and the objective realm of ends and means.

Our list could be extended; but we must turn now to the peculiarities of Husserlian transcendental phenomenology.

III

At least ordinarily, as every phenomenologist would allow, one experiences the stream of one's own consciousness as but one process among others in the world. One finds and accepts it as existing on a par with the rest of the world. If, being intent on establishing the most evident possible basis for a "pure" psychology, one abstracts from everything in the world except the presented part of one's own stream of consciousness (the specious present), one still means the latter as inherently "worldly." And this remains the case, even if one goes on to dissociate oneself (*qua* "eidetic" psychologist) from one's ineradicable believing in the actual existence of one's psychic processes and, in a secondary attitude, accepts them as only possible individual examples of the universals which they exemplify. Even then one means their possibility as a worldly possibility, either in *the* world or in some ideally possible variant of it. Correlatively, the exemplified universals (*something, individual, conscious process, perceiving, judging, loving, willing,* etc.) are meant as extending to essentially worldly affairs, ideally possible instances in some ideally possible world.

And now for the crucial Husserlian theses:

While reflectively grasping the speciously present part of my stream of consciousness and refraining from acceptance of anything beyond it, I can dissociate myself from my natural and inevitable believing in its (possible and actual) worldliness, its being-in-the world. When I actually do so, I can still grasp that process as somehow *being* (though not as being worldly) and as having the inherent determinations that it still presents: notably its intentionality as believing-in "the world" and as believingly intending "itself as worldly." And I can still describe that consciousness, not only with respect to its inherent parts and moments, but also with respect to its intentional objects, with respect to "the world," to which it is inherently intentive, and with respect to the "worldliness" which *I* no longer apprehend as inherent in it but which *it* inherently intends as belonging to itself. For I do still find "the world," not indeed as simply there, and most assuredly not as an inherent part of my non-worldly stream of consciousness, but precisely as the latter's intentional object. Similarly, I still find the "worldliness" of my stream of consciousness, not indeed as an inherent determination, but precisely as an intentional objective sense which my non-worldly stream of consciousness has for itself as its own intentional object—a status that it necessarily and rightly apperceives itself as having.

In explaining all this, Husserl frequently used technical terms, some of which we shall define here: One's underlying attitude of believing in the world and in the worldliness of one's stream of consciousness is *the natural attitude*. An active *refraining* from participation in the natural attitude (and therefore in all the other attitudes and processes—of believing, valuing, or striving—which it underlies) is *transcendental-phenomenological epoché* (restraint). As actual or possible worldly existents, streams of consciousness, egos, attitudes, subjective habits and abilities, etc., are *psychic* or *mental*. In their fundamental, non-worldly being, as disclosed by transcendental-phenomenological epoché, they are *transcendental*. The world, in its fundamental status, *i.e.*, as an intentional object of transcendental consciousness, is a *transcendental phenomenon*. The process that "leads me back to," and enables me to see, my stream of consciousness as transcendental, and the world as a transcendental phenomenon, is transcendental phenomenological *reduc-*

tion. And, finally, reflective observational analysis of transcendental consciousness, particularly with respect to its intentionality and its intentional objects, is *transcendental phenomenology*.

The systematically fundamental transcendental science is an eidetic phenomenology. This should be supplemented, however, by a phenomenology of transcendental matters of fact; and eventually a transcendental science may include inductive generalizations and hypotheses about transcendental being.

Most of the content of a pure psychology (whether empirical or eidetic) can be purified of its "worldly" implications and translated into (either empirical or eidetic) transcendental phenomenology. Conversely, most of transcendental phenomenology (but obviously not the theory of transcendental phenomenological reduction) can be deprived of its transcendental, and so of its philosophical or metaphysical, significance and be understood "naturally," *i.e.*, as pure psychology. Furthermore, pure psychology as a whole, and all other theories of essentially worldly affairs, both real and ideal, can be reinterpreted as theories of "the same" affairs *qua* transcendental phenomena, intentional objects-of transcendental consciousness.

Phenomenological analysis discovers that the reflectively graspable part of one's stream of consciousness has a bewilderingly complicated intentional structure, with a correspondingly complicated intentional-objective "sense." Consider, for example, the essential structure of even so elementary a process as sensuous perceiving. The everyday physical thing itself is indeed presented, but only as an ideal objective unity, actually and potentially intended through a multiplicity of quasi-objective appearances under various perceived or apperceived circumstances in the perceiver's co-intended body and in other co-intended things—appearances as far or near; visual appearances, tactual appearances, etc.—and all on the ultimate basis of a complex harmonious flow of sensation. Each momentary temporal part of the stream of perceptive consciousness must be intentionally "retentional" of preceding, and "protentional" of succeeding, parts. Moreover, since perceived things are intended as perceivable by others, the intricate system of intentionalities by virtue of which other psychophysical beings are there, for the perceiver, is also involved. And, if one's stream of consciousness did not have this whole complex structure (only hinted at here), one could not in any way intend so much as a pebble.

But the structure of a present consciousness points back to a "genesis"; and, as transcendental, it points back to a transcendental genesis, a transcendental historical process whereby it has become what it is and whereby, correlatively, the actual world has been "generated" as its intentional object. The transcendental phenomenologist must therefore undertake "genetic" analyses of transcendental consciousness, its implicit "history" and its implicit "traditionariness."

In the evident detailed results of these "static" and "genetic" analyses, rather than in arguments, the truth of transcendental phenomenological idealism—the eidetic truth that any possible world, or other possible object, is fundamentally an ideal intentional object of transcendental consciousness—is *demonstrated*. Everything of which anyone could conceivably be in any way conscious (and, *a fortiori,* everything of which anyone could speak)—everything that might be intended, directly or indirectly, clearly or obscurely, correctly or incorrectly, as existent or non-existent, possible or impossible, real or ideal; every possible object of belief or doubt, of love or hate, of desire or aversion, of care, anxiety, or any other attitude—can be *shown,* in detail and in gross, to be the purely intentional objective sense of some synthesis of possible transcendental intendings. The specious realistic tenet that ready-made things-in-themselves can swim into one's ken is incompatible with the evident structure of consciousness.

On the other hand, any "psychological" or "anthropological" idealism, any theory implying that the world is somehow dependent for its existence on some consciousness in the world, involves the vicious circularity of making the whole depend for its existence on something that itself can exist only as a dependent part of the whole.

From the point of view attained by transcendental phenomenological reduction one can see that, although the worldliness of consciousness is indeed a derived status, every consciousness must be worldly, in addition to being transcendental. Accordingly one can also see the necessary falsity of any theory that implies the possibility of a consciousness which is not, so to speak, the "core" of the psychic component in a psychophysical entity.

And, finally, any solipsistic idealism is also necessarily false. Inevitably and rightly I intend my world, not as mine alone, but as everyone's. Moreover, every mind in the world, every psychophysical component of every psychophysical entity, is *ipso facto* a "mundanized" transcendental consciousness.

IV

Already, before the first world war, Husserl was attracting both attention and students from abroad. Afterwards, in the years before the National Socialist Revolution, the number of foreigners studying under Husserl, Scheler, or Heidegger, greatly increased. On some of these students phenomenology exercised a decisive influence. It does not yet appear, however, that they in turn have exercised a decisively phenomenological influence on the course of philosophy outside Germany, except in France. On the whole, they have functioned abroad chiefly as translators, expositors, interpreters, or critics, of "German" phenomenology. Following the Revolution of 1933, a number of German and Austrian phenomenologists found refuge abroad; and, as the shadow of Nazi power spread, more of them came to the United States and became members of the American philosophical community. In 1939, with native Americans under the leadership of Marvin Farber, they joined in founding the International Phenomenological Society and, in the following year, a quarterly with the reminiscent name, *Philosophy and Phenomenological Research*. This organ has given its readers not only essays about phenomenology but also phenomenological (and non-phenomenological) essays. Thus strengthened and implemented, phenomenology has survived and perhaps increased its influence in America; whether it will also propagate itself remains to be seen. So far, it continues to be an exotic.

BIBLIOGRAPHY

(English)

DORION CAIRNS, "Abstract of Husserl's *Die Frage nach dem Ursprung der Geometrie,*" *Philosophy and Phenomenological Research,* vol. i, no. 1 (September, 1940), pp. 98-109.

———, "The Ideality of Verbal Expressions," *ibid.,* vol. i, no. 4 (June 1941), pp. 453-462.

———, "Phenomenology," *A Dictionary of Philosophy* (New York, 1942), pp. 231-234.

MARVIN FARBER, *The Foundation of Phenomenology: Edmund Husserl and the Quest for a Rigorous Science of Philosophy* (Cambridge, 1943).

———, "Phenomenology," *Twentieth Century Philosophy* (New York, 1943).

———, et al., *Philosophical Essays in Memory of Edmund Husserl* (Cambridge, 1940).

JAMES STREET FULTON, "The Cartesianism of Phenomenology," *The Philosophical Review*, vol. xlix (1940), pp. 285-308.

MORITZ GEIGER, "An Introduction to Existential Philosophy," *Philosophy and Phenomenological Research*, vol. iii, no. 3 (March, 1943), pp. 255-278.

———, "The Philosophical Attitudes and the Problem of Subsistence and Essence," *Proceedings of the Sixth International Congress of Philosophy* (London, 1927).

ARON GURWITSCH, "A Non-Egological Conception of Consciousness," *Philosophy and Phenomenological Research*, vol. i, no. 3 (March, 1941), pp. 325-338.

JEAN HERING, "Concerning Image, Idea, and Dream," *ibid.*, vol. viii, no. 2 (December, 1947), pp. 188-205.

EDMUND HUSSERL, *Ideas: General Introduction to Pure Phenomenology*, tr. by W. R. Boyce Gibson (London; New York, 1931).

———, "Phenomenology," tr. by C. V. Salmon, *The Encyclopedia Britannica*, 14th ed. (1929), vol. xvii, pp. 699-702.

FRITZ KAUFMANN, "Cassirer, Neo-Kantianism, and Phenomenology," *The Philosophy of Ernst Cassirer* (Evanston and Chicago, 1949), pp. 801-854.

———, "In Memoriam Edmund Husserl," *Social Research*, February, 1940, pp. 61-91.

———, "The Phenomenological Approach to History," *Philosophy and Phenomenological Research*, vol. ii, no. 2 (December, 1941), pp. 159-172.

LUDWIG LANDGREBE, "The World as a Phenomenological Problem," *ibid.*, vol. i, no. 1 (September, 1940), pp. 38-58.

V. G. MCGILL et al., "Symposium on the Significance of Max Scheler for Philosophy and Social Science," *ibid.*, vol. ii, no. 3 (March, 1942), pp. 269-358.

PHILIP MERLAN, "Time Consciousness in Husserl and Heidegger," *ibid.*, vol. viii, no. 1 (September, 1947), pp. 22-53.

ALFRED SCHUETZ, "Sartre's Theory of the Alter Ego," *ibid.*, vol. ix, no. 2 (December, 1948), pp. 181-199.

HERBERT SPIEGELBERG, "Critical Phenomenological Realism," *ibid.*, vol. i, no. 2 (December, 1940), pp. 154-176.

———, "Phenomenology of Direct Evidence," *ibid.*, vol. ii, no. 4 (June, 1942), pp. 427-456.

CHAPTER TWENTY-NINE

EARLY PHILOSOPHIES OF EVOLUTION

RAY H. DOTTERER

THE EVOLUTIONIST philosophies of the nineteenth century represent a continuation of the perennial war of attrition between naturalism and supernaturalism, and of a progressive encroachment of the former upon the preserves of the latter. By the middle of the century, in the thought of almost everybody who thought about the question at all, eclipses and comets, the movements of the planets, the formation of the solar system and of the earth's crust, in principle even the weather, had been transferred from the domain of the supernatural to that of the natural; and, for the bolder minds, the inclusion of everything else in all-embracing Nature was an obvious next step.

These bolder minds were, however, still few. To most men the human soul seemed to require a supernatural explanation; and the realm of plant and animal life remained as a screen between the physical domain and the human. Here the theologians still found their chief data for the argument from design. The hand and the eye of man, together with similar wonderful adaptations in the lower animals and in plants, all enforced the necessity of admitting a Great Plan.

Securely entrenched in the realm of life, teleology was able to sally forth and annex some provinces of regions commonly regarded as natural. Thus one lecturer after another on the foundation established by the Earl of Bridgewater (1756-1829) was able to amass a multitude of details illustrative of the goodness and power of God in designing his creation. The earth's distance from the sun was just what was required to produce the right temperature for the maintenance of life. The shape of its orbit, the inclination of its axis to the plane of the ecliptic, and the period required for its revolution around the sun were all intended to provide an agreeable and beneficent variety of seasons. Even the rate of the earth's rotation on its axis was so adjusted as to give the proper amount of darkness for soothing and restful slumber.

Moreover, whatever examples of *progress* or *process* might be recognized in the inanimate world, as, for example, the "uniformitarian" explanation of the strata of the earth's crust introduced by Lyell (1797-1875) and other geologists, it was still thought necessary to appeal to supernatural causation to explain how the natural order got started in the first place.

In the biological realm there were, to be sure, provinces in which development was too obvious to be denied. The babe grew to be a man. The seed became an herb, a shrub, or a tree. Varieties of plants and animals had admittedly arisen in historical times. Yet, it was held, there were limitations to the possibility of modification in nature. *Species* did not change. Varieties, as the name indicated, were the result of variation; but species, as this name also was meant to indicate, remained always the same. They, indeed, were among those permanent realities by reference to which change and becoming were to be explained.

There had of course been dissenters. Erasmus Darwin (1731-1802) and Lamarck (1744-1829) had suggested that the various species of plants and animals had arisen by the modification of earlier and different species; but the case made by them did not seem convincing to their contemporaries. The weight of authority could not be overcome without a good explanation of new species. The suggestion of Lamarck that the effects of use and disuse might be transmitted to offspring, and his still more vague idea that the need of an organism for a certain structure might somehow cause this structure to appear, seemed less probable to critical minds than the traditional doctrine of independent creation by the Deity.

It remained for Charles Darwin (1809-1882) and Alfred Russell Wallace (1823-1913) to present the conception of natural selection as the principal explanation of the origin of the species which have appeared on the face of the earth. This, together with the steady accumulation of supporting data drawn from geology, geographical distribution, and embryology soon led to the acceptance of the "Darwinian theory," as it came to be known, by all who were familiar with the difficulties encountered by botanists and zoologists in deciding which groups of plants and animals were "true" species, and which but sub-species or varieties. Thus the developmental conception, which came to be known more commonly as the "theory of evolution," obtained wide currency.

Before going on to consider the broader significance of the idea of evolution, it may be well to make a little clearer what Darwin meant by "natural selection," or by the phrase which he took over from Herbert Spencer (1820-1903), "survival of the fittest." The point to be emphasized is that we should not think of Nature as an entity which consciously selects. "I mean by Nature," says Darwin, "only the aggregate action and product of many natural laws, and by laws the sequence of events as ascertained by us." (pp. 70 ff.)[1] The doctrine is, then, that in nature there is a "struggle for existence," resulting from the universal tendency of organisms to produce more offspring than can survive; and that those who do survive are able to do so in consequence of some superior fitness to live in the environment in which they are produced. Thus there may be said to be a "selection" analogous to that by which breeders improve strains of domesticated plants and animals. The phrase "survival of the fittest" has the advantage of not suggesting a personification of Nature, but rather the superior health, strength, or cunning which enables some to survive while most of their generation perish. It has the disadvantage, however, of suggesting to many minds irrelevant kinds of *fitness*, thus leading to the misunderstanding that evolution is always in the direction of aesthetic, ethical, or other "progress."

Both Spencer and Ernst Haeckel (1834-1919), whom we shall take as typical representatives of evolutionist philosophy, acknowledged indebtedness to Carl Ernst von Baer (1792-1876), who was a pioneer in modern embryology. The former derived from him the conception of a progressive change from homogeneity to heterogeneity (v. II, pp. 9 ff.).[6] It became a central thesis of Spencer's that *in general* the homogeneous is unstable; that a trend toward heterogeneity is characteristic of evolution in all its phases, whether we are thinking of individual organisms or groups of organisms, of the earth, the solar system, or the entire cosmos.

In working out the implications of this principle, however, Spencer soon realized that it could not stand alone (v. II, pp.

180 ff.),[6] but must be recognized as incidental to a more fundamental process which he speaks of as the "integration of matter and the concomitant dissipation of motion." In accordance with the law of gravitation diffused matter tends to become more consolidated; at the same time, the energy or motion, whether sensible or insensible, which the matter contains, tends to be more and more uniformly diffused.

We must next distinguish between *simple* and *compound* evolution. The former is the uncomplicated integration of matter and dissipation of motion which we have been describing. The latter covers the vast multitude of cases in which the primary redistribution of matter and motion is accompanied by secondary redistributions. While the whole in question is consolidating it is also differentiating into parts in each of which the double process of integration and dissipation proceeds with some degree of independence. We thus have a change from a less coherent to a more coherent structure as well as from a more homogeneous to a less homogeneous state.

It must be admitted, however, that not all changes from less to greater heterogeneity come within what we call evolution. To constitute evolution there must also be a change from the indefinite to that which is clearly demarcated. We thus arrive at the complete statement of Spencer's formula: *"Evolution is an integration of matter and concomitant dissipation of motion, during which the matter passes from an indefinite, incoherent homogeneity to a definite, coherent heterogeneity; and during which the retained motion undergoes a parallel transformation."* (p. 396.)[4]

Spencer presents this, not merely as a *definition* of what one may choose to call evolution, but also, it would seem, as a statement of what is constantly taking place in nature. The reader may wonder whether there are any exceptions to this "law" of evolution. The best answer to such a question would be to point out that a "natural law," whatever else it may be, is a rule for expecting events; and that, even if there should be some exceptions, the law so regarded is worth formulating, provided the exceptions are not too numerous.

Having arrived at the law of evolution inductively, Spencer goes on to present it as an inference from the persistence of matter and force; or, as we might prefer to say, from the conservation of mass and energy. The energies which have chief place in the argument are the kinetic energy of sensible or insensible masses and the potential energy of such masses at greater or smaller distances from one another, but subject to mutual attraction.

If, then, we assume the existence of a homogeneous aggregate which is acted upon by some force or forces, it is easy to show that its various parts would be acted on unequally, and that these inequalities would be multiplied as time passed. For even a uniform external force acting upon the previously homogeneous aggregate would, on account of its varying effectiveness upon parts at different distances and angles of incidence relative to its source, produce different effects upon these parts; and, inasmuch as each part would then be a source of action upon every other part, the multiplication of effects would proceed in geometrical progression.

Taking our cue from the nebular hypothesis of Kant (1724-1804) and Laplace (1749-1827), let us now think of a region filled with extremely diffuse matter. Under the influence of gravity, this nebula would contract. Thus the predominant movement of each particle would be toward the center of the whole; yet not in every case exactly toward the center. For, in some cases, the mutual influence of the particles would produce curvilinear movements; and it is very improbable that at any given instant these would be exactly balanced relatively to all possible axes. Consequently, as the nebula contracted, any advantage of one axis over the others would be increased until eventually some one axis would become *the* axis about which the nebula would be rotating at a constantly accelerating rate. Also, on account of the segregation of similar units resulting from the operation of a uniform force upon a mass composed of different kinds of units, local integration would accompany local differentiation. It is obvious, too, that a generation of heat would accompany increase of density.

These principles Spencer applies to explain, not only the origin of the solar system, the geological evolution of our planet, the development of plants and animals, but also the production of life and consciousness and, indeed, everything that characterizes animals and human beings, regarded either as individuals or as societies. What are known to us subjectively as states of consciousness are objectively, Spencer maintains, modes of force.

This explanation of all phenomena, biological, psychological, and sociological, as well as those usually thought of as chemical and physical, by reference to no laws other than those commonly called "natural," is paralleled very closely in the system of Haeckel. The latter derives everything from the "law of substance," which embraces the persistence of both matter and force. In accounting for the appearance of life and consciousness in the later stages of evolution he, however, attributes a primitive rudimentary vitality and mentality to the constituent atoms. He thus arrives at a quasi-religious position, somewhat similar to that of Spinoza (1632-1677) or of Goethe (1749-1832). (p. 331.)[7]

To this world-view Haeckel gives the name "monism." Whether or not monism has room for the idea of God depends upon the definition we choose to employ. If the word "god" is understood to mean a personal extra-mundane entity, Haeckel's position agrees with that of the atheist. He quotes approvingly Schopenhauer's remark, "Pantheism is only a polite form of atheism. The truth of the position lies in its destruction of the dualist antithesis of God and the world, in its recognition that the world exists in virtue of its own inherent forces." (p. 291.)[7]

Haeckel crowns his evolutionist philosophy with a "monistic religion" and a "monistic ethics." While he finds definite contradictions between the "revealed truths" of Christianity and the results of scientific inquiry, the monistic and the Christian ideas of virtue are, he says, in essential agreement. In granting this, he is thinking primarily, however, of the humanist principles of charity and toleration, which, as he points out, are by no means original with Christianity. Moreover, according to Haeckel, Christian ethics has been marred by too much insistence upon altruism, and a denunciation of egoism; while monistic ethics lays equal emphasis upon the two, and finds perfect virtue in the just balance between love of self and love of one's neighbor (pp. 350 ff.).

Monistic philosophy destroys the three central dogmas of dualistic systems: the personality of God, the immortality of the soul, and the freedom of the will. Monism, however, does not try to explain the fundamental law of substance, in the sense of attempting to tell *why* it is as it is. Haeckel readily grants that the innermost character of nature is not understood even by the greatest scientists and philosophers. We learn to know more and more about the phenomenal forms of the mysterious underlying substance; but we do not know the "thing in itself" that lies behind the knowable phenomena. (p. 380.)[7]

A HISTORY OF PHILOSOPHICAL SYSTEMS

This agnostic conclusion of Haeckel's philosophic enterprise reminds one of Spencer's doctrine of the *Unknowable*, which is presented in Part I of the latter's *First Principles*. It seems to have come from the "apophatic" theology of the Neoplatonists by way of a long line of medieval and modern thinkers, including Kant, Hamilton (1788-1856), and Mansel (1820-1871). (39 ff. and 65 ff.)[4] However, no matter how venerable may be the appeal to an ultimate incomprehensibility, whether made to shield traditional theology from destructive criticism or to relieve evolutionist science from embarrassing questions about *origins* and ultimate *grounds*, it is hard to attach any meaning to the notion of a "reality" which is said to be unknowable.

For if we know nothing about "it," how can we know that "it" is real? Or, if we know that what we are talking about exists, *i.e.*, if we use the term "reality" as a collective name for the totality of all existents, do we not know at least that much about it? And, granted that by "reality" we are to mean all that exists, is it not probable that we know *something* about *some* existents, in addition to the bare fact that they exist? It may be objected that to have a knowledge of existents is not the same as to have knowledge of the whole to which they belong. But do we know whether the all constitutes a *whole* or is merely an *aggregate*? To know *this* would be to know a great deal about reality. In short, at any given stage of scientific advance, reality is partly known and partly unknown. And, as concerns what is not yet known, we have no sufficient reason to assert that it is *unknowable* rather than simply *unknown*.

It may be said, perhaps, that science treats only of our *ideas*. But our ideas, if we really "have" them, are real. Thus even a dream, if it actually occurs, must be included among the constituents of reality. Consequently, even if science were nothing more than a correlation of groups of earlier and later human ideas (that is to say, of "phenomena"), it would be, so far forth, an investigation of the nature of reality.

Returning to the positive content of the nineteenth century philosophies of evolution, let us, in conclusion, inquire very briefly how we might wish to supplement them in view of recent advances in the sciences.

One of the developments which must be taken into account is the discovery of radioactivity and the consequent release of intra-atomic energy. It can no longer be taken for granted that the principal source of the energy of an aggregate of material particles is their drawing together in accordance with the law of gravitation. Thus the sun may be expected to radiate energy into surrounding space at approximately its present rate much longer than would be possible if, as was formerly supposed, the only source of its energy were the contraction of its mass. Also the release of energy from within the atom makes it unnecessary to suppose, in order to explain hot springs and geysers, volcanic eruptions and lava flows, that the earth was originally molten (although it is not impossible that it was).

A closely related scientific advance has been the discovery of the theoretical inter-convertibility of mass and energy. As a consequence, Spencer's "persistence of matter" and "persistence of force" are, neither of them, quite true. Strictly speaking, we should now refer to the conservation of *mass-energy* rather than of either mass or energy considered separately. As our sun, or any of the stars, radiates energy, its mass is diminished in the process. If this were all that can be said, while Spencer's "dissolution" would proceed somewhat differently, it would nevertheless arrive ultimately at the indicated end. There is, however, more to be said. According to the relativity theory, space is finite. This means that energy is not radiated away indefinitely, but eventually returns to the region from which it came. Thus Spencer's cautiously expressed speculation that, as existing systems dissolve, their debris may ultimately be reintegrated to form new ones, would seem to be substantiated.

It may be significant that Spencer does not mention the "second law of thermodynamics"; and that Haeckel refers to the principle that "the entropy of the universe approaches a maximum," (p. 247)[7], only to protest against it as erroneous. Combined with the idea of the convertibility of matter into energy, this second law asserts, in effect, that "matter" is simply a *high-level* form of energy, which under certain conditions tends to be transformed into energy of lower and still lower levels. The tragic conclusion would then be that all high-level energies, including matter, would ultimately be transformed into energy of the lowest level, which is uniformly distributed heat.

If, however, we may suppose that under appropriate conditions energy changes back again into matter, it is conceivable that in far distant regions of the relativists' finite space the dissipated energy of our system reappears as electrons and protons, or whatever may be the ultimate units of matter. This extremely diffuse matter would then be gradually integrated to form new evolving systems.

This conception would, to be sure, run afoul of another "discovery" of recent science, the "expanding universe." According to this doctrine, which in our present context may be regarded as a reinforcement and extension of the "second law of thermodynamics," while space is finite, its total volume is constantly increasing. Thus "dissolution" would continue indefinitely, and the present evolutionary cycle must have been initiated by a creative act.

Against this it should be pointed out (1) that on the available evidence a pulsating universe is just as probable as an expanding one; (2) that as still more distant star clusters are revealed by improved telescopes it is possible that *their* light will not show the shift toward the red; and (3) this shift need not be interpreted as indicating a motion away from us, since it might be merely a function of distance or a result of many successive encounters with particles of cosmic dust.

Another advance of recent science which should be taken into account is the "principle of indeterminacy." This supports the empiricist theory of natural law, and strengthens the evidence for the doctrine of emergent causation. If this view be accepted, Haeckel's attribution of rudimentary life and mind to the ultimate units of matter is unnecessary. For the "higher" or non-mechanical features of the natural order may be thought of as supervening—in accordance with specifiable uniformities—upon the occasion of describable configurations of those which are "lower" or mechanical.

Thus the evolutionism of the nineteenth century survives in the twentieth as a pluralistic naturalism, which "explains" life and mind and values in the only sense in which anything can be explained, that is, by formulating empirical laws for the correlation of earlier and later observed states of affairs.

NOTES AND BIBLIOGRAPHY

1. C. R. Darwin, *The Origin of Species* (New York, 6th edition, 1872).
2. A. R. Wallace, *The Theory of Natural Selection* (London, 2nd edition, 1870).
3. J. J. Romanes, *Darwin and After Darwin* (Chicago, 1892).
4. H. Spencer, *First Principles* (New York, 1885).
5. ———, *Principles of Biology* (New York, 1891).
6. ———, *Autobiography* (New York, 1904).
7. E. Haeckel, *The Riddle of the Universe* (New York, 1900).

CHAPTER THIRTY
VITALISM

ARTHUR BERNDTSON

I. INTRODUCTION

IN ITS narrower sense, Vitalism is a theory in biology and in philosophy of science, which holds that living processes cannot be explained by physico-chemical laws. In its broader and present sense, Vitalism is a group of ideas which brings to the whole of philosophy the image, as it were, of life. As thus understood, Vitalism is anti-rationalistic and pragmatic, holding that universals and fixed principles are not factors in the real, but merely instruments for the action of living things. It is idealistic both in the ontological sense, identifying the real with something akin to spirit, and in the epistemological sense, classing many of the objects of knowledge as appearances dependent on cognition. It regards time and change as fundamental, and favors an evolutionary and historical outlook. It is revisionist in its ethics, and rejects eternal norms and external imperatives. It is explicitly non-theistic: partially pantheistic: and endowed with a profoundly religious sense in its feeling for a universal and self-transcending creativity.

The leading representatives of vitalistic philosophy are Friedrich Nietzsche (1844-1900) and Henri Bergson (1859-1941). Immediate and extensive anticipations of their doctrines are to be found in Schopenhauer, whose system appears to be distinguished from theirs mainly in its nihilism; and lesser roots appear in the voluntaristic idealism of Fichte. In recent decades resemblances may be found in American pragmatism and in A. N. Whitehead (1861-1947), without evidence of historical influence; in Existentialism; and in three Latin-American philosophers who have consciously accepted much of Bergson and not a little of Nietzsche: Alejandro

Korn (1860-1936), José Vasconcelos (1882-   ), and Antonio Caso (1883-1946).[1]

Despite this historical context, Vitalism is not an historically articulated movement. Bergson's first important work appeared in the year of Nietzsche's collapse, but closer continuity is not apparent. The reason for this lack of identification may lie in the fact that Bergson's major work, in theory of knowledge and in metaphysics, was completed before Nietzsche's scattered work in these fields was given definitive publication by his editors. Nietzsche's prevailing interest, reflected in the many titles which appeared in the 1870's and 1880's, was ethical, social and esthetic; and Bergson wrote little in these fields until late in life. There are differences, therefore, in points of emphasis in the two philosophies. There are also differences in doctrine. The two men agree in the attack on intellect, but Bergson is alone in the formulation of a positive theory of knowledge, embracing the activity of intuition. There is a greater appearance of dualism in Bergson's metaphysics, and his ethics approaches creativity in terms of love rather than of what Nietzsche called power. But neither the historical discontinuity, nor the differences of emphasis and of doctrine, negates the impressive extent of their common participation in the body of ideas defining Vitalism.

II. FRIEDRICH NIETZSCHE

Friedrich Nietzsche was born near Leipzig in 1844, wrote the precocious and original *Birth of Tragedy* in 1870, collapsed on a street in Turin in 1889, and died in 1900 after eleven years of insanity. In the twenty productive years of youth and early maturity thus allotted to him, Nietzsche wrote extensively, passionately and under increasing difficulties, with results which are evident in the unusual scope of his thinking and in the breadth of his influence and adumbrations. His instrumental theory of knowledge presages recent pragmatism. His criticism of nineteenth century atomism resembles recent tendencies in physics, and his emphasis on time and change is renewed in the philosophy of Alexander (1859-1938). His ethics is the strongest recent statement of relativism in values; this notwithstanding, it has had influence on the ethics of Nicolai Hartmann (b. 1882). His esthetics afforded an important interpretation of Greek tragedy, and his personality and philosophy have had great influence in recent art. He was a close student of human culture: both in its historical perspectives, with influence on Spengler (1880-1936), and in its diseases, with anticipations of Freud (1856-1940). And beyond the pale of philosophy, Nietzsche was a finished artist, as indicated by *Thus Spake Zarathustra*; a prophet, who proposed to create as well as to clarify values; and an oracle frequently misunderstood, as by Hitler.

The value-motif which dominates Nietzsche's philosophy makes its first appearance in his theory of knowledge.[2] In opposition to a realistic interpretation of experience and reason, Nietzsche holds that our knowledge is subjective and instrumental. In its empirical foundations our knowledge involves sense organs, whose operation is relatively crude, and sensory qualities, which cannot strictly be known since they elude quantification. In its structure our knowledge involves concepts, categories and the laws of logic, all of which center around the invented factor of identity. Concepts imply abstraction and simplification, and these imply the reduction of diverse becoming to stable and self-identical being. This reduction is consummated in the principle of non-contradiction, which forbids the assignment of contradictory predicates and leads ultimately to a Parmenidean metaphysic. The methods of identity belong primarily to intellect, but intellect cannot be evaluated by itself without circularity, and it can not be compared with other intellects for evaluation of its results. We must therefore refrain from assigning to objective reality the deliverances of sense and of reason. But this does not imply the rejection of what is usually called knowledge. Our methods of knowing have developed in the evolutionary process as methods of adjustment and mastery in relation to the world, and it is precisely their subjective character which underlies their utility. Thus the crudeness of our sense organs reflects our need rather than the character of objective reality, and the qualitative status of sensations is tied up with their emotional tone or value-character. The affiliation of intellect with principles of identity gives the organism a stable context in which to operate, and the law of non-contradiction is a prescription by the organism in the interest of coherent action.

In keeping with his relativistic methodology, Nietzsche supplies a metaphysic whose major tendency is to deny every form of the absolute.[3] No basic reality can be found in psychical states, for these are schematized in the interest of simplicity, and furthermore they are powerless. We commonly think that our feeling of effort, which we identify with volition, is the effective cause of our actions; but this feeling, like all states of consciousness, is a mere epiphenomenon to a set of forces of which we have no awareness. The apparent causality of our feeling of effort is the archetype of our general notion of causality, whose essence is not a formula of uniformity in nature, but an identification of events in nature with volition in human action: natural events are regarded as effects of purposive forces. But such forces can not be lodged in thin phenomena: they require substantial agents. As the source of our idea of causality is to be found in human action, so the source of the idea of substance is to be found in the idea of a psychical agent or subject. But this idea is a fiction of our logical demand for identities and of our grammatical habit of constructing sentences whose predicates are referred to subjects. The general conception of substance must therefore be rejected, and with it the derivative conception of causality.

A further consequence is the rejection of substantial materialism or atomism.[4] The contemporary mechanics of solid particles in extrinsic motion should be replaced with a doctrine of dynamic quanta in intrinsic tension with each other. These forces are not to be understood in the nominal sense currently held in mechanics, but in the literal sense of urges or willings. These urges constitute, or manifest, the universal ontological entity: the will to power. It appears that here Nietzsche does have an absolute, for which there is no anticipation in his principles of method. It may also be argued that the will to power is a substance, since it is not conditioned by anything prior, and a cause, since it is the power conditioning everything posterior. But it is likely that Nietzsche rejects substance and causality primarily in the sense of detached principles of Being which are externally invoked to explain Becoming; and his will to power is not such a principle. On the contrary, the will to power is Becoming considered as endowed with its own principle of fertility. The will to power thus expresses the absolute character of immanent change. But even here the absolute is qualified by the doctrine of eternal recurrence. Power or energy is limited, time is infinite, and the result is the repetition of the history of the world through cycles identical in kind and infinite in number.

A HISTORY OF PHILOSOPHICAL SYSTEMS

The will to power is more basic than the will to live, and the second is an interesting localization of the first. Like its sponsor, life is in continual process, which takes the form of the evolution of new types.[5] The aim of evolving life is not to secure self-preservation through relatively passive adjustment to environment, but to secure increased power involving mastery and transformation of the environment. In its native and healthy form life does not so much seek to preserve itself as to consummate itself in a creative transcending which may involve perishing. This principle is illustrated in the case of exceptional individuals, whose genius is power highly developed and unstable. Such individuals are the protagonists of evolution, but they have less survival value than do the masses; and they must reckon in addition on the destructive effect of the envy and resentment of the masses. The many therefore are more likely to survive, though in a profound sense they are less fit for living.

Various of these evolutionary principles are developed in Nietzsche's ethics. Value and power are the same; conduct, personality and moral codes are valuable only insofar as they promote power.[6] Pleasure and pain are not standards of value: they are accessory phenomena. Pleasure is a feeling accompanying increase of power; but the value lies in the increase of power, not in the pleasure. Pain does not necessarily imply decrease of power; it signifies resistance, whose overcoming is necessary for increase of power. An ethic oriented toward pleasure will uniformly wish to avoid pain, and will readily fall into a "pessimism of sensibility" because of the great extent of pain in life. An ethic of power will readily embrace painful situations as part of its program of power-expansion, and will not be seduced into pessimism by considerations of mere feeling. But the rejection of pleasure as standard does not imply asceticism or formalism in the power-philosophy. Such consequences are affiliated rather with a third view, which identifies value with the processes and dictates of conscience. For Nietzsche, the entire apparatus of conscience must be rejected.[7] Fixed rules violate the principle of flux, and commands divorced from the power-formula imply a source acceptable only to a transcendent metaphysics. The illusion of "moral" freedom and responsibility stems from the introversion among subject peoples of their thwarted impulse for external power. And the sense of guilt variously implies introversion of the sadistic impulses which are so common among men, and success on the part of the ascetic priest in relieving the depression and redirecting the resentment of a sick people.

Not the "wickedness" of those condemned by conscience, but sickness of spirit in individuals and groups, is the concern of the enlightened moralist. The essence of sickness is fear and apathy. It is illustrated in the morality of the slave, who preaches "pity, the obliging, helping hand, the warm heart, patience, diligence, humility," [8] in order to help solve the problem of fear and envy of the master, who would live according to the equation of the "good, noble, powerful, beautiful, happy," [9] were it not that he is hoodwinked, in Christian and democratic society, by the preachments of the slave. Sickness is found also in contemporary nihilism, whose apathy expresses profound uncertainty and disillusionment about the value of life. For these forms of sickness the remedy is to be found generally in the acceptance of the power philosophy, and specifically in the cultivation of values in their terrestrial and changing character, in the practice of the code of the master, and in the creative directing of our energies toward the production of Superman.

A further remedy is to be found in art, which may be regarded as Nietzsche's alternative to doctrinal religion.[10] In a godless and purposeless world there is much occasion for disgust and terror, which art can deal with by transformation into the comic and sublime. The virtues of art are optimally illustrated in tragic drama, whose function most assuredly is not to teach resignation, nor to arouse pity and fear. In its Dionysian basis tragedy uses the pain of becoming as a catalyst, and presents the consoling union of the individual with the universal becoming. In its Apollonian form these values are clarified through presentation to objective contemplation. Art thus presents the fusion of vital and mysterious existence with ordering mastery. Such fusion acts as a tonic; it is a sign of a strong and creative people; it indicates the direction in which men must move if they are again to find meaning in life.

III. HENRI BERGSON

Henri Bergson shares with Descartes (1596-1650) and Comte (1798-1857) the honors of French philosophy, and adds to the rationalism of the first and the empiricism of the second an equally distinctive intuitionism. His philosophy is set forth, in its basic positions, in *Time and Free Will* (1889), *Matter and Memory* (1896), and *Creative Evolution* (1907); to which should be added the brief and summary account of method in the *Introduction to Metaphysics* (1903), and the late application to axiology in *The Two Sources of Morality and Religion* (1932). It is difficult to summarize the philosophy expounded in these volumes: a philosophy singularly rich in suggestion but unconcerned with literal proof; which proceeds, like the reality it describes, with an interpenetration of parts which defies delimitation in ready formulas; and which qualifies the seemingly rigorous opposition of its basic terms with hints at fusion. With these cautions in mind, it may be said that Bergson is a direct realist in epistemology, with concessions to dualism in his view of invented appearance; a dualist in ontology, with hints of a monism favoring mind; a temporalist and particularist; an evolutionary vitalist in biology, who does not quite accept teleology; a mystic in theology; and a libertarian in his view of duration, memory, the evolutionary process and personality.

The theme running through the various parts of Bergson's philosophy is that of the opposition of the like and the unlike. The problem makes its first appearance in *Time and Free Will,* which distinguishes quite sharply between two orders of reality: space and duration, which are the archetypes respectively of the homogeneous or mechanical and the heterogeneous or vital. Space is external, that is, alien in essence, in relation to perceiving mind; it is indefinitely divisible into homogeneous parts which are external to each other; in its homogeneity it is without quality and thus it is pure quantity. Duration is internal to mind; it is not intrinsically divisible, since its heterogeneous parts interpenetrate; it is fundamentally qualitative. Space is a theatre of change without succession: events in space arise and perish in a continually re-created present, with no factor of continuity to bind moment with moment. Duration is indistinguishable from change; but change in duration involves succession, whereby different moments are bound together by memory in a continuous order of past, present and future: in duration the past survives organically in the present. Space is the locus of mathematical or deterministic causality: the homogeneity of space permits events to be repeated, and the absence of qualitative succession causes the future to inhere in the present and therefore to follow necessarily from the present. Duration is the locus of dynamical or free causality: events in duration have the character of spontaneous forces, which avoid sheer accident by virtue of the endurance of the past in the novel future. Space and duration are therefore antithetical and equally real; and time, which represents an attempt to impose the homogeneous form of space upon succession, is a spurious conception reducible to space.

A closer determination of the spatial and durational orders, with indications of a monistic tendency, is to be found in the account of matter and spirit in *Matter and Memory*. Spirit is esentially memory; it implies the coloration of events by the survival of preceding events. Spirit is independent of matter: memory is not a function of the brain, whose minute movements are not the cause or receptacle of memory-images, but merely the conditions of rapport between memory and the practical action of the body; and perceptions are not representations manufactured in the brain, but parts of material reality directly presented to consciousness and there somewhat transformed. This material reality seems to be irreducibly opposed to states of consciousness, since the latter are fluid, qualitative, indivisible and apparently unextended, while material particles are static, shorn of qualities, inherently divisible and extended. But the unextended character of psychical states is not inherent: psychical states take on extensity in proportion as they evolve toward action. And certain of the characters of bodies require re-interpretation. Bodies are not static entities identified with space and externally related to motion; they are themselves motions, in the form of minute vibrations endlessly repeated. These motions, though extended, are indivisible; and their high degree of homogeneity, which underlies their calculability, is not without a tincture of quality. In pure perception these motions would be apprehended in their virtually unqualified homogeneity, as a disjunct multiplicity of billions of vibrations. But in ordinary perception memory comes into play, causing the earlier vibrations to be carried over into the experience of the later and condensing the entire set into a unitary experience of fully developed quality. The difference between the material and the psychical, between homogeneous motion and heterogeneous quality, is therefore one of tension or duration: a minimum of duration in matter, and varying degrees of duration in spirit. Space is thus seen to be irrelevant to the distinction: extensity belongs alike to mind and matter, but the notion of a purely homogeneous and infinitely divisible medium belongs to neither; and space, which is this medium, becomes a useful fiction of intellect.

With mind and matter in nicely balanced distinction from each other, permitting mutual independence but not prohibiting interplay, it is not surprising that life, the topic of *Creative Evolution,* should be lodged in physico-chemical ensembles and yet be independent in some measure of them. The species of living organisms change: the course of evolution is based on mutations in the germ cells, but these mutations are not accidental; evolution seems to move in a fairly definite direction, but the cause is not to be found in the mechanical yielding of the organism to its physical environment; effort is involved in evolution, but the effort is not one of individuals, with acquired characteristics passed on to offspring: it is in the species and its seat is the germ plasm. This effort is the vital impetus (*élan vital*), which is the source of mutations and of the directed character of evolution. The vital impetus is not an attribute of body, but a kind of kinetic substance whose being lies in its ceaseless becoming. In relation to body the impetus is a tendency to advance in novelty and complexity, in contrast to the retrograde movement of body, which is subject to the principle of the degradation of energy. Because of its ceaseless becoming, the vital impetus is not subject to mechanistic determination, which negates duration from the past, nor to teleological determination, which negates duration from the future. But though not bound by a blue-print from the future, the impetus is basically telic; it is duration endowed not only with memory, through which the past survives, but also with appetency, through which the future is created.

In its self-development and in its struggles with matter the vital impetus brings forth two modes of action: instinct, perfected in insects, and intelligence, developed especially in man.[11] Instinct is a "faculty of using and even of constructing organized instruments," or parts of the animal body. Instinct involves a kind of feeling of life for life, but its direction remains outward and practical. Intelligence is the "faculty of manufacturing artificial objects"; it is not at home with life, or ends, but with matter, or means. As a sophisticated instrument of action, intelligence deals with "the unorganized solid," since fluidity and life are not amenable to fabrication; it regards motion as a relation of stationary points in space, since such points or places can be acted upon, and thus loses sight of essential mobility, which does not concern action; and it conceives the fiction of an infinitely divisible and homogeneous space as the pattern of our unlimited possibility of acting, through decomposition and recomposition, on matter. Intelligence is therefore a power of analysis, which breaks down heterogeneous and puzzling wholes into homogeneous parts which invite planned action. It is also a power of forming concepts, which express the homogeneity of particulars and disregard individualizing differences. Intelligence is therefore a tool for action, through spatial devices, rather than a mode of knowing, whose object must be durational reality. But when intelligence has become sufficiently familiar with its own operations, which are inward and ideational, it becomes interested in ideas as such, apart from relation to action. Intelligence thus acquires a contemplative factor, which instinct lacks. The fusion of the virtues of the two methods results in intuition, or "intellectual sympathy," which has the affinity for life and for durational reality of instinct, and the contemplative character developed by intelligence: "by intuition I mean instinct that has become disinterested, self-conscious, capable of reflecting upon its object and of enlarging it indefinitely."[12] From the opposition of instinct and intelligence in organic evolution we are led, then, to the opposition of intuition and analysis in human history.

According to the *Introduction to Metaphysics,* the method of analysis belongs to science, which is therefore confined to symbols or appearances. This is illustrated not only in geometry, the science of space, but also in biology, the science purporting to deal with life; biology studies organs and anatomical elements, which are only the "visual symbols" of life. But at the end of the *Introduction* Bergson is willing to grant some status to intuition in science: modern mathematics endeavors to follow the generation of magnitudes, and modern physics dates from Galileo, who regarded mobility as prior in reality to immobility. This notwithstanding, the definitive use of intuition is assigned to metaphysics, which has stumbled among artificial problems generated by the belief that intelligence is a method of knowing. In this respect metaphysics may learn from art, which characteristically expresses its intuitions of the depths of human personality in a form which is intuited.

A HISTORY OF PHILOSOPHICAL SYSTEMS

And intuition extends finally to religion, whose highest and mystical exercise, as shown in the *Two Sources,* consists in the saints' intuition of God, who is the vital impetus identified as creative love.[13]

NOTES

1. Alejandro Korn, leading philosopher of Argentina, is characterized by intellectual negation and moral affirmation. He is anti-rationalistic, holding that concepts are symbolic inventions and that metaphysical systems are "dialectical poems." He is antipositivistic, believing that science, committed to mechanism, is hostile to ethics, which pre-supposes liberty. Rejecting direct realism, dualistic realism and subjective idealism, he tends to accept a voluntaristic form of absolute idealism, which centers on a theory of a basic and universal "acción consciente." This analogue of the will to power seeks increased liberty but posits no other norms: Korn's ethics is cheerfully relativistic. See his *Libertad Creadora.*

José Vasconcelos, of Mexico, is anti-rationalistic and voluntaristic. He opposes Platonism, for its fixed and independent ideas; mathematics, for seeking unity by elimination of quality and heterogeneity; and mechanism, for its omission of creative impulse. He praises art for its conciliation of qualitative heterogeneity and unity, and for its sense of organism and of creative desire; he finds these virtues codified in the esthetic principles of rhythm, melody and harmony, and believes that recent science tends to vindicate these insights of the artist. His religious orientation is shown in his preference for "revelatory" over "terrestrial" and "metaphysical" ethics, and in his adding to the Nietzschean forms of Apollonian and Dionysian art a third and culminating category of mystical art. See his *Lógica Orgánica, Realismo Científico, Estética* and *Ética.*

Antonio Caso, also of Mexico, is likewise anti-rationalistic, favoring intuition rather than the imposition of logical forms for the discernment of plastic reality. Freedom is a basic principle in his philosophy: he welcomes recent signs of indeterminism in physics, and deplores both individualistic and state-centered forms of social servitude. His esthetics finds the source of art in a "vital excess," from which stems a creative process involving intuition and empathy. Such creative projection is not limited to art proper: it extends to religion in the form of myth, and to epistemology in the form of the logical construction of a world of ordered experience. See his *Problemas Filosóficos, La Persona Humana y el Estado Totalitario,* and *Estética.*

2. *Will to Power,* Book 3, Part I (*Werke,* v. 16).
3. *Ibid.*
4. *Ibid.,* Part II, #618-639.
5. *Ibid.,* #640-687.

6. *Ibid.,* #688-715.
7. *Genealogy of Morals,* Second and Third Essays (*Werke,* v. 7).
8. *Beyond Good and Evil,* p. 242 (*Werke,* v. 7).
9. *Genealogy of Morals,* p. 313.
10. *Birth of Tragedy,* #1-8 (*Werke,* v. 1).
11. *Creative Evolution,* ch. 2.
12. *Ibid.,* p. 176.
13. *Two Sources of Morality and Religion,* ch. 3.

BIBLIOGRAPHY

Works of Nietzsche:
 The Birth of Tragedy, Thus Spake Zarathustra, Beyond Good and Evil, Toward the Genealogy of Morals, and *Ecce Homo* are available in the Modern Library *Philosophy of Nietzsche.*
 The Complete Works of Friedrich Nietzsche, 18 vols., ed. Oscar Levy (New York, 1909 ff.).
 Nietzsche's Werke, 20 vols. (Leipzig, published in part by Naumann and in part by Kröner, 1894-1926).

Works on Nietzsche:
 A. H. J. KNIGHT, *Some Aspects of the Life and Work of Nietzsche* (Cambridge, England, 1933).
 H. L. MENCKEN, *The Philosophy of Friedrich Nietzsche* (Boston, 1908).
 G. A. MORGAN, *What Nietzsche Means* (Cambridge, Mass., 1941).
 CHARLES ANDLER, *Nietzsche, sa Vie et sa Pensée* (Paris, 1920-31).
 ERNST BERTRAM, *Nietzsche: Versuch einer Mythologie* (Berlin, 1918).
 KARL JASPERS, *Nietzsche* (Berlin, 1936).

Works of Bergson:
 Time and Free Will (London, New York, 1910). The French Original is *Essais sur les données immédiates de la conscience.*
 Matter and Memory (London, New York, 1911).
 Laughter: An Essay on the Meaning of the Comic (New York, 1911).
 Introduction to Metaphysics (New York, 1912, 1949).
 Creative Evolution (New York, 1911).
 Mind-Energy (New York, 1920).
 The Two Sources of Morality and Religion (New York, 1935).

Works on Bergson:
 H. W. CARR, *Henri Bergson* (New York, 1912).
 EDOUARD LE ROY, *The New Philosophy of Henri Bergson* (New York, 1913).
 JACQUES MARITAIN, *La philosophie Bergsonienne* (Paris, 1930).
 BEN-AMI SCHARFSTEIN, *Roots of Bergson's Philosophy* (New York, 1943).

CHAPTER THIRTY-ONE

PRAGMATISM

DONALD S. MACKAY

"THE PRAGMATIC movement, so-called—I do not like the name, but apparently it is too late to change it—seems to have rather suddenly precipitated itself out of the air. A number of tendencies that have always existed in philosophy have all at once become conscious of themselves collectively, and of their combined mission." [1] William James (1842-1910), one of the founders of American pragmatism, so described the movement in 1907, when it was already in full swing and had become a topic of lively debate in philosophical circles. The word, "mission," was used advisedly, for James and his fellow-pragmatists had much of the spirit of the moral reformer in their teachings.[2] The "combined mission" was to be, indeed, a transformation of philosophy and its methods in the interest of all that is "profitable to our lives." The several tendencies, so combined, would gain significance through the new orientation of thought toward practical consequences. Pragmatism was said to be "a new name for some old ways of thinking," but it involved much more than the novelty of the name, and we may be in a better position to understand the movement as a whole if we start with the "combined mission," and then consider the several tendencies involved in it.

I

The pragmatic movement had "precipitated itself" thirty years earlier in a paper by Charles Sanders Peirce (1839-1914) on "How to Make Our Ideas Clear." [3] Peirce was the son of a celebrated mathematician, Benjamin Peirce, and himself a creative genius in the fields of mathematical logic and the philosophy of science. The essay had received scant attention at its publication, but it was popularized by James in a lecture entitled "Philosophical Conceptions and Practical Results," which he delivered before the Philosophical Union of the University of California in 1898.[4] In the criticism and defense of pragmatism, which were to follow in this country and abroad, Peirce's original statement of the theory was widely misrepresented. The name was often used, so he complained, "to express some meaning that it was rather designed to exclude." Wishing to disassociate himself from those who were, in his opinion, making a travesty of the movement, he publicly renounced the name and substituted *Pragmaticism,* a name which, as he remarked, "is ugly enough to be safe from kidnappers." [5]

In the meantime, a group of philosophers at the University of Chicago had been working along similar lines under the leadership of John Dewey (1859-   ). The members of this group, the "Chicago School of Thought," had independently adopted the philosophical method that Peirce had named "pragmatic." They emphasized the efficacy of ideas, as intellectual tools, employed in experimental operations for the solution of problems. The movement gave rise to a logical theory known as *Instrumentalism*. It was a generalized theory of human intelligence as a name for the competent procedures of reflective thinking wherever it may occur. The experimental techniques of the laboratory sciences could be extended into all fields of inquiry, and more effective controls and safeguards of inference could be instituted in the practice of solving problems.

A third phase of the movement was in the philosophy of Ferdinand C. S. Schiller (1864-1937) who strove to make the pragmatic method and its implications intelligible to the British mind under the name of *Humanism*. Schiller traced the movement back to the teaching of the Greek sophist, Protagoras, in the fifth century B. C.[6], and to the utilitarian ethics of the nineteenth century. The true is said to be that which works in the way of human belief, although, as Schiller was careful to point out, the converse does not hold, and not every belief that works is true. With utility as a criterion, absolute certainty is manifestly impossible. Truth is *relative*—relative to the felt satisfaction of human needs and desires. On these assumptions Schiller carried on a sustained polemic against the critics of pragmatism, most of whom adhered to Kantian notions of *a priori* necessities and Hegelian notions of the Absolute. These critics he castigated as "intellectualists." He went beyond James and other pragmatists in his contention that true ideas and beliefs are only those that "work,"—indeed, he went so far as to maintain that a belief may be true for one person and false for another, if it should lead to satisfactory consequences in the experience of the former and to unsatisfactory consequences in the experience of the latter. Subjective conditions of personal preference and private feelings of satisfaction enter into the "verification" of beliefs for Schiller in a way that is difficult to reconcile with Peirce's original account of the pragmatic method. However, Schiller's emphasis on the practical differences in human conduct that are consequent on the truth and falsity of beliefs brings out an important aspect of the movement.

Peirce described pragmatism as a "reconstruction of philosophy." [7] He was contrasting it with previous attempts in the 16th and 17th centuries and in particular with the intellectual reforms attempted by Bacon and Descartes. These two thinkers had formulated rules for methods of inquiry by which fruitful discoveries could be made and knowledge placed on firmer foundations. Bacon's "Great Instauration" of learning anticipates Peirce's proposed "reconstruction," with its emphasis on the practical consequences of ideas as employed in the solution of human problems. In much the same way that Bacon had attacked the "distempers" of learning, "fantastical, contentious, and delicate," in the 16th century,[8] Peirce attacked the empty abstractions of "pure intellectualism" in the 19th century. Learning could be advanced and positive knowledge acquired insofar as human life was in Bacon's phrase "endowed with new discoveries and powers." [9] In the same spirit, Peirce deplored the spider-like spinning out of speculations from philosophical conceptions, such as ideas of "substance," or of "mind" or "matter," that were chronically vague and ambiguous. In contrast to these speculative ideas were the clear and precise meanings that attached to terms in scientific reasoning. The point of the contrast was that philosophers *dispute* whereas scientists *investigate*. Disputation tends only to increase differences of opinion among those who participate, while experimental inquiry must lead to eventual agreement among all who investigate.[10] Philosophers are inclined to dispute instead of investigating because the persistent problems of philosophy have been formulated in traditional terms. The meanings of these terms had long since become obscure or even unintelligible to later generations, however clear they might have been, or at least *seemed* to be, to the philosophers who had first thought about the problems.

Descartes rebelled against the traditional teaching of the schools in his day for similar reasons. He was doubtful of the validity of methods that could have given rise to so many conflicting opinions "regarding the self-same matter, all supported by learned people, while there can never be more than one which is true." [11] He had no intention of prescribing to others a method of "rightly conducting the reason and seeking truth in the sciences," but he was convinced that he had found one for himself in the operations of mathematical analysis. There was need of a radical reconstruction of philosophy if it were to meet the rigorous and exact requirements of such a method.[12]

These attempted reconstructions in the 16th and 17th centuries are mentioned only in order to bring out their sharp contrasts with the reconstruction that Peirce contemplated in the 19th century. He thought that previous efforts had failed in the long run, and for two reasons. One was a misconception of the *sources* of knowledge and the other was a misconception of its *nature* and *validity*. The sources of knowledge had been ascribed to particular sensations, passively received from an "external" world, or to particular feelings, arising within the consciousness of an individual mind.[13] The nature and validity of knowledge had been conceived in terms of inner states of consciousness and activities of thought that were entirely subjective. The assumptions of this subjectivism or mentalism had led to hopeless confusions between the logical validity of knowledge and the psychological compulsiveness of belief.[14] Bacon's celebrated theory of induction was vitiated by his nominalistic assumptions about the sources of knowledge. Notwithstanding his insistence upon the need of experiment, he had little or no acquaintance with scientific procedure. He supposed that knowledge could be obtained by generalizing from a few crude experiments without any deductive analysis of the hypotheses and guiding principles that warrant the generalizations.[15] More serious, however, were Descartes' misconceptions of the nature and validity of knowledge. He assumed that knowledge consists of ideas, and that ideas are modifications of the mind, conceived as a "thinking substance." Truth was for him a psychological property of judgments, tested by the "clearness and distinctness" of ideas. The validity of knowledge was supposed to depend on the connections of ideas as modes of *thinking*, and not on the connected facts. Thus, the nature of knowledge and the grounds of its validity are in the intuitive and introspective feelings of clearness that ideas possess as mental modifications, so that there is in final analysis no distinction between an idea as *seeming* clear, subjectively, and an idea as *being* clear, objectively.[16]

Pragmatism was primarily a method of clarifying ideas objectively.[17] It was a method of clarifying ideas by extending the techniques of experimental inquiry from the physical and biological sciences into the field of logical analysis.[18] As such, it was sharply opposed to the nominalism of Bacon, on the one side, and to the subjectivism of Descartes, on the other, because these two tendencies had combined to make a logic of science virtually impossible. Theories of knowledge had been debated by philosophers with little or no understanding of procedures in the modern laboratory. To insist with Bacon and other empiricists that all knowledge comes from experience is not only futile, but positively misleading, so long as the "experience," from which knowledge is said to be derived, is conceived in terms of separate and distinct sensations or sense-data. Such data, supposedly "given" to the receptive mind without any prior activity of selection, comparison, and discrimination, were quite unlike the data of science, which had to be sought out and isolated under the controls of experimental analysis. To insist with Descartes and other rationalists that knowledge consists only of clear and distinct ideas is even more futile and misleading, for the supposed tests of their validity were ascribed to the mere presence of ideas in an attentive mind. Scientific data are discovered in a process of inquiry, under deliberately planned conditions of observation, and not casually received as separate impressions on the several senses. The validity of ideas, for scientific purposes, is determined in the consideration of their consequences when employed experimentally in the course of inquiry, and not by fixing attention upon the ideas themselves in order to make them appear to be clear, introspectively.

Instead of assuming that ideas are distinct by being subjectively different from one another, that is, having nothing "unclear" in them, pragmatism holds that ideas are different in meaning only when they *make* an objective difference in conduct. How does an idea "make a difference," practically? In an obvious sense, an idea might be said to make a difference in my conduct when, in taking some action on the idea, I cause different results to follow. If I have the idea that a pencil for which I am looking is in the top drawer and not in a lower drawer of my desk, then I shall probably open the top drawer instead of the others. In acting on that supposition, my conduct will be different from that which would probably have occurred had I entertained a different idea of the pencil's location. Pragmatism is not reducible to truisms such as this, the obvious fact that ideas have practical consequences. Ideas are said to "make a difference," not in the trivial sense that different results follow when we act upon them, but in the important sense that there is no discernible difference between one idea and another excepting in the different effects that might *conceivably* have practical bearings on our conduct. Pragmatism is a method of clarifying the significant differences among ideas through the anticipation of their future consequences in practice. The "pragmatic maxim" was formulated by Peirce as follows: "Consider what effects, that might conceivably have practical bearings, we conceive the object of our conception to have. Then, our conception of these effects is the whole of our conception of the object." [19]

As a test of significance in the clarification of meanings, the pragmatic rule had its difficulties, which critics were quick to point out, but when James and Schiller proposed that it be used as a criterion of truth, the proposal was deluged with objections. By what test, it was asked, could the significance of the *conception* of the effects be determined according to the pragmatic rule? Was it by considering the further effects of conceiving the effects of our conception of the object, and then considering the effects of conceiving the effects *ad infinitum*? Or were the pragmatists not tacitly assuming an *a priori* test for the validity of their conceptions of future consequences—a test of relevance, coherence, or consistency,—when distinguishing between effects that were consequences, and effects that were not consequences of the idea in question? These and similar difficulties were aggravated in the attempts to make the pragmatic test apply to the truth of judgments as well as to the meaning of ideas. The traditional opposition of the useful to the true, the good, and the beautiful, the separation of "instrumental" from "intrinsic" values, and the ingrained prejudice against the "practical" in favor of the "theoretical" were now to be transferred from the earlier attacks on utilitarianism to the attacks on pragmatism. To say that the truth of a belief or judgment depends on its practical consequences was to debase truth to considerations of personal profit or to other mercenary aims (and James's use of an easily misunderstood slang expression, "the practical cash value" of an idea, as well as his insistence that ideas are true in being "profitable to our lives," gave support to this criticism), while the attempt to enlarge the scope of the practical so as to include the abstract results of mathematical analysis or theoretical conclusions in pure physics was to deprive the word, *practice*, of any distinctive meaning. One of the most pertinacious critics of pragmatism, commenting on its alleged ambiguity, was led to ask, as though in mock despair, "Am I and have I been always myself a Pragmatist?" [20]

Looking back at the debate that was to continue for a quarter of a century or more, one wonders how much was merely verbal and how much was concerned with real difficulties, whether in the use of the pragmatic method for the clarification of meanings or in applying the test of anticipated consequences for determining the truth or falsity of ideas. There may have been "thirteen pragmatisms" [21] and as many different "pragmatic" criteria by formula, but the proposed method of philosophical analysis, in whatever terms it may have been formulated, is plain enough from Peirce's illustrations.[22] What is meant by saying that a thing is *hard*? What is a clear idea of *weight*? What, in general, is the meaning of *force*? Applying the pragmatic rule, we consider the effects which we conceive a hard object to have when it is pressed; we consider the effects which we conceive a heavy object to have when its support is removed; we consider the effects which we conceive a force to have in the acceleration (change of the velocities) of bodies or particles of bodies in motion. "What we mean by force is completely involved in the effects." [23] The meaning is distinguishable only through the consideration of differences among the possible consequences of the idea in operation. Diamonds are notably brilliant, transparent, and hard; what is the meaning of hardness in distinction, say, to brilliancy or transparency? If, in our experience, all transparent objects were hard, and all hard objects transparent, then transparency and hardness would mean the same, since there could be no discernible difference in their conceived effects. In order to make clear the meaning of hardness, or any other idea, by the pragmatic method, we must, as James says, "try to interpret each notion by tracing its respective practical consequences." [24] Instead of looking for some inner coherence or consistency of meaning in the ideas of the several properties, we must consider the possible effects of overt operations, such as cutting the smooth surface of a piece of glass with a diamond, or testing the stone's resistance under increasing pressure. Had diamonds never been observed in contact with anything but soft cotton, and their hardness never put to the test, no analysis of their properties of brilliancy and transparency could have disclosed any necessary connection with the property of hardness. Under such hypothetical conditions, it would have made no difference in meaning (unless for convenience of language) to have said that a diamond was soft while in contact only with cotton, and that it remained so until brought into contact with a hard object, the hardness of the diamond then increasing under heavier and heavier pressure. "There is no difference between a hard thing and a soft thing so long as they are not put to the test." [25]

II

What were the leading tendencies of thought involved in the pragmatic movement? The most obvious is the attitude and way of thinking that characterized British empiricism from Bacon to Mill, and which the latter had described as "the method of detail." Concrete and denotable matters of observation are the necessary condition in apprehending the meaning of ideas as well as testing the truth of beliefs or supposed forms of knowledge. James dedicated his lectures in *Pragmatism* to the memory of John Stuart Mill "from whom I first learned the pragmatic openness of mind and whom my fancy likes to picture as our leader were he alive today." Peirce bears witness to Mill's importance by frequent reference to his *System of Logic,* although usually with adverse criticism of his theory of induction, his doctrine of the association of ideas, and his uncritical assumption that all knowledge is derived from particular sensations. While the *a priori*, transcendental conditions assumed in the Kantian theory of knowledge were rejected by Peirce quite as emphatically as by Mill, the objections to the logic of Mill's empiricism ran along the same lines as Kant's criticism of Locke and Hume. It should be remembered that the name, *pragmatism*, was suggested to Peirce by Kant's distinction between the *praktisch* and the *pragmatisch*.[26] Some of Peirce's friends had wished him to call his method, *practicalism*, "but for one who had learned philosophy out of Kant, . . . and who still thought in Kantian terms most readily, *praktisch* and *pragmatisch* were as far apart as the two poles, the former belonging in a region of thought where no mind of the experimentalist type can ever make sure of solid ground under his feet, the latter expressing relation to some definite human purpose." [27]

Another major tendency in pragmatism was the evolutionary interpretation of life as represented chiefly by Charles Darwin in his theory of natural selection. *Continuity of development* was a postulate of pragmatism in its analysis of experience and thought. The concept of evolution meant that there is no break or gap between the organic and the inorganic, and likewise no separation could be assumed between a mind and the conditions of its development, both physical and biological. "Minds inhabit environments which act upon them and on which they in turn react," wrote James in partial agreement with Spencer's evolutionism, and such a psychology "takes mind in the midst of all its concrete relations," as opposed to "the old-fashioned 'rational psychology,' which treated the soul as a detached existent, sufficient unto itself, and assumed to consider only its nature and properties." [28] With a similar emphasis on continuity, although from the standpoint of a behavioral instead of an introspective analysis of thought, Dewey held (1) that ideas and logical forms of inquiry have been evolved out of biological processes, (2) that thought or inquiry is itself a continuing process, an "ongoing activity," "an enterprise continually renewed," (3) that the later stages of the process are continuous with the earlier stages, and (4) that the temporal continuity of experience and inquiry has a definite biological basis in the modification of structures in the nervous system, which "condition" further responses of the organism to its changing environment.[29] Experience is not primarily cognitive—a *knowing*-affair. It is rather an affair of undergoing, having, enjoying, suffering things and events through the interactions of a living being with its surroundings. In the experiential adjustments of organism to environment, and of environment to organism, "a future is implicated in a present" and the "reality" of the present is the continuous transformation of a past into a future. From the standpoint of pragmatism, experience "is primarily what is undergone in connection with activities whose import lies in their objective consequences—their bearing upon future experiences." [30] With this postulate of continuity went a complete and unquestioning reliance on *the genetic method of explanation*, which had proven so successful in accounting for the organization, functions, and species of living beings. Here, again, the influence of Darwin was marked in the shift of investigation from questions concerning the reason *why* things are characterized as they are to questions as to *how* they came to be so characterized in their origins and development.[31] No further explanation of an object was necessary, and none was possible, beyond a descriptive account of the process of development together with verifiable predictions of the future consequences. "Once admit that the sole verifiable or fruitful object of knowledge is the particular set of changes that generate the object of study together with the consequences that then flow from it, and no intelligible question can be asked about what, by assumption, lies outside." [32]

A third tendency in the pragmatic movement, which goes back at least as far as Aristotle's psychology, was the naturalistic interpretation of the mind as a function of the living organism.[33] This functional theory was reinforced by the results of modern physiology, with its more exact knowledge of the basis of mental activities in the central nervous system. As Whitehead has remarked, "The effect of physiology was to put mind back into nature. The neurologist traces first the effect of stimuli along the bodily nerves, then integration at nerve centres, and finally the rise of a projective reference beyond the body with a resulting motor efficacy in renewed nervous excitement." [34] The influence of physiology and experimental psychology was evident in Peirce's theory of inquiry as a "struggle," arising out of an initial "irritation of doubt," to the end of attaining a "calm and satisfactory" state of belief. In other words, thinking is a response to a stimulus that interrupts the habitual routine of activities, thus causing a state of perplexity and hesitation from which "we struggle to free ourselves and pass into a state of belief." Peirce compares this to "the irritation of a nerve and the reflex action produced thereby; while for the analogue of belief, in the nervous system, we must look to what are called nervous associations—for example, to that habit of the nerves in consequence of which the smell of a peach will make the mouth water." [35] He was among the first to apply the notion of the conditioned reflex to the psychology of learning and inquiry, but in the logical analysis of meanings he was careful to employ the notion only by way of analogy. While the drawing of inferences in the process of inquiry is conditioned *psychologically* by concepts, operating as "habits of mind," the validity of an inference depends *logically* on the fact that the particular habit, which determines it, is or is not "such as to produce true conclusions in general." The implications of this theory for pragmatism become apparent in the ensuing statements that "the whole function of thought is to produce habits of action," and that in order to develop the meaning of a thought, "we have simply to determine what habits it produces, for what a thing means is simply what habits it involves." [36]

A fourth tendency was in the experimentalism of the scientific outlook as expressed in the techniques of the modern laboratory. It is no exaggeration to say of the pragmatic movement that it was simply an attempt to extend the experimental attitude and habits of action into other areas of human interest and other fields of inquiry, including philosophy. It was not that laboratories could be set up and experiments performed in these fields, for this was manifestly impossible, but the experimentalist's type of mind and approach to problems promised to make the inquiries at once more factual and more fruitful. The experimentalist is one who strives to understand things only through their observable behavior. When he is not clear about the meaning of a proposition, hypothesis, or theory, he turns to possible operations on the materials of inquiry under their specific conditions. If there are two rival hypotheses or theories, presumably about the same matters, the experimentalist asks, "What particular experimental fact could have been made different by one or the other view being correct?" or "In what respects would the world be different if this alternative or that were true?" If no observed or observable difference can be discerned in the concrete consequences, the alternative "has no sense." [37]

The "mission" of the pragmatic movement in philosophy appears, negatively, in its opposition to intellectualism and all forms of totalitarian thinking. It appears, positively, in the attitude, described by James, *"of turning away from first things, principles, 'categories,' supposed necessities, and of turning towards last things, fruits, consequences, facts."* [38] Among the several tendencies that have "become conscious of themselves collectively," we have mentioned only the more obvious trends of traditional empiricism with its "method of detail," the evolutionary interpretation of life, experience, and thought, the functional theory of mind in the light of modern physiology, and the experimentalism of the laboratory sciences. Through their joint influence the rôle of intelligence and its habitat in nature have come to be more clearly understood. Instead of elaborating theories about passive "states" of knowledge in a knowing mind, or "contents" of knowledge within its own fixed and immutable "forms," pragmatism offered a working hypothesis concerning the *practice* of knowledge in "the real business of living." The pragmatic method of clarifying ideas and testing the validity of propositions by the conceived effects of experimental operations is justifiable in the long run only by its own pragmatic tests. It will be amply justified if it helps to clarify the issues in the social and political conflicts of each generation through a more informed and confident intelligence.

NOTES

1. W. James, *Pragmatism: A New Name for Some Old Ways of Thinking* (New York, 1907), p. vii.

2. This is exemplified in his chapter on Habit with its "ethical implications and pedagogical maxims" (*Principles of Psychology,* [New York, 1890], Vol. I. Chap. IV), in his criticism of Royce's theory of the Absolute as permitting "moral holidays," and in the rejection of determinism as inhibiting moral effort ("The Dilemma of Determinism" in *The Will to Believe, and Other Essays in Popular Philosophy* [New York, 1897]).

3. *Popular Science Monthly* (January, 1878); reprinted in C. S. Peirce, *Chance, Love, and Logic,* edited with an introduction by M. R. Cohen (New York, 1923), and in C. S. Peirce, *Collected Papers,* edited by C. Hartshorne and P. Weiss (Cambridge, Mass., 1934), Vol. V, pp. 248-271.

4. *The University Chronicle* (Berkeley, California, September, 1898); reprinted in W. James, *Collected Essays and Reviews* (New York, 1920).

5. *Collected Papers,* V, p. 277.

6. The *Homomensura* principle that "man is the measure of all things, of the things that are that they are, of the things that are not that they are not."

7. *Collected Papers,* V, pp. 249-251.

8. "In reason as well as in experience, there fall out to be these three distempers . . . of learning; the first, fantastical learning; the second, con-

tentious learning; and the last, delicate learning; vain imaginations, vain altercations, and vain affectations." *The Works of Francis Bacon,* edited by Spedding and Ellis (New York, 1870), Vol. 3, p. 382.

9. *Ibid.,* Vol. 4, p. 79: "Now the true and lawful goal of the sciences is none other than this: that human life be endowed with new discoveries and powers" (*Novum Organum,* Aphorism LXXXI); *cf.* p. 47: "Human knowledge and human power meet in one; for where the cause is not known the effect cannot be produced. Nature to be commanded must be obeyed; and that which in contemplation is as the cause is in operation as the rule" (Aphorism III); and pp. 20–21: "Lastly, I would address one general admonition to all; that they consider what are the true ends of knowledge, and that they seek it not either for pleasure of the mind, or for contention, or for superiority to others, or for profit, or fame, or power, or any of these inferior things; but for the benefit and use of life" (*The Great Instauration,* preface).

10. *Collected Works,* V, p. 268: "The opinion which is fated to be ultimately agreed to by all who investigate is what we mean by the truth, and the object represented by this opinion is the real."

11. *The Philosophical Works of Descartes,* translated by Haldane and Ross (Cambridge, 1911) Vol. I, p. 86.

12. *Ibid.,* p. 9: "It were better never to think of investigating truth at all, than to do so without a method. For it is very certain that unregulated inquiries and confused reflections of this kind only confound the natural light and blind our mental powers" (in Rule IV of *Rules for the Direction of the Mind*).

13. Peirce refers to this view as "nominalism" (he speaks of "a tidal wave of nominalism" in philosophy since Descartes, and says that "every sect has been nominalistic," *Collected Papers,* I, pp. 19–20), and again, more specifically, as "English sensationalism."

14. "The question of validity," says Peirce, "is purely one of fact and not of thinking" (*Collected Papers,* V, p. 226). He described his own position as "extremely unfavorable to the use of psychology in logic," and he sharply dissented from the position of J. S. Mill (1806–1873) that the theoretic grounds of logic are derivable from the science of psychology (*ibid.,* II, p. 25). "Psychology must depend in its beginnings upon logic in order to be psychology and to avoid being largely logical analysis. If then logic is to depend upon psychology in its turn, the two sciences, left without any support whatsoever, are liable to roll in one slough of error and confusion" (*ibid.,* II, p. 29). In view of these statements, it is surprising to find pragmatists so frequently charged with this same confusion. It is, as Peirce put it, "the fundamental mistake of confounding the logical question with the psychological question. The psychological question is what processes the mind

goes through. But the logical question is whether the conclusion that will be reached, by applying this or that maxim, will or will not accord with the *fact*" (*ibid.*, V, p. 226).

15. "Superior as Lord Bacon's conception is to earlier notions, a modern reader who is not in awe of his grandiloquence is chiefly struck by the inadequacy of his view of scientific procedure. That we have only to make some crude experiments, to draw up briefs of the results in certain blank forms, to go through these by rule, checking off everything disproved and setting down the alternatives, and that thus in a few years physical science could be finished up—what an idea! 'He wrote on science like a Lord Chancellor,' indeed, as Harvey, a genuine man of science, said" (*ibid.*, V. p. 224).

16. "The distinction between an idea *seeming* clear and really being so, never occurred to him. Trusting to introspection, as he did, even for a knowledge of external things, why should he question its testimony in respect to the contents of our minds? But then, I suppose, seeing men, who seemed to be quite clear and positive, holding opposite opinions on fundamental principles, he was further led to say that clearness of ideas is not sufficient, but that they need also to be distinct, *i.e.*, to have nothing unclear about them" (*ibid.*, V, pp. 249-250).

17. In view of later developments this remains its major contribution to contemporary philosophy, more important than any of its highly debatable formulas for "the meaning of truth" or "the meaning of meaning."

18. T. H. Huxley (1825-1895) the English biologist, had a considerable influence on the pragmatic movement. In his many popular lectures and essays, he strove to combine the aims of a liberal education with the aims and methods of natural science, but not as an end in itself. "Obviously, it is one thing to say that the logical methods of physical science are of universal applicability, and quite another to affirm that all subjects of thought lie within the province of physical science. . . . Assuredly I have never given the slightest ground for the attribution to me of the ridiculous contention that there is nothing true outside the bounds of physical science" (*Evolution and Ethics and Other Essays* [New York, 1903], p. 126).

19. *Collected Papers*, V, p. 258. James's version introduces a reference to "thoughts," "sensations," and "reactions" which strongly suggests the nominalism or sensationalism rejected by Peirce (see note 13, above). "To attain perfect clearness in our *thoughts* of an object," wrote James, "we need only consider what effects of a conceivably practical kind the object may involve—what *sensations* we are to expect from it, and what *reactions* we must prepare. Our conception of these effects, then, is for us the whole of our conception of the object, so far as that conception has positive significance at all" (*Collected Essays and Reviews* p. 411, italics added).

20. F. H. Bradley (1846-1924), *Essays on Truth and Reality* (Oxford,

1914), p. 127: "While reading the lectures on Pragmatism, I, doubtless like others, am led to ask, 'Am I and have I been always myself a Pragmatist?' This question I still find myself unable to answer. The meaning of 'practice' and 'practical' is to my mind with Prof. James most obscure and ambiguous. On the one side he insists on a doctrine acceptable perhaps only to the minority. On the other side he extends so widely the limits of his creed that few indeed would in the end be left outside the fold."

21. A. O. Lovejoy, "Pragmatism *versus* the Pragmatist" (Durant Drake et al., *Essays in Critical Realism* [New York, 1920], p. 37).

22. *Collected Papers*, V. pp. 259-265.

23. *Ibid.*, p. 262.

24. *Pragmatism*, p. 45.

25. *Collected Papers*, p. 260. One of the two most important developments of Peirce's pragmatism, aside from those in James and Dewey, was the "operational" theory of meaning, formulated in P. W. Bridgman, *The Logic of Modern Physics* (New York, 1927): "In general, we mean by any concept nothing more than a set of operations; *the concept is synonymous with the corresponding set of operations*" (p. 5). The other was the "prediction" theory of law, propounded by the late Justice O. W. Holmes, Jr.: "The prophecies of what the courts will do in fact. . . . are what I mean by the law. The primary rights and duties with which jurisprudence busies itself again are nothing but prophecies. . . . a legal duty so called is nothing but a prediction that if a man does or omits certain things he will be made to suffer in this or that way by judgment of the court; and so of legal right. . . . The duty to keep a contract at common law means a prediction that you must pay damages if you do not keep it—and nothing else. . . . You see how the vague circumference of the notion of duty shrinks and at the same time grows more precise when we wash it with the cynical acid and expel everything except the object of our study, the operations of the law" (*Collected Legal Papers,* pp. 167-202, quoted in M. H. Fisch, "Justice Holmes, the Prediction Theory of Law, and Pragmatism," *The Journal of Philosophy*, Vol. XXXLX, No. 4 [Feb. 12, 1942], p. 87). The operational theory has since been taken up in many different quarters with the familiar refrain: "The meaning of a proposition is its verifiability."

26. On this distinction, see Kant's *Critique of Pure Reason,* A827 (B855); *cf.* N. Kemp-Smith, *A Commentary to Kant's Critique of Pure Reason* (New York, 1923), p. 577: "When a belief is contingent (*i.e.,* is affirmed with consciousness that on fuller knowledge it may turn out to be false), and yet nevertheless supplies a ground for the employment of means to certain desired ends, it may be called *pragmatic* belief." Moral belief, on the contrary, is not contingent and hypothetical, but required by the necessary postulates of the *practical* reason.

27. *Collected Papers,* V, p. 274.

28. *Principles of Psychology,* I, p. 6. His picturesque but often misleading phrase, "the stream of thought," was used to describe the fact that thought "goes on" in a continuous process. "Within each personal consciousness thought is sensibly continuous" (*ibid.,* p. 225).

29. J. Dewey, *Logic: the Theory of Inquiry* (New York, 1938), pp. 8-9, 11, 245 ff.

30. J. Dewey, *Creative Intelligence* (New York, 1917), p. 20; *cf.* his *Experience and Nature* (Chicago, 1925), p. 393: "In creative production, the external and physical world is more than a mere means or external condition of perceptions, ideas, and emotions; it is subject-matter and sustainer of conscious activity; and thereby exhibits. . . . the fact that consciousness is not a separate realm of being, but is the manifest quality of existence when nature is most free and active."

31. The introduction of Darwinian ideas of evolution and the genetic method of explanation into the theory and method of pragmatism was due in large part to the suggestions of Chauncey Wright (1830-1875) who had taken a leading part in the "Metaphysical Club," where he, James, Peirce, O. W. Holmes, Jr., and others used to meet for discussion in the early '70's. See especially Wright's essays, "Evolution by Natural Selection" and "Evolution of Self-Consciousness" (*Philosophical Discussions,* [New York, 1878], pp. 168-266).

32. J. Dewey, *The Influence of Darwin on Philosophy* (New York, 1910), p. 14.

33. Cf. *Aristotle's Psychology,* translated with introduction and notes by W. A. Hammond (New York, 1902), Book II, Chap. 1, pp. 44-46: "The soul. . . . is the form of a natural body endowed with the capacity of life . . . Soul, therefore, will be the completed realization of a body such as described. . . . As cutting is the realization of the axe, and vision the realization of the eye, so is the waking state the realization of the living body; and as vision and capacity are related to the organ, so is the soul related to the body. . . . It is, therefore, clear that the soul is not separable from the body." Previously, he had said "that the properties of the soul do not exist apart from the physical matter of living things, in which such qualities as courage and fear are expressed" (Book I, Chap. 1, p. 9).

34. A. N. Whitehead, *Science and the Modern World* (New York, 1925), p. 206.

35. *Collected Papers,* V, p. 231.

36. *Ibid.,* pp. 256-257.

37. W. James, *Pragmatism,* pp. 48-49; *cf.* P. W. Bridgman, *op. cit.,* p. 151: "The most elementary examination of what light means in terms of direct experience shows that we never experience light itself, but our

experience deals only with things lighted. This fundamental fact is never modified by the most complicated or refined physical experiments that have ever been devised; from the point of view of operations, light means nothing more than *things lighted*."

38. *Pragmatism,* pp. 54-55.

BIBLIOGRAPHY

C. S. PEIRCE, *Collected Papers,* ed. by C. Hartshorne and P. Weiss (Cambridge, Mass., 1934), Volume V. Pragmatism and Pragmaticism.

———, *Chance, Love, and Logic: Philosophical Essays,* ed. with an introduction by M. R. Cohen, with a supplementary essay on the pragmatism of Peirce by J. Dewey (New York, 1923).

W. JAMES, *The Principles of Psychology,* 2 vols. (New York, 1890).

———, *Pragmatism: a New Name for Some Old Ways of Thinking* (New York, 1907).

———, *Collected Essays and Reviews* (New York, 1920). Chapters IV, X, XXVIII, XXXI, XXXII, XXXVI.

J. DEWEY, *Studies in Logical Theory* (Chicago, 1903).

———, *How We Think,* rev. ed. (New York, 1933).

———, *The Influence of Darwin on Philosophy* (New York, 1910).

———, *Essays in Experimental Logic* (Chicago, 1916).

———, *Reconstruction in Philosophy,* rev. ed. (New York, 1948).

———, *The Quest for Certainty* (New York, 1929).

———, *Philosophy and Civilization* (New York, 1931), Chapters II, III, VI.

———, *Logic: The Theory of Inquiry* (New York, 1938).

F. C. S. SCHILLER, *Humanism* (New York, 1903).

———, *Studies in Humanism* (New York, 1925).

J. BUCHLER, *Charles Peirce's Empiricism* (London, 1939).

S. HOOK, *The Metaphysics of Pragmatism* (Chicago, 1927).

C. I. LEWIS, *Mind and the World Order* (New York, 1929).

A. O. LOVEJOY, *The Revolt Against Dualism* (Chicago, 1930).

———, and others, *Essays in Critical Realism* (New York, 1920), pp. 35-81.

G. H. MEAD, *The Philosophy of the Present* (Chicago, 1932).

———, *Mind, Self, and Society* (Chicago, 1934).

W. P. MONTAGUE, *The Ways of Knowing* (New York, 1925).

C. MORRIS, *Six Theories of Mind* (Chicago, 1932).

A HISTORY OF PHILOSOPHICAL SYSTEMS

R. B. PERRY, *The Thought and Character of William James*, 2 vols. (Boston, 1935).

H. W. SCHNEIDER, *A History of American Philosophy* (New York, 1946).

H. G. TOWNSEND, *Philosophical Ideas in the United States* (New York, 1934).

F. J. E. WOODBRIDGE, *Nature and Mind* (New York, 1937).

CHAPTER THIRTY-TWO

EXISTENTIALISM

HELMUT KUHN

I. THE PRINCIPLE OF EXISTENTIALISM. We distinguish the nature or essence of a thing from its existence. By essence we denote *what* a thing is, by existence, *that* it is. Evidently the two terms are irreducible to each other. To use Kant's well-known illustration: the definition of the essence of a hundred dollars has no bearing on the question as to whether or not this sum exists. Yet its existence or non-existence (in my pocket) does make a difference to me. To explain what is meant by existence is by no means easy. An attempt at explanation would involve the paradoxical task of defining the essence of existence. There is no difficulty, however, in explaining with reference to essence what existence is *not*. Essence and definition are correlative terms. That which is definable in a thing we call its essence. Existence, on the other hand, is undefinable, though not necessarily incomprehensible. Furthermore, essence, in every particular case, implies an infinite wealth of structures and relations. The essence of man, *e.g.*, according to the classic definition, involves a participation in "reason" and "life," and such participation admits of degrees. A man can be more or less reasonable and accordingly he can be more or less of a man. Existence, on the contrary, is unanalyzable and posits an alternative. A thing either exists or does not exist and there is no intermediate position between existence and non-existence, or Being and not-Being.

Essence and existence, though irreducible, are not unrelated to each other. It may rather be affirmed that every philosophical position involves a more or less explicit idea as to the nature of this relation. Systems of thought which award a superior rank to essence, perhaps even to the point of letting existence be absorbed into essence, will be classified as instances of "essentialism." The counter-position, then, will receive the name of "existentialism." Existentialism, we define, is a philosophical doctrine which gives priority to existence over essence.

To this definition of the essence of existentialism we may now give a concrete historical or existential sense. In the sequence the word "existentialism" will be chiefly used as a proper name, referring to a philosophical movement rather than as a general term denoting a timeless philosophical possibility. The movement called Existentialism took its origin shortly before and during the war of 1914-1918 and it is still in progress. Largely though not exclusively it is a revival, interpretation, and adaptation of the thought of the Danish writer, philosopher and theologian, Sören Kierkegaard (1813-1855).

Essentialism at its boldest is expressed in Hegel's philosophy. By constructing Becoming as a passage from non-existence (not-Being) to existence (Being) Hegel (1770-1831) completes the absorption of existence into essence: his dialectical logic overcomes through mediation the either/or which sets an absolute separation between existence and non-existence. Kierkegaard's existentialism, a counterthrust to Hegel's essentialism, is aimed at the core of Hegelian dialectic, the idea of mediation. Kierkegaard's thought might be styled an anti-Hegelian Hegelianism, and this paradoxical description applies also to most of twentieth century Existentialism.

The adaptation of Kierkegaard by modern Existentialism is a creative rather than an imitative process. In the *Unscientific Postscript* Kierkegaard expatiates on the idea of "subjective truth," an important corollary to his conception of existence, and in his *Philosophical Fragments* some applications to the general theory of being (ontology) are suggested. But only modern Existentialism develops Kierkegaard's passionate affirmations, semi-poetical hints, and psychological analyses into systems of philosophy and theology. The movement comprises a bewildering variety of thought, particularly in regard to its theological implications. It ranges from determined atheism to Protestant Biblicism and Catholic theism. In the maze of contradictory theorems the mere name of Existentialism is no sufficient guide. For it is claimed by some who are hardly entitled to it, and it is disclaimed by others whom we consider prominet representatives of the movement.

Amidst the diversity of points of view, however, we notice a unity of basic conviction and attitude. The authentic Existentialist is known by the *pathos of existence,* the affirmation of the uniqueness of the concrete and real as over against the abstract and possible, and the repudiation of the attempt to construct a picture of the world by means of a self-sufficient intellect. Whatever existence be, it is surely something actually encountered rather than something thought. The emphasis on irreducible existence goes hand in hand with a critical attitude towards the essentialism regnant in modern thought. Existentialists are unanimous in rejecting idealist rationalism of Cartesian origin, and they level their criticism especially against the body-mind dualism prevalent in the Platonic-Cartesian tradition. Therein they follow the lead of another school of thought which can be considered the immediate predecessor of Existentialism: the Philosophy of Life (Vitalism, *Lebensphilosophie*) as represented by Friedrich Nietzsche (1844-1900), Henri Bergson (1859-1941), and Wilhelm Dilthey (1833-1912). Aside from Kierkegaard these three thinkers rank first among the influences which have shaped Existentialism.

The diversity of modern Existentialist thought must be understood as resulting from the underlying principle. Existence as such, we remember, is indefinable. In defining existence we would have to define the essence of existence, and this again would be tantamount to an absorption of existence into essence. A definition of existence can be undertaken only from a radically essentialist point of view. Yet the word "existence" carries an intelligible meaning. In addition it is a key-word which permeates the whole of human discourse and which cannot be safely ignored by any philosophy. Hence we must assume that existence is understood by virtue of a trans-rational act, an "encounter." What is the nature of this act of comprehension? What is the form under which existence is met with or encountered? According to the various answers to this question Existentialism becomes diversified into a number of conflicting types of thought. "Existence is met with through crisis," and, "Existence is met with through communion"—these two answers stand out, and correspondingly we discern two main types of Existentialism: Critical Existentialism and Social Existentialism. The treatment of these two versions of Existentialism must be prefaced by a few general remarks.

We remember the difference between a hundred dollars "as such," according to their essence, and the question of their existence—a difference not included in the definition of a hundred dollars. In order to settle the question of existence *in concreto* we take a look into our wallet. In this case as in all similar cases we solve the problem by the evidence of our senses. Generally it is true that within a large area of experience existence is discovered through the impact of things upon us as bodily, sentient beings. So the most obvious answer to the question as to the mode of experiencing existence is surely: through the senses. Yet a Sensationalist Existentialism is not among the currents of thought which compose the Existentialist movement. In post-Cartesian philosophy essentialism has developed in close alliance with physicalism. Hence the anti-naturalistic and anti-sensationalist temper which characterizes the Existentialist protest.

Crisis is an extraordinary experience clearly set off against ordinary human life, whereas communion (with other persons) is a strand in the tissue of all human experience. It follows that existence discovered through crisis will differ more radically from essence than existence discovered through communion. Insight gained in the anguish of crisis will be separated by a gulf from everyday knowledge, while the understanding of persons through communion has a marked affinity to rational understanding in general. Consequently, Critical Existentialism will be more emphatically existentialist, more uncompromising in subordinating essence to existence, more violently anti-traditionalist and anti-rationalist than Social Existentialism. As a matter of fact the latter shades off into theories whose classification as existentialist is doubtful.

Admitted that existence lies outside the realm of essences and that, by the same token, it is undefinable, little more than tautologies can be advanced in speaking about it. On the other hand a great deal can be said about our human mode of comprehending existence. So a shift of attention takes place from existence as such to our way of encountering existence, from an objective interest in an existence which is indifferent in regard to the multiple existents, to a subjective interest in that peculiar existent which everyone of us is. Attention focuses on the human self as the locus where existence is discovered or even where it originates. A shift of terminology follows, with Kierkegaard taking the lead. For him the word "existence" denotes chiefly that mode of being which is characteristic of man or, even more narrowly, that passionately intensified form of human life which makes the mind susceptible to experiencing a crisis, and through crisis, existence (or transessential Being).

II. Critical Existentialism. Definitions define essences, and essences, in turn, are ideal possibilities. They lack that plenary status of Being, which would entitle us to classify them as existents along with the universe or the pen in my hand. Hegel constructs the essential structure of the universe, including the course of world history. Is this construction anywhere in touch with the universe as it actually exists? Or is it not rather a self-interpretation of Hegel's mind disguised as a metaphysics? By raising these questions Kierkegaard becomes the founder of Critical Existentialism. His questions are such as to cast a doubt not only on Hegel's philosophy but on the Platonic or essentialist tradition of which Hegel is a representative.

Kierkegaard's sceptical query is actuated by two fundamental affirmations. The human individual, he affirms, with his vital concern for himself, his own salvation, is content with nothing short of real existence. As disembodied intelligences we might be put off with a realm of essences or ideal possibilities. As concrete individuals we hanker after existence. So the link is discovered which connects the abstract ontological problem of the meaning of existence with man's metaphysical-religious aspiration.

But how can this thirst for existence be assuaged? Kierkegaard's attempt to answer this question brings into play a second conviction of his, no less fundamental than the first one. The intellect by itself, Kierkegaard holds, is unable to transcend the sphere of essences. The experience of this inability induces a crisis of despair. Heart and mind are at variance with each other. As an intelligent being man sees himself debarred from ever filling his metaphysical-religious need. This despair becomes the peripetia of an inner drama, or, to change the metaphor, the healing crisis of a metaphysical sickness. The surrender of all hope, which is the surrender also of the pride of intellect, is followed by a miraculous disclosure of existence. What the methodical advance of the intellect is incapable of achieving is reached inadvertently, suddenly, by a "leap." In the crisis of despair an answer is offered which, far from being supported by reason, is an affront to reason—a paradox or an absurdity. But precisely the shock administered to our intellect (an intellect naturally at home among ideal possibilities) marks the encounter with trans-essential existence. The individual, set adrift by his intellect among possibilities, is at last vouchsafed a firm ground to stand upon. But whatever the nature of this new certainty be, it surely is not of philosophical origin. At the climax of the crisis, the individual is thought of by Kierkegaard as paralyzed by dread (*Angst* or anguish)—a dread not of any concrete danger or any particular dreadful thing, but rather a dread of nothing, a giddiness in the face of infinite possibilities which engulf the determinate and existent. For if everything is possible nothing is determined and certain. And this experience of dread is at the same time man's awareness of his freedom—not the freedom to choose between good and evil but that more fundamental freedom which precedes and renders possible his commitment to a scale of values.

This theory of crisis, expressed chiefly in Kierkegaard's *Either/Or* and *The Concept of Dread*, is taken over, lock, stock and barrel, by modern Critical Existentialism. But the conclusions drawn from this theory by our contemporaries point in different directions. We list three conclusions represented by three schools of thought respectively: (a) Dialectical Theology, (b) Kantian Existentialism, (c) Phenomenological Existentialism.

(*a*) *Dialectical Theology.* In 1919 Karl Barth (1886-   ) published his famous commentary to the Epistle to the Romans. In the same year Karl Jaspers (1883-   ) submitted a work on the *Psychology of World Views.* The two publications together mark the beginning of the Existentialist Movement. Barth, faithful in this to Kierkegaard's intentions, looks upon crisis as the triumph of faith won through the discomfiture of reason. The reality disclosed in the anguish of despair is for him God—not, however, the God of the savants and philosophers but the God of Abraham, Isaac, and Jacob, the God who spake through the prophets and was revealed in Jesus Christ. The surrender of autonomous reason at the climax of the inner drama becomes the contrite hearing of the Word. The conclusion drawn by Barth from the theory of crisis is itself no philosophical theory but a biblicism which denounces philosophy as an inept guide towards faith. Since the publication of Barth's revolutionary book Dialectical Theology has profoundly affected, one might say, resuscitated, Protestant theological thought. The general trend has been towards mitigating the harshness of Barth's irrationalism. Especially in America, where Reinhold Niebuhr (1892-   ) stands out as the chief representative of so-called neo-orthodox thought, the crisis theory has been transformed under the influence of the prevailing pragmatic temper and the interest in social problems.

(b) *Kantian Existentialism.* The honor of first advocating Existentialism in our time belongs to Karl Jaspers. He has presented his views in books of vast scope, and his literary work is still growing. The pivot of his thought is a modern adaptation of Kierkegaard's theory of crisis. The climactic moment of the crisis he likes to describe as a "foundering" (*Scheitern*), and the situations productive of crisis are labelled by him "limit situations" (*Grenzsituation*). In all this Jaspers faithfully follows Kierkegaard, and his contribution consists chiefly in the wealth and subtlety of applications both to the inner life of the individual and the cultural life of our society. But the philosophical conclusions which he draws from the Kierkegaardian premises depart widely from Kierkegaard's intent.

An ineluctable limit contains man's search for truth and induces a crisis of intellectual despair—the limit being set by the perspective character of his knowledge. According to his standpoint and his dominant interests he sees segments only of reality. The "Encompassing" (*das Umgreifende*) eludes his grasp. In passing through crisis, however, he may establish a contact with that unknown something that lies beyond the perspective limitations of his knowledge. This encounter is described by Jaspers as the "rise into transcendence" (*Aufschwung in die Transzendenz*)—an experience which is to result not in knowledge proper but in a symbolic equivalent of knowledge, the "decodification" (*Entziffern*) of rationally unintelligible "signs" (*Chiffren*). Communication, on this level, becomes possible as "evocation." Through stimulating a crisis also in the collocutor a meeting of minds can be achieved.

Jasper's Existentialism is Kantian both in conception and execution. Kant's dualism of appearance and "thing in itself," or phenomenon and noumenon, has its counterpart in Jaspers' distinction of limited perspectives of knowledge and the Encompassing which is unlimited but also unknowable. In spite of its serious and morally elevated tone Jaspers' Kantianism is reminiscent of Vaihinger's (1852-1933) positivistic philosophy of the "As If," and one might speak of an "Existentialist Fictionalism."

(c) *Phenomenological Existentialism.* The problem of existence and its relationship to essence is an aspect of the vaster problem of Being. Both Dialectical Theology and Kantian Existentialism turn away from the philosophical core of the question, the former by a leap to divine revelation, the second by substituting for the full problem the narrower one of the part-whole relationship. Within the camp of Critical Existentialism only the Phenomenological School attacks the ontological center of the problem. As such Edmund Husserl's (1859-1938) Phenomenology, with its emphasis on the discovery of "essences" (*Wesenheiten*) through "intuition" (*Anschauung*), seems to run counter to any existentialist tendency. However, the resolute separation of intuited essences as pure meanings from the question of their status as real or non-real is helpful in bringing the ontological problem in focus. Husserl's method of *epoché* "brackets" the question of existence which, by this suspension, becomes all the more pressing.

The master of Phenomenological Existentialism is Martin Heidegger (1889-   ) whose fragmentary main work *Sein und Zeit* appeared in 1927. Jean-Paul Sartre (1905-   ), author of *L'Etre et le Néant* (1947), who has acquired fame in more recent years, transforms Heidegger's deeply searching and suggestive but unfinished ideas into a subtly but paradoxically constructed system.

The Kierkegaardian crisis, re-interpreted in the light of Wilhelm Dilthey's historicism, continues a fundamental presupposition in Heidegger's thought. But the emphasis shifts from the crisis as such, as a passage or transitory event, to the ontological insight won through this passage. Despair, leap, anguish—all the conceptual paraphernalia of Kierkegaard's religious pathology of the mind—become instrumental in attaining an understanding of Being. The situation of crisis itself is subjected to an ontological interpretation. It is understood as an encounter with Nothingness, the prerequisite, according to Heidegger's *Was ist Metaphysik?*

(1929, 5th edition 1949), for the grasp of Being. But what is meant by Being?

Heidegger offers no clear and consistent answer. He considers his philosophy a move toward rejoining Being but he does not claim to have completed this act of recovery. At any rate the Being in question is an existentially unabridged Being in contradistinction to its essentialist foreshortening which, Heidegger believes, originates as early as with the Platonic conception of Idea. In pre-Socratic thought, among the ancient Ionians, he finds a more authentic vision of Being. But in his published writings he fails to disclose that pre-Socratic truth which has been betrayed by Occidental philosophy under the leadership of Plato. The emphasis on the historical character of the self-disclosure of Being in his more recent writings suggests the suspicion that the conception of Being toward which Heidegger tends might actually be post-Hegelian rather than pre-Platonic.

With Being placed magnificently above God or gods, the subjective and Kierkegaardian elements are eclipsed in Heidegger's thought. Along this path Jean-Paul Sartre does not follow his master. With Sartre, the Existentialist *par excellence,* the principle "existence precedes essence" is truly fundamental. The human self, he maintains, has existence but it has no essence or nature. In order to show that the self's existence is prior to the realm of essences Sartre adopts the Hegelian distinction of Being-in-itself and Being-for-itself. The former is undifferentiated, "massive," timeless self-identity. A tautology describes it best: it is what it is. Being-for-itself, on the contrary, never *is* but continually *has to be.* And since there is no moment at which it is, in the sense of being identical with itself, it may be called a "hole" amidst the density of being. It is "its own naught." It is only in the perpetual act of escaping from itself, and that precisely means: it "exists." Through determinative negations the For-it-self carves out of the block of the In-itself the shifting patterns of the multiple things which constitute the world, thus revealing itself as an active, a "naughting" naught. In performing these acts of cosmogonic negation the For-itself is free. For there is nothing either outside itself or within which could determine its activity. Thus through a dialectic reminiscent of Fichte, the concrete world is made to arise out of an interaction playing back and forth between a passive pole and an active pole.

But this cleverly constructed system is marred by a flaw so fatal as to reduce it to a brilliant *jeu d'esprit*. The subtle balance between essence and existence within the concept of Being is not disregarded with impunity. Sartre tries to make existence great at the expense of essence. Existence is to be the fountain-head of essential Being. Actually he ends up with essentializing existence itself: existence is surreptitiously identified with a particular essence or nature—with human nature.

III. Social Existentialism. Within an essentialist frame of reference, the particular existent is relevant only as a "case." Its individuality is determined by way of negation as that which is *not* definable in terms of essence. Essence and species belong together and it is, to say the least, extremely difficult to imagine an "individual essence." There is, however, one particular class of existents which are not amenable to so disparaging a treatment: persons. In a sense persons like other things can be dealt with as mere cases illustrating or embodying an essential possibility. I can, *e.g.*, count or weigh persons. But in doing so I deliberately set aside their specific nature as persons. For practical purposes I assimilate them to things. I focus on certain qualities which they *have* instead of attending to what they *are*. Once more we discover a bond between existence and the human self. The living person, we remember, is not to be put off with ideal possibilities: he insists on existence. Now we broaden and modify this earlier statement. The person, we suggest, while it demands existence, affords also the prototype of existence. The person, however, must not be understood as an isolated entity but as an ego in communion with an *alter ego*. As long as we deal with things which we measure, manipulate and subject to our dominion by use we are debarred from access to reality proper. The encounter with Being in its existential fullness takes place where, by an act which transcends the distinction between volition and cognition, we open ourselves in genuine communion to the impact of another person.

This approach to Being through the I-thou relationship is advocated by Gabriel Marcel (1877-) whose *Journal Métaphysique* antedates both the re-discovery of Kierkegaard by the Germans and the author's acquaintance with the Danish proto-Existentialist.

Marcel's dichotomies—the "I-thou" *vs.* the depersonalizing "he," the free abandon of communion *vs.* the constructive-aggressive attitude of scientific knowledge, the mystery of Being *vs.* the problems of theoretical-practical life, the "participation" in Being *vs.* the contemplation of objects—all show clearly the influence of Bergson. Just as the Bergsonian distinction between *élan vital* and its crystallizations takes on a religious significance, so also Marcel's parallel disjunctions. By introducing the idea of an absolute person his Social Existentialism rejoins the tradition of Christian metaphysics and theology. A *rapprochement* is effected between Existentialism, the most revolutionary of all contemporary schools of philosophy, and the traditionalist Thomism of Etienne Gilson (1884-   ) and Jacques Maritain (1882-   ). It is again Bergson who has opened the eyes of these Catholic thinkers to the distinction in St. Thomas between the super-essential act of existence which is God, and the realm of essences which depend for their existential incarnation upon that act. "I Am that I Am." The God of Exodus is not *a* being (every being may, or may not, exist)—He is Being. In Heidegger or Sartre Existentialism seems a rebel philosophy. With Thomistic theo-ontology the prodigal son returns to his father's house.

BIBLIOGRAPHY

I. The Principle of Existentialism.
    1. General Studies on Existentialism.
Marjorie Grene, *Dreadful Freedom* (Chicago, 1948).
Ralph Harper, *Existentialism, A Theory of Man* (Cambridge, 1948).
Helmut Kuhn, *Encounter with Nothingness*, A Study on Existentialism The Humanist Library (Hinsdale, Illinois, 1949).
———, "Existentialism—Christian and Anti-Christian," *Theology Today* (October, 1949), 311-23.
Karl Löwith, "Problem and Background of Existentialism," *Social Research*, 15:345-69 (September, 1948).
Paul Tillich, "Conception of Man in Existential Philosophy," *Journal of Religion*, 19:201-15 (July, 1939).
Jean Andre Wahl, *A Short History of Existentialism.* Translated by Forrest Williams and Stanley Maron (New York, 1949).
    2. Sören Kierkegaard, Founder of Existentialism.
Robert Bretall, editor, *A Kierkegaard Anthology* (Princeton, 1946).

SÖREN KIERKEGAARD, *The Concept of Dread*. Translated by Walter Lowrie (Princeton, 1944).
———, *Concluding Unscientific Postscript*. Translated by David F. Swenson and Walter Lowrie. Princeton: Princeton University Press. For the American-Scandinavian Foundation, 1941.
———, *Either/Or*, A Fragment of Life. Translated by David F. Swenson and Lillian M. Swenson. Princeton: Princeton University Press, 1944. 2 vols. (Vol. 2 translated by Walter Lowrie).
———, *Fear and Trembling*, A Dialectical Lyric. Translated by Walter Lowrie. Princeton: Princeton University Press, 1941.
———, *Philosophical Fragments*. Translated by David F. Swenson. Princeton: Princeton University Press. New York: American-Scandinavian Foundation, 1936.
———, *Stages on Life's Way*. Translated by Walter Lowrie. Princeton: Princeton University Press. London: H. Milford, Oxford University Press, 1940.
WALTER LOWRIE, *Kierkegaard* (London, New York, 1938).
JAMES COLLINS in recent issues of *The Modern Schoolman*.

II. Critical Existentialism.
    1. Dialectical Theology.
KARL BARTH, *The Epistle to the Romans*. Translated from the Sixth Edition by Edwyn C. Hoskyns (London, 1933).
HEINRICH EMIL BRUNNER, *The Theology of Crisis*. Swander Lectures, 1928 (New York, 1929).
REINHOLD NIEBUHR, *Beyond Tragedy,* Essays on the Christian Interpretation of History (New York, 1937).
———, *The Nature and Destiny of Man*, A Christian Interpretation. Gifford Lectures, 1939 (New York, 1941-43). 2 vols. I. "Human Nature"; II. "Human Destiny."
    2. Kantian Existentialism.
KARL JASPERS, *Psychologie der Weltanschauungen*. 3. Gegenüber der 2 unveränderte aufl. (Berlin, 1925).
———, *Die Geistige Situation der Zeit* (Berlin, Leipzig, 1931).
———, *Philosophie* (Berlin, 1932). 3 Vols. 1. bd. Philosophische Weltorientierung. 2. bd. Existenzerhellung. 3. bd. Metaphysik.
    3. Phenomenological Existentialism.
MARTIN HEIDEGGER, *Sein und Zeit*. 1. Hälfte (Halle, 1927).
———, *Vom Wesen des Grundes* (Halle, 1929).
———, *Was ist Metaphysik?* (Halle, 1929. Fifth edition, Frankfurt, 1949).
———, *Platons, Lehre von der Wahrheit,* Mit einem Brief über den "Humanismus" (Bern, 1947).

A HISTORY OF PHILOSOPHICAL SYSTEMS

Jean-Paul Sartre, *L'Etre et le Néant* (Paris, 1943).
———, *L'Existentialisme est un Humanisme* (Paris, 1946).
Albert Camus, *Le Mythe de Sisyphe* (N. p. 1942).

III. Social Existentialism.

Gabriel Marcel, *Journal Métaphysique* (Paris, 1927).
———, *Être et Avoir* (Paris, 1935).
———, *Du Refus à L'Invocation* (Paris, 1940).
———, *Homo Viator,* Prolégomènes à une métaphysique de l'espérance (Paris, 1945).
———, *The Philosophy of Existence.* Translated by Manya Harari (New York, 1949).
Martin Buber, *Between Man and Man* (New York, 1948).
Etienne Gilson, *Being and Some Philosophers* (Toronto, 1949).
Jacques Maritain, *Existence and the Existent* (New York, n.d.).

CHAPTER THIRTY-THREE

THE NEW MATERIALISM

ROY WOOD SELLARS

IT HAS become quite the custom to add the adjectives, new or modern, to fundamental philosophical positions to indicate that some basic transformation has taken place. The broad principles are the same; and yet methods and concepts have been brought up to date. The new materialism exemplifies this identity with difference. It represents a thorough overhauling of traditional materialism in the light of developments in both science and philosophy.

For quite understandable historical and cultural reasons, it so happened that materialism became a "suppressed alternative" in academic philosophy. Philosophers took no pains to bring it into line with their technical analyses in logic and theory of knowledge or to make it more presentable. In fact, its refutation had become economically schematized. This was made fairly easy in the nineteenth century because of the dominance of Kantianism and idealism. And, after all, science had not yet penetrated far beyond the macroscopic level of the inorganic world. Matter was a term largely symbolic of mass, movement, and blind mechanism. The notions of levels, organization and fields were hardly glimpsed. In my own lifetime, the transformations in both science and philosophy have been astonishing. And I am impressed by those in philosophy almost as much as by those in science. It keeps me on my toes, for instance, to keep up with linguistic analysis. Everything must be stated clearly and analytically.

This development is all to the good. While, however, it was, at first, attached to the Humian type of empiricism with its inclination to sensationalism and phenomenalism, there are many indications that more recognition is being given recently to the realistic meanings of perception and to the rôle of reference and indicative words. What I called "critical realism" and "physical realism" will, I take it, be again explored. But this leads to space-time corporealism; and then a reconstruction of the essentials of materialism does not seem far off. It must, of course, be an empirically-minded and plastic materialism. It must avoid both traditional reductionism and mystical holism and work out its categories carefully. Phrases like "blind mechanism" and "epiphenomenalism" betray their background of Cartesian dualism, with life and mind stuck on, as it were, on the outside. That is, clearly, *not* the right beginning.

In the present paper, I shall stress an empirical type of perceptual and referential realism in epistemology, an exploratory ontology which stresses categories and levels, and an axiology which seeks to do justice to valuations and intelligent action. All of which will sum up to a kind of new deal for materialism. Or shall I call it a fair deal?

This program assumes that it is invalid to start with an *a priori* notion of materialism and then to belabor it. But it is rightly demanded that materialism do justice to all the facts from the inorganic to the human and the social. Thus, personality and ethical choice must be a part of the picture. But psychology and the social sciences are helping the philosopher here. *What materialism intrinsically rejects is the incorporeal and dualism.*

It is interesting to note that, in academic philosophy, the term naturalism was, first of all, widely used, particularly in the United States. Curiously enough, this country was a pioneer. Naturalism signified a rejection of theism and transcendentalism and a stress upon empiricism. On the technical side it was often very vague. Those idealists who became naturalists tended to put emphasis upon human experience in opposition to the notions of absolute idealism. And this could lead to a stress upon scientific method as the defining characteristic of naturalism. It was this direction that American pragmatism took under the leadership of John Dewey (1859-   ).

But, on the positive side, naturalism could be materialistic. This was the older tradition going back to the Ionians and culminating in the ancient world in Democritus (fl. 421 B.C.), Epicurus (343-270 B.C.), and Lucretius (99-55 B.C.). In the modern world it had had continued revivals and reformulations in the eighteenth and the nineteenth centuries. One of the most interesting of these was the dialectical materialism of the Marxists. Here the stress was upon the rejection of idealism, the acceptance of science, the importance of history, and the replacement of mechanical postulates by what were called dialectical ones. In the English-speaking world academic philosophy was dominated by epistemological questions as the ante-chamber to ontological ones. The American realists wrestled with the problem of the physical world and our human knowledge of it. To make a long story short, the critical realists were more explicit in their confrontation with traditional problems, such as those of psychophysics. Here there was a division between the dualists, represented by Lovejoy (1873-) and Pratt (1875-1944) particularly, and the monists, represented by the panpsychists, Drake (b. 1878) and Strong (1862-1940) and the materialists, Santayana (1863-) and Sellars (1880-). The panpsychists became increasingly materialistic in their outlook but rightly emphasized the psychophysical problem: What is the ontological status of sentience? Santayana made much of the realm of essence as additional to that of the realm of matter. "That matter is capable of eliciting feeling and thought follows necessarily from the principle that matter is the only *substance, power,* or *agency* in the universe: and this, not that matter is the only *reality,* is the first principle of materialism." [1] In his article, "What is Materialism?" Sidney Hook (1902-) has raised much the same question in a more pragmatic context. How can the materialist categorize generic properties, consciousness and logical implications? In what sense can they be existentially allocated?

In the Preface of my first book, *Critical Realism,*[2] I used the expression, the "new materialism"—in this, I believe, antedating Santayana's proclamation of materialism. I here developed both the notion of levels in nature and the double-knowledge approach to an identity theory of the mind-brain. I distinguished, but related, mind and consciousness and spoke of mind, henceforth, as a physical category of an emergent level. It may be of interest to state that, in my conversations with Drake and Strong, I found that Drake was opposed to the idea of levels and emergence as mystical, while Strong admitted that he had not, perhaps, recognized sufficiently the importance of organization. This was in 1937 in Fiesole, Italy. Strong had swung away from the notion of essences by this period.

Now it is clear, I take it, from all this that the modern materialist who is a technical philosopher has a big job on his hands in the way of analysis, categorization, and systematic putting together of his results. He must do a job comparable to that of Aristotle's in the framework of modern realism and patterned dynamics. He will, of course, reject the too Platonic conceptions of matter and form of Aristotle for whom there could be incorporeal and meta-physical forms. Fortunately, he will find leads in modern science and in linguistics.

The coöperative book, *Philosophy for the Future*,[3] reflects an exploratory program for the development and the clarification of an adequate materialism. The stress laid in this volume, edited by McGill, Farber and Sellars, is upon "The broad, programmatic, and self-corrective character of modern materialism."

Broadly speaking, then, materialism has always stood for the rejection of the *meta*-physical or the incorporeal. It is generically continuous with the Ionic approach to *physis* or nature. In contrast to the mythologists who wanted a "likely story" of origins the Ionians sought, in the main, to find out what things are made of and what the particular "go" of them could be. They were guided by the practical arts of the time and arrived in some measure at experimental methods. But there was, in addition, persistent, rational reflection in the way of supplementation. This tended to be intuitive and somewhat pictorial. One can compare in this respect the atomism of Democritus with that of Dalton with his evidential discovery of combining numbers. In modern science the interplay of constitutive and operational factors is still undergoing clarification. Laws, theories and predictions are interconnected. And what we may call the *texture* of nature is being gradually deciphered. What stands out is its dynamic quality and architectonic subtlety. A perceptual imagination based on macroscopic things is left far behind. Mathematical symbols must now support conception. One other point must be kept in mind, namely, that relations and equilibria are as much a part of the concept of physical systems as are particles. It is the order and patterns of things and processes which science is comprehending; and, as we shall note, such knowledge does not involve any *acquaintance* with what we may call the stuff, or being, of the external world. Human knowing has to have its verification and confirmation but its disclosures about the world must then be tentatively taken at their face-value. That, we must say, is the kind of world it is. The alternative is an emotionally motivated agnosticism.

Modern materialism moves up and down from the human to the biological and the inorganic; and back again. Only so can the proper balance be kept. Personality is what it is; and full justice must be done to it. At the same time, this beautiful apple, resting on my desk, ripened by the summer sun is what it is. The new materialism is thoroughly empirical but not positivistic and phenomenalistic. It retains the natural, human awareness of a knower who is also an agent. It handles as it observes.

Plato, it will be recalled, asked the question in the *Laws*: Which came first, soul or body? His answer was soul. It was the self-mover. Modern dynamism and evolutionism no longer sees point to the disjunction. Aristotle still retained the vitalism implied and worked out his philosophy of nature in terms of matter and form as largely correlatives. This, we know, was taken up by Thomism and given a more creationalistic framework in terms of the Judeo-Christian God as the source of creaturely existence. But modern materialism is more empirically minded and begins with primary existence. Thus, it undercuts the Aristotelian construct of matter *vs.* form. Thought presupposes being and action. It is. itself, largely a form of symbolic action.

Any systematic insight into the perspective of the new materialism must rest upon developments in theory of knowledge, ontology and cosmology, and axiology. It is to these that I now briefly turn.

I

In its rejection of scholasticism, modern philosophy passed to a vague complex of dualism and subjectivism. Mind, vaguely conceived, was set over against matter; and mechanism was opposed to teleology. At the same time, a puzzling, psychological subjectivism was inaugurated by both Descartes and Locke. What a quagmire for thought and culture! No wonder that it has taken centuries of scientific growth and philosophical analysis to escape from it.

There are two reasons why epistemological clarification is so much needed. First, because one easily gets puzzled in ontology unless one is guided by a clear conception of the nature and reach of human knowing. And, second, because modern philosophy got off to a too subjectivistic start with Descartes, Locke, Berkeley, Hume and Kant. It seemed to philosophers that they were shut up into their own minds and left to the contemplation of what were usually called *ideas*. The corporeal world, even that of their own bodies, retreated and became transcendent as extra-mental. It has been a fairly complicated business to work back to a proper, realistic framework of a designative and manipulative sort tied in with behavior and language. Man had to discover again that he was primarily an organism, alert to the things around him, and not a disembodied mind or soul.

Much of the original difficulty sprang, as we have indicated, from an overstress upon the causal approach to perception, unbalanced by the supplementary emphasis upon response, manipulative meanings, pointing, and linguistic symbolization. There can be little doubt that the soul-body dualism of the Platonic-Christian tradition supported this simplification. With the supplanting of Scholasticism by scientific method, even what was valuable in Aristotelianism was ignored. As against the Thomists, I think that, in the long run, it was for the best; for it meant that the whole complex had to be thought through in the light of the growth of science and of an accompanying effort at philosophical analysis.

Since I must make a long story short, I think it best to emphasize the perplexities associated with the concept of matter. While scientists, like the ordinary run of men, kept on thinking in terms of denotable and manipulatable things and their constituents, philosophers were dominated by their subjectivistic gambit, which had switched attention from the actual references and claims of human knowing to such entities as sensations, images and concepts. Now there are, no doubt, such entities; and they play their part in human knowing. But concentration of attention on them and on mental processes in general eclipsed the primary task which should have been a study of perceptual references and assertions. The result was both bad psychology and bad epistemology. Berkeley's *to be is to be perceived* symbolizes the mistake. It ignores the designations and manipulative meanings basic to perception and assumes that knowing is a kind of acquaintance, a sensing. On these terms, material things become x's. But is not the whole perspective perverted? If we can designate the things around us and confirm facts about them, does science ask for more? Matter is that which can be designated, located and manipulated; and *not* that which ought to be intuited, as sensations can be.

The false gambit is exposed in Mill's definition of matter as the permanent possibility of sensation. In our own day, phenomenalistic positivists have sought to reduce material-thing sentences to a string of sentences about future sensations, obtainable conditionally. I have the impression that the failure of this effort is leading them to take the realism of language more seriously.[4] It will, I think, be found that critical realism can avoid Santayana's realm of essences along these lines.

Just one other point and I must end this episteomological section, which is designed to prepare the way for a materialistic ontology. The physical realist cannot accept Hume's treatment of causality, logical as it is, within his framework. Are there not executive meanings of agency and action for both percipient and thing perceived? Extreme rationalists have sought to identify executive meanings with logical necessity. I can see, at most, an analogy. The modern materialist rejects both Humian psychologism and logical rationalism. Causal activity is an ontological category. But, of course, specific causal laws must be empirically discovered.

II

Modern ontological materialism is tied in closely with science. Its job is clarification of categories. As I have indicated, it must do to-day what Aristotle sought to do in his day. What is the status of relations and processes? How shall we think of the generic? How shall we conceive organization? What is the existential basis of properties? What shall we mean by dispositions and habits? Here we have, I think, the possibility of a new kind of nominalism which stresses similarity but has nothing in common with psychologism of the Berkeley-Hume type. Things can have similar natures. We can then think of these generically. But we must not project our verbalized distinctions into nature and make entities of them. Even to call them *entia rationis* may easily be misleading.

Now the materialist is clearly a substantialist so far as this signifies rejection of phenomenalism. But, as I have indicated, his substantialism makes room for processes and relations. It is, likewise, evolutionary and holds that novel wholes can arise through integrative causality. Physics and biology seem to be on the threshold of new insights with regard to texture and processes. The relation of the macroscopic, or molar, to the microscopic must be thought through carefully, especially when the molar object is an organism. The whole *is* the parts in their spatio-temporal relations. True; but as biology shows, there may be centers of dominance both genetically and functionally. The disregard of this architecture in terms of isolated factors is what is usually called reductionism, that is, a *nothing-but a priorism*. Modern materialism is not epiphenomenalistic and reductive after the fashion of the scientific materialism based on classical physics. Relations, processes, integrative involvement are recognized.

And so we must be careful about terminology. For me, novelty and levels are associated with integrative causality. For Professor Donald Williams [5] reduction seems to be a synonym for analysis. Analysis *in situ*, so to speak, does not preclude comprehension of relations and patterned processes. No modern materialist impugns what is empirically confirmable. But is there good reason to speak of evolved properties as epiphenomenal to the spatio-temporal? I grant that they involve these categorial characteristics and are, to that extent, always spatio-temporal. But the substantialist holds space-time to be a categorial characteristic of matter and energy. I suspect the influence of S. Alexander's neo-realism to be operative here. But I am in hearty agreement with Williams's rejection of positivism. Is not the nuclear physicist still trying to probe into the particles and forces which constitute the kernel of the atom?

In ontology, then, the modern materialist stresses *aseity* as against the contingence notion of creationalism. And he is an ontologist as against phenomenalism and experientialism. In order to be all this, he must be a competent epistemologist as well as have a sense for categories. It is indeed a challenge and promises to give new vitality to philosophy.

There remains in this section one crucial topic for discussion, namely, the mind-consciousness-organism problem. In my own writings I have used the formula, the double-knowledge and emergence approach.

In essentials, it is this. Mind stands for processes and operations and their dispositional conditions. Consciousness for sentiency and awareness; and the organism for the living locus. The highest level of mind involves the use of symbols, worked out in cultures.

In each one's experiencing and awareness he is, I think, literally participating in the neuro-mental activities of his organic self and, in reflexive self-knowledge and introspection—not quite the same—can become aware of them—but never exhaustively. Here, and here alone, is each human being, on the inside of nature, his bit of nature. The essential preliminary is to be openminded and not to begin with the Cartesian gambit.

It is important to realize that the sciences, developed around external perception and its manipulative meanings, do not pretend to any *intuition* of the stuff, or being, of things and events. Those not well trained in epistemology are easily confused. Since neural events must have an intrinsic nature, why not accept the fact that this intrinsic nature rises to a feeling-*quale,* say, in the thalamus and to discriminated data in the visual center? Conceptualization of this situation and the proper syntax need to be worked out. The brain-event is not colored, as we say a surface is colored, but includes a color-sensation as a qualitative dimension, isolated in awareness. How this is taken up in the complexities of perception and conditioned thereby will gradually be worked out, as more is known of the method of cerebral activity.

In concluding this section I would point out that modern philosophy is very language-conscious. The new materialism can hardly be new enough unless it can allocate a status for symbols and their meanings. But this does not seem hard to do in the light of the growth of semantics and the psychology of language. Words are reproducible patterns of sound or sight used in syntactical ways and linked with designations and discriminations. Man is a tool-using animal; and language is his most delicate tool.

There are, of course, all sorts of fascinating questions, such as the relation of logic to ontology, which cannot be taken up in this brief outline. The thesis of the materialist is that any satisfactory analysis can be fitted into his realistic epistemology and ontology. Thus implication is a propositional relation and not, *by itself,* a bit of matter. The relation of logic to psychology and this to the functioning, symbolizing organism is involved.

A HISTORY OF PHILOSOPHICAL SYSTEMS

III

I have left myself small space for the discussion of values and ethics; but can, I hope, bring out the essential points.

First of all, there is no logical connection between ontological materialism and so-called "ethical materialism." Historically, philosophical materialism has mainly been humanistic and reformist. Concern with power and possessions has been a cultural phenomenon.

It is customary these days to distinguish between simple, natural values and moral valuations connected with the idea of right and of obligation. The latter presupposes the former.

Human beings have drives, wants, desires and purposes in relation to things, events, other persons and situations. Designative cognitions make possible the linkage of these drives with the objective situation. The result is an appraisal of objects and objectives in the light of their bearing upon the self. We develop pro-attitudes and anti-attitudes and verbalize them. So far as I can see, there is nothing mysterious about all this. Values are, then, appraisals founded on the affective-volitional side of the self. They are not arbitrary but testable. It would be a mistake to make them external and observational for they are essentially relational and reflexive.[6]

In the moral life, the justification of choices among values becomes focal. It is the very nature of the moral life to be sensitive to the long run and to the lives of others. Man is a socialized animal. What arises in customary morality is heightened in reflective morality. Reason and sympathetic imagination play an important rôle.

Naturally, the materialist works hand in hand with the social scientist but refuses to ignore the normative question. It is clear that right and good are connected terms. Right expresses responsibility with respect to maximizing good in a given situation and involves agency and responsible choice.

It can be said, then, that the materialist simply deepens the naturalistic outlook in these matters and, like him, rejects the isolation of values from the human situation. There is no sense in speaking of *what ought to be* apart from needs and purposes. The materialist is more concerned with the perspective of increasing the good than with rigorism for its own sake. With this criterion in mind, it seems to him that moral judgments can be *justified*, even as empirical statements are *confirmable*. In the strict sense he is led to distinguish between pure cognition and appraisal as different goals. Appraisal is tied in with human living as a going concern. No more than cognition is it arbitrary.

NOTES

1. *The Philosophy of George Santayana* (New York, 1940), edited by P. A. Schilpp, 497 ff. The primary difficulties are his doctrine of essence and his epiphenomenalism.

2. *Critical Realism* (Chicago, 1916). See, also, *Evolutionary Naturalism* (Chicago, 1921) and *The Philosophy of Physical Realism* (New York, 1932).

3. *Philosophy for the Future,* The Quest of Modern Materialism (New York, 1949). This is a coöperative book in which scientists and philosophers explore a materialistic outlook of an evolutionary sort.

4. The development of semantics has led away from Humian phenomenalism to a greater stress upon symbols and designation. Russell is a transition figure here. The emphasis should be upon the *use* of words.

5. Donald Williams, "Naturalism and the Nature of Things," *Philosophical Review*, Vol. LIII (1944). I suspect that Williams is hesitating between neo-realism and critical realism. See, also, in this connection the article by Dewey, Hook and Nagel, "Are Naturalists Materialists?" in the *Journal of Philosophy,* Vol. XLII (1945). A recent summary is to be found in *Philosophy and Phenomenological Research,* Sept., 1949, in an article by Harry Ruya and Monroe Shapiro called "Pluralism and Contemporary Naturalism."

6. Much of the ethical discussion of values follows the wild-goose chase inaugurated by the so-called "naturalistic fallacy" of G. E. Moore, which he now acknowledges not to be a fallacy. Simple, natural values are presupposed by moral questions. Appraisals are empirical and justifiable. By their very nature values are reflexive and situational. Here the modern materialist is humanistic and cultural.

CHAPTER THIRTY-FOUR

VARIETIES OF NATURALISM

VERGILIUS FERM

NATURALISM is a type of philosophy which cuts across the historical stream of Western thought. Like all philosophies it has many antecedents but unlike the majority it can claim no long course of consecutive development. Only recently can it be said to form a school or system. Up until our own day it was a synonym for materialism because it had its recent re-birth within the framework of the development of the physical and biological sciences—particularly beginning with and continuing from the late nineteenth-century—when interpretations of the world were moulded out of the categories familiar to those sciences. Naturalism, too, became popular by reason of a bankrupt type of metaphysics called by the name of positivism which developed out of the intense interest in scientific ways of thinking, a type of thought which circumscribed the area of philosophy to the more immediate focus of man's assured vision.

Today naturalism has taken on a much wider meaning than that of materialism and positivism. In fact, its possibilities invite a great variety of metaphysical interpretation. This broadening of its area is a part of the widening visions of contemporary advocates who, although they see in the scientific temper the hope for a sound philosophical inquiry, are aware that there are areas in which nineteenth-century conceptions of science offered too limited views of the world and that there are realms of experience which lie untouched by strictly physical categories, experiences which lay valid claim to inclusion in any sound metaphysical vision. The world of space and time and mind contains values and even purposes and ideals which reach out beyond purely quantitative and mechanical measurements creating a new type of naturalistic theory of reality and at the same time laying hold upon many of the virtues claimed as a peculiar possession by those of the traditional non-naturalistic schools.

A summary definition of naturalism would be: Nature is the sum and substance of all that is and to know Nature is to come to terms with it in the most promising way, *i.e.*, by social and tested experience, by scientific methods, by reflections based on such experience and methods. The antithesis to this view of the world would be: Nature is explained by Something-Beyond-Itself and that one comes to terms with this extra-Nature by some major premise of reasoning which is *deductive* rather than inductive *in emphasis,* speculative rather than empirical, or, by an appeal to a supposed special form of knowledge such as revelation or faith or authority or to a preconceived set of explanatory principles. Naturalism, in other words, is based on a One World of discourse and rests upon a method of arriving at knowledge and philosophic vision which can be said to be basically empirical.

The term Nature itself is not qualitatively clear. Whereas the early modern naturalists emphasized the world of space and time and things-seen-and-measured, recent naturalists interpret Nature more broadly, as something *more* than merely physical and tangible, richer in possibilities than that of a machine or even a complicated organism. Nature, moreover, is not necessarily a closed system; within it there may be many systems however loosely conjoined; or, it may be a closely-knit Whole into which all parts function for ends. Naturalists are agreed that the pattern of the world is to be found *within* the World and for the understanding of its functioning and explanation there is need for no structure or frames of reference beyond Itself.

The most common view that stands in opposition to the naturalistic platform is that of supernaturalism (of whatever form), particularly the supernaturalism long dominant in Western classical thought. Sporadic attempts have been made by naturalistically-minded thinkers of one kind or another in the course of Western thought to repudiate the metaphysical pattern of supernaturalists. For the most part, these attempts have been weak and halting and inconsequential. The established household of supernaturalistic philosophy could not easily be affected by such heresies on the part of minor prophets. Only when the might of a scientific culture swept in like a torrential tide, did supernaturalism begin to shake from off its allegedly unshakable foundations. Only today, with naturalism moving beyond the confines of materialistic and positivistic interpretations, has the school reached a stature which is recognized by all orthodox schools as a major threat. Naturalists are convinced that their general view will sweep the field since a scientific culture demands a philosophy appropriate to it.

* * *

Early expressions of naturalism occurred in ancient Greek thought. In fact, the very beginnings of Greek philosophy among the Ionians was a naturalistic challenge against entrenched views of the day. If one were to ask: "Why is the beginning of Greek philosophy dated with them?", the answer is easy to give. When questions were directed critically to the orthodox explanations of the nature and events of the world, when thinkers began to look away from the gods and from forces beyond the realm of Nature and focus their attention upon Nature Itself, this was the beginning. The Ionians sought to answer their own questions within the framework of Nature. In this sense, they were the first naturalists in the historic stream of Western philosophy. We know that they were not consistent nor even successful in following through their premises but their method of inquiry was a beginning of a "new deal." The Ionians were not materialists (so-called by some historians); they were dynamists (or more strictly, hylozoists) since they interpreted nature to be alive with forces within, of one kind or another.

Revolutionary as was the method of the Ionians relative to the thought of their day, it must be pointed out that even their naturalism was not new in the story of man's earliest reactions to his world. Whatever the theory of the earliest forms of philosophy and religion, whether animism, dynamism, vitalism, polytheism, anthropomorphism—it would seem, at least a plausible hypothesis, that prehistoric man may well have fashioned his earliest supernaturalistic explanations out of the matrix of an implicit naturalism. For, whatever goes on in a world outside of his experience, it was experience with himself and others, with the elements of nature, that formed the base of whatever rudimentary speculations he formed. A supernaturalistic explanation, indeed, may have come early in man's view of existence; but at the foundation of all his supernaturalism lay the world of his immediate and pressing environment. And surely it was the real world of day-to-day existence that counted! The gods became the reflection of that nature, wild and kind, unpredictable and dependable, ungracious and generous, terrifying and mild. Even early astral metaphysics with its pointing to a world far beyond the horizons was framed in a world of observation within the ken of an experienced imagination. The very origin of magic (defined as the manipulation of the forces of nature to conform to man's will) was, at least, a nascent naturalism. Of course, the antiquity of naturalism, even its refinement by the ancient Ionians, argues neither one way nor another. It only suggests that the long span of an overshadowing supernaturalism in the course of Western thought extending down to our very day may well have rested upon an original "orthodoxy" of Naturalism, with a history much longer.

Eastern speculative thought, by and large, converted the original naturalistic temper by a peculiar inversion of philosophical emphasis. While its conclusion of Unity was naturalistic its method of approach was non-naturalistic. Philosophical Hinduism conceived the world as one—an ever present spiritual Reality shining equally in the highest outreaches of the human spirit and in the lowliest of creatures. But this was a conclusion *to be experienced*. The empirical *followed* upon the philosophy. Naturalists would agree to some Unity to all existence but the unity is a result of empirical method rather than the condition to it. Even those who speak of systems of Nature (pluralism) have one frame of reference: Nature.

Ancient Greek atomism gave naturalism a materialistic turn and is generally considered the earliest prognostication of nineteenth-century materialistic naturalism. The Greek philosophers, however, were unable to shake off their mythologic heritages and supernaturalistic entities, entities retaining other-world *logoi* and *theoi* in their heretical speculations.

The sharpened dualism of Persian thought (a moot question whether or not the interpretation of dualism was correctly given by Zoroastrian priests) entered Greek thought by cultural and ideological infiltration and set its indelible mark through popular religions (*e.g.* Orphism) into the big philosophies of Western culture. Plato's two-world view (so interpreted in the long tradition which followed him) and Aristotle's twin-world of Form and Matter set the pace for the centuries to follow. Both philosophies were more congenial to the accepted Greek view of life as a bifurcation between the changing and the changeless, the latter beckoning to a more satisfying and enduring existence and to their ideals of Beauty. Socrates who preceded both was too preoccupied with ethics to engage in strictly metaphysical inquiry. Moral questions he posed as sufficiently independent of the gods to be discussed in dialectic and thus gave to ethics a strongly naturalistic flavor. It was his illustrious disciple—so the traditional interpretation—who turned the eyes of man philosophically to a world that was more real in a sphere beyond. And, while Aristotle nurtured naturalism in his scientific inquiries, he also was too steeped in the tradition to free his metaphysics by a comprehensive naturalism. True, he effected a compromise of a kind by bringing the two worlds together into a greater intimacy and claimed to improve upon the teaching of his teacher. Yet he did not completely extricate his philosophy from the tradition of his predecessors.

Logos theologies which crowded the speculative world in ancient times, grasped eagerly by early Christian thinkers, were half-hearted attempts to bring the broken metaphysical world together and dull the edge of traditional dualism. Had the logos ideology been taken more seriously as the grand unification of split worlds and had the Aristotelian scientific naturalism been taken more seriously as a philosophic method—these two factors alone might have achieved a naturalistic philosophy of enormous consequences to the development of Western thought. Logos, however, increasingly took on the rôle of mediator and emissary between a super-and a nether-world rather than as a fundamental unifying principle. From our perspective, it may be seen as an admission of the weakness of the two-world idea and an attempted corrective by a quasi-unification of both. Early Christian thinkers wedded their own Mediator to the Logos and thus continued the supernaturalistic emphasis, although they softened the dichotomy of two worlds by the doctrine of incarnation (God entering into this world). Holding to the view that human nature was too wanting and frail in the light of ideals of perfection, the Christian Logos became the bridge between two worlds offering the means of escape from one world to the other. Moreover, Christians were too close in origin to Hebraic and Judaistic anthropomorphic cosmology to be receptive to a one-world idea.

Neoplatonism with its One World thus stood as a heresy to Christian thought (although there were "Christian Neoplatonists" among the mystically inclined) much as Hinduism with its Grand-Whole-Reality is still a heresy to Westerners.

John Scotus Eriugena (*ca.* 800-880) who produced the first great philosophical system of the Middle Ages (in the Christian tradition) set up a system of thought which, in its philosophy of the unity of Nature and its emphasis upon the claim of reason to grasp the nature of Nature, may be said to be an expression of naturalism. The threat of the church did keep him within the bounds of respect for orthodox supernaturalism; but, taken as a whole, it was a strong philosophical witness to naturalistic heresy. Neoplatonism had influenced him in this direction, no doubt. But common empirical sense kept this philosopher from the extreme ideas of mystical theology. The empirical for Eriugena was like that of the disciplined rationalism of Spinoza. The two philosophies have much in common.

Spinoza's (1632-1677) cosmic neutralism (universal Substance) or spiritualistic monism ranks high among the historic naturalistic threats against supernaturalism. For him the metaphysical world is of one weave and there is no outside factor needed to explain what is explicable within Nature. The dualism of *natura naturans* and *natura naturata* fades before the one underlying Substance or God. Whether we view the world as creative process or the created result, it is still the same world. All things belong together. Although Spinoza's method was rationalistic it was a philosophy which welled out of disciplined wisdom and was empirical *in this sense.*

The towering philosophy of Kant (1724-1804) casting its shadow into subsequent schools of modern thought delayed the day for the revival of naturalistic philosophy by its implicit dualism of the real as over against the phenomenal world. Kant's metaphysics was steeped in the orthodox tradition both in theology and philosophy. Only the so-called NeoKantians with their lofty idealistic excursions within the limits of the phenomenal world of ideas and some post-Kantian Absolutists succeeded in constructing a Unified World but such a view was too diluted to carry force except among those whose love for speculative metaphysics could dim the rugged realities of the every-day world.

The rise of naturalism as something more than a sporadic protest against the established two-world views, of course, came naturally and easily with the rise of the physical sciences, first in the eighteenth century and then with increasing vigor in the nineteenth.

Hobbes (1588-1679), the materialist, had already helped to crowd the supernatural into the natural, the sacred into the secular. Hobbes belonged to the day which learned with surprise about an expanded physical Universe and the corresponding provincialism of the cosmic science of ancient and medieval heritage. La Mettrie (1709-1751) and baron von Holbach (1723-1789) added zest to a materialistic naturalism. Büchner (1824-1899) shifted the emphasis to a dynamic theory of the world and invited popular support to a more softened materialistic naturalism. The expanding vistas of scientific knowledge increasingly placed in demand a type of philosophy more in tune with its method and spirit. The laws of the conservation of mass and energy enclosing the physical world within itself, suggesting that perhaps mind and its outreaches belong within its framework—a powerful scientific hypothesis—stimulated a naturalistic view; physiological studies and, above all, the inescapable report of Darwin (1809-1882) and the evolutionary account of man spoke loudly for a philosophy of a world that held within itself its own factors of explanation. Even mathematics helped in the same direction with the growing success of the application of its principles of quantitative measurement. And then came the voice of Haeckel (1834-1919) announcing a dramatic picture of the unity of the world in one grand biological principle of evolution and dissolution.

Thus, to the late modern mind, naturalism was born again— but in the full dress of materialism. Naturally, it came to be associated synonymously with materialism. The physical and biological sciences nurtured the philosophy and the philosophy was clothed with all their limitations, particularly of the nineteenth-century variety. To many minds the two are still held together indissolubly. Only recently has this provincialism of interpretation been corrected.

Nineteenth-century naturalism, however, contained one corrective of its supposed indissoluble relation with materialism. This was the more modest affirmation of the positivists of whom Auguste Comte (1798-1857) was the early major prophet. Said Comte (in paraphrase): philosophy has finally grown up after its infant stage of theological explanations and its adolescent stage of metaphysics to the mature stature of concern with only such matters as can be dealt with. Positivism is the philosophy of the future and man and his social world are its main characters. What lies beyond the distant hills lies beyond the distant hills. The world of philosophy is the world bounded by a circumscribed human experience. Naturalism of this type became fenced in and for it the old philosophy with its speculations into the wider reaches of the human mind became an anachronism. Positivistic naturalism was a strong deterrent against materialistic naturalism and helped to keep in check the notion of their synonymity. To this camp have come many wearied philosophical souls, high-minded in the pursuit of the ideals of the scientific temper and in moral and social earnestness but, nevertheless, souls barren of that true delight of all philosophers: speculation about the wider horizons of existence. Positivism continues in many places and under different forms in contemporary thought. In religion it goes under the name of religious humanism or, more particularly, the religion of humanity.

Not so easily can human imagination be thus cribbed and confined. It would be better, thought others (still clinging to naturalism), that materialism be got rid of or softened by making more of the unique claims of the human spirit upon the nature of reality, claims which reach out beyond the positivistic short-circuits. Methodologically, the sciences prove their worth to the philosopher; but they fail to satisfy the hunger of the truly metaphysical spirit. So we have Herbert Spencer (1820-1902), a revisionary naturalist, seeing the world as a grand Unity of the "Persistence of Force," systematizing the appearances and paying polite respect to the encompassing Unknowable by a kind of mystic religious silence. So we have, also, recent non-positivistic naturalists revising the inherited materialism toward a "new materialism" by skilful reconstructions (incorporating some features imported from idealism) but still clinging to it. There are the graded level-systems of S. Alexander (1859-1938) and R. W. Sellars (contemporary)—each level calling for appropriate categories but all resting upon the fundamental base of the physical. There is the naturalistic materialism of Santayana (contemporary) which gives full acknowledgment of the unique though limited sphere of mind or spirit in its own "flowering" order of existence, although issuing out of the physical framework of the soil (or, to change the figure: as the spark of light issues from the friction of matter)—all one system of Nature. There is the animistic materialism of W. P. Montague (contemporary), its materialism softened by reference to dimensions and force, reserving for the mind a unique place as potential energy but belonging within the self-enclosed order of physical existence, the two (mind and matter) playing a kind of hide-and-seek game of potential versus kinetic energy—in the same world.

William James (1842-1910) whose philosophy possessed so many facets of implication taught (at one major point) a species of naturalism in his doctrine of mind as a part of the same world to which physical bodies belong. Each, he held, was a kind of context within a larger whole of neutral stuff—best understood as "pure experience" which is neither the none nor the other. Bertrand Russell (a contemporary Pythagorean) in one of his metaphysical excursions clearly drew a naturalistic picture of the world in his doctrine of logical atomism in which physical events and psychical experiences merge into a compresence. Both James and Russell were far removed from materialism but they were naturalists in certain phases of their philosophies, *viz.*, their doctrine of nature as qualitatively of one weave in a *tertium quid*. And their method was to follow through from experience—a method peculiarly emphasized in the philosophy of the former. To this list of neutralistic naturalists may be added such names as Mach (1838-1916), Avenarius (1843-1896) and, more recently, E. B. Holt and R. B. Perry (contemporary).

But there is still another type of naturalism. H. Bergson's (1859-1941) biotism is a case in point. For him Nature is a pulsating life getting expressed in a movement up, in creative becoming, and in a movement down in the deposits of matter and intellection. God is to be identified with the ceaseless activity and creative becoming of Nature, not as Something apart in another sphere. Similarly, J. E. Boodin (b. 1869) with his doctrine of metaphysical energism described the world as activity-systems or processes beyond physical and spiritual explanations. Both may be classified as dynamistic naturalists. Both philosophies reflect respect for the natural sciences and for empirical method.

We do not generally think of absolute idealism as a form of naturalism. However, if we find in certain idealisms a method of rationalism which can be said to be empirical in the broadest meaning of that term and if we find the world (on such a basis) being interpreted as of One Weave, One Reality, we may have here a species of naturalism. On the other hand, certain absolute idealisms belong with Hinduism in the category of inverted naturalism since *the conclusion* (not hypothesis) of a Unifying Principle is first asserted and then a confirmatory experience appealed to.

Hegel's (1770-1831) encompassing spiritualistic Absolutism may be said to be a form of naturalism if we understand his rationalism (as do some of his interpreters) as grounded in empiricism. However, Hegel's whole method of approach appears to have been so largely committed to deductive principles as to render his empiricism less acceptable to naturalists. Schopenhauer's (1788-1860) *World as Will and Idea* and Münsterberg's (1863-1916) encompassing world of Ideal-Value may be classified as spiritualistic naturalism because for them there is no order of existence apart from the one that is self-contained and their approaches came by way of psychological empiricism. More on the side of an inverted type of naturalism is Fichte's (1762-1814) doctrine of the One Great Self or God permeating everything with its restless assertings, an experience of unity *to be achieved*. So also, contemporary Theosophists and those of the school of New Thought—all claiming Eastern thought as their *fons et origo*. Divinity is within not outside; the supernatural is within the natural. This Divinity is there: something to be experienced.

*　　*　　*

A naturalist in philosophy, then, may belong to one of several camps. He may be a materialist, a positivist (metaphysically agnostic), a neutralist, a dynamist or an idealist—all depending on how Nature is interpreted. Or, he may hold that many systems (pluralism) are contained within a System which Itself is not definable by any one category.

How, then, in summary, do naturalists, of whatever stripe, argue their cause?

As indicated throughout, there are two major premises upon which naturalism rests: the belief that reality is a unity *of some kind* (at the minimum: a single frame of reference) which does not permit a metaphysical dualism in which the world as we know and experience it is to be explained by some extraneous order; and the belief that the philosopher's approach to his task must begin and work out from experience and not from some major metaphysical or theological premise which imposes itself upon experience to minimize its fundamental significance by an appeal to some special form of knowledge such as a superimposed faith or "existential" authority or supernatural revelation. Empiricism is a broad concept and now generally means more than it did for earlier modern thought (such as sensationalistic empiricism). Experience is not something apart from reason. Reason itself is empirical when it observes and respects experience and weaves it into some coherent meaning. Of course, no empirical method can today ignore the methods of responsible scientific inquiry; but such inquiry does not mean an enslavement to laboratory techniques nor to purely inductive procedure. Scientific methods continually employ hypotheses and critical deductions.

Naturalists, it is clear, find good company with the philosophical monists in their arguments—although not all monists are naturalists nor are all naturalists monists (*e.g.,* metaphysically agnostic positivists). Monists argue for the principle of interdependence and interpenetration as necessary to intelligibility and understanding (and most naturalists agree, some differing by holding only to a plurality of systems within a given system). Monists appeal to the law of parsimony of explanation, *viz.,* that a simple explanation is to be preferred to the more complicated. The appeal of supernaturalists and others to another order of existence is unnecessary since the world of experience is sufficient for its own explanation. Naturalists claim that all dependable knowledge comes through natural channels and that the world is amenable to such inquiry. For how can what is beyond such knowledge be known—unless recourse is dogmatically made to some special form of knowledge (such as imparted "faith" or "authority" or "revelation")?

It is possible to construct a form of naturalism which will encompass the valuable insights of certain features of idealism. Such spiritualistic naturalism will not necessarily surrender by virtue of its ontologic position a belief in Divinity. The Divine for such naturalism will, of course, be non-deistic and less anthropomorphic. The charge made by supernatural theists of the orthodox tradition that the Divine thus becomes impersonal may be met by the assertion that such Divinity may well turn out to be *more* than personal (as humans understand personality). Impersonal pantheism follows from strict immanence. But a spiritualistic naturalist may well claim that Nature reveals levels transcendent upon others *within its framework* (as argued by Santayana and others) and that Divinity like that of a self may be within the body of Nature although transcending each and all of its separate experiences. Such a doctrine of Divinity is panentheistic.

Nor does spiritualistic naturalism necessarily rule out ontologic values even though they be related to situations—nor the scale of values. Nor does such a view necessarily minimize the possibility of purpose or the significance of the claims of the human spirit. Nor does such a view necessarily deny revelation if by revelation is meant the complementary side of discovery. Nor does such a view necessarily destroy the religious spirit which is seen to be an altogether natural response to the totality of things nor the values of a valid religion made valid by an appeal to the best in human hopes and experiences.

Supernaturalism has long been tried and it is not without its philosophical respectability. But supernaturalism thrives best in a traditional cosmology, and/or a bankrupt view of human knowledge and power and/or in an atmosphere of obeisance to a circumscribed theology. Many of the values of supernaturalism can well be preserved by a spiritualistic naturalistic metaphysics. A naturalistic philosophy of this type may well encourage man to feel much more at home in his world and provide the incentive to make that home a better place in which to live. Man may, moreover, have wider areas of experience ahead in an extension of his life (as suggested by his experience); but that extension need not imply a flight from all that has been part and parcel of his present experience. To believe in personal continued existence does not require a world altogether different any more than do newer emergents in biological evolution require a plurality of Natures.

What is the most compelling drive to the support of some form of naturalism is the desire to fashion a kind of constructive philosophy which is akin to our present culture. Practically all disciplines of contemporary inquiry—be they educational, programs of social reform, scientific, technological, psychological, ethical, economic—are committed to the empirical method and unity of understanding—and with phenomenal success! A scientific culture calls for a philosophy (and even a theology) which will match its reality-feeling. Naturalism, say its exponents, is the answer to this need for a vital philosophy suggested by the kind of world now being disclosed to the modern disciplined mind.

BIBLIOGRAPHY

On the Varieties of Naturalism:
 VERGILIUS FERM, *First Adventures in Philosophy* (New York, 1936), p. 210 ff., and *passim*.

Y. H. KRIKORIAN, ed., *Naturalism and the Human Spirit* (New York, 1944).
H. BERGSON, *Creative Evolution* (New York, 1913).
S. ALEXANDER, *Space, Time and Deity* (London, 1920).
G. SANTAYANA, *Life of Reason*, 5 vols. (New York, 1905-1906).
———, "Brief History of My Opinions" in G. P. Adams and W. P. Montague, editors, *Contemporary American Philosophy*, Vol. II (New York, 1930).
J. DEWEY, *Reconstruction in Philosophy* (rev. ed., Boston, 1949).
———, "From Absolutism to Experimentalism" in *Contemporary American Philosophy*, Vol. II.
F. J. E. WOODBRIDGE, *Nature and Mind* (New York, 1937).
J. B. PRATT, *Naturalism* (New Haven, 1939).
M. C. OTTO, *The Human Enterprise* (New York, 1940).
J. F. BOODIN, "Nature and Reason" in *Contemporary American Philosophy*, Vol. I.
W. P. MONTAGUE, "Confessions of an Animistic Materialist" in *Contemporary American Philosophy*, Vol. II.
R. W. SELLARS, "Realism, Naturalism and Humanism" in *Contemporary American Philosophy*, Vol. II.
R. W. SELLARS, V. J. McGILL, M. FARBER, editors, *Philosophy for the Future* (New York, 1949).
H. N. WIEMAN, *Normative Psychology of Religion* (New York, 1935).
VERGILIUS FERM, "Christianity—A Naturalistic Point of View" in *Crozer Quarterly*, Vol. XVII, No. 3, July, 1940.
CORLISS LAMONT, *Humanism as a Philosophy* (New York, 1949).

CHAPTER THIRTY-FIVE

PANPSYCHISM

CHARLES HARTSHORNE

PANPSYCHISM (from the Greek for "all" and "soul") is the doctrine that everything is psychic or, at least, has a psychic aspect. It is sometimes held in the guise of a "two-aspect theory," that everything is both physical and psychical. In its more significant form, panpsychism is rather the view that all things, in all their aspects, consist exclusively of "souls," that is, of various kinds of subjects, or units of experiencing, with their qualifications, relations, and groupings or communities. The view has been accepted by a good many philosophers and scientists.

In contrast to "idealism," as this term is often used, panpsychism is not a doctrine of the unreality of the spatio-temporal world perceived through the senses, or its reduction to mere "ideas" in the human or divine mind. The constituents of this world are, for panpsychists, just as real as human minds or as any mind. Indeed, they are minds, though, in large part, of an extremely low, subhuman order. Thus panpsychism is psychical realism; realistic both in the sense of admitting the reality of nature, and in the sense of avoiding an exaggerated view of the qualities of its ordinary constituents. "Souls" may be very humble sorts of entities—for example, the soul of a frog—and panpsychists usually suppose that multitudes of units of nature are on a much lower level of psychic life even than that.

Panpsychism also contrasts with the monistic tendency of much idealism. It does not depreciate individual distinctness, and in its most recent forms it admits some degree of freedom or self-determination, even in the lowest orders of psyches. In so far, it is pluralistic. This pluralism of panpsychism is evidently connected with its realism. When Berkeley (1685-1753) reduced the physical world to "ideas" in human and divine minds, he was saying that the inorganic world lacks reality in the full sense of individuality—for an idea is a function of individuals rather than itself an individual. Hindu monism (Sankara, 8th century) is a more extreme denial of individuality to the constituents of nature. Panpsychism, in contrast, is able to admit all the variety of levels of individuality, including the ultramicroscopic, which are suggested by the discoveries of science.

On the other hand, the theory can do justice to the motif of monism. For Whitehead (1861-1947), Royce (1855-1916), Fechner (1801-1887), Varisco (1850-1933), Haeberlin (1878-   ), and other panpsychists have agreed that the system requires a God, and that individuals other than God, in spite of this otherness, are *in* God, not simply outside him. This does not have a one-sidedly monistic implication, because—as Whitehead has most clearly seen —individuals generally are not simply outside each other (the fallacy of "simple location") but in each other, and God's inclusion of all things is merely the extreme or super-case of the social relativity or mutual immanence of individuals. Thus the monistic principle of inclusiveness itself is given a pluralistic aspect. There are as many cases of "including other individuals" as there are individuals.

As approaches to panpsychism among the ancients, one might mention Plato's doctrine that soul is the principle of all motion; Aristotle's statements that the soul is in a manner all things, that all things are moved by God as the lover by what he loves (implying that all things love, and thus are sentient subjects, *i.e.*, in the widest sense souls), that a soul is the form of any organized, self-moving body (implying that if—as there are reasons to think—nature consists entirely of more or less organized, self-moving bodies, and their aggregates or groupings, then nature consists entirely of besouled constituents); and certain echoes of the foregoing in Plotinus. However, Plato seems to regard Space, or the Receptacle, as seemingly irreducible to soul, and he does not expressly state that universal Forms or Ideas are essentially functions of souls. Aristotle has a bias —going even beyond Plato's—in favor of unchanging actuality which leads him to identify soul primarily with what is in principle actual and fixed, and to account for change and potentiality in terms of some other principle or "matter"—as though the creativity of soul, its will to produce novel values, were not as striking a characteristic of it as any! Indeed, the more conspicuous this character the higher the level of soul! The Greeks could not make up their minds whether soul were essentially a principle of change, *the* principle of change indeed; or whether it was essentially a principle of fixity; again, whether soul was essentially a principle, the principle, of variation and particular individuality, or of identity and universality. This rather implies an obscure apprehension on their part that soul is *all* these things, *the* principle of reality in its aspects of being *and* becoming!

The first clear statement of the panpsychist theory seems to have been the Leibnizian (1646-1716) monadology. But it must be understood that many features of this earliest formulation are extrinsic to panpsychism as such. That monads are percipient subjects, which collectively constitute the universe, is the panpsychic element in Leibniz. This philosopher seems also to have been the first to develop clearly the insight (as it has seemed to most panpsychists) that "extension," spatiality, is primarily a group character, that groups must have members, and that such members need not be extended, at least not in the same sense as the groups. Groups have characters not possessed by their members, and perhaps extension is such a character. An extended thing may be really many things, one here, another there, a third in a third place, the totality being indistinctly perceived by us as one "thing" with different parts in different places. That ordinary extended things are such indistinctly perceived groups—the old atomistic conception of the Greeks—has been more and more verified by science, especially since Leibniz; what Leibniz contributed was the insight, almost entirely lacking previously, that there is no reason favoring, and strong reasons opposing, the supposition that the constituents of extended (*i.e.*, composite) "physical" things are simply much smaller, extended physical things. As against this materialistic interpretation of atomism, Leibniz proposed a psychical one. And indeed, if *all* the objects of external perception are, as atomism maintains, composites rather than singulars, then we cannot look to such perception to tell us what in principle it means to be a singular entity. It is only the image we have of a stone that is unitary, not the stone; therefore, it is illogical to regard atoms (the real units) as merely very small stones, or anything of a nature which we can know in the manner in which we know stones. What other sort of nature, otherwise known, can be pointed to? Leibniz replies, the human self is a singular entity with real unity, a unity which is known to us by immediate feeling. Here is the model, and the only one available, for an idea of the singular reality as such. The singulars, whose groupings form extension, in that diverse members of a group are in diverse places, are conceivable only as analogous to the self. What Leibniz thus discovered is the immensely important fact (by which all materialism is rendered suspect) that it is not the function or within the capacity of external perception to tell us *what* things are, but only to tell us where they (and especially, where groups of them) are, in how small or large an area, and how they are changing their relative positions. If we wish to know *what* the things thus distributed in the spatial system may be, we must supplement external perception by that which alone remains, internal perception, self-perception, intuitive grasp of the unitary nature of our experience. We do know to some extent what and not merely where and when, this experience is. If a man did not know what "experience" is, he could not claim to verify any assertion. Furthermore, psychology can give a fair description of how experiences are integrated into the unity of a personality. Thus the "psychic" is a datum.

Of course, we cannot directly apply our internal experience to the characterization of things in general; we must generalize, extend into an infinitely flexible analogy, the basic traits thus accessible to us. Panpsychism does not undertake to tell us what particular sorts of souls other than the human there are; only comparative psychology can attempt to do that. Panpsychism merely says that ultimately comparative psychology is the inclusive science, with "physics" its most elementary branch; "physical" laws being (as one would put it today) statistical or group aspects of the psychological laws of the most elementary and widely distributed types of psyches. The place of biology in this scheme is dealt with by the Australian biologist, W. E. Agar (1882-   ).

If extension is due to groups, does this mean that a singular corresponds to a geometrical point? Leibniz seems not wholly clear in his answer to this question. Many of his successors, *e.g.*, Peirce (1839-1914) and Whitehead, would say that even a singular does occupy a space-volume, but the "extension" of this volume is different from that of visual objects, which are never singulars, and which always consist of indistinctly perceived members occupying diverse areas. Moreover, the volume even of singulars would be meaningless apart from some community of singulars, since space is essentially a system of relations. Extendedness is then not a property capable of distinguishing "mere matter" from mind, since minds, as entering into communal relations with one another, must exhibit extendedness. A mind, according to most panpsychists, is not simply outside the space-time world. It is also not at a mere point in that world, and nothing remains than that it be in an area of the world. And indeed, if our experience had no spatial character, it could not acquaint us with extended things.

The panpsychist argument is thus not that extension must consist of inextended units. The argument is rather: physical objects, as perceived, are not singulars; the singulars of which they must be composed are conceivable only as more or less remotely resembling the human self (since this is for us the only distinctly intuited singular) but differing from that self in the immensely smaller area of its effective presence and operation, in the enormously greater number of its instances in a given world area, in the more monotonous character of its temporal changes. Such differences can be explained as meaning that the singulars in question are, taken individually, drastically subhuman in scope, importance, and power. Only through their enormous numbers do they sometimes collectively seem superior to us, at least in brute power. Taken one by one, they are unimaginably trivial, in comparison with ourselves. (Haeberlin and Royce deny this, for reasons that seem obscure.)

An alternative to the atomistic form of panpsychism was developed by Fechner, and later by Royce. Fechner contrasts the atomistic or "monadological" view, which we have sketched above, to the "synechological." Whereas the former considers such things as atoms (or molecules, perhaps protons and electrons) as each a sort of rudimentary psyche or unit of experiencing, Fechner holds that these minute entities are merely the ultimate elements of "systems," such as animal organisms, and only these systems as wholes are sentient subjects. However, he classes among such systems not only animals, but plants, the earth and the other planets, and other such large bodies. This is to some extent a return to the primitive and Greek view which saw in the heavenly bodies conscious and indeed divine beings. Fechner is the greatest modern defender of this ancient conception. But he adds to it an astonishingly eloquent exposition of the theory that plants—for example, trees—are to be regarded as sentient and conscious. Whatever can be said for this view must, it seems, have been said by Fechner. And his account of the earth-soul is similarly eloquent. Since Fechner was a master of the scientific knowledge of his time, an authority in physics as well as "founder" of experimental psychology, one cannot but be impressed with his advocacy of the synechological alternative to monadological panpsychism. It seems, nevertheless, doubtful if the advances of science since his time have served to support him. On the one hand, the discoveries in microscopic life suggest that comparative psychology must in principle be extended indefinitely downward toward the minute. A book has even been written on the *Psychic Life of Microorganisms*. And the cellular structure of the higher organisms implies that such "systems," to use Fechner's term, consist of simpler systems, and certain analogies between cells and molecules, together with the phenomena of viruses, imply that the principle does not end with cells. So we begin to see nature as consisting of organisms composed of organisms, on many levels, and Whitehead and others hold that even an electron is a rudimentary organism or systematic unity. It seems arbitrary to halt the analogy which is basic to comparative psychology at any particular level (for other than practical reasons of scientific convenience relative to the given state of investigation). But, on the other hand, some of the larger systems Fechner dealt with so enthusiastically seem to contemporary knowledge rather too loosely integrated to be accepted as sentient subjects. Thus it is arguable that a tree has less unity than one of its own cells; and even more, that the earth has less unity than the animals inhabiting it.

Royce's panpsychism followed Fechner's in some respects, but added the remarkable notion that not only individual animals, along with heavenly bodies, are sentient individuals, but that each species of animal as a whole is a single conscious individual. Here Royce exploits the impression that naturally arises in the lover of nature that a single species of bird (let us say) has its own individuality, which is much more striking than the individuality of single members of the species. Each wood thrush sings much like all the others, but none sings at all like any other kind of bird. "The song of the wood thrush" has a more impressive individuality than the song of this or that wood thrush. Variations among the members of the species seem like moment to moment variations within one individual. However, in drawing the inference that such a species is conscious, Royce has not so far had followers.

A more important contribution of Royce was the conception of diverse tempos of psychic life or of diverse spans of the specious present. Thus whereas a man experiences events lasting over something like a tenth of a second as a series of events, and cannot distinguish distinctly those lasting much less than a tenth of a second, there might be individuals who would experience a millennium as a single happening, and others for whom a millionth of a second would be a distinct experience. In this way, Royce tries to deal with the objection which his and Fechner's form of panpsychism tends to arouse, that a planet does not seem to be doing anything very exciting or worth having feelings about. On our time span, says Royce, nothing may happen to a planet worth being conscious of, but if the planet experiences a long period of time as a single happening, enough change may occur in such a period to provide contrasts dramatic enough for the planet consciousness. This principle is also stressed by Whitehead, and it seems scarcely possible to doubt that it has validity, whether or not it justifies attribution of "souls" to heavenly bodies. It is contrary to all reasonable analogies to think that even all animals have just the same span to their specious presents; much less, that the higher animals and microbes, or microbes and atoms, could do so. It is such dimensions of variation as this, in principle infinite in extent—for if there be a specious present of a tenth of a second, why not one of a millionth of a second, or of a million years, or a billion—it is such unlimited variabilities as this that furnish the answer to the objection sometimes made to panpsychism as such, that it underestimates the variety of nature. Before we could justify this objection we must first have established the limits of the variety of possible psychic life. And who has been able to set such limits? Until and unless they can be set, the objection has no definite meaning. And it is always to be borne in mind that what a panpsychist cannot interpret as a single sentient subject he may be able to deal with as a group or crowd of subjects (the Leibnizian principle) or as an element in a more comprehensive single subject (the Fechnerian principle).

An important question is, how psychic singulars can interact or be related to one another, and thus constitute the extended world of "physical" reality. Leibniz denied literal interaction, and substituted "preestablished harmony" through the divine fiat. He has not been followed in this notion, which involves forbidding paradoxes. Interaction has since been accepted by every representative panpsychist. But the problem is, to point to something in experience that gives a basis for the concept of interaction. Lotze (1817-1881) wrestled with the problem, but his solution is merely to posit that we are all parts of One spiritual being, whose parts interact, since they are not separate entities but are unified through the whole inclusive of them. But this is largely verbal, as it stands. Fechner's view was similar. Peirce and Whitehead are the thinkers who really effect an advance here.

According to Peirce, one of the three universal aspects of experience, or supreme categories, is "reaction," which means, an element of experience containing intrinsic reference to something other than itself. Peirce points out that experience is pervaded by a sense of duality, of dynamic relatedness to another, as in such pairs as effort-resistance, struggle-obstacle, "the *novel*—the *expected*," present-past, feeling—thing felt, subject-object. Peirce maintains cogently that this dynamic duality cannot be treated as a mere illusion, a mere feeling of reaction, but must be accepted as a felt reaction of feelings, a real transaction between an experience and something other than itself. This real reference to another, Peirce calls Secondness or the Dyad. His three categories are, Feeling-quality, Striving or Reaction, Meaning or Representation. These correspond to the monadic, dyadic, and triadic elements of all experience respectively. In this scheme panpsychism acquires greater precision of language than it formerly possessed. That all is psychic means, all is feeling, in reaction with other feeling, and more or less shot through with meaning or sign-character. (To reach Peirce's conception, we must take Feeling to include all the qualitative content of sensation, often classed under cognition.)

An important contribution involved in Peirce's view is his uniquely vivid sense of the spontaneous, creative, or chance-character of the life of feeling; the radical absurdity of looking for a reason for blue or green or sour or any other quality of feeling. Process in its details issues from no necessity, but is a continual influx of unpredictable novelty. Law is everywhere only statistical and approximate, and on the higher levels of mind the regularities are even less complete. Another contribution is in the recognition of the basic rôle of sympathy in reality. Feelings react with other feelings, but in this reaction is involved some degree of participation in the qualities of these other feelings. A feeling feels the feelings to which it reacts. Feelings echo to some extent the feelings around them, and this is the basis of the possibility of relationships among realities by which they constitute a world of things relevant to one another.

Similar ideas (developed independently) along with many new ones in a much more fully articulated system are found in the panpsychic metaphysics of Whitehead, who, it is probably safe to say, will stand out, with Leibniz, as one of the two great artificers of the panpsychic philosophy in its present form.

We have seen that the contribution of Leibniz to our theme was primarily his freeing atomism from its illogical alliance with materialism. Atomism here means topological pluralism, the principle that in diverse perceived "places" are not merely parts of one extended thing, but always diverse things, collectives of which are what are perceived as extended. Now the same principle can be applied to time as to space. In different experienced moments of time are not merely different states, or temporal parts, of one thing enduring through time, but different things, and it is only sequences of these things that have extension or endurance through time. This temporal atomism or chronological pluralism is termed "epochalism" by Whitehead. A single temporal unit or epoch is not a mere instant, but a "specious present," a unitary experience or quantum of process, just as even the least thing in space, say an electron, is not a mere physical point. In both cases, there is a unit which is not actually divided into, or composed of, smaller units; but, although not divided, it is conceptually divisible. It is a least actual, but not a least possible, part of space or time. The mathematical continuum of point-instants is the system of all possible divisions of space-time; the atomic-epochal units are the actual divisions at a given moment. The human specious present is the only epoch we directly experience with any vividness, just as the spatial spread of a human experience is the only atomic unit. In perceiving the non-human world we are always apprehending collectives, both spatial and temporal. To form even a vague conception of the singulars composing these collectives our only resource is to generalize analogically the epochal and atomic characters of human experiences.

The units of reality, then, are unit-experiences, "experient-occasions," or "actual entities," not "souls." It may seem that the name panpsychism should no longer be applied (it is, to be sure, never used by Whitehead himself). However, "psychology without a soul" has long been with us, and the word "psychic" cannot conveniently be restricted to a certain theory of the temporal structure of experience rather than another. Moreover, the analogy between the human soul and other individuals is still in force in Whitehead; it is merely given a more subtle, complex, and carefully generalized formulation. The tendency for experiences to occur in integrated sequences, expressive of enduring individual characteristics, is not confined to human beings. The higher animals have something analogous, though the modes of integration, through memory and persisting purposes and so on, are much simpler and radically inferior in degree of consciousness. And even the sequences of occasions constituting a cell or an atom may have some bits of memory-echoes and flashes of rudimentary anticipation, and certainly there must be some continuity of quality running through these sequences. *So far as nature thus consists of enduring individuals, with self-identity through time, this identity will be analogous to that of souls.* But whereas the old theory admitted two forms of change, irreducible to any common principle: the creation of new actualities (such as souls), *and* the production of new states of an already existing actuality (such as new experiences of a soul), chronological pluralism or epochalism has but the creation of new actualities, *i.e.*, unit experiences. New souls do indeed come into being, but that is not an additional principle but a special application of the universal principles by which occasions supersede one another in time. For every such occasion has intrinsic reference (somewhat as in Peirce's theory of reaction) to preceding occasions, with which it has some degree of sympathetic participation, echoing their qualities, but with a new over-all quality of its own as it reacts to them. Ordinary "memory" is merely a privileged case of this intrinsic reference of experiences to their predecessors, and the persistence of personality traits is a privileged case of the qualitative echoing of old experiences in new ones. Some occasions form single strand sequences, each member of which echoes certain qualities common to the whole sequence. This type of sequence is said to have "personal order," since it is analogous to the stream of experiences constituting the inner life of a human person. In other cases the relations of reaction

A HISTORY OF PHILOSOPHICAL SYSTEMS

(Whitehead's term is "causal efficacy," or "conformation of feeling to feeling," or "physical prehension") form multiple strand sequences structurally not analogous to a soul. But always there is analogy to the unit experience from which all knowledge starts.

We can barely mention once more the new synthesis of theistic and pantheistic insights by which, especially in Fechner and Whitehead, God as supreme psyche completes the panpsychic system. God includes the lesser subjects, but so that their freedom is preserved and his responsibility for the details of their acts is not unlimited. This involves an aspect of passivity and process toward novelty in God, despite the eternal necessity of his existence and essential character.

BIBLIOGRAPHY

W. E. AGAR, *The Theory of the Living Organism* (Melbourne, London, 1943).

——, "The Wholeness of the Living Organism," *Philosophy of Science,* vol. xv (1948), pp. 179-91.

A. BINET, *The Psychic Life of Microorganisms* (Chicago, 1903).

G. T. FECHNER, *The Religion of a Scientist:* Selections from G. Th. Fechner. Ed. and trans. by W. Lowrie (New York, 1946).

——, *Zend-Avesta oder über die Dinge des Himmels und des Jenseits.* Vol. I (especially chs. x, xi) (Hamburg, Leipzig, 1851).

V. FERM, *First Adventures in Philosophy* (New York, 1936).

P. HAEBERLIN, *Naturphilosophische Betrachtungen* (Zürich 1939-40).

——, *Logik* (Zürich, 1947).

C. HARTSHORNE, *Beyond Humanism* (Part ii), (Chicago, 1937).

——, *Man's Vision of God* (Chicago, 1941; New York, 1948).

G. W. LEIBNIZ, *Discourse on Metaphysics, Correspondence with Arnauld,* etc. (Chicago, 1902).

——, *Monadology* and Other Writings (New York, 1898).

W. P. MONTAGUE, *The Ways of Things* (New York, 1940).

F. PAULSEN, *Introduction to Philosophy,* tr. by F. Thilly (New York, 1912).

C. S. PEIRCE, *Collected Papers,* Vol. I, VI (Harvard, 1931-35).

——, *The Philosophy of Peirce: Selections,* J. Buchler, ed. (New York, London, 1940).

——, *Chance, Love and Logic* (New York, 1923, 1949).

J. ROYCE, *The World and the Individual,* Vol. II (New York, 1901).

C. A. STRONG, *Essays on the Natural Origin of the Mind* (London, 1930).

B. VARISCO, *Know Thyself* (London, 1915).

A HISTORY OF PHILOSOPHICAL SYSTEMS

A. WENZL, *Wissenschaft und Weltanschauung* (Leipzig, 1939, 1949).
A. N. WHITEHEAD, *Science and the Modern World* (New York, 1925).
——, *Process and Reality* (New York, 1929, 1949).
——, *Adventures of Ideas* (New York, 1933, 1948).
——, *Modes of Thought* (New York, 1938).

CHAPTER THIRTY-SIX

CONTEMPORARY THOMISM

DONALD A. GALLAGHER

> Restore the golden wisdom of Saint Thomas . . .
> extend and perfect the old by new truths.

THE INTELLECTUAL character of contemporary Thomism is set forth in the above words of Pope Leo XIII in his letter On the Restoration of Christian Philosophy, (*Aeterni Patris*, 1879). In this chapter we are concerned with Thomism as a philosophical movement of the twentieth century and with its twofold task of restoration and progressive development. Thomism—the term Neo-Thomism, like Neo-Classicism, has unsatisfactory connotations—is the most prominent philosophical synthesis in the far from homogeneous movement which is called for convenience the New Scholasticism.[4]* The term refers also to a definite school of theology in the Catholic Church with characteristic doctrines on divine grace, human freedom and the end of man.[8] Nevertheless, as one may be a Thomist without following this particular theological school, for my present purpose I take the term Thomist to designate anyone who accepts Thomas Aquinas as his master in philosophy and the basic teachings of Thomas as philosophical truth.[15,16]

There are certain doctrines which all Thomists hold (for example, the famous twenty-four theses).[15] It is unnecessary to resume here the doctrines of Thomistic philosophy; the student may consult introductory works with profit, as well as advanced commentaries, and the writings of Saint Thomas himself.[8,10,27,30,33] From the historical standpoint, we understand by Thomism that Christian philosophy whose principles and basic doctrines were first set forth

---

Note: To avoid the use of footnotes, the numbers in the chapter refer the reader to the items in the bibliography.

A HISTORY OF PHILOSOPHICAL SYSTEMS

by Saint Thomas Aquinas (1224-1274), principally in his theological *summas*; which was developed by such commentators as Cajetan (1470-1534) and John of Saint Thomas (1589-1644); and which was revived by Leo XIII (pontificate: 1878-1903) and Cardinal Mercier (1851-1926). In our time, it has been expounded by such men as Martin Grabmann (1875-1948) in Germany, F. Olgiati (1886-) in Italy, G. Manser (1866-1949) in Switzerland, Léon Noel (1888-) in Belgium, R. Garrigou-Lagrange (1877-), Jacques Maritain (1882-) and Etienne Gilson (1884-) in France. In our country and Canada, it is expounded by Yves Simon (1903-), Anton Pegis (1905-), L. M. Regis (1903-), and C. de Koninck (1906-). It furnishes inspiration also for the Aristotelian and realistic philosophies of men like M. J. Adler (1902-) and John Wild (1902-).*

In this chapter we have been asked to discuss the thought of Jacques Maritain and Etienne Gilson as outstanding examples of Thomism. We shall also consider briefly the background of contemporary Thomism, and Thomism in the U.S.A.

I

It is part of the paradox of Thomism that it claims to be an exception to the generally valid principle that the proper name of no philosopher should be used to circumscribe perennial philosophy because it is not a system but a wisdom, a synthesis and a spiritual organism capable of assimilating truth wherever it may be.[1,19,16] This is, in fact, the first important observation I would make about Thomism—I trust not ungraciously in this history of philosophical systems—that it is not a system among systems. Although few philosophies bear such a systematic appearance as Thomism—for example, the *Summa* with its hundreds of articulated parts—anyone who is familiar with the living thought of Saint Thomas knows that we simply miss the point of his philosophic wisdom if we classify his doctrine as a system. As Aimé Forest points out in his *La structure*

---

*Note: Thomism cannot be fully appreciated apart from its relations with other Catholic philosophies such as Suarezianism and Scotism in the past, and at the present day, the modified Augustinianism of M. Blondel (1861-1949) and the Catholic existentialism of G. Marcel (1869-). The theological thought of H. de Lubac (1896-) opens up new horizons for the future of Thomist philosophy.

metaphysique du concret selon S. Thomas, Thomism is not a system because it is not a philosophy of ideas but a philosophy of being; it does not enclose being in a formula but rather seeks that which is formal and actual in being (*esse*).

There is not space in this chapter to discuss all the important objections to our point of view.[36] The recent forceful criticisms of Thomism by Professors Wild and Northrop and the replies to them deserve mention.[14] All we can do here is to indicate the general procedure of the Thomist in meeting objections and explaining his position. Many objections to Thomism rest on misconceptions. After these have been disposed of, there will remain some basic disagreements about the fundamental issues in philosophy. The question then becomes one of determining to what extent and with whom intellectual cooperation is feasible.[18]

Almost twenty-five years ago Zybura reported the reactions of non-Scholastics to Scholastic philosophy.[36] Much progress towards a better understanding has been made since, but, as Prof. Collins observes, the general attitude toward Scholasticism still appears to be one which questions the philosophical relevance of the historical study of Scholasticism, and doubts the completeness of the Scholastic commitment to the contemporary philosophical effort.[5] While the Thomist holds that the most basic questions in philosophy have been solved (such as the demonstrability of the existence of God), nevertheless, he does believe that there remains a significant sense in which these questions must constantly be restated and rethought, and that there are many important questions which still await definitive solution. The Thomist need not be apologetic about his convictions. With Oswaldo Robles (1904-   ), the Mexican Thomist, he can say that he is a Thomist because he finds in the doctrine of Thomas Aquinas a pure and absolute objectivity.[30] But for this very reason the difficulty persists. Many sincere minds find Thomism's claim to be *the* catholic philosophy pretentious, a barrier to freedom of inquiry.

To this central objection there is no simple answer, surely none which can be stated in a few paragraphs. Here we can only state honestly what we are convinced the answer is and then, as evidence that Thomism can be genuinely philosophical, point to the works of Thomas and of his present-day followers. Does the Thomist claim that Saint Thomas has all the answers? To answer yes to this naive question would rule one out as a genuine philosopher automatically. Yet, the Thomist would hold that the teachings of Saint Thomas do provide the most true and comprehensive expression of perennial philosophy. He believes that the philosophy of Saint Thomas does contain the solutions to the major questions of philosophy, as well as a host of lesser ones, and that it contains the principles in terms of which all true solutions can be organically assimilated. The Thomist does not regard the contributions of other philosophers as valueless,—far from it. Many men besides Saint Thomas have discovered truth and attained deep insight into reality, and accordingly they are, as he himself viewed them, his collaborators in the quest for wisdom. His philosophy is capable of integrating the insights of his great rivals and compeers into a coherent whole. Such integration is one of the tasks of the contemporary Thomist.

II

The only answer to the suspicion that Thomists are not earnest inquirers into truth and reality is to point out some representative Thomists who are genuine philosophers. It is not possible in this survey even to mention the names of all the contemporary Thomists who have made important contributions to the movement.[5,13,22,36] In accordance with the plan of this volume, our purpose is rather to select representative Thomists who illustrate the trends of thought in contemporary Thomism and who symbolize the movement most dramatically. There is no intention of minimizing the importance of divergent points of view, even within Thomism itself, which cannot be given adequate attention here.

In his epoch-making document, *Aeterni Patris,* Pope Leo XIII granted official approval and gave much impetus to a movement towards reviving Scholastic philosophy which had been gathering momentum since the middle of the nineteenth century.[5,32] The study of the philosophy of Saint Thomas was particularly encouraged and his doctrine was accorded an approbation given to that of no other Catholic philosopher.[15] Due to Papal encouragement, Catholic institutes of higher learning were founded or expanded at Louvain, Milan, Fribourg, and the Catholic University of America. Outstanding personalities like the American Edward Pace (1861-1938) who studied under Wundt at Leipzig, and Agostino Gemelli (1878-   ) of Milan who came to the Church from militant positivism deserve mention, but Cardinal Mercier is the most significant figure in this early period.[36] Without him, the Neo-Scholastic Revival, as it was then generally called, would not have been the vital movement it was. There is no place here to recount the dramatic story of Mercier's endeavor to rethink Thomism in function of contemporary problems or to recall the encouragement he gave Catholic laymen in particular to do serious research in all branches of knowledge. Besides his work of organizing and inspiring the school of philosophy at Louvain, Mercier's own most important contributions were in epistemology and psychology.

The very fact that there was a lively interest in the new science of psychology at the Scholastic centers we have mentioned shows that they were not indifferent to modern science. If anything, there was some over-eagerness about harmonizing Thomism and modern thought, in a sincere effort to show the value of both. This tendency was apparent not only in science but also in epistemology. Léon Noel, Mercier's disciple at Louvain, has said that it is difficult to exaggerate the importance of his master's *Critériologie*.[36] But Mercier's criteriological realism has been strongly criticized in recent years for not being an authentic Thomistic realism and for conceding too much to the Cartesian and Kantian statements of the epistemological problem.[29] One may agree with Gerard Smith and G. B. Phelan that Gilson in *Réalisme thomiste* has decisively settled the matter, showing that the starting point of the realist must be the evidence of being and not the data of thought, and that the problem of the bridge is a pseudo-problem.[20,25] Nevertheless, one cannot deny that without the genius and inspiration of Mercier the achievements of later Thomists might not have been possible. Entangled in the all-pervading "Cartesianism" he fought against, it was difficult for Mercier at the turn of the century to achieve completely what he urged all Thomists to do—to rethink Thomism by first rediscovering the genuine and undiluted thought of Thomas himself.

III

At the present time there are numerous centers in Europe and North and South America where the historical and doctrinal study of Saint Thomas is vigorous. Among the large number of Thomists doing work which deserves attention, perhaps a dozen might be ranked with the most prominent philosophers of our time. In the forefront of these stand Jacques Maritain and Etienne Gilson. Without the historical research and the doctrinal reassessment of the pioneers of the Thomistic revival, the achievements of these men would hardly have been possible, yet it is they who have made the greatest impact upon the present-day world and given us the contributions most likely to be judged of enduring value.[12,19,20]

What is most dramatic and significant about the philosophical adventures of Maritain and Gilson is that both began their intellectual journey from the very center of modern French culture. These Thomists were no strangers to modern thought; they started from it and won their way back to the living center of European tradition—Catholic wisdom. They then proceeded to interpret the Catholic heritage to the contemporary mind and made Thomism a part of the intellectual life of our time.[24,26]

The life-story of Maritain is familiar to all who have read the beautiful volumes of Raïssa Maritain.[21] He himself says that after voyaging eagerly among all the modern philosophies, when he came at last to Saint Thomas he experienced a sort of illumination of the intellect. He wrote the famous line, "Woe to me if I do not thomisticize," and accepted his philosophical vocation under the standard of Saint Thomas.[17] Since that time Maritain has looked upon Saint Thomas as the "apostle of our time," a truly universal and contemporary spirit who offers us a wisdom and a method in terms of which we can save intellectual values in the theoretical order and human values in the practical order.[16] For over forty years Maritain has pursued this vocation, and in over forty volumes and scores of essays has touched upon every aspect of modern thought. He has spent much time teaching in the U. S. A. and at present is on the faculty of Princeton University.

It is impossible to do justice to the wealth and variety of Maritain's thought in the scant space at our disposal. If our brief discussion encourages the student to go to Maritain's works, our efforts will be amply repaid. The advanced student must eventually master the *Degrees of Knowledge* and *True Humanism,* but at first it may be profitable to consult his "text-books" *Logic, Preface to Metaphysics,* and *Introduction to Philosophy* for a general outline of Thomistic philosophy.

Although Maritain's moral philosophy rests upon his metaphysics, the student may find it easier to begin with the former. In *Things that are not Caesar's,* and *Christianity and Democracy,* Maritain gives a statement of his political thought. His social philosophy, and in particular his doctrine of personalism, which is at the heart of his social and political thought and subject to much controversy, will be found in *Freedom in the Modern World* and *Person and the Common Good.* In *Education at the Crossroads* the student will find a remarkable treatment of contemporary educational problems. To the student interested in art, *Frontiers of Poetry, Art and Scholasticism,* and *Art and Faith* will prove illuminating. In these books Maritain applies the principles of Thomism to contemporary art for which he has a rare appreciation. Although Maritain is not a historian of philosophy, the student will find in his studies of Bergson, Descartes, and Saint Augustine many rich historical insights.

The student who pursues the study of Maritain to the realm of theoretical philosophy should read his works on metaphysics, particularly his recent book, *Existence and the Existent,* in which he gives a penetrating analysis not only of Saint Thomas' metaphysics of existence but also of modern existentialist doctrines. His most complete treatment of the epistemological problem is to be found in the *Degrees of Knowledge.*[12,19,25] Unlike Gilson, who rejects the term critical realism, Maritain thinks an authentic critique of knowledge is possible, provided it does not begin with the *cogito* but with *scio aliquid esse,* and provided it is not set up as the precondition to metaphysics. In *La philosophie de la nature,* the student will find his distinction between the empiriological and the ontological approach to the physical world, that is, between the natural sciences and the philosophy of nature. Of Maritain's philosophy of the sciences, Y. Simon has observed that it marks the first time the science of phenomena was given a justification which owes nothing to an idealistic philosophy.[20]

Maritain is primarily a philosopher and not a theologian. Yet he has written so profoundly and beautifully on the spiritual life and mystical experience that Abbé Journet calls him *un théologien immense et fécond.*[19] Besides his studies on natural mystical experience, action and contemplation, and some chapters on John of the Cross in the *Degrees of Knowledge,* the student will find *Prayer and Intelligence* particularly helpful.

A HISTORY OF PHILOSOPHICAL SYSTEMS

Due in part to the demands of the practical order to which he has given himself so generously, Maritain has never synthesized all the themes we have mentioned into one comprehensive masterwork. The grand outlines of such a synthesis are available, however, in the *Degrees of Knowledge* and *True Humanism,* his most ambitious works in the spheres of speculative and practical philosophy, respectively. M. J. Adler discerns in the first the outlines of a *Summa* for our time, and Y. Simon believes no more authentically Thomistic book has ever been written.[20]

In the sphere of theoretical philosophy, Maritain utilizes the principle *distinguer pour unir,* first, to explain the diversity of specifically distinct disciplines in philosophy and the sciences, and second, to unify them in terms of an all-embracing wisdom. In the sphere of practical philosophy, he recognizes the diversity of ends pursued by men in the practical order. While recognizing the autonomy of the temporal order and of zones of action in the political and social areas, he orders these activities and their "infravalent" ends to the one absolutely ultimate end of man, the Beatific Vision. For Maritain, moral philosophy is autonomous and distinct from moral theology, but since moral philosophy must consider the only ultimate end which actually exists for man, his supernatural end, any moral philosophy to be truly adequate must be a Christian moral philosophy.

In terms of this moral outlook, and attentive to the suggestions of common sense and popular wisdom, as well as to the most scientific investigations into man, Maritain has labored to restore political and social thought to the plane of wisdom.[19] He shows the intimate links between man's nature, liberty, and the meaning of history. He shows the evangelical inspiration behind the age-long struggle for democracy, and the need for a spiritualization of the means of temporal action. He outlines a pluralist society for the modern age which would be at once personalist and communitarian. To the anthropocentric humanist doctrines which degrade instead of liberating man, Maritain opposes theocentric humanism. In his inquiry into social thought, he gave serious attention to the actual course of history under the influence of Christianity and was led to develop a Christian philosophy of history and culture. Journet holds that Maritain was the first to formulate explicitly (especially in *True Humanism*) a Christian philosophy of history as distinct from the Christian theology of history to be found in Augustine's *City of God*.[19]

The thought of Maritain has been orientated by his ideal of Christian philosophy. For him, (in *De la philosophie chrétienne*), Christian philosophy is not a contradictory notion but a reality. In terms of its guidance and its fruitful union with theology the Thomist is enabled to accomplish a truly philosophical and universal work.

In spite of his immense labors in the universe of thought, Maritain has not confined himself to the theoretical statement of his moral doctrines. Convinced that the philosopher has the right and the duty, if need be, to enter the political domain and as a philosopher to judge questions that involve moral decisions, he has often taken a stand on problems of immediate practical concern. His moving indictment of Anti-Semitism and his defense of all brothers in the human family as children of the same Father are among the pages for which history will do Jacques Maritain most honor. He has not merely written about these problems; he has participated in action, often at great personal sacrifice. He has been reproached for devoting so much of his time to practical concerns and not pursuing the speculative fields for which he has such extraordinary gifts. The simple answer is that he has followed his conscience; he has shown that the philosopher's vocation is not interrupted fruitlessly by these incursions into the practical order, but that, if need arise, it is part of that very vocation and can only do honor to philosophy.

Maritain is mindful of the importance of the historical study of Thomism, but his philosophical genius is at its best in the area of doctrinal philosophy and in his chosen task of extending, elaborating, and deepening the Thomistic synthesis. His interpretations of Saint Thomas have sometimes been challenged, but no one has denied that his profound and original thought sheds light upon every topic it touches. In virtue of his great accomplishments, G. B. Phelan has hailed him as *the* philosopher of the twentieth century.[26]

Etienne Gilson has spoken sparingly of his personal experiences as a seeker of wisdom.[11,12] But enough is known to reveal a man who from the outset has been passionately devoted to the pursuit of wisdom and yet capable of the immensely patient and painstaking labors of historical investigation. Inspired by Bergson and taught historical method by Lévy-Bruhl, Gilson began his career by tracking down the Scholastic sources of Descartes' thought. As a result of this work, he came to the conclusion that the only context in which the metaphysics of Descartes made sense was the metaphysics of Saint Thomas. More than that, he found in Thomas' thought the substantial nourishment of metaphysical certitude.

In the first stages of his career, it appeared that Gilson was more the historian than the philosopher, reporting positions with rare fidelity rather than embracing and defending them. But, as A. C. Pegis points out, Gilson never believed that one could be an historian of philosophy without being a philosopher as well.[24] In reality, as Henri Gouhier shows, Gilson's work developed along three lines, erudite research, historical synthesis, and lastly, philosophy itself.[12] This development was not chronological, but emphasis shifted from the first and second stages to the third as his maturing vision enabled him to advance with sureness to the philosophical level.

Any complete assessment of Gilson's thought would have to take account of his erudite appraisals, permeated with rare understanding, of great individual figures in philosophy—Augustine, Bonaventure, Dante, Scotus. It would have to take account of his over-all interpretation of mediaeval philosophy, (*The Spirit of Mediaeval Philosophy, La philosophie au moyen age*). It would consider his interpretation of the philosophical significance of the history of philosophy in such works as the *Unity of Philosophical Experience*. It would consider his extremely important work in epistemology (*Réalisme methodique, Réalisme thomiste et critique de la connaissance*). Such an estimate would give a central place to Gilson's conception of Christian philosophy, (*The Spirit of Mediaeval Philosophy,* and *Christianity and Philosophy*), described by him as that philosophy which, while keeping the orders of reason and revelation formally distinct, considers revelation an indispensable auxiliary to reason. (On this question many Thomists have taken sharp issue with Maritain and Gilson.) Finally, no account of Gilson would be complete which failed to consider his views on social order, humanism, art and letters, and on the apostolate of the intellect which he eloquently describes as the dedication of the intelligence to the service of Christ the King.

The crowning achievement of Gilson's life-work is the rediscovery and restatement of Saint Thomas' metaphysics of existence. His latest book, *Being and Some Philosophers,* provides a sketch of the crucial experiments in the history of metaphysics from which metaphysics itself emerges. Let us enlarge upon this basic theme in order to sum up the central point of all Thomistic metaphysics.

In previous works, Gilson devoted considerable attention to what he regarded as Saint Thomas' central intuition, namely, that it is impossible to do justice to God without doing justice to nature, and that doing justice to nature is at the same time the surest way of doing justice to God. As Saint Thomas himself puts it, "The First Cause from the abundance of its own goodness confers upon other things not only that they be but that they may be causes." God, then, causes (1) the very existence of things, and (2) He causes them to be *efficacious* second causes. Previously, Gilson concentrated on the second point and explained with deep insight the causality of creatures in the orders of natural action, moral action, and knowledge. He came to perceive more and more that this central intuition of Saint Thomas should be expressed with emphasis upon point one. It is because God, who is being itself, gives to creatures the gift of being that they are true existents and are able to be efficacious causes.

If being is the act of acts and the first object of the human mind, Gilson inquires, why have so few philosophers seen it as the first principle of philosophic knowledge? He finds the answer in the overwhelming tendency of the intellect to sterilize being and reduce it to an abstract concept. Various philosophies have deep perceptions corresponding to fundamental aspirations of the mind, but it is Thomas' metaphysics which, Gilson believes, is able to assimilate the insights of all the great doctrines of being. For Gilson, Thomas' insight into being as the perfection of perfections and the act of existing was a rare moment in history, but its significance was never fully appreciated until the present.

Why is it, indeed, that Thomas' philosophy appears as the emptiest of metaphysics to many thinkers? Gilson replies that it may appear as either the emptiest or the richest. If we take Thomist metaphysics as one of *ens* (being) in a purely formal way—and some of Thomas' followers have been guilty of spreading this misconception—then it is the most abstract of abstractions or what Gilson terms a "thingism." It should rather be understood as a metaphysics of *esse* (being as the *act* of existing, as the to-be of things). In this view, being is the very act of existing enjoyed by subjects (*supposita*). As an individual substance of a rational nature, man the person is endowed with knowledge and is capable of responding to act, to the act of existence in finite things and to the Infinite Actuality, *Ipsum Esse*, in whom Essence and Existence are identical, whose name is I AM WHO AM. When man faces toward God, the image towards its Maker, an act responds to the Act and gives itself to the One Who has given it everything.

In his autobiographical essay, "Compagnons de route," as well as in his Aquinas Lecture, Gilson records the story of his own personal rediscovery of the meaning of *esse*.[11,12] One of the tasks of contemporary Thomists is to assist in the full recovery of this metaphysics of existence and to lead others to do the same. Etienne Gilson reminds us that if we are to achieve this end, we must realize that the object of Thomism is not Thomism but the world, man and God attained as existents.[10]

Precisely because Maritain and Gilson are contemporary figures, the time has not come for a definitive evaluation of their philosophical significance. Although they differ on certain points, in particular on the question of critical realism, they are at one on all fundamental issues in Thomism. Today when the various existentialist philosophies are among the most vital developments in philosophy, Maritain and Gilson hold that Saint Thomas' is the truly existential philosophy.[6,28] Today when philosophers are concerned with working out a humanistic philosophy, these Thomists declare that only a God-centered humanism confers upon man his true dignity and discloses the secret of his being. The life-work of Maritain and Gilson, who have labored side by side in the related fields of philosophical doctrine and its history, has been, then, in a real sense a collaboration. Recently Gilson said of Maritain that we are all indebted to him in the same way that he is to our common master, Saint Thomas.[19] For his part, Maritain has called Gilson one of the greatest missionaries France has ever given to Christianity.[12]

IV

It seems appropriate in this volume designed for students in American colleges to turn next to the American scene and survey the local state of Thomism. It is true that American Thomism has a meager past compared with the European, and at present can hardly match the work being done in European countries. The situation, however, is far superior to what it was in 1933 when Fr. McCormick of Loyola University in Chicago said that the great need of American Catholic philosophy was more scholarship.[22]

For evidence of scholarship of increasing worth, the student may turn to reviews such as *New Scholasticism, Modern Schoolman, Thought, The Thomist, Mediaeval Studies,* and the *Review of Politics,* which come from the leading centers for graduate study in this country and Canada. The *Proceedings* of the American Catholic Philosophical Association, founded a quarter of a century ago, also contains representative essays.[3,13,30,28] Outstanding among lecture series is the Annual Aquinas Lecture of Marquette University. Published since 1937, these lectures provide an excellent sampling of American Catholic philosophers.[1,11,23,29,34]

Two of the most outstanding representatives of Thomism in America are A. C. Pegis and Yves Simon. Pegis, who began his teaching career at Marquette University and is now President of the Institute of Mediaeval Studies at Toronto, is one of the leading disciples of Gilson and is particularly noted for his research in mediaeval philosophy.[23] He discerns in the history of philosophy the unfolding of philosophy itself and, ultimately, a vindication of philosophical truth. As Dr. Beatrice Zedler puts it, Pegis is not a Thomist in the sense that he started with the position of Aquinas and made of the history of philosophy a series of examples to verify his convictions. "Rather, taking history as his point of departure, he has seen justified those ideas with which we associate the name of Saint Thomas.[37] Pegis' "Dilemma of Being and Unity" is perhaps his deepest, and "The Mind of Saint Augustine" is perhaps his most literary study. His editions of the *Basic Writings of Saint Thomas* and *The Wisdom of Catholicism* have brought Catholic thought to many who might never have become acquainted with it.

Yves Simon was born in France. He came to the U.S.A. in 1938, and has taught at Notre Dame and at the University of Chicago since 1948. Deeply influenced by Maritain, he has endeavored to extend the frontiers of Thomism by exploring new regions in theoretical and practical philosophy. His principal works, *Ontologie du connaître, Trois leçons sur le travail, Critique de la connaissance morale, March to Liberation, The Nature and Functions* of *Authority, Prévoir et savoir,* show the range of his interests. Endowed with remarkable powers of exposition, Simon is able to present with equal deftness penetrating metaphysical analyses and realistic evaluations of practical problems. In his recent work, *Community of the Free,* he describes the secret sources of racist ideology and makes a notable contribution to the theory of democracy. But he has not stopped with analyzing moral problems. He has also committed himself to action in the practical order, for he believes that it is the duty of the scholar to do what he can, as man and as thinker, to help solve the burning questions of our time.

To Pegis, the convert, and Simon, a native of France, may be added M. J. Adler of Chicago University, who is neither a Catholic nor, strictly, a Thomist, as an outstanding disciple of Saint Thomas in America. Criticized by Thomists for being too Aristotelian, criticized by other philosophers who find it hard to forgive his adherence to Saint Thomas on grounds of reason alone, Adler has often waged a lonely battle for his convictions. Influenced by Aristotle, Saint Thomas and Maritain, he has made important contributions to the cause of American as well as of Thomist philosophy,[1,3]

V

It is too early to appraise the significance of Thomism in the U.S.A. Despite some laudable efforts, Thomism still remains outside the main currents of philosophical thinking in this country. To some extent, this is unavoidable, for Catholic scholars have had to turn to Europe in order to get into contact with their intellectual traditions. In future years, however, the prospects for Thomism may well be greater in this country than in Europe. Such is the opinion of Yves Simon. But he believes that unless Thomism measures up to its opportunities, it will collapse as a movement of contemporary import. It should develop, he thinks, various secondary centers of organization within the metaphysics of being, such as a metaphysics of knowledge, of love, of consciousness, of life. If this were done, the basic doctrines of Thomistic philosophy would be seen with fresh awareness; if this were done in our country, American philosophers, often more interested in these secondary areas, might be drawn to the central area of the metaphysics of existence itself.

Maritain has pointed out the necessity for young Thomists to enter not only the various fields of philosophy but also fields closely related to it and to become competent in them. Looked at from the vantage-point of Thomism, these fields would be seen in a perspective no other doctrine affords. (The exposition of Freudianism by Dalbiez is an excellent case in point.) It may be added that American Thomists should do more extensive research in the areas of psychology, symbolic logic and semantics, and in the critical study of American philosophies, especially pragmatism.

No one man, perhaps, would be able to accomplish the many-sided and complex work confronting Thomists today in their aim of unifying philosophical and scientific knowledge. The state of the sciences is so far developed beyond anything the thirteenth century knew that it may be conjectured that the grand synthesis will be the achievement of a body of trained investigators, led by men of commanding vision, who would co-ordinate their results. To some extent this is already being done, and there is no doubt the work will continue.

What would the mission of a future Thomas Aquinas be? There are some critics of Thomism who say its habit of literal interpretation of the text of Thomas is so narrowing that there is no room within it for a man of intellectual stature equal to that of Aquinas himself. The answer is that if another Aquinas ever did appear, and was truly catholic, he would work, no doubt, *within* the wisdom of Saint Thomas as the latter worked within the wisdom of Saint Augustine. He would differentiate, without dividing, philosophy and theology even more fully than the author of the *Summa Theologiae* who gave philosophy more autonomy than did the "eminently theological and virtually philosophical" Father of the Church, Augustine. A new Thomas, (perhaps a layman well trained in theology as well as in philosophy), would not be the great theologian of the twentieth or twenty-first century—for that is another, and a greater, vocation—but pre-eminently the Christian philosopher. Another Aquinas would relive Aquinas' ultimate reason for greatness; he would be another Aquinas because he would not simply follow the Common Doctor but would tread with him the path to reality itself.

In the meantime, the collective enterprise of contemporary Thomism will continue, and if it measures up to its responsibilities and opportunities, will be significant and vital. We stand in need of more men of high professional competence. We need a Catholic William James or a philosophical Merton in this country. We need men who can speak the language of American philosophy and utter in our tongue the freshness and contemporaneousness of the man who was very much of his own time and who offers very much for ours and who will be, when our concerns are outmoded, still alive and perennial.

NOTES AND BIBLIOGRAPHY

(Note: The principal works of Maritain and Gilson are listed in the chapter. The items included here are either of immediate utility to students or were directly used for this study.)

1. M. J. Adler, *Saint Thomas and the Gentiles* (Milwaukee, 1938).
2. V. J. Bourke, *A Thomistic Bibliography,* 1920-1940 (Saint Louis, 1945).
3. R. E. Brennan, ed., *Essays in Thomism* (New York, 1942).
4. *Catholic Encyclopedia.* See articles on Scholasticism, Neo-Scholasticism and Thomism by W. Turner, M. De Wulf and D. Kennedy.
5. J. Collins, "For Self-Examination of Neo-Scholastics," *The Modern Schoolman* (Saint Louis University), XXI (May, 1944).
6. "Esistenizialismo," *Acta Pont. Academiae Romanae S. Thomae* (Rome, 1947). (Symposium on Existentialism by Maritain, Gilson, etc.)
7. R. Garrigou-Lagrange, "La puissance d'assimilation du thomisme," *Revue thomiste,* XXII (1939).
8. R. Garrigou-Lagrange, "Thomisme," *Dictionnaire de théologie catholique,* tome XV (book length study).
9. Bro. Gerardus, "Jacques Maritain, Doctus Angelico," *Journal of Arts and Letters,* I, nos. 1-3 (1949).
10. E. Gilson, *Le thomisme,* (5th ed., Paris, 1944). *The Philosophy of Saint Thomas Aquinas,* trans. of 3rd ed. (Saint Louis, 1937).
11. E. Gilson, *History of Philosophy and Philosophical Education* (Milwaukee, 1947).
12. *Etienne Gilson—Philosophe de la Chrétienté* (Paris, 1949). (See for Gilson bibliography and studies on his philosophy.)
13. C. A. Hart, ed., *Aspects of the New Scholastic Philosophy* (New York, 1932).
14. R. J. Henle, "Professor Northrop's Idea of Thomism," *The Modern Schoolman,* XXIV (Jan., 1947). *See ibid* (May, 1947) for discussion of Wild's views.
15. E. Hugon, *Les vingt-quatre thèses thomistes* (Paris, 1926). (Explanation of the 24 basic theses of Saint Thomas' philosophy.)

16. J. Maritain, *Saint Thomas Aquinas* (London, 1933).
17. J. Maritain, personal credo in *I Believe,* ed. by C. Fadiman (New York, 1939).
18. J. Maritain and W. Sheldon on philosophical co-operation and intellectual justice in *Modern Schoolman,* XXI and XXII (1944-1945).
19. *Jacques Maritain: son oeuvre philosophique, Revue thomiste,* XLVIII (Paris, 1949). (See for Maritain bibliography and studies on his philosophy.)
20. *The Maritain Volume of the Thomist* (New York, 1943). (See for Maritain Bibliography, 1910-1942 and studies on his philosophy.)
21. R. Maritain, *We Have Been Friends Together,* and *Adventures in Grace* (New York, 1942 and 1945).
22. "Neo-Scholasticism—a World View," *The Modern Schoolman,* X (May, 1933). (Symposium by leading Scholastics in Europe and America.)
23. A. C. Pegis, *Saint Thomas and the Greeks* (Milwaukee, 1939).
24. ———, "Gilson and Thomism," *Thought,* XXI (1946).
25. G. B. Phelan, "Verum sequitur esse rerum," *Mediaeval Studies,* I (1939).
26. ———, *Jacques Maritain* (New York, 1937).
27. R. Phillips, *Modern Thomistic Philosophy* (London, 1934). (Good introduction for students.)
28. *Proceedings of the American Catholic Philosophical Association,* see volumes XX, XXI, XXIII, on Democracy, Philosophy of Being, Finality (1945-49).
29. L. M. Regis, *Saint Thomas and Epistemology* (Milwaukee, 1946).
30. O. Robles, *The Main Problems of Philosophy* (Milwaukee, 1946).
31. P. Rousselot, *The Intellectualism of Saint Thomas* (London, 1935).
32. J. H. Ryan, "The New Scholasticism and its Contribution to Modern Thought," ed. by D. S. Robinson, *Anthology of Recent Philosophy* (New York, 1929).
33. A. D. Sertillanges, *Foundations of Thomistic Philosophy* (Saint Louis, 1931). (*Vd.* his two vol. La philosophie de S. Thomas d'Aquin.)
34. Y. R. Simon, *The Nature and Functions of Authority* (Milwaukee, 1940).
35. W. Walton, "Aquinas," *Collier's Encyclopedia.* (Excellent brief article.)
36. J. S. Zybura, ed., *Present-day Thinkers and the New Scholasticism* (Saint Louis, 1927).
37. B. Zedler, "Anton Pegis," *The Thinker's Digest,* (Summer, 1943).

CHAPTER THIRTY-SEVEN
LOGICAL POSITIVISM

GUSTAV BERGMANN

LOGICAL POSITIVISM is a movement rather than a school, in the sense that those to whom the label is currently applied represent a broad range of interests and, on questions of common interest, often disagree with respect to what constitutes the right answer or about the proper method to arrive at it. Thus a systematic and critical account, preceded by a minimum of historical remarks, becomes preferable to a simple narrative. In the case of a far-flung, complex, and still very active movement, a report of this kind must to some extent reflect the opinions of the reporter; in a sense, it is merely a proposal as to what body of doctrine may reasonably be called Logical Positivism.

The difficulties one encounters in isolating a sufficiently comprehensive core of sufficiently detailed agreement are not unrelated to the circumstance that the writers who are, in fact, called Logical Positivists derive intellectually and, in most cases, also biographically from one of two centers, the Cambridge School of Analysis and the Vienna Circle. One might even say, though not without qualification, that what has come to be called Logical Positivism—the term appeared for the first time in 1930—is the result of the interaction that took place between the two centers during a formative period of not much more than ten years, which, broadly speaking, coincides with the third decade of the century.[1] The qualification needed is this. As things now stand, most Continental positivists (though many of them now live and teach in the United States, I shall, for convenience, call them so) seem to have entered upon a retrogressive development away from epistemological analysis and toward a more or less naive realism. Logical Positivism, though enriched by the Continentals' continuing contributions to fields of their original interest (mathematical logic and the philosophy of science), thus appears today as the contemporary form of British empiricism.

All this is not to deny that *as long as one sticks to cautious generalities* all Logical Positivists could still agree that they (a) hold Humean views on causality and induction; (b) insist on the tautological nature of logical and mathematical truths; (c) conceive of philosophy as logical analysis, *i.e.*, as a clarification of the language which we all speak in everyday life; and (d) that such analysis leads to the "rejection of metaphysics" in the sense that, *e.g.*, the points at dispute among the *traditional* forms of idealism, realism, and phenomenalism could not even be stated, or, at least not be stated in their original intent, in a properly clarified language. Meager as such diplomatic formulae appear beside a large and often controversial literature, it is worth noticing that these four points can all be found in the *Tractatus*; two of them, (b) and (d), state, no matter how inadequately, Wittgenstein's decisive contribution, the "new turn" by which Logical Positivism distinguishes itself from the earlier empiricist philosophies which could not account for the peculiar truth claim of logic and mathematics and hovered uneasily between Humean scepticism and the traditional ontological positions. This new turn makes Wittgenstein, in the eyes of many, the dominant figure of the movement. Be that as it may, there is no doubt that the formative period of interaction began when both Cambridge and Vienna fell under the spell of the *Tractatus*. But Wittgenstein himself had already been in England and come into contact with G. E. Moore and Betrand Russell. This brings us back to the differences between the two centers.

What happened at Cambridge [2] was the second phase of a revolution that had begun at the turn of the century. The first phase, led by G. E. Moore, had already replaced the "speculative" and "metaphysical" temper of British Hegelianism by an atmosphere of literal-minded "analysis" and cautious "empiricism." To be sure, Moore has always been a realist; nor did he ever accept the Humean denial of intuited connections between simple characters (which is probably one of the reasons why British positivists still strangely consider such truths as, say, the transitivity of temporal succession or the mutual exclusiveness of colors as analytic). Yet Moore's insistence that the task of philosophy is not either to prove or to disprove common sense but merely to make clear what it is that we know and how we know it when we assert such propositions as "tables are real" or "lions exist"—this insistence lies half-way between the old "metaphysics" and the "antimetaphysical" turn of the new. This continuity had important effects on the British positivists, many of whom are students of Moore. (The flavor of his incomparable style still lingers in their writings.) It led some of them to embrace a phenomenalism not unlike, in spite of Humean and Wittgensteinian overtones, the neutral monism of William James. Thus they are disturbed by the notion of unsensed sensa, whose paradoxical air they cannot resolve by the casuistic analysis of ordinary usage to which, under the influence of Moore, they tend to limit themselves. Others, combining Moore's technique with the Wittgensteinian contention that philosophers always attempt to say the unsayable, have taken to practicing some sort of grammatical psychotherapy. Thus, perhaps not all the effects of the British continuity are desirable. Yet it is probably this continuity that saved virtually all British positivists from the implicit materialism (physicalism [3]) which in Vienna led to the proclamation that philosophy was coextensive with the methodology of the special sciences, *i.e.*, that the meaningful core of *all* philosophical questions could be *completely* recovered through what has since become known as the operational analysis [4] of the special sciences in terms of physical objects and some of their immediately observable properties and relations. This "scientistic" radicalism of Vienna (which Schlick, the personal center of the group, never shared) had its causes. To simplify for the sake of suggesting a pattern, Vienna tried to achieve in one step what in England had been accomplished in two. For, with the exception of some relatively isolated figures, the heavy hand of Kantianism and Hegelianism still lay over German academic philosophy, particularly in the Protestant North; empiricism, ever since the *Materialismusstreit* and the days of the great Helmholtz, has found its best refuge, such as it was, among the method-conscious and mathematically inclined scientists. Thus one understands why the members of the Circle (and their associates in Berlin and Prague) drew most of their inspiration from the development of axiomatics (Hilbert), the anti-Kantian implications of relativity (Einstein), Poincaré's conventionalism, the rising American school of behaviorism in psychology and the social sciences, and most important, from *Principia Mathematica*.[5] Nor is it surprising that the break occurred in the

Catholic South, never quite conquered by idealism, where Husserl (whose antipsychologism in logic and whose conception of philosophy as descriptive are relevant antecedents), Meinong (who stimulated Russell), and other students of Brentano cultivated logic and their own peculiar brand of Aristotelian "empiricism." Even Mach, whose phenomenalism was, except for Wittgenstein and Russell, the strongest single philosophical influence, owed much to this atmosphere in which he lived and taught.

Turning to a more systematic treatment, I explain first in what sense Logical Positivism is an empiricist philosophy and why it considers the analysis of language its principal tool. Consider the account a traveller ordinarily gives of a geographical region or an experimentalist's description of his apparatus. If one does not mind the trouble, one can, at least in a schematic manner or, as one also says, in principle, transcribe such an account so that (1) the transcript contains, besides grammatical particles, only a small number of "undefined" terms, also called undefined descriptive constants, and (2) everybody who understands these terms and the "grammar" of the language knows, after reading the transcript, what he would know had he read the original account. If given the "definitions" of the terms that occur only in the original, such a person could even reconstruct the latter. If one says 'simple ideas' instead of 'undefined terms,' one sees that, broadly speaking, this is but a linguistic version of Locke's basic vision, provided one extends—as one must, if the thing is to be philosophically significant—the claim for the possibility of such a linguistic "reconstruction" to the whole of our experience. But everything still depends on the choice of the undefined terms! To be an empiricist means to adopt an "empiricist meaning criterion" or "principle of acquaintance," *i.e.*, to assert the sufficiency of a class of undefined terms that refer to the sort of thing philosophers call the phenomenally given in contradistinction to, say, physical objects. Logical Positivists are empiricists in this sense; and they also hold that the grammatical schema of *PM* is adequate for the purpose, which implies that all undefined descriptive constants (with whose referents we must be acquainted) are either proper names or predicates. (Again, this latter thesis, Russell's "logical atomism," commits one to a Humean view on causality and induction, a frequency theory of probability and, as will be seen, a syntactical interpretation of the modalities.) On the other hand, empiricists need not restrict their basis, as Hume did without appreciating the need for both proper names and predicates, to (the names of) nonrelational sense data; leaving aside the niceties of precise formulation, all Logical Positivists would probably admit the necessity of including some relational predicates, *e.g.*, some spatial and temporal ones, among the undefined terms. (The new logic's emphasis on relations as well as Mach's and Meinong's preoccupation with the introspective irreducibility of some relational characters are here relevant antecedents.) Nor does an analysis that penetrates "down" to those very simple and, alas, very fragile givennesses philosophers call sense data have any particular virtue in itself. The point is, rather, that one needs it if one wants to answer the questions philosophers have asked about space, time, substance, and change, and also for that *partial* resolution of the realism thesis, which Berkeley anticipated in his theory of physical objects. So I must next say what I mean by the phrase 'resolution of the realism thesis' and why and under what conditions the linguistic turn is essential for this purpose. I shall begin by explaining what is meant by an ideal language. An ideal language must be (1) *complete,* (2) *formally constructed* [6], and (3) it must allow for the *resolution of all philosophical puzzles*.

Our natural languages, English, French, German, etc., are complete in the obvious sense that "everything" can be said in any one of them. The analyst's ideal language is not complete in this literal sense; in fact, it is not at all a language actually to be spoken but merely the blueprint or schema of one, complete only in the sense that it shows, in principle, the structure and systematic arrangement of all areas of our experience. To illustrate what this means, we do not, in designing such a schema, attempt to invent and catalogue names for all discriminable hues, brightnesses, pitches, tastes, etc.; we simply stipulate that a sufficient number of such predicates is to be included among its undefined terms. Similarly, when we retrace in such a schema Berkeley's analysis or, if you please, definition of a physical object, we are content with a reconstruction "in principle," leaving the rest to the scientific study of perception. In an obvious and obviously innocuous sense, the ideal language is thus a fiction. Yet the British Positivists, probably under the influence of Moore's close adherence to idiomatic English and his suspicion of all systematizing, tend on the whole to reject it as unjustifiably speculative and, therefore, but another excrescence of the Teutonic furor. Many differences in formulation, as well as some which are not merely matters of formulation, stem, I believe, from this difference. Be that as it may, the idea, implicit in Russell's writings, was most vigorously taken up by the Continentals. Carnap, in particular, saw clearly that the grammatical schema of *PM*, supplemented with descriptive constants, was a likely candidate for the ideal language. No matter how mistaken otherwise, his book of 1928 [1] remains an impressive attempt at such a reconstruction (*Aufbau, Konstitution*) of the world.

With respect to the last of the three criteria for an ideal language, it turns out that *in* the *PM* language the traditional philosophical assertions cannot be stated, or, to say the same thing differently, that attempts to state them lead to grammatical nonsense. To show by an example how this works, it is sufficient to mention that, depending on their context, the forms of the idiomatic 'to be' appear in at least four different transcriptions corresponding to predication ('John *is* a man'), class inclusion ('a man *is* a mammal'), identity ('the father of John *is* the husband of Mary') and the existential clause ('there *is* an x such that . . . x . . .'). Taken together with the rule that the existential clause joined to a constant yields, not a sentence, but grammatical nonsense, this simple observation is enough to reject what the Viennese called metaphysical realism. However, this "resolution" of a traditional position is, so far, both *partial* and *negative*. To complete it, one must also, positively, identify the structural features of the ideal language that reflect those aspects of our experience on which the realists insisted when they engaged in the traditional dialectic with their idealistic and phenomenalistic opponents. Such a positive feature is, for instance, the occurrence of the all-clause and the existential clause in the grammatical apparatus, which, together with the undefined temporal relations of the specious present, permits a treatment of the past, the future and, generally, "the unperceived," which is free from the echoes of "metaphysical" phenomenalism. This, of course, merely illustrates what must be done with respect to the realism issue, just as this issue itself, though historically rather central, serves merely to illustrate what must and can be done, negatively and, since they all have a common sense core, positively for all philosophical positions or, as the Mooreans would rather have it, puzzles.

This raises the question how the claim of everything being expressible *in* the ideal language can be reconciled with a method of philosophizing by means of statements *about* it. One way out of this difficulty is to assert, with Wittgenstein, (1) that all "statements of empirical fact," *i.e.*, nontautological statements which fulfill our meaning criterion, can be transcribed into the ideal language, and (2) that even our own philosophy, strictly speaking, cannot be stated, that it merely "shows itself," so that the reader of this essay, for instance, insofar as it is not purely historical, must "throw away the ladder after he has climbed up on it." It is important to distinguish the principle involved in (2) from the question of a sufficiently broad conception of "empirical fact." The facts of awareness, for instance, and of moral and ethical experience were either ignored by most Logical Positivists—in this they followed James Mill, who taught that to be aware of something and to be aware of this awareness is one and the same thing; or they reconstructed them only partially, from without, as it were, within the framework of behavioristic science, thus rashly denying the status of empirical facts to the phenomenal givennesses involved. To remedy such shortcomings which, as will be seen, can be done, is one thing; to face the principle involved in (2) is another. Now there is one thing, I believe, that can be done, not to avoid eventual withdrawal into Wittgensteinian silence, since at some time talk must come to an end, but at least to postpone it as long as something can perhaps still be said. This solution hinges on the second criterion, which requires that the ideal language be constructed formally. First, all one does in so constructing it is to lay down rules about geometrical designs; thus one stays safely in the realm of the speakable. (The mathematical niceties involved need not concern us.) Second, by constructing a pattern, without any explicit reference to its use, that can, in fact, serve as the ideal language, one makes sure that in exhibiting its structure one exhibits the basic structure of the world. If at this point I am told that this answer makes that basic strucure itself "merely a matter of fact," I should counter that in so broad a sense everything is a fact and that my critic has, therefore, not said anything. If I am told that ultimately I must rely upon the significance of this geometrical treatment of language "to show itself," I would not argue.

I turn now to the discussion of two "metaphysical" tendencies, the one toward *logical constructionism,* the other toward *logical structuralism,* which Logical Positivists have not always avoided.

One who says that all "there is" are sense data and that a physical object, say, *e.g.,* a chair is a "construction" out of sense data, is, obviously, a traditional phenomenalist rather than a Logical Positivist. Yet some Logical Positivists, probably under the influence of Russell, come dangerously close to saying this. Thus it may pay to dispel the illusion. Since what one asserts in denying that chairs are constructions is usually expressed by 'chairs exist,' this can be done by analyzing the latter statement. The point, then, is that the transcription of this statement into the ideal language reads, roughly, 'there is something such that this something is a chair.' A little more accurately, in a sense data analysis this transcription contains, not one, but very many existential clauses; and the relational predicate, 'chair,' whose referent these clauses assert to be exemplified, has a very complicated definition. However, this definition, though it contains existential clauses, does not involve "existence" in the sense of the argument between constructionists and realists. After all, no definition does. All one can say about a definition is, first, that it is grammatically correct and second, that it stays, like our Berkeleyan definition of 'chair,' within the limits of the principle of acquaintance. On the other hand, the existential clause could not conceivably apply, either falsely or truly, to such a predicate as 'chair,' since to apply it to a constant, whether defined or undefined, whether proper name or predicate, yields, not a sentence, but grammatical nonsense. All one can say is that correctly defined predicates are or are not "exemplified"; in this sense there is, of course, no reasonable doubt that chairs "exist." What goes for chairs and mermaids, who do not happen to "exist," goes also for densities, forces and all the other "abstract entities" of science. The old poser, whether they are "fictitious" or "real," simply never arises. (This is not to say that there are not certain questions as to how the entities of a scientific model theory, such as electrons, are to be accounted for. But then, this is a very technical matter within the philosophy (logical analysis) of science and, as such, devoid of properly philosophical import. All basic philosophical questions can be argued in terms of chairs and mermaids. Who believes otherwise is a victim of that unfortunate scientism so strong among most Continental Positivists.)

A HISTORY OF PHILOSOPHICAL SYSTEMS

The axioms of, say, Euclidean geometry are sometimes called the "implicit definitions" of the descriptive constants ('point,' 'straight line,' 'coincide,' etc.) that occur in them. This means that somebody unfamiliar with points, lines, their coincidence, etc., or with any other empirical interpretation of the axiomatic system, may yet be said to be familiar with all of them in the sense that (1) he could, within the limits of inductive uncertainty, recognize one, and (2) he can derive, or check the derivation, of any geometrical theorem. The gist of logical structuralism is the extension of this idea to the whole of our experience. Its hope is to provide grounds for the view that while "the quale of our experience is subjective, private, ineffable, its form or structure is objective, public, communicable." The naivete of this short-cut to avoid the classical problems is patent. The main document of structuralism in the positivistic literature is Carnap's *Aufbau*.[1] Historically, structuralism echoes the old dichotomy of content and form and, from recent sources, Schlick's distinction between *Erkennen* and *Erleben*, and, also, Russell's between knowledge by acquaintance and by description. (For a consistent Logical Positivist there is, of course, no such thing as knowledge by description, in the sense that nothing needs to be added to what has been said about chairs, mermaids, and forces.) The intent of all this, particularly with Carnap and Russell, is quite clearly realistic. However, when structuralists insist that the "meaning" of an undefined predicate, say 'green,' not exhausted by the ineffable quale, comprehends the laws of color, they fall, no matter how unconsciously, into the idealist-pragmatist thought pattern. Insistence on the self-containedness of the given is the very foundation of all nonidealistic philosophy, positivist and realist alike.

With respect to the problem of tautological (analytical) truths (logic and arithmetic), which occupies a very prominent place in the literature, I can here only say that it is *possible* to characterize their transcriptions into the ideal language formally [6]—at least, this is the basic idea, whatever technical modifications it may have to undergo in the hands of the mathematical logicians. This *distinguishes* them from so-called statements of empirical fact, for which the formalist can only certify grammatical correctness. From the viewpoint here taken, the clarification of what we mean when we say that certain propositions express necessary or nonfactual truths

479

consists in pointing at this possibility and this distinction. But it is readily seen that this answer does not appeal to the nontechnical, casuistic, and often psychologizing temper of the British Positivists. Thus some of them, impressed by the arbitrariness of definitions *within* a language and by the importance of recognizing statements not ordinarily so recognized as definitions or conventions, have tended to speak of necessary truth as truth by definition or convention. This is not only inadequate in itself; it also blurs—as in the aforementioned case of the transitivity of temporal succession—the distinction between analytical truth (logical form) and the incidental grammatical form of idiomatic speech.

In ethics and aesthetics all Logical Positivists are, in a nontechnical sense of the term, relativists. Most Continentals are of the opinion that everything one can say on these subjects belongs, in principle, to the social sciences. The British, though more traditional in tone, follow by and large the same line. Sometimes these views are argued by means of a distinction between "cognitive" and "noncognitive," which is both irrelevant and spurious, since our givennesses do not come with these labels and since, as James observed, they are, in an obvious sense, all cognitive. However, there is no reason why one should not, as the facts seem to warrant, admit an undefined predicate with the root meaning of, say, 'good.' In a careful *Aufbau,* which avoids the genetic fallacy,[7] this is certainly compatible with the common sense core of relativism. But apparently most Logical Positivists fear that if they admit such characters are "there," they will also have to admit that something else is "out there," perhaps even in a "non-natural" manner. These fears are the wages of unexamined realistic residues.

With respect to the Self, the British Positivists hold views very similar to those of Hume, James Mill, and William James. Most Continentals, with the typical foreshortening of perspective due to their scientism, are satisfied with that partial clarification of related issues that lies in a correct statement of behaviorism. Some others cling to the so-called double aspect theory, which is merely a statement of (scientific) common sense, not its analytical clarification. Recently, however, an attempt [8] has been made to include in the ideal language an undefined predicate of immediate awareness. This has three consequences. First, it does justice to the phenomena which provide the ground for the "act" philosophies of Descartes,

Locke, Brentano, and Moore. Second, one needs it to dispel completely the apparent phenomenalistic implications of a consistent empiricism. Third, in completing the ideal language, it strives, in its own way, toward the ideal of that "complete" description of the world which is, and always will be, the business of *philosophia prima et perennis*. But this, to be sure, is a far cry from the iconoclasm of the early Positivists.

NOTES AND BIBLIOGRAPHY

1. The beginning of this period is marked by the appearance, in both English and German, of Ludwig Wittgenstein's *Tractatus Logico-Philosophicus* (London, 1922); its peak by Rudolf Carnap's *Der Logische Aufbau der Welt* (Berlin, 1928), the work in which the author comes closest to the classical empiricist tradition; its end by Carnap's *The Logical Syntax of Language* (German: Vienna, 1934; English: New York, 1937) and Moritz Schlick's *Gesammelte Aufsaetze* 1926-1936 (Vienna, 1938), which show him under the influence, not to say fascination, of Wittgenstein. Much of the later writings of the Continental group is contained in the eight volumes of the journal *Erkenntnis* (1930-39).

2. Most of the work of this group is to be found in the main English journals. A. J. Ayer's *Language, Truth and Logic* (London, 1936) and *The Foundations of Empirical Knowledge* (London, 1940) have almost the status of textbooks.

3. The prime mover behind this tendency was Otto Neurath, an important member of the Circle whose manifold activities and encyclopedic, if not always profound, interests defy classification. The programmatic pamphlet, *Wissenschafliche Weltauffassung: Der Wiener Kreis* (Vienna, 1929) owes its existence to his initiative, social actionism, and reformist zeal.

4. To understand why 'operational' is sometimes used in such phrases as 'operational analysis' and 'operational definition,' consider the definition of, say, length in terms of the laying-off of a yardstick. It is a so-called definition in use, *i.e.*, roughly, what it gives a synonym for, in terms already understood, is not 'length,' but the simplest kind of sentence in which 'length' occurs; the synonym given is a compound sentence describing the operations performed and the result obtained in ascertaining the length of an object. However, this does not mean that length is a product of, or in any other sense dependent on, these operations. To say anything of the sort is to take an instrumentalist position. Generally instrumentalism, which is essentially an idealistic metaphysics, and logical positivism, which stands in the tradition of British empiricism, are irreconcilable opposites. Attempts to engineer a

rapprochement, made when the Continentals first came to America, were thus bound to fail.

5. B. Russell and A. N. Whitehead, *Principia Mathematica,* 3 vols. (Cambridge, 1910-13, 2nd ed., 1925-27), frequently quoted as *PM.* During the first phase of the British development Russell's logical analyses parallel Moore's work. His influence on the Continental Positivists is second only to Wittgenstein's. Russell himself, deeply committed to realism, has never accepted the positivistic turn, which he did so much to bring about. Yet he says, in *An Inquiry into Meaning and Truth* (New York, 1940), that he is "as regards method, more in sympathy with the logical positivists than with any other existing school."

6. Such a construction, also called syntactical, makes no reference whatsoever to the prospective use of the language or the "meaning" of its terms. Its first step (in the case of a written language) consists in choosing classes of geometrical shapes which are to serve as the *signs* or symbols of the language. In the second step one lays down the rules by which certain finite series of signs are singled out as *sentences.* Every other string of signs corresponds to what I have, in the text, called grammatical nonsense. Logic in the narrower sense is further interested in formally characterizing that subclass of the class of all sentences which corresponds to what we mean by tautological (analytic) truth.

7. To explain this phrase, assume, for the sake of the argument, a scientific theory of the psychoanalytic type to be true. On what occasions we feel, say, moral disapproval depends causally, according to such a theory, on what other occasions in our early childhood we experienced or anticipated pleasure or pain. But this does not mean that what we now experience when we morally disapprove of something is either pleasure or pain, or their anticipation, or perhaps their memory. Who neglects this distinction commits the genetic fallacy.

8. G. Bergmann, "A Positivistic Metaphysics of Consciousness," *Mind,* 54 (1945), and "Professor Ayer's Analysis of Knowing," *Analysis,* 9 (1949).

CHAPTER THIRTY-EIGHT
SEMANTICS

GUSTAV BERGMANN

SEMANTICS is not a philosophical system; nor is there any group of philosophers or any philosophical movement whose work is semantical in a technical sense that requires a technical term. Thus one cannot speak of a philosophical semanticist or a semantical philosophy as one speaks, say, of a philosophical realist or an idealistic philosophy. Yet the opposite impression has been created by the frequency with which some philosophers as well as some students of other fields, traditionally and on historical grounds considered closely allied with technical philosophy, now use 'semantics' and 'semantical'. Perhaps this justifies a brief account of the different things different writers mean by these terms. It is well to realize, though, that if it is to be of any use to philosophers, such an account must state its own philosophical presuppositions. The standpoint here taken is that of Logical Positivism.[1] The bias this introduces is in practice much less pronounced than one might fear on principle. For many of the "semanticists" who have an explicit philosophical position are either Logical Positivists or rather close to Logical Positivism. Those who are not share at least some traits of the positivistic temper. Their inclination is analytical rather than speculative; and they have a high regard for the significance, or potential significance, of behavior science on the one hand and of mathematical logic on the other.

The word 'semantics,' derived from a Greek root signifying *sign,* has come to be used for certain studies of *language.*[2] Derivatively, studies that use the results of such investigations as *tools* for their own purposes are then also called semantical. In this derivative sense a good deal of philosophy has been semantical ever since the Platonic Socrates taught his disciples to speak precisely and to distinguish between the meanings of words. This emphasis on language, common to all analytical philosophy, has been particularly strong in British Empiricism, as anyone who glances through Locke's Essay can see for himself. But it is also true that Logical Positivism, the contemporary form of British Empiricism, attributes to one kind of linguistic study—the one which has been called *formal* [1]—a tool position of such centrality and excellence as has never been claimed before. However, Logical Positivism is not in any other sense a philosophy of language or a linguistic philosophy. What now sometimes goes by these names is a systematically impure mixture of anthropology, psychology, criticism, and philosophy proper.

The historian of philosophy is probably justified in connecting the linguistic turn of Logical Positivism with the rise of modern or mathematical logic, which began around the middle of the last century. From the viewpoint of the general historian of ideas this development is but part of a larger pattern. Our civilization as a whole has, during this century, become increasingly language-conscious. Since I cannot spend much space on speculating about the broader social dynamisms which produced this result, I shall content myself with the hint that this language-consciousness of ours grew simultaneously with our ideology-consciousness. Whatever the social forces involved, the intellectual sources of this growth were, systematically speaking, scientific rather than philosophical or logico-mathematical. The central phenomenon there is the development of the social or, as I shall call them, behavior sciences which, modest as their present achievements are if compared with physics or even biology, have yet during this period reached a level that makes the idea of a real science of man something more than a utopia. The scientific study of linguistic behavior, that is, its adequate description and the search for its causes and effects in and on the group and the individual belongs to behavior science. It occupies by now a strategic position in psychology, anthropology, sociology, and, also, in such intellectual pursuits as literary criticism, to which these traditional divisions of behavior science are of auxiliary service. Semantics, in one sense of the term, is this science of language or, perhaps better, linguistic behavior. To avoid confusion I shall, in this sense, always speak of *scientific semantics*. (In view of the fundamental position of psychology among the traditional divisions of behavior science 'psychological semantics' would also be a good name.)

All Logical Positivists and virtually all scientific semanticists are behaviorists. The behaviorist insists that all the technical terms of his field are defined in terms that refer to what he himself, the scientist, immediately observes. To understand this, imagine a laboratory situation in which a subject S is, as one usually says, expected to discriminate between two shades of green. In describing this situation the behaviorist may, without further elaboration, say that *he* sees two different shades of green. But when he says, on the basis of what he observes, 'S *sees* two different shades of green,' then he considers 'sees' as a technical term and, very roughly speaking, the whole sentence as the left side of its definition; the right side consisting of a statement of what he, the scientist, has observed.[3] The same procedure is followed in the case of "linguistic" behavior. Words spoken or written by his subjects are, to begin with, for the behaviorist just physical events. It is his business to define the conditions under which a noise or a gesture becomes a "word" or "sign"; what he means by saying that his subject "understands" a "language," that some "sentences" of this language "designate," and therefore "inform" his subjects about their physical environment, while others merely "express" or "direct" their "attitudes." To say the same thing differently, the words in this paragraph around which I put double quotes are all technical terms of behavior science. Or one could also say that the behavior scientist and his subjects do not, in principle, speak the same language.

No argument is needed to show that the actual resources of a behavior science thus strictly conceived are as yet very limited and, for all we know, may always remain so. Certainly it would be foolish to reject, for *practical* purposes, less reliable knowledge which we possess about human behavior (though behaviorists in this case prefer to speak of prescientific insight). To admit this is one thing. To agree, as virtually all scientific semanticists do, that behavior science can, *in principle,* be behavioristically construed and, for all purposes of *methodological* analysis, must be so construed, is another thing. Yet this agreement has at least two far-reaching consequences. Assume, first, for the sake of the argument, that a scientific semanticist has succeeded in distinguishing between "factual" or "cognitive" sentences which "designate" *matters of fact* and others, called "nonfactual" or "noncognitive" because they do not so "refer." It will be noticed that the phrase 'matters of fact,' which I have italicized but not put between double quotes, belongs to the scientist's own language. His achievement presupposes, therefore, that he already knows what *he* means by matters of fact and is thus, rather obviously, completely irrelevant for what is meant by a philosophical analysis of this, philosophically speaking, very difficult phrase.[4] What has been shown in this case could be shown in all others. I conclude that scientific semantics has no direct philosophical import or significance whatsoever. The mistaken belief that this is not so can probably be traced to the interest Deweyan pragmatists (instrumentalists) have taken and still take in scientific semantics. For the tendency to substitute scientific (causal and genetic) for philosophical analysis and, even worse, to mistake the former for the latter is one of the hallmarks of instrumentalism.

Consider, second, the definitions which "semanticists" who are not themselves practicing scientists but "philosophical" writers[5] offer for the technical terms of scientific semantics. It is often said, *e.g.*, that A is a "sign" of B if it promotes behavior that B would promote but that is not appropriate to A alone. Plausible as this sounds, it must not be taken too seriously. Or is the behavior promoted in me by 'murder' really always of the kind I would display when I witnessed murder? Generally, the very difficult job of framing adequate definitions for the terms of scientific semantics (and of finding the laws in which they occur) is better left to the practicing behavior scientist. For, if the principle of the thing has once been established, it is hard to see what value there is in anticipatory armchair science. All one does if one does this sort of thing is restate, sometimes rather pretentiously, common sense.

The *formal* study of language consists in the construction of artificial sign systems; as I explained in introducing the notion of the ideal language[1] such an artificial or formal language, also called *calculus,* is really but the grammatical schema or skeleton of a language and one must not in constructing it have explicit reference to anything but the shapes and arrangement of the signs themselves.[6] 'Formal semantics' would be a good name for this discipline; as it happens it is most commonly known as *logical syntax.* Formal, pure, or, if you please, philosophical semantics is a branch of logical syntax. To explain what it deals with some preparatory remarks are needed.

A sign, its name, and what it is the name of are three different things. Commonsensical as it is, the distinction is fundamental and of far-reaching import. In idiomatic speech we neglect it. We say, *e.g.*, 'Paris is the capital of France' as well as 'Paris has five letters,' employing the same sign once as the name of the city, once as the name of this name. Or, as one also says, once we *use* it, once we *mention* it. We would do better if we wrote the second time ' 'Paris' has five letters,' making 'Paris' and ' 'Paris' ' two different words.[7] In ordinary speech our understanding of the context saves us from the confusions which, on principle, must arise if one neglects such precautions. On the other hand, it should be clear that in constructing a calculus to be interpreted as containing these two sentences one must see to it that it contains two different signs; and, generally, that in a calculus an expression must be distinguished from that other expression that one wishes to interpret as its name. To make one obvious point, if we have a formal classification of signs in which the names of individual objects are called particulars while the names of characters are called universals, then the name of a universal is, of course, a particular, and so is the name of any word, expression, or sentence.[8] A related distinction is that between language and *metalanguage*. Just as the behavior scientist does not himself, in principle, use the language of his subjects, so the formalist does not in designing and discussing a calculus himself speak it—whatever it could mean to speak an artificial language. Rather, he speaks about it in, say, English; or, as one also says, English is his (syntactical) metalanguage. A mathematician could, *e.g.*, invent a rule that coordinates to each sentence of a calculus a number depending only on the shapes and the arrangement of its signs; he could then use these numbers, which are of course English words, instead of proper names, as in prisons numbers are used instead of proper names, when he speaks in his English metalanguage about the sentences of the calculus. Such a rule has in fact been invented, for *PM* and related calculi, by the mathematician K. Goedel. Mathematicians, who are not primarily concerned with philosophical accuracy, have been misled by Goedel's rule into saying that calculi containing expressions (number signs) which can be interpreted as numbers contain the names of their own sentences. This is inaccurate for at least three reasons. First, the number signs of the calculus must be distinguished from the (English) numbers which the logician, like the prison warden, uses instead of proper names. Second, in philosophically interesting calculi number signs are never particulars, as they would have to be if they were proper names. Third, and most important, there is no reason whatsoever why a calculus that contains number signs should also contain sentences that could be interpreted as '. . . designates (is the name of) . . .,' where the first blank is filled by a number and the second by the (English) interpretation of a sentence of the calculus.

The prime concern of logical syntax has long been (1) to construct calculi which contain for *every* English sentence (including arithmetical identities) which we consider intuitively as a tautological (analytical) truth [9] a corresponding sentence; and (2) to characterize formally the class of *all* these sentences. It was Goedel who showed, in a justly celebrated paper that appeared in 1931, that if one insists on certain ways of carrying out this characterization the problem (2) is insoluble. His proof makes use of sentences which, *with the inaccuracy pointed out in the last paragraph,* can be interpreted as saying about themselves that they possess a certain syntactical property, that is, to repeat, a property that depends only on the shapes and the arrangement of their signs.

Formal semantics is the syntactical construction of calculi that can be interpreted as containing the word 'true,' some expression of "naming," such as 'designates' as it occurs in ' 'Peter loves Mary' designates Peter loves Mary' and, therefore, also the names of at least some of its expressions, say, *e.g.*, of its sentences. If one succeeds in constructing such a calculus, then one has, upon the positivistic view of philosophical analysis, the proper tool for the resolution or, if you please, reconstruction of the philosophical issues that revolve around truth, designation, and related ideas. Among these notions truth is, no doubt, the one that troubled philosophers most. For a philosophical analysis of truth three points are of primary importance.

1. Since truth is predicated of sentences and since the names of sentences are particulars *in* the calculus, 'true' will be a predicate *in* the calculus that takes particulars as its subjects. 'True,' in a philosophically relevant sense of the term, is, therefore, not a syntactical property of the sentences of a calculus. In other words, the main task of formal semantics is not to "define truth" by finding a formal characterization of all true sentences but, rather, to frame, within

the calculus it constructs, a definition of 'true.' The point needs emphasis because the mathematician Tarski,[10] who in a sense founded the discipline of formal semantics, preoccupied as he was with mathematical rather than with philosophical issues, conceived of truth as a syntactical property. This was particularly unfortunate because philosophers, who did not really understand him, thought Tarski had proved "that the words 'true' and 'false,' as applied to the sentences of a given language, always require another language, of higher order, for their adequate definition." [11] All that can be proved is that if one considers truth as a syntactical property of the sentences of a calculus, then this calculus is either inconsistent or it cannot contain a predicate that could, *with the inaccuracy pointed out in the discussion of Goedel's rule,* be interpreted as 'true.' The proof proceeds, analogously to Goedel's, by constructing, within the calculus, a sentence that may, *with the same inaccuracy,* be interpreted as saying about itself that it is false and which has, therefore, been *mis*taken for a formal reconstruction of the famous Lier paradox ('I am now lying'—If the speaker does not lie, then he lies; if he lies, then he does not lie).

2. One of the reasons why it is philosophically absurd to consider truth as a syntactical property is that one can assert a sentence to be true if and only if one knows (a) what it says or means and (b) whether what it says is the case (which, of course, is a matter of fact, not of words, syntax, or what have you). Philosophers refer to this piece of common sense as the correspondence view of truth. Realists, grounding this view in their peculiar conception of objective fact, sometimes claim that Logical Positivists cannot consistently adopt it. It seems thus desirable to reconstruct formally the common-sense core of the correspondence view. To do this one has to construct a calculus in which, say, the sentence ' 'Peter loves Mary' is true if and only if ('Peter loves Mary' designates Peter loves Mary) and (Peter loves Mary)' and all similar sentences are analytic. In the sentence just mentioned the clause in the first parenthesis corresponds to condition (a) above, the second to condition (b).

3. Since truth is a matter of thought or language and since, in contradistinction to idealistic views, the object of thought is not in any way affected by being thought about, it seems desirable to distinguish truth and designation from such "natural" properties and relationships as, say, greenness and fatherhood. Casting about for a

formal expression of this idea one finds that in calculi similar to PM^{12} one can formally distinguish between so-called *descriptive* signs and expressions on the one hand and so-called *logical* ones on the other. *E.g.,* 'green' and 'is the father of' belong to the first category, 'and,' 'not' and 'transitive' to the second.

It follows that the philosophically most interesting task of formal semantics is solved if one can supplement the schema of *PM* by a logical sign of designation and, in terms of it and in agreement with the condition in 2, define a predicate 'true.' This, it turns out, is not at all difficult.[13]

Though it is not necessary for an adequate definition of truth, one may attempt to refine the formalization of designation so that the calculus also contains sentences that can be interpreted as, say, ' 'Peter' designates Peter' or ' 'green' designates green.' In calculi which do not have a certain property known as extensionality, such attempts meet with difficulties first pointed out by G. Frege as early as 1892. Carnap [14] has recently undertaken a systematic treatment of such questions. Investigations of this kind may be of some formal interest; their philosophical significance is doubtful. If, *e.g.*, one were to explore "what there is" by trying to determine what "entities" can be "named" in a calculus that embodies certain features of the ordinary usage of 'name' and 'naming,' he would, it seems to me, grievously overestimate the philosophical import of this usage. At any rate, I do not see what insight one could gain in this way that could not also be gained by a syntactical study of the (nonlinguistic) part of the ideal language.

It appears, then, that aside from its usefulness for a positivistic statement of the correspondence view and, perhaps, aside from some problems of intrinsic mathematical interest, formal semantics is philosophically not important. The same, it has been seen, holds for scientific semantics, again aside from questions that are of intrinsic scientific interest. I conclude, therefore, that the current rage for "semantics" is but a passing moment in the history of philosophical thought.

NOTES AND BIBLIOGRAPHY

1. Explanations of ideas and terms to be found in the article on Logical Positivism in this volume will not be repeated. Familiarity with that article is assumed.

2. Within philology, which in the broadest sense is also a semantical discipline, 'semantics' is the name for the study of the historical development of the meanings of words.

3. This does not commit us to the opinion that S has no data or that it is "meaningless" to speak of them. Indeed, if our scientist were to say 'If I have two green data and S sees them (in the behavioristic sense of 'seeing'), *then* there are also two similar data (numerically different from mine and perceived by S),' his statement could be shown to satisfy the principle of acquaintance. But the behavioristic approach is desirable in the interest of reliability and objectivity in the ordinary, nonphilosophical sense of these terms. Nor does it impose any limitations on behavior science since all the evidence we can, *in fact*, ever have for what is asserted, in statements like the one just mentioned, by the clause following 'then' is asserted by clauses of the kind that precedes it. Behaviorism, in short, is a methodological not a philosophical position. And, as indicated by the phrase 'in fact,' that I cannot have your data is upon this view not an analytical truth.

4. In other words, language analysis which is philosophically significant must be analysis from the standpoint of the speaker, that is, in the illustration given, of the scientist. Also, as has been shown in the article on Logical Positivism, it proceeds formally, not scientifically.

5. Probably the best-known work in this vein is C. W. Morris, *Signs, Language and Behavior* (New York, 1946), containing a good bibliography of what is by now a voluminous literature. Morris himself was originally a pragmatist.

6. This, as has been seen, is also the condition upon which the actual similarity of such a calculus with our natural language (or, as one also says, its *interpretation*) is philosophically significant.

7. Single quotes are customarily used to mark the distinction. The single quotes after 'making' and the outer pair of such quotes after 'and' are due to the circumstance that the sentence in the text does not use but mention what they surround.

8. This is not quite correct since when we speak of a word we do not ordinarily mean any single one of its occurrences or *tokens*, whose name would be a particular, but all occurrences of a certain *type* (roughly, similar marks on paper, similar noises). The name of a word would then be a universal. However, the simplification I have introduced is harmless.

9. Since 'true' will presently be used precisely, it should be noted that 'true' and 'analytically true' are not technical terms of the syntacticist. All he does is design definitions that reflect formally what is meant intuitively by the latter term.

10. A. Tarski, *Der Wahrheitsbegriff in den formalisierten Sprachen*. (This monograph appeared in Polish in 1933, in German translation in the Polish

journal "Studia Philosophica" in 1936.) R. Carnap's *Introduction to Semantics* (Cambridge, 1942) suffers philosophically from the author's dogmatic realism, technically from the tendency to subsume syntax under semantics.

11. Quoted from B. Russell, *An Inquiry into Meaning and Truth* (New York, 1940), p. 75.

12. The *PM* schema being the only likely candidate for the ideal language, it is not necessary to consider other calculi. Carnap was apparently the first to recognize the philosophical significance of the formal distinction between logical and descriptive expressions.

13. Formally this can be done as follows: 1. *PM* (unramified) is supplemented by descriptive constants and it is stipulated that only closed expressions are sentences. 2. For each sentence there is a particular obtained by surrounding the sentence with single quotes. 3. The sign 'Des' is added with the proviso that all substitution instances of 'x *Des* p' are sentences. 4. All sentences '' . . .' *Des* . . .,' all sentences obtained from these through rewriting of bound variables, and the negations of all other substitution instances of 'x *Des* p' are added to the primitive sentences. 5. '*true* (x)' is defined by '(E p) (x *Des* p . p).' Contexts containing '*Des*' are not extensional.

14. R. Carnap, *Meaning and Necessity* (Chicago, 1947). For an incisive criticism see G. Ryle's review in *Philosophy* (24) (1949), pp. 69–76.

CHAPTER THIRTY-NINE

A BRIEF HISTORY OF GENERAL THEORY OF VALUE

STEPHEN C. PEPPER

THEORY OF value is generally regarded as having its official origin in the debate between Alexius Meinong (1853-1920) and Christian Ehrenfels (1859-1932) during the '90's and the first two decades of the present century. Behind them was the work of Franz Clemens Brentano (1838-1914) and issues over value discussed by economists. Previous to this time there was, of course, a long history of ethical, aesthetic and economic problems of value. Value did not emerge as a new infant problem in the '90's. It had a long past history. What emerged was a notion that there was something common to all these problems which could be gathered into one central problem of value in general. And because this notion emerged in the context of a rather special sort of issue within the sphere of the total subject, general theory of value has never as yet been able to extricate itself entirely from that sort of issue.

The issue greatly simplified was whether the source of all value is to be attributed to desire or to feeling. Ehrenfels espoused the former view, Meinong the latter. Both agreed, however, upon another matter which could have been an even deeper issue—namely, that value had its locus in an object. For both of these writers value was a property of an object. But what endowed the object with value for Ehrenfels was that somebody desired it or could desire it, whereas it was the expectation or possibility of pleasure in an object that instituted value for Meinong. The publicity of value was assumed by both these men, as also its relativity to a subject.

General theory of value thus became associated with naturalistic issues in the tradition of Hobbes, Hume, Bentham, and Mill, not to mention earlier hedonists. The naturalistic side of Spinoza came also into this movement, and he is frequently referred back to as having had particular insight in declaring that things are good because they are desired, not desired because they are good.

At the same time these early men were careful to distinguish their views from simple hedonism. One of the unquestionable merits of the general value theory movement is that it led to a very intensive study of the details involved in hedonistic and conative conceptions of value. For one thing it made this distinction between feeling and desire exceedingly sharp, and at the same time brought out many internal discriminations (as between wishing, striving, desiring), whereas formerly the distinction was vague and largely undiscerned. Once the distinction is made, most of the work of the earlier hedonists appears primitive. J. S. Mill (1806-1873), for instance, switches from pleasure to desire and from desire to desirability with utter unconcern, almost as if they were all synonyms. Mill was just simply unaware of the distinctions that later unfolded as a result of the intensive study forced upon this subject matter by the probing of Meinong and Ehrenfels and of those who followed. Such analytical discriminations and the increasing complexities exhibited in the field of this subject will quite possibly be viewed as the principal contribution of general value theory to philosophy in the first fifty years of its development.

In briefly following this development, it will be possible to name only a few of the men most influential in its course. From the standpoint of American philosophy, W. M. Urban (1873-   ) is of first importance. His book *Valuation, Its Nature and Laws*, published in America in 1909 and written as a result of his studies in Austria where he absorbed the issues of the new subject, did much to plant these issues in American soil. Being of idealistic bent, he stressed particularly the problem of meaning and judgment related to value. Because of the Meinong-Ehrenfels assumption that value was a property of an object arising from a subject's desire or feeling about the object, it was inevitable that some judgment on the part of the subject should be inferred to figure in the value situation. How far, then, is the value of an object dependent on a subject's judgment about it or meanings ascribed to it? In what respect are there value errors? What sort of judgment mediates sound values? Is the mediating judgment also evaluative? How far does a value judgment involve a judgment about the existence of the object? What happens to a valuing judgment if the object of reference of the judgment does not exist spatio-temporally? What happens to the value then? Are subsistent "objectives" distinct from existent objects required to anchor the references of valuing judgments, and to give a locus for values not referred to existent objects—for instance the valuing of a house as yet unbuilt, a utopia, a perpetual motion machine? These are the sort of questions Urban's *Valuation* brought into American philosophy.

I shall not attempt to state Urban's position beyond repeating his pregnant definition of value as "funded affective-volitional meanings." His term "affective-volitional" became a widely accepted term of reference to the whole field of the Meinong-Ehrenfels controversy conveniently avoiding the exclusion of either side, or the necessity of taking sides. And the term "funded," on the metaphor of interest accumulating to capital in a bank, became a fertile term in value theory much exploited by contextualists such as Dewey, particularly in explaining some characteristics of aesthetic value. The main significance of Urban's work lies not so much in his theoretical conclusions, which are admittedly difficult to make clear, as in his introduction to America of the new issues in value theory, mostly undigested as yet because so new. The book is certainly not a typical idealistic or organistic treatment of value, though Urban brought to the issues the added complication of an idealistic attitude.

The typical idealistic (organistic) treatment will be found in Bernard Bosanquet's (1848-1923) Gifford Lectures, *The Principle of Individuality and Value* (1911) and *The Value and Destiny of the Individual* (1912). These were a very nearly (if not a completely) definitive summary of the Hegelian movement on this subject. It is pertinent to observe that for the Hegelians value was always treated as a general theory. The core principle of coherence in their philosophy was intrinsically a universal value principle. Value for them permeated the universe. They had a general value theory long before the name was invented, which once more shows how philosophically provincial the issues of the special "general value theory" movement are. Bosanquet's, Bradley's, Royce's, and other idealists' writings on value all fall within our field of study, and yet they antedate in their sources the Meinong-Ehrenfels movement, and have been practically entirely uninfluenced by it. This indicates to me (what is anyway rather obvious) that the Meinong-Ehrenfels movement presupposes a set of metaphysical categories (the naturalistic) under which this school's issues have almost no impact at all upon the idealistic movement in its treatment of value, and *vice versa*.

In the last twenty years, monumental books of the sort associated with the classical idealists have ceased to appear. But it should not from this fact be assumed that the movement is dying out or even weakening. A surprising amount of specialized writing, particularly in the field of aesthetic criticism, is organistic in principle. Much of it is not noticeable because it no longer appears in the traditional Hegelian vocabulary. I. A. Richards (1893-   ), for instance, in most of his later writings has developed organistic principles. Theodore M. Greene's *The Arts and the Art of Criticism* (1940) is a predominantly organistic theory. So are James Feibleman's (1904-   ) writings. Bertram Morris's (1908-   ) *The Aesthetic Process* (1943), perhaps the most consistently organistic work in aesthetics since Bosanquet, contains a number of important novel insights. There is a lot of organicism in Whitehead. Organic conceptions of value seem to have settled so completely into much of the thought of our time that we no longer notice them any more unless we go out specially looking for them.

To return to the general theory of value movement originated by the Meinong-Ehrenfels debate. This culminated in R. B. Perry's (1876-   ) *General Theory of Value* (1926), which is the most complete and systematic treatment of the subject in English and probably in any other language. It was so thorough that it seemed to close progressive study of the subject for a while, at least in America. It took time for the younger men to absorb it, and find out where its internal difficulties lay. For most of these difficulties underlay his level of criticism by as much as his level of analysis probed beneath the level of nineteenth century studies of the subject.

He defined value as "any object of any interest." It is possible that he meant this term "interest" to mediate between Ehrenfels' "desire" and Meinong's "feeling." He also sought to lift the study out of the introspective bog of the continental issues by espousing a behavioristic approach, allying himself with some of the early analyses of the behavioristic psychologist E. C. Tolman. He embedded "interest" in a biological setting by locating it in the area of docile animal behavior. He then gave a detailed psychological analysis of "interest" in behavioristic terms distinguishing between "governing propensity," "subordinate acts," and "object of reference." There was then an extensive analysis of purely cognitive activity as contrasted with interested activity, and of the rôle of the mediating judgment in determining the object of interest. Various forms of value changes were exhaustively described. Finally Perry suggested four ultimate value criteria, intensity, comprehensiveness, preference and correctness. He did not regard value as precisely an attribute of an object. For him it was a relation holding between an interest and an object. But he did find himself involved in the problem of the "objective," which troubled Meinong so greatly, in order to have an object for an interest when the object did not literally exist.

Closely associated with Perry's view at this time in the minds of many was that of D. W. Prall (b. 1886), which was summarized in *A Study in the Theory of Value* (1921). So closely were these two men popularly associated together that the theory was often called the Perry-Prall theory. There were indeed wide areas of agreement. But actually within the general naturalistic area of motor-affective responses they were almost as opposed in attitude and emphasis towards matters at issue as Ehrenfels and Meinong, and along the same line of cleavage. Perry's theory in the last analysis is a conative or desire theory of value, which comes very near to explaining feeling or pleasure away. Prall's view is essentially an affective or feeling view, developed on the whole introspectively rather than behavioristically, with a tendency toward the exploration of desire in terms of pleasure and pain. Perry's theory is particularly weak on the aesthetic side, and particularly strong on the ethical side. Prall's is particularly strong on the aesthetic side. His feeling theory was expanded into two excellent works on aesthetics, *The Aesthetic Judgment* (1929) and *Aesthetic Analysis* (1936). His ethical views ran somewhat parallel to Santayana's, whose influence can often be sensed in Prall's writings.

Perry belonged to the school of American realists. The principal rival school in this country at that time was that of the pragmatists, which found its maturest exponent in John Dewey (1859-   ).

Through Dewey's long life, he has been constantly concerned with value problems. But not until very late did he appear to conceive these problems in terms of a general theory of value. His most important single work on the subject is a monograph entitled *Valuation* prepared for the *Encyclopedia of Unified Science*. His approach is utterly foreign to Perry's and hardly joins issue at all except on the categorial level underlying their characteristic pronouncements.

The sphere of the value problem for Dewey is the "situation" (more specifically the social situation) in which an environment and a number of persons, possibly a whole society, are involved. A value problem develops when a conflict arises within a situation. The conflict is bad. A reestablishment of harmony in the situation is good through satisfying the various conflicting interests. "Satisfaction" for Dewey, however, is not a mental state, but rather a state of integration or harmony. And "interest" for Dewey is not Perry's individual conative interest but rather some broader social interest such as a shipping interest, a worker's interest, an academic interest, a parental or child interest. Dewey and Perry are at one, however, in preferring a behavioristic approach to value problems so as to avoid imputations of privacy or subjectivity for their studies. Value theory for them is a scientific enterprise open to observation, hypothesis, and verification just like any other branch of science.

In the name of scientific precision, however, another school of value theory has come to the front which reaches just opposite conclusions. The logical positivists' school emphasizes the privacy of value judgments, and consequently makes a great deal of the contrast between value judgments and scientific judgments. The former are not strictly speaking open to verification but only to harmonization by way of persuasion. Only scientific judgments are susceptible of objective verification. Value is located in feeling, in this respect reminiscent of Meinong's stand. But the value is confined to the feeling, not a property of an object endowed with value through feeling, as Meinong maintained. The relation to an object as definitional of value is dropped out by the typical logical positivists, and consequently for them all anchorage in the external factual world is abandoned and value becomes entirely subjective.

The sources of this theory are various. The originators of logical positivism should, of course, be referred to, particularly Maurice

A HISTORY OF PHILOSOPHICAL SYSTEMS

Schlick (1882-1936) and Rudolf Carnap (1891-   ). Their interests were mainly in logic and the philosophical analysis of scientific method and results. But Schlick on a summer cruise on the Dalmatian coast took a little time off and wrote down his reflections on ethics (*Fragen der Ethik,* 1930, trans. by S. Rynin as *Problems of Ethics,* 1939). This is a hedonistic approach to the subject quite traditional in tone and consonant with the Hume, Bentham, Mill tradition. Value is identified with pleasure and a maximization of pleasure and minimization of pain are the ethical objectives. There are a number of original details in his working out of the theory. One of these is his method of answering the usual criticisms of the hedonistic calculus by a special mode of maximization. But I shall not go into these details, since this traditional hedonistic approach to ethics was quickly abandoned for something else which might be called the official positivistic doctrine. Schlick's little book for its tense clarity and brilliance will probably remain a milestone in the history of ethics. But the direction it was going was almost immediately abandoned by Schlick's followers. All that was retained was the identification of value with feeling and an important reference back to Hume.

The official declaration of logical positivistic tenets appeared in 1936 with the publication by Alfred S. Ayer (1910-   ) of *Language, Truth and Logic.* This book has been much criticized by members of the logical positivistic school for a variety of reasons. But it has steadily held its place in the minds of the philosophical public as the single document which most clearly announced the cluster of concepts associated with the logical positivistic position. Here one will find the categorical distinction made between the value judgment and the scientific or factual judgment, between emotive expression and description of fact, the one private and unverifiable, the other open to public verification.

One of the men most responsible for this shift of emphasis seems, strangely enough, to have been G. E. Moore (1873-   ) through his doctrine of the indefinable good. This doctrine will be found in Moore's *Principia Ethica* (1903). The arguments for his position are mainly linguistic, to the effect that the meaning of the word "good" cannot be identified with pleasure or adaptation or anything else without loss of some of its connotation. Accordingly, he dubbed all such identifications (or, if you will, reductions) illustrations of a "naturalistic fallacy." To avoid such a "naturalistic fallacy" he argued that the meaning of "good" cannot be identified with anything else than the reference of its own meaning, just as the meaning of "yellow" cannot be identified with physical vibrations but only with an irreducible and in that sense indefinable quality, yellow. So G. E. Moore, partly by the meaning reference argument and partly by analogy with references to introspectively irreducible sensory qualities, took the view that the word "good" referred to an "indefinable," irreducible quality "good." This quality he held could be intuited in good acts, much as we can observe yellow in yellow tulips.

This view of G. E. Moore's was developed along the traditional line of studies of nineteenth century moral philosophers. It is improbable that G. E. Moore had even heard of a general theory of value when he was first struggling with his analysis of "good." But the ease with which his conception of an indefinable "good" could be taken over into a general theory of value is patent.

Now as it happened G. E. Moore was at the University of Cambridge. Thus he was associated with Russell and Whitehead. Wittgenstein later settled in Cambridge. The researches of the Viennese positivists were congenial to the Cambridge logicians. G. E. Moore was right there with his analytical semantic methods. These were congenial to the conceptual habits of analysis of the growing school of young logical positivists and many converts seem to have been made.

G. E. Moore's doctrine of the indefinability of good was extremely attractive to these young logical analysts. It should be remembered too that I. A. Richards was also resident in Cambridge and in his early writings (*e.g.*, Ogden and Richards, *The Meaning of Meaning*, 1923) had made a great deal of the distinction between emotive meanings or statements and statements of fact. There was one element in common between G. E. Moore's indefinable "good" and I. A. Richards' emotive meanings, namely, that both were intuitive occurrences immune to inductive processes of verification. Now, conceive a young convert to Moore's indefinable good, who through the very rigor of his own methods of conceptual analysis convinces himself that Moore is not justified in a notion of a quality, good, that can be factually predicated of acts. But consider that the young student retains his habits of thought toward value statements, and does not concede them to be statements of empirical probability. Quite naturally in the intellectual environment of Cambridge he will identify value statements with I. A. Richards' emotive meanings, and then all the consequences of logical positivistic doctrine on the subject follow.

Unquestionably, the most carefully worked out treatment of the positivistic doctrine of the value judgment as an emotive expression is to be found in Charles Stevenson's (1908-   ) *Ethics and Language* (1944). The consequence that such judgments are not regarded as subject to error in the same manner as scientific statements leads to a study of how persons may be induced to change their value judgments. Out of this study Stevenson develops the concept of the "persuasive definition" as the pivotal instrument of moral persuasion. Whatever one's final view may be of this species of emotive theory of value, Stevenson's meticulous study of various types of emotional persuasion in the ethical field will remain of permanent worth.

In this book Stevenson explicitly connects the emotive value judgment theory with Moore's indefinable good. "Almost all those who now emphasize the emotive aspects of ethics," he writes, "have at one time been greatly under Moore's influence. It is not easy to believe that this is an accident. The parallel between his views and the present ones—which in spite of all differences remains surprisingly close—will be evident from this observation: 'Wherever Moore would point to "naturalistic fallacy" the present writer . . . would point to a persuasive definition' " (pp. 272-3).

It is probably safe to say that the emotive theory of the positivistic species has passed its peak of attractiveness. The most repugnant aspect of this theory to those who found it unacceptable was that it placed ultimate questions of value beyond the pale of rational enquiry. There has been a steady and increasing opposition to this disposition of issues concerning matters of value.

A comprehensive reinstatement of the problem of value in a rational empirical setting can be found in C. I. Lewis's (1883-   )*An Analysis of Knowledge and Valuation* (1947). Only half of this book treats of value, but it treats the subject just as it treats any epistemological problem. It distinguishes between "intrinsic" and "inherent" value. The former is an immediate datum regarded as indubitable and on a par with the immediate data of sight or touch which are attributable to objects through correlation. The latter, inherent value, is a property of objects which are said to have value and consists in the capacity of such objects to produce "intrinsic" values. This capacity is verifiable by inductive method. The result is that values are conceived as embedded in the world of natural events subject to scientific treatment. A value judgment is just as scientific and empirical as any judgment of immediacy or of the properties of an object. And general principles of evaluation are empirically derivable and verifiable. True statements can be made about the greater inherent value of certain objects. These statements are not mere emotive expressions which one might hope to persuade others also to feel, but are cognitive judgments which one may expect others to believe on scientific grounds of rational evidence.

This brings us up to the present day. A fair cross-section of the present status of thought on the subject of value can be found in *Value, a Cooperative Enquiry* (1949), edited by Ray Lepley (1903-   ). It takes its departure from a series of questions asked by Dewey probing at the heart of the principal contemporary issues on the subject. The fourteen contributors spread over a wide range of philosophical attitude. Their essays make it clear that there is no great unanimity on the subject. They also make it clear that there is a lot of vigorous thinking on the matter at levels of enquiry much deeper than those characteristic of the thought of the nineteenth century or earlier. It looks as though we are entering upon an exceedingly fertile period of enquiry on the subject. New contributions from anthropology, sociology, economics, and from social, behavioristic, and clinical psychology are all pouring into the field and being gradually digested. Whatever comes out of this material by way of guidance in human problems of choice and evaluation will be much more complicated than anything envisaged in earlier periods, but it will also be much more firmly established in fact and possibly more effective in the attainment of better judgments for individual and social health and harmony.

A HISTORY OF PHILOSOPHICAL SYSTEMS

BIBLIOGRAPHY

A. Meinong, *Psych.-ethische Untersuch. z. Werttheorie* (1894).
C. Ehrenfels, *System der Werttheorie* (1897).
F. C. Brentano, *Psychologie vom empirischen Standpunkte* (1874).
W. M. Urban, *Valuation, Its Nature and Laws* (New York, 1909).
B. Bosanquet, *The Principle of Individuality and Value* (London, 1912).
———, *The Value and Destiny of the Individual* (London, 1913).
I. A. Richards, *Principles of Literary Criticism* (1926).
T. M. Greene, *The Arts and the Art of Criticism* (1940).
Bertram Morris, *The Aesthetic Process* (1943).
R. B. Perry, *General Theory of Value* (New York, 1926; reprint, 1950).
D. W. Prall, "A Study in the Theory of Value" in *University of California Publications in Philosophy*, III, No. 2 (1918), 179-290.
———, *Aesthetic Judgment* (New York, 1929).
———, *Aesthetic Analysis* (New York, 1936).
J. Dewey, *Theory of Valuation* (*International Encyclopedia of Unified Science* Series), Vol. II, No. 4 (Chicago, 1939).
C. L. Stevenson, *Ethics and Language* (New Haven, 1944).
Maurice Schlick, *Fragen der Ethik* (1930) trans. by S. Rynin as *Problems of Ethics* (New York, 1939).
Alfred A. Ayer, *Language, Truth and Logic* (New York, 1936).
G. E. Moore, *Principia Ethica* (Cambridge, 1903).
C. K. Ogden and I. A. Richards, *The Meaning of Meaning* (New York, 1923).
C. I. Lewis, *An Analysis of Knowledge and Valuation* (LaSalle, 1946).
Ray Lepley, editor, *Value, A Cooperative Inquiry* (New York, 1949).
S. C. Pepper, *Aesthetic Quality* (New York, 1938).
———, *A Digest of Purposive Values* (New York, 1947).
John Laird, *The Idea of Value* (Cambridge, England, 1929).
Wolfgang Köhler, *The Place of Value in a World of Facts* (New York, 1938).

CHAPTER FORTY

RECENT SCHOOLS OF LOGIC

ALBERT E. AVEY

THE MOST fundamental value is truth; and the prime distinction with which we are always concerned is the distinction between truth and falsehood. Logic is concerned with the question whether it is possible to formulate principles which will serve as criteria of correct thinking, and so enable us to avoid error.

In the attempt to formulate such logical principles there have been different approaches to the field, leading as a consequence to different schools of interpretation of what logic should be. To some interpreters it is primarily a set of rules, essentially practical, for guiding the process of thinking in common sense, the sciences, and philosophy. For others the basic task of logic is to clarify the place and function of thinking in the process of knowing, and to interpret thought as a phase of the structure of reality. To a third group the primary question is how analysis arrives at broad generalizations by means of which thought can be guided, and experience organized. A fourth school sees in formal principles only one aspect of the process of facing experience; to them concrete procedures are more significant than general principles. Methods of solving problems so as to gain ends valued constitute for them the significant aspect of thinking. A fifth group is not satisfied with broad statements of method; it wishes to know in detail how the thought process works, what explicit assumptions it takes for granted, and how it is related to the detailed formal laws employed in special fields of knowledge.

The earliest roots of Occidental Logic are found in Pre-Socratic philosophy, in the dialectical arguments of the Eleatic School, (which saw in identity, contradiction and excluded middle attributes of reality), and in the skeptical tendencies of certain Sophists. But

A HISTORY OF PHILOSOPHICAL SYSTEMS

whereas much of the discussion by the Sophists was based upon ambiguities in concepts the positive advance toward significant results began in the *Dialogues* of Plato (427-347 B.C.) where Socrates is represented as clearing away ambiguities by an inductive inquiry into the basic meaning of terms. In his later dialogues Plato came to the conclusion that by dichotomous division thought might proceed from the most inclusive concept 'Being,' to the definition of such specific classes as 'the Sophist' and 'the Statesman,' by arranging the content of the realm of thought in a classificatory system.

I. Aristotelian Tradition with Emphasis on Deduction.

The suggestions of Plato were carried to a larger systematic development by Aristotle (384-322 B.C.), though the condition in which his treatises have come down to us is confused and incomplete. The phases of the field with which Aristotle dealt were chiefly: the categories, the structure of language, types of propositions of the subject-predicate form; formal rules of consistency of propositions, the categorical syllogism, fallacies, scientific proof and the distinction between essential and unessential attributes. At times he used a very elementary type of symbolism.

After Aristotle a further step in logical theory was made by the Stoics in the discussion of hypothetical and disjunctive forms of argument, and in consideration of certain linguistic questions.

The Aristotelian tradition has been carried on with emphasis on different aspects down to the present day. Hobbes (1588-1679) in his *Leviathan* (1651) and Locke (1632-1704) in his *Essay Concerning Human Understanding* (1690) wrote in the Aristotelian tradition, but their doctrines were strongly marked by nominalism. Reasoning was regarded as a process of manipulating verbal signs, and as akin to the operations used in mathematics (addition, subtraction, etc.). This in a sense anticipated aspects of investigation which have become increasingly prominent in recent decades. These men gave an interpretation of the place of language in experience rather than an advance in the process of calculation.

1884 saw in the *Studies and Exercises in Formal Logic* of J. N. Keynes (b.1852) a thorough treatment of the same tradition with consideration of the exact interpretation of the meaning of the accepted forms (*e.g.*, the question of existential import of the A, E, I, and O propositions). In an appendix he considered numerous problems of the sort dealt with by symbolic logic, but without developing a technical symbolism. H. W. B. Joseph (1867-1943) gave in his *Introduction to Logic* (1906) a substantial treatment of the Aristotelian tradition, to which many students of the essentials of the subject have felt a debt. And again in the *Science of Logic* (1918) of Peter Coffey (b.1876) the tradition received an extensive and detailed restatement from the scholastic point of view, covering both deductive and inductive procedure, and their connection with scientific method.

II. *Metaphysical Logic*

Another aspect of logic was hit upon by St. Augustine (353-430) in his search for final truth. This was the recognition of the presuppositions one is taking for granted in any thinking, even the asking of a question. (*Cf. Soliloquies,* II, 1 ff.; *De Trin.* X, 14, etc.) Descartes (1596-1650) in his *Discourse on Method* (1637) applied the same procedure and formulated his dictum which declares the act of thinking to be the prior presupposition of all further experience.

This turn of thought led to a new development in the work of Immanuel Kant (1724-1804). From this came what Kant called *Transcendental Logic.* (*Critique of Pure Reason,* 1781). It was logic since it considered the general forms of thought. It was transcendental since it went to the very outer edge of experience.

Kant's doctrine was a statement of the innate structure of a mind, which must be presupposed, and possessed, in order that any thinking should be possible. His analysis carried him back to the categories of Aristotle, and to the basic forms of traditional logic, which he reconsidered in his own way. But the significance of his work lay in the fact that it dealt not primarily with the question: "What forms does thought take?" but: "How is any thinking possible?" The turn he gave to the field influenced strongly the work of his followers.

The point which Kant made in his *Critique of Pure Reason* that experience must conform to the structure of thought in order to be knowable, led to the *Logic* (1817) of Hegel (1770-1831). To Hegel it seemed necessary to conclude that the order of thought and the order of reality are the same, and the study of the one is identical with the study of the other. As a consequence the unfolding of reason is the course of the real. Logic and ontology are one; hence what Hegel calls Logic is really Metaphysics.

In his *Principles of Logic* (1883) F. H. Bradley (1846-1924) presented a theory of the judgment as the fundamental unit of thought structure, and an interpretation of the nature of inference. This was a discussion of the meaning of the processes employed in reasoning, not a statement of the specific forms which thought takes in its activity. Bradley's study supplements the work of detailed analysis, looking in the general direction of Hegel but keeping closer to logic itself.

B. Bosanquet (1848-1927) in his *Logic* (1888) worked farther in the spirit of Bradley, considering the meaning of the topics characteristic of the Aristotelian tradition, but relating them to the general background of thought and knowledge, coming to a formulation of the coherence theory of truth.

W. E. Johnson in his *Logic* (1921-1924) gave another thoroughgoing review of the subject as inherited from Aristotle, and as affected by basic concepts originating among the symbolic logicians.

III. Aristotelian Tradition with Emphasis on Induction.

No attempt was made to break away from the past until Francis Bacon (1561-1626) raised the question about the establishment of the major premises used in deduction. The answer seemed to be: "by induction," and in the *Novum Organum* (1620) he gave attention chiefly to the question of mental attitudes which act as obstacles in the way of impartial observation, and summarization in the form of general laws. These obstacles were designated 'Idols of the tribe, the cave, the marketplace and theater.'

In 1843 appeared the *System of Logic,* of J. S. Mill (1806-1873). It was a notable attempt by a mind continually growing in breadth and incisiveness to face the problem of the procedures of thought, as seen from the standpoint of associationist psychology on the one hand and an interest in social welfare on the other. But the associationist theory could not do justice to mathematics, and consequently not to the subtle details of logical theory which were developing. It was only by radical departure from his early training that in his later work he could entertain the problem which Kant had in mind in his *Critique*. Out of the interest in a method for tracing social causes came the set of Methods of Experimental Inquiry,—Agreement, Difference, Joint Method, Concomitant Variations, and Residues. This is the phase of Mill's study that has made the most lasting impression.

IV. Instrumentalist Logic.

W. Wundt (1832-1920) canvassed the entire field of philosophy, including *Logic* (1880-1883). His approach was psychological and epistemological, concerned with the function which thought performs as a phase of human experience, rather than as a set of formal principles from which can be deduced a symbolic and mathematical system. In *Studies in Logical Theory* (1903) John Dewey (1859-   ) and his students presented their interpretation of logic as primarily methodology. The psychological aspect of life they held prior to the formal-logical, and of more universal interest. Thought occurs in the face of a problem, and it is more essential to devise an instrument of attack than to elaborate the details of deductive forms. From Dewey comes the five-fold description of a thought process: Sense of a problem, clarification of the issue, survey of the possibilities, deduction of consequences of a hypothesis, and verification by experience.

An interest akin to that of Wundt and Dewey is manifested by J. M. Baldwin (1861-1934) in his *Thought and Things, A Genetic Theory of Reality* (1906-1912). He presented an evolutionary interpretation of the growth of the thinking process and its place in biological development.

V. Symbolic Logic.

The most recent development in logic began with Leibniz (1636-1716). A mathematician as well as a man learned in other lines, he saw the limitations of the Aristotelian tradition and conceived a much broader study of the processes of thought. It occurred to him that if one could single out the fundamental elements of experience and the irreducible forms of relation which hold among them one could by successive combinations of these anticipate all possible knowledge. If a suitable system of symbols could be devised it would be possible to construct a universal language. The language was to be ideographic, each symbol with a single meaning, and each term and relation possessed of its appropriate symbol. The language would thus be completely free from ambiguity, a perfectly scientific language. It would offer a complete calculus of reasoning, a combinatorial art with which was to be constructed an encyclopedia of all knowledge, a system of unified science such as has been re-emphasized in recent years. He devised symbols for the elementary relations 'and' 'or' 'implies' 'inclusion' 'equivalence,' etc.

Leibniz attempted to deal with logical problems on the basis of intension but sensed the difficulties which presented themselves in this connection, and which led him increasingly to an extensional view. He also was aware of certain problems in the interpretation of universals and particulars, and anticipated a number of basic principles and rules accepted by later systems of symbolic logic, such as: the laws of simplification, transposition, tautology, composition and identity. He distinguished 'inclusion' from the 'part-whole' relation. He also regarded the elements of a logical sum as not mutually exclusive, and gave some consideration to quantification of the predicate.

J. H. Lambert (1728-1777) continued the type of doctrine suggested by Leibniz and elaborated certain details further. He used mathematical symbols to indicate logical processes: $=$, $+$, and others which were not later adopted by general practice, and symbolized the common properties of the concepts a and b by ab. He distinguished different cases of the universal "All A is B," *i.e.*, where A and B are equal and where they are not. He used :: to signify relative products; and faced the problem of the powers of relations. (Cf. *Briefwechsel*, pub. 1782.)

Augustus DeMorgan (1806-1871) in his *Formal Logic* (1847) extended the traditional theory by constructing new types of compound propositions, with immediate inferences and syllogisms based upon them, and introduced a numerical factor of probability into premises and conclusion of syllogisms. He laid a foundation for later work on the logic of relations, used a symbol for relative products, developed formulas for the compounding of relations, and introduced the concepts of 'universe of discourse,' 'transitivity' of relations, 'ancestor' and 'descendant.' He is best known for the formula for developing dual theorems, which also gives an expression for negatives of complex terms: *viz.*, the negative of a sum is the product of the negatives of the elements, the negative of a product is the sum of the negatives of the factors.

In 1854 came George Boole's (1815-1864) *Laws of Thought*.

Boole was primarily a mathematician, but was interested in a formulation of logical study which would do justice to the processes employed in mathematics. His theory was placed definitely on a basis of extensional interpretation, and consisted in a two-valued algebra, representing existence or non-existence, when applied to classes, and truth or falsehood, when applied to propositions. In interpreting alternation, he held the elements to be mutually exclusive; the negative of x was represented by "1-x"; there was no reference to "inclusion" of one class in another, or of "implication" of one proposition by another. The fundamental relation was equivalence ($=$) of one expression to another.

In the course of his discussion he recognized the laws of commutation ($xy = yx$), distribution $[x(y + z) = xy + xz]$; added determinants; if $(x = y)$ then $(xz = yz)$; and absorption ($xx = x$). He was especially interested in the theory of probability, and his formulas serve well to indicate the distribution of possible chances of occurrence under given conditions. His law for the distribution of a term ($x = xy + xy'$, $x = xyz + xyz' + xy'z + xy'z'$), and for the universe ($1 = x + x'$, $1 = xy + xy' + x'y + x'y'$, etc.) is especially useful in this connection, and as an extension of the Aristotelian process of division and classification.

Difficulties which resulted from Boole's interpretation of alternatives as mutually exclusive were avoided by W. S. Jevons (1835-1882) when he rejected this limitation (*Pure Logic,* 1864), thus starting the interpretation which has continued to the present. He revised Boole's symbolism for negatives of classes by omitting the symbol for the universe; $1 - x$ became simplified to $- x$, $=$ was adopted from mathematics as the symbol for identity; contradictions were equated to zero; and the law of absorption was employed in a more extended form ($a + ab = a$). He emphasized also the substitution of similars as a fundamental process in the generalization of formulas.

G. Frege (1848-1925) developed a rigorous theory of the logic of mathematics, (*Begriffschrift,* 1879) running into basic problems regarding the nature of number, concepts, symbols, etc., which had great influence upon the ideas of B. Russell (1872-   ). But his notation was so space-consuming that it was not adopted by later logicians.

The preliminary steps of DeMorgan and Boole bore more perfect fruit in the work of Charles Peirce (1839-1914). For him the logic of relations assumed a more central position, and broke away from close connections with arithmetical processes, as these had been indicated in the work of Boole; (*Johns Hopkins Studies in Logic,* 1883). Their application to the logic of classes was emphasized. Peirce employed the symbol ($<$) for 'inclusion' and 'implication.' He introduced a method of treating 'particular' and 'universal' propositions as sums and products of propositions containing variables, and employed Σ and Π in this connection. He elaborated the theory of relative terms, developing the forms of relative multiplication, association, addition, distribution, inclusion, etc. He derived the processes of mathematical demonstration from the more general procedures of logic, by introducing limitations and special assumptions, and thus interpreted mathematical concepts in terms of logical relations. He also developed a theory of propositional functions, used 'implication' in the sense of 'material' implication, and also began the use of a truth-table to represent the relations of propositions.

John Venn (1834-1883) generalized the representation of the relations of classes by means of circles by adding a fourth circle to the traditional three and indicating the universe of discourse as a whole (*Symbolic Logic,* 1881). By means of Boole's law of development, he was able to describe, in terms of subject and predicate and their negatives, the sub-divisions of the universe indicated by a proposition or a combination of propositions up to four. By this means he was able to solve problems which could not readily be dealt with through syllogisms.

In 1883 Mrs. Christine Ladd Franklin (1847-1930) devised a formula for testing the validity of syllogisms, by means of an 'antilogism.' It is composed of a triad of propositions, two universals and a particular, such that if two of them are true the third will be false. By taking any two of the propositions and the contradictory of the third a valid syllogism will be constructed. And since there are three ways in which to do this each antilogism represents three valid syllogisms. Applying this procedure to $a<b$, $b<c$, $sa\bar{\vee}c$ there result: $a<b$, $b<c$, $\therefore a<c$; $sa\bar{\vee}c$, $b<c$, $\therefore sa\bar{\vee}b$; and $a<b$, $sa\bar{\vee}c$, $\therefore sb\bar{\vee}c$. (Cf. *Johns Hopkins Studies in Logic.*)

Ernst Schroeder (1841-1902) brought the entire field of the *Algebra of Logic* (1890-1895) to a well-rounded presentation to his date, dividing his discussion among classes, propositions, and an extensive treatment of relations.

G. Peano (1858-1932) began a new phase of the science, developing a symbolism which was not only more exact than previous symbolisms, but much more convenient. He introduced the symbol ε, indicating the irreducible relation of the individual member to the class as defined by a concept. This was a recognition of a problem which had puzzled even Plato, and had been obscured in the later discussions. It was a clear recognition of a relation distinct from that of a subclass to an including class, and from that of implication. The concept of *existence* was also recognized in a way unknown before, and new symbols introduced which have continued in use in later work. (Introduction to *Formulaire*, 1894.)

A. N. Whitehead (1861-1947) in his *Universal Algebra* (1898) revived the aim of Leibniz to construct a calculus which might facilitate reasoning in every field of thought. In the more specialized interest of mathematics it was to bring recent developments of algebra and geometry together. But his interpretation was never merely formal and mathematical; it was conceived as related to the general field of knowing.

In his *Grundlagen* (1904) David Hilbert (b.1862) presented a formalization of mathematics which did not regard logic as prior. He took the position that many theorems of the system are mere formulas, without meaning in themselves but introduced to complete the formal structure of the system. A central problem is the proof of consistency of a logistic system, resting on the demonstration that there is no formula such that both it and its negative are theorems in the system.

Josiah Royce (1855-1916) was also thoroughly interested in logical theory and, acting upon a suggestion of Peirce, he undertook to formulate the conception of a comprehensive system, Σ, and of an order of relations so inclusive that any particular system of entities in some order might be derived by a process of selection (*Trans. Amer. Math. Soc.* Vol. 6, 1905). This he stated as a system which would apply not only to classes and propositions, but to the wider area of the possible modes of action open to a rational being who can act and reflect upon action. This suggestion has been regarded as promising, but it was never worked out into extensive detail.

In 1908 L. E. J. Brouwer (b.1881), in opposition to the formalism of Hilbert, in a Dutch periodical maintained a view called 'intuitionism,' and held that mathematics has no presuppositions, not even logic. There remains no other source than intuition. He also held that there are instances (propositions requiring a variable whose range is infinite) in which the law of excluded middle is rejected; and similarly double negation, and indirect proof.

1910 was the epochal year which saw the publication of *Principia Mathematica Vol. I* by Whitehead and Russell. Its symbolism was derived from Peano, and its theory based upon six primitive ideas: elementary propositions, elementary propositional functions, assertion, assertion of a propositional function, negation, disjunction, plus the idea of equivalence by definition, which is not on a par with the other ideas, merely indicating possible substitutions. It then employs three definitions: of implication, product (negative of a sum), and material equivalence. Then with five primitive propositions and five rules of inference the basis is laid for the derivation of the systematic calculus of elementary propositions.

The treatment of propositional functions requires additional definitions and primitive propositions. From the calculus of propositional functions is derived the calculus of classes, and the calculus of relations. On these as a basis is developed a theory of Cardinal Arithmetic, Relation-Arithmetic, Series and Quantity.

In 1913, in the *Transactions of the American Mathematical Society*, H. M. Sheffer showed that it is possible to replace two primitive propositions of *Principia* (regarding negation and disjunction) by a single primitive idea and proposition in terms of a binary rule of combination interpretable as "rejection." This he called the "stroke" function, represented by the symbol (/). On this basis the number of fundamental operations can be reduced and the symbols of *Principia* redefined.

Between 1913 and 1918 C. I. Lewis (1883-) developed a variation from the Whitehead-Russell system, through what he calls 'strict implication,' as contrasted with the 'material implication' of *Principia Mathematica*. There the meaning of "p implies q" is that "p is false or q is true" as a matter of fact. While this definition is thoroughly in accord with the demonstrations of mathematics, it seems not to be exactly what is usually meant by "implication." Lewis revised the definition by taking account not merely of the *true* and the *false*, but also of the *possible* and *impossible*. His symbolism is modified accordingly. (See his *Survey of Symbolic Logic,* 1918.) Suitable postulates, many analogous to those of *Principia Mathematica* are stated, but with some additional ones necessary in order to recognize the relation of truth to possibility, impossibility, falsehood, etc. The system contains a partial system which may be called a *Calculus of Consistencies,* another, a *Calculus of Ordinary Inference* which omits certain theories which seem strange from the common point of view, retains the notion of "consistency," and avoids certain complexities of "strict implication." It is also capable of extension to propositional functions, classes and relations, though since strict implication is a matter of intension, certain relations which hold of extension are missing.

L. Wittgenstein demonstrated the importance of a study of language. His *Tractatus Logico-philosophicus* (1922) is concerned with determining the conditions which symbolism must satisfy.

F. P. Ramsey (1903-1930) proposed modifications of *Principia Mathematica,* in the treatment of functions, which made possible among other things the omission of the Axiom of Reducibility and a simplification of the theory of types. (*Foundations of Mathematics,* 1931.)

A. Tarski represents a Polish school. His chief work is contribution to the technical details of the logic of mathematics, and the interpretation of fundamental concepts, such as 'truth functions,' 'truth,' 'meta-language,' 'meta-mathematic,' etc. (Cf. *Fund. Math.* Vol. 5, 1924.)

Kurt Gödel (b.1906) pointed out the impossibility, under certain circumstances, of formalizing a consistency proof for a logistic system within that system. This indicated a difficulty for Hilbert's position. (Cf. *Monatsh. Math. Phys.* Vol. 38, 1931.)

R. Carnap (b.1891) has contributed to the refinement of symbolic structure and interpretation; and in his *Logical Syntax of Language* (1934) has placed emphasis upon the recognition of a hierarchy of languages, and the problems attendant upon passing from one to another. Thus he recognizes the problems dealt with by Russell in his theory of types, but follows Ramsey in developing a simplified theory as contrasted with the ramified theory of Russell.

From this brief review it will be evident that the field of logic has sustained a continuing interest, and bids fair to continue to do so in the years ahead.

A HISTORY OF PHILOSOPHICAL SYSTEMS

BIBLIOGRAPHY

Historical Surveys:
  C. I. LEWIS, *A Survey of Symbolic Logic* (Berkeley, 1918).
  F. ENRIQUES, *The Historic Development of Logic*, Trans. by J. Rosenthal (New York, 1929).
  Encyclopedia of the Social Sciences, article "Logic" (New York, 1933).
  Encyclopedia Britannica, article "Logic, History of" (New York, 1947).

Important Systematic Works:
  ARISTOTLE, *Works*, translated into English. Volume I. W. D. Ross, ed. (Oxford, 1928).
  F. BACON, *Novum Organum*, ed. by Ellis, Spedding and Heath (London, 1857-70).
  G. W. LEIBNIZ, *Philosophische Schriften*, ed. by C. I. Gerhardt (Berlin, 1887).
  I. KANT, *Critique of Pure Reason*, trans. by N. Kemp Smith (London, 1929).
  G. W. F. HEGEL, *Logic*, trans. by W. Wallace (Oxford, 1874).
  G. BOOLE, *Laws of Thought* (Cambridge, 1854; Chicago, 1914).
  A. N. WHITEHEAD and B. RUSSELL, *Principia Mathematica* (Cambridge, 1910-1913).
  J. DEWEY, et al., *Studies in Logical Theory* (Chicago, 1903).
  J. ROYCE, *Principles of Logic*, in *Encyclopedia of the Philosophical Sciences*, ed. by Windelband and Ruge, Vol. I (New York, 1913).
  R. CARNAP, *The Logical Syntax of Language* (New York, 1937).

CHAPTER FORTY-ONE

RECENT EPISTEMOLOGICAL SCHOOLS

LEDGER WOOD

EPISTEMOLOGY has occupied a central position in the philosophical speculations of modern philosophers from Descartes to the present day. In this long and continuous development three phases may be distinguished: (1) the first phase—embracing the seventeenth and eighteenth centuries—was the period of controversy between the rival schools of rationalism and empiricism. In this controversy the great Continental Rationalists, Descartes, Spinoza and Leibniz were arrayed on the one side; the British Empiricists, Locke, Berkeley and Hume on the other. (2) The second phase, inaugurated by the Critical Philosophy of Immanuel Kant, effected a reconciliation of rationalism and empiricism with, however, rationalism in the ascendancy. The idealistic rationalism developed by the classical German idealists, Fichte, Schelling and Hegel, was the dominant epistemological school of the 19th century. (3) The third phase is the revolt against idealism which began early in the present century and from which stem the influential schools of the present day.

Considered in this historical context, it will be convenient to regard as "recent" the epistemological movements which had their inception in the revolt against idealism early in the present century. The historical causes of the early twentieth century revolt in epistemology are exceedingly complex and elusive. The new epistemologies were, on the negative side, the expression of a profound dissatisfaction with the dogmatism, formalism and rigidity of the idealism of Francis Herbert Bradley (1846-1924) and Bernard Bosanquet (1848-1923). British idealism was a German importation which held temporary sway over the British mind, but the empirical and analytic temper of mind inherited from Bacon, Locke, Berkeley, Hume and J. S. Mill, soon reasserted itself.

The new movements in epistemology, however, owe their rise chiefly to scientific developments. Of great epistemological significance is the establishment of psychology as an experimental science; the first psychological laboratory was founded by W. M. Wundt (1832-1920) at Leipzig. The experimental investigation of sensation undertaken in Wundt's laboratory and its successors achieved a remarkably exact correlation between intensity of stimulus and resultant sensation and forced upon philosophers the task of the epistemology of perception. The rapid growth of mathematics during the nineteenth century—particularly the elaboration of systems of non-Euclidean geometries by Bolyai and Lobachevsky early in the century—constituted a challenge to rationalism in both its early dogmatism and later critical forms. As a result of developments in mathematics and mathematical logic, the epistemological problem of the *a priori* is presented in a new and baffling form. Developments in the physical sciences likewise had their epistemological repercussions: the picture of the inner constitution of the physical object which emerges from physical investigations at the atomic and sub-atomic levels is so completely at variance with the object of ordinary sense perception, that it becomes a crucial task of epistemology to give a plausible account of the relation between perceptual and physical objects. Biology, likewise, helped to determine the complexion of recent epistemology. Knowledge, in the biological context, is viewed not as a passive mirroring of the outside world, but as an instrument of adaptation of the organism to its environment. Pragmatic and instrumentalist epistemologies are, as their exponents fully appreciate, treating the problem of knowledge in a biological context.

In our account of twentieth century epistemology in England and America, two phases may be readily distinguished. (1) The first phase is represented by the various schools of realism and pragmatism which spearheaded the revolt against the prevailing absolute idealism and which flourished for the first two or three decades of the century. This first phase, which may be characterized as the period of the proliferation of the schools, was a period of ferment and controversy. Such schools as new realism, critical realism, pragmatism, pragmatic humanism and instrumentalism vied with one another and were united principally by their common antagonism to idealistic epistemology and their employment in epistemological enquiry of the techniques and results of the sciences—especially mathematics and logic, psychology, physics and biology. (2) The second stage of recent philosophy, the contemporary phase, began in the late twenties and early thirties and is the period of the positivistic invasion. During this period the Anglo-American realism in a variety of forms, including critical realism, "objective relativism" and perspectivism, retain their adherents but realistic epistemology has been radically transformed through the assimilation of the analytical techniques of the positivists. Pragmatism, which has differentiated into such subvarieties as instrumentalism, conceptual pragmatism, has persisted with undiminished vitality. Pragmatism, because of its natural affinities with positivism, has even more than realism benefited from contact with positivism. Closely allied with both pragmatism and positivism is the operationalism, promulgated by certain physicists and psychologists. There is also in contemporary epistemology a resurgence of idealism—an idealism of a very different type, however, from the absolutism dominant at the turn of the century. It is evident that the proliferation of the schools is still continuing apace, but there are also hopeful indications in the present of a consolidation of the schools: there are many signs of convergence and interplay and cooperation among the various "isms" of contemporary epistemology.

MONISTIC OR PRESENTATIVE REALISM

Epistemological realism in England and America owes its inception to a vigorous article by G. E. Moore (1873-) entitled "Refutation of Idealism." In this essay, Moore, following the German phenomenologist A. Meinong (1853-1921), distinguishes between the *act* of awareness and the *object* of which we are aware and then, in terms of this distinction, gives a precise formulation of the thesis of epistemological realism. Realism is the epistemological position which asserts the object of knowledge is distinct from and independent of the act of awareness; the object of awareness, "when we are aware of it, is precisely what it would be, if we were not aware." [1] The distinction between act and object of knowledge underlies Moore's refutation of idealism; he argues that epistemological idealism because of its failure to distinguish sharply between knowing and the object known falsely assumes that objects exist only in so far as they are known. Berkeley (1685-1753) in equating "to be" with "to be perceived" was a victim of this confusion; Berkeley is indeed correct in asserting that the *act* of perceiv*ing* is a mental process but the *object* perceiv*ed,* since it may be divorced from the act, is not necessarily mind-dependent. G. E. Moore's version of realism, which provided the point of departure for later realism, may be summed up in the statements: (1) act and object are distinct and separable constituents of the knowledge-situation; (2) the object is independent of the act of knowing in that the object may continue in existence and retain its qualities unmodified when no longer present to the act of awareness; (3) the mind, in acts of awareness, directly and immediately apprehends objects of knowledge.

American New Realism is a school which had its inception in "The Program and First Platform of Six Realists," which appeared in *The Journal of Philosophy* in 1910, and in a cooperative volume, *The New Realism,* by the same authors, E. B. Holt, W. T. Marvin, W. P. Montague, R. B. Perry, W. B. Pitkin and E. G. Spaulding. The new realism, on its negative side, attacks the Berkeleyan argument along lines similar to Moore's refutation of idealism. W. P. Montague casts the principal Berkeleyan argument in syllogistic form as follows: *"Ideas are incapable of existing apart from a mind. Physical objects in so far as they are perceived or known at all are certainly 'ideas.' All physical objects are, therefore, incapable of existing apart from a mind,"* [2] and then diagnoses the Berkeleyan fallacy as an ambiguous use of the term 'idea,' which "is used in the major premise to denote an act or process of perceiving, while in the minor premise it is used to denote the object of that act, *i.e.,* the thing or content that is perceived." [3] Montague imputes a similar fallacy to the absolute idealist of the Bradleyan type which is guilty of an ambiguous use of the term experience: "the constant use of the one word *experience* to denote an *experiencing* and an *experienced,"* says Montague, "has produced in the mind of the idealist the curious delusion . . . that the objects that we experience can only exist at the moments when they are experienced." [4]

The epistemology of the new realism, on its constructive side, offers an analysis of the knowledge-situation which closely resembles the realism of G. E. Moore. The new realists formulate their main realistic theory in terms of the theory of independence: independence is defined by R. B. Perry in his essay entitled "A Realistic Theory of Independence" as non-dependence or absence of dependence with respect to a specified relation. When the notion of independence is applied to the case of knowledge, Perry finds at least *some* physical things, logical and mathematical entities and other minds are independent of a knowing consciousness and that they may become objects of consciousness without sacrificing their independence. "Realism," says Montague, "holds that things known may continue to exist unaltered when they are not known, or that things may pass in and out of the cognitive relation without prejudice to their reality, or that the experience of a thing is not correlated with or dependent upon the fact that anybody experiences it, perceives it, conceives it, or is in any way aware of it." [5]

A second characteristic thesis of new realism is epistemological monism: epistemological monism is the doctrine that knowledge is presentational, that the object of knowledge is directly given to consciousness. The issue here is between epistemological monism and epistemological dualism—between presentationalism and representationalism. Epistemological dualism is the doctrine that the "object" of knowledge is known only through the mediation of "ideas" or "content" of knowledge; that content and object of knowledge are two numerically distinct elements in the knowledge situation. Perhaps the most typical historical exponent of dualistic realism is John Locke (1632-1704); the world of ideas, according to Locke, contains images, copies, or representations of the real world outside the mind. The new realism in its monistic aspect is a revolt against the Lockean epistemology. "Epistemological monism," says R. B. Perry in *Present Philosophical Tendencies,* "means that when things are known they are identical element for element, with the idea or content of the knowing state . . . That which is commonly called the 'object' of knowledge merges, according to this view, with the idea, or is the whole thing of which the idea is a part. Thus when one perceives a tulip the idea of the tulip and the real tulip coincide, element for element; they are one in color, shape, size, distance, etc." [6]

Error, illusion and hallucination are crucial phenomena for monistic realism: if all knowledge is immediate and presentational, it is difficult to see how any distinction can be drawn between veridical and non-veridical forms of knowledge, and yet such a distinction is unavoidable. The new realists have not tried to evade the epistemological difficulties raised by the fact of delusive knowledge. E. B. Holt in his essay in *The New Realism,* entitled "The Place of Illusory Experience in a Realistic World," and in his chapter on "Error," in *The Concept of Consciousness* (1914), comes to grips with this problem. We cannot here consider the ingenious devices by which Holt and other monistic realists assimilate delusive cognition to their theory; we observe merely, for the most part, that they have the courage and consistency to ascribe reality of a sort to illusory and hallucinatory objects.

The neo realism of Bertrand Russell (1872-   ) shows the influence of G. E. Moore and also has many affinities with American New Realism. In *Our Knowledge of the External World* (1914), which also appeared under the title *Scientific Method in Philosophy,* Russell analyzes the perceptual knowledge into the two factors: (1) "consciousness" or the act of mental awareness and (2) the "sense data" or "sensible objects" of which we are aware. The "sensible object" is not a thing such as a table but the color patch or feeling of hardness of which I am momentarily aware when I look at or touch the table.[7] The perceptual object, the table, is nothing but a "logical construction" from the different appearance of the table to the same observer at different times or to different observers at the same or different times; "all the aspects of a thing are real, whereas the thing is a mere logical construction." This epistemological position is clearly monistic realism: the "sensible objects" are "perceptions" or aspects of the world which exist when no observer is perceiving them but which are immediately apprehended when consciousness is directed upon them. In the *Analysis of Mind*, published in 1921, Russell develops in modified form and in a changed terminology the theory outlined in *Our Knowledge of the External World*. The pure acts of awareness of the earlier work are completely eliminated in the later version of the theory; and the "sense data" or "sensible objects" of the earlier essay are frequently referred to as "sensations" in the later. The "sensations" are neutral entities—*i.e.,* neither mental nor physical—which as parts of one class or collection constitute physical objects and as belonging to another collection constitute physical objects. "Sensations," he says, "are what is common to the mental and the physical worlds; they may be defined as the point of intersection of mind and matter." [8] The epistemological hypothesis of the *Analysis of Mind* and of the *Analysis of Matter* (1927) is both realistic and monistic—realistic because the neutral entities constituting material objects may exist as perspectives even when they are not constituents of any mind; monistic because in any instance of actual knowledge identical sensations constitute a mind and a material object.

The epistemological theories of A. N. Whitehead (1861-1947) and S. Alexander (1859-1938) belong in the tradition of monistic realism but in each case epistemological doctrines are embedded in a system of metaphysics and expressed in the peculiar terminology of the system; it is consequently very difficult to formulate the epistemological theories apart from their metaphysical context. Among the factors into which the knowledge-complex is analyzable Whitehead includes: (1) "the 'subject' which feels," (2) "the 'initial data' which are to be felt"; (3) "the 'objective datum' which is felt." [9] He illustrates his analysis by a simple example, the audition of sound. "In order to avoid unnecessary complexity, let the sound be one definite note. The audition of this note is a feeling." "Secondly, there is the complex ordered environment composed of certain other actual entities which . . . is felt by reason of this audition. This environment is the datum of this feeling. It is the external world, as grasped systematically in this feeling." [10] The foregoing triadic analysis might suggest that Whitehead in distinguishing between the 'initial datum,' and the 'objective datum' is committed to epistemological dualism, but the two are so completely integrated in his organic conception of reality that his position is predominantly monistic. "The actual entity which is the initial datum is the actual entity perceived, the objective datum is the 'perspective' under which that actual entity is perceived, and the subject of the simple physical feeling is the perceiver." [11] In Whitehead's realistic epistemology, epistemological monism prevails over dualism.

Alexander's epistemology, although expressed in an entirely different terminology, closely resembles Whitehead's. In *Space, Time and Deity* (1920), Alexander distinguishes between two forms of knowledge which he calls "enjoyment" and "contemplation": enjoyment is the mind's direct awareness of itself, the mind's living through of its own activity; "contemplation," is the mind's apprehension of an object other than itself and involves an inner duality of subject and object.[12] The mind "enjoys" itself in the process of "contemplating" a foreign object. Alexander has little to say about "enjoyment": he presumably accepts it as an ultimate, irreducible and unanalyzable fact; the mind can "enjoy" itself because it is itself.[13] Contemplation, however, is more complex: it involves the togetherness or, as he calls it, the "compresence" of the two constituents of knowledge, namely consciousness and its object. The knowledge relation has for Alexander no special dignity or preëminence; it is simply an instance of the relation of compresence when one of the terms of the relation happens to be a conscious mind. The doctrine of knowledge as the mind's contemplation of an object is clearly realistic: the object of contemplative knowledge is an independent existent which has entered into a cognitive relation with a mind. Moreover, his realism, despite his admission of the inner duality of consciousness and its object, is epistemologically monistic: he considers all sense qualities as inherent in the object contemplated by the mind; the content and the object of knowledge are completely identified.

John Laird's (b. 1887) *A Study in Realism* and Norman Kemp Smith's (1872-) *Prolegomena to an Idealistic Theory of Knowledge*—both of which appeared in 1924—contain realistic epistemologies along lines indicated by Moore and Russell. Laird's realism is of an extreme form, which may be characterized as a "searchlight" theory of knowledge. Mind is a pure activity, which illumines and discovers preexistent objects, without altering them in the process. Laird's realism emphasizes the directness and immediacy of knowledge of all types. In perception we literally gaze out on the sense data which are constitutive of the perceptual object and he construes as objective the meaning-relation whereby we infer from directly perceived objects the existence of unperceived objects. Laird carries the doctrine of presentational immediacy to extreme limits in claiming that in memory the mind directly apprehends past objects in their pastness without the mediation of memory images and he even asserts that imaginary objects, which reside in a world of fictions, are no less "real" than the world of perceptual objects, and that they are directly apprehended by the mind. Laird's theory is radical and consistent monistic realism—his critics would urge that it is the *reductio ad absurdum* of this type of epistemology.

Kemp Smith's theory of knowledge is, despite the misleading title of his principal epistemological work, predominantly realistic rather than idealistic—though he does make some concessions to epistemological idealism. He holds that the sense-data with which the mind is directly confronted in perception are not made of mental stuff though their occurrence may be in part psychologically conditioned, the sense-data are "private" in that they are accessible only to a single percipient, yet they are "objective" in that they belong to the physical rather than the psychical world. The sense-data as such are unextended, but are projected upon the spatial continuum which is directly intuited by the mind. The spatial continuum is like the painter's canvas upon which the colored pigments (the qualitied sense-data) are spread. Despite the obvious concessions to idealism, Kemp Smith's theory is a novel variant of monistic realism: the perceptual object, both in its qualitative and its spatio-temporal aspects, is a true part of the physical world and is immediately or intuitively apprehended by the mind. His admission of the partial, causal dependence of the sense-data on the mind and of their "privacy" dilutes but does not negate his realism. This diluted realism has disparagingly been called anemic realism and it is certainly not so red-blooded as the Laird-type of theory.

Monistic realism was the dominant epistemology of the first quarter of the present century; it reached its climax in the writings of Russell, Whitehead and Alexander and, although it continued to have its adherents during the last quarter century, the movement has now lost considerable of its vitality. Though Russell has not entirely repudiated the position, his epistemological interests have radically shifted and in his chapter on "Perception and Knowledge" in his *An Inquiry into Meaning and Truth* (1940), there is scarcely a trace of the earlier epistemology of *The Analysis of Mind*. Realism, the development of which has just been traced, may now be viewed with considerable historical detachment; it is a movement of the recent past which continues to permeate epistemological discussion of the present but it is a phase of realism which has run its course. This phase of realism has been christened in retrospect "objective relativism": it is so-called because it assigns an objective status to the multiple, relative perspectives in which the object of knowledge may be apprehended.[14]

A HISTORY OF PHILOSOPHICAL SYSTEMS

DUALISTIC OR REPRESENTATIVE REALISM

The theory of representative perception is epistemologically dualistic in that it insists on the numerical duplicity of the sense-data directly present to the mind and the real external object. The theory had its historical origin early in the modern period in the causal theories of perception of Descartes (1596-1650) and Locke. In both Descartes and Locke the epistemological dualism of representative ideas and of external object was associated with and fostered by a metaphysical dualism of mental and physical orders but this association of epistemological with metaphysical dualism is not logically necessary and in the present section we shall ignore psycho-physical dualism and be concerned solely with epistemological dualism. Epistemological dualism was advanced in America by a group of Critical Realists which was composed of G. Santayana, C. A. Strong, A. K. Rogers, A. O. Lovejoy, R. W. Sellars, J. B. Pratt and Durant Drake. These thinkers differed greatly among themselves in general philosophical orientation and metaphysical allegiance, but in their coöperative volume *Essays in Critical Realism* (1920), they attacked the monistic tenets of the new realism and agreed on the bare essentials of a dualistic epistemology, which may be summarized as follows: (1) the mind is directly confronted with sense-data which constitute the content or vehicle of knowledge; (2) physical objects exist independently of the mind and are known through the mediation of the sense-data; (3) material objects are numerically distinct from the data by which they are known.

As in the case of new realism, the several critical realists instead of continuing their coöperative epistemological enquiries, developed their individual theories frequently along diverging lines. A. O. Lovejoy's (1873-   ) *The Revolt Against Dualism* (1930), and G. Santayana's (1863-   ) *Scepticism and Animal Faith* (1923), represent two such divergent developments of critical realistic epistemology. Lovejoy's work is largely critical: the early lectures in the volume contain detailed exposition and criticism of "objective relativism," particularly of Whitehead and Russell; only in the last two lectures does Lovejoy formulate in positive terms his own epistemology. The characteristic tenets of Lovejoy's version of dualistic realism are: (1) The mind is directly aware of "ideas." By "ideas"

Lovejoy means "non-physical experienced particulars"; he used the term "idea" in essentially the same sense as did Descartes and Locke. (2) The ideas afford evidence for inference to "an order of existences or events which persist when unperceived" and which are "causally related to our sensa." The external object "cannot be identical with our sensa." [17] "Whatever knowledge we have of real objects is indirect or representative; the datum whereby you know any such object is not identical with the object known." [18] (3) Memory and anticipation are even more obviously than perception, representative not direct modes of apprehension: "In memory and other retrospection there is a conscious and intrinsic reference to a reality other than the content given. . . ." [19] Indeed, "retrospection is . . . a case in which the duality of the datum and the thing known is immediately manifest . . ." "Of the other form of intertemporal cognition, actual or supposed—that is, foreknowledge or expectation—the dualistic implications are, if possible, even more manifest . . ." [20] "Future events not only are not now being experienced, but they have never entered into existence *as* events; and upon them no sane mortal can suppose his cognitive grasp to be direct and assured." [21]

Santayana's epistemological position as formulated in *Scepticism and Animal Faith* has little in common with Lovejoy's save its advocacy of representative realism. (1) Lovejoy characterized the immediate data of knowledge as existent whereas Santayana rejects existential data entirely; ". . . the notion that the datum exists," says Santayana, "is unmeaning, and if insisted upon is false." [22] The immediate and indubitable data of knowledge are according to Santayana essences, which, "although (they) have the texture and ontological status of Platonic 'ideas,' . . . are infinite in number and neutral in value." [23] (2) The essences function in Santayana's epistemology as the vehicles of knowledge; "essences," he says, "are indispensable terms in the perception of matters of fact, and render transitive knowledge possible." [24] Santayana is as vehemently opposed as Lovejoy to any form of presentation-realism; he speaks of "the absurdity of wishing to have intuitions of things. . . ." [25] His realism is representative, but not the less confident; "knowledge is knowledge because it has compulsory objects that preëxist." The objects are not inferred from the data—no causal inference from the essences to existent things is possible; the existence of physical objects is accepted and believed on the basis of animal faith. "Knowledge accordingly is belief: belief in a world of events . . . This belief is native to animals and precedes all deliberate use of intuitions as signs or descriptions of things . . ." [26] (3) Santayana, like Lovejoy, considers memory as affording a crucial instance of representational knowledge; in examining "the cognitive claims of memory," he insists that "memory itself must report facts or events in the natural world, if it is to be knowledge and to deserve the name of memory." [27]

An epistemological position which seeks a compromise between the radically dualistic epistemology inherited from Locke and Kant and an equally extreme monism of the type exemplified by the neo-realists, was advanced by D. C. Macintosh (1877-1948) in *The Problem of Knowledge* (1915). Macintosh was originally considered a member of the group of Critical Realists, but, because of his rejection of what he called "absolute dualism" in epistemology, he chose to label his own view "critical epistemological monism." In his opinion "any absolute dualism in epistemology is foredoomed to agnosticism" [28]; knowledge of the qualities or even of the existence of a transcendent object is precluded by a radical dualism of ideas and physical objects such as was asserted by Locke or a dualism of phenomena and things-in-themselves as maintained by Kant. The chief weakness of extreme monistic realism is, according to Macintosh, its inability to give a satisfactory account of error and illusion; if all sense qualities including illusory and hallucinatory experiences are independently real, the distinction between veridical and non-veridical perception, between truth and falsity loses all meaning.[29] Macintosh's compromise between the two extreme versions of realism holds "the doctrine that the object perceived is existentially, or numerically, identical with the real object at the moment of perception, although the real object may have qualities that are not perceived at the moment; and also that this same object may exist when unperceived, *although not necessarily* with all the qualities which it possesses when perceived." [30] The additional qualities which emerge in the process of perception are the result of the productive activity of consciousness.[31] Macintosh in affirming that consciousness is a productive activity makes an important concession to idealism. In the main, however, his epistemology is unequivocally realistic—in part monistic and in part dualistic.

A HISTORY OF PHILOSOPHICAL SYSTEMS

PRAGMATIC AND INSTRUMENTALIST THEORIES

The epistemological issues which divide the idealists from the realists and the various schools of critical and new realism from one another are for the pragmatist and instrumentalist largely pseudo-problems. The pragmatic theory of knowledge is a method of inquiry, a theory of meaning and a criterion of truth which may, to be sure, be fruitfully applied to the traditional issues of epistemology but which drastically alter the form and import of the epistemological problem rather than decide between the conflicting epistemological hypotheses. The detailed examination of the pragmatic theories of inquiry, meaning and truth lies beyond the scope of the present chapter, but we cannot avoid reformulating the pragmatic verifiability principle if we wish to understand the pragmatic attitude toward the central problems of epistemology. C. S. Peirce (1839-1914) enunciated the pragmatic maxim in his epoch making article: "How to Make Our Ideas Clear" which appeared in *Popular Science Monthly,* 1878: "Consider what effects that might conceivably have practical bearings, we conceive the object of our conception to have. Then our conception of these effects is the whole of our conception of the object." William James (1842-1910) in his address before the Philosophical Union of the University of California in September, 1898, recast Peirce's formula in these words: "To attain perfect clearness in our thoughts of an object, then, we need only consider what effects of a conceivably practical kind the object may involve—what sensations we are to expect from it, and what reactions we must prepare. Our conception of these effects, then, is for us the whole of our conception of the object, so far as that conception has positive significance at all." [32] The consequences for epistemology of taking seriously the pragmatic maxim of Peirce and James are fully worked by John Dewey (1859-   ). Dewey labels his position instrumentalism or experimentalism and enunciates its basic aim and method as follows: *"Instrumentalism is an attempt to constitute a precise logical theory of concepts, of judgments and inferences in their various forms, by considering primarily how thought functions in the experimental determination of future consequences."* [33]

Just how does the instrumentalist principle bear on the focal epistemological issues which divide the realists and idealists into rival schools? Dewey gives a forthright answer to this question in his contribution to the Pragmatists' cooperative volume, *Creative Intelligence,* 1917. The issues which divide the epistemologists are pseudo-problems arising from an artificial separation of subject and object of knowledge and then addressing themselves to the pragmatically meaningless question as to how the two are related in knowledge; ". . . the chief divisions of modern philosophy, idealism in its different kinds, realism of various brands, so-called common-sense dualism, agnosticism, relativism, phenomenalism, have grown around the general relation of subject and object. . . . Is it not time that philosophers turned from the attempt to determine the comparative merits of various replies to the questions to a consideration of the claim of the questions?" [34] Questions regarding subjective and objectivity of sense qualities, images, dreams, illusions and the like arise from the false assumption "that consciousness is outside the real object; that it is something different in kind"—an assumption which "makes consciousness supernatural in the literal sense of the word." [35] The conception of consciousness as something standing outside nature, as an otiose spectator of nature "depends upon the isolation of mind from intimate participation with other changes in the same nexus" [36] and is thus at variance with the biological continuity of man and nature.

The professional epistemologists are according to Dewey guilty not only of isolating sense-data from their causal nexus in nature, but of a fragmentary and isolated treatment of the sense-data themselves. Sense-datum epistemology is committed to "a doctrine of the disconnected atomicity of sense-data," a doctrine "common to sensationalism and to some form of new realism." [37] "As a matter of fact," insists Dewey, "smells, tastes, sounds, pressures, colors, etc., are not isolated; they are bound together by all kinds of interactions or connections . . ." [38] Dewey acknowledges that sense-datum analysis may be legitimate for certain purposes, but to base a theory of knowledge on atomistic sense-data rather than on ordinary perceptions is to generate artificial and pragmatically insoluble problems.

Although Dewey's application of the instrumentalist principles renders meaningless the epistemological disputes between the idealists and the realists and between monistic and dualistic realism, it does not preclude epistemological enquiry altogether. Indeed, Dewey's instrumentalist analysis throws considerable illumination on certain problems concerning knowledge. The point of departure for Dewey's own examination of knowledge is found in "the objects of everyday experience, the concrete things of the world in which we live and which, from the standpoint of our practical affairs, our enjoyments and sufferings, form the world we live in." [39] Perception of ordinary objects provides then the basis and ground of knowledge, but, insists Dewey, perception as such is not itself knowledge. "Many realists . . . have treated the perceptions as *cases of knowledge,* instead of simply natural events having in themselves (apart from the use that may be made of them) no more knowledge status or worth than, say, a shower or a fever." [40] Although perceptions are non-cognitive natural events, they have a unique cognitive function. "They are the sole ultimate data, the sole media, of inference to all natural objects and processes. While we do not, in any intelligible or verifiable sense know *them,* we know all things that we do know *with* or *by* them." [41] Dewey gives particular attention to the inferences from perceptions to so-called scientific objects, such as atoms and electrons; to say that a scientific or physical object exists and has specific metric properties, is merely to make predictions that such and such perceptions will occur under specified conditions. Dewey speaks characteristically of the "metric character of the physical object," and notes that "metric traits are reached by a series of operations of which they express the statistically constant outcome . . ." [42] "In other words, the conception of the physical object is, in considerable degree, the outcome of complex operations of comparison and translation." [43] This operationalist interpretation of the physical object renders meaningless the problem so baffling to many realistic epistemologists of determining the relation between the perceived object and its physical counterpart. "The problem which is supposed to exist between two tables, one that of direct perception and use and the other that of physics (to take the favorite illustration of recent discussion) is thus illusory. The perceived and used table is the only table. . . ." [44] The so-called "physical table" is reducible to a set of predictive statements to the effect that if certain operations are performed, perceptions of a determinate character will be had. While it is contrary to the spirit of the instrumentalist interpretation of knowledge to assimilate it to any one of the typical epistemological theories, it will perhaps not be amiss to point out that Dewey's theory paved the way for and has close affinities with the phenomenalistic hypothesis to which we now turn our attention.

PHENOMENALISTIC AND IDEALISTIC THEORIES

The most influential theories of the second phase of contemporary epistemology may be described as phenomenalistic; the first phase of contemporary epistemology was a realistic revolt against nineteenth century idealism, the second phase a phenomenalistic counter-revolution. Contemporary phenomenalism is not a school comparable to the schools of new and critical realism, but it is a well-defined tendency of contemporary epistemological thought. Contemporary phenomenalists, though they may differ from one another, agree in restricting knowledge to the phenomenal order of sense-data; they reject the realistic hypothesis of a trans-phenomenal object of knowledge.

Contemporary phenomenalism may be traced to the eighteenth and nineteenth centuries and early twentieth century sources: Hume (1711-1776) and Leibniz (1646-1716) gave utterance to phenomenalistic doctrines; Kant's analysis of knowledge contained in the *Critique of Pure Reason* is, if the transcendental paraphernalia and the doctrine of the thing-in-itself are eliminated, and Hegel's analysis of cognition in his *Phenomenology of Mind* (1807), are special forms of phenomenalistic epistemology. J. S. Mill's (1806-1873) dictum that matter is nothing but a "permanent possibility of sensation" [45] is another classical formulation of phenomenalism. F. Brentano's (1838-1917) theory of intentional reference in his *Psychologie vom empirischen Standpunkt* (1874) and the "Phenomenology" of Husserl [46] (1859-1938) contain many phenomenalistic insights.

The contemporary revival of phenomenalism to which we now turn our attention is largely a reaction to realism expressed, however, in the sense-datum terminology of new realism. Though the thinkers whom we shall examine would not all apply the term phenomenalism to their theories and certainly would not consider themselves as belonging to a school, nevertheless they have much in common.

C. I. Lewis (contemporary), who labels his point of view "conceptualistic pragmatism" and expresses his philosophical indebtedness to "Peirce, James, and Dewey—especially Peirce," [47] seems committed to a phenomenalist epistemology. He sums up his epistemology in *Mind and the World-Order* (1929) in these words: "The two elements to be distinguished in knowledge are the concept, which is the product of the activity of thought, and the sensuously given, which is independent of such activity," [48] and in his recent volume *An Analysis of Knowledge and Valuation* (1946), he applies this analysis to perception: "Perceptual knowledge has two aspects or phases; the givenness of something given, and the interpretation which, in the light of past experience, we put upon it. In the case of perceiving the white paper, what is given is a complex of sensa or qualia—what Santayana calls an 'essence.'" [49] The perceptual knowledge of an object is interpretative activity of the mind operating on the data of sense and "is neither coincidence of mind and object in the momentary experience nor any duplication of the object in the mind.[50] Lewis thus explicitly rejects realism in its presentative and representative forms [51] but nevertheless insists that there is a significant sense in which the perceived thing is real and objective: "To ascribe an objective quality to a thing means implicitly the prediction that if I act in certain ways, specifiable experience will eventuate: if I should bite this, it will taste sweet, if I should pinch it, it will feel moderately soft; if I should eat it, it would digest and not poison me; if I should turn it over, I should perceive another rounded surface much like this—these and a hundred other such hypothetical propositions constitute my knowledge of the apple in my hand. *These are the meaning which this presentation has to me now,* but it may be that neither now nor in the immediate future do I actually verify these possibilities." [52] The meaning of objectivity of perceptual knowledge is again defined in terms of a set of statements: ". . . a statement of objective empirical fact is translatable into some set of predictive statements each of which formulates some possible confirmation in direct experience, the whole set of such statements being inexhaustible in number . . ." [53] Lewis disavows "a phenomenalistic interpretation of the relation of mind to reality in cognition," since "it is still possible, in terms of the conception here presented, to affirm that the content of presentation is an authentic part or aspect or perspective which is ingredient in the objective reality known." [54] Yet his unwillingness to commit himself to a realism of either a presentational or representational sort places him in the phenomenalistic camp; the only objectivity which Lewis' theory unequivocally assigns to the perceived thing is the phenomenal objectivity expressible by a set of predictive hypothetical statements.

A phenomenalistic position so extreme that it is scarcely distinguishable from Berkeleyan subjective idealism is advanced by W. T. Stace (contemporary) in *The Theory of Knowledge and Existence* (1932). Stace in his Preface expresses his "kinship of spirit" with Poincaré and Vaihinger. The underlying assumption of his empirical and fictionalistic epistemology is: "Whatever belief I hold on whatever subject must be either a datum of *my* consciousness or else an inference or mental construction which *I* base upon *my* data." [55] My sense data constitute the starting point of all knowledge; [56] "the solitary mind is confronted with a phantasmagoria of private presentations." [57] The sense data exist only in so far as they are perceived; "the solitary mind cannot be aware of any distinction between the *esse* and the *percipi* of its presentation. It cannot, for example, draw any distinction between 'blue' and 'awareness of blue.' " [58] The sense data are private or subjective, but this does not, in Stace's opinion, mean that they are 'mental'; ". . . the question whether the presentation is 'mental' or 'non-mental' . . . is itself meaningless, and the dispute which is supposed to center round it is a mere quarrel over words." [59]

Physical objects since they are not immediate data must, on Stace's view, be constructions: "Our thesis is that belief in an external world is a mental construction." [60] A mental construction is an arbitrary invention of the mind which "can never be either proved or disproved, nor can there ever be the slightest evidence for or against it. . . . The whole mental construction (of an external world) is a work of the imagination which supposes its experience extended into a void where there is in fact no experience." [61] The external world then is a mental construction; it is a pure creation of the mind to which no existential facts correspond.[62] Stace denies real or literal objectivity to things perceived and assigns to them what may be called phenomenal objectivity. The essential feature of the concept of phenomenal things is its predictive function. "The concept (of a thing) contains a great deal more than what is given in perception. This element of interpretation enables us to regulate our actions. Suppose I see before me a round yellowy-red object. I recognize this on sight as an apple . . . all that I *see* is the color and the shape. But the concept 'apple' means much more than this. It implies, for example, that the object will taste sweet, will have a white, juicy interior when cut open, etc. . . . The concept enables me to predict future possible experiences in various ways." [63] The essential meaning of perceptual objectivity for Stace as for Lewis is expressed by a set of predictive statements about sense data.

A phenomenalistic theory of knowledge which has much in common with the positions of Stace and Lewis, will be found in the present author's *The Analysis of Knowledge* (1941). I have there analyzed the knowledge-situation into three factors: (1) knowing subject; (2) content present to the subject and consisting of sense qualities which possess the function of "intent" or reference; and (3) the phenomenal object referred to or envisaged by the content. This triadic pattern is exemplified not only in perception, but also in memory and the knowledge of other selves. The "phenomenal" object is not an existent entity but an "object" thought about or entertained by the knowing mind. Since this theory does not preclude the existence of a physical object in addition to the perceptual or phenomenal object, it may be called referential realism, rather than phenomenalism.

Professor H. H. Price (1899-) of Oxford University in his *Perception* (1933), develops a position which is phenomenalistic up to a point, but which then veers off in the direction of monistic realism. He asserts, in the first place, that the mind, by an act of sensing, has an awareness of sense-data. "When I am in the situation which is described as seeing something, touching something, etc., it is certain in each case that a colour-patch, or a pressure, or a noise exists at that moment and that I am acquainted with this colour-patch, pressure or noise. Such entities are called sense-data, and the acquaintance with them is called sensing . . ." [64] The sense-data may or may not exist through the intervals when they are not being sensed; we have no assurance that identical sense-data are sensed by different minds; we are not committed to any special view as to their 'status'—they may be physical, they may be mental or they may be neutral, *i.e.*, neither mental nor physical; we are not committed to either a psychological or a physical explanation of their origin.[65]

Price examines the relation between sense-data and finds that they belong to "families"—a "family" is a group of sense-data, actual and obtainable, consisting of a standard solid together with an indefinite number of distortion-solids.[66] The discovery of "families" of sense-data is a necessary stage in the process of gaining an apprehension of material objects;[67] it is the phenomenalistic stage of knowledge and if Price had stopped at this point and defined a material object as a family of sense-data or a system of causally interrelated families or as the "object" envisaged by the family or system, his position would have been thoroughgoing phenomenalism.[68] But his epistemological analysis does not stop here; he proceeds to examine the relation between sense-data as numbers of families and material objects[69] and thereby to establish that "Phenomenalism is false."[70] In not very convincing fashion, he seeks to show that there is a sense in which families of sense-data "belong to" physical objects; "the family is related to the material thing by delimiting or coinciding with the physical . . . portion of the thing."[71] His final epistemological position may thus be described as a basic phenomenalism with strongly neo-realistic overtones.

THE RESURGENCE OF IDEALISM

We conclude our summary of twentieth century epistemology with a brief reference to the contemporary resurgence of idealism. The boldly realistic epistemologies of the early decades of the century attacked the very foundations both of Berkeleyan subjective idealism and the Bradley-Bosanquet-Royce versions of absolute idealism. Moore and the American new realists were the vanguard of the revolt against idealism and were followed by the constructive realisms of Alexander, Whitehead and the Russell of *The Analysis of Mind* and the *Analysis of Matter*. The doctrine of representative ideas, prominent in the critical realism of Lovejoy, introduced an idealistic element into an otherwise realistic epistemology. The phenomenalistic epistemologies of Lewis, Price and Stace marked further inroads of the idealistic analysis of knowledge and the healthy resurgence of idealism during the last decade amply refutes those who predicted idealism's early demise.

A truly monumental contribution to idealistic epistemology is to be found in Brand Blanshard's two volume work *The Nature of*

Thought (1940). Blanshard begins his analysis of knowledge at the level of perception and in the course of a penetrating critique of sense-datum epistemology seeks to show that even at this level, the sensuously given is suffused with thought and judgment. Blanshard's discussion of perception is no mere reiteration of familiar idealistic arguments; it is a vigorous treatment of the problem of perception which takes full cognizance of realistic contributions to the epistemology of perception. Likewise, in his interpretation of the functioning of ideas in knowledge he formulates his position with full knowledge of the current pragmatic and behavioristic interpretations of ideational thought. The catholicity of his epistemology is manifest in his attitude toward scientific psychology; his psychology is more sophisticated than that of realistic epistemology. Blanshard, however, never loses sight of the central idealistic insight that ideal elements are constitutive of knowledge at all its levels; he is in the main tradition of German and Anglo-American idealism but *The Nature of Thought* is no mere recapitulation of earlier insights and arguments.

NOTES

1. *Philosophical Studies,* p. 29.
2. *The New Realism,* p. 258.
3. *Ibid.*
4. *Op. cit.,* p. 260.
5. *Op. cit.,* p. 474.
6. *Present Philosophical Tendencies,* p. 126.
7. *Our Knowledge of the External World,* p. 80 ff.
8. *Analysis of Mind,* p. 144.
9. *Process and Reality,* p. 337 ff. *Cf.* also *Science and the Modern World,* p. 103 ff.
10. *Op. cit.,* p. 357.
11. *Op. cit.,* p. 361 ff.
12. *Cf. Space, Time and Deity,* Vol. I, p. 12.
13. I have criticized Alexander's doctrine of "Enjoyment" in *The Analysis of Knowledge,* p. 97.
14. *Cf.* A. E. Murphy's article in the *Philosophical Review,* XXXVI (1927), p. 122, and A. O. Lovejoy, *The Revolt Against Dualism,* Lects. III, IV.
15. *The Revolt Against Dualism,* p. 260n.
16. *Cf. op. cit.,* p. 264.
17. *Op. cit.,* p. 298.

18. *Op. cit.,* p. 303.
19. *Op. cit.,* p. 305.
20. *Op. cit.,* p. 308.
21. *Op. cit.,* p. 309.
22. *Scepticism and Animal Faith,* p. 45.
23. *Op. cit.,* p. 77 ff.
24. *Op. cit.,* p. 80.
25. *Op. cit.,* p. 88.
26. *Op. cit.,* p. 179.
27. *Op. cit.,* p. 150.
28. *The Problem of Knowledge,* p. 14.
29. *Cf. op. cit.,* p. 232 ff.
30. *Op. cit.,* p. 310 ff.
31. *Cf. op. cit.,* p. 315.
32. William James, *Collected Essays and Reviews,* p. 411. *Cf.* William James, *Pragmatism,* Lecture II. *Cf.* also John Dewey, "Development of American Pragmatism" in *Twentieth Century Philosophy,* ed. by D. D. Runes (1943).
33. *Op. cit.,* p. 463.
34. *Creative Intelligence,* p. 34.
35. *Op. cit.,* p. 35.
36. *Op. cit.,* p. 37.
37. *The Quest for Certainty,* p. 126.
38. *Ibid.*
39. *Loc. cit.,* p. 195.
40. "Naive vs. Presentative Realism" in *Essays in Experimental Logic,* p. 253 ff.
41. *Op. cit.,* p. 259.
42. *Op. cit.,* p. 240 ff.
43. *Ibid.*
44. *Op. cit.,* p. 240.
45. J. S. Mill, *Examination of Sir Wm. Hamilton's Philosophy,* ch. 11.
46. *Cf. Ideen zu einer reinen Phaenomenologie* (1913). English translation by B. Gibson entitled *Ideas.*
47. *Mind and the World-Order* (1929), p. xi.
48. *Op. cit.,* p. 37.
49. *An Analysis of Knowledge and Valuation,* p. 188.
50. *Mind and the World-Order,* p. 134.
51. *Cf. op. cit.,* p. 135.
52. *Op. cit.,* p. 187n.
53. *Op. cit.,* p. 190.
54. *Op. cit.,* p. 187n.
55. *Theory of Knowledge and Existence,* p. 67.

56. *Cf. op. cit.,* p. 307.
57. *Op. cit.,* p. 73.
58. *Ibid.*
59. *Op. cit.,* p. 74.
60. *Op. cit.,* p. 95.
61. *Op. cit.,* p. 111.
62. *Cf. op. cit.,* p. 168.
63. *Op. cit.,* p. 245.
64. *Perception,* p. 18.
65. *Cf. op. cit.,* p. 18 ff.
66. *Op. cit.,* p. 272.
67. *Cf. ibid.*
68. *Cf. op. cit.,* p. 282.
69. *Cf. op. cit.,* p. 273 ff.
70. *Cf. op. cit.,* pp. 287, 293.
71. *Op. cit.,* p. 303.

BIBLIOGRAPHY

G. P. ADAMS and W. P. MONTAGUE, editors, *Contemporary American Philosophy,* 2 Vols. (1930).

S. ALEXANDER, *Space, Time and Deity* (2nd ed., 1928).

A. J. AYER, *The Foundations of Empirical Knowledge* (1940).

———, *Language, Truth and Logic* (1936).

B. BOSANQUET, *The Meeting of Extremes in Contemporary Philosophy* (1921).

B. BLANSHARD, *The Nature of Thought,* 2 Vols. (1940).

C. D. BROAD, *Mind and its Place in Nature* (1925).

———, *Perception, Physics and Reality* (1914).

———, *Scientific Thought* (1923).

J. DEWEY and Others, *Creative Intelligence* (1917).

J. DEWEY, *The Influence of Darwin on Philosophy* (1910).

———, *Essays in Experimental Logic* (1916).

———, *The Quest for Certainty* (1921).

———, *Logic, The Theory of Enquiry* (1938).

D. DRAKE and others, *Essays in Critical Realism* (1920).

D. DRAKE, *Mind and its Place in Nature* (1925).

M. FARBER, *The Foundation of Phenomenology* (1943).

E. B. HOLT and others, *The New Realism* (1912).

E. B. HOLT, *The Concept of Consciousness* (1914).

E. HUSSERL, *Ideas: General Introduction to Pure Phenomenology.* Trans. by W. R. Boyce Gibson (1931).

W. JAMES, *Pragmatism* (1907).

———, *Essays in Radical Empiricism* (1912).
———, *Collected Essays and Reviews* (1920).
J. LAIRD, *Knowledge, Belief and Opinion* (1930).
———, *A Study in Realism* (1920).
———, *Recent Philosophy* (1936).
C. I. LEWIS, *Mind and the World-Order* (1929).
———, *Analysis of Knowledge and Valuation* (1946).
A. O. LOVEJOY, *The Revolt against Dualism* (1930).
D. C. MACINTOSH, *The Problem of Knowledge* (1915).
R. NIETZ, *A Hundred Years of British Philosophy* (1938).
W. P. MONTAGUE, *The Ways of Knowing* (1925).
G. E. MOORE, "Refutation of Idealism" in *Mind*, NS. Vol. xii (1903); republished in *Philosophical Studies* (1922).
J. H. MUIRHEAD, ed., *Contemporary British Philosophy* (1924).
R. B. PERRY, *Present Philosophical Tendencies* (1912).
H. H. PRICE, *Perception* (1933).
D. D. RUNES, ed., *Twentieth Century Philosophy* (1943).
B. RUSSELL, *The Problems of Philosophy* (1912).
———, *Scientific Method in Philosophy* (1914).
———, *The Analysis of Mind* (1921).
———, *An Inquiry into Meaning and Truth* (1940)
———, *Human Knowledge: Its Scope and Limits* (1948).
G. SANTAYANA, *Scepticism and Animal Faith* (1923).
P. A. SCHILPP, ed., *The Philosophy of Bertrand Russell* (1944).
———, *The Philosophy of John Dewey* (1939).
N. K. SMITH, *Prolegomena to an Idealist Theory of Knowledge* (1924).
E. G. SPAULDING, *The New Rationalism* (1918).
W. T. STACE, *The Theory of Knowledge and Existence* (1932).
———, "Russell's Neutral Monism" in *The Philosophy of Bertrand Russell*, ed. by P. A. Schilpp.
J. E. TURNER, *A Theory of Direct Realism* (1925).
A. P. USHENKO, *Power and Events* (1946).
H. VAIHINGER, *The Philosophy of "As If,"* Eng. trans. (1924).
W. H. WERKMEISTER, *The Basis and Structure of Knowledge* (1948).
A. N. WHITEHEAD, *Principles of Natural Knowledge* (1919).
———, *The Concept of Nature* (1933).
———, *Process and Reality* (1929).
———, *Science and the Modern World* (1925).
L. WOOD, *The Analysis of Knowledge* (1940).
———, art. "Epistemology" in *The Dictionary of Philosophy*, ed. by D. D. Runes (1942).
———, art. "Philosophy" in *The American Year Book* for the years 1947-50., ed. by W. M. Schuyler.

CHAPTER FORTY-TWO

PHILOSOPHY OF THE SCIENCES

A. CORNELIUS BENJAMIN

ALTHOUGH philosophical activity has been characterized in the last quarter century by the publication of numerous and substantial books and articles in an area which has come to be called the "philosophy of the sciences," there is little reason to believe that either the method or the subject-matter of this field of problems should be considered novel. Philosophers have always been interested in the sciences, as they have been concerned with the other major phases of man's activity, and they have felt a certain responsibility to investigate its nature and presuppositions for the same reason that they have considered it their task to examine art, religion, and morality.

Consequently, one would be extremely rash to assign a date when the philosophy of the sciences began to exist as a discipline. The publication of a significant book in the area would afford a convenient starting point, but the choices would be many and any selection more or less arbitrary. Undoubtedly the writings of the logical positivists in recent years have contributed greatly to the refinement and advancement of certain problems. But *Science et Hypothèse*, by Jules Henri Poincaré (1854-1912), which antedates these publications by some years, is certainly a classic in the field. This suggests that one might go back to the work of some of the mathematical logicians, such as Guiseppe Peano (1858-1932), Gottlob Frege (1848-1925), and George Boole (1815-1864); but one is then promptly led to the earlier work of Johann Bolyai (1802-1860) and Nicholaus Lobachewski (1793-1856). On the side of the inductive sciences important books were written by John Stuart Mill (1806-1873), by Auguste Comte (1798-1857), and by William Whewell (1795-1866). However, the productions of these men were no more startling or definitive than, say, the *Principia* of Sir Isaac Newton (1642-1727), or the *Novum Organum* of Francis Bacon (1561-1626).

In view of this uncertainty about origins the only reasonable attitude is to refrain from announcing the birth of a new discipline, and admit that, like Topsy, it just "growed up." What is important is that within the past twenty or thirty years certain problems have emerged from the broader philosophical background, and are with increasing sharpness distinguishable from those of closely related areas.

Perhaps all that one can do even today is to define the field empirically, *i.e.*, list the actual problems which are being examined and discussed by certain writers, without any attempt to predetermine the area by intensional definition or to organize the special problems within the general field. The main characteristic of all these investigations is that while they are philosophical in spirit and method they take their point of departure from the sciences, individually or collectively. Thus they are "about" the sciences, yet not strictly scientific; they examine the experimental method, yet they do not themselves use the experimental method in the narrow sense; they accept science as a going concern, yet they attempt to criticize and evaluate the sciences from the point of view of their presuppositions, methods, and implications for a larger view of the world. The studies are pursued most effectively by scientists well trained in philosophy and philosophers who are competent in science. This is not to deny that many studies have been published in recent years which purport to make important contributions to the field and which are the work of philosophers who have inadequate understanding of science and of scientists who consider that philosophy is mere "generalization and speculation" which, as Darwin suggested, any fool can carry on. But the insignificance of such writings can usually be detected; many of them fall into the area of popularizations of science, written for the layman, and frequently prove to be erroneous in their portrayal of scientific facts and definitely misleading in their conception of what the philosophical task is.

If one does not insist on too rigid an application of logical categories the problems of the philosophy of the sciences may be classified in three fairly well defined fields. These overlap to a great extent, and there is some reason to believe that there may be important problems within the general field which are not included in any of these subdivisions. Furthermore, one of these areas, as will be shown presently, itself consists of a fairly heterogeneous collection of problems which are grouped together not so much because they have something in common as because they do not seem to find proper location in either of the other regions.

The first field includes all problems related directly or indirectly to a consideration of the method of science. Whatever else science may be it is an attempt, by means of a regulated and controlled method, subject to errors which must be avoided if possible, to achieve a systematic knowledge of a certain subject-matter. The use of the term "science," in the singular, should not be considered as prejudicing the issue as to whether there is or is not *one* method for all the sciences. If the commonly accepted distinction between the rational sciences (mathematics, rational mechanics) and the empirical sciences (physics, chemistry, biology, psychology, sociology) is correct there are at least *two* such methods. One of the problems of the philosophy of the sciences is precisely that of examining and criticizing this dichotomy, and of determining the exact sense in which it holds. In the vocabulary of the rational sciences, for example, there occur such words as *axiom, postulate, definition, theorem, corollary, deduction, proof, consistency, independence,* and *interpretation*. It is the task of the philosophy of the sciences to examine these notions, to define them if possible, to give them the maximum clarity if they cannot be defined, and to formulate the criteria which can be taken as measures for the adequacy of the sciences in which they occur. Among the words which appear in the description of the empirical siences are *data, hypothesis, theory, law, classification, measurement, induction, deduction, experimentation, verification,* and *idealization*. The philosophy of the sciences must subject these terms to a similar analysis, and endeavor to show how they are interrelated in the method which has proved so successful in providing us with knowledge of the world in which we live.

As an example of such a problem consider the difference between *proof* as employed by the mathematician and *verification* as employed by the empirical scientist. The former is based on the deductive method, the latter on the inductive, or, as it is sometimes called, the inductive-deductive method. A system of geometry consists of a body of statements and concepts which can be subdivided into two classes—the underived notions and the derived notions. The former constitute the logical foundation of the entire scheme; they consist of axioms, postulates, undefined terms, and definitions. All the basic "ideas" which enter into the system are undefined terms and definitions, and all the "true" propositions of the scheme are included among the axioms and postulates. The latter group of notions consists of the theorems and corollaries; the essential feature of this group is that each and every member can be derived by strict logical deduction from certain of the former group. All the derived propositions are true *if* the postulates and axioms are true; this is the defining characteristic of deduction. Thus the significant feature of a deductive scheme is its independence of external considerations; no idea may be introduced into the theorems which is incapable of definition in terms of the primitive ideas, and no theorem must be introduced which is incapable of proof either in terms of other theorems in the scheme or in terms of certain of the axioms and postulates. Whether the axioms and postulates are true in any empirical sense is irrelevant to the deductive truth of the theorems, though it may have a bearing on the application of the system of propositions to a certain subject-matter. Mathematicians formerly held that the axioms and postulates must be "self-evident" or "intuitively true"; recent thought has tended to look upon them as mere "conventions," which may or may not have concrete interpretations; thus the formal cogency of a mathematical system is considered to be independent of its application, and proof consists merely in showing the deducibility of theorems from the underived notions much as a game of checkers consists in the working out of the positions of the men according to rules, without regard for any meaning which might be attached to the counters or to the moves.

Verification of an empirical hypothesis is something quite different. Nothing in the nature of proof, in the strict sense, enters into the natural sciences; all that can be established is probability of a higher or lower degree. Verification is an operation performed on a hypothesis. In its original form a hypothesis is simply a guess. It is not, of course, a purely random guess, for it is based on data which, because of their presumed bearing on a certain problem, have been previously collected, classified, and measured if possible. Thus the empirical sciences take their origin in observed phenomena—things, movements, changes, and processes which go on in the world about us. Some one of these natural events puzzles us; we desire to know more about what it is, how it takes place, or why it takes place, or what effect it has on other natural happenings. This leads us to observe it carefully for the purpose of forming a conjecture as to what is happening behind the scene. Such a hypothesis is, in its first form, a mere hunch, and arises as a flash of insight or a sudden inspiration. Verification then goes to work to remove the doubt which is inevitable in connection with an idea arising under such conditions. This involves making predictions as to what further events would occur in the situation *if* the hypothesis were true. These anticipated events are then sought either in the situation as it stands or in the situation as modified through experimental controls. If they are found, the hypothesis is to that extent considered to be confirmed; if they are not, the hypothesis is rejected. The significant point is that the hypothesis is never proved by its anticipated consequences but only rendered more and more probable; the degree of credence to be given to the hypothesis is proportionate roughly to the number and variety of the confirming instances. Thus hypotheses increase in probability, gradually taking on the status of generally accepted theories, but subject always to disconfirming predictions, which require either that the conjectured explanations be completely rejected, or that they be radically modified.

Problems in the second area of the philosophy of the sciences are somewhat less well defined than problems of method. In a sense, many of these are also problems of method. But the reference is more directly to subject-matter than to procedure, so that they involve what are commonly called metaphysical considerations in a way in which the former do not. They have to do with the analysis of the basic concepts and presuppositions of the sciences. Each of the sciences has three types of concepts which enter into consideration. First, there are the concepts of a science which are peculiar to its subject-matter, *e.g., force, matter,* and *motion* for the physicist. Second, there are the concepts which are presupposed by a science but not subjected to analysis by the science itself, since they are taken over from another science, *e.g., number, order* and *quantity* as used by the physicist. Third, there are the concepts which are presupposed by a science but not subjected to analysis by any science, *e.g., time,* as used by the physicist. While the problem of analysis in the case of each type of concept is different, there are common features. Each concept, provided it is not purely methodological, is presumed to have some empirical reference; *force, matter, motion, number, order, quantity,* and *time* designate features of our world, and it is an important problem to determine as clearly as possible exactly what the empirical content of these terms is and how they refer to aspects of our experience. But the concepts as used by the scientist may acquire meanings which are quite remote from their empirical foundation. Through various operations of idealization, abstraction, extrapolation, and generalization the concepts take on other interpretations which are more useful, perhaps, for the purposes of the scientist, but are so removed from the empirical and descriptive meaning that they are in many cases properly called "fictions" or "constructs." Examples can be found in the notions of *mathematical infinity, mathematical zero, perfect levers* and *gases, frictionless motion, the economic man,* and *the ideal state.* The problem in the case of each of such concepts is to show precisely what it means empirically, what it means as a functioning concept in science, and through what operations the latter meaning may be derived from, or tested by, the former. Such considerations are necessary in order that the empirical reference of the natural sciences may be justified and the abstract character of the rational sciences properly evaluated.

An example of such a problem is afforded by the concept of time. Let us call the time which is experienced by all of us in our daily lives "empirical time," and the time which enters as t in the formulas of physics "physical time." At first glance these might appear to be one and the same thing. But a moment's consideration will show that this is not the case. For example, empirical time—your time—has a beginning and an end; the beginning is your first remembered event, and the end will be the last conscious event of your life. Physical time, on the other hand, extends infinitely into the past and the future; for physics there is always a moment before any moment, and always a moment after any moment. Again, empirical time is not infinitely divisible; in a sense it is not divided at all but runs along in an unbroken stream; but even if divisible it can only be broken up into elements which are finite in duration— say the length of a span of attention—and anything shorter than this cannot be detected as a duration at all. Physical time, however, is capable of infinite division; there are seconds, tenths of a second, hundredths of a second, and so on indefinitely. Furthermore, empirical time has a definite "arrow"; past and future are quite different from one another, and time passes from the future into the past, never the reverse. For physics, or at least for certain types of physical process, the distinction between past and future exists only as the difference between $+t$ and $-t$; the formula for falling bodies enables us to compute either how far a body must have fallen to reach a certain point at a certain time, or how far it will fall from this point in the same time, but it does not tell us which the body has done or will do. Finally, empirical time flows unevenly; it speeds up as we are interested and absorbed, and slows down as we are bored. As Newton said, physical time, *i.e.*, the absolute time of pre-relativity, "flows equably throughout." Just how we can measure this absolute flow, since our measuring instruments may be subject to variations, is another matter and a question which is not relevant here.

We may say, consequently, that the t of physics is something quite different from time as we experience it, and the problem arises as to how physics can be said to have any application to the world since the time which it employs in its formulas is in a clear sense something fictional. The answer consists in showing through what logical operations the time of physics can be derived from empirical time. A. N. Whitehead [1] (1861-1947), for example, has shown through his method of extensive abstraction how instants of time can be considered to be certain functions of concrete durations which we all experience in our everyday lives. Thus physics may be shown to have an application to our world, though a somewhat more abstract and involved application than we had supposed. Similarly, through a consideration of certain processes of correlation, extrapolation, and isolation the other features of physical time may be shown to be derivable from empirical time.

The third area of the philosophy of the sciences consists, as was indicated above, of a miscellaneous group of problems, which are not susceptible of any systematic classification. They may all be roughly described as concerned with the implications which science has, either in its content or in its method, for the other aspects of our lives. Among these problems are, first, those which are concerned with the theoretical relations of the sciences to one another, and of the sciences to man's other attempts to understand, evaluate, and control the world. This has come down in the history of philosophy as the general problem of the classification of the sciences. While almost all great philosophers have attempted a solution of the problem, seldom have they restricted it to the sciences in the narrow sense of the word. Bacon called his classification a "description of the intellectual globe," and the problem has usually been conceived in terms of an attempted organization of all the so-called disciplines —sciences, humanities, arts and technologies, philosophy, and history. Its aim is to show the logical relations which hold among these various modes of inquiry and evaluation—how some are general and others are specific, some abstract and others concrete, some rational and others empirical, some pure and others applied; how understanding resembles and differs from appraising; how composite studies may be formed from more elemental studies; how studies about studies, *e.g.*, the philosophy of the sciences, may emerge; and so on. A second type of problem in this area concerns the theoretical implications of certain truths in science insofar as they modify our judgments in other areas of our experience; *e.g.* whether we can admit free will even though science has shown that the world is guided by necessary law, or whether we can still believe in the existence of a human soul when psychology has shown the concept to be unnecessary, or whether we can retain faith in God when the natural sciences seem to be increasingly capable of accounting for all natural processes. Finally, there are the problems of the practical effects, *i.e.*, effects on our form of government, manner of living, cultural products, health, comfort, etc., of the discoveries of science. The outstanding example of this in recent years is, of course, the problem of the atomic bomb; but the broader problem is as old as science itself, for science has always affected our lives favorably (telephones, radios, automobiles, medicines) as well as adversely (poisons, gunpowder, instruments of torture).

As an example of a problem in this area brief reference may be made to a situation which has arisen in recent quantum mechanics. The traditional mechanics had assumed, not without justification, that the world was, so far as its mechanical properties were concerned, a deterministic system guided by necessary law. This meant that on the basis of knowledge of the laws of mechanics and of the state of any particle at any moment, *i.e.*, knowledge of its position and velocity, accurate prediction could be made as to its state at any later moment. It is summed up in the famous remark of P. S.

Laplace [2] (1749-1827) that if he knew the state of every particle in the universe at any time he could predict the entire course of the universe. Prior to about 1925 it had been supposed that there was nothing theoretically impossible in ascertaining the state of any particle, though practically there might be serious difficulties. But about this time W. Heisenberg [3] (1901-   ) demonstrated that where the particle concerned is very small, accurate observation of its state is impossible. In order to record its position some form of energy, for example, light, must be used. But light has a definite momentum, and the particle is knocked out of its position by the impact of the light wave; thus we observe it not where it was prior to the illumination but where it is after it. If the attempt is made to avoid this by using light with a longer wave and thus less momentum, a new difficulty appears—we disturb the particle less but because of the greater wave length we no longer have determinate information about its position. Heisenberg formulated this by saying that the product of the uncertainty in position and the uncertainty in velocity is a constant; this means that if we know accurately where the particle is we know only very inaccurately what its velocity is, and conversely. But since prediction depends upon accurate knowledge of both, we can never know exactly what any future state of the particle will be.

The presumed implications of this conclusion, both for science and for the broader aspects of experience, have been many and various. Some writers, such as Albert Einstein (1879-   ) and Max Planck [4] (1858-1947) have felt that the consequences for science were not serious, and that it is still possible to believe in causal laws and a deterministic world. Others, such as A. S. Eddington [5] (1882-1944) and A. H. Compton [6] (1892-   ), have suggested that the consequences are more far-reaching. If the two conditions required for a particle to be in a certain state are incompatible then the particle cannot be in such a state; hence it cannot itself, so to speak, know where it is going. This is equivalent to saying that the future state of a particle is not completely determined by its present state. The only conclusion, therefore, is an abandonment of the principle of causality, at least in certain areas. When this result is transferred to the realm of human behavior belief in freedom of the will is presumed to receive strong support; for if the will is free it is uncaused, and if there are breaks in causality in the natural world we may expect them as well in the human world. Eddington says that what we mean by a choice may be, so far as the brain is concerned, the unpredictable movement of one of its tiny particles; such a possibility is perfectly compatible with science, and the freedom of the will is thus preserved.

Although the above account of the problems of the philosophy of science has been much over-simplified, and there has been no opportunity for critical evaluation, it may suffice, in the limited space available, as an indication of the type of consideration which has engaged writers in this important area. In conclusion, brief reference may be made, first, to an important controversial issue in the field, and, second, to the direction in which further developments may be expected in the future.

The publication, in 1927, of *The Logic of Modern Physics* [7] by P. W. Bridgman (1882-) marked an important event in the development of the philosophy of the sciences. In this book the position which has come to be known as "operationalism" was first clearly expressed. It is a theory for the definition of concepts—primarily scientific concepts, but having broad possibilities of generalization into all areas of thinking. Bridgman objected to the absolutes which had crept into physics, *e.g.*, absolute space and time, and insisted that such concepts can have no place since all the processes by which they are ascertained are relative. He therefore suggested that a concept should always be defined in terms of operations; *"a concept is synonymous with the corresponding set of operations."* [8] The concept of time, for example, is meaningless apart from the concrete and specific operations which are employed in the measurement of time. Similarly, the concept of length is relative since the operations for the measurement of length vary according to whether we are measuring very small lengths, very great lengths, distances of the stars, lengths of moving objects, etc.

Operationalism has spread from physics to the other sciences, particularly to psychology. While the point of view has something important to contribute, especially to the theory of meaning, it has serious limitations if not properly generalized. Certainly operations should not be restricted to those of measurement, since this is only one way we have of knowing objects. Furthermore, operationalism runs the danger of eliminating all generalization from science and preventing all prediction. For every operation is performed at a time and a place, and if performed at another time and place is, strictly speaking, another operation; thus if a concept is defined in terms of an operation it ought to be defined in terms of the specific operation performed at the time and place. But in this case all generality disappears. Similarly with predictability, since when I predict I anticipate the *kind* of event which is going to occur; but if operationalism is strictly correct there are no *kinds* of events, for every event is, in a sense, unique. Operationalism is significant in having called our attention to operations, but it tends to forget that the meaning of a concept is determined both by an operation performed upon something and something on which the operation is performed.

Recent publications in the area suggest the direction for future studies. No specific reference to the developments in mathematical logic need be made, since the topic is more adequately treated elsewhere in this volume. In the first place, there is reason to believe that the movement toward the formalizing of scientific doctrine will gain momentum; with the development of a more adequate logical symbolism it becomes possible both to express the newer scientific theories more precisely, and to formulate the scientific method itself in a less ambiguous manner. Secondly, as indicated by the article entitled "Testability and Meaning" [9] by R. Carnap (1891-   ) and *Experience and Prediction* [10] by Hans Reichenbach (1891-   ), the criteria of the meaningfulness and verifiability of scientific theories deserve further study; some attempt should be made, if possible to measure what can be called "degree of confirmation." Studies in this area merge imperceptibly with problems of semantics and general theory of signs. Finally, in spite of noteworthy contributions by such men as Reichenbach,[11] D. C. Williams [12] (1899-   ), and Bertrand Russell [13] (1872-   ), the problem of the grounds of induction demands further investigation. While it would, perhaps, be unfair to say that the situation is exactly what it was in Hume's day, frankness demands recognition of the fact that progress since his time has consisted not so much in solving the problem as in discovering and clarifying the possible alternative solutions.

A HISTORY OF PHILOSOPHICAL SYSTEMS

NOTES

1. *Concept of Nature* (Cambridge, 1920), Chaps. III, IV, V.
2. *Philosophical Essay on Probabilities* (New York, 1902), p. 4.
3. See his *Physical Principles of the Quantum Theory* (Chicago, 1930).
4. For the views of both Einstein and Planck see the latter's *Where is Science Going?* (New York, 1932).
5. *Nature of the Physical World* (New York, 1929), Chaps. X, XIV.
6. *The Freedom of Man* (New Haven, 1935).
7. (New York).
8. *Ibid.*, p. 5.
9. *Philosophy of Science,* vol. 3, no. 4, and vol. 4, no. 1.
10. (Chicago, 1938).
11. *The Theory of Probability* (Berkeley, 1949).
12. *Ground of Induction* (Cambridge, 1947).
13. *Human Knowledge, its Scope and Limits* (New York, 1948).

BIBLIOGRAPHY

BERNHARD BAVINK, *The Natural Sciences* (New York, 1932).
A. CORNELIUS BENJAMIN, *An Introduction to the Philosophy of Science* (New York, 1937).
C. D. BROAD, *Scientific Thought* (New York, 1923).
MORRIS COHEN, *Reason and Nature* (New York, 1931).
E. W. HOBSON, *The Domain of Natural Science* (New York, 1923).
W. S. JEVONS, *The Principles of Science* (London, 1907).
V. F. LENZEN, *Physical Theory* (New York, 1931).
EMILE MEYERSON, *Identity and Reality* (New York, 1930).
W. H. WERKMEISTER, *The Basis and Structure of Knowledge* (New York, 1948).
A. N. WHITEHEAD, *Science and the Modern World* (New York, 1925).

CHAPTER FORTY-THREE

RECENT SCHOOLS OF AESTHETICS

VAN METER AMES

AESTHETICS goes back at least to Plato (427-347 B.C.) in the West, as reflection upon beauty and upon the production, appreciation and criticism of art. But the systematic and specialized development of this reflection is modern, coming with a new interest in questions of art after they were separated in the Renaissance from those of morality and religion; and stimulated by sharper discrimination of the different fields of value.

Recent aesthetics has developed largely in relation to the successive aims and theories of French painting and literature in the latter half of the nineteenth century and since. The striving for realism on the part of French painters and writers is more or less in line with the idea of art as imitation in the thought of Plato and Aristotle (384-322 B.C.). But whereas Plato depreciated art for rendering the visible world, although he suggested Aristotle's view that art could indicate the universal and ideal, Courbet (1819-1877) urged the artist to stick to what he perceived in his own time and place, without trying to improve upon it. Charles E. Gauss (1909-   ), in his book *The Aesthetic Theories of French Artists* (1949), links Courbet's realism with the rise of experimental science, positivistic philosophy, and realism in literature. Manet (1832-1883) followed, then the impressionists, neo-impressionists, and Cézanne (1839-1906), all "concerned with the appearance of the external world." Gauss holds that even the subsequent symbolists and surrealists were searching for a kind of realism. But he shows the shift, coming with Gauguin (1848-1903) and other symbolists, toward the idea of art as not a rendering of outer reality but "a symbol of the state of the artist's soul."

A HISTORY OF PHILOSOPHICAL SYSTEMS

Meanwhile, in literature, there was the romantic reaction against the mechanism and classicism of the seventeenth and eighteenth centuries; followed by a period of naturalism, as in Zola (1840-1902), and of objective severity in the Parnassian poets. At the close of the nineteenth century came another swing away from the felt limitations of the scientific influence. This was the literary symbolist movement set off by Baudelaire's (1821-1867) translation of Poe (1809-1849), spreading through Mallarmé (1842-1898) and Rimbaud (1854-1891) to a number of subsequent poets and novelists.

Modern art and aesthetics have not always been antagonistic to science. There is an interesting parallel between cubism and the work of Whitehead (1861-1947) and Russell (1872-) on the logic of mathematics and the interpretation of science as rational constructions through which to view the world. Their *Principia Mathematica* (1910) came out about the time that Bracque (1881-) and Picasso (1881-) were beginning to paint in geometric forms, under the influence of Negro sculpture, and bearing in mind Cézanne's saying that nature should be seen in terms of the cylinder, the sphere, the cone. Other influences were at work to suggest that the world as seen was less real than one built up intellectually, abstractly. The flitting motion pictures, the increasing use of machinery and of speeding conveyances habituated people to perspectives that had not been familiar to the retina. So it was natural for many thinkers to regard beauty as design resting upon an order of balance and rhythm that was mathematical.

But the attempt to reduce art to a highly rational formula was opposed by irrational movements which also recognized that science and its use had broken the continuity with the past. Dada, initiated in Switzerland in 1916, was a disillusioned glorification of nonsense on the part of painters and writers. It was derived from futurism, launched in France and Italy half a dozen years earlier, which was violent against the culture of the past, its logic and sentiment. Futurism sought to plunge forward with the force and movement of the machine, and with the intuitions of an utterly original self.

Emphasis upon intensely personal expression goes back into the nineteenth century and is not confined to a few schools or fads. Eugène Véron (1825-1889) said in his book *L'Esthétique* (1878) that the artist's personality cannot be kept out of his work and that its expressiveness is what counts. Tolstoy (1828-1910) developed this idea in *What Is Art?* (1896). The theories of Hirn (1870-   ) and Nietzsche (1844-1900) are in the same vein. But they all agree that artistic expression is more than a reflexive overflow of what is felt. There must be the use of a medium, involving mastery of technique and materials, and a consequent modification of original impulse, a control toward form. The tendency is to reject the word beauty as too abstract and too suggestive of a value already given. The interest is rather in what man can create.

Santayana (1863-   ), although retaining the word beauty in his book *The Sense of Beauty* (1896), gives there what has been a most useful account of the three aspects of a work of art, which the expressionist theories more or less recognize as distinguishing artistic expression: sensuous stuff, formal arrangement, representation. And contemporary theories of aesthetics can in general be classified as stressing one or more of these aspects, or as attempting to deal with them all. In view of these three phases of art, and the alteration of previous experience as it enters into them, it becomes clear that art cannot be identified with expression as a simple transmission of emotion, any more than it can be regarded as just the imitation of something that aroused emotion. The sensuous stuff of art must involve a transposition from the different or mixed medium of a life-experience into the chosen material of a particular art. When form is grasped, it is always the form of something, and the materials of which artistic form is made are primarily the pleasures of sense. But Santayana is careful to say that beauty appears when the pleasure of sense is objectified: focused on the formal relations which constitute an object for contemplation. Finally, the associations in their turn become aesthetic only when they also are fused with the object.

Sense, form and association are indissoluble in aesthetic experience, because, as Dewey (1859-   ) has explained in his *Art As Experience* (1934), form and association are processes which spring from the materials and grow out of or become involved in their inherent relationships. Then Kant (1724-1804) was mistaken, along with many later thinkers, in supposing a pure form in art which could avoid any representation of reality. But form can involve a more or less extreme transformation of the given; and distortion of it, or considerable abstraction from it, has been appealing to Clive Bell (1881-   ) and others in reaction against too much pictorial realism in the painting of the nineteenth century. In form the pleasures of sense are not rejected but refined. And associated meanings may be so reduced or absorbed in the sensuous formal structure that they are not felt to be added on.

Elaborate analysis of form has been made by a number of recent aestheticians in terms of unity and variety, harmony, proportion, equilibrium, and the like. But people differ as to what constitutes harmony, right proportion, and so on. In a broad sense whatever in the make-up of an object helps one to perceive it as a whole may be called its form; and this will depend somewhat upon the interest and training of the perceiver. In a narrow sense form is just the bare outline or surface of a thing, conceived in such a disembodied way as to leave out the feel of it as well as the larger structure of its meanings. If form cannot fuse with the values of sense and society it is hard to explain interest in it. If form is not an organization of natural and social energies, or a device for bringing them together effectively, one may wonder about the worth of anything apparently so empty as sheer unity and variety.

The play theory suggested by Kant, developed by Schiller (1759-1805) and others, was an attempt to explain pleasure in mere form, apart from reference to actual life. But the play theory was found inadequate because, much as there is in common between play and art as outlet for thwarted energies, the fact remains that art is more serious and significant.

Another attempt to explain a seeming interest in empty form is the theory of *Einfühlung* or empathy. Crudely stated it is practically a variation of the play theory: holding that art forms stimulate an incipient play of muscles and affect the heart-beat and breathing. Forms which do this in a refreshing manner are beautiful; those which do it in a frustrating way are ugly. Up to a point the theory is that animation of geometric figures by projection of the appreciator into them enables him to unify and vary the content of his psychic life more or less agreeably. But it turns out, at least in the "official" version of Lipps (1851-1914), Volkelt (1848-1930), and Vernon Lee (1856-1935), that the identification of the self with the not-self of artistic form must not involve the biological, practical or social self. The self of aesthetic experience is not that of other experience, but a shadowy contemplative self. And the personality of the artist is likewise reduced: his normal feelings and interests have to be left out or sublimated in artistic production. Thus the empathy theory, which would show how the form of art is interesting as an expression of life, renders expression so formal as to shut out life. Although purporting to be a theory of the self's identification with the object, empathy turns out to have something in common with Bullough's (1880-   ) theory of psychical distance which stresses the need of a certain aloofness for aesthetic effect. So far, however, as empathy does mean a meeting of subject and object, the object is reduced to a symbol for the most subjective kind of content.

Also akin to the subjectivity of symbolism, also regarding art as escape from everyday social reality and from the self that functions there, is the aesthetics of Croce (1866-   ). Beauty is not in objects, shapes or colors, except as they stand for intuitions which alone have actual aesthetic value. A work of art is really an intuition, a vision, a piece of pure imagination, and is the basic stage of the human spirit. On it rest the logical, economic, and ethical levels. But art is envisaged as so independent of the other levels that it is hedged with negations. It is not a physical fact, for the physical-animal-natural aspect of things is regarded as sub-aesthetic and inchoate except as shaped by intuition. Secondly, art has nothing to do with logic, with questions of reality or unreality, truth or falsity. In the third place, art has nothing to do with questions of use or pleasure. Finally, art has nothing to do with morality. Croce's theory joins that of the formalists in equating art with form, and excludes the sensuous or physical aspect of the object from the aesthetic fact, thereby neglecting communication which depends upon a material means. He does not take seriously the questions of material and technique. He thinks of them as presenting no difficulty to a person capable of the inner synthesis that is the heart of art for him. Any material difficulty is merely practical and not aesthetic.

But actually each art is what it is largely on account of the problems peculiar to its medium. For Dewey and an increasing number of authors the art-work expresses the qualities of a material as well as the intuition of an artist. The fact is that theories of pure form, of empathy, and of intuition have been so dominated by the approach of the more or less passive appreciator of works regarded as ethereal, that awareness of the medium and of the artist's struggle with it has tended to be lost. Indeed, modern aesthetics in general has seemed so abstract that Utitz (1883-) and Dessoir (1867-1947) in Germany wanted another name for the study of the artist, the particular arts, and the material and social aspects of artistic production. To cover all this they chose the term "general science of art." Dessoir linked aesthetics and the science of art in 1906 in the title of his book, *Aesthetik und allgemeine Kunstwissenschaft,* and used the same double title for the journal he edited for thirty years. A modification of this title is that of the American *Journal of Aesthetics and Art Criticism,* founded in 1941 and ably edited by Thomas Munro (1897-) for The American Society for Aesthetics. But in the usage of this Society the word "aesthetics" is consciously broadened "to include all studies of the arts and related types of experience from a philosophical, psychological, scientific, historical, critical, or educational point of view." The same is true of The French Society for Aesthetics and their *Revue d'Esthétique,* launched in 1948.

In this amplified and more scientific conception of aesthetics it is impossible to assume (with Croce) that the artist always knows what he is going to accomplish before he makes a move, or that he does nothing which cannot be repeated in the intuition of an appreciator. Creative work must be worked out, and the artist learns what he is going to do as he goes along. He takes notes, he sketches, he tries this and that, and he tries again. The work of execution is much more important than the original idea, and determines the greatness of the artist, according to Dessoir. Agreeing with this, Dewey holds that what distinguishes the artist is his patience and perseverance in developing an idea which cannot become clear except in the medium that is coaxed to embody the idea while modifying it.

A thing counting against the artist in the modern world has been the tendency to associate him with the dead and gone. But Dewey, I. A. Richards (1893-), and others have viewed artistic success as simply an ordering of ordinary experience with striking originality. Obviously in commercial art the artist is involved in the common world; and while this may hamper him it enables him to have influence. The art-for-art tendency to work in private or for a coterie, with an injured sense of being misunderstood by most people, is offset by growing recognition of the life-importance of modern architecture, interior design, music and literature.

This wider artistic interest raises afresh the question of standards of taste and criticism. Here we find new rivals in the old division between those who exalt form and technique in a strict way and those who take a looser view. The former would base judgment upon the authority of the past, demanding that contemporary work conform to norms exemplified in classics of other days. The opposing position is impressionistic, relativistic, and encourages the critic to rely upon his own responses. This stand is appealing in a time of impatience with the past and a sense of developing types of expression which cannot be fairly judged by ancient categories. But could we still speak of criticism if it were dissolved into individual reactions not to be correlated? If anyone is to be considered a critic, or more of a critic than the next man, it must be because in some fashion his impressions are more reliable. And if, like Anatole France (1844-1924), he professes just to record his adventures among masterpieces, why should he speak of masterpieces? Even if he avoided such a question-begging term his selection of some things for comment, rather than others, would imply a criterion.

Dewey avoids the apparent deadlock between the camp of hard and fast rules and that of personal impressions by pointing out that even personal criticism in the field of aesthetics is a kind of judgment, while every aesthetic judgment is an effort to state impressions articulately. All that can be asked is that a critic's perceptions be sensitive, have the benefit of a broad experience, and be stated coherently. And the proper function of the critic is not to give grades, to praise, pass or condemn, which tends to shut off appreciation in another, but rather to open his eyes and encourage his own perception. This view does not abolish norms but regards them as feelers. They are guides to help make fresh discoveries, not guards against straying out of bounds.

Critics with similar equipment and training have relatively little difficulty in criticizing an artwork's internal structure, as compared with judging its social import, as D. W. Gotshalk (1901-) has pointed out in *Art and the Social Order* (1947). If this import is to be gauged according to the values of the critic's time, must he not also be critical of them? And is it not in the rôle of art to suggest that larger criticism? Thus social progress as well as the advancement of art depends upon the artist's freedom, as Kallen (1882-) has shown in his monumental *Art and Freedom* (1942). And Milton

C. Nahm (1903-   ) in his *Aesthetic Experience and its Presuppositions* (1946) regards art as a kind of "emergency action" to generate courage for facing life's difficulties; and to give energy for unspecified ends and purposes.

Such belief in the continuing viability and social effectiveness of art contrasts with Spengler's (1880-1936) thesis that art must die out in an age of science and technology; and reaches back to the teaching of William Morris (1834-1896) who said that "the cause of art is the cause of the people." Lewis Mumford (1895-   ) sees the use of science and the machine as bringing a new set of aesthetic canons: of precision, simplicity and economy. The use of new materials and processes by modern architecture, and its service in decently replacing slums, and joining with engineering to build dams and power plants that make whole valleys more livable, is visibly introducing a new age. It is an age in which art's vaster sweep calls for a more ample philosophy of art, which would restore the ancient integration of art with life and morals.

Aesthetics is just beginning to do justice to the freedom and responsibility of creative activity, in science as well as what is called art, and in the whole enterprise of developing a democratic society. What must be sought is not only an order but a freshness of values. Whitehead has said that in its proper environment an organism should achieve and appreciate an "infinite variety of vivid values." If this is so, aesthetics can scarcely be separated from the effort of the physical and social sciences to improve the environment of men. Whitehead and Malraux (1903-   ) have suggested that the factory, which has been unlovely as compared with a sunset or a country cottage, might become such an organization of machinery, workers, and service as to be a synthesis of values in our time as rich and vivid as the cathedral was in the Middle Ages. Aesthetics, although still interested in art of the past, is following the love of shaping things toward planning on a grand scale. Aesthetics touches reflection upon science on the one hand, and moral and political philosophy on the other, in asking how to arrange the environment without destroying freedom, by fostering values that are not frozen, official or obligatory.

The moot question is whether art can be judged according to a criterion of the socially valuable without suffering from unaesthetic and unfair restrictions. The answer depends upon the extent to which we are willing to let art stand apart as art, or insist upon integrating it with the rest of life. When social problems are serious and pressing there is a temptation to resume Plato's concern that art serve the public interest. If, on the contrary, the special nature and value of the aesthetic quality depend upon the isolation of art, the thought of crushing it with the burden of the time is distressing. The sensuous and formal aspects of art cannot be separated from the representative phase which gains force from dealing with human problems. Much of art is intended merely to pass the time. Advance guard art, however, is a protest against existing conditions, whatever else it is, and even if it seems absurd. This has been true of cubism, futurism, Dada, and devotion to pure form. Under Nazism and Fascism such tendencies were rightly suspected of having something to do with liberalism and rejection of imposed authority.

For Freud (1856-1939) the artist is one who can reverse the day-dreaming escape from life, by realizing his dreams in a way to help other people and so succeed in life after all. This involves mastery of form. And the Freud-influenced surrealist group, officially founded in 1924, brought a fresh emphasis on form, along with free association and flight from logic to the irrational in poetry and painting. Surrealism has meant a combination of unconscious and deliberate control, for discrediting what is called the world of reality in order to substitute a reality of desire. It is not clear what that further reality is, except that it involves revulsion against convention and eagerness to scandalize the bourgeois. The surrealist movement has had a political strain of opposition to nationalism and capitalism and at times has sided with revolutionary socialism. But often the idea seems merely to break up familiar patterns of experience and, in the words of Dali (1904-   ), to "systematize confusion."

Less ambiguous is the Marxian conception of art as properly dedicated to the proletarian cause, and the belief that art can change man (with the help of other forces) in order to change society. In France this view has attracted a number of former surrealists, and now finds its chief rival in existentialism which Sartre (1905-   ) considers to be even more revolutionary in the struggle for a classless society. Existentialism has taken over much of the surrealist emphasis upon the irrational, partly as an ideal and partly as identified with the sickening absurdity to be rejected in bourgeois society. Art should help the individual realize that he has absolute freedom to detach himself from any situation, yet is responsible for his own predicament and that of everyone else; also that his authentic existence can begin only beyond a despair that wipes out excuse and regret.

The irrationality of this position, which has spread surprisingly, calls for a more constructive and scientific aesthetics like that of Lalo (1877-), Souriau (1892-) and Bayer (1898-), the leaders of The French Society for Aesthetics. Meanwhile in the United States Santayana's writing still sums up and correlates the main themes of aesthetics, so as to provide a practical basis for agreement and for differences to be discussed: with regard to the sensuous and formal aspects of art, and concerning whatever may be its further significance.

The controversy over the nature of this significance is freshly presented by John Hospers (1918-) in *Meaning and Truth in the Arts* (1946). His conclusion is that, while art is related to life-experiences, its distinctive contribution is in transforming them into something new which is intrinsically rewarding. The suggestion is that, although it is not the rôle of art to reconstruct society in any direct way, cultivation of art might help our ailing civilization to offset a dangerous over-devotion to abstract knowledge.

We come back to Aristotle's belief that art is healing; but no longer so much in the contemplation of it as in the freer practice of it by children and adults; and in the use of art to make houses and offices, cities and valleys, more livable. Historians of art are helping us to realize that this was the function of art in ancient civilizations, and in medieval Europe before the modern separation of art from life.

BIBLIOGRAPHY

W. ABELL, *Representation and Form* (New York, 1936).
S. ALEXANDER, *Beauty and Other Forms of Value* (London, 1933).
B. BOSANQUET, *Three Lectures on Aesthetic* (New York, 1915).
L. BUERMEYER, *The Aesthetic Experience* (Merion, Pa., 1924).
E. F. CARRITT, *The Theory of Beauty* (New York, 1914).
———, *Philosophies of Beauty* (Oxford, 1931).
R. W. CHURCH, *An Essay on Critical Appreciation* (Ithaca, N. Y., 1938).
H. DELACROIX, *Psychologie de L'Art* (Paris, 1927).

A HISTORY OF PHILOSOPHICAL SYSTEMS

M. Dessoir, *Aesthetik und Allgemeine Kunstwissenschaft* (Berlin, 1906).
J. Dewey, *Art as Experience* (New York, 1934).
C. J. Ducasse, *The Philosophy of Art* (New York, 1929).
I. Edman, *The World, The Arts, and The Artist* (New York, 1928).
C. E. Gauss, *The Aesthetic Theories of French Artists* (Baltimore, 1949).
K. E. Gilbert, *Studies in Recent Aesthetic* (Chapel Hill, 1927).
K. E. Gilbert and H. Kuhn, *A History of Esthetics* (New York, 1940).
K. Gordon, *Esthetics* (New York, 1909).
D. W. Gotshalk, *Art and the Social Order* (Chicago, 1947).
T. M. Greene, *The Arts and the Art of Criticism* (Princeton, 1940).
E. Hanslick, *The Beautiful in Music* (New York, 1891).
J. Hospers, *Meaning and Truth in the Arts* (Chapel Hill, 1946).
H. M. Kallen, *Art and Freedom* (New York, 1942).
H. N. Lee, *Perception and Aesthetic Value* (New York, 1938).
C. I. Lewis, *An Analysis of Knowledge and Valuation* (La Salle, Ill., 1946).
Earl of Listowel, *A Critical History of Modern Aesthetics* (London, 1933).
T. Munro, *The Arts and Their Interrelations* (New York, 1949).
M. Nadeau, *Histoire du Surréalisme* (Paris, 1945).
M. C. Nahm, *Aesthetic Experience and its Presuppositions* (New York, 1946).
D. H. Parker, *The Principles of Aesthetics* (New York, 1920, 1946).
S. Pepper, *Aesthetic Quality* (New York, 1938).
D. W. Prall, *Aesthetic Judgment* (New York, 1929).
———, *Aesthetic Analysis* (New York, 1936).
E. D. Puffer, *The Psychology of Beauty* (Boston, 1905).
M. M. Rader, *A Modern Book of Esthetics.* An Anthology. (New York, 1935).
L. A. Reid, *A Study in Aesthetics* (New York, 1931).
D. D. Runes and H. G. Schrickel, *Encyclopedia of the Arts* (New York, 1946).
G. Santayana, *The Sense of Beauty* (New York, 1896).
———, *Reason in Art* (New York, 1905).
M. Schoen, *Art and Beauty* (New York, 1932).

CHAPTER FORTY-FOUR

RECENT SCHOOLS OF ETHICS

GLENN NEGLEY

THE TERM "school" denotes a systematic position in philosophy. System implies, within the limits of reasonable variation, a common framework of principle and method which characterizes the school. On the basis of such definition, the description of recent and contemporary ethical speculation in terms of "schools" would necessitate a tour de force classification which would be both untrue and unfair. Under certain conditions, inability to arrange philosophic thought in neat traditional categories may well indicate vigor and progress in that thought rather than sterility. In fact, were there not now evident general dissatisfaction with traditional schools of ethics, if there were not a considerable amount of ethical analysis which is admittedly negative and unsystematic, the inescapable inference would be that ethicists of the present day are content to celebrate established theories. It has been clear for some time that the systematic moral views represented in the traditional ethical schools have been already exploited to the limit of tolerance, and while one may still elect such a position and relax within its pre-fabricated shelter, such retirement is not likely to add anything to the structure.

There is one outstanding exception to this generalization that recent ethical thought has extended beyond the confines of traditional systems. That exception is, of course, Thomistic or scholastic morals, which remain systematic and traditional and may indeed be said to constitute a "school." It seems reasonable, however, to assert that scholastic moral theory is, under the circumstances of its exploitation, essentially dogma rather than speculation; the discipline appropriate to the exposition of this or any other authoritarian system is therefore apologetics, with which we are not here concerned.

A HISTORY OF PHILOSOPHICAL SYSTEMS

Any statement of recent ethical theory which attempted to force the philosophers of the contemporary period into pre-established systems not only would result in a distortion of the thought of individuals, but would preclude recognition and understanding of the contributions of recent critical analysis to the progressive reformulation of the moral problem. If recent work in ethics were without observable direction as it is in most cases without definable system, a brief survey could attempt little more than to catalogue an arbitrary selection of men. It seems to me that recent ethical theory has not been as random as many have supposed; rather, I should say that there is evident a describable direction of development in the breakdown of traditional patterns of ethical analysis. The continuity with traditional schools has been maintained to the extent that critical reformulations of the moral problem have come as the result of inquiries into the premises and assumptions of systematic positions. I doubt that many contemporary moralists could find a label with which they could long be content as an adequate description of their ethical positions, if in fact they are quite sure what their ethical positions are.

The general process of reduction to which traditional schools have been subjected by recent ethical thought has unquestionably been stimulated by the vigorous attack of positivistic analysis. While the efforts to systematize the positivist position, in ethics and elsewhere, have been noticeably and increasingly unsuccessful, when not actually embarrassing, the critical accusation that certain basic assertions in ethical systems are meaningless has had a valuable and much needed cathartic effect. On the other hand, the positivist claim that only empirical statements are sensible is considered by most ethicists an unwarranted and unverifiable assertion. Such imposed restriction to sense data dogmatically declares meaningless a large area of experience which the ethicist has good reason to consider real and observable. Whether the experience can be described as sensory, or whether it necessitates description in some other terms, is itself the problem of ethics. The ethicist might remark, and sometimes does, that the positivist position evidences either a blindness induced by unhealthy preoccupation with formal systems or a remarkable insensitivity to one very real area of experience. Criticism need not be restricted, however, to such "moralistic" comments; attempts to sustain the positivist view have indicated clearly that the experience with which the ethicist is concerned is not ignored by positivist analysis, nor is it treated as meaningless. What the original dogmatic attitude seems to evidence is ignorance of what the ethical problem really is. This failure to meet the problem becomes apparent when one notes the cavalier manner in which arbitrary definitions and distinctions are assumed to be exhaustive without explanation or justification. Vituperation of traditional ethical speculation does not clarify the problems of ethical analysis, nor is clarification to be anticipated from constructions which erect a superstructure on assumed and arbitrary dichotomies such as that of "attitude" and "belief," or of "descriptive" meaning and "emotive" meaning.[1] This kind of procedure does not contribute to ethical speculation because the assumptions here so casually made are precisely the subject-matter of the ethical problem. At any rate, these distinctions appear to be the subjects of attention for those who are aware of developments in recent ethical thought.

The problem to which the attention of ethicists has been directed by the analysis of traditional theory may be rather loosely stated as concerned with the nature of primitive moral experience, if primitive is understood as analytically and not anthropologically elementary. Now it is always very easy to find in any such formulation simply a restatement of an old problem, but the nature of the restatement is of the greatest importance. To be sure, it is not only in the modern period that ethicists have recognized that the choice necessary to moral action proceeds from attitude, disposition, or something equally ambiguous in designation. Kant recognized that the good will of his theory depended upon a disposition (*Gesinnung*), and his inability to describe this elementary fact of moral experience in other than rhetorical synonyms brought him to an impasse when he finally asked himself how such a disposition could be cultivated.[2] The important development of recent ethical thought has been the demonstration that critical analysis has reduced every ethical school to this same premise of a primitive fact which is demonstrable but not definable. In the course of this critical reduction, recent ethicists have considerably clarified the nature of the moral act and especially have given attention to certain methodological requirements which were not satisfied in the traditional schools of ethics. In this connection, it is extremely important to note the increasing attention of logicians to the fundamental character of "persuasive" definitions, so-called, or "selection." [3] Recognition of the coördinate normative and methodological nature of definition can contribute much to the clarification of ethical problems. Ethical speculation seems blocked by the recognition that unless selection or choice is given the weight of metaphysical status, it is difficult to describe that primitive moral experience as other than arbitrary. Yet, it seems equally difficult to avoid arbitrariness by substantiation in metaphysical substance without becoming involved in the Hegelian tautology.

It is to be expected, then, that utilitarianism, with its persistent anti-metaphysical tendency, should be reduced to the arbitrary by its critical exponents. The naive definitions of hedonism would hardly be acceptable to any but the most uncritical of behaviorists, and we shall not here concern ourselves with any current versions of that school, if such there be. The critical view of utilitarianism is, briefly, that moral choice is the act of a self which discriminates according to criteria of self-interest. According to one exposition, for example, a self chooses in the moral situation what kind of a self he would like to become.[4] That there is anything so substantial and invariant in man's nature as to determine this choice is rejected by the utilitarian as not factual. On the other hand, the contemporary utilitarian stresses the importance to moral choice of rational deliberation, but he finds it necessary to admit that deliberation can never determine choice. A limit must be placed on reflection if action is to ensue, and eventuation in action is the assumption of moral choice.[5] It is beyond the limitation upon reflection that the actual choice is made, and unless some ground other than the nature of the individual or the nature of reflection can be discovered, the actual choice itself must be declared arbitrary. It is thus non-rational, although influenced by rational analysis. The implication of this analysis seems clear, that any criteria of action can hardly help but be equally arbitrary and non-rational. The utilitarian may put his trust in political processes of agreement, hoping that "arbitraries" will prove amenable and adjustable in the social process. Bentham (1748-1832) also indulged in the dubious and optimistic assumption that satisfaction of private "arbitraries" would automatically, miraculously, result in greater social collectivities of good. As a kind of final reduction, arithmetical counting may be substituted for moral criteria, and mere multiplicity of "arbitraries" accounted as somehow good in itself.[6]

One of the unpleasant corollaries of this acceptance of the arbitrary is the violence done to prediction and control of action. The justification of coercion as a method is always unappetizing to the moralist, but the justification of coercion as a *moral* method is a *reductio*.[7] Yet, it seems difficult to see just what other method is available to influence the arbitrary when influence is in practice necessary. The moral problem could hardly be resolved less happily, and none of the spokesmen for this general point of view seem particularly happy about the predicament in which their analysis has landed them. The reduction, however, is an unavoidable consequence when the self-interest school is subjected to analysis, and unless this description of the primitive moral experience as immediate, non-rational, and arbitrary can be qualified by further construction, it must be admitted that it is a *reductio ad absurdum* as far as ethical theory is concerned.

One of the most serious and painstaking efforts in recent ethical theory has been the attempt to overcome the arbitrariness of the moral act by describing moral experience in its entirety as a mediate process, subject to definition and description. This direction of attack has involved an extensive reinterpretation of the nature and function of rational inquiry.[8] The dichotomy between the immediacy of the primitive moral experience and the mediacy of rational analysis has resulted, so this view holds, from a too rigid and formalistic description of the processes of logical inquiry. These latter are not, as has been generally assumed, merely a set of formal procedures which are applied to given data. Such a definition, it is contended, not only falsifies the nature of logical inquiry but exiles all data, including those of moral experience, to an unknowable and arbitrary realm of immediacy. It is necessary to understand that the processes of rational inquiry and of moral choice are interactive, mutually corrective elements of the complex of thought and action. It would be an understatement to remark that this insistence upon the recognition of logical inquiry as instrumental to the purposes of moral action has met with mixed reactions from philosophers. For our purposes here, we must restrict our attention to consideration of the success of this analysis in describing the primitive moral experience as other than arbitrary. In respect to this problem, it must be reported that this departure from traditional patterns fares no better than those ethical analyses which develop from critical examinations of the ethical schools. Apparently the best that can be done by this effort to reinterpret rational inquiry as an essential but integral part of moral action cannot resolve the problem of the arbitrary. When faced with the final blunt necessity for describing the ground upon which elementary moral choice is made, the answer given by this theory turns out to be very ambiguous. One effort to answer the question has resulted in an extended and tortuous distinction of "desire" and "desirable"; but linguistic changes do not create objectivity. The direction of thought here seems to be toward a definition of the "desirable" in terms of sytematic reflection as a social process, on the assumption that varied "desires" will find some common objectivity in the "desirable." [9] This is the happy-thought assumption again, already exemplified by utilitarian analysis; unless it can be demonstrated that "desire," as it is being used in this argument, is a distinguishable and amenable element of the reflective process, and not immediate in nature, then the primitive moral experience remains undefined and arbitrary. In fact, this direction of analysis involves an additional disturbing implication, for if logical inquiry is an integral part of the process of moral action, and the primitive datum of moral action remains arbitrary, then rational inquiry and analysis are unavoidably subject to determination by the arbitrary.

The traditional school of ethical theory known as intuitionism is distinguished by its very insistence upon the immediate nature of the primitive moral experience, although here again it must be allowed that contemporary ethicists who have developed their positions from a critical analysis of the intuitionist school would probably not agree to be classified in terms of the classical theory. The inability of other ethical analyses to avoid an ultimate admission that some basic part of the moral experience is immediate, and hence arbitrary, has resulted in renewed interest and attention to the intuitionist argument. It may safely be asserted that this ethical position has had very little influence, up to the present time, on ethical speculation in the United States, although it is of interest to note that the intuitionist school, together with the scholastic, constitute almost the whole source of tradition and influence in the philosophy of Latin-America.[10]

The most systematic development of the intuitionist theory in recent philosophy began as a reaction against metaphysical abstraction.¹¹ The original reliance upon psychological observation was, however, quickly transcended in the construction of a theory which demanded "autonomic" insight into the nature of the good.¹² The important contribution of this analysis to the problem of the immediate in moral experience is that the intuitionist is not content to admit that a mere disposition is the sole product of this primitive immediacy. The intuitionist insists that immediate moral experience is "insight," or in other words, that it provides knowledge. Such a description of the primitive moral datum would indeed remove the curse of the arbitrary from the immediate, for such experience gives not mere feeling but knowledge of values, or at least knowledge from which a value-system or axiology can be constructed. Thus, the intuitionist is not satisfied with Kant's immediately given disposition (*Gesinnung*), restrained by a formal categorical imperative; the resultant dichotomy is a surd and can be resolved only if the moral experience is understood as somehow transcending the limitations of mediate and immediate in an apprehension of reality (*Wesensschau*).¹² Systematic intuitionist theory would then consider naive and wholly unsatisfactory the mere assertion that goodness is not analyzable because it is intrinsic and self-evident; ¹³ this is another reduction to the arbitrary, for it asserts that no rational explanation can be given of moral experience.¹⁴

That the intuitionist analysis has worked back to the necessity of a supporting metaphysic is apparent. In further development of this position, values come to be described as self-existent essences, for some such declaration of objectivity is necessary in order to avoid relapse into complete subjectivity with all of its concomitant difficulties of the arbitrary.¹⁵ It is interesting to note what happens to the intuitionist view when the determination to avoid being pushed into metaphysics is maintained to the bitter end. When forced to describe a criterion of action—which clearly does not follow from the immediately intuited disposition—the non-metaphysical intuitionist can only assert that the "success or failure" of the act in question is the only available criterion.¹⁶ That this view does not avoid the subjective arbitrariness of the utilitarian reduction is clear when it is realized that the determination of "success or failure" is a matter of individual opinion as to what is "morally suitable."

The direction of speculation in recent ethical theory to which reference has been made clearly indicates a general failure to avoid subjectivity and arbitrariness of a degree that practically reduces the moral criterion to arithmetical counting or impulsive, psychological delight. The aesthetic view implied in the latter alternative has been stated, although not systematically formulated as an ethical theory. Such an examination of the moral problem would in fact reduce ethical theory to formulation in essentially aesthetic terms, an alteration so radical that nothing recognizable would remain of the moral or ethical problem as it has generally been understood.[17]

One major "school" of ethical theory remains to be considered, and here again it is necessary in small compass to lump together under one generous and ambiguous genus a large group of divergent ethicists.[18] The philosophical position from which this ethical speculation develops is that of objective idealism, and it is characterized by an initial demand for a metaphysical foundation to substantiate any possible value structure. This school, if such it can be called, is unquestionably the most systematic of those we have observed as well as closer to the lines of traditional thought. While the philosophical position of objective idealism has taken many varied forms when applied to an examination of the moral problem, it is possible to summarize the view in such manner as to indicate its pertinence to the problem under consideration here. One form of the intuitionist school advances very close to the view of objective idealism when, in search of objectivity, it admits that the value consciousness is not infallible, that concreteness is a necessary characteristic of the moral situation, and that ethical propositions are therefore true only in "context." [15] The objective idealist goes much further than this hesitant admission of factual context, to a proclamation that action makes moral sense only if that action is an integral part of an organic whole. By organic whole is meant the structural order of relations in the world or universe, inescapably the proper subject of metaphysical speculation.

The objective idealist thus considers all other ethical theories essentially subjectivistic and meaningless. Perhaps the only theory which the idealist considers with any approval at all is that which has been termed "naturalism." Naturalism is perhaps the most ambiguous of all ambiguous designations in philosophy, and it seems particularly difficult for philosophers to maintain a consistent naturalistic position in ethical theory.[19] While appreciating the naturalist's emphasis on continuity and wholeness, the idealist objects to naturalism's description of "organic" as biological; for the idealist, this limited description involves a substitution of "self-preservation" for "self-realization." Naturalism, according to the idealist, is therefore subject to the same reduction implicit in the utilitarian position.

The present position of objective idealism, at least in respect to ethical theory, represents more a refinement and less a critical reduction of the traditional and systematic school from which it developed than is true of any other current ethical theories. The refinement or development of this metaphysically grounded ethic has been evident mainly in efforts to clarify the nature of objectivity. The metaphysical objectivity demanded can be found only in a systematic order of relations which is external to the individual as such. The concrete manifestation of these ordered relations in experience is what the idealist means by "institutions," and the idealist ethical position can properly be called "institutionalism" as over against the "individualism" of the ethical theories which it opposes.

The problem of the immediate and arbitrary is thus rather skillfully skirted by the theory of objective idealism, but it is questionable whether the idealist has, as he appears to assume, defined the problem out of existence. The idealist position maintains that the most primitive datum of moral experience is not intention or disposition or any subjective experience; it is the *act* itself. The act has achieved objectivity, has transcended subjectivity, by embodiment in objects which are ordered according to principles implicit in the nature of things; this principled order is logical and hence knowable through rational metaphysical speculation. The moral act, therefore, has metaphysical rather than mere individual or social status; as such, the only criteria which are applicable to it are criteria derived by metaphysical speculation.

The objective idealist is therefore essentially a rationalist, but the critical exponents of this position admit readily enough an irreducible quality of immediacy or feeling as a necessary element in moral action. Feeling performs the moral function of empirical anticipation of the moral act, and this apparently adds motivation to rational analysis. As an explanation of the function of the arbitrary within the moral process, such description seems reasonable enough, but it does not describe the primitive datum as other than immediate and arbitrary. If the immediate is to be understood simply as a concrete instance expelled by metaphysical order through institutional forms, the implied reduction is to a determinism just as arbitrary whether social or metaphysical. If, on the other hand, the immediate is not really the immediate, but incipient reason, then it must operate at this level as intuition or *Wesensschau*. If, finally, the immediate is really immediate, it seems an excess of optimism to assume that the arbitrary will gracefully adjust to control by reason.

I should be very sorry indeed if the result of this rapid glance at recent ethical theory were assumed to be negative or pessimistic. On the contrary, it seems to me that the forthright critical attitude of contemporary ethicists has so clarified the atmosphere of ethical speculation that there is now promise of systematic construction which will constitute a real development in moral theory. I would not, in fact, be surprised if positivists and objective idealists one day discover a mutual level of intercourse at which they can fruitfully discuss the nature of the good.

NOTES AND BIBLIOGRAPHY

(References are necessarily selective, intended only to suggest more extended discussions.)

1. C. L. Stevenson, *Ethics and Language* (New Haven, 1945).
2. I. Kant, *Religion Within the Limits of Reason Alone*, trans. by Greene and Hudson (Chicago, 1934).
3. *E.g.*, Max Black, "The Definition of Scientific Method," in *Science and Civilization,* ed. by R. C. Stauffer (Madison, 1949).
4. C. M. Perry, "The Arbitrary as Basis for Rational Morality," in *The International Journal of Ethics,* XLIII (1933).
5. *Cf.*, C. S. Peirce, *Collected Papers,* ed. by C. Hartshorne and P. Weiss (Cambridge, Mass., 1931); esp. Vol. I, Bk. IV.
6. R. B. Perry, *General Theory of Value* (New York, 1926).
7. R. Niebuhr, *Moral Man and Immoral Society* (New York, 1932).
8. John Dewey, *The Quest for Certainty* (New York, 1929).
 ————, *Logic, The Theory of Inquiry* (New York, 1938).
 ————, "Logical Conditions of a Scientific Treatment of Morality," reprinted in *Problems of Men* (New York, 1946).
9. John Dewey, *et al., Journal of Philosophy,* Vol. XL (1943).
10. *E.g.*, L. Recasens Siches, *et al., Latin-American Legal Philosophy* (Cambridge, Mass., 1948).
11. H. O. Eaton, *The Austrian Philosophy of Values* (Norman, Okla., 1930). F. Brentano, *The Origin of the Knowledge of Right and Wrong* (Westminster, 1902).

12. M. Scheler, *Die Wissensformen und die Gesellschaft* (Leipzig, 1926).
———, *Von Ewigen im Menschen* (Berlin, 1933).
13. G. E. Moore, *Principia Ethica* (Cambridge, 1929).
14. H. A. Prichard, *Interest and Duty* (Oxford, 1932).
15 N. Hartmann, *Ethics*, trans. by S. Coit, 3 vols. (New York, 1932); esp., Vol. I, Sec. V.
16. W. D. Ross, *The Right and the Good* (Oxford, 1930).
17. G. Santayana, *Works* (New York, 1937); esp. Vol. I.
———, "A General Confession," in *The Philosophy of George Santayana*, ed. by P. Schilpp (Evanston, Ill., 1940).
18. H. W. B. Joseph, *Some Problems in Ethics* (Oxford, 1931). E. Jordan, *The Good Life* (Chicago, 1949).
19. H. A. Larrabee, "Naturalism in America" in *Naturalism and the Human Spirit*, ed. by Y. H. Krikorian (New York, 1944).

CHAPTER FORTY-FIVE

PHILOSOPHIES OF HISTORY

ELIZABETH FARQUHAR FLOWER

THE PHILOSOPHY of history has enjoyed a variety of reputations. Often welcomed at the boards of history and philosophy, it has sometimes become the guest of honor; frequently enough it has been sent away only to reenter unnoticed, as Croce (1866-) suggested, by another door. Its definitions are as diverse as its respectability, and perhaps we shall be forced to accept the somewhat unpalatable implication in Aristotle's remark that poetry is more philosophic than history, since its statements are of the nature of universals rather than of accidentals. The task of the philosophy of history would appear from this to be the search for generalizations or patterns in the unique and non-recurrent. In any case, the following review of the problems and the history of the philosophy of history is directed toward the clarification of its definition.

Of the manifold issues facing the philosopher of history—and modesty is not his calling card—there are at least three persistent problems. They concern the nature of social change, social causation and historical knowledge. The first two problems are metaphysical, the last is methodological.

That there exists some sort of process, and that it is knowable in some sense, is postulational to a philosophy of history. For if there are those who entertain a position like Parmenides' (c. 500-425 B.C.) denial of change, they must be content with an "historical nihilism." But once having accepted the notion of change or process, philosopher-historians are exhaustive in their descriptions of it. Empedocles (c. 494-434 B.C.), Spengler (1880-1936), and Sorokin (1889-) seem to believe that history unfolds in broadly recurrent cycles which lack any over-all direction; on the other hand, teleological theories define either a direction or an end. Optimistic faith in the perfectibility of man like that which Vico (1668-1744) shared with Turgot (1727-1781) and Condorcet (1743-1794) is even challenged today in the *Partisan Review*. Polybius (201-120 B.C.) and Augustine (354-430) believed that the process of history is transcendental; while others, *e.g.*, the contemporary Naturalists and Marx (1818-1883), would have us believe that it is immanent in the growth of institutions and cultures. Still others have read the history of man as his progressive realization of freedom—although the term itself has all the wealth of meaning that a Hobbes (1586-1697), a Kant (1724-1804) or a Croce might assign it. Whatever the nature of the process is taken to be (optimistic or pessimistic, inevitable or achievable, idealistic or naturalistic), the choice usually carries with it particular conclusions as to the nature of value in history.

A decision about the nature of the historical process also influences the interpretation of social causation. The determination of the factors of social change is easier for those who affirm the Design of God or any other transcendental idea, since they have only to relate these forces to the execution of the plan. Thus, for Bossuet (1627-1704), God's plan was to be worked out through the influences of geography; while for Herder (although the basic force of history is the *Geist* in its changing expressions) its expressions seemed to be modified by analyzable environmental factors. But for Montesquieu (1689-1755), F. Boas (1858-1942) and others, who do not hold an *a priori* or transcendental view, the precise relevance of such determinants as geography, race, environment, tradition, great men, group inter-reaction, motivation, and even the "irrational" is the most important issue to be defined.

However, a thorough examination of the problem of social causation immediately leads to more orthodox philosophic problems. It is clear that no analysis of causal factors in history can be complete until tested in terms of a more general causal theory; and similarly, that the existence and the nature of an historical process depend on what one accepts as evidence for it.[1] In other words the problem of historical knowledge is but a part of the more general problem of methodology, a point which may be overlooked by the working historian.

Take Ranke's (1795-1886) precept, so long enjoined upon historians, to present history "as it really is." Such a maxim, even when regarded as an ideal, is not easy to apply. It presupposes some theory of the relation between psychological understanding and objective explanation. The problem is not only, as Ranke himself recognized, to discount the prejudices that are peculiar to the observer and to his particular intellectual climate—the idols of the cave, theater and tribe,—but also to take account of the idols of the market place, if we may amplify Bacon's imagery to include an analysis of judgments of law and fact in history and of fact and value. This latter issue split the historians of the 19th century; for Anglo-French empiricism argued that the methods of physical sciences could be extended to the social sciences, while the Germans generally held that the content of the social sciences is unique and requires a distinct method.

Let us not anticipate the 19th century, however, until we consider it in a brief historical review. In the three centuries between Cusanus (1401-1464) and Newton (1642-1727) and Leibniz (1646-1716), man's notion of himself and his relation to the universe was drastically altered. Even while men were accustoming themselves to the expanding frontiers of astronomical space, geographic horizons were being enlarged; while they were learning a new sense of time from the study of planetary origins, they were also gaining new temporal perspectives of primitive cultures; while they were formulating universal laws of terrestrial mechanics, they sought universal laws in social phenomena.

The immediate reaction to the developing science was an optimistic faith in the capacity of man's reason to understand this mechanical or near-mechanical world, and through understanding to control it. The social ideas of the 17th and 18th centuries accepted this thesis and they may be summarized as an effort to translate the method of Descartes, Newton, and Leibniz to the interpretation of the natural world. "The last reconciling synthesis of the ideas of Enlightenment is the endeavor to understand the previous course of human history itself as the natural development of human nature; in this the philosophy of the 18th century strips off all its one-sidedness and realizes its highest consummation." [2]

Such was the intellectual atmosphere in which the modern notion of history was born. Just how great the innovation was may be seen in the contrast with the Medieval Christian views it succeeded. With respect to the notion of man himself, one need only consider the Augustinian and Calvinistic doctrine together with Rousseau's (1712-1778) moral dignity, Kant's maxim of the human worth, and the sharp insistence of Helvetius (1715-1771), Condorcet and Godwin (1756-1836) on man's perfectibility. Turgot expressed this faith: "The progress of humanity is the gradual evolution of man's nature as a whole—the enlightenment of his intelligence and the purification of his feelings." [3]

A second contrast appeared in the nature of the historical process. In the Christian view, history is part of a cosmic struggle between good and evil; although the design of God transcends the world, it is deducible from His nature and knowable through revelation and the Church. The 'Moderns' argued (as Locke did) against the Fall and Redemption; God's pattern is there, it is true, but it operates only in natural laws and causes, not in miracles. In fact, according to Condorcet, when man gains the knowledge of the laws of historical process, he will be able to direct the course of humanity toward the achievement of absolute equality among nations and individuals.

Perhaps the most important change was the redefinition of natural law. The Medievalists had distinguished clearly between the *lex naturae,* physical law, and *jus naturale,* the law common to all peoples at all times. Now the 17th and 18th centuries took these two ideas and developed them separately, but did not lose sight of their initial connection as aspects of the eternal law. However, the methods of the natural sciences had been so successful in finding universal principles that there was an understandable tendency to apply the physical sciences to the social ones; *i.e.,* to view the *jus gentium* in terms of *lex naturae.*[4] This accounts for the overwhelming flavor of the mechanistic interpretation of social data. Condillac (1715-1780), for example, spoke of the mechanics of passion; and the notion of natural rights really had the quality of physical properties. Natural law was distinguished both from particular law and from the supernatural. The mechanistic interpretation infiltrated the social contract and political theories. The analysis of the state, for example, was artificial in the extreme inasmuch as it was considered as a sum of its irreducible elements—the natural man, whose properties were certain inalienable rights, and who was manipulated by natural laws to form society.

Vico is ordinarily considered the European founder of the philosophy of history, although many anticipated him. Bossuet's description of the 12 stages and the continuity of God's will as historical process, Grotius' (1583-1645) secularization of law, and Suarez' (1548-1617) redefinition of sovereignty and equality, were important to the 18th century definition of natural man. It is in Bodin's (1530-1596) *Method for Easily Understanding History*, however, that we see the promise of a genuine philosophy of history. He discussed each of the three problems that were posed at the beginning of this chapter. Utilizing the historical data that were available, he attempted to induce the nature of the historical process as it is determined by conflict and the physical environment.

With Vico, though, we first come to a complete philosophy of history. He began with a kind of pragmatism. Truth is a mental construct because verifying and doing are the same insofar as they both make things come true. Historical knowledge proceeds from this conjunction of the subject and object of knowledge, and it is scientific when it succeeds in recreating the facts of society ideally. Thus, history is identified with historical knowledge and is "humanity's living consciousness of what it has done." Divine Providence is the cause of history. According to Croce's interpretation,[5] it is immament in the world and works out its recurring cycle of three stages by natural means and through man's moral consciousness. Vico's was the first complete philosophy of history. He formulated a method which depended on empirical evidence; he examined the extent to which historical knowledge was possible; and he analyzed the notion of process and of causation. For the most part, French and English ideas that relate specifically to the philosophy of history were elaborations of problems he had set until the 19th century formulations of scientific method.

Kant's contribution to the philosophy of history places him between the 18th and 19th centuries. He was allied with Kepler and Newton in intention, since he sought laws guiding the development of human action, *i.e.*, of man's will viewed phenomenally and historically. With his predecessors, Kant continued to regard that extreme abstraction, the natural man, as the ultimate political and social unit and to interpret international relations as an expansion of individual morality. In contrast, the later Empiricists and Romanticists emphasized the organic nature of society even when investigating cultural differences. In other respects, Kant belonged to the 19th century. He moved away from the mechanistic analysis of the state: the social contract and the state of nature are speculative principles of the understanding rather than actual moments of history, and natural right has become regulative maxim rather than a property of the individual. Even Kant's idea of progress joins him to later views. For the 18th century, progress was possible, largely rational and directed toward happiness; the 19th century regarded it as inevitable, and frequently irrational and indifferent to one's desires.

The Kantian dualism between man viewed as a free, autonomous agent and man as a determined object of the physical order is carried over into the philosophy of history in the distinction between physical and social causation. Historical knowledge is possible because its objects are noumenal.

For Kant the process of history is the unfolding of Nature's secret design in the development of the natural rational capacities of man's will; the dynamics of history arise from his 'unsocial sociability.' Selfish and social forces are at work within him. Natural antagonism forces men to compete and thus breeds innovation, invention, and progress along with lawful order. Thus the end of political evolution is a civil constitution which allows scope for the benefits of conflict but provides against dissolution by it—*i.e.*, it must allow the greatest liberty of the individual consonant with the liberty of others. Since national governments cannot cultivate the moral potentialities of their citizens while wasting their resources in war and defense, a world federation guaranteeing peace among nations is the *sine qua non* for progress.

The catastrophies of the French Revolution seemed to be a concrete refutation of the main tenets of the Enlightenment. The reaction against the undue prominence of Reason as the instrument of progress, evident in Montesquieu, was clearly expressed by Rousseau, whose influence on Herder was largely responsible for translating Romanticism to Germany. The philosophy of history from Herder (1774-1803) to Hegel (1770-1831) is marked by a progressively unscientific (*i.e.*, non-empirical) attitude. At the beginning, *Zeitgeist* and *Volksgeist* were at least tempered by analyzable environmental factors, but ultimately *Weltgeist* became the sole determinant of history.

Herder, for example, developed Montesquieu's lead and analyzed the effects of external forces like topology, climate, and culture-contacts upon the formation of culture groups. In addition, in an effort to explain how diverse institutions arose under similar external conditions, he postulated the *spirit* or genius of a people which interacted uniquely with the environment. History, then, is a pure natural history of human powers, actions, and propensities modified by time and place. With an optimism that aligned him with the Enlightenment, Herder believed that nature, by divine harmony of the cosmos, is preparing the way for the goal of history, humanity. All things are good—institutions, heroes, etc.—as they develop that end. Imperfections are vanishing; rationality and justice are being realized as man is educated by history.

H. E. Barnes (1889-   ) noted that Lamprecht (1856-1910) developed a part of the Romanticist Doctrine in his theory of the collective-psychology of nation and humanity.[6] Herder's relevance is apparent. Lamprecht also anticipated Dilthey (1833-1911) when he insisted that scientific investigation should proceed not according to abstract principles but through a sympathetic understanding of life in its manifold aspects. However, his stress on nationality, *Volksgeist,* humanity and the social nature of man's personality were immediately related to Fichte (1762-1814), F. Schlegel (1772-1829), Schelling (1775-1854) and Krause (1781-1832) (whose importance was tremendous in the Spanish-speaking world). The contribution of each is generous—to *Kulturgeschichte*, to analyses of the stages of history, to quasi-mystical dynamics, and to the increasing part of the philosophy of history in systematic thought. But, of course, their virtues and their defects were written largest in Hegel, who organized those tendencies into a systematic whole.

Hegel's philosophy of history traces the rational development of Spirit in society as it works out its potentialities through its own inner dialectic of positive, negative, and negation of the negative. Now since the essence of *Geist* is freedom, human progress consists in the progressive consciousness of liberty. Developing the thesis that the real is rational and the rational real, Hegel followed the movement of the Spirit as it is developed by men and their institutions. The ruler alone was free in the Oriental world, yet his freedom was so undisciplined that it became sheer capriciousness. The Graeco-Roman world advanced only the limited realization that some are

A HISTORY OF PHILOSOPHICAL SYSTEMS

free, since slavery was an intrinsic part of their civilization. Finally Western Europe, under the impact of Christianity, realized that man *as such* is free. This freedom is neither capricious nor subordinate; it can arise only in an organized constitutional state, *e.g.*, Prussia, which unites subjective familial love and objective community interest and which alone can provide the opportunity to its citizen to develop his artistic, intellectual, and social potentialities—in other words to become a true personality.

From the foregoing, it is clear that Hegel was at once more conservative and more progressive than Kant. Not only did he replace the Kantian transcendental freedom by an objective dialectic, but by so doing he forfeited the notion of natural law as an ideal standard to the reactionary view that positive law *ought* to be because, in fact, it is, *i.e.*, its reality insures its rationality. This latter argument unfortunately colored Hegel's treatment of international relations. The more advanced state is limited by no such morality as Kant had imagined when it meets in a more primitive state an obstacle to the realization of its own freedom. The true object, then, of the philosophy of history is the dialectic advance of the consciousness of freedom in the historical succession of states.

Hegel's grandiose scheme and his cavalier selection of facts to fit an *a priori* mold are not particularly fashionable today. Cosmic drama it may well be, but empirical and sturdy history it is not. On the other hand, it is not wisdom to dismiss lightly a philosophy of history which outweighs all others in influence. Dialectical materialism, totalitarianism, and socialism drew chiefly upon it. From the German nationalistic history of Droysen (1808-1884) and Treitsche (1834-1896) to the biblical criticism of D. F. Strauss (1808-1874); from the aesthetics of Bosanquet (1848-1923), the sociology of Ratzenhofer (1842-1904), and the ethics of T. H. Green (1836-1882) to *Geisteswissenschaften* scarcely a related field was left untouched (or unscathed) by Hegel.

Benedetto Croce (1866-   ) follows in the main line of Hegelian tradition, but his philosophy of history is much more than lip-service. Liberty again plays the leading rôle, for it is the moral ideal of humanity, the eternal creator, and explanatory principle of history. Reality is also the spirit developing through conflict, but Croce stresses its unity and adventure as it roves beyond the narrow Hegelian rationality into the unconscious, nature, art, and intuition.

A HISTORY OF PHILOSOPHICAL SYSTEMS

Croce shatters the dualism between historical events and knowledge of them. This means, in a mood as reminiscent of St. Thomas (1225-1274) as of Hegel, that the Absolute both enacts the world process and reflects upon it. From the standpoint of human understanding, history is always contemporaneous: it exists only as the historian-philosopher thinks it—as he relives and recreates it in terms of the past and evaluates it in terms of the future—but it is always present. Thus, concrete philosophy is the same as history, and abstract philosophy is its methodology, the directive principle of interpretation.[7] Collingwood restates this negatively: history is not the past at all; it is, rather, the past as it is reformed in the consciousness of the historian. He goes on to say that it cannot be understood as facts, but only as the reasons why such facts occurred.[8]

Now the contrast between Collingwood's pursuit of the *why* and Comte's (1798-1857) earlier explicit disavowal of it as the aim of positive science highlights the distinction between the romantic and naturalistic conceptions of history which divided the 19th and 20th centuries. Even within Germany the historical school of Savigny (1779-1861), B. Niebuhr (1776-1831), and von Ranke opposed what they regarded as the capricious treatment of historical objectivity, the disregard of historical analysis, and the rejection of traditional logic. Nevertheless, von Ranke, the greatest of these, could not entirely free himself of the Hegelian influence.

In England and France, the intellectual environment created a different attitude toward social data. Tacitly (or explicitly) they accepted the Enlightenment's identity of mechanical and social law and made a comprehensive effort to apply the methods of physical science to social science. Moreover, the principles of mechanics were finding ever-widening application within the physical sciences themselves. Chemistry was generalized by the breakdown of the distinction between organic and inorganic; biologic discoveries implied that the organism could be regarded as an object of empirical research. Wherever natural science had been extended to the interpretation of social facts it had been uniformly successful: had not Cartesian mathematics and Newtonian physics provided an adequate basis for the economics of Ricardo (1772-1823), Adam Smith, Malthus (1766-1834) and the Physiocrats; did not psychology continue to advance under the methods of the Classic Empiricists! There seemed to be no reason why the methods that had yielded so much knowledge of the natural world might not be extended to social facts generally and even to the problem of social growth. In effect, this is what Spencer and Comte tried to do. They agreed on a naturalistic interpretation of social phenomena based on induction and observation; the frame of reference is nature viewed as a mechanical system, but it gives up social ends. They also agreed that the basis of history is the breadth of social phenomena and not political or otherwise specialized. But on the whole, Comte examined the assumptions of his method more critically and self-consciously.

The two positivists differ widely in the working out of their ideas. Comte correlated the phases of social organization with those of intellectual development: thus the theological stage (explanation in terms of gods) corresponds to society under an unlimited authority; the metaphysical stage (explanation in terms of final causes) is society under government by such abstract principles as equality, natural right and freedom; and finally the positive stage of descriptive explanation is correlated with industrialism. Society is analogous to a body at rest; opposed forces, such as egoism and altruism, liberalism and conservativism, maintain it; but progress depends upon strengthening the social forces that move society toward increased humanity.

Spencer (1820-1903), on the other hand, was not a social reformer. His conception of moral and social process as part of an inevitable cosmic evolution was consistent with the *laissez-faire* of the utilitarian-liberal policy which he supported. Although denying that evolution was synonymous with progress, he generally regarded the movement from homogeneity to heterogeneity as a movement from lower to higher; thus, for example, the history of social development through tribal, military and industrial stages.

The influence of evolution and positivism on empirical method may be summarized in Charles Beard's (1874-1948) comment on Spencer to the effect that that "child of a Utilitarian age, applied after a fashion at least, what purported to be rigid canons of thought to the origins of religion, to the rise and development of ceremonials, to social, military, and industrial institutions, and to current political practice." [9] Buckle (1821-1862) set up a scheme for historical induction on the basis of which he made generalizations about moral, intellectual and physical history. In the most famous of these, he analyzed the effects of too many and too few environmental obstacles and pointed to the optimum conditions pertaining in Europe. Bagehot (1826-1877) continued the interest in empirical method and utilized the data of Darwinianism and the new anthropology in his analysis of custom, revolt and conflict. In this century, Henry (b.1838) and Brooks Adams (b.1848), influenced by Bagehot, Gibbs (b.1877), Turgot and Comte, tried to base a history of socio-physical laws of phases and thermodynamics. This empirical trend influenced such German scholars as Tonnies and Lamprecht who studied the evolution of social groups. Lamprecht also anticipated the 'new history' of James Harvey Robinson (1863-1936), H. E. Barnes and other Americans who believed that all social, intellectual and cultural phenomena are relevant to the study of the past, the 'dynamic mold of the future.' Teggart even subjected the methods of history and its standards of impartiality to historical analysis.

Another twentieth century figure of importance is Arnold Toynbee (1889-   ). His analysis of societies, their growth, challenge and response, breakdown and disintegration, and ultimate withdrawal, was reminiscent of Spengler. Indeed, Toynbee noted his agreement with the German pessimist on two cardinal points: . . . "that the smallest intelligible fields of historical study were whole societies and not arbitrarily limited insulated fragments of them like the nation-states of the modern West" . . . and that "the histories of all societies of the species called civilization were in some sense parallel and contemporary." But Toynbee felt that Spengler was "unilluminatingly dogmatic and deterministic" regarding the evidence for his cycle of youth, maturity, old age and death. "And here I became aware of a difference of national traditions. Where German *a priori* method drew a blank let us see what could be done by English Empiricism." [10] Yet his analysis did not profoundly revise the assumptions of history, and Toynbee's virtue (as well as Spengler's) lay in his breadth of perspective.

In this chapter we have traced some of the problems as they were posed by the 17th and 18th centuries and as they were later developed in empirical and idealistic terms. Unless one is ready to accept Marx' union of the method of Hegel and the materialism of Feuerbach (1804-1872), most attempts at synthesis seem unsatisfactory. However, it is possible that contemporary reexaminations of the basic problems of philosophy may indicate new lines of research and new statements of the problems. In Germany, for example, the interpretation of history has been enriched by the concept of *Geisteswissenschaften* and the effort to take into account ideal factors such as psychological states and values.[11] Windelband (1848-1915) and Rickert (1863-1936) held that the events are unique groupings of value and a space-time setting; clearly a method (ideographic), distinct from the physical sciences, is required to handle the particularity of social phenomena and their relation to transcendental value. Spranger (1882-) and Dilthey emphasized rather the psychological categories of historical knowledge. History is not a series of facts; it is action, feeling, willing. The historian himself is a creature of emotions and values. Hence, he who would understand the past must relive it and be capable of relating subjective and objective insights. Now a technique for studying the preferences and choices of men and their resultant cultural expressions is the formulation of ideal psychological types, *e.g.*, the economic, religious and the political, in terms of which we may study real personalities.

Removed from the humanistic orientation of modern German idealism, logical empiricism and formal logic are focusing attention on the problems and techniques of analysis; [12] and critiques of scientific method generally not only increase the awareness of our assumptions but also the power to achieve ends. As a spokesman for the Naturalists puts it, "History is, then, not only the conserving, the remembering, and the understanding of what has happened: it is also the completing of what has happened. . . . For him (man), consequently, the purpose of history is not a secret he vainly tries to find, but a kind of life his reason enables him to live." [13]

NOTES

1. J. H. Randall, Jr. and George Haines, "Controlling Assumptions in the Practice of American Historians." *Theory and Practice*, No. 54, Social Science Research Council. See also F. J. Teggart, "Causation in Historical Events," *Journal of the History of Ideas*, III (1942), pp. 3-11.

2. Robert Flint, *The Philosophy of History in France and Germany* (New York, 1874), p. 356.

3. A. Turgot, *On the Progress of the Human Mind* (Hanover, Vt., 1929), p. 12.

A HISTORY OF PHILOSOPHICAL SYSTEMS

4. Arthur Nussbaum, *A Concise History of the Law of Nations* (New York, 1947).
5. B. Croce, *The Philosophy of Giambattista Vico*. Trans. by R. G. Collingwood (New York, 1913).
6. H. E. Barnes, *A History of Historical Writing* (Norman, Okla., 1937), pp. 180, 316.
7. B. Croce, *History as the Story of Liberty* (New York, 1941), p. 60.
8. R. G. Collingwood, *The Idea of History* (Oxford, 1946).
9. Charles Beard, "Introduction," *Encycl. of the Social Sciences* (New York, 1937), I, p. 160.
10. A. J. Toynbee, *Civilization on Trial* (New York, 1948), pp. 10-11. See also A. J. Toynbee, *A Study of History,* abridged by D. C. Somervell (New York, 1947).
11. For summary see H. L. Friess, "The Progress of German Philosophy in the Last One Hundred Years," *Journal of Philosophy* (Lancaster, Pa., 1930), XXVII, pp. 396-415.
12. For example, C. G. Hempel, "The Function of General Laws in History," *Journal of Philosophy,* XXXIX (1942), pp. 35-48, and E. Zilsel, "Physics and the Problem of Historico-sociological Laws," *Philosophy of Science,* VIII (1941), pp. 567-579.
13. F. J. E. Woodbridge, *The Purpose of History* (New York, 1916), p. 89.

BIBLIOGRAPHY

HENRY ADAMS, *Degradation of the Democratic Dogma* (New York, 1919).
W. BAGEHOT, *Physics and Politics* (New York, 1940).
HENRY T. BUCKLE, *History of Civilization in England* (New York, 1903).
A. COMTE, *The Positive Philosophy,* 2 vols. (New York, 1921).
W. DILTHEY, *Einleitung in die Geisteswissenschaften* (Berlin, 1922).
G. P. GOOCH, *History and Historians in the 19th Century* (London, 1913).
G. W. F. HEGEL, *Lectures on the Philosophy of History* (London, 1909).
──────, *Philosophy of Right* (London, 1896).
J. G. HERDER, *Ideen Zur Philosophie der Geschichte der Menscheit* (Berlin, 1879).
I. KANT, *Eternal Peace and Other International Essays*. Trans. by Wm. Hastie (Boston, 1914).
──────, *Idea of a Universal History*. Trans. by Thomas de Quincey (Hanover, Vt., 1927).
KARL LAMPRECHT, *What is History?* (New York, 1927).
H. SPENCER, *The Study of Sociology* (New York, 1877).
OSWALD SPENGLER, *Decline of the West,* 2 vols. (New York, 1926-28).

E. Spranger, *Lebensformen* (Halle, 1925).
E. W. Strong, "Materials of Historical Knowledge," *Naturalism and the Human Spirit* (New York, 1944).
F. J. Teggart, *Theory and Process of History* (Berkeley, Cal., 1941).
J. W. Thompson, *A History of Historical Writing*, 2 vols. (New York, 1942).
W. Windelband and H. Rickert, Articles in *Die Philosophie im Beginn des 20 Jahrhunderts. Festschrift für Kuno Fischer* (Heidelberg, 1904–05).

CHAPTER FORTY-SIX

PHILOSOPHIES OF CULTURE

HORACE L. FRIESS

THE TERM "culture," as used today in social science, includes all the ways and conditions of living invented by human societies. From remote times man has been conscious of himself as a culture-builder. The culture-hero myths of early peoples attest this. Each of the ancient civilizations shows its distinct and preferential awareness of a cultural heritage. The historians, poets, and philosophers of Athens reflected on the merits and liabilities of Athenian culture. In China it was the estimation of Chou dynasty culture and of still older traditions that largely occupied both the early Confucian school and its rivals. Human beings always live in some cultural environment as necessarily as in a physical one. There is no possibility for them of a complete detachment from culture. Only the character of their attachment to culture—what they get of it and make of it—can vary.

Intellectual attitudes toward culture can be grouped into three very general kinds. The first kind is characterized by acceptance of some given culture as normative. The second attempts a general critique of culture and of all cultures from some universal base assumed to transcend all cultural conditions. The third kind of attitude is concerned with comparative and immanent criticism of cultures. It seeks to interpret the significance of specific cultural changes in terms that remain culturally conditioned, though they need not be static on that account. These three different attitudes can be found operating to some degree in every historic period of philosophy. But it was the Hellenistic period—with its meeting of many local cultures, its universal religious movements and its philosophies of nature—that first furnished a particularly favorable context, in the western world, for transcendent critiques of culture. This orientation remained productive not only in the Middle Ages, but also in early modern times through the eighteenth century. With the industrial changes of the nineteenth and twentieth centuries unprecedented dynamic transformations of everyday life and of technical knowledge were introduced. These have provided the context in which a relatively new comparative and immanent kind of culture analysis and criticism has begun to flourish.

The great Athenian philosophers stood clearly at a boundary, where their thinking partook of both the first and second attitudes. They turned powerfully away from the cave of custom toward the sunlight of eternal ideas and principles of nature. Yet it is also clear, and even explicit, how much Greek cultural traditions and values were taken to be normative in their theories of the cosmos. To Plato (427-347 B.C.) "the universe could never be anything but a crystal case to hold the jewel of a Greek city." [1] And Aristotle (384-322 B.C.) thought of no better human society for it to contain. But, in the late Roman era, for St. Augustine (354-430) the distinction between an eternally normative "City of God" and every earthly city of man had become radical and fundamental, at least in theory. Concretely Rome and the Latin culture very deeply influenced Augustine's conceptions of the one divinely established Church, as well as his views of human error and pride. And all Roman Catholic argument continued to find God's ordinance in specific institutions, such as the Papacy, which infidels commonly saw as cultural, *i.e.*, as inventions of human society. Both the Eastern schism and the Protestant revolt involved charges that Rome upheld as divinely ordained some institutions of fallible human origin.

For several centuries after the Reformation philosophers still usually referred their critiques of culture to some transcendent, extracultural base. But since religious sects were burning each other up over special revelation, while natural science was brilliantly entering a new path of secure progress, the most promising source for such a universal standard and base of criticism now seemed to be in the light of nature. "Nature establishes unity," it was held, "and everywhere settles a few invariable principles; the soil is still the same, but culture produces various fruits." [2] The philosophers could indeed point to a contrast between the inconsistent patchwork of human culture and the beautiful order of natural action so simply and precisely comprehended in the new physics. But the more they sought the moral of the contrast, the more problematic certain questions proved to be. If it was unnatural, how did culture get that way? Was it some early cultural mistake, perhaps the invention of private property, that introduced antagonism and selfishness into human society? Or was human nature laden with discordant passions at bottom? Was nature also more complicated than current "systems" revealed? The eighteenth century *philosophes* did not lose their great faith in human progress through natural enlightenment, reason, and sociability, but they ended with more than one view of nature, man, science, and cultural advance. Diderot (1713-84) and Montesquieu (1689-1755) especially emphasized the importance of considering the variety in both nature and culture. Kant (1724-1804), toward the end of the period, concluded that the antagonisms in human society were nature's ways of bringing all of man's capacities into development, and of leaving the production of a world-wide civil order to moral reason and free will rather than to instinct.

Among modern philosophers Hegel (1770-1831) can claim the distinction of having tried to satisfy in his ambitious synthesis all the main attitudes in the interpretation of culture. He presented a huge historical survey, in which a dialectic of development and criticism internal to each culture was exhibited as the principle of progress. At the same time, since the dialectic was also the universal and comprehensive logic of nature and of spirit, its coming to self-knowledge in culture was the progressive revelation of Absolute Truth. And lastly, since the process was cumulative, modern western culture now held the essentials of all earlier invention, and possessed the perfected norm of human wisdom and freedom. Europe was thus offered historic criticism, eternal justification, and present self-assurance all in one doctrine.

But the package was too big; and it fell apart at once in a time that was beginning to feel the critical impact of most unprecedented changes in cultural conditions and problems. Some of the younger generation in Hegel's audience cried out. Karl Marx (1818-1883), pointing to the condition of the working-classes in the new factory towns, wrote: what is needed now is to change the world, not a philosophy comprehending its past. Sören Kierkegaard (1813-1855) protested that the eternal anguish at the heart of Christianity could not be put at peace with any culture. The Schopenhauerians submitted that culture should be estimated in relation to deliverance from, rather than reconciliation with life. From this viewpoint Eduard von Hartmann (1842-1906) achieved the most ingenious and elaborate account of culture as a long way around to nirvana. A soteriological interest, and more or less of the transcendent attitude, was present in the very contrasting culture-critiques of all these men.

In the age of Darwin (1809-1882) comparative study of cultures was for a time directed, from various angles, toward tracing the presumed general evolution of human society and its institutions. One line of such inquiry focussed much on family and kinship relations, another on political and economic organization, and still another on the mind and ideas of man. Along the first line the hypothesis that patriarchal relations had been generally preceded by matriarchal ones was developed by J. J. Bachofen (1815-1887) in *Das Mutterrecht,* 1861. The hypothesis was taken over in *Ancient Society,* 1877, by L. H. Morgan (1818-1881) who held that man, in the stage of "savagery," had evolved from promiscuous communism in sex to matriarchal relations, from these to patriarchal relations in the next stage of "barbarism," and from patriarchal polygamy to the monogamic family in the "civilized" stage. Though this doctrine was accepted by Marx and Engels in *The Origin of the Family, Private Property, and the State,* 1884, their own interest was focussed on their distinctive doctrine of the dialectic evolution of property relations from primitive communism, through various forms of private property and class-conflict, to the overcoming of exploitation again in advanced industrial communism. In the same era individualism found its great champion among these cultural evolutionists in Herbert Spencer (1820-1903). In his many volumes he taught that a universal development from kinship and custom-ruled societies, through militaristically governed and finally industrially ordered societies meant progressive opportunity for individuality, freedom, and peace.

The intellectual aspects of culture have received great attention from anthropologists as well as from philosophers. The French positivist, Auguste Comte (1798-1857), distinguished three great stages in the development of all human thought: a theological or animistic one, a metaphysical, and a positive scientific stage. J. S. Mill (1806-

1873) in the concluding part of his *System of Logic,* 1843, stated that study of culture should postulate a psychological unity of man, and pay attention to the discovery of new ideas as the most powerful forces in human development. Among anthropologists, E. B. Tylor (1832-1917) in his *Primitive Culture,* 1871, drove home the ubiquitous rôle of animistic thinking in man's heritage. In the next generation, Franz Boas (1858-1942) and his school of American anthropologists avoided over-all generalization about cultural evolution in favor of gathering more specific information on various cultures. But they also affirmed basic unity of the mind of man, and searched for the course of specific inventions and ideas to explain the important developments in cultural history and progress.

L. Levy-Bruhl (1857-1939) and other European scholars, who stressed the rôle of "pre-logical" and "mythical thinking" in primitive culture, apparently did not intend to question the continuity of man's intellectual development, although argument was raised on this issue. A sustained philosophical critique of the thought-forms involved in language, myth, and knowledge was presented by Ernst Cassirer (1874-1945) in his *Philosophie der symbolischen Formen,* 1923-29. The contribution which Cassirer made to cultural science by his rich understanding of man as *animal symbolicum* was somewhat offset by a relative neglect of the tool-making *homo faber.* Just the opposite one-sidedness can be found in the writings of a contemporary American anthropologist, Leslie White (1900-   ). He holds that "culturology" as a distinct science should abstract itself from psychological considerations, and that it can arrive at a satisfactory understanding of the general evolution of "culture" by studying technological changes and their effects.

Unilinear accounts of cultural evolution in general are extremely exceptional, however, in contemporary scientific literature. Though the field of cultural facts exhibits many continuities, it seems to obstruct rather than to aid comprehension to approach culture as if it were some single entity. Current emphasis falls rather on the great variety of specific facts, on the need to understand particular cultures and their irreducible patterns, and on the study of many specific problems by cross-cultural analysis. This pluralistic emphasis has been accompanied by some shift of interest from genetic to functional problems, but also by more exact concern with specific culture areas and their relations in dealing with genetic problems. Rather unique is the position of F. Graebner (1877-1934) and his "culture-historical school of ethnology," which attempts to reconstruct cultural history in terms of the diffusion of culture-traits and complexes from a few great original "culture circles" (*Kulturkreise*) of early mankind. But no school of thought today would deny the importance of diffusion and acculturation problems for the history and interpretation of culture. They must inevitably play a part in any adequate approach from a pluralistic basis.

Cycles and recurrent rhythms in culture changes have also received renewed attention as the idea of unilinear evolution of culture has waned. The ancient belief in historical cycles had always been kept alive in the traditions of European humanism. In the eighteenth century the Italian philosopher G. B. Vico (1668-1744) opposed prevailing ideas of progress with a "new science" of cultural and political cycles, largely inspired by Greek sources but applied to modern as well as ancient nations. In recent times Oswald Spengler (1880-1936) described some nine historic cultures as going through similar cycles of growth and decay, and diagnosed western civilization as having entered its last phase. In the last work of Henri Bergson (1859-1941), *The Two Sources of Morality and Religion,* 1932, a more complex picture is given of forces in the human psyche and in culture making for static recurrences, and of other more dynamic tendencies accounting for creative advance. Both Spengler and Bergson have influenced the contemporary British historian, A. J. Toynbee (1889-   ) in *A Study of History,* 1934-   , which notes the rhythms of rise and fall in some twenty-nine cultures, yet holds out a hope of continuation for western civilization through a process of religious renascence and moral expansion. The contemporary sociologist P. Sorokin (1889-   ), influenced by traditions of Eastern Orthodoxy, finds alternating trends to "sensate" and to "idealogical" cultures, and sees salvation for current ills as depending on a swing of culture from its present sensate values to repossession by a dominating spiritual ideal.

Manifold influences went far and wide from the high-charged criticisms Friedrich Nietzsche (1844-1900) offered of cultural traditions. More fertile than either his eternal recurrence or superman teachings, was his acute sense for the hidden psychological implications of moral and cultural norms. The interrelations of culture patterns and types of moral personality have since become a major theme of contemporary research. The aim of understanding life by an interweaving of biographical study and culture analysis inspired the work of Wilhelm Dilthey (1833-1911) and many others. But it was the psychoanalytic methods and ideas developed first by Sigmund Freud (1856-1939) in clinically probing the more unconscious reactions and motivations of his patients that brought the current enterprise of psycho-cultural research to a new level of intensive cultivation. The post-Freudians, working along these lines, are not bound by Freud's own culture theories and still less by his "myth" of cultural origins (*cf. Totem and Taboo,* 1913; *Civilization and its Discontents,* 1930). They are anything but united in their many psychological systems and methods, to say nothing of being agreed in matters of philosophy and culture theory. Even their names and major differences are too numerous to be listed in the brief compass of this discussion. But the equipment they are developing should eventually make it possible for men to explore the psychodynamics of their institutions more cooperatively over a greater range and with more intensive sights than ever before.

Important efforts have also been made recently, in anthropology and in philosophy, to focus culture analysis more upon functions and human needs than upon problems of origin as such. In anthropology Bronislaw Malinowski (1884-1942) espoused a "functionalist" theory of culture. Its motivations, especially in contrast to genetic emphases, are clear and intelligible enough. But it seems to tie the understanding of culture and cultures to a prescribed little system of essential functions, and not to get processes and possibilities of change sufficiently into the picture. In this very respect, where Malinowski's "functionalism" seems weak, the reconstruction of method, worked out by John Dewey (1859-   ) in philosophy, is strong. Dewey would regard culture analysis as integral with ongoing social inquiry; and such inquiry he conceives as: (i) directed to specific conditions and problems, (ii) requiring social communication and access to ideas and information, (iii) including scrutiny and revaluation of aims and values, and (iv) being experimentally controlled and validated by consequences in reconstructing specific situations. So conceived, social inquiry prescribes no over-all theory of culture, but examination and appraisal of specific cultural conditions is always of its essence. The very heart of this method is to give maximum attention to the cultural factor in human problems, *i.e.,* to the results and possibilities of social invention. Criticism of culture is for Dewey the central function of philosophy, which approaches it by way of the reflective examination of beliefs and intellectual methods. And effective knowledge of culture is expected to be gathered best in the ongoing social process of specific and cooperative problem-solving.

This brings us back to the point raised in the beginning that the kind of attachment which men develop to culture can vary, though no complete detachment from it is possible. Attachment may be more active or contemplative, conventional or peculiar, narrow or broad, and may have many qualities besides. In today's physically unified world many common problems are faced by men attached in one way or other to different cultural backgrounds. This situation stimulates cross-cultural inquiry, by which is meant an attempt to examine problems and propositions as they appear when viewed in more than one cultural context. It is a difficult process that contains no guarantee of success with any problem. But it should in time deeply affect philosophic and perhaps all cultural construction. For by more inclusive consideration of the actual and possible range of social invention—in other words, of cultural variety—the formulation and treatment of moral and other philosophic questions should be greatly enriched. And the following words of one who was skillfully engaged in forwarding cross-cultural studies may suggest some of mankind's possible gains from this source for the practical living of life. "We may hope a little, that whereas change has hitherto been blind, at the mercy of unconscious patternings, it will be possible gradually, in so far as we become genuinely culture-conscious, that it shall be guided by intelligence." [3]

The thought of gaining more intelligent control of culture has indeed lured many philosophers from the days of Plato to our own. The kinds and the amount of knowledge available have grown tremendously, but their employment for so complex an end is perhaps more difficult to oversee than ever. One suspects that even so elaborate an attempt as the recent one by F. S. C. Northrop (1893-   ) to find the key to cultures in the logic of their sciences generalizes far too simply, and invites a modern version of control by philosopher-kings. The actual increase of intelligent control must necessarily be piecemeal, and while intellectuals have their indispensable functions in it, the work is such as "can be done only by the resolute, patient, cooperative activities of men and women of good will, drawn from every useful calling, over an indefinitely long period." [4]

NOTES

1. G. Santayana, *Platonism and the Spiritual Life*, p. 27.
2. Voltaire, *Works*, IX, p. 152.
3. Ruth F. Benedict, *Race: Science and Politics* (rev. ed., 1943); *Patterns of Culture* (1946).
4. J. Dewey, *Reconstruction in Philosophy*, enlarged edition (1948), p. xxxv.

BIBLIOGRAPHY

Encyclopaedia of the Social Sciences: articles by F. Boas on "Anthropology"; B. Malinowski on "Culture"; and J. Dewey on "Philosophy."
H. E. BARNES and H. BECKER, *Social Thought from Folklore to Science* (1938).
R. F. BENEDICT, *Patterns of Culture* (1934).
H. BERGSON, *The Two Sources of Morality and Religion* (1935).
F. BOAS, ed., *General Anthropology* (1938).
V. F. CALVERTON, ed., *The Making of Man* (1931).
E. CASSIRER, *An Essay on Man* (1944).
J. DEWEY, *Logic, the Theory of Inquiry*, ch. 24 (1938); *Reconstruction in Philosophy*, enl. ed. (1948); *Freedom and Culture* (1939).
T. S. ELIOT, *Notes Towards the Definition of Culture* (1949).
S. FREUD, *Civilization and Its Discontents* (1930).
E. FROMM, *Man For Himself* (1947).
HERSKOVITS, *Man and his Works* (1948).
S. HOOK, *The Hero in History* (1943).
A. L. KROEBER, *Configurations of Culture Growth* (1944).
R. LINTON, ed., *The Science of Man in the World Crisis* (1945).
R. H. LOWIE, *The History of Ethnological Theory* (1937).
B. MALINOWSKI, *A Scientific Theory of Culture and Other Essays* (1944).
M. MANDELBAUM, *The Problem of Historical Knowledge* (1938).
J. MARITAIN, *Freedom in the Modern World* (1935).
J. S. MILL, *A System of Logic*, Bk. VI (1843).
F. S. C. NORTHROP, *The Meeting of East and West* (1946); *The Logic of the Sciences and the Humanities* (1947).
T. PARSONS, *The Structure of Social Action* (1937).

A HISTORY OF PHILOSOPHICAL SYSTEMS

S. A. Rice, ed., *Methods in Social Science* (1931).
W. Schmidt, *The Culture Historical Method of Ethnology* (1939).
P. Sorokin, *Society, Culture, and Personality* (1947); *Contemporary Sociological Theories* (1928).
A. J. Toynbee, *A Study of History* (1946).
M. Weber, *From Max Weber*, Gerth and Mills, trans. (1946).
L. White, *The Science of Culture* (1949).
A. N. Whitehead, *Adventures of Ideas* (1933); *Modes of Thought* (1938).

CHAPTER FORTY-SEVEN

PHILOSOPHIES OF RELIGION

VERGILIUS FERM

THE STUDY of the philosophy of religion has become a highly specialized discipline. Those who aspire to work in this field must acquire a comprehensive grasp of many areas of inquiry: the history of religions (or what was once called "comparative religion"), ancient cultural history and the history of religious institutions, historic and systematic theology (Christian and non-Christian), psychology of religion, social anthropology and social psychology, besides, of course, those areas of philosophy covered by metaphysics, cosmology, philosophical psychology, historical and systematic ethics, value theory, epistemology, the history of philosophy as well as sufficient acquaintance with the history and development of the physical sciences. To all this are now added even the more technical requirements such as a general acquaintance with researches in archaeology and the critical studies carried on in the fields of "sacred" literatures—not to mention the working tools of the trade, the basic languages, both classic and modern, and some grasp of language-meanings of cultures far removed from that of one's own.

Even the minimum requirements call for so large an order of preparation and so long a period of apprenticeship that no conscientious worker in the field today will hesitate to confess his deep feeling of incompetence. There is perhaps no other area of specialized interest in the wide reaches of philosophical inspection that demands more in the way of catholic training and outlook. Among professional philosophers there is today a tendency to circumvent this requirement of long discipleship and to enter into more promising fields of limited and prescribed philosophical inquiry with the result that the subject is left occupied by relatively few persons of sufficient qualifications to carry on mature and disciplined inquiry. It is not strange, then, to find not a few professional philosophers passing careless judgments upon religious questions, sometimes dismissing them as somewhat trivial or a subject-matter of interest only to dogmatic theologians. Added to this is that vast horde of lay-preachers (ordained or unordained) orating from pulpits or in the market-places for whom religion is a subject upon which anyone may speak with authority who has a "call" and those theologians whose estimates of religion are constricted by a commitment to their own brand, their own cult or their own type of theology. And still more are the run-of-the-mill discussions, in clubs, in class-rooms, on street-corners—which toss the subject of religion to and fro as if it were as simple a topic as an opinion about the state of the weather. It is no wonder that this field—old in ancient interest (although not called by the name)—has been debauched by charlatans, quacks and by dogmatic academicians and unripe intelligentsia.

For centuries in the history of our Western culture the field was occupied and controlled by vested interests: church-men and priests and theologians and philosophers under the constraints of their own religious cultus. And even to this day, what goes for philosophy of religion in some reputable circles is but a disguised form of ecclesiastical or theological apologetics. It was a particular religion's philosophy of religion; but it was more than that: it was a particular sectarian's philosophy of religion in terms of a particular sect of a particular religion.

The field of the philosophy of religion may be defined as an in-inquiry into the general subject of religion without bias to any particular one, employing the tools of critical analysis and evaluation. It is a part of free philosophical inquiry using data from whatever source. Its field is not only that of general evaluation but also of considered interest in those topics usually occurring in the frame-work of religion: the nature and function of religion; its value; the validity of the claim of religious knowledge as a particular kind; the relation of religion with ethics; the problems of evil, theodicy, purpose, prayer; the existence or non-existence of Deity and Its character; the nature of faith and belief and their relation to reason; institutional expressions of religion and their import; the problem of continued existence after the experience of death; and a host of others.

* * *

A HISTORY OF PHILOSOPHICAL SYSTEMS

Among professional philosophers it may be said that the subject of religious philosophy took on its character of distinctiveness in the nineteenth-century in Germany. From there it took its flight to English speaking countries with France following only slowly thereafter. For some point of beginning, it is easy to start with Hegel (1770-1831). He may be credited with having treated his subject with greater catholicity and larger sweep than those who came before him in the long tradition of Christian theology. His philosophy of religion, however, followed upon his philosophy of history with the typical Hegelian premise of a dialectical development of religions toward an absolute religion—thus placing the subject squarely in the frame-work of a particular philosophy. There were predecessors who had made suggestive contributions. Hume (1711-1776) had, for example, made the observation that religion did not rise out of mere rational reflection and had pointed to psychological factors as marking its universal characteristics. Such heretical observation, however, was too great for the times. Kant (1724-1804), too, had made his observations not without great influence. By his sharp analytic approach he had placed the subjects of his discourse upon a plane somewhat independent of the claims of traditional theology. The moral nature of man became for him an *a priori* principle sufficient to explain and erect a theory of religion. There was lacking in him an appreciation of those subtle factors which motivate the mind (now commonplaces of observation in religious psychology) due to his own structural and analytic type of psychology; and there was no regard for the enormous rôle in the whole phenomenon of religion played by social and cultural influences (now commonplaces of observation). Hegel's contemporary, F. D. E. Schleiermacher (1768-1834), corrected the narrow emphasis which Kant had given to the subject proclaiming a counter-position which, while seeming as narrow, had implications of breadth. Said Schleiermacher: man's beliefs about the Universe are not at all characteristics of the religious spirit; rather, it is out of his inner *feeling* toward life and reality that religions spring. Doctrines are to be seen as results of experience; religious institutions (*e.g.*, the church) are only the media for provoking such experience; and, theology is but the reflection upon it all.

Among such thinkers (and there were others) are found the origins of the modern inquiry into the philosophy of religion as a special discipline. Such thinking was a radical departure from the traditional view that religion was something apart from the natural modes of response, something unique in origin and value, a supernaturally grounded body of beliefs and expected reactions exempt from the peerings of secular inquiry. Religion had always been taken *normatively* from some particular religious point of view rather than *descriptively*; for Catholics and conventional Protestants it had to do with a revelation centered in a tradition by which all religious phenomena were to be judged. To Hegel it became a field of wider perspective, including religion in its earliest expressions, in its variety of forms—all, however, as leading to a universal and absolute ideal. To this insight of universality, Hegel was driven not by an objective study of historic religions as such, but by his method of dialectic (which, however, he thought was empirical). Schleiermacher, on the other hand, became the father of what is now called "religious empiricism" and a fore-runner of that special field of inquiry known as the "psychology of religion." And as for Hume and Kant, both contributed to the spirit of critical investigation, so strongly characteristic of the philosophical approach. All had their short-comings, each viewing the subject from his own particular theory or limited perspective. And all were well within their own religious tradition.[1]

The subsequent development of the subject followed naturally upon the presuppositions of the *kind* of philosophy to which thinkers felt themselves committed. Philosophy of religion continued as a branch of a *particular* philosophy. Since absolute idealism was long regnant, of the type which moved out from Hegelian influences, the subject became colored by it. Otto Pfleiderer's (1839-1908) contribution to the subject, although grounded in Hegelianism, was a more serious attempt to consider the history and variety of religious expressions and the psychological features involved. So also did Eduard von Hartmann's (1842-1906) emphasis upon the unconscious mind illuminate factors of religious psychology—almost up-to-date in some of its insights. A. Dorner's (1846-1920) idea of the gradual preponderance of the ideal elements in the world over the real betrayed his Hegelian premises; nevertheless, the historical and psychological came in for emphasis. Philosophy of religion thus followed the course of speculative idealism in the land of its birth; a parallel development got expressed in writings elsewhere, *e.g.*, John Caird (1820-1898), John Watson (1847-1939) and Josiah Royce

A HISTORY OF PHILOSOPHICAL SYSTEMS

(1855-1916) in America. A turn toward an emphasis upon personal values was given in the religious philosophies of H. Lotze (1817-1881), R. Eucken (1846-1926), H. Siebeck (1842-1920), Hastings Rashdall (1858-1924), G. T. Ladd (1842-1921)[2] and more particularly of B. P. Bowne (1847-1910).[3] Personal idealism although flowing from other channels thus followed in more or less reaction against absolute idealism.

A marked departure, however, was given in the thought of Albrecht Ritschl (1822-1889)[4] whose doctrine of value-judgments set a course which developed into a school. Religion, said Ritschl, moves in a realm of its own, independent of scientific judgments, of speculation, of mystic or intuitive claims. The religious spirit is an *independent* value-judgment which asserts a deliverance of man from whatever theory of the world and assures him of a destiny and worthy meaning to life and reality. Religion, said A. Sabatier (1839-1901)[5]—following the Ritschlian general point of view—is a matter of the heart, not of reason. Ideologies in religion are, at best, symbols. And so, too, H. Höffding (1843-1931)[6] followed this trend in his famous religious theory resting upon his famous phrase "the conservation of value." It is man's awareness of value, which he seeks to preserve for himself and society—not a mere knowledge of the world—that forms the basis of the whole religious structure.

Close to the value-judgment theories was the development of pragmatic philosophies of religion. Does not the religious experience share with all experience a functional value for man? Does it not presumably render service, promoting enduring satisfactions and holding out a stable grasp of life? Do not religious ideas belong with other ideas in the same category of functioning for human ends? Are not the various religious expressions indications of various needs and experience? So argued the pragmatists of various types and schools. Divinity there may well be, said some; if so, It does service as an ideal. Said William James (1842-1910):[7] it may well be that there is; in fact, there *ought* to be such a Divinity which is a personal *Thou* and we do well to act on this belief as a live option.

One more step was easy. This step had been taken by A. Comte (1798-1857)[8] in his "religion of humanity," a philosophy of religion which held that the worship (worth-ship) of man is quite sufficient since the values which count are those which are human. L. Feuerbach (1804-1872)[9] went further to assert that religion is but the mirror of man's ideals and the gods the product of the human imagination. The end-result of this course of religious thought drifted into the various forms of "religious humanism" which has attracted some of the best spirits to its ideals.

Fifty to sixty years ago, just at the turn of the century and before, two developments in the study of religion took place which began to set a distinctive stamp to the study of religious philosophy.

The one was the trend of speaking of a "science of religion" based upon an objective study of historic religions including archaeology and primitive beginnings. Max Müller had had translated *The Sacred Books of the East* in fifty-one volumes (1875-   ) showing how widespread and universal were many religious ideas and practices although cultural differences were marked. Anthropological studies with their far-reaching implications for religion brought out a host of books treating the subject from the point of view of origins with special theories of the nature of religion, of magic, of spirits, of gods, of totems, etc.,—books by such familiar names as E. B. Tylor, B. Spencer and F. J. Gillen, J. G. Frazer (famed for his *Golden Bough*), C. H. Toy, A. Lang, W. Wundt, I. King, M. Jastrow, N. Söderblom, R. Otto, and others [10]—all suggesting on more scientific grounds the long evolutionary history of religious ideas and practices and how cultural circumstances (geography, climate, economic status, social isolation or communication) play into man's religious thinking. A host of books appeared dealing with special cultures, such as on India, Iran, the Graeco-Roman world, etc. But, instead of thinking of religions ethnologically or nationally, they were now seen to be broadly cultural phenomena. The old classification of divisions of religions according to racial or national groups or in terms of their generic names called sooner or later for revision. More knowledge, for example, of Hinduism or Buddhism or even of Christianity reveal these "big" religions to be plural, of great variety—all reflecting stages of culture. Religions became viewed as functional expressions of life. Anthropological studies led naturally to social theories of the origin and nature of religion. Said E. Durkheim (1858-1917),[11] religion starts and ends with group behavior, a product of social interaction. The American "Chicago School" of thought with its emphasis on functionalism in psychology drew heavily upon the anthropological and social studies and gave emphasis to this social interpretation. The writings of such men as E. S. Ames, G. B. Foster, G. B. Smith and S. Mathews [12] became enormously influential. The truth of religious ideas became a lesser question; functional value in social interaction became the prime interest and principle of explanation.

The second and parallel development was the beginning of the specialized inquiry of the psychology of religion, with pioneer work done by E. D. Starbuck, J. Leuba, G. A. Coe, J. B. Pratt, G. S. Hall and others.[13] By means of questionnaire methods of study data were collected and interpreted, with the net result that the phenomenon of religion was found to be of the same psychological stuff as any other human reaction. Particular religious ideas became illuminated by this approach—ideas of god (their moral evolution), of conversion, of cult practices, and the like. Very little has been done in this area of inquiry since these earlier days—largely because of the shifting schools of psychology with the long interim reign of behaviorism from about the second decade of the century and after. Since then, religious phenomena have come under the shocking scrutiny of Freudians and neo-Freudians. During and after the first World War studies in various forms of psychoses appeared, offering valuable insights into the subtle motivations of overt behavior. A definite school of religious thought developed by this British school of dynamic psychologists got itself expressed in numerous volumes of wide reading, by such writers as J. A. Hadfield, T. W. Pym, R. H. Thouless, C. E. Hudson, E. R. Micklem, and others.[14]

* * *

The state of the subject of the philosophy of religion today judging by the output of books may be described as revisionary, due to the rise of more disciplined studies in philology, cultures, historic religions, social psychology, anthropology and related subjects. Philosophers, qualified in the field, now carry on their studies with a growing sense of independence of ecclesiasticism, theology and apologetics. There are, of course, the continuing exceptions of those who move in and out of the field with their minds still loyal to some given theology. During the first quarter of the century there appeared such widely read books as G. Galloway's *Philosophy of Religion* (1914), D. Drake's *Problems of Religion* (1916), W. E. Hocking's *The Meaning of God in Human Experience* (1916) (a neo-idealistic account), and W. K. Wright's widely popular *A Stu-*

dent's Philosophy of Religion (1922). Then followed treatments of the subject which moved within the orbit of particular philosophies. Among these may be mentioned: D. C. Macintosh [15] who envisaged a philosophy of religion tied to an empirical theology; Henry N. Wieman [16] whose many books sought to link the field within the framework of a theocentric naturalism; S. Radhakrishnan's [17] comprehensive picture of a philosophic Hinduism as the pinnacle of the truth of religious thought by which Occidental philosophies of one kind or another are to be judged; Rufus Jones [18] who defended the way of the mild mystic on the wave of a revival of mystical interpretations (W. R. Inge, E. Underhill, S. Dasgupta, E. W. Lyman); [19] E. S. Brightman's [20] vigorous defense of rationalism in religion (in the face of current irrationalistic thought) and of theistic personalism.

During the first World War and with increasing vigor after the Second, scholars who might well have turned their energies to the pursuit of religious philosophy as a discipline of free rational inquiry, turned away and sought, instead, to revitalize traditional theologies. The alleged dilemma of man aspiring towards ideals and his alleged incompetence to fulfil them in social living created a new interest in ancient dogmas of religion for which this was an old theme. Existential philosophies based upon pathos experience came to the fore and heralded a day of the revival of the more sombre features of Protestant orthodoxy. Philosophically-minded theologians joined traditionalists in singing songs of despair and anguish. The mind with its attempted channeling of ultimate truths through the dialectic of reason was to be taken to be engaged in futile enterprise; the only way open to that which is fundamentally real is by an "encounter" with the all-transrational existence. A theology founded on revelation (interpreted anew) was again to hold sway over religious philosophy. Philosophy of religion was to be relegated to a second-rate status by reason of its impossible attempt to deal with that which is reality.

In the middle of this century the peak of this movement has probably been reached even though the chorus in praise of "faith" and "communion" and "authority" and "revelation" is still strong. Voices of protest have been heard all along—particularly from the camp of religious philosophers—and they will sooner or later again be heard in increasing numbers, for the simple reason that reason itself is man's only way of ever coming to non-dogmatic terms with the world. The One-World idea into which this era has come since the last World War will call a new generation of religious thinkers to the tasks of religious philosophizing. But the tasks will not be quite the same as in older generations. The religions of the world—in the plurality of their forms—better known with the world of contact grown smaller through technological advances—will come with their offerings and gifts. There will be less of the patronizing spirit of those of past generations who felt themselves "called" to a circumscribed and hallowed theology. It will be a meeting of East with West and West with East. Religions will no longer seem divided into hard and fast divisions. All of them will be seen to be essentially plural, as plural as is the Christian religion in all its varieties. Values which wear the air of the universal will be stressed; differences of ideologies and practices will be understood in terms of culture and circumstance. There will be a grasp toward unity without uniformity; but a unity of value-appreciation and not of some superiorly inspired theology or tightly closed system of philosophy. The divisions of men will be seen cutting across horizontally with the levels of their culture and not vertically in terms of the steps of history out of which each has climbed. All the greater prophets will be invoked; and those will be chosen for higher seats whose insights into life transcend provincialities of time and locality.

As yet this day has not seen the full dawn. But the signs are unmistakable. Conventional theologians as such—those with committed views—are not the prophets of tomorrow. They belong with the priests who enjoy the full splendor of popular following and applause. It will be those religious philosophers who are true to the philosopher's vision of seeing things broadly and together; those who see sanely in man's religious spirit something that is part and parcel of his mental frame; those who see a kind of world which stimulates the values of common and shared experience. Those books are not yet written. Their preparation will come only by way of an academic discipline gained by a cultivation of what is called the "liberal arts." Their specialized training will be longer and of a type different from that which has been customary, for the field is rich in complexity. For such preparation distinctive graduate schools of religion will appear which will cultivate the kind of scholarship now demanded by other leading professions.[21] Theological schools will probably continue as propagandizing instruments for religious organizations and they will have their mission understood as such. But from them cannot be expected the height nor the depth nor the spread of vision required for the understanding of religious phenomena unless they are ready to submit to the more catholic approach peculiarly required in the study of religious philosophy. Even as systematic theology once rightly enjoyed the central place in a theological curriculum of a partisan theological school, so will philosophy of religion become the pivotal subject among the many disciplines in the schools of religion tomorrow.

NOTES

1. For bibliography of G. W. F. Hegel, see p. 304. D. Hume, *Natural History of Religion* (1757); *Dialogues concerning Natural Religion* (1751–1761). For bibliography of Kant, see p. 289. I. Kant, *Religion within the Bounds of Mere Reason* (1793–1794). F. D. E. Schleiermacher, *Reden über Religion*, Eng. tr. by J. Oman (1892). John Locke's *The Reasonableness of Christianity* (1695), an earlier work, should not be overlooked.

2. For bibliography of this group of post-Hegelian religious philosophers see Bibliography in G. Galloway, *The Philosophy of Religion* (reprint, N. Y., 1921).

3. For bibliography of B. P. Bowne, see p. 351. *Cf.* p. 344.

4. His notable book entitled, *The Christian Doctrine of Justification and Reconciliation* (Eng. tr., 1872).

5. *Philosophy of Religion* (1901); *Religions of Authority and the Religion of the Spirit* (1903).

6. *Philosophy of Religion* (1901, Eng. tr., 1906).

7. "Reflex Action and Theism" (1881), "The Will to Believe" (1896) in *The Will to Believe* (1897); *The Varieties of Religious Experience* (1902).

8. *Cours de Philosophie positive,* 6 vols. (1830-1842).

9. *Wesen der Religion* (1845).

10. For bibliography see H. L. Friess and H. W. Schneider, *Religion in Various Cultures* (1932); Vergilius Ferm, *First Chapters in Religious Philosophy* (N. Y., 1937).

11. *The Elementary Forms of the Religious Life* (London, 1915).

12. G. B. Foster, *The Function of Religion in Man's Struggle for Existence* (1909); E. S. Ames, *Psychology of Religious Experience* (1910); G. B. Smith, *Social Idealism and the Changing Theology* (1912); S. Mathews' autobiography and bibliography in *Contemporary American Theology*, edited by Vergilius Ferm, Vol. II (New York, 1933), p. 163 ff.

A HISTORY OF PHILOSOPHICAL SYSTEMS

13. For bibliography see *First Chapters in Religious Philosophy*. Also see *Religion in Transition*, edited by Vergilius Ferm (London, 1937).

14. For an account of this school and bibliography see *First Chapters in Religious Philosophy*.

15. For an autobiographical account and bibliography see *Contemporary American Theology*, Vol. I (New York, 1932), p. 277 ff.

16. For similar information see same work, Vol. I, p. 339 ff.

17. See *Religion in Transition* (above cited); *The Reign of Religion in Contemporary Philosophy* (1920).

18. For an autobiographical account and bibliography see *Contemporary American Theology*, Vol. I, p. 191 ff.

19. W. R. Inge, *Christian Mysticism* (London, 1899); E. Underhill, *Mysticism* (1911); S. Dasgupta, *Hindu Mysticism* (1927); E. W. Lyman's autobiography and bibliography in *Contemporary American Theology*, Vol. II, p. 105 ff.

20. For an autobiographical account and bibliography see *Contemporary American Theology*, Vol. I, p. 53 ff. Also his *A Philosophy of Religion* (1940).

21. Some universities have already begun pioneer work in this direction.

BIBLIOGRAPHY

(Works mentioned in the above NOTES are not repeated in the Bibliography.)

E. S. WATERHOUSE, *Modern Theories of Religion* (London, 1910).
C. W. REESE, ed., *Humanist Sermons* (Chicago and London, 1927).
E. LEROUX, "Philosophy of Religion" in *Philosophy Today* (Chicago, 1928),
   E. L. Schaub, editor, p. 224 ff. An account of the philosophy of religion in France up through the first-quarter of this century.
R. W. SELLARS, *Religion Coming of Age* (New York, 1928).
H. BERGSON, *The Two Sources of Morality and Religion* (New York, 1932).
H. N. WIEMAN and B. E. MELAND, *American Philosophies of Religion* (Chicago, 1936).
C. HARTSHORNE, *Beyond Humanism* (Chicago, 1937).
P. ORTEGAT, *Philosphie de la Religion* (Paris, 1937).
J. S. BIXLER, ed., *The Nature of Religious Experience* (New York, 1937).
S. SANTINATHA, *The Critical Examination of the Philosophy of Religion*, in 2 vols. (Poona City, India, 1938).
J. M. MOORE, *Theories of Religious Experience* (New York, 1938).
E. A. BURTT, *Types of Religious Philosophy* (New York, 1939).
D. L. SCUDDER, *Tennant's Philosophical Theology* (New York and London, 1940).
E. GILSON, *God and Philosophy* (New York, 1941).

A HISTORY OF PHILOSOPHICAL SYSTEMS

A. E. HAYDON, *Biography of the Gods* (New York, 1941).
A. C. GARNETT, *A Realistic Philosophy of Religion* (Chicago, 1942).
J. A. MARTIN, JR., *Empirical Philosophies of Religion* (New York, 1945).
CORLISS LAMONT, *Humanism as a Philosophy* (New York, 1949).
VERGILIUS FERM, ed., *An Encyclopedia of Religion* (New York, 1945).
———, ed., *Religion in the Twentieth Century* (New York, 1948).
———, *What Can We Believe?* (New York, 1948).
———, ed., *Forgotten Religions* (New York, 1950).

INDEX*

Abailard, Peter, 193, 194, 216, 220.
Abbasid caliph al-Mamun, 161; caliphate, 160.
abhāva, 9.
Abhidharmakośa, 40, 42.
Absolute, the, 4, 13, 52, 177, 292 ff., 308, 316 ff., 320, 324 ff., 343, 346, 347, 377, 378, 388, 398, 582, 590.
absolute idealism, absolutism, 39, 292 ff., 307, 315, 342, 345, 346, 385, 419, 434, 437, 438, 518, 535, 536, 570, 601, 602; Classical German Idealism, Chap. XXIII; English and American, Chap. XXV; absolutism, main argument, 324. See idealism; speculative idealism.
abu-al-Hasan al-Ashari, 161.
a contingentia mundi, 324.
Academy, the, 94, 102, 141, 188, 232, 233.
Achilles and the tortoise, 79.
acosmism, 79.
actuality, 108, 109, 111.
Adam, 154, 155.
Adams, Brooks, 584.
Adams, Henry, 584.
Adharma, 7, 9.
Ādhibhautika, 12.
Ādhidaivika, 12.
Adhidharma, 34, 35.
Ādhyātmika, 12.
Adler, Max, 313.
Adler, M. J., 455, 461, 467.
Advaita, 13, 15.
Advaita Vedānta, 14.
Advaitists, 14.
Advancement of Learning, 235.
adventitious ideas, 242, 250.
Aenesidemus, 125.
Aesthetic Analysis, 497.

Aesthetic Experience and its Presuppositions, 559.
Aesthetic Judgment, The, 497.
Aesthetic Process, The, 496.
Aesthetic Theories of French Artists, The, 552.
aesthetics, 97, 103, 116, 141, 281, 282, 288, 295 ff., 302, 349, 376, 377, 380, 384, 385, 460, 480, 496, 497, 570; recent schools of, Chap. XLIII. See art.
Aesthetik und allgemeine Kunstwissenschaft, 557.
Aeterni Patris, 454, 457.
Afshana, 165.
Against the Heresies, 146.
Agar, W. E., 445.
agni, 3.
agnosticism, 277, 371, 422, 436, 438, 439, 527.
Agur, 159.
Aham Brāhma asmi, 5.
Ahankāra, 11.
Ahimsā, 7.
Ahuna-Vairya, 22.
Ahunavaiti, 22.
Ahurā, 28.
Ahurā-Mazdā, 21, 23, 24, 26.
Aion, 137.
Ajīva, 7.
Ākāṣa, 7, 9.
akhyāti, 13.
alaukika, 10.
ālaya-vijñāna, 39, 41.
Albert of Saxony, 223.
Albert, St., the Great, 200-203, 208.
Albertus Magnus, 166, 168, 169.
Albo, Joseph, 182.
Alcalà, Coimbra, Salamanca, universities, 228.
Alcott, Bronson, 343, 351.

*Authors and Book Titles listed in the Bibliographies appending each Chapter are not indexed.

611

INDEX

Alexander, the Great, 118, 160.
Alexander of Aphrodisias, 228.
Alexander of Hales, 208.
Alexander, S., 376, 425, 436, 522-524, 536.
Alexandria, 65, 135, 136, 146, 148, 149, 151, 160; Alexandrian philosophy, 129, Chap. XI; Alexandrian school of Christians, 144, 146, 148 ff.; Alexandrism, 228.
al-Farabi, 161, 165, 183.
Algazel, 162.
Algebra of Logic, 511, 512.
al-Ghazzali, 162, 166, 167, 178.
al-Kindi, 161, 162, 165.
allegorical method, 65; allegorization, 150, 151, 232.
Allport, G. W., 347.
Almohades, 166.
Amalric of Bènes, 194.
Amelios, 135, 136.
Ameretāt, 25, 26.
American Catholic Philosophical Ass'n., 466.
American New Realism, 518 ff., 521, 535. See Neo-Realism; realism, American.
American Society for Aesthetics, 557.
Ames, E. S., 604, 607.
Ames, Van Meter, 552 ff.
Ameshā-Spentā, 21 ff.
Ammonius Saccas, 135 ff., 151.
Amos, 57, 58.
analogical, 213.
Analysis of Knowledge, The, 534, 536.
Analysis of Knowledge and Valuation, An, 325, 501, 532, 537.
Analysis of Matter, 522, 535.
Analysis of Mind, 521, 522, 524, 535, 536.
analytic-synoptic method, 345.
anamnesis, 108.
anarchism, 269.
Anaxagoras, 77 ff., 84, 101, 341.
Anaximander, 71, 73, 74, 99, 132.
Anaximenes, 71, 72.
Ancient Society, 591.
Anekāntavāda, 7.
angels, 133.
angst, 410.
animal faith, 527.
animal symbolicum, 592.

animism, 431, 592.
anirvacanīya, 14.
Anquetil du Perron, 19.
Anschauung, 412.
Anselm, 191 ff., 195, 208, 242.
antahkarana, 11, 13.
anthropology, 98, 591, 592, 594, 603.
anthropomorphism, 58, 59, 65, 149, 173, 431.
anti-Gnostic, 151, 156; anti-Gnostic Fathers, 145 ff.
anti-naturalism, 408.
antipsychologism, 474.
anti-rationalism, 147, 173, 174, 375, 385.
anti-semitism, 147, 462.
anti-trinitarianism, 236.
Antigone, 83.
antilogism, 511.
antinomies, 286.
Antioch, 160.
anyathā-khyāti, 10.
Apeiron, 132.
Appearance and Reality, 316, 320, 322.
apologetics, 599.
Apologists, Christian, 144 ff.
Apostolic Constitutions, 148.
Apostolic Fathers, 144 ff.
Aprathak-Siddhi, 15.
a priori, 249, 283-286, 425.
Aquinas, Thomas, 168, 169, 171, 198 ff., 202 ff., 212, 213, 216, 223, 228, 229, 238, 256, 341, 415, 422, 454-468, 582. See Thomism.
Aquinas Lecture, 466.
Arabic philosophy, 171, 193, 194, 197, 204, 212, 213, 217, 221, 234; Chap. XIII; essence of, 162 ff.; influx into Western thought, 168 ff.
Āranyakas, 3, 4.
arbitraries, 566 ff., 569-572.
Arcesilaus, 125.
arche, 132, 134.
Archelaus, 87, 91.
archetypal type, 282, 287, 288.
"Are Naturalists Materialists?", 428.
arhan, 8.
Arians, the, 156.
Aristeas, Letter of, 65, 66.
Aristides, 145.
Aristippus, 101.

612

INDEX

Aristotelian logic, 114, 348, 505, 506, 510. See logic.
Aristotelianism, 132, 170, 172, 173, 181, 197, 208, 341, 423, 455, 474; Chap. IX; condemnation by church, 198, 212; renaissance, 227-229, 231, 232, 234, 237, 238; tradition and induction, 507. See realism, Aristotelian; Revived Aristotelianism.
Aristotle, 78, 88, 94, 95, 97, 103, 105 ff., 118, 119, 125, 129, 133, 135-137, 139, 145, 161-166, 168, 169, 171, 175, 179, 182, 183, 185, 186, 188, 193, 194, 197-202, 204, 206-209, 212, 213, 217, 227-230, 232-234, 237, 256, 257, 341, 396, 402, 421, 422, 424, 432, 433, 443, 467, 505, 506, 552, 561, 574, 589; basic notions of, 108; basic distinctions in his physics and metaphysics, 111, 112; and the pontifical decree of 1231, 168.
arithmetic, 511, 513.
ārmabha-vāda, 10.
Ārmaiti, 25, 26, 28.
Arnauld, 247.
arrow in flight, 79 ff.
art, 116, 288, 377, 380, 384, 385; the arts, 237; Chinese, 53. See aesthetics.
Art and Faith, 460.
Art and Freedom, 558.
Art as Experience, 554.
Art and Scholasticism, 460.
Art and the Social Order, 558.
Arts and the Art of Criticism, The, 496.
Arya Samaj, 17.
asamprajnāta Samādhi, 12.
Asanga, 39-41.
Asatkāryavāda, 10.
asceticism, 119, 187, 379, 380.
aseity, 425.
Asha, 22, 24, 25, 28.
Asha Vahishta, 23.
"as if" philosophy, 412. See Vaihinger, H.
Asomaton, 139.
association, principle of, 96.
astral metaphysics, 432.
Atar, 23.
ateleology, 121, 380.

Atharva-Veda, 3.
atheism, 7, 12, 254, 277, 341-343, 370, 406.
Athenagoras, 145.
Athens, 147; Athenian culture, 588, 589.
Ātman, 5, 17, 40.
atomic energy, 372.
atomism, 9, 78, 80, 120, 121, 163, 175, 248, 376, 378, 421, 425, 432, 444, 446, 450.
Aufbau der Welt, Der Logische, 479-481.
Aufschwung in die Transzendenz, 411.
Augustine, 127, 148, 152 ff., 164, 169, 170, 185, 186, 189, 194, 197, 199, 200, 204, 205, 208, 460, 462, 463, 466, 468, 506, 575, 577, 589.
Augustinianism, 152 ff., 191, 199, 201, 203, 205, 206, 232; modified, 455.
Avadhi, 7.
Avenarius, R., 336, 437.
Avendeath, 168.
Averroës, 161, 162, 164-167, 169, 181, 198, 202, 203, 208, 212, 228; and Western thought, 169.
Averroism, 168, 198, 203-206, 209; Latin, 202, 203, 212, 228.
Avesta, 23, 28-31.
Avey, A. E., 504 ff.
Avicebron, 177.
Avicenna, 161, 162, 164-166, 168, 169, 179, 198-202, 208, 213, 214, 217; and Thomism, 168, 169; his influence on the West, 168 ff.; Avicennian-Augustinianism, 200.
avidyā, 8, 14, 16.
axiology, 348, 349, 422, 569. See value.
axioms, 268, 473, 543.
"Axioms as Postulates," 343.
Ayer, A. J., 481, 482, 499.

Bachofen, J. J., 591.
Bacon, F., 89, 235, 236, 253, 262, 291, 389-391, 394, 398-400, 507, 517, 541, 547.
Bacon, Roger, 200.
Bādarayaṇa, 13.
baddha, 7.
Baer, Carl, von, 367.
Bagehot, 584.

INDEX

Baghdad, 158, 160-162, 166.
Bahya Ibn Paquda, 176.
Baldwin, J. M., 508.
Barnes, H. E., 580, 584, 586.
Baron, S., 183.
Barth, Karl, 410, 411.
Bartholomae, 31.
Basic Writings of Saint Thomas, 466.
Basilides, 146.
Basra, 161, 162.
Baudelaire, 553.
Bauer, 308.
Bayer, 561.
Beard, Charles, 583, 586.
beatific, 233; vision, 213, 461.
beatitude, 210.
beauty, see art; aesthetics.
Becker, Oskar, 354.
becoming, 99, 134, 164, 298, 378, 380, 383, 406.
Begriffschrift, 510.
behavior sciences, 484, 485, 487.
behaviorism, 347, 357, 395, 473, 480, 485, 491, 496-498, 536, 566, 604.
being, 75, 77, 79, 80, 93, 111, 113, 114, 131, 132, 137, 139, 142, 165, 166, 169, 190, 193, 207, 208, 213, 222, 292, 298, 309, 340, 378, 406, 413, 414, 456, 464, 465, 467, 505; being and essence, 169 See essence and existence; existence; ontology.
Being and Some Philosophers, 464.
Being and Time, 354.
Bell, Clive, 555.
Ben Sira, 64, 67.
Bene Qedem, 159.
Benedict, Ruth, 595, 596.
Benjamin, A. C., 540 ff.
Bennett, John, 349.
Bentham, 264, 270, 494, 499, 566.
Berdyaev, N., 343, 349-351.
Bergmann, G., 471 ff., 482, 483 ff.
Bergson, H., 303, 341, 343, 347-349, 375, 376, 380 ff., 407, 415, 437, 460, 462, 593.
Berkeleianism, 315.
Berkeley, G., 142, 253, 254, 257, 262-264, 291, 316, 340, 342, 344, 346, 423, 424, 442, 443, 475, 478, 516, 517, 519, 533, 535.
Berndtson, A., 375 ff.
Bernstein, Ed., 313, 314.

Bertocci, P. A., 344, 347, 349.
Beyond Good And Evil, 386.
Bhagvad-Gītā, 5 ff., 13.
Bhakti, 6, 15, 16.
Bhakti-Yoga, 6.
Bheda, 15.
Bible, the, 173, 174, 176, 179, 197; Biblicism, 406. See New Testament; Old Testament.
Bigg, C., 156.
biology, 366, 367, 375, 381, 384, 395, 425, 445, 447, 517, 518, 529, 582.
biotism, 437. See vitalism.
Birth of Tragedy, 376, 386.
Bixler, J. S., 344, 350.
Blanshard, B., 346, 535, 536.
Blondel, M., 455.
Boas, F., 575, 592.
Bochenski, I. M., 344.
Bodhisatta, 9.
Bodin, Jean, 236, 578.
body and mind, see mind and body.
Boehme, Jacob, 236.
Boethius, 185, 187-189; of Dacia, 202, 203, 216.
Bolin, W., 339.
Bolyai, 517, 540.
Bonaventure, St., 169, 199-201, 208, 209, 463.
Boodin, J. E., 344, 348, 350, 437.
Book of Wisdom, 169.
Boole, G., 509-511, 540.
Bosanquet, B., 315-317, 321-327, 495, 496, 507, 516, 535, 581.
Bossuet, 575, 578.
boundless, the, 71.
Bowne, B. P., 303, 340-342, 344-351, 602, 607.
Boyle, 247.
Bracque, 553.
Bradley, F. H., 100, 315-317, 320-325, 400, 401, 495, 507, 516, 519, 535.
Brahe, Tycho, 237.
Brāhmaṇ, 5, 13-15, 17; Brahmans, 136; Brahmanism, 33.
Brāhmaṇas, the, 3, 4, 12.
Brahmo Samaj, 17.
Bréhier, E., 136.
Brentano, F., 474, 481, 493, 531, 572.
Brethren of Purity, 183.
Brethren of Sincerity, 162.

INDEX

Bridgman, P. W., 401, 402, 549.
Briefwechsel, 509.
Brightman, E. S., 340 ff., 342, 344, 345, 348-351, 605, 608.
Brihādaraṇyaka, 4.
British school of dynamic psychologists, 604.
brotherhood, 67.
Brouwer, L. E. J., 512, 513.
Bruno, Giordano, 235, 341.
Büchner, 435.
Buckle, 583, 584.
Buddha, 8, 9, 33, 35-38.
Buddhahood, 40.
buddhi, 11.
Buddhism, 6, 8 ff., 56, 155, 603; Buddhist philosophical systems, Chap. III.
Bukhara, 165.
Bulesis, 137.
Bullough, 556.
Buridan, John, 223.
Burnet, J., 91, 102.
Butler, Joseph, 271.

Cabala, the, 234.
Caird, Edw., 343.
Caird, John, 343, 601.
Cairns, Dorion, 353 ff.
Cajetan, cardinal, 169, 455; Cajetanus, Thomas de Vio, 228.
calculus, 486-491, 509, 512, 513.
Calculus of Consistencies, 514.
Calculus of Ordinary Inference, 514.
Calkins, M. W., 340, 342, 343, 347, 350.
Callicles, 88.
Calvin, John, 577.
Cama, K. R., 30.
Cambridge school of analysis, 471, 472.
Cambridge university, 500, 501.
Campanella, Thomas, 235.
Candide, 276.
Candrakīrti, 39.
canon, 156; of Marcion, 147.
Canon, 165.
capitalism, 310, 311.
Cardan, J., 234.
Carnap, R., 476, 479, 481, 490, 492, 499, 514, 550.
Carneades, 125, 127.

Carpocrates, 146.
Carr, H. W., 342, 350.
Carthage, 146.
Caso, Antonio, 344, 376, 385.
Cassirer, Ernst, 592.
Castor and Pollux, 126.
catechetical schools, 148.
categorical imperative, 295, 342, 569.
categories, 12, 97, 98, 100, 136, 137, 293, 298, 309, 342, 346, 377, 419, 424, 425, 429, 436, 505, 506, 542, 544, 545; Kantian, 264, 285, 286, 288; of Peirce, 449; Aristotle's *Categories,* 161.
Catholic Reformation, 236.
Catholic university of America, 457.
Catholicism, see Aquinas; Neo-Thomism; Thomism.
causality, cause, 10, 11, 35, 38, 93, 102, 103, 108-111, 128, 242, 244, 249, 260-263, 285, 331, 336, 346, 347, 373, 378, 381, 382, 423-425, 464, 472, 474, 548; causation, social, 575, 579; "causal efficacy," 452; cause-effect, 229, 246, 250, 261, 283; efficient and final, 110; material, efficient, formal, final, 102 ff. See final causes.
"Causation in Historical Events," 585.
Cell, G. C., 350.
certainty, 205, 241, 244, 282.
Cetana, 7.
Cézanne, 552, 553.
Chalcidius, 186.
Chaldean astrology, 70.
Chalmers, Lord, 42.
chance, 449.
Chance, Love and Logic, 398.
Chāndogya, 4.
change, 8, 11, 13, 34, 35, 37, 72, 73, 83, 84, 99, 108-110, 116, 167, 375, 381, 444, 475. See motion.
Charlemagne, 158.
Charles de Saint-Evremond, 270.
Chartres and other schools, 192.
Chārvāka, 6 ff.
Ch'eng wei Shih Lun, 41.
ch'i and *chih,* 50.
Chicago school, the, 388, 603, 604.
Chiffren, 411.
Chinese culture, 588; philosophy, 42; Chap. IV.

615

INDEX

choice, 566 ff. See freedom.
Christian Doctrine of Justification and Reconciliation, The, 607.
Christian Mysticism, 608.
Christian philosophy, early, Chap. XII.
Christian view of history, 577.
Christian Wisdom, 186.
Christianity, 603. See under specific chapter headings.
Christianity and Democracy, 460.
Christianity and Philosophy, 463.
Christianity as Old as Creation, 276.
Christology, 152.
Chronos, 137.
Chrysippus, 118, 122.
Chu Hsi, 56.
Chuang Tzŭ, 51-53.
church and state, 236.
Cicero, 127, 186, 197.
circular reasoning, 242.
cit, 13.
City of God, 152, 462, 589.
City of the Sun, 235.
Civilization and its Discontents, 594.
Civilization on Trial, 586.
Clark, G. H., 70 ff., 118 ff.
Clarke, Samuel, 276.
class struggle, 309-312, 591.
Cleanthes, 122.
Clement, 146, 148-151, 156.
Coe, G. A., 344, 347, 351, 604.
Coffey, P., 506.
cogito ergo sum, 89, 154, 241, 345, 460.
Cohen, Hermann, 303.
Cohen, M. R., 398.
coherence theory, 325, 326, 345, 348, 392, 394, 495, **507.**
Cohon, S. S., 57 ff.
Collected Essays and Reviews, **398,** 400, 537.
Collected Legal Papers, 401.
Collected Papers, 398-402.
Collingwood, R. G., 582, 586.
Collins, J., 456.
Commentary on the Epistle to the Romans, 194.
communism, 312, 591. See Marx.
Communist Manifesto, 309.
Community of the Free, 467.
"Compagnons de route," 465.

compresence, 523.
Compton, A. H., 548.
Comte, A., 264, 273, 330 ff., 380, 435, 540, 582-584, 591, 602. See law of three stages; positivism.
Concept of Consciousness, The, 521.
Concept of Dread, The, 410.
Concept of Nature, 551.
conceptualism, 218.
Concise History of the Law of Nations, A, 586.
concrete universal, 324, 326, 327. See universals.
Condillac, E. de, 270, 577.
conditioned reflex, 396.
Condorcet, marquis de, 273, 332, 575, 577.
Confessions, 153.
Confucianism, 44 ff., 55, 56.
Confucius, 44 ff., 53.
conscience, 379.
consciousness, 357 ff.
conservation of mass and energy, 435.
conservation of value, 602.
Consolation of Philosophy, 188.
Constantinople, 159.
Constitutionalism, 274, 275.
contemplation, 140 ff., 233.
Contemporary American Theology, 607, 608.
contextualism, 307, 495.
contingency, 249, 324, 401, 425.
Contra Celsum, 151.
"Controlling Assumptions in the Practice of American Historians," 585.
Copernicus, N., 237, 280; view, 235; astronomy, 240; revolution in knowledge, 284.
Cordova, 167.
correspondence theory, 489.
cosmological argument for God, 276.
cosmology, 70 ff., 128, 134, 163, 166, 176, 177, 181, 187, 422, 433.
Courbet, 552.
Cours de Philosophie Positive, 607.
Cousin, V., 343.
creatio ex nihilo, 164, 167, 174, 176, 209, See *ex nihilo.*
creation, 10, 20, 21, 27, 57, 59-62, 102, 146-149, 154-156, 163, 167, 168, 173, 174, 176, 177, 179-182,

INDEX

188-190, 209, 217, 220, 249, 346, 365, 373, 422, 425, 434, 451; creativity, 376, 383, 385, 449.
Creative Evolution, 381, 383, 386.
Creative Intelligence, 402, 537.
Creel, H. G., 44 ff.
Creighton, J. E., 315-317, 321, 322, 324.
Crescas, Hasdai, 182.
crisis, 407-412.
criteriological realism, 458.
Critériologie, 458.
critical existentialism, 407 ff.
critical monism, 527.
critical philosophy of Kant, Chap. XXII; 292, 516.
critical realism, 303, 345, 401, 419, 420, 424, 428, 460, 465, 517, 518, 525, 527, 528, 531.
Critical Realism, 420, 428.
criticism, 558.
Critique de la connaissance morale, 466.
Critique, the Kantian Critiques, 281, 282, 284, 285, 289, 346, 401, 506, 507, 531.
Croce, B., 556, 557, 574, 575, 578, 581, 582, 586.
cubism, 553, 560.
culture, 272, 273, 377, 461, 579, 580, 584, 585, 589, 603; philosophies of, Chap. XLVI; scientific, 440. See Greek culture; Latin culture.
culturology, 592.
Cunningham, G. W., 315 ff.
Cursus Philosophicus Thomisticus, 169.
Cusanus, Nicolaus, 234, 235, 576.
cycles, 236, 373, 378, 574, 578, 593.
Cynics, the, 118, 119, 123.
Cyprian, 148.
Cyrenaics, 118, 119.

Dada, 553, 560.
Dalbiez, 468.
D'Alembert, J., 267, 278.
Dali, 560.
Dalton, 421.
Damascus, 158.
Daniel, 67.
Dante, 169, 203, 233, 463.
Dark Ages, 185, 231.

Darwin, Charles, 366, 367, 395, 396, 435, 541, 591.
Darwin, Erasmus, 366.
Darwinism, 277, 367, 402, 584. See natural selection.
Dasgupta, S., 605, 608.
Dayananda, swami, 17.
De Anima, 112, 193.
death, 120.
Declaration of Independence, 269.
Declaration of the Rights of Man and the Citizen, 269.
Decline and Fall of the Roman Empire, The, 273.
deduction, 390, 430, 542, 543.
De Ente et Essentia, 169.
degree of confirmation, 550.
Degrees of Knowledge, 459-461.
deism, 276, 342.
Deists' Bible, the, 276.
De la philosophie chrétienne, 462.
De l'esprit, 270.
De l'homme, 270.
De Maistre, J., 332.
Demiurge, 101, 128, 146, 147.
Democritus, 78, 80, 104, 139, 163, 232, 345, 419, 421.
De Monarchia, 203.
De Morgan, A., 509, 510.
De Oratione, 151.
De Principiis, 151.
De Republica, 186.
Descartes, René, 89, 96, 154, 223, 238, 240 ff., 245-247, 250, 253, 255, 291, 341, 345, 380, 389-391, 399, 407, 408, 419, 422, 423, 426, 458, 460, 463, 480, 506, 516, 525, 526, 576, 582.
design, 579; design argument, 365. See teleological argument for God.
desire, 123, 247, 493 ff., 568; desire and good, 245.
despair, see crisis.
despotism, enlightened, 274.
Dessoir, 557.
destiny, 59.
determinism, 124, 125, 245, 247, 249, 250, 280, 379, 383, 548; economic, 308-310.
De tradendis disciplinis, 231.
De Trinitate, (Augustine), 152; (Boethius), 188.

INDEX

Deutero-Isaiah, 59.
Deuteronomy, 60.
"Development of American Pragmatism," 537.
Devotio Moderna, 236.
Dewey, John, 264, 313, 337 ff., 339, 388, 395, 401, 402, 419, 428, 486, 495, 497, 498, 502, 508, 528 ff., 531, 532, 537, 554, 556-558, 594-596.
DeWolf, L. H., 344, 349.
dharma, 6-10, 13, 16; *dharmas,* 35, 40, 41.
dharma-bhūta-jnāna, 15.
Dharmakīrti, 42.
dialectic, 99, 132, 161, 189, 191, 193, 194, 351, 413, 433, 504, 581, 600, 605; Hegelian, see Hegelian dialectic; meaning of, 306 ff.; three laws of, 313.
Dialectic, the, 231.
dialectical materialism, 420, 581; Chap. XXIV.
dialectical theology, 410 ff., 412.
Dialogues concerning Natural Religion, 607.
Dialogues on Love, 233.
Diatessaron, 145.
Diccionario de la Filosofía, 344.
Didache, the, 144, 148.
Diderot, D., 267, 277, 590.
Digāmbaras, 7.
Dignāga, 42.
"Dilemma of Being and Unity," 466.
"Dilemma of Determinism," 398.
Dilthey, W., 407, 412, 580, 585, 594.
Diogenes Laertius, 230.
Diogenes of Sinope, 119.
Discourse on Method, 204, 506.
Discourse on the Moral Effects of the Arts and Sciences, 271.
Discourse on the Origin of Inequality, 271, 272.
Discourses, 236.
Disputationes metaphysicae, 229.
distinguer pour unir, 461.
Divine, the, 103 ff., 136, 438, 439, 602. See God.
divine madness, 237.
Dodds, E. R., 141.
dogmatism, the new, 127 ff.
Dominican order, 168, 169, 228.

Dorner, A., 601.
Dotterer, R. H., 365 ff.
double aspect theory, 480.
double truth theory, see truth.
doubt, 240, 241. See scepticism.
Drake, D., 342, 401, 420, 525, 604.
Dravyas, 9.
Dream of Scipio, 186.
Dreyer, H., 340.
Droysen, 581.
dualism, 7, 9, 11, 21, 59, 104, 128, 244, 250, 292, 314, 342, 370, 376, 381, 419, 420, 422, 423, 432-434, 438, 449, 525, 579. See epistemological dualism.
dualistic realism, 525 ff.
Dunham, J. H., 93 ff.
Duns Scotus, see Scotus.
duration, 381-383.
Durkheim, E., 335, 603.
duty, 6, 13, 47.
Du Vair, Guillaume, 232.
Dvaita, the, 15.
dyad, 127, 449.
dynameis, 133, 138.
dynamism, 307, 422, 431. See naturalism, dynamistic.
dyos, 133.
dysteleology, 155.

Earl of Bridgewater, the, 365.
Eastern Orthodoxy, 593.
Eastman, Max, 314.
Ebreo, Leone, 233.
Ecclesiastes, book of, 63, 66.
eclecticism, 153, 231, 234.
ecstasy, 176 See *ékstasis.*
ectypal type, 282, 284-288.
Eddington, A. S., 548, 549.
Edessa, 159, 160.
Education at the Crossroads, 460.
Ego, the, as Absolute, 295.
egocentric predicament, 345.
egressus, the, 135, 137, 139.
Ehrenfels, C., 493-497.
eidetic truths, 356 ff.
eidos, 96, 101, 135, 355.
Eikon, 138.
einfühlung, 555.
Einstein, A., 473, 548, 551.
Either/Or, 410.
Eklampsis, 137.

618

INDEX

ékstasis, 134, 141.
elan vital, 383, 415.
Eleatic school, 74 ff., 306, 504; Eleatics, 307.
Elementary Forms of the Religious Life, The, 607.
elements, 71 ff., 76-78, 93, 164, 235.
emanation, 139, 166, 175-177, 180, 181, 187, 200.
emergence, 420, 425, 440. See levels.
empathy, 555, 556.
Empedocles, 76 ff., 104, 574.
empiricism, 235, 236, 268, 270, 336, 345, 346, 380, 391, 394, 398, 418, 419, 422, 425, 428, 430, 432, 437-440, 472-474, 477, 479, 481, 484, 516, 533, 576, 578, 582, 584, 585; early modern, Chap. XX; Aristotelian, 112, 113; of Ockham, 222, 223; Thomistic, 206; empirical theology, 605. See instrumentalism; logical empiricism; religious empiricism; sensationalism.
encounter, 407, 408, 410, 411, 414, 605.
Encyclopaedia, the (French), 267, 268; Hegel's, 293.
Encyclopedia of Unified Science, 498.
encyclopedic, 231; encyclopedists, 162.
energeia, 141.
energy, 372, 373; metaphysical energism, 437. See dynamism.
Engels, F., 299, 309, 313, 336, 591.
English New Realism, 518, 521 ff. See Neo-Realism.
Enlightenment, 576, 579, 580, 582, 590; the philosophy of, Chap. XXI. See religion of the Enlightenment.
Enneads, the, 136 ff., 140 ff., 162.
Enoch, 67.
ens, 464.
entelechy, 168.
entia rationis, 424.
entities, actual, 451.
entropy, 372.
Entziffern, 411.
Epekeina, 132.
Ephrem, St., 160.
Epictetus, 122, 123, 230.
Epicureanism, 6, 64, 119 ff., 122-127, 232, 270.
Epicurus, 118, 119, 125, 232, 419.

epiphenomenalism, 378, 419, 425, 428.
epistemological dualism, 321, 345, 347, 520, 522, 525, 527, 530.
epistemological idealism, 518, 519, 524, 527-529, 531 ff., 535. See mentalism.
epistemological monism, 347, 518, 520-525, 527, 529, 534. See critical monism.
epistemological realism, 517 ff., 528, 536.
epistemological schools, recent, Chap. XLI.
epistemology, 10, 12, 14, 37, 118, 120, 187, 206, 253 ff., 307, 322, 337, 345 ff., 356 ff., 360 ff., 376, 381, 418-420, 422-426, 458, 463, 471; phenomenalistic theories, 531; representationalism, 520, 533. See Kant's critical philosophy; knowledge.
Epistrophe, 141.
epochalism, 450.
epoché, 412.
Erasmus, D., 231, 236, 267.
Erdmann, J. E., 88.
Eriugena, John Scotus, 189-191, 194, 216, 434.
Erkennen and *Erleben*, 479.
Erkenntnis, 481.
error, 12-16, 96, 246, 347, 520, 521, 527.
ESP, 347.
Essay Concerning Human Understanding, 505.
Essay on Forms of Government, An, 278.
Essay on Universal History, 273.
Essays in Critical Realism, 401, 525.
Essays in Experimental Logic, 537.
Essays on Truth and Reality, 321, 400.
esse, 465.
essence(s), 188, 355, 356, 359, 421, 428, 526, 532, 569; realm of, 420, 424.
essence and existence, 202, 204, 207, 208, 213, 214, 217, 309, 405 ff., 413, 414; essence and being, see being and essence.
essentialism, 214, 406-408, 413.
Estética, 385.

619

INDEX

eternalism, eternity, 102, 104, 138, 163, 164, 167, 168, 174, 200, 203, 209.

ethics, 97, 119 ff., 140, 176, 180, 182, 194, 227, 270, 295, 296, 301, 335, 338, 348, 349, 370, 376, 379, 380, 385, 388, 401, 427, 428, 433, 461, 480, 499-501; Aristotelian, 115, 116; recent schools of, Chap. XLIV. See hedonism; moralists, early Greek; natural rights; *summum bonum*; utilitarianism.

Ethics, the, 244, 247.

Ethics and Language, 501.

ethnology, 593.

Ética, 385.

Euathlus, 87.

Eucken, Rudolph, 299, 300, 602.

Euclid, 165, 479.

euphemia, 141.

Europäische Philosophie der Gegenwart, 344.

Eustochius, 136.

evil, 62 ff., 66, 82, 120, 121, 123, 128, 134, 139, 146, 347; Augustine's solution to the problem of, 154, 155. See good and evil; theodicy.

evocation, 411.

evolution, 11, 15, 307, 348, 375, 379, 381 ff., 395, 398, 402, 422, 425, 435, 440, 583, 584, 591; early philosophies of, Chap. XXIX.

Evolution and Ethics, etc., 400.

"Evolution by Natural Selection," 402.

"Evolution of Self-Consciousness," 402.

Evolutionary Naturalism, 428.

Examination of Sir Wm. Hamilton's Philosophy, 537.

existence, 202, 371, 464, 478, 512; pathos of, see pathos of existence. See being; essence and existence.

Existence and the Existent, 460.

existentialism, 309, 312, 354, 375, 439, 455, 458, 464, 465, 469, 560, 605; Chap. XXXII; social existentialism, 407, 408, 414 ff.; Thomistic, 208, 209, 214, 223. See Kantian existentialism.

ex nihilo, 110, 148, 154; *ex nihilo nihil fit*, 76. See *creatio ex nihilo*.

experience, 253; pure, 437. See empiricism.

Experience and Nature, 402.

Experience and Prediction, 550.

"experient occasions," 450, 451.

experimentalism, 396-398, 528. See instrumentalism.

expressionism, 554.

Exodus, 208, 415.

extension, 444 ff., 450.

extensive abstraction, 546.

Ex Uno Plura, 131.

Ezekiel, 57, 60.

Fable of the Bees, the, 270.

Fackenheim, E. L., 171 ff., 183.

faith and reason, 153, 161, 172-174, 181, 185-187, 189, 191, 194, 199, 203-205, 229, 410.

falasifa, 161.

Farber, Marvin, 363, 421.

Farmer, H. H., 349.

fate, 48, 121, 124, 125, 154.

Fechner, G. T., 443, 446-449, 452.

Federalist Papers, 274, 275.

feeling, 450, 452; as category, 449.

Feibleman, James, 496.

Ferm, Vergilius, preface, 144 ff., 156, 429 ff., 598 ff., 607, 608.

Ferré, N.F.S., 349.

fetishism, 311.

Feuerbach, L., 299, 308, 336, 339, 584, 602, 603.

Fichte, J. G., 291-293, 299, 302, 304, 343, 348, 350, 375, 413, 438, 516, 580; on aesthetics, 296; on morality, 295, 296; on nature, 294; on religion, 297.

Ficino, Marsilio, 233.

fictionalism, 533. See "as if" philosophy.

fideism, 222.

fides quaerens intellectum, 191.

final causes, 583. See causality.

finalism, 132.

finiteness of God, see God.

First Chapters in Religious Philosophy, 607. 608.

First Principle, 177.

First Principles, 371.

Fisch, M. H., 401.

INDEX

Flewelling, R. T., 342, 344, 347, 350, 351.
Flint, R., 585.
Florence, 232, 233.
Flower, E. F., 574 ff.
force, 370.
foreknowledge, 249.
Forest, Aimé, 455, 456.
Forgotten Religions, 156.
form, 108, 132, 188, 201, 284, 348, 356, 443.
form and matter, 94, 99, 102, 104, 109, 110, 112, 125, 127, 177, 206-208, 235, 421, 422, 432.
Formal Logic, 509.
formalities, 215.
Formulaire, 512.
Fosdick, H. E., 349.
Foster, G. B., 604, 607.
Foundations of Mathematics, 514.
Fountain of Life, 177.
Four Noble Truths, 33 ff.
Fragen der Ethik, 499.
France, Anatole, 558.
Francis de Vitoria, 229.
Francis of Mayronne, 222.
Franciscan order, 222.
Frankel, Charles, 266 ff., 329 ff.
Franklin, Mrs. C. L., 511.
Fránquiz, A., 344, 350.
Frazer, J. G., 603.
Frederick, the Great, 274, 278.
freedom, 60, 121, 124, 137, 154, 160, 210, 236, 245, 247, 249, 250, 280, 288, 342, 346, 349, 351, 370, 379, 385, 410, 413, 442, 452, 454, 548, 549, 575, 579-581.
Freedom of Man, The, 551.
Freedom in the Modern World, 460.
Frege, G., 490, 510, 540.
Freiburg, 354.
French Constitution, 273, 274.
French Encyclopedists, 332.
French painters, 552.
French Revolution, 579.
French Society for Aesthetics, 557, 561.
Freud, S., 50, 106, 277, 333, 377, 560, 594.
Freudianism, **468, 604.**
Fribourg, 457.

Friess, H. L., 586, 588 ff., 607.
Frontiers of Poetry, 460.
Frye, R. M., 348.
"Function of General Laws in History," 586.
Function of Religion in Man's Struggle, etc., 607.
functionalism, 396, 398, 508, 517, 592, 594, 603, 604. See instrumentalism; pragmatism.
Fund. Math., 514.
futurism, 553, 560.

Gabirol, Solomon Ibn, 171, 177, 183.
Galileo, 223, 229, 238, 284.
Gallagher, D. A., 454 ff.
Gallienus, emperor, 136.
Galloway, G., 604, 607.
Gandhiji (Gandhi), 17.
Gangesa, 9.
Garnett, A. C., 342, 349.
Garrigon-Lagrange, R., 455.
Gassendi, Pierre, 232.
Gathās, the, 20 ff., 31.
Gauguin, 552.
Gaunilon, 192.
Gauss, C. E., 552.
Gautama, 9.
gāv, 31.
Gay, John, 270.
Geiger, Moritz, 353.
Geist, 575, 580.
Geisteswissenschaften, 581, 585.
Gemelli, Agostino, 457, 458.
Genealogy of Morals, 386.
General Theory of Value, 496.
general will, the, 275.
genetic fallacy, 480, 482.
genetic method, 396, 402.
Genetic Theory of Reality, A., 508.
geology, 366.
geometry, 542, 543.
Gerard of Cremona, 165.
German idealism, 141, 350, 516; classical German idealism, Chap. XXIII.
Gerson, Levi Ben, 181.
Gersonides, 181, 182.
Gesinnung, 565, 569.
Gestalt psychology, 264, 347.
Geulincx, 244.

621

INDEX

Gibbon, Edw., 273.
Gibbs, 584.
Gibson, B., 537.
Gilbert of La Porrée, 192.
Gilbert, Wm., 238.
Gilson, Étienne, 223, 340, 344, 350, 415, 455, 458-460, 462 ff., 466, 469.
Gītā, 6, 15.
Glorious Revolution, the 274.
gnosis, 146, 150, 151.
Gnosticism, 68, 146, 147, 151, 156; Christian, 144.
God, 3, 4, 6, 7, 10, 12, 15, 16, 20 ff., 57 ff., 60, 62, 64, 65, 73, 121, 138, 163, 168, 175, 176, 178, 179, 181, 182, 187-190, 192, 195, 202, 208-210, 217, 220-222, 242, 243, 246, 249, 250, 259, 308, 341, 342, 346, 348, 349, 365, 370, 434, 437, 443, 452, 575, 578, 603; as substance, 244 ff.; existence, 456; finiteness of, 349; for Plato, 102 ff. See Absolute, the; cosmological argument for; Divine, the; ontological argument for; ontological-cosmological argument for; pantheism; pan-entheism; teleological argument for; theism.
Godwin, 577.
Goedel (Gödel), K., 487-489, 514.
Goethe, 27, 299, 340, 370.
Golden Bough, 603.
good, the, 50, 427, 499, 500, 566, 569; and desire, see desire and good; the Platonic idea of, 100 ff., 132.
good and evil, 26 ff., 155, 245, 247, 577. See evil.
Gordianus, emperor, 135.
Gorgias, the, 132, 133.
Gospel of John, See John, Gospel of.
Gotama, see Buddha.
Gotshalk, D. W., 558.
Göttingen, 353, 354.
Gouhier, Henri, 463.
Grabmann, Martin, 455.
grace, 58, 154, 155, 210, 236, 454.
Graebner, F., 593.
Great Instauration, The, 389, 399.
Greatness and Decadence of the Romans, 273.
Greek culture, 588, 589.
Greek philosophy, the beginnings of, Chap. VI; early Greek moralists, Chap. VII; Hellenistic schools of philosophy, Chap. X.
Green, T. H., 343, 348, 350, 581.
Greene, T. M., 496.
Greene, W. G., 82.
Gregory IX, pope, 198.
Grenzsituation, 411.
Grote, John, 340.
Grotius, Hugo, 236, 578.
Ground of Induction, 551.
Grundlagen, 512.
Guide for the Perplexed, 179.
Guillaume d'Auvergne, 168.
guilt, 379.
Gundisalvus of Seville, 168.
Guttmann, J., 183.

habit, James on, 398.
Hades, 73.
Hadfield, J. A., 604.
Haeberlin, 443, 446.
haecceity, 214, 215.
Haeckel, Ernst, 300, 367, 370-373, 435.
Haggadah, the, 67, 68.
Haines, George, 585.
Halachah, the, 67, 68.
Haldane and Ross, editors, 399.
Hall, G. S., 604.
Hallevi, see Jehudah Hallevi.
Hamilton, Alexander, 274.
Hamilton, C. H., 33 ff.
Hamilton, W., 371.
Hammond, W. A., 402.
Han, 55.
Han Fei Tzŭ, 55.
happiness, 119, 120, 210, 270, 301. See pleasure.
Hardie, W. A., 105.
Harkness, G., 349.
harmony, 167.
Harrington, 274.
Harris, W. T., 318, 319.
Hartley, D., 270.
Hartmann, von, Ed., 302, 591, 601.
Hartmann, Nicolai, 376.
Hartshorne, Charles, 342, 344, 347, 349, 398, 442 ff.
Harvey, W., 237, 400.
Haurvatāt, 25, 26.
He Who Is, 208.
Healing, 165.

622

INDEX

hedonism, 494, 499, 566.
Hegel, G.W.F., 141, 264, 291-293, 302, 304, 306-308, 310, 311, 318-320, 340, 342-344, 348-350, 406, 409, 413, 438, 506, 507, 516, 531, 579-582, 584, 590, 600, 601, 607; Hegelian dialectic, 141, 298, 308, 310, 319, 406, 580, 590; on aesthetics, 296; on history, 298, 302; on morality, 296; on nature, 294; on religion, 297, 307.
Hegelianism, 307, 309, 319, 335, 388, 413, 472, 473, 495, 496, 566; and four lines of development, 299; right and left wings, 299 ff.; left wing, 308; re-Hegelianization, 313. See Neo-Hegelianism.
Hegelians, the young, 308, 309.
Heidegger, M., 354, 363, 412, 413, 415.
Heidelberg school, 303.
Heisenberg, W., 548.
Heisenberg principle, 103.
heliocentric theory, 237.
Hellenism, culture, 588; Hellenistic schools of philosophy, Chap. X. See Judaism, Hellenistic.
Helmholtz, von, H. F. L., 473.
Helsel, P. R., 82 ff., 344.
Helvetius, C., 270, 278, 577.
Hempel, C. G., 586.
Heptad, 22.
Heraclitus, 70 ff., 72 ff., 74, 83, 84, 87, 93, 99, 110, 116, 124, 132, 133, 145, 306, 308, 341.
Herder, von, J. G., 273, 575, 579, 580.
Hermeneutics, 161.
Hermes Trismegistus, 129, 234.
Hesed, 58.
Hesiod, 82, 85.
Hexapla, the, 151.
Hilbert, 473, 512-514.
Hildebrand, C. D. W., 344.
Hīnayāna, 9, 34, 37, 38, 41, 42; school of, 8.
Hindu Mysticism, 608.
Hinduism, 3 ff., 9 ff., 42, 155, 432, 434, 438, 443, 603, 605.
Hippocrates, 85.
Hippolytus, 148.
Hirn, 554.
historical criticism, 230.

historicism, 412.
historiography, 272.
history, humanistic theory of, 236; philosophies of, see philosophies of history; Renaissance-humanist conceptions of, 231; of philosophy, 350.
History as the Story of Liberty, 586.
History of Historical Writing, A, 586.
Hitler, 377.
Hobbes, Thomas, 47, 237, 246 ff., 269-271, 435, 494, 505, 575.
Hocking, W. E., 343, 346, 347, 349, 350, 604.
Höffding, H., 602.
Holbach, baron von, 277, 435.
Holcroft, T., 278.
holism, 419.
Holmes, O. W., Jr., 401, 402.
Holt, E. B., 437, 519, 521.
Holy Immortals, 21 ff., 25, 26.
homo faber, 592.
homo-ousios, 151, 156.
homonensura, principle, 398.
Homer, 82, 118.
Homeric religion, 73, 74.
Hook, S., 313, 420, 428.
Horne, H. H., 351.
Hosea, 58.
Hospers, John, 561.
House of Wisdom, 161.
"How to Make Our Ideas Clear," 387, 528.
Howison, G. H., 340, 343.
Hsüan Tsang, 41.
Hsün Tzŭ, 53-55.
Hubaysh, 161.
Hudson, C. E., 604.
Hulē, 139.
Human Knowledge, its Scope and Limits, 551.
humanism, 267, 278, 308, 343, 370, 388, 427, 428, 461, 465, 517, 593; classical, 229 ff.; in the Renaissance, 229 ff., 234, 237. See religious humanism.
Hume, D., 96, 250, 253, 254, 257, 262-264, 273, 276, 283, 286, 291, 331, 345, 418, 423, 424, 428, 472-475, 480, 494, 499, 516, 517, 531, 550, 600, 601, 607; and utilitarianism, 271.
Hunayn ibn-Ishaq, 161.

623

INDEX

Husserl, E., 353ff., 363, 412, 474, 531.
Hutcheson, Francis, 271.
Huxley, T. H., 400.
Huygens, 247.
hylomorphism, 109. See form and matter.
hylozoism, 73, 77, 431.

I Am That I Am, 415, 465.
I-thou, 414, 415.
Ibn Gabirol, Solomon, see Gabirol, Solomon.
ibn-Rushd, 161.
ibn-Sina, 161, 183.
Ibn Zaddiq, Joseph, 177.
id quod est, 188.
Idea of History, The, 586.
idealism, 11, 12, 221, 300, 309, 336, 343, 350, 375, 418, 420, 434, 436, 442, 460, 472, 474, 479, 489, 495 ff., 516, 518, 531 ff., 570, 571, 575, 584, 585; idealism, absolute, see absolute idealism; idealism, Berkeleianism, see Berkeley, Berkeleianism; German, see German idealism; Classical German, see absolute idealism; English and American, see absolute idealism; subjective, 8, 533, 535, see subjectivism; idealism, speculative, see speculative idealism; definition and varieties, 315, 316; idealism, transcendental, 292; idealism, epistemological, see epistemological idealism. See Buddhism; Hegelianism; Hinduism; Neo-Hegelianism; naturalism, idealistic; panpsychism; personalism; Platonism; transcendental phenomenology.
Idealist Argument in Recent British and American Philosophy, The, 317.
ideas, innate, 244, 255, 262, 264.
ideas, Platonic, 94 ff., 108, 128, 132, 133, 188, 205, 413, 526.
ideas, Plotinus', 137 ff.
Ideas pertaining to a Pure Phenomenology, etc., 353.
Ideen zu einer reinen Phänomenologie, etc., 353, 537.
identity, 346; identity theory, 420.
idols of the cave, etc., 89, 507, 576.
Ignatius, 144.

ignorance, 8, 16, 90, 274, 347; learned, 234.
illumination, 181, 200, 201, 204.
Imitation of Christ, 236.
immortality, 25-27, 66, 74, 104, 105, 148, 163, 168, 169, 174, 175, 180-182, 187, 203, 229, 233, 247, 297, 342, 351, 370, 440.
impersonalism, 345.
Implication and Linear Inference, 322-324.
incarnation, 210, 433.
Incoherence of Incoherence, 166.
Incoherence of the Philosophers, 166.
indeterminacy, principle of, 373.
indeterminism, see freedom.
Indian philosophy, Chap. I; 301, 432, 438. See Hinduism.
Indra, 3.
induction, 235, 253, 261, 336, 390, 394, 430, 439, 472, 474, 540, 542, 550, 583.
inductive logic, 235, 348, 507.
infinite, infinity, 80, 132, 182, 235, 545.
infinite regress, 126.
infinitesimal calculus, 247.
Influence of Darwin on Philosophy, The, 402.
Inge, W. R., 605, 608.
inner voice, 91.
Inquiry into Meaning and Truth, 524.
instinct, 383, 384.
Institute of Mediaeval Studies, 466.
instrumentalism, 375-377, 383, 384, 388, 392, 395, 481, 486, 517, 518, 528 ff., 567.
instrumentalist logic, 508.
intellectualism, 397; pure, 389.
intelligence, 383 ff., 388.
intentio, 166.
intentionality, intentionalism, 357 ff., 360 ff., 531.
interaction, 347, 448, 449.
interest, 496 ff., 498.
internality of relations, see relations, internal.
International Phenomenological Society, 363.
Introduction to Logic, 506.
Introduction to Metaphysics, 381; 384.
Introduction to Philosophy, 459.

624

INDEX

Introduction to Semantics, 492.
Introduction to the Categories of Aristotle, 188.
intuition, intuitionism, 11, 100, 125, 220, 221, 244, 250, 282, 321, 381, 384, 385, 412, 426, 445, 500, 513, 526, 556, 568-570, 572. See illumination; mysticism.
Ionians, 93, 99, 432; Ionia, school of, 70 ff; philosophy, 421, 431.
Irenaeus, 145, 146.
irrationalism, 312, 313, 411, 605.
Isaiah, 57, 58, 67, 186.
Ishaq, 161.
Islam, 30, 171, 174, 177, 179, 180, 183, 202; Islamic philosophy, Chap. XIII.
Israeli, Isaac, 171, 176.

Jacobites, the, 160.
Jaeger, W., 82.
Jahrbuch für Philosophie, etc., 353, 354.
Jainism, 6 ff., 8, 33.
Jain logic, 7.
Jakeh, 159.
James, William, 264, 317, 341, 387-389, 392-395, 397, 398, 400-403, 437, 469, 473, 480, 528, 532, 537, 602. See pragmatism.
Jansenism, 236, 268.
Jaspers, Karl, 410-412.
Jastrow, M., 603.
Jay, John, 274.
Jehudah Hallevi, 173, 178.
Jeremiah, 57, 59, 60.
Jerusalem, 147.
Jesuit order, 228; Jesuits, 268.
Jesus, 22, 89, 90, 154.
Jevons, W. S., 510.
Jewish people, 159, 168; Jewish philosophy, 171 ff.; ancient Jewish philosophy, 57 ff.; mediaeval Jewish philosophy, Chap. XIV; three periods of mediaeval Jewish philosophy, 173 ff. See Judaism.
Jin, 6.
Jīva, 7, 11, 15.
Jñāna-mārga, 4.
Joannitius, 161.
Job, book of, 61-63.
Jodl, F., 339.

John of the Cross, 460.
John, Gospel of, 145, 156.
John of Jandum, 203.
John of St. Thomas, 169, 455.
Johns Hopkins Studies in Logic, 511.
Johnson, P. E., 344, 347.
Jones, Rufus, 605.
Joseph, H. W. B., 506.
Joseph Ibn Zaddiq, 177.
Josephus, 66, 67.
Journal of Aesthetics and Art Criticism, 557.
Journal of the History of Ideas, 585.
Journal Métaphysique, 414.
Journal of Philosophy, 586.
Journal of Speculative Philosophy, The, 318.
Journet, Abbé, 460, 461.
Judaism, 145, 147, 155, 160, 433; Hellenistic, 65 ff.; Rabbinic, 67 ff.
Jundishapur, 159, 160.
Jurji, E. J., 158 ff.
jus gentium, 577.
jus naturale, 577.
justice, 58, 61.
Justin Martyr, 145, 148.
Justinian, emperor, 141.
jyāna, 13.

Kāla, 7.
kalam, 161, 173 ff., 177, 183.
Kallen, 558.
kalon, 141.
Kames, Lord Henry, 276.
Kant, I., 100, 229, 250, 253, 262, 264, 273, 274, 291-293, 295, 301-303, 313, 314, 331, 340, 342-344, 346, 348-350, 369, 371, 395, 401, 405, 423, 434, 506, 507, 516, 527, 531, 554, 555, 565, 569, 575, 577-579, 581, 590, 600, 601, 607; Kant's critical philosophy, Chap. XXII; and morality, 295; and the use of *pragmatisch*, 394, 395.
Kantianism, 336, 342, 388, 394, 418, 458, 473; Kantian existentialism, 410-412. See Neo-Kantianism.
Kapila, 11.
karma, 5-7, 9, 10, 13, 15, 38; laws of, 27, 28.
karma-mārga, 4.
Karma-Yoga, 6.

625

INDEX

katharsis, 140.
Kepler, Johannes, 238, 280, 578.
Kerstetter, W. E., 344.
Kevala Jyāna, 7.
Keynes, J. N., 505, 506.
Khyāti, 13.
Kierkegaard, S., 406, 407, 409-414, 590.
King, I., 603.
kleśas, 36.
knowledge, 7, 8, 10-16, 80, 95 ff., 97, 100, 108, 112, 113, 125, 126, 187, 190, 201, 205, 206, 208, 212, 220, 221, 229, 241, 244, 253, 255, 262, 282 ff., 292, 345, 376, 377, 390, 391, 394, 398-400, 421, 467, 479. See epistemology; illumination; revelation; truth.
Knudson, A. C., 341, 342, 344-346, 349, 350.
Koninck, de, C., 455.
Koran, the, 159-161, 165, 173, 174.
Korn, A., 348, 350, 375, 376, 385.
Krause, 580.
krishna, 6.
Kristeller, P. O., 227 ff.
kṣaṇa-bhangvāda, 8.
kṣaṇika, 37.
kshathra, 24-26.
Kuhn, H., 405 ff.
Kullmann, E., 131 ff.
kulturgeschichte, 580.
Kulturkreise, 593.
Kumārila, 13.
Kumārila Bhatt, 12.

Ladd, G. T., 344, 348, 602.
Laird, John, 523, 524.
Lalo, 561.
Lamarck, 366.
Lambert, J. H., 509.
Lamprecht, 580, 584.
Lang, A., 603.
language, 482, 483, 505, 508, 509; ideal language, 475-481, 486, 490, 492. See semantics.
Language, Truth and Logic, 499.
Lankāvatāra, 39.
Lao Tzŭ, 51.
La Persona Humana, etc., 385.
La philosophie au moyen age, 463.

La philosophie de la nature, 460.
Laplace, 369, 547, 548.
Larger Logic, 319.
La structure metaphysique du concret selon S. Thomas, 455, 456.
Latin America, 344 ff., 458; philosophy, 350, 375, 385, 456, 568.
Latin Averroism, see Averroism, Latin.
Latin culture, 589.
Lavely, J. H., 350.
law, 401; Jewish, 67, 172, 173, 174, 176, 178, 179, 182; Jewish and the prophets, 57 ff.
law of parsimony, 439. See Ockham's razor.
law of substance, 370.
law of three stages, 273, 332, 334, 435, 583, 591.
Laws, the, 102, 103, 128, 134, 422.
Laws of Thought, 509.
learning, Bacon on, 398, 399.
Lebensphilosophie, 407.
Lee, Vernon, 555.
Legalists, the, 54 ff.
Leibniz, G. W., 229, 247 ff., 291, 340, 342, 344, 346, 350, 444, 445, 448-450, 508, 509, 512, 516, 531, 576. See monads.
Lemuel, 159.
Leo XIII, pope, 454, 455, 457.
Leonardo da Vinci, 237.
Lepley, Ray, 502.
Lessing, G. E., 273.
L'Esthétique, 553.
L'Etre et le Neant, 412, 413.
Leuba, J., 604.
Leucippus, 262.
levels of mind, 449; in nature, 420, 425, 436, 439, 440, 442 ff. See emergence.
Leviathan, 505.
Levy-Bruhl, L., 335, 339, 463, 592.
Lewis, C. I., 264, 325, 501, 513, 514, 531-535.
lex naturae, 577.
Li Ssŭ, 55.
Libertad Creadora, 385.
libertinism, 270.
Lier paradox, 489.
ling-śarīra, 11.
Lipps, 555.

INDEX

Lipsius, Justus, 232.
live option, 602.
Lobachewski, 517, 540.
Locke, John, 253, 254, 257, 262-264, 268-270, 274, 276, 291, 394, 422, 423, 474, 481, 484, 505, 516, 517, 520, 525-527, 577, 607.
Loemker, L. E., 350.
logic, 41 ff., 94, 140, 193, 194, 218, 222, 227-229, 231, 249, 348, 391, 399, 418, 426, 472, 487, 517, 518, 585; recent schools of, Chap. XL; pure, 356. See Aristotelian logic; inductive logic; instrumentalist logic; Jain logic; mathematical logic; metaphysical logic; pragmatism; symbolic logic.
Logic (Bosanquet), 325, 507; (Maritain), 459; (Mill), 334; (Wundt), 508.
Lógica Orgánica, 385.
logical atomism, 437, 474.
logical constructionism, 478.
logical empiricism, 338.
logical entities, 115, 319, 520.
Logical Investigations, 353.
logical positivism, 338, 483, 490, 498-501, 540, 564 ff., 572; Chap. XXXVII.
logical structuralism, 478, 479.
logical syntax, 486-489, 491, 492.
Logical Syntax of Language, 514.
Logic of Modern Physics, The, 401, 549.
logic of relations, see mathematical logic.
Logic or the Morphology of Knowledge, 321.
Logic: the Theory of Inquiry, 402.
Logische Untersuchungen, 353.
logistic, 104, 514.
logoi, 432.
logon, 92.
logos, 66, 73, 93, 123, 124, 132, 133, 137, 145, 146, 149-151, 433.
Lokāyata, 6.
Lombard, Peter, see Peter Lombard.
Long, W., 344.
Lotze, H., 303, 304. 340, 343, 344, 346-349, 449, 602.
Louis de La Vallée Poussin, 35, 39.

Louvain, 457, 458.
love, 23, 24, 28, 46, 376, 385, 467; love and hate, principles of, 77. See Plato, Platonic love.
Lovejoy, A. O., 401, 420, 525-527, 535, 536.
Loyola, Ignatius, 336.
Loyola university, 466.
Lubac, de, H., 455.
Lucena, 167.
Lucian Martyr, 148.
Lucretius, 120, 232, 235, 262, 270, 419.
Lukacs, Georg, 313.
Luke, 147.
Luminar, 344.
Luqman, 159.
Luther, M., 236.
Lyell, 366.
Lyman, E. W., 605, 608.

Mably, Abbé, 273.
Mach, Ernst, 336, 339, 437, 474, 475.
Machiavelli, N., 236, 237.
Macintosh, D. C., 342, 349, 527, 605.
Mackay, D. S., 387 ff.
Macrobius, 186.
Mādhva, 13.
madhyama, 38.
Mādhyamika Śāstra, 38.
Mādhyamikas, 34, 37, 41; school of, 8.
Madison, James, 274.
magic, 60, 432.
Magna Moralis, 161.
Mahābhārata, 5.
mahat, 11.
Mahavīra, 7.
Mahāyāna, 9, 34, 37, 39, 42; school of the, 8.
Māhayāna-sūtrāla-mkāra, 39.
Maimon, Solomon, 182.
Maimonides, 168, 171, 179-183.
Maine de Biran, 343.
Majjhima Nikāya, 42.
Malebranche, N., 244, 247.
Malinowski, B., 594.
Mallarmé, 553.
Malraux, 559.
Malthus, 582.
manahprayāya, 7.

627

manas, 10, 11, 16, 41.
Mandeville, Bernard de, 270, 271.
Manet, 552.
Mani, 155.
Manichaeism, 155, 156.
mano-vyñāna, 41.
Mansel, H. L., 371.
Manser, G., 455.
mantras, 3.
Marburg, 354; school, 303.
Marcel, Gabriel, 223, 414, 415, 455.
March to Liberation, 466.
Marcion, 147; Marcionism, 147.
Marck, S., 306 ff.
Marcus Aurelius, 122, 123.
mārga, 8, 16.
Maritain, J., 340, 344, 349, 350, 415, 455, 459-463, 465-467, 469.
Maritain, Raïssa, 459.
Mark, 145.
Marlatt, E. B., 347, 351.
Marquette university, 466.
Marrakesh, 166.
Marsilius of Padua, 203.
Martin, B. N., 344.
Marvin, W. T., 519.
Marx, K., 277, 278, 299, 309-314, 333, 336, 575, 584, 590, 591; Marxism, 308, 310, 312, 313, 420, 560; orthodox, 312, 313; revisionist, 314; schools of, 312 ff.
Mashal, the, 61.
materialism, 78, 80, 99, 121, 124, 232, 246 ff., 254, 262, 277, 303, 315, 335, 336, 342, 346, 347, 378, 429, 431, 435-437, 444, 445, 450, 473, 584; ancient, 120; new materialism, 436, Chap. XXXIII; the term, 309. See naturalism, materialistic.
materialism, dialectic, Chap. XXIV.
Materialismusstreit, 473.
mathematical logic, 114, 115, 387, 472, 479, 484, 517, 540, 550. See symbolic logic.
mathematics, 74, 114, 115, 128, 237, 238, 240, 241, 243, 247, 259, 260, 282, 283, 333, 356, 384, 385, 390, 421, 435, 450, 487, 489, 508-514, 517, 518, 542, 543, 545, 553, 582.
Mathews, S., 604, 607.
Mati, 7.
matriarchy, 591.

matter, 7, 108, 139, 163, 181, 187, 243, 258, 259, 368-370, 372, 373, 383, 418, 420, 423, 424, 443, 544, 545.
matter and form, see form and matter.
matter and mind, see mind and matter. See mind and body.
Matter and Memory, 381, 382.
Matthew of Aquasparta, 200, 201.
Maurer, A., 197 ff.; 212 ff.
Maximus Confessor, 189.
Māyā, the, 14.
Mazdā, 23, 27, 28.
Mazdā-Ahurās, 22.
McConnell, F. J., 344, 349, 350.
McCormick, Fr., 466.
McGill, V. J., 421.
McTaggart, J. M. E., 316, 341-343, 349.
Mead, G. H., 337.
meaning, external and internal, 324.
Meaning of God in Human Evperience, 604.
Meaning of Meaning, The, 500.
Meaning and Necessity, 492.
Meaning and Truth in the Arts, 561.
Mecca, 158.
mechanics, 547, 582.
mechanism, 78, 243, 347, 348, 385, 418, 419, 422, 577, 583.
mediaeval philosophy, 141. See under special chapter headings.
Mediaeval Studies, 466.
mediator, 133, 134.
Medina, 158.
Meditations, 246.
Meinong, A., 474, 475, 493-498, 518.
Meister Eckhart, 169.
Melanchthon, Philip, 229.
Melekh, 135.
Melito, 145.
memory, 382.
Mencius, 49-51, 54.
Mendelssohn, Moses, 182.
Meno, 113.
mentalism, 322, 390. See epistemological idealism.
Mercier, cardinal, 455, 458.
Merton, 469.
metalanguage, 487.
metaphysics, 107, 108, 111, 114, 165, 213, 227, 346 ff., 472, 473.

628

INDEX

Metaphysics, 111, 112, 133, 193.
"Metaphysical Club," 402.
metaphysical logic, 506, 507.
Method for Easily Understanding History, 578.
Mettrie, La, 435.
Michael Scotus, 167.
Micklem, E. R., 604.
Middle Ages, 185 ff., 188, 197 ff., 222, 230, 232, 262, 434, 576, 577, 589.
Midrashim, 67.
Milan, 457.
Milesians, 70 ff., 93.
Mill, James, 270, 477, 480.
Mill, J. S., 264, 334, 336, 339, 394, 399, 424, 494, 499, 507, 508, 517, 531, 537, 540, 591, 592.
Mīmāmsā, 12, 13.
mind, 425, 426, 437.
mind and body, 244, 340, 347, 358, 407, 420. See soul and body.
mind and matter, 243, 244, 382, 383, 422, 446.
"Mind of Saint Augustine," The, 466.
Mind and the World-Order, 532, 537.
Minucius Felix, 145.
miracles, 155, 179, 180, 203, 229, 409, 577.
Mo Tzŭ, 45 ff.
Modern Schoolman, 466.
modes, 244 ff., 247.
Mohammed, 29 ff., 158.
Mohammedanism, see Islam.
Moism, 45 ff., 51, 52, 55.
mokasa, 16.
mokṣa, 5, 6, 10, 13.
Molinism, 236.
monads, 247 ff., 340, 342, 346, 444, 446, 447.
monogamy, 591.
Monatsh. Math. Phys., 514.
Mone, 141.
monism, 4, 9, 15, 17, 75, 76, 79, 80, 93, 128, 131 ff., 133 ff., 136, 137, 139, 141, 162, 246, 307, 308, 314, 346, 347, 381, 382, 420, 434, 439, 442, 443, 473; monism of Haeckel, 370. See epistemological monism; unity.
Monologium, 195.
monos, 133.

monotheism, 4, 21, 128, 176; ethical, 58, 60.
Montague, W. P., 436, 437, 519.
Montaigne, Michel de, 230, 232, 270.
Montesquieu, baron de, 272-275, 575, 579, 580, 590.
Moore, G. E., 428, 472, 473, 475, 481, 482, 499-501, 518, 519, 523, 535.
Moore, J. S., 344, 347, 349.
Mora, J. F., 344.
moral sense, 271.
moral sentiments, 271; morals, see ethics.
moralists, early Greek, Chap. VII.
morality, Stoic, 122 ff.
More, Sir Thomas, 231.
Morgan, D. N., 253 ff.
Morgan, L. H., 591.
Morris, Bertram, 496.
Morris, C. W., 491.
Morris, Wm., 559.
Moses, 60, 66, 149, 181, 208.
motion, 77-80, 93, 96, 98, 101, 102, 127, 132, 137, 138, 243, 244, 246, 346, 368, 373, 382, 443, 544, 545.
Mounier, E., 340, 344, 350.
Muelder, W. G., 344, 349, 350.
Muirhead, J. H., 319.
mukta, 7.
Müller, Max, 603.
Mumford, Lewis, 82, 559.
Munich, 353.
Munk, A. W., 349, 350.
Munro, Thomas, 557.
Münsterberg, H., 438.
Murphy, A. E., 536.
Mutakallimun, 161, 163, 168.
mutations, 383.
Mutazilite, 161.
Mutterrecht, Das, 591.
mystery cults, 62, 74.
mysticism, 36, 40, 91, 134, 162, 176, 194, 222, 236, 293, 381, 434, 605. See intuition.
Mysticism, 608.

Nāgārjuna, 38-40.
Nagel, E., 428.
Nahm, M. C., 558, 559.
nairātmya, 39.
"Naive vs. Presentative Realism," 537.

629

INDEX

Nālandā, 41.
nāma, 8.
nāma-rūpa, 8.
Nārāyan, 15; Nārāyana, 15.
Natorp, P., 94.
natura naturans and natura naturata, 434.
natura tantum, 214.
natural knowledge, 200.
natural law, 274.
natural religion, 276 ff.
natural rights, 268-272, 277, 278, 577, 583.
natural selection, 366, 367, 395. See Darwinism.
Natural History of Religion, 607.
naturalism, 346, 365, 373, 396, 427, 428, 493, 494, 496, 497, 553, 570, 571, 575, 582, 583, 585; ancient, 72, 121; animistic, 436, 437; dynamistic, 437; idealistic or spiritualistic, 434, 438-440; inverted, 432, 438; materialistic, 294, 295, 299, 300, 309, 419, 420, 429, 431, 432, 435, 436, 438; neutralistic, 434, 437, 438; non theistic, 419; positivistic, 337, 419, 431, 435, 436, 438; scientific, 319, 433; theocentric, 605; varieties of naturalism, Chap. XXXIV.
"Naturalism and the Nature of Things," 428.
naturalistic fallacy, 428, 500, 501.
nature, 346, 357, 358, 367, 422, 425, 426, 430, 431, 447, 448, 451; and God, 464.
Nature and Functions of Authority, 466, 467.
Nature of the Physical World, 551.
Nature of Thought, The, 535, 536.
naughting naught, 413.
Naville, Pierre, 313.
Near East, 160, 161.
nebular hypothesis, 369.
necessity, 103, 221.
necessitarianism, see determinism.
negation, 27.
negative evil, 155.
negative infinity, 139.
Negley, Glenn, 563 ff.
Neo-Classicism, 454.
Neo-Confucianism, 56.

Neo-Hegelianism, 315 ff., 317, 319, 346.
Neo-Kantianism, 302 ff., 434; Chap. XXIII.
neo-orthodoxy, 411, 605.
Neoplatonism, 119, 124, 131 ff., 150, 152, 155, 156, 166, 172, 173, 175 ff., 179, 187-190, 197, 199, 204, 230, 232, 233, 235, 434; Neoplatonists, Christian, 434; early Neoplatonism, 133 ff.
Neopythagoreanism, 127, 128, 133.
Neo-Realism, 345, 420, 425, 428, 517, 520, 521, 525, 527, 529, 531, 535, 589. See American New Realism; English New Realism.
Neo-Scholasticism, 454, 458; Hispanic, 228.
Neo-Thomism, 340, 344, 349, 350, 415; contemporary Thomism, Chap. XXXVI.
nescience, principle of, 14.
Nestorians, 160, 161.
Neti, Neti, 5.
Nettleship, R. L., 95.
Neurath, Otto, 481.
neutral entities, 521; neutral sense data, 534. See essences.
neutralism, 434, 437, 473, 521, 522. See naturalism, neutralistic.
new materialism, see materialism, new.
new realism, see Neo-Realism.
New Realism, The, 519, 521, 536.
new scholasticism, see Neo-Scholasticism.
New Scholasticism, 466.
New Testament, 149, 150, 156.
New Thought, school of, 438.
Newhall, J. E., 344.
Newton, I., 77, 163, 247, 267, 280, 282, 342, 541, 546, 576, 578, 582.
Nicea, council of, 152, 156.
Nicene Fathers, 144.
Niceno-Constantinopolitan creed, 152.
Niebuhr, B., 582.
Niebuhr, R., 411.
Nietzsche, F., 302, 375 ff., 385, 407, 554, 593.
Nigidius Figulus, 127.
nihilism, 8, 375, 380; historical, 574.
Nirguṇa, 15.

630

INDEX

nirvāṇa, 8, 33, 36, 38, 591.
Nisibin, 159, 160.
niṣkāma-karma, 6.
Noel, Léon, 455, 458.
nominalism, 192, 218, 222, 223, 390, 391, 399, 400, 424, 505.
nomos, 91.
non-contradiction, principle of, 377.
non-existence, 9, 12, 13, 16, 75, 76, 100, 139, 362.
normative sciences, 348.
Norris, L. W., 344.
Northrop, F. S. C., 456, 595.
nothing, 412, 413.
Notre Dame university, 466.
noumenal, 346, 579. See Kant.
Nous, 78, 100, 133, 137, 138.
novelty, see creativity; emergence.
Novum Organum, 235, 399, 507, 541.
numbers, 74, 80, 101, 103, 128.
Numenius, 134.
Nussbaum, A., 586.
Nyāya, 9.
Nyāya Sūtras, 9.
Nyāya-Vaiśesika, 10, 12.

objective idealism, 570-572; see idealism, absolute.
objective relativism, 518, 524, 525.
Observations on Man. 270.
Observations on the History of France, 273.
Ockham, Wm. of, 216 ff.; Ockhamism, 228, and Scotism, Chap. XVII; Ockham's razor, 217.
Ogden, 500.
Old Testament, 57 ff., 147, 151, 159.
Olgiati, F., 455.
Oman, J., 607.
omnipotence, 221, 222.
On Incantations, 229.
On the Division of Nature, 189.
On the Immortality of the Soul, 229.
On the Progress of the Human Mind, 585.
On the Soul, 168.
one world, 595, 606.
ontological argument for God, 191 ff., 195, 250.
ontological-cosmological argument for God, 241 ff.
Ontologie du connaître, 466.

ontology, 100, 356, 357, 406, 409, 420, 422, 424-426, 460. See being.
operational analysis, 473.
operationalism, 481, 518, 530, 549, 550; operational theory of meaning, 401.
optimism, 123, 124.
Oration, 233.
Oresme, Nicholas, 223.
organistic conceptions, 495 ff.
organon, the, 114; *Organon* of Aristotle, 186, 188, 193.
Origen, 146, 148, 150 ff., 156, 186.
Origin of the Family, etc., 591.
original sin, 154, 155, 213.
Orpheus, 233.
Orphic cults, 127; Orphism, 432.
orthogenesis, 348.
Otto, R., 603.
Our Knowledge of the External World, 521, 536.

Pace, Edw., 457.
Padua, university of, 229.
Paedagogus, the, 149.
Pahlavi, 30, 31.
pain, 119, 121, 379. See pleasure; suffering.
Paley, William, 270.
Panaetius of Rhodes, 122.
pan-entheism, 440.
panpsychism, 315, 342-344, 346, 420; Chap. XXXV.
Pantaenus, 148.
pantheism, 73, 162, 190, 194, 293, 297, 299, 304, 307, 342, 370, 375, 439, 452.
Paracelsus, Theophrastus, 234.
paradeigmata, 138.
paradox, 270; 18th century, 268; paradoxes of Zeno, 79 ff.
parergon theorias, 141.
Parmenides, 73 ff., 76-79, 83, 93, 99, 100, 103, 110, 116, 132, 137, 139, 345, 377, 574.
Parmenides, the, 104, 132, 307.
Parnassian poets, 553.
particulars, 8. See universals.
Partisan Review, 575.
Pātaṇjali, 11.
pathos of existence, 407, 590, 605. See existentialism.

631

INDEX

Patrizzi, Francesco, 235.
Paul, 144, 146, 147.
Peano, G., 512, 513, 540.
Pearson, Karl, 336.
Pegis, A., 455, 463, 466, 467.
Peirce, Benjamin, 387.
Peirce, C. S., 264, 344, 387-390, 392-394, 396-402, 445, 449, 451, 511, 512, 528, 532.
Pelagianism, 155.
Pelagius, 155.
Pentateuch, 59, 65.
Pepper, S. C., 493 ff.
Perception, 534, 537.
perception, pure, 382.
"Perception and Knowledge," 524.
perfectibility, 273, 575, 577.
perfection, 7, 9, 16, 25-27, 210.
Péri, Noël, 39.
Pericles, age of, 84 ff., 104.
peripateticism, 127, 129, 145, 163, 188.
permanence, 72, 73, 80.
Perry, R. B., 345, 437, 496-498, 519, 520.
Perry-Prall theory, 497.
Persian Letters, 273.
person, 341. See self.
Person and the Common Good, 460.
personal idealism, Chap. XXVII; 303, 343, 602.
Personal Idealism, 343.
personalism, 315, 460, 461, 605; Chap. XXVII.
Personalism, 340.
"Personality, Human and Divine," 343.
pessimism, 63, 122, 124, 301, 302, 379.
Peter Lombard, 218, 228.
Peter of Spain, 218.
Petrarca, Francesco, 230.
Pfänder, Alexander, 353.
Pfleiderer, Otto, 601.
Phaedo, 101, 104, 133.
Pharisaism, 147; Pharisees, 67.
Phelan, G. B., 458, 462.
phenomenalism, 302, 342, 418, 422, 424, 425, 428, 434, 472-474, 476, 478, 481, 529, 531 ff.; see Kant.
phenomenology, 518; Chap. XXVIII;

632

phenomenological existentialism, 410, 412 ff.
Phenomenology of Mind, 319, 531.
Philebus, 94, 100, 101, 139.
Philo, 66, 128, 133 ff., 138, 149, 150.
philology, 230, 491. See language.
philosophes, the, 329, 590.
Philosophical and Political History of the Indies, The, 273.
"Philosophical Conceptions and Practical Results," 388.
Philosophical Discussions, 402.
Philosophical Essay on Probabilities, 551.
Philosophical Fragments, 406.
Philosophical Studies, 536.
Phil. Union of the Univ. of Calif., 528.
Philosophie der Symbolischen Formen, 592.
philosophies of culture, Chap. XLVI.
Philosophy for the Future, 421, 428.
philosophy of education, 351.
Philosophy of George Santayana, The, 428.
Philosophy of G. Vico, 586.
philosophy of history, 58 ff., 153, 154, 272-274, 298, 309-312, 334, 350, 351, 378, 461, 462; philosophies of history, Chap. XLV.
Philosophy of History in France and Germany, 585.
Philosophy and Phenomenological Research, 363, 428.
Philosophy of Personalism, The, 341, 350.
Philosophy of Physical Realism, 428.
philosophy and religion, 178, 203.
philosophy of religion, 349; philosophies of religion, Chap. XLVII.
Philosophy of Religion, The, 604, 607.
Philosophy of Religion, A, 608.
Philosophy of Right, 296.
philosophy of the sciences, 347 ff., 387, 472; Chap. XLII.
Philosophy of Science, 551, 586.
Physical Principles of the Quantum Theory, 551.
physical realism, 419, 442.
physicalism, 473.
"Physics and the Problem of Historico-sociological Laws," 586.

INDEX

Physics, the, Aristotle's, 111, 112, 161, 182.
physics, 518; the new, 238. See philosophy of the sciences.
Physiocrats, the, 582.
physis, 91, 421.
Picasso, 553.
Pico della Mirandola, 233, 234.
Piper, R. F., 347, 348.
pistis, 151.
Pitkin, W. B., 519.
"Place of Illusory Experience in a Realistic World," 521.
Planck, M., 548, 551.
Plato, 46, 61, 66, 77, 80, 85, 87, 88, 93-105, 118, 124, 125, 127, 128, 132-137, 139, 141, 145, 148-150, 156, 161-165, 169, 175, 186, 188, 193, 199, 201, 205, 207, 230, 232, 233, 237, 255, 281, 306-308, 316, 341, 348, 407, 409, 413, 422, 432, 443, 484, 505, 512, 552, 560, 589, 595; Platonic ideas, see ideas, Platonic; Plato's line, 95-97, 99, 105; Platonic love, term coined, 233. See Platonism.
Platonic Theology, 233.
Platonic Tradition in Anglo-Saxon Philosophy, The, 319.
Platonism, 108, 128, 145, 156, 169, 179, 186, 189, 191, 192, 194, 195, 199, 216, 281, 311, 315, 385, 421, 423; Chap. VIII; Platonic renaissance, 232 ff.; Christian Platonists, 216. See ideas, Platonic.
Platonism and the Spiritual Life, 596.
Platonopolis, 136.
play theory, 555.
pleasure, 101, 118-121, 123, 271, 379, 493 ff. See happiness; hedonism.
Plethon, Georgios, 232, 233.
Plotinus, 127, 128, 132 ff., 135 ff., 151, 152, 162, 164, 165, 183, 186, 341, 443. See Neoplatonism.
pluralism, 7, 9, 12, 15, 16, 76-80, 104, 128, 248, 314, 343, 346, 347, 373, 432, 438, 439, 442, 443, 450.
"Pluralism and Contemporary Naturalism," 428.
Plutarch, 128, 129, 134, 230.
Pneuma, 133.

Poe, 553.
Poincaré, 473, 533, 540.
Poinsot, J., 169.
political philosophy, 274, 275, 309, 335, 461, 462, 577, 579. See philosophy of history.
Politicus, 128.
Polybius, 575.
polytheism, 431.
Pomponazzi, Pietro, 229.
Popular Science Monthly, 398, 528.
Porphyry, 135, 141, 165, 186, 188.
Posidonius, 122.
positing, 293, 449.
positivism, 112, 113, 264, 346, 422, 425, 429, 431, 435, 436, 439, 518, 552, 583, 591; Chap. XVI. See naturalism, positivistic.
positivism, logical, see logical positivism.
potentiality, 108-111.
Poussin, see Louis de la Vallée.
power, 376, 378-380, 385.
Prabhākara, 12, 13; Prabhākar Miṣra, 12.
practicalism, 395.
pragmateia, 133.
Pragmaticism, 388.
pragmatism, 10, 264, 272, 277, 313, 329, 337, 338, 343, 375, 419, 420, 468, 479, 486, 497, 517, 518, 528 ff., 536, 578, 602; Chap. XXXI; conceptualistic, 532; pragmatic epistemological theories, 528 ff.; pragmatic maxim, 392; thirteen pragmatisms, 393.
Pragmatism, 394, 398, 401-403, 537.
"Pragmatism *versus* the Pragmatist," 401.
Prajāpati, 4.
Prajnā, 8.
Prajnāpāramitā, 38.
Prakriti, 11, 12, 15, 16.
Prall, D. W., 497.
Pramānas, 10.
Prapatti, 15.
prasāda, 6, 16.
Prasasta Pāda, 9.
Pratt, J. B., 342, 347, 349, 420, 525, 604.
Prayer and Intelligence, 460.

INDEX

predestination, 174, 236; double predestination, 154.
prediction theory of law, 401.
pre-established harmony, 248, 342, 449.
pre-existence, 66.
Preface to Metaphysics, 459.
prehension, 452.
Present Philosophical Tendencies, 520, 536.
Prévoir et savoir, 467.
Price, H. H., 534, 535.
Priestly Code, 59.
primary qualities, 257, 259, 263.
Primitive Culture, 592.
primitivism, 272.
Prince, the, 236.
Principia, 541.
Principia Ethica, 499.
Principia Mathematica, 473, 474, 476, 482, 487, 490, 492, 513, 514, 553.
Principle of Individuality and Value, The, 326, 327, 495.
principle of non-contradiction, 327.
principle of uncertainty, 548.
Principles of Logic, The, 323, 507.
Principles of Psychology, 398, 402.
Pringle-Pattison, A. S., 303, 349.
privation, 139, 164.
probabilism, 222.
probability, theory of, 474, 510, 543, 544.
Problem of Knowledge, The, 527, 537.
Problemas Filosóficos, 385.
Problems of Ethics, 499.
Problems of Religion, 604.
Process and Reality, 536.
Proclus, 141, 142, 230.
"Program and First Platform of Six Realists," 519.
progress, 366, 367, 579, 580, 590, 593; theories, 273, 274.
"Progress of German Philosophy," etc., 586.
Prohodos, 141.
Prolegomena, 281.
Prolegomena to an Idealistic Theory of Knowledge, 523.
proof *vs* verification, see verification.
Proslogium, 191.
Protagoras, 85-87, 91, 95, 388.
Protrepticus, 149.

Proudhon, P. J., 335.
Proverbs, the book of, 61, 63, 66, 159.
providence, 62, 168, 174, 179-181, 187, 203, 351, 578; general, 274.
Pseudo-Dionysius, 186, 189.
Psyche, 138 ff.
psychic life, see panpsychism.
Psychic Life of Microorganisms, 447.
Psychologie vom empirischen Standpunkt, 531.
psychology, 347, 399, 423, 458, 468, 518; associationist, 507; comparative, 445, 447; dynamic, 604; empirical, 517; experimental, 447; pure, 358, 359, 361; rational, 395. See behaviorism; Gestalt psychology.
psychology of religion, 601, 604.
Psychology of Religious Experience, 607.
Psychology of World Views, 410.
psychological idealism, 362. See idealism, subjective.
psychophysics, 420.
Ptolemy, 165.
Pudgala, 7.
Pure Logic, 510.
purpose, 346-348. See teleology.
Purpose of History, 586.
Puruṣa, 5, 11, 12.
Pūrva, 12.
Pūrva mīmāmsā, 12.
Pym, T. W., 604.
Pyrrho, 125.
Pythagoras, 66, 83, 99, 103, 133, 233, 284.
Pythagoreans and Pythagoreanism, 73 ff., 145, 162, 437. See Neopythagoreanism.

Qadarites, 160.
Quadratus, 145.
quaestio form, 194.
qualities, see primary qualities; secondary qualities.
quantum mechanics, 547.
Quest for Certainty, The, 537.
questionnaire, the, 604.

racism, 467.
Radhakrishnan, S., 605.
radioactivity, 371 ff.

INDEX

Ram Mohan Roy, 17.
Ramakrishna Paramahamsa, 17.
Rāmānuja, 13-15, 341.
Ramsdell, E. T., 349.
Ramsey, F. P., 514.
Ramsperger, A. G., 240 ff.
Ramus, Peter, 231.
Randall, J. H., Jr., 585.
Ranke, 575, 576, 582.
Rashdall, H., 340, 343, 348, 349, 602.
rationalism, 268, 302, 313, 380, 391, 407, 424, 434, 438, 516, 580, 581; early modern, Chap. XIX; principal thesis, 241. See anti-rationalism; Hegel.
Ratnakīrti, 42.
Ratzenhofer, 581.
Raymond, archbishop, 168.
Raynal, Abbé, 273.
realism, 192, 193, 218, 472, 476. See Platonism; ideas, Platonic.
realism, American, 420, 497. See critical realism; American New Realism.
realism, Anglo-American, 518. See American New Realism; English New Realism.
realism, Aristotelian, 113, 114, 116.
realism, dualistic, see dualistic realism.
realism, epistemological, see American New Realism; English New Realism; epistemological realism; critical monism; critical realism; criteriological realism; Neo-Realism; religious realism. See following headings.
realism, naive, 471, 517.
realism, physical, 424.
realism, presentative, 518-521; 523, 526-528, 530, 533, 537.
realism, referential, 534.
realism, representative, 520, 525 ff.
realism thesis, 475.
Réalisme methodique, etc., 463.
Réalisme thomiste, 458.
Realismo Cientifico, 385.
"Realistic Theory of Independence, A," 520.
realitates, formalitates, 215.
reason and faith, see faith and reason.
Reasonableness of Christianity, The, 276, 607.

rebirth, doctrine of, see reincarnation; transmigration.
reconstruction of philosophy, 389, 390.
Reconstruction in Philosophy, 337, 596.
recurrence, 378.
Reden über Religion, 607.
rediscovery of Aristotle, 197 ff. See Aristotelianism; Revived Aristotelianism.
"Reflex Action and Theism," 607.
Reformation, Protestant and Catholic, 236.
'Refutation of Idealism," 518.
Regis, L. M., 455.
regressus, the, 139, 140.
regula veritatis, 146.
regulative ideas, 292.
Reichenbach, Hans, 550.
reification, 311, 312.
Reign of Religion in Contemporary Philosophy, The, 608.
Reinach, Adolf, 353.
reincarnation, 28 ff.
relations, external, 358; internal, 325, 327.
relativism, 376, 377, 385, 480, 529.
relativity, 98, 473, 549; principle, 87; theory, 372.
relativity of truth, 388.
religion and philosophy, 297 ff.; philosophies of religion, Chap. XLVII.
religion of humanity, 335, 436, 602.
religion of the Enlightenment, 275 ff.
Religion in Transition, 608.
Religion in Various Cultures, 607.
Religion within the Bounds of Mere Reason, 607.
Religions of Authority and the Religion of the Spirit, 607.
religious cults, 432.
religious empiricism, 601.
religious humanism, 335, 337, 436, 602, 603. See religion of humanity.
religious realism, 342.
Renaissance, 160, 185, 189, 192, 552; renaissance philosophies, Chap. XVIII.
Renouvier, C., 340, 342, 343.
Republic, the, 95, 96, 100, 103, 104, 132, 136, 161, 186, 281.
resurrection, 64, 67.

635

INDEX

revelation, 57 ff., 146, 162, 171 ff., 174, 176, 178, 180, 181, 185, 189, 190, 199, 203, 204, 208-210, 213, 276, 412, 415, 439, 463, 589, 601, 605; and discovery, 440; and reason, 463.
Review of Politics, 466.
Revived Aristotelianism, 163, 164, 179, 193, 194; Revived Aristotelianism and Thomistic philosophy, Chap. XVI. See Aristotelianism, renaissance; rediscovery of Aristotle.
Revolt Against Dualism, The, 525, 536.
Revue d'Esthétique, 557.
Rhine, J. B., 347.
Ricardo, 582.
Richards, I. A., 50, 496, 500, 501, 557.
Rickert, H., 303, 348, 585.
Riddles of the Sphinx, 343.
Rig-Veda, 3.
Rigveda Samhitā, 3.
right, 427; righteousness, 62.
rights, natural, see natural rights.
Rimbaud, 553.
Riṣabha, 6.
Ritschl, Albrecht, 303, 602.
Robinson, D. S., 344.
Robinson, J. H., 584.
Robles, O., 456.
Rogers, A. K., 525.
Roman Catholicism, 589. See Catholicism.
Roman schools of philosophy, Chap. X.
Roman Stoicism, 122. See Stoicism.
romanticism, 578-580, 582.
Romero, F., 344, 345.
Rousseau, J. J., 269, 271-273, 275, 577, 579; Rousseauanism, 311.
Royce, Josiah, 303, 315-317, 324, 342, 343, 345, 349, 351, 398, 443, 446-448, 495, 512, 535, 601, 602.
Rta, 3, 4.
Ruach, 133.
Ruge, 308.
Runes, D. D., preface, 537.
rūpa, 8.
Russell, B., 264, 327, 428, 437, 472, 474, 476, 478, 479, 482, 492, 500, 510, 513, 514, 521-525, 550, 553.

Ruya, H., 428.
Ryle, G., 492.
Rynin, S., 499.

Saadia Ben Joseph, 174, 175.
Sabatier, A., 602.
Sacred Books of the East, The, 603.
Sadāsat-Kārya-Vāda, 16.
Sadducees, 67.
Saint-Simon, Claude Henri, de, 332.
Śaivism, 6, 14.
Saksena, Shri K., 3 ff.
Salonina, 136.
Sāma-Veda, 3.
Samādhī, 8.
Sāmānya, 9.
Samavāya, 9.
Samdhinirmocana, 39.
Samghata, 8.
Samhitās, 3.
Sāmkhya-Yoga, 15.
Samsāra, 8.
samtāna, 37.
Samyag Cāritra, 7.
Samyag Darshan, 7.
Samyag Jyāna, 7.
Sanborn, H. C., 344, 346, 347.
Sanchez, Francisco, 232.
Śankara, 13, 14, 443.
Sānkhya, 11, 12.
Sānkhya-Yoga, 11.
Sāntam, Sivam, Advaitam, 17.
santāna, 8.
Santayana, G., 420, 424, 428, 436, 439, 497, 525-527, 532, 554, 561, 596.
Śāntideva, 39.
Sanyāsa, 13.
Sartre, Jean Paul, 223, 341, 349, 412-415, 560.
Sarvam Khalvidam, Brahma, 14.
sarvamasti, 34.
Sarvāstivādins, 34, 35, 40.
Sasanians, 29-31.
Sassanid Persia, 160.
Satkāryavāda, 11.
Sautrāntikas, 34, 35, 37.
scepticism, 53, 63, 64, 66, 80, 125 ff., 221, 222, 232, 240, 263.
Scepticism and Animal Faith, 525, 526, 537.
Scheitern, 411.

636

INDEX

Scheler, Max, 353, 363.
Schelling, F. W. J., 291-293, 299, 302, 304, 343, 516, 580; on aesthetics, 296; on nature, 293, 294, 296; on religion, 297.
Schiller, F., 555.
Schiller, F. C. S., 340, 343, 348, 349, 388, 389, 392.
Schilling, S. P., 349.
Schilpp, P. A., 428.
Schlegel, F., 580.
Schleiermacher, F. D. E., 340, 600, 601, 607.
Schlick, M., 473, 479, 498, 499.
Schneider, H. W., 607.
scholasticism, 114, 422, 423, 456-458, 563; early Christian, Chap. XV; schoolmen, 218, 222; scholastic method, 228; new scholasticism, 454; scholastic philosophy, 229. See Neo-Scholasticism.
Schopenhauer, A., 300 ff., 341, 343, 370, 375, 438, 591; Chap. XXIII; on history, 302; on religion, 302.
Schroeder, E., 511, 512.
Science and the Modern World, 402, 536.
Science et Hypothèse, 540.
Science of Logic, 506.
Science of Knowledge, The, 292.
science of religion, 603.
sciences, the, 357; classification of 332 ff., 546 ff.; empirical, 542, 543, 545; rational, 542, 545. See under specific headings.
sciences, the philosophy of, Chap. XLII.
scientific method, 541, 542, 544, 550, 585; and positivism, 330.
Scientific Method in Philosophy, 327, 521.
scientism, 335, 473, 478, 480.
scio aliquid esse, 460.
Scotism, 228, 455; and Ockhamism, Chap. XVII.
Scotus, Duns, 212-217, 219-221, 223, 463.
scriptures, 147, 151, 156, 209.
Searles, H. L., 344, 348.
secondary qualities, 257, 259, 263.
Secret of Hegel, The, 318.
Sein und Zeit, 354, 412.

self, 261 ff., 340, 345, 426, 444-446, 480; or spirit, 382; and person, 341. See soul.
self-evident, see axioms.
Sellars, R. W., 418 ff., 420 ff., 436, 525.
semantics, 263, 418, 424, 426, 428, 468, 472, 474, 475, 500; Chap. XXXVIII. See language.
Semite, 159.
Seneca, 122, 197.
sensationalism, 390, 394, 399, 400, 418, 439, 529.
Sense of Beauty, The, 554.
Sentences, 218, 228.
Sententiae, 194.
Septuagint, 65, 133.
sex, 155, 349.
Sextus Empiricus, 125, 230.
Shaftesbury, Lord, 271, 276.
Shang Yang, 55.
Shankara, 345.
Shapiro, M., 428.
Sheffer, H. M., 513.
Shepherd of Hermas, 144.
Siebeck, H., 602.
Siger of Brabant, 202, 203, 208.
sign, 487-488, 490, 492, 505; signs and symbols, 482. See semantics; symbols.
Signs, Language and Behavior, 491.
Śīla, 8.
Simon, Yves, 455, 460, 461, 466, 467.
Simonides, 83.
simple location, fallacy of, 443.
singularism, see monism.
siope, 141.
Śiva, 6.
skepticism, see scepticism.
Skeptics and the Academy, 125 ff.
Sketch of the Progress of the Human Mind, 273.
slave morality, 380.
Smaller Logic, 319.
Smith, Adam, 271, 278, 582.
Smith, Gerard, 458.
Smith, G. B., 604, 607.
Smith, N. Kemp, 401, 523, 524.
Social Contract, The, 272, 275.
social contract theory, 247, 267, 579.
social existentialism, see existentialism, social.

637

INDEX

Social Idealism and the Changing Theology, 607.
social philosophy, 350, 461.
socialism, 269, 312, 314, 581.
sociology, 333, 334.
sociology of knowledge, 337.
Socrates, 78, 85, 87-91, 94, 101, 105, 113, 118, 135, 150, 162, 413, 433, 484, 505.
Socratic method, 89, 90, 98, 307.
Socratics, Pre, 131, 504.
Söderblom, N., 603.
Soliloquies, 506.
solipsism, 362.
Solomon, 64, 66.
Solomon, Wisdom of, 66.
Somervell, D. C., 586.
Sommerville, John, 313.
Sophist, the, 96, 99, 100, 124, 137.
Sophists, 80, 84-90, 125, 162, 329, 504, 505.
Sophocles, 83.
Sophroniscus, 94.
Sorley, W. R., 340, 342, 343, 348, 350.
Sorokin, P., 574, 593.
Sotion, 127.
soul, 167, 175, 201, 207, 233, 249, 340, 395, 402, 442 ff.; Augustine's conception of, 154; and body, 201, 206, 207, 422, 423. See mind and body; self.
Soul Universal, 138, 139.
Souriau, 561.
Soviet philosophy, 313, 344.
space, 7, 9, 17, 80, 102, 128, 138, 163, 182, 235, 283, 285, 346, 372, 373, 381-384, 443, 446, 450, 475, 549, 550.
space-time, 419, 425, 450.
Space, Time and Deity, 522, 536.
Spaulding, E. G., 519.
specious present, 359, 360, 448, 450.
speculative idealism, 322, 324, 601. See idealism.
Spedding and Ellis, editors, 399.
Speeches to the German Nation, 295.
Spencer, B., and Gillen, F. J., 603.
Spencer, Herbert, 336, 350, 367-369, 371, 372, 395, 436, 583, 591.
Spengler, O., 350, 377, 559, 574, 584, 593.

Spinoza, B., 119, 182, 235, 244 ff., 247, 250, 291, 307, 330, 345, 370, 434, 494, 516.
Spirit of Laws, The, 272, 273.
Spirit of Mediaeval Philosophy, The, 463.
spiritual life, 19 ff.
spiritualism, 343. See idealism.
Spranger, E., 585.
Sraosha, 26.
Sri Aurobindo Ghosh, 17.
Sri Ramana Maharishi, 17.
Śruti, 7.
Stace, W. T., 533-535.
stages of thought, the law of, 273. See law of three stages.
Stalinism, 312.
Stallknecht, N. P., 280 ff.
Starbuck, E. D., 604.
statistical laws, 445, 449.
Sterling, J. H., 318.
Stern, W., 340, 342, 343, 347, 350.
Stevenson, Charles, 501.
Stewart, J. A., 95.
St. Louis school, the, 318, 319.
Stoa, 133.
Stoicism, 66, 119, 121 ff., 125-127, 145, 147, 150, 232, 505.
Strauss, D. F., 299, 581.
Strauss, L., 183.
stream of thought, 402.
Strickland, F. L., 347.
Stromateis, the, 149.
Strong, C. A., 342, 420, 421, 525.
Student's Philosophy of Religion, A, 604, 605.
Studies and Exercises in Formal Logic, 505.
Studies in Logical Theory, 508.
Studies in Speculative Philosophy, 321, 322.
Study of History, A, 586, 593.
Study in Realism, A, 523.
Study in the Theory of Value, A, 497.
Suarez, F., 229, 578; Suarezianism, 455.
sub specie aeternitatis, 246, 307.
subjectivism, 390, 422, 423.
subordination, doctrine of, 156.
substance, 233, 248, 258, 259, 263, 347, 378, 424, 425, 434, 475.

INDEX

suffering, 8, 11-13, 15, 33, 36, 37, 46, 59, 61 ff., 297. See pain.
sufficient reason, principle of, 249, 250.
Sufis, 30, 162.
suicide, 121, 122, 126.
Summa Theologiae, 204, 228, 455, **468**.
summum bonum, 15, 16, 27, 44, 101, 116, 148, 180, 182, 454, 461.
Sung dynasty, 56.
Śūnya, 9, 38.
Śūnyavāda, 9; Śūnyavādins, 34, 38.
super-personalism, 439.
Superman, 380, 593.
supernaturalism, 173, 181, 203, 210, 277, 365, 366, 415, 419, 430-435, 439, 440, 461, 529, 577. See revelation.
superspace, 80.
suppositio, 218.
surrealism, 552, 560.
Survey of Symbolic Logic, 514.
survival of the fittest, see natural selection.
Sūtras, 13, 34, 35, 37-39.
sva-dharma, 6.
Śvetambaras, 7.
Syad, 7.
syllogism, 114, 326, 505, 509, 511.
symbolic logic, 348, 468, 475, 506, 508 ff. See mathematical logic.
Symbolic Logic, 511.
symbolism in religion, 303.
symbols, 132, 384, 385, 426. See sign; symbolic logic.
sympathy, 271, 301.
Symposium, 233.
syncretism, 145, 155, 161.
synechological view, 446, 447.
synthetic judgments, 283.
synthetic philosophy, 336.
Syrian, 159; Syrian Christians, 159, 160.
System of Logic, 394, 507, 592.
System of Nature, 277.

Tagore, 17.
Talmud, 67.
Tanmātras, 11.
Tao, 52, 53.
Taoism, 51 ff.; **55, 56**.
Tao Tê Ching, 51.
Taraporewala, I. J. S., 19 ff.; 156.
Tarski, A., 489, 491, 514.
taste, 558.
Tat Ekam, 4.
Tatian, 145, 149.
tat tvam Asi, 5.
Teggart, F. J., 584, 585.
teleology, 78, 103, 281, 288, 304, 343, 381, 383, 422, 574, 575, 577. See design argument.
teleological argument for God, 276. See design.
telepathy, 347.
Telesio, B., 235.
telos, 132.
temporalism, 381. See time.
Tennant, F. R., 343, 349.
Tennyson, 22.
tertium quid, 437.
Tertullian, 145-147, 153, 154.
"Testability and Meaning," 550.
thalamus, 426.
Thales, 70, 71, 75, 76, 138.
Theaetetus, 77, 95, 96, 98.
theism, 5, 13-16, 58, 340, 343, 344, 346, 406, 439, 452.
theocentric humanism, 461, 465.
theocracy, 47, 60.
theodicy, 62 ff., 154, 155, 175, 249, 297; Gnostic, 146.
Theognis, 82, 83.
theoi, 432.
theology, 133, 134, 150, 161, 169, 173, 186, 191, 194, 203, 213, 228, 334, 349, 365, 599, 606, 607; and philosophy, 203, 222.
Theology of Aristotle, 162.
theological schools, 606, 607.
theo-ontology, 415.
theophany, 190.
Theophilus, 145.
theoria, 141.
Theory of Knowledge and Existence, The, 533, 537.
Theory of Moral Sentiments, 271, 278.
Theory of Probability, The, 551.
theosophy, 236, 438.
thermodynamics, 584; second law of, 372, 373.
thingism, 464.
Things that are not Caesar's, 460.

639

INDEX

Thomas à Kempis, 236.
Thomas, St., see Aquinas.
Thomism, 168, 169, 214, 228, 342, 422, 423, 563; contemporary Thomism, Chap. XXXVI. See Aquinas; Neo-Thomism.
Thomist, The, 466.
Thompson, R. J., 185 ff.
Thought, 466.
Thought and Things, 508.
Thouless, R. H., 604.
Thrasymachus, 88, 90.
three stages of thought, law of, see law of three stages.
Thucydides, 85.
Thus spake Zarathustra, 377.
Tillotson, J., 276.
Timaeus, 98, 101-103, 128, 133, 134, 186, 230.
time, 7, 9, 17, 101, 102, 137, 138, 163, 283, 285, 303, 346, 375, 382, 448, 450, 451, 475, 544-546, 549, 550. See duration; eternity; space-time; specious present.
Time and Free Will, 381.
Tindal, M., 276.
Tirthānkara, 6, 7.
Toland, J., 276.
Tolman, E. C., 497.
Tolstoy, 554.
Tonnies, 584.
Torah, 64-68.
Totem and Taboo, 594.
Toy, C. H., 603.
Toynbee, A. J., 584, 586, 593.
Tractatus Logico-Philosophicus, 472, 481, 514.
traducianism, 154.
Transactions of the American Mathematical Society, 512, 513.
transcendence, 149. See Gnosticism; supernaturalism.
transcendental method, Kant's, 285.
transcendental phenomenology, 360 ff.
transmigration, 4, 5, 15, 38.
Treatise on Man, A, 278.
Treitsche, 581.
triadic dialectic, see dialectic, Hegelian.
triadic element of experience, 449.
trichotomy, 129.

Trimśikā, 40.
trinity, 134, 151, 152, 175, 191, 219; first used in Christian literature, 145.
Troeltsch, E., 303.
Trois leçons sur le travail, 466.
Trotzkyites, 312.
tṛṣṇā, 8.
True Humanism, 459, 461.
truth, 10, 16, 22, 24, 26, 28, 39, 75, 80, 101, 125 ff., 146, 241, 245, 249, 264, 319-322, 325, 326, 345, 347, 355, 356, 389, 390, 392, 393, 397, 399, 400, 472, 480, 488-491, 504, 514, 528, 543, 570, 578; analytic, 480; double truth theory, 173, 203, 229; necessary, 250; relative, 388; subjective, 406; tautological, 479, 488; universal, 234. See coherence theory; correspondence theory; pragmatism.
Tucker, A., 270.
Turgot, A., 273, 332, 575, 577, 584, 585.
twelve stages, 578.
Twentieth Century Philosophy, 537.
twenty four theses, 454, 469.
two aspect theory, 442.
Two Sources of Morality and Religion, The, 381, 385, 386, 593.
"Two Types of Idealism," 321.
Tylor, E. B., 592, 603.

Ulrici, H., 343.
Umgreifende, das, 411.
uncertainty principle, see principle of uncertainty.
Underhill, E., 605, 608.
uniformitarian theory, 366.
unio mystica, 134.
Universal Algebra, 512.
universal harmony, 276.
universal ideas, 278.
universal principles, 268, 269.
Universal Will, 302. See Soul Universal.
universalism, 151, 178.
universals, 8, 9, 12, 94 ff., 188, 193, 214-216, 218-220, 355, 356, 359, 375, 487, 491, 509, 511; universal, concrete, see concrete universal.

INDEX

universe, the expanding, 373.
University Chronicle, The, 398.
unity, 103, 104, 127, 131 ff., 133, 137; man's unity, 207. See monism.
unity of apperception, 289.
Unity of Philosophical Experience, 463.
Unknowable, the, 371.
Unscientific Postcript, 406.
Upaniṣads, the, 4-8, 12, 13, 15, 17, 301.
Urban IV, 198, 199.
Urban, W. M., 494, 495.
utilitarian age, 583.
utilitarianism, 269-271, 388, 392, 566, 569.
Utitz, 557.
utopia, 235, 312, 332.
Uttar mīmāmsā, 12.

vah-, 31.
Vaibhāṣikas, 34-37.
Vaihinger, H., 303, 336, 412, 533.
Vaiśeṣika, 9.
Vaiśeṣika Sūtras, 9.
Vaiṣnavism, 6, 14.
Vajracchedika, 38.
Valla, Lorenzo, 231, 232.
Valentinus, 146.
Valuation, 498.
Valuation, its Nature and Laws, 494, 495.
value, 326, 337, 338, 346, 348-350, 359, 376, 377, 379, 380, 427-429, 569, 606; a brief history of General Theory of Value, Chap. XXXIX; four criteria, 497; scheme of values, 271; value theory of Ritschl, 303. See axiology; conservation of value; value judgments.
value judgments, 498, 499, 501, 602.
Value, a Cooperative Enquiry, 502.
Value and Destiny of the Individual, The, 495.
varieties of naturalism, Chap. XXXIV.
Varieties of Religious Experience, The, 607.
Varisco, 443.
Varuṇa, 3.
vas, 31.
Vasconcelos, José, 344, 376, 385.

Vasubandhu, 39-41.
Vātsyāyna, 9.
Vaughan, R. M., 349.
vāyu, 3.
Veatch, H., 106 ff.
Vedānta, 4, 13 ff.
Vedānta-Sūtra, 15.
Vedas, 3 ff., 6, 8, 13, 17, 19.
vehicles of knowledge, 525 ff.
Venn, J., 511.
vera ratio, 189.
Verdenglichung, 310.
vere es, 192.
verification, 543, 544; *vs.* proof, 542.
Véron, Eugène, 553.
verum ens, 193.
Vesalius, Andreas, 237.
Vibhāṣa, 35.
vicāra, 12.
Vico, G., 575, 578, 593.
Victorines, the, 194.
Vidyā, 14.
Vienna Circle, 471-473, 476; school of, 500.
vijñāna, 39.
Vijñāna-vāda, 8.
Vijñānavādins, 34, 39 ff.
vijñapti, 40.
vijñaptimātra, 40.
Vijñaptimātratāsiddhi, 41.
Vimśatikā, 40.
Vinaya, 34.
Vinci, da, Leonardo, see Leonardo da Vinci.
virtues, 50.
visesa, 9.
Vishnu, 6, 15.
Viśiṣtādvaita, 14, 15.
vitalism, 407, 422, 431; Chap. XXX.
viveka, 12.
Viveka-jnāna, 11.
Vivekananda, swami, 17.
Vives, Juan Luis, 231.
Viyoga, 11.
Vlachos, N. P., 84.
vohu, 23, 25.
Vohu-Manō, 23, 24, 26, 28, 30, 31.
void, 9, 37 ff., 78, 121, 138, 139, 141.
Volkelt, 555.
Volksgeist, 579, 580.
Voltaire, 267, 268, 272, 276, 596.

641

INDEX

voluntarism, 221, 296, 301, 302, 341, 375, 385; of Scotus, 217 ff.

Wahrheitsbegriff in den formalisierten Sprachen, Der, 491.
Wallace, A. R., 366.
Ward, James, 303, 343, 347, 348.
Was ist Metaphysik?, 412, 413.
Watson, John, 601.
Way to the Blessed Life, The, 295.
Weiss, P., 398.
Weltgeist, 579.
Werkmeister, W. H., 345, 348, 350.
Wesen der Religion, 607.
Wesenheiten, 412.
Wesensschau, 569, 572.
What is Art?, 554.
"What is Materialism?", 420.
Where is Science Going?, 551.
Whewell, W., 540.
White, Leslie, 592.
Whitehead, A. N., 342, 344, 345, 347-349, 375, 396, 402, 443, 445, 447-452, 496, 500, 512, 513, 522, 524, 525, 546, 553, 559.
Whitman, Walt, 340, 343, 350.
Widgery, A. G., 291 ff., 349.
Wieman, H. N., 605.
Wild, J., 455, 456, 469.
Will, Universal, 301.
Will to Believe, The, 398, 607.
will to live, 379.
will to power, 378 ff., 385.
William of Alnwick, 222.
William of Auvergne, 199, 200, 202, 208.
William of Auxerre, 198.
William of Champeaux, 216, 220.
William of Moerbeke, 199.
Williams, B., 350.
Williams, D., 425, 428, 550.
Wilson, G. A., 344, 346.
Windelband, W., 303, 585.
wisdom, 101, 122.
Wisdom Literature, 60 ff.
Wisdom of Catholicism, The, 466.

Wittgenstein, L., 264, 472-474, 477, 481, 482, 500, 514.
Wolfson, H. A., 183.
Wood, Ledger, 516 ff.
Woodbridge, F. J. E., 586.
World and the Individual, The, 316.
World as Will and Idea, The, 300, 438.
worship, 602.
Wright, Chauncey, 402.
Wright, W. K., 349, 604.
Wundt, W. M., 342, 457, 508, 517, 603.
Wu wei, 52.

Xenocrates, 102.
Xenophon, 94.

Yahweh, 58 ff.
Yajur-Veda, 3.
Yang Chu, 52.
Yao and Shun, emperors, 48.
Yaśomitra, 42.
Yathārtha-Vāda, 16.
Yearbook for Philosophy and Phenomenological Research, 353.
Yoga, 10-12, 17.
Yogācāras, school of, 8.
Yogin, 10.
Youtz, H. A., 349.

Zabarella, Jacopo, 229.
Zaddiq, see Joseph Ibn Zaddiq.
Zarathushtra, see Zoroaster.
Zedler, Beatrice, 466.
Zeitgeist, 579.
Zeno of Elea, 79 ff., 145, 306, 308.
Zeno, founder of Stoicism, 118, 119, 122, 125.
Zilsel, E., 586.
Zola, 553.
Zoroaster, 19 ff.
Zoroastrianism, 155, 432; Zoroastrian philosophy, Chap. II.
Zybura, J. S., 456.

SCHEELE MEMORIAL LIBRARY

3 6655 00009343 5
B72 .F4
Ferm, Vergilius Tur/History of

DATE DUE

OCT 10 '64			
DEC 18 '64			
MAY 12 '65			
MAR 16 '67			
JAN 6 '69			

DATE DUE	BORROWER'S NAME		
	APR 0 4 2007		
	APR 1 0 2007		
	MAY 0 4 2007		

B
72
.F4

1794

CONCORDIA COLLEGE LIBRARY
BRONXVILLE, N. Y. 10708